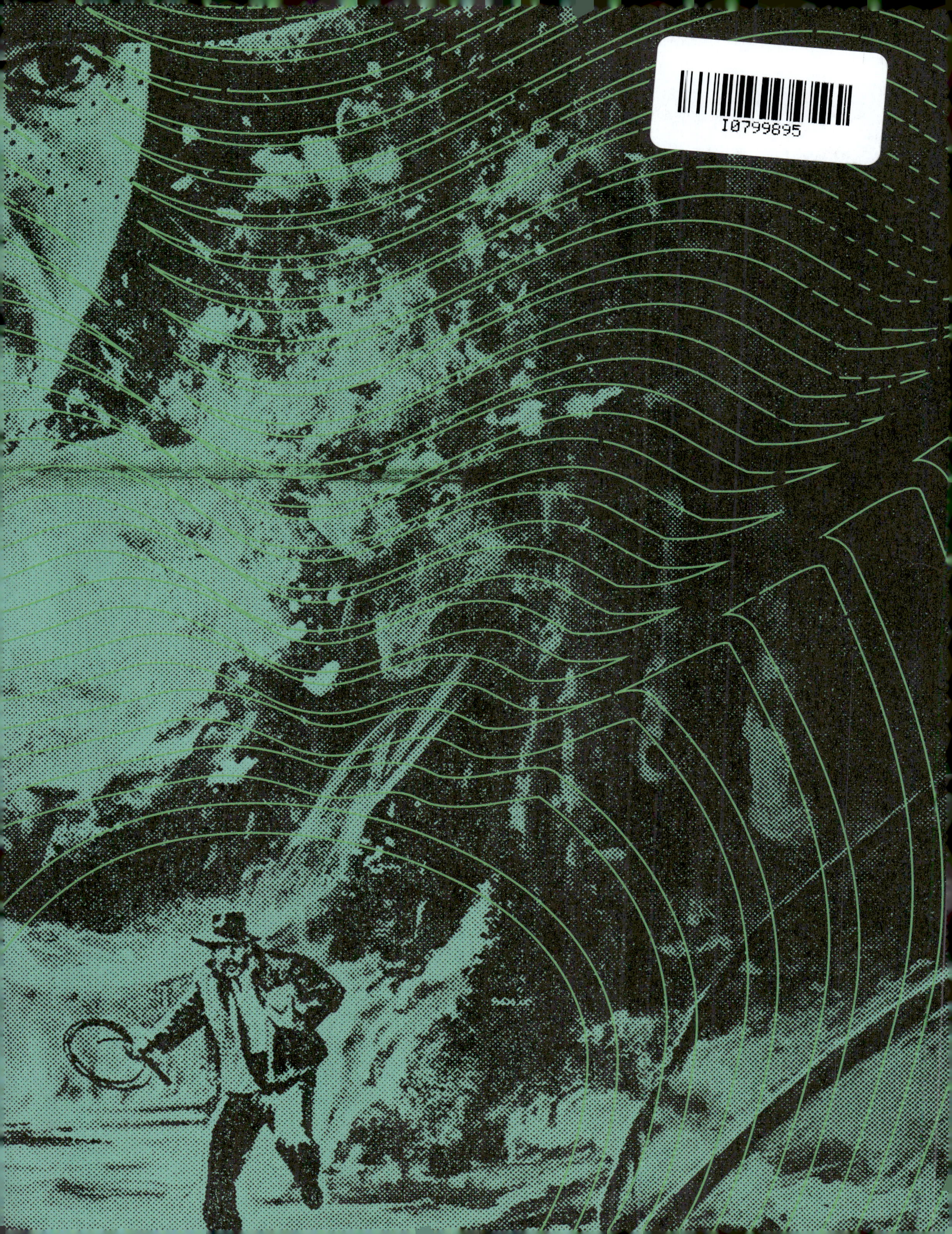

AD ASTRA

20 YEARS OF NEWSPAPER ADS FOR SCI-FI & FANTASY FILMS

BY

MICHAEL GINGOLD

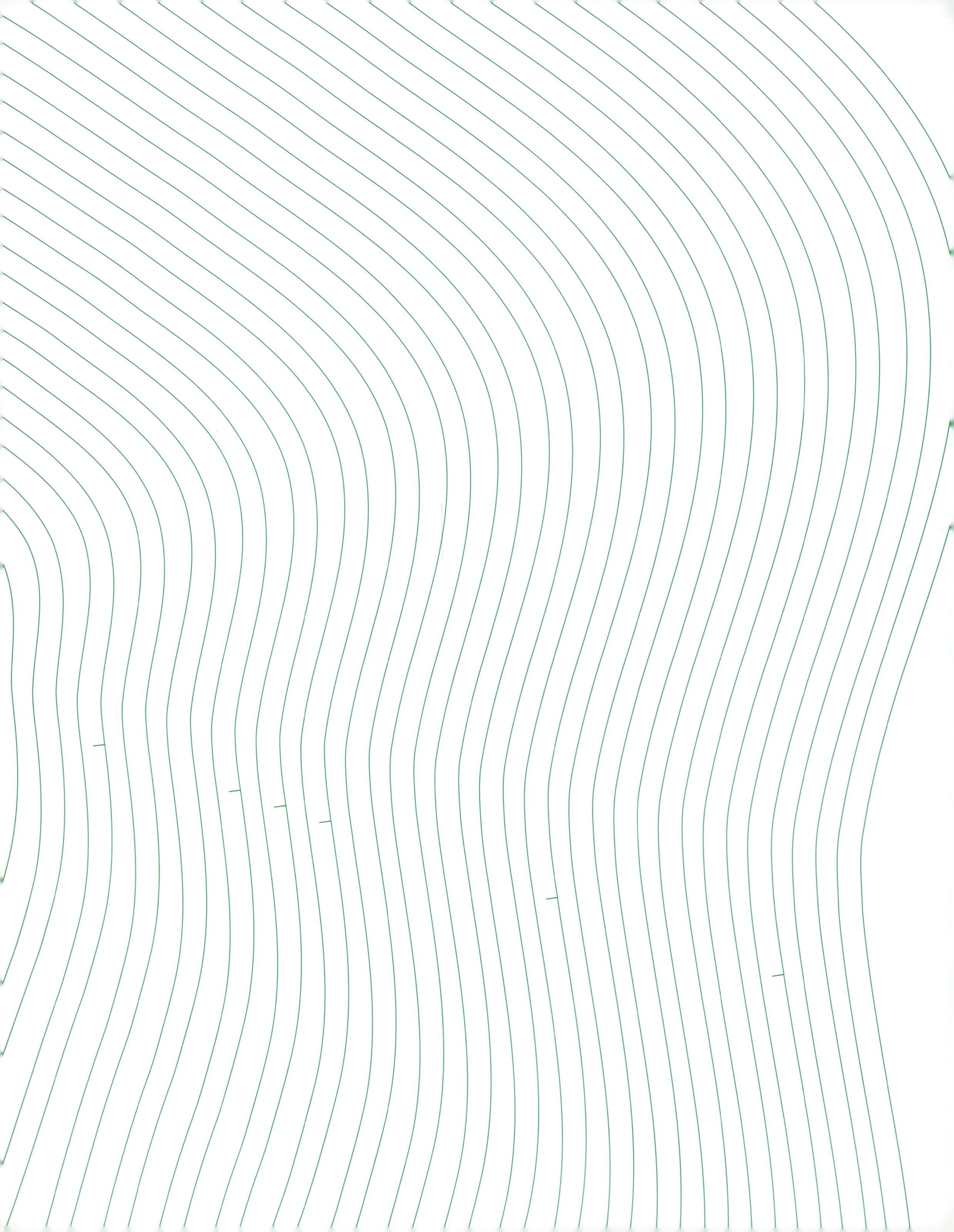

CONTENTS

INTRODUCTION

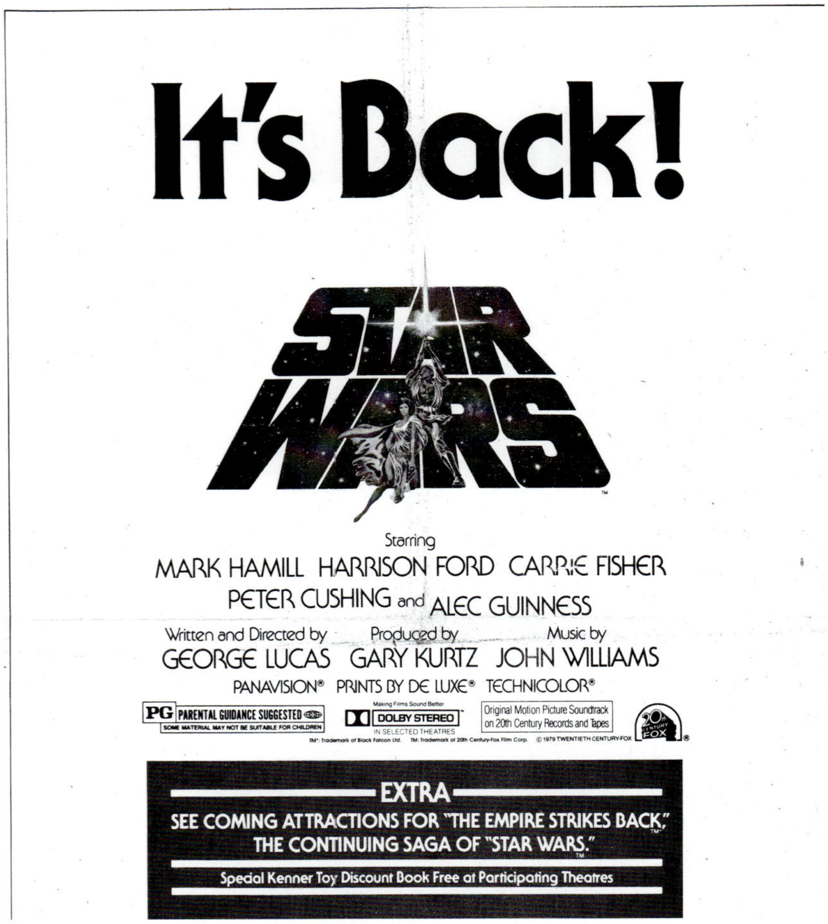

I WAS EXACTLY THE RIGHT AGE WHEN *STAR WARS* WAS FIRST RELEASED.

IT WAS THE SUMMER OF 1977 AND I WAS TEN YEARS OLD. I was already a science fiction fan, though my favorite films weren't space adventures, but rather monster movies – specifically, the stop-motion epics featuring the pioneering effects of Willis O'Brien and Ray Harryhausen, and the exploits of Godzilla, Gamera and their brethren from Japan's Toho and Daiei studios. I had almost exclusively experienced these creatures on television, running home after school to catch "Monster Week" and similarly themed showcases on WABC Channel 7's *The 4:30 Movie*, and looking forward to Thanksgiving, not just for the family feast but also for WOR Channel 9's triple feature of *King Kong*, *Son of Kong* and *Mighty Joe Young* on Turkey Day, and then three or four Godzilla flicks the following day. And sure, once in a while I'd see something like *Godzilla vs. Megalon* or the 1975 re-release of *The 7th Voyage of Sinbad* in a theater, but my life-altering experience on the big screen happened in a galaxy far, far away, in May of '77.

My family and I were on our annual Memorial Day Weekend outing to a campsite in upstate New York, and one day we took a day trip to a nearby town. There, we found that the local theater (whose name is lost in the mist of my memory) was playing *Star Wars*, which was already being hailed as a major step forward

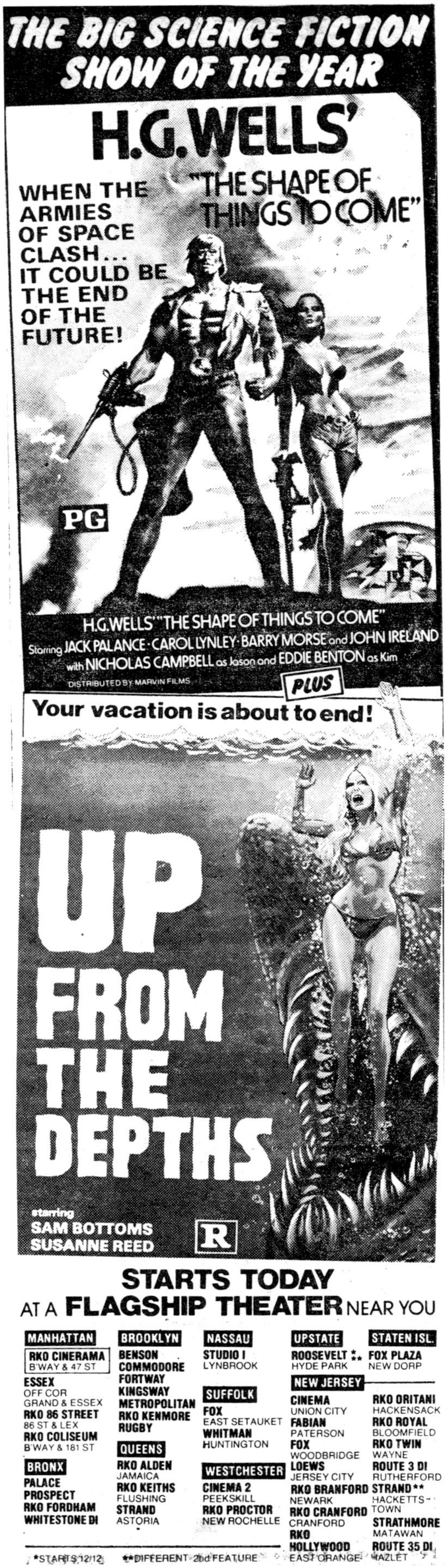

in cinema. So we went... and discovered this particular screening wasn't quite what we'd hoped for. *Star Wars* was one of the first major films to be presented in 70mm and six-track Dolby Stereo in select engagements, but ours certainly wasn't one of them. The projector was situated on the balcony, and the image went blurry about half a dozen times during the showing, prompting shouts of "Focus!" from the audience. The seats weren't all that comfortable either.

Despite all that, we loved the movie, and I was particularly entranced. Here was a film that opened up all kinds of new possibilities for imaginative cinema, while feeling like it was made just for kids like me. After all, the hero wasn't an intrepid scientist or square-jawed soldier, but a youth who dreamed of adventure and bigger things in his future. A week or so later, we saw *Star Wars* again at a better theater closer to home, and I must have seen it another ten times over the course of its long theatrical run. I was part of that first generation to be captivated by George Lucas' vision in its purest form, and because of it, was compelled to seek out more science fiction and fantasy on the big screen. But it wasn't just movies...

Another formative event feeding my nascent fandom occurred a little later that season. During a July 4th Weekend trip to the Finger Lakes area, I was perusing a pharmacy magazine rack when I came across *Famous Monsters of Filmland* #136, featuring none other than the latest Harryhausen picture, *Sinbad and the Eye of the Tiger*, on the cover. Before this, I had somehow managed not to discover the "World's Most Amazing Magazine" and immediately snapped it up. (I only found out later I'd just missed *Godzilla vs. Bionic Monster* – re-titled *Godzilla vs. the Cosmic Monster* after the issue went to press – on the cover of #135.) *FM*, which devoted three successive covers to *Star Wars*, was another revelation, and proof there was a whole subculture of "monster kids" just like me who were anxious to read more about these movies we loved.

In December '77, another groundbreaker, Steven Spielberg's *Close Encounters of the Third Kind*, came out, and I was taken with its equally dazzling visuals and uniquely optimistic view of the possibilities of alien visitation. In April 1978, I watched my first Oscar telecast, hoping to see *Star Wars* grab a few golden men; it wound up nabbing seven, with *Close Encounters* sneaking in a Best Cinematography win. Christmas season '78 brought *Superman* and *Invasion of the Body Snatchers*... and then, in 1979, sci-fi and fantasy truly exploded out of Hollywood as multiple projects put into the works in the wake of *Star Wars* and *Close Encounters*' box-office success saw the light. The long-anticipated *Star Trek: The Motion Picture* emerged; James Bond went to outer space in *Moonraker*; *Alien* brought hardcore horror to the cosmos; Walt Disney Pictures went PG for the first time with *The Black Hole*; the waning disaster-movie genre sought to milk the trend with *Meteor*, and an old hero attempted new relevance in *Buck Rogers in the 25th Century*.

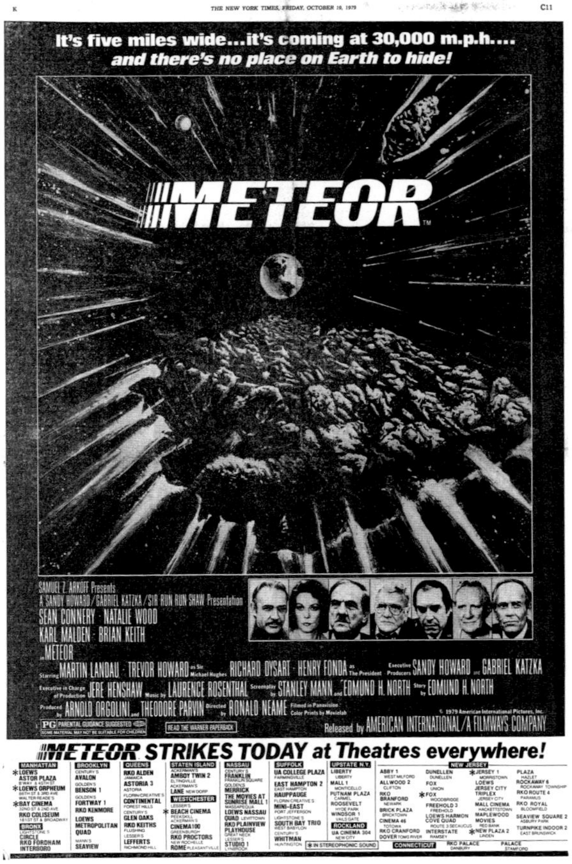

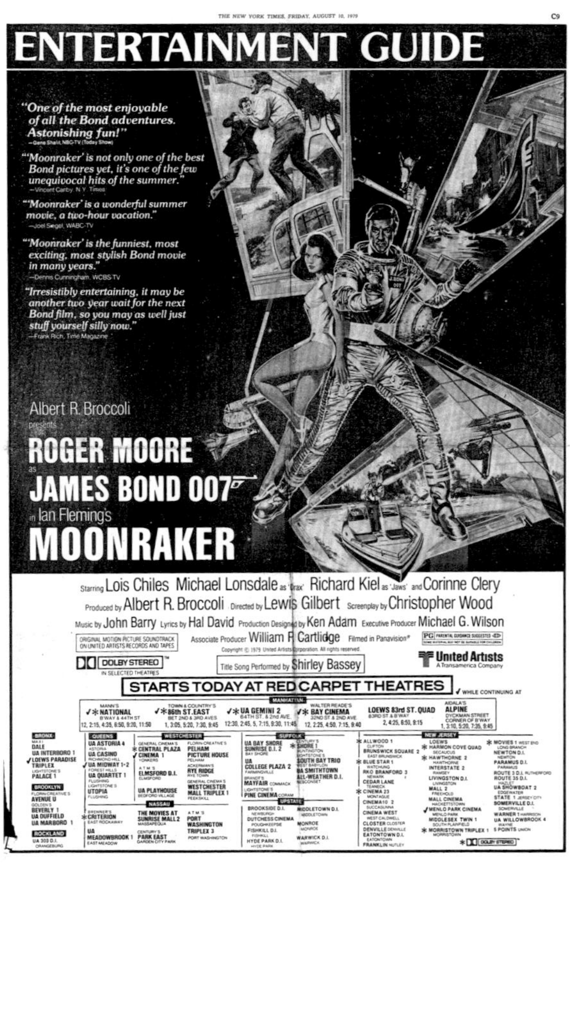

As detailed in my previous volume, *Ad Nauseam: Newsprint Nightmares from the 1980s*, '79 was also the year I began collecting newspaper ads for genre films. While horror became my first love that year, thanks to John Carpenter's *Halloween* and others, I was enthusiastic enough about science fiction and fantasy to clip those ads too. As opposed to fright flicks, which were often issued by small distributors that could only afford limited space in New York's tabloids – the *Daily News* and *Post* – sci-fi and fantasy were necessarily the bigger-budgeted province of the studios, which had more to spend to promote them, often taking full pages (and sometimes more than one) in the larger-scale *New York Times*. I still sought out the smaller pictures, though – the oddities from independent distributors and the many low budget *Star Wars*/*Alien*/*Mad Max* knockoffs and sword-and-sorcery flicks. Once in a while, the campaign for a non-genre film would reference a popular movie within the genre: When New World Pictures released Francois Truffaut's drama *The Green Room*, the ad included the tagline "In The Green Room, *everyone* can hear you scream. But no one will help," a variation on *Alien*'s classic slogan.

The first half of the '80s was a golden age for fantastical films, starting with 1980's *The Empire Strikes Back* and continuing with classics and cult favorites, including *E.T. the Extra-Terrestrial*, *Return of the Jedi*, *Raiders of the Lost Ark*, *Blade Runner*, *Superman II*, the first two *Star Trek* sequels, *The Terminator*, *Ghostbusters*, the U.S. release of *Mad Max* and its sequel *The Road Warrior*, *Escape from New York*, *Flash Gordon*, *Conan the Barbarian*, *The Adventures of Buckaroo Banzai*, *The Last Starfighter*, and *The NeverEnding Story*. The genre arguably hasn't seen such a rich and diverse era since, though as it continued through to the '90s, interesting and creative works still managed to escape the studio sausage factories. You'll find all these big-ticket titles here, along with plenty of smaller, idiosyncratic movies and, for fun and variety, a number of sci-fi- and fantasy-tinged comedies. (If there's an '80s film from the scarier side of those genres you can't find here, you'll probably find it represented in *Ad Nauseam*.)

Following the form of that book, this one also assembles snippets from daily-newspaper reviews of many significant films large and small, back when they first hit theaters. Unlike the '80s' horror output, which was often tossed to second-stringers to cover, major-studio sci-fi fare from that decade and the next was considered more "legitimate" and tended to be written up by the major critics of the time. So here you'll find takes on the movies from *The New York Times*' Vincent Canby, the *Chicago Sun-Times*' Roger Ebert and that noted contrarian Rex Reed, among others. Their reactions range from raves for enduring hits to dismissals of films that would be more favorably reassessed in the ensuing years… along with scorn for legendary turkeys such as *Howard the Duck*.

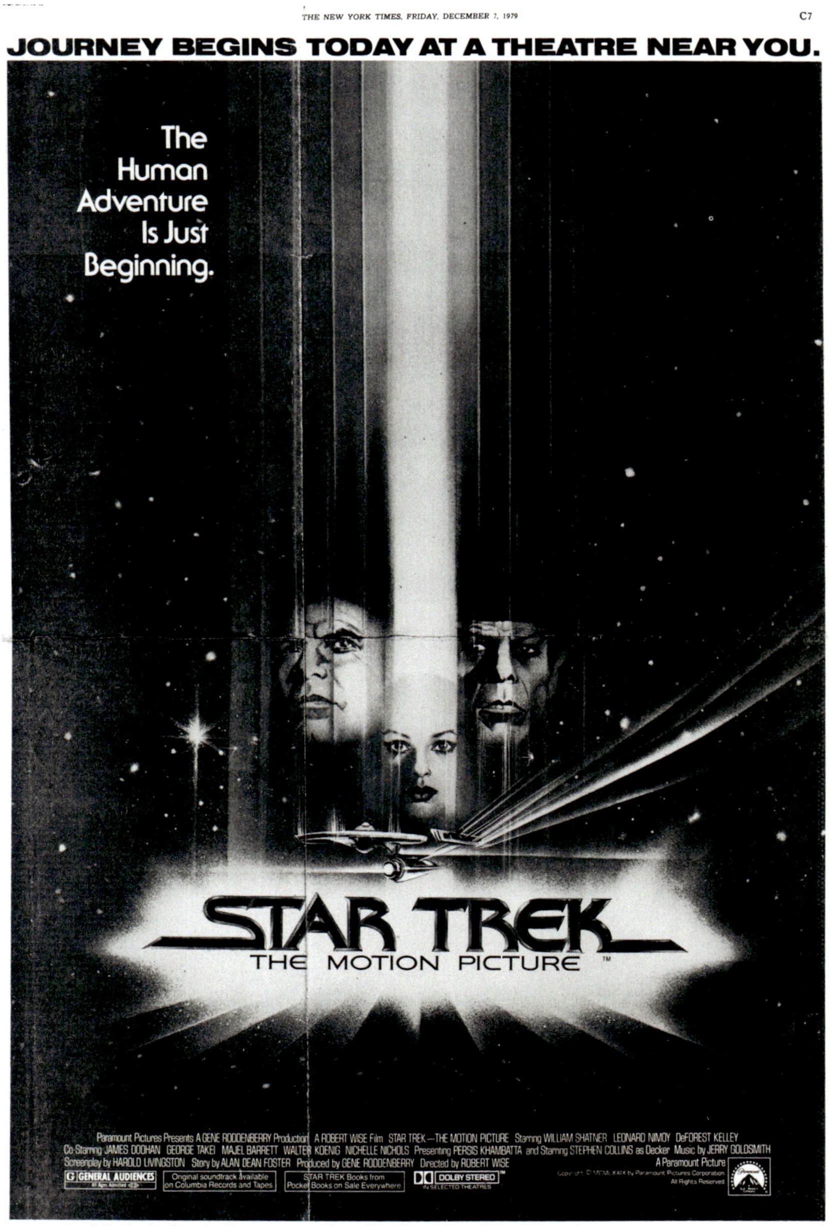

Through the pages of *Ad Astra* (that's Latin for "to the stars"), you can trace the history of science fiction and fantasy from the post-*Star Wars* boom through the rise of CGI—and the period when some papers started running the ads in full color. As such, it's appropriate that it starts with the year of *The Empire Strikes Back*, with its gritty physical environments and creatures, and ends with the one that saw the debut of the digital-effects-saturated *Star Wars: Episode I – The Phantom Menace*. You'll see trends rise and fall, and, in the ads for the first *Batman* franchise, the seeds planted for the current superhero movie boom. And a good portion of the book will take you back to a time before the Internet mainstreamed geek culture, when studios seeking to lure audiences to their expensive flights of fantasy had to depend, to a large degree, on black-and-white print imagery. Putting this collection together, I became that young fan again, poring over the daily papers to find out what adventures through other realms awaited me at local theaters. Whether you were around back then or are a younger devotee of these films, turn the page and join me on the journey...

— MICHAEL GINGOLD

FOREV

MOVIE ADS ARE WHAT MADE ME WANT TO BE A FILMMAKER.

I CAME OF AGE IN THE LATE '60S/EARLY '70S, WHEN THE FRONT PAGES OF NEWSPAPERS WERE FULL OF ASSASSINATIONS, RESIGNATIONS, WAR, AND INFLATION. But if you headed to the back of the paper, there was a page or two of complete fantasy. This was in the early days of the rating system, when X movies still bought ads next to Disney entertainment. People think of that era as this golden age of Hollywood auteurs such as Coppola/Scorsese/Altman – but if you were going to the drive-in, it was more a time of Hammer horror, Japanese monsters and Filipino women's prisons.

I began a lifelong habit of reading newspapers and magazines in reverse order from the back to the front because those ads became my top priority. Staring at those black-and-white pages, studying every photo and piece of copy, I became obsessed. I wanted to live in those ads. I was a very weird kid. In my first wallet, I didn't carry any pictures of my family; instead, there was a small cutout of a newspaper ad for *The Getaway*, with "my friends" Ali MacGraw and Steve McQueen. I'd even dumpster dive in the big garbage bins behind the local movie houses, searching for discarded pressbooks and posters that were not stained with buttered popcorn.

I bought a book that came out in 1972 called *Those Great Movie Ads*, which was exactly what the title says: a collection of newspaper ads from the classic days of Hollywood. It put the form in historical context. It's where I learned the difference between the hard sell and the soft sell, and what an ad looks like when both leading men have been promised top billing. This was in the pre-VCR days when the only way to revisit a film was to look at the ad. The book quickly became my favorite bathroom reading.

Old movie ads still fascinate me – so much so that after I found some success in the film business, I hired a relative to go into the microfilm section of my Indiana hometown library and take screen grabs of every movie ad from the Friday edition of *The South Bend Tribune* from 1969-1974. Hundreds of images – all mind-blowing. They painted a real-time picture of how movies were actually consumed. I put a few of these shots on social media, and they quickly became my most popular posts. Proustian memories of childhood days poured out, triggered by remembrances of entertainment sections past. Apparently, there are a lot of other movie-ad freaks out there.

The huge response led to me appearing on the *Trailers from Hell*-affiliated podcast *The Movies That Made Me*, hosted by Josh Olson and Joe Dante. The three of us took the wine concept of *terroir* – how a specific area's soil and climate affect the taste of the grape – and applied it to the filmgoing experience. We did that by looking at my old hometown movie ads to examine how films were locally released and sold: genre trends, weird double features, midnight movies, sneak previews, kiddie matinees and surreal drive-in triple bills. We saw how my cinematic obsessions as a kid morphed into the actual movies I've made in Hollywood – *Ed Wood* and *Dolemite Is My Name* being the obvious examples.

In the Internet age, I wonder if this has all gone away. People no longer decide what movie to see based on a small black-and-white image in a newspaper. Even in Hollywood, the only time the entertainment section gets interesting is during awards season, when full pages are bought "For

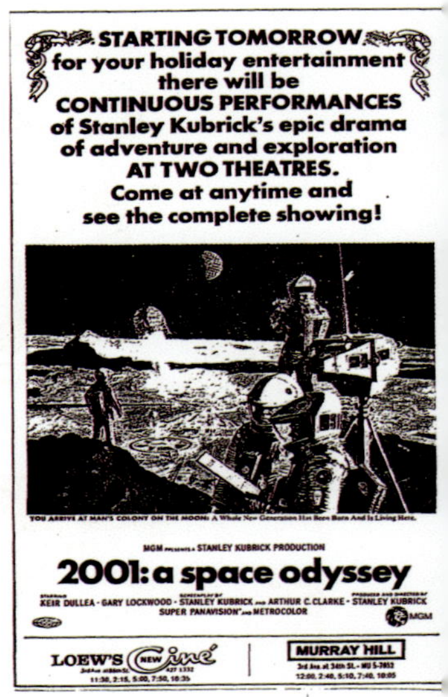

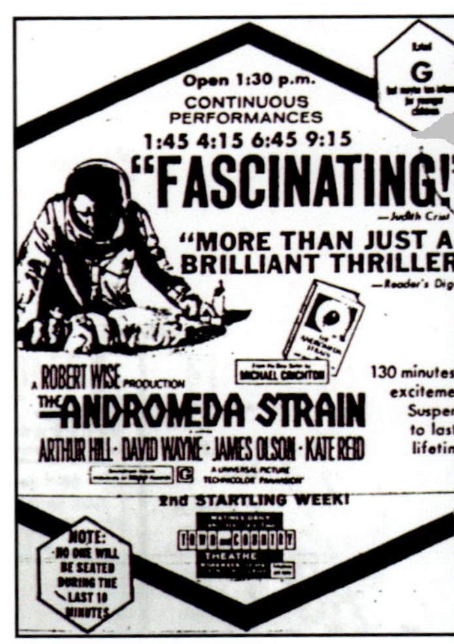

WORD

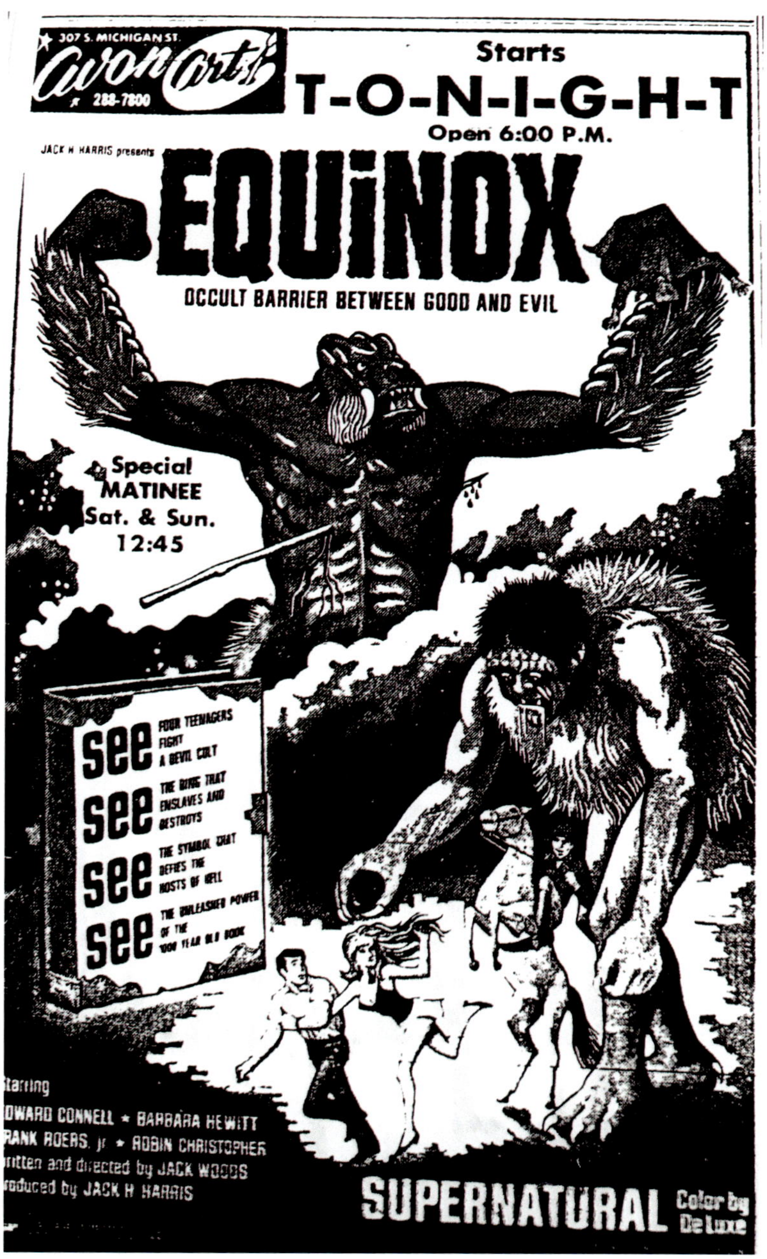

Your Consideration." Those ads can be insanely indulgent, and deserve their own coffee-table tome. But in most remaining newspapers, the movie ad page is nonexistent.

All the more reason to celebrate the fantastic job author Michael Gingold has done to celebrate the lost art of movie advertising. His glorious volume *Ad Nauseam* took us deep into the newsprint nightmares of the 1980s: slasher films, Italian terror and big-studio schlock. It was delightfully entertaining. So many forgotten films – *Dracula Blows His Cool*?!? And so many great taglines – "You don't have to go to Texas for a chainsaw massacre!" "By sword. By pick. By axe. Bye bye." And who knew *The Legend of Boggy Creek* had a sequel?

Now Michael is back with *Ad* Astra – a look at ads from the science fiction genre. Going through this collection, I instantly had a case of PTSD as I remembered lining up at a theater for the first showing of David Lynch's *Dune*. We were all so excited… until an usher started passing out a printed glossary of *Dune* terminology that we were supposed to quickly learn before we entered the theater. Here's an example: "GOM JABBAR (Gom Jab-bar): a poison needle tipped with meta-cyanide used by the Bene Gesserit." I've never seen an audience go from enthusiastic to perplexed *that* fast. This kind of memory awaits you on every page of this book. You'll flip back and forth and shout, "Oh wow! I totally forgot about that one!"

Enjoy!

LARRY KARASZEWSKI

Screenwriter
Ed Wood / The People vs. Larry Flynt
Man on the Moon / Big Eyes

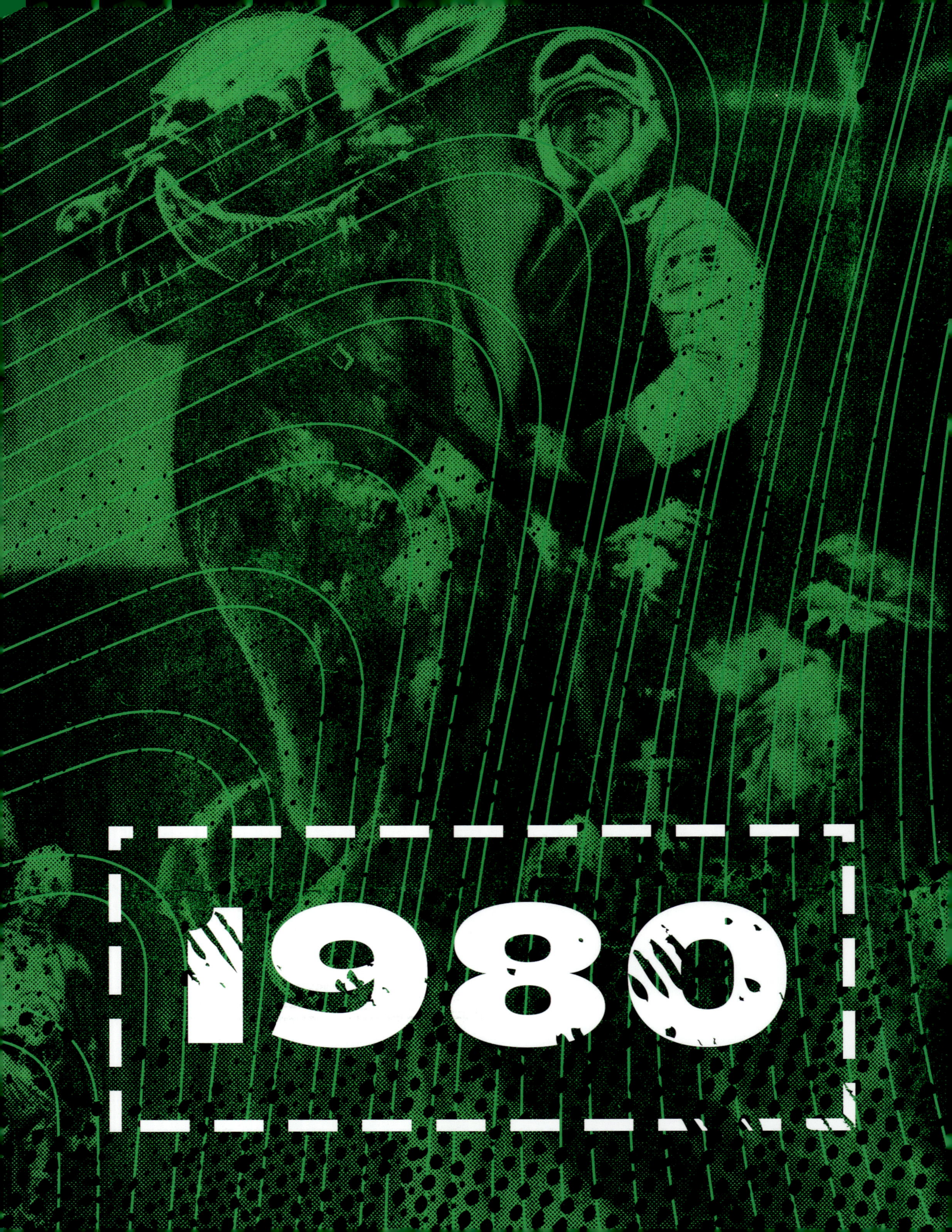
1980

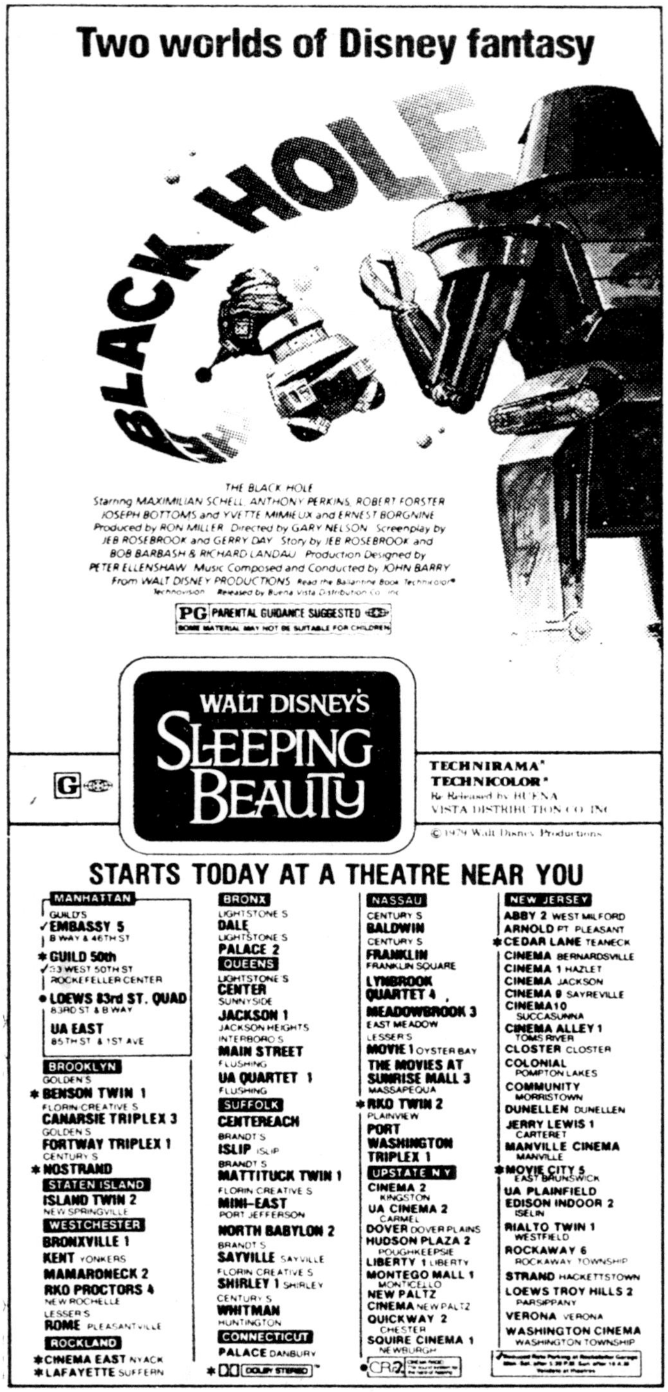

Two worlds of Disney fantasy
THE BLACK HOLE
THE BLACK HOLE
Starring MAXIMILIAN SCHELL, ANTHONY PERKINS, ROBERT FORSTER
JOSEPH BOTTOMS and YVETTE MIMIEUX and ERNEST BORGNINE
Produced by RON MILLER Directed by GARY NELSON Screenplay by
JEB ROSEBROOK and GERRY DAY Story by JEB ROSEBROOK and
BOB BARBASH & RICHARD LANDAU Production Designed by
PETER ELLENSHAW Music Composed and Conducted by JOHN BARRY
From WALT DISNEY PRODUCTIONS Read the Ballantine Book Technicolor®
Technovision Released by Buena Vista Distribution Co. Inc
PG PARENTAL GUIDANCE SUGGESTED
SOME MATERIAL MAY NOT BE SUITABLE FOR CHILDREN
G
WALT DISNEY'S
SLEEPING BEAUTY
TECHNIRAMA®
TECHNICOLOR®
Re-Released by BUENA
VISTA DISTRIBUTION CO. INC
© 1979 Walt Disney Productions
STARTS TODAY AT A THEATRE NEAR YOU
MANHATTAN
GUILD'S
✓EMBASSY 5
B'WAY & 46TH ST
*GUILD 50th
✓33 WEST 50TH ST
ROCKEFELLER CENTER
•LOEWS 83rd ST. QUAD
83RD ST & B'WAY
UA EAST
85TH ST & 1ST AVE
BROOKLYN
GOLDEN'S
*BENSON TWIN 1
FLORIN/CREATIVE'S
CANARSIE TRIPLEX 3
GOLDEN'S
FORTWAY TRIPLEX 1
CENTURY'S
*NOSTRAND
STATEN ISLAND
ISLAND TWIN 2
NEW SPRINGVILLE
WESTCHESTER
BRONXVILLE 1
KENT YONKERS
MAMARONECK 2
RKO PROCTORS 4
NEW ROCHELLE
LESSER'S
ROME PLEASANTVILLE
ROCKLAND
*CINEMA EAST NYACK
*LAFAYETTE SUFFERN
BRONX
LIGHTSTONE'S
DALE
LIGHTSTONE'S
PALACE 2
QUEENS
LIGHTSTONE'S
CENTER
SUNNYSIDE
JACKSON 1
JACKSON HEIGHTS
INTERBORO'S
MAIN STREET
FLUSHING
UA QUARTET 1
FLUSHING
SUFFOLK
CENTEREACH
BRANDT'S
ISLIP ISLIP
BRANDT'S
MATTITUCK TWIN 1
FLORIN/CREATIVE'S
MINI-EAST
PORT JEFFERSON
NORTH BABYLON 2
BRANDT'S
SAYVILLE SAYVILLE
FLORIN/CREATIVE'S
SHIRLEY 1 SHIRLEY
CENTURY'S
WHITMAN
HUNTINGTON
CONNECTICUT
PALACE DANBURY
* DOLBY STEREO™
NASSAU
CENTURY'S
BALDWIN
CENTURY'S
FRANKLIN
FRANKLIN SQUARE
LYNBROOK
QUARTET 4
MEADOWBROOK 3
EAST MEADOW
LESSER'S
MOVIE 1 OYSTER BAY
THE MOVIES AT
SUNRISE MALL 3
MASSAPEQUA
*RKO TWIN 2
PLAINVIEW
PORT
WASHINGTON
TRIPLEX 1
UPSTATE N.Y.
CINEMA 2
KINGSTON
UA CINEMA 2
CARMEL
DOVER DOVER PLAINS
HUDSON PLAZA 2
POUGHKEEPSIE
LIBERTY 1 LIBERTY
MONTEGO MALL 1
MONTICELLO
NEW PALTZ
CINEMA NEW PALTZ
QUICKWAY 2
CHESTER
SQUIRE CINEMA 1
NEWBURGH
•CR2
NEW JERSEY
ABBY 2 WEST MILFORD
ARNOLD PT. PLEASANT
*CEDAR LANE TEANECK
CINEMA BERNARDSVILLE
CINEMA 1 HAZLET
CINEMA JACKSON
CINEMA 9 SAYREVILLE
CINEMA 10
SUCCASUNNA
CINEMA ALLEY 1
TOMS RIVER
CLOSTER CLOSTER
COLONIAL
POMPTON LAKES
COMMUNITY
MORRISTOWN
DUNELLEN DUNELLEN
JERRY LEWIS 1
CARTERET
MANVILLE CINEMA
MANVILLE
*MOVIE CITY 5
EAST BRUNSWICK
UA PLAINFIELD
EDISON INDOOR 2
ISELIN
RIALTO TWIN 1
WESTFIELD
ROCKAWAY 6
ROCKAWAY TOWNSHIP
STRAND HACKETTSTOWN
LOEWS TROY HILLS 2
PARSIPPANY
VERONA VERONA
WASHINGTON CINEMA
WASHINGTON TOWNSHIP

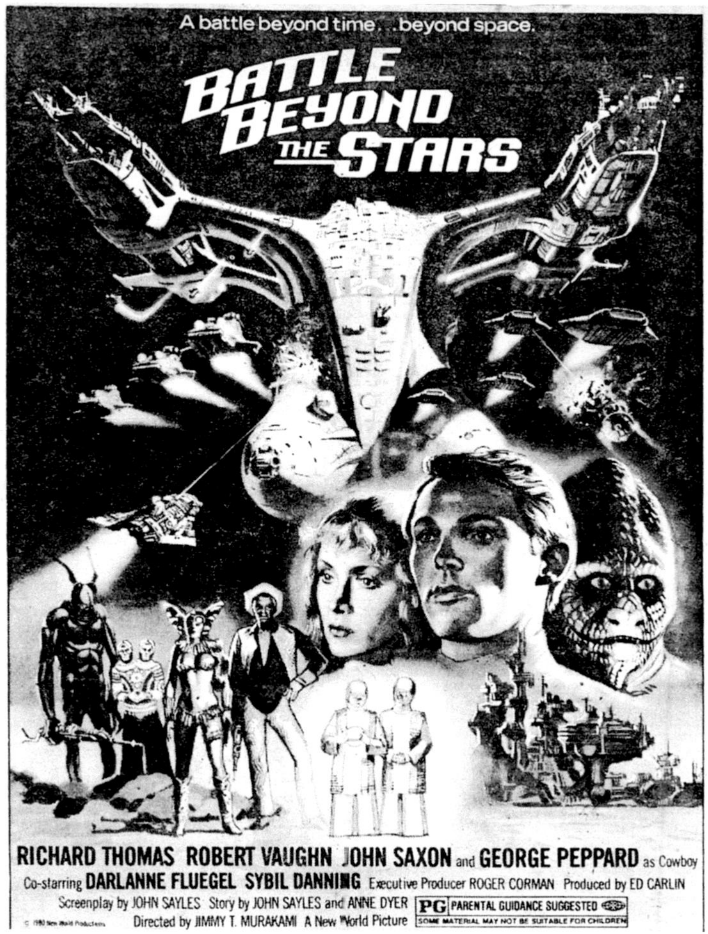

A battle beyond time... beyond space.
BATTLE BEYOND THE STARS
RICHARD THOMAS ROBERT VAUGHN JOHN SAXON and GEORGE PEPPARD as Cowboy
Co-starring DARLANNE FLUEGEL SYBIL DANNING Executive Producer ROGER CORMAN Produced by ED CARLIN
Screenplay by JOHN SAYLES Story by JOHN SAYLES and ANNE DYER
Directed by JIMMY T. MURAKAMI A New World Picture
PG PARENTAL GUIDANCE SUGGESTED
SOME MATERIAL MAY NOT BE SUITABLE FOR CHILDREN

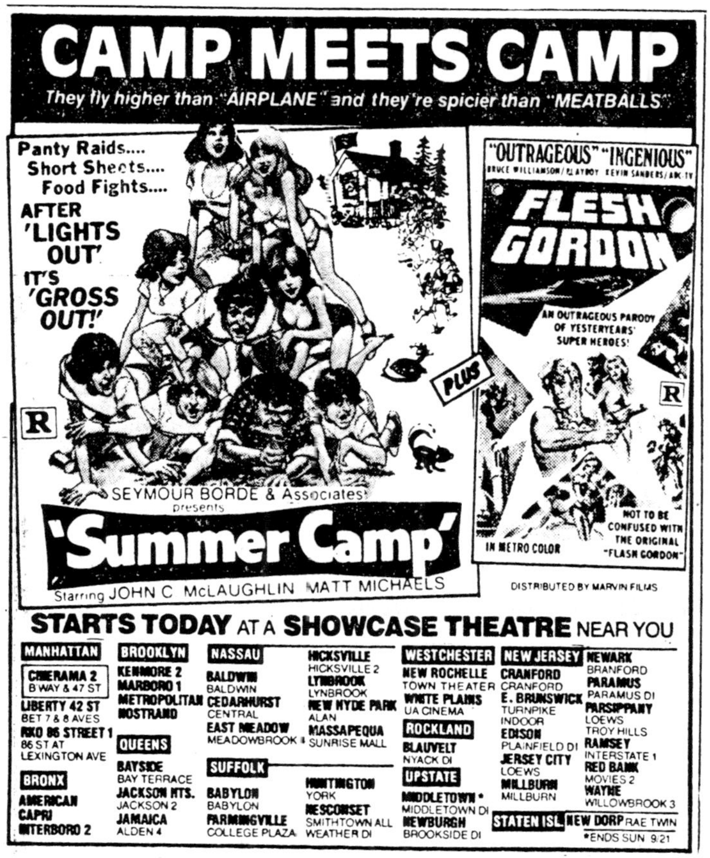

CAMP MEETS CAMP
They fly higher than "AIRPLANE" and they're spicier than "MEATBALLS"
Panty Raids....
Short Sheets....
Food Fights....
AFTER 'LIGHTS OUT' IT'S 'GROSS OUT!'
R
SEYMOUR BORDE & Associates presents
'Summer Camp'
Starring JOHN C. McLAUGHLIN MATT MICHAELS
PLUS
"OUTRAGEOUS" "INGENIOUS"
FLESH GORDON
AN OUTRAGEOUS PARODY OF YESTERYEARS' SUPER HEROES!
R
NOT TO BE CONFUSED WITH THE ORIGINAL "FLASH GORDON"
IN METRO COLOR
DISTRIBUTED BY MARVIN FILMS
STARTS TODAY AT A SHOWCASE THEATRE NEAR YOU
MANHATTAN
CINERAMA 2
B'WAY & 47 ST
LIBERTY 42 ST
BET 7 & 8 AVES
RKO 86 STREET 1
86 ST AT
LEXINGTON AVE
BRONX
AMERICAN
CAPRI
INTERBORO 2
BROOKLYN
KENMORE 2
MARBORO 1
METROPOLITAN
NOSTRAND
QUEENS
BAYSIDE
BAY TERRACE
JACKSON HTS.
JACKSON 2
JAMAICA
ALDEN 4
NASSAU
BALDWIN
BALDWIN
CEDARHURST
CENTRAL
EAST MEADOW
MEADOWBROOK
HICKSVILLE
HICKSVILLE 2
LYNBROOK
LYNBROOK
NEW HYDE PARK
ALAN
MASSAPEQUA
SUNRISE MALL
SUFFOLK
BABYLON
BABYLON
FARMINGVILLE
COLLEGE PLAZA
HUNTINGTON
YORK
NESCONSET
SMITHTOWN ALL WEATHER DI
WESTCHESTER
NEW ROCHELLE
TOWN THEATER
WHITE PLAINS
UA CINEMA
ROCKLAND
BLAUVELT
NYACK DI
UPSTATE
MIDDLETOWN*
MIDDLETOWN DI
NEWBURGH
BROOKSIDE DI
NEW JERSEY
CRANFORD
CRANFORD
E. BRUNSWICK
TURNPIKE
INDOOR
EDISON
PLAINFIELD DI
JERSEY CITY
LOEWS
MILLBURN
MILLBURN
NEWARK
BRANFORD
PARAMUS
PARAMUS DI
PARSIPPANY
LOEWS
TROY HILLS
RAMSEY
INTERSTATE 1
RED BANK
MOVIES 2
WAYNE
WILLOWBROOK 3
STATEN ISL. NEW DORP RAE TWIN
*ENDS SUN 9/21

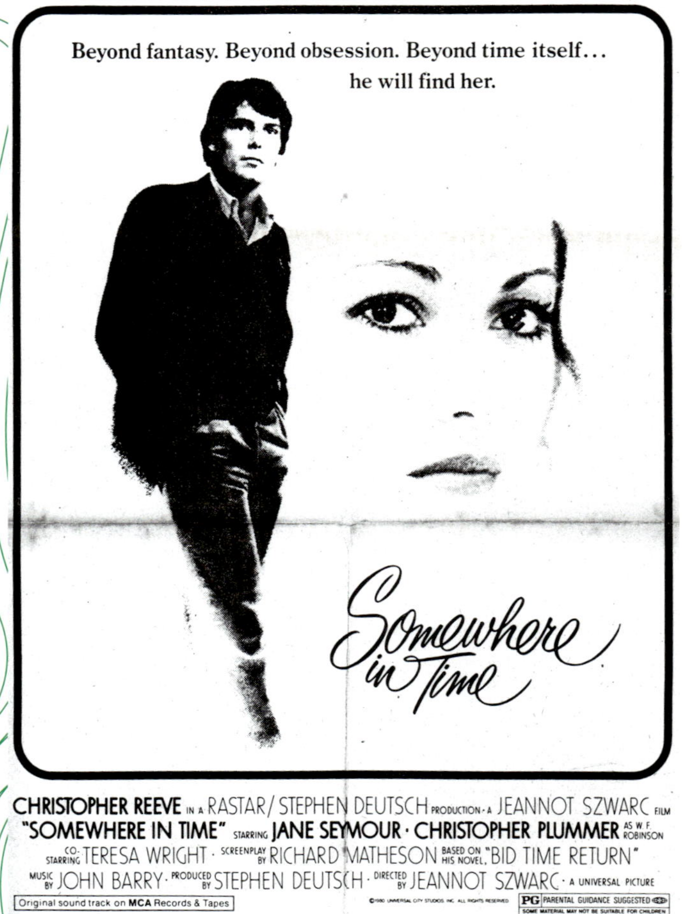

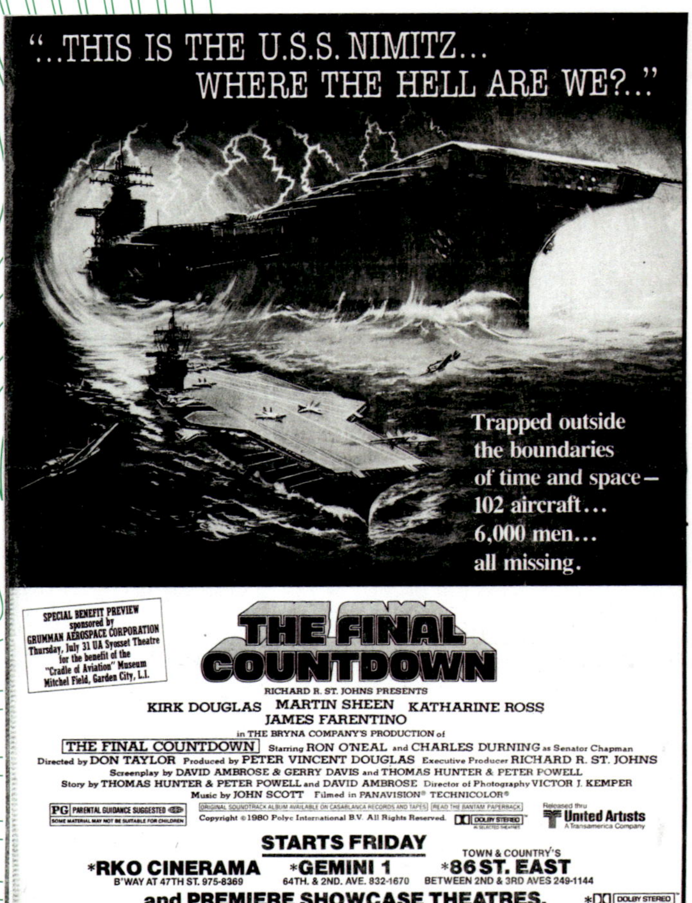

THE EMPIRE STRIKES BACK

As the '80s sci-fi boom took hold, the most eagerly awaited film was the follow-up to the commercial and critical favorite *Star Wars*. (And yes, despite the popular misconception, *Star Wars* received a number of raves upon its first release.) Today considered by many to be the very best film of the saga, *The Empire Strikes Back* was also described that way by some critics at the time, and many appreciated its more serious tone and expansion of its universe – though others had issue with its more downbeat elements.

"...[T]his sequel to *Star Wars* is more fun, more human, and more dazzling than the original. ... The excitement is without pause, the twists and bizarre characters are blends of the best technology the screen can offer."

–Rex Reed, New York *Daily News*

"I wish it were a handful of minutes shorter, but this is my single caveat about another richly imaginative, engrossing, and spectacular motion picture from the redoubtable George Lucas."

–Charles Champlin, *Los Angeles Times*

"*The Empire Strikes Back* joins *The Godfather, Part II* as one of the rarest of films – a sequel that lives up to and expands upon its original. ... It's not an exaggeration to compare the world of *Star Wars* to the Land of Oz. The *Star Wars* saga – a series of nine planned films – promises to be an even more complete world than Oz, and just as enduring."

–GENE SISKEL, *CHICAGO TRIBUNE*

"The picture isn't as funny as *Star Wars*, and its different sections aren't as smoothly coordinated. On the other hand, Kershner gives the material a sense of peril and tension that the original conspicuously lacked. If the first film was adventure-as-a-lark, *Empire* is adventure with menace and meaning."

–John Hartl, *The Seattle Times*

THE STAR WARS SAGA CONTINUES

Starring
MARK HAMILL · HARRISON FORD · CARRIE FISHER
BILLY DEE WILLIAMS · ANTHONY DANIELS as C-3PO

Co-starring DAVID PROWSE · KENNY BAKER · PETER MAYHEW FRANK OZ as Yoda

Directed by IRVIN KERSHNER Produced by GARY KURTZ

Screenplay by LEIGH BRACKETT and LAWRENCE KASDAN Story by GEORGE LUCAS

Executive Producer GEORGE LUCAS Music by JOHN WILLIAMS

PG PARENTAL GUIDANCE SUGGESTED
SOME MATERIAL MAY NOT BE SUITABLE FOR CHILDREN

ORIGINAL SOUNDTRACK ON RSO RECORDS
NOVELIZATION FROM BALLANTINE BOOKS

A Lucasfilm Ltd. Production — A Twentieth-Century Fox Release
Filmed in Panavision® — Color by Rank Film Laboratories — Prints by Deluxe®
TM: ©LUCASFILM LTD. (LFL) 1980

STARTS WEDNESDAY, MAY 21st. AT THESE SELECTED THEATRES in 70mm & DOLBY STEREO

IN MANHATTAN

LOEWS ASTOR PLAZA
44th ST. west of B'WAY • 869-8340

LOEWS ORPHEUM
86th ST. near 3rd AVE. • 289-1332

A CINEMA 5 THEATRE
MURRAY HILL
34th ST. near 3rd AVE. • 685-7652

IN NASSAU

LOEWS NASSAU QUAD
LEVITTOWN • (516) 731-5400

RKO LAWRENCE
LAWRENCE • (516) 371-0203

IN WESTCHESTER

GENERAL CINEMA
CENTRAL PLAZA CINEMA
YONKERS • (914) 793-3232

IN NEW JERSEY

GENERAL CINEMA
MENLO PARK CINEMA
EDISON • (201) 549-6767

RKO PARAMUS
PARAMUS • (201) 487-7909

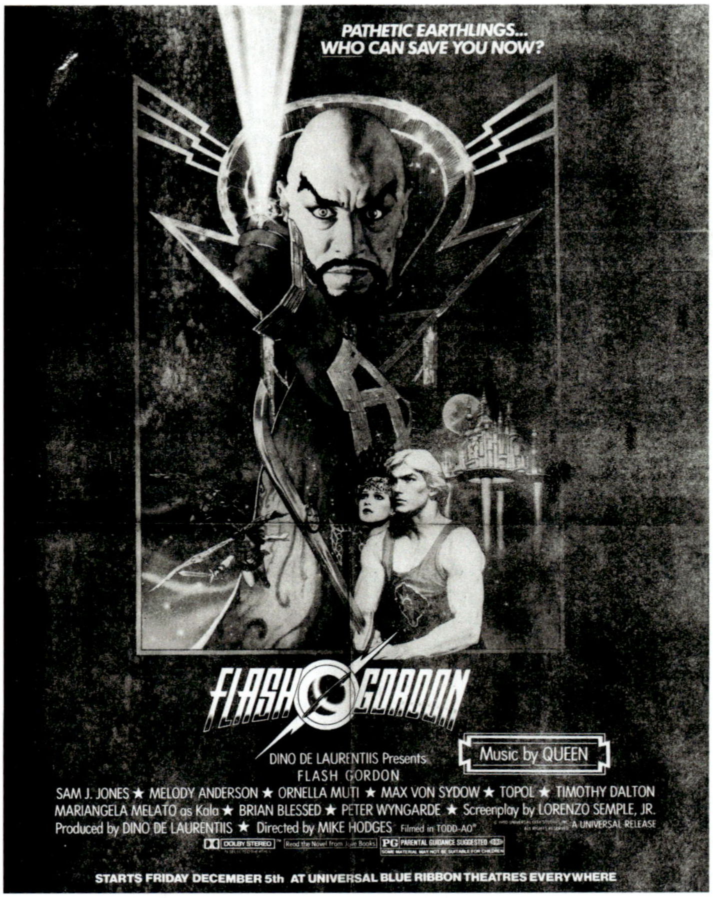

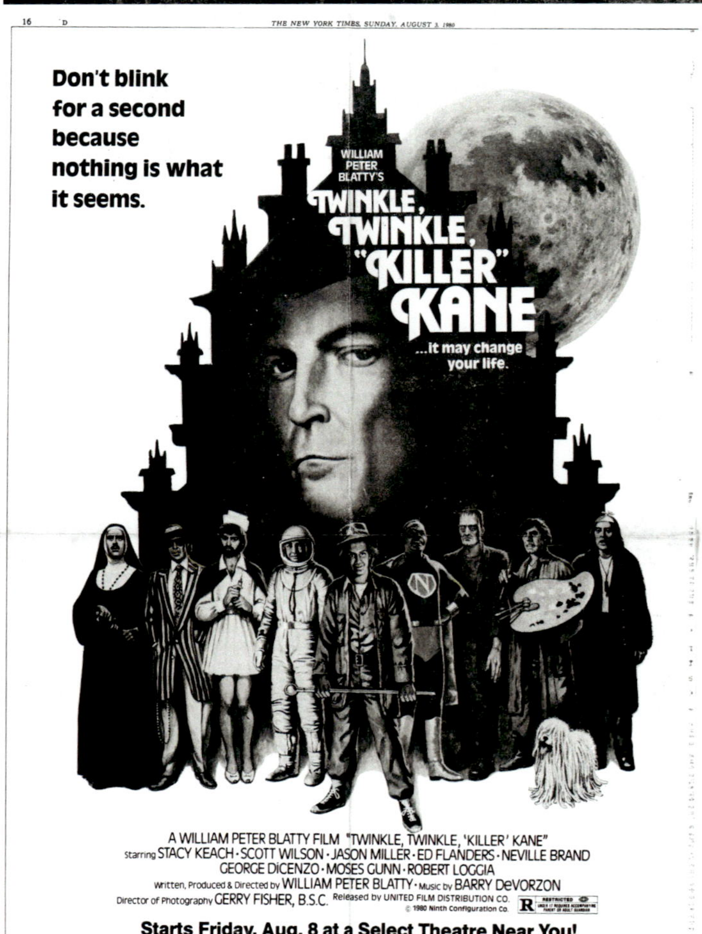

FLASH GORDON

It's said that George Lucas developed *Star Wars* because he was unable to secure the rights to make a new movie featuring comic-strip and serial hero Flash Gordon. Once Lucas' movie became a box-office force, veteran producer Dino De Laurentiis did succeed in bringing Flash back to filmdom, and he, writer Lorenzo Semple Jr. (who also penned the screenplay for the producer's 1976 *King Kong*) and director Mike Hodges (the last in a string of potential helmers that included Federico Fellini and Nicolas Roeg) did so with a full serving of camp and music by Queen. The eclectic cast led by slab of beefcake Sam J. Jones – whose performance was largely dubbed – competes with outlandish production and costume design, and the result has won a strong cult following, which appreciates it in a way many reviewers of the time did not.

"Screenwriter Lorenzo Semple has provided an energetic, if mindless, script that bounds along like a happy gazelle."

–Jack Mathews, *Detroit Free Press*

"Nothing in *Flash Gordon* is meant to be taken seriously. The villains are so evil they're ludicrous. And the heroes in their goodness generally seem stupid. ... I enjoyed every minute of it."

–R.H. GARDNER, *THE BALTIMORE SUN*

"The new, revised $20-million *Flash Gordon* is a condescending parody. It's not even as funny as the old *Batman* TV series. ... The parody of superheroes in a 30-minute TV format or a 20-minute serial was fun, but the mood can't be sustained for a 108-minute feature."

–Michael Blowen, *The Boston Globe*

"[Jones'] blond hair is so perfectly rinsed and brushed that when he falls into quicksand and is about to disappear, one worries not about Flash or [sidekick] Dale or even Earth, but about the hairdresser."

–Vincent Canby, *The New York Times*

An epic adventure filled with nonstop action!

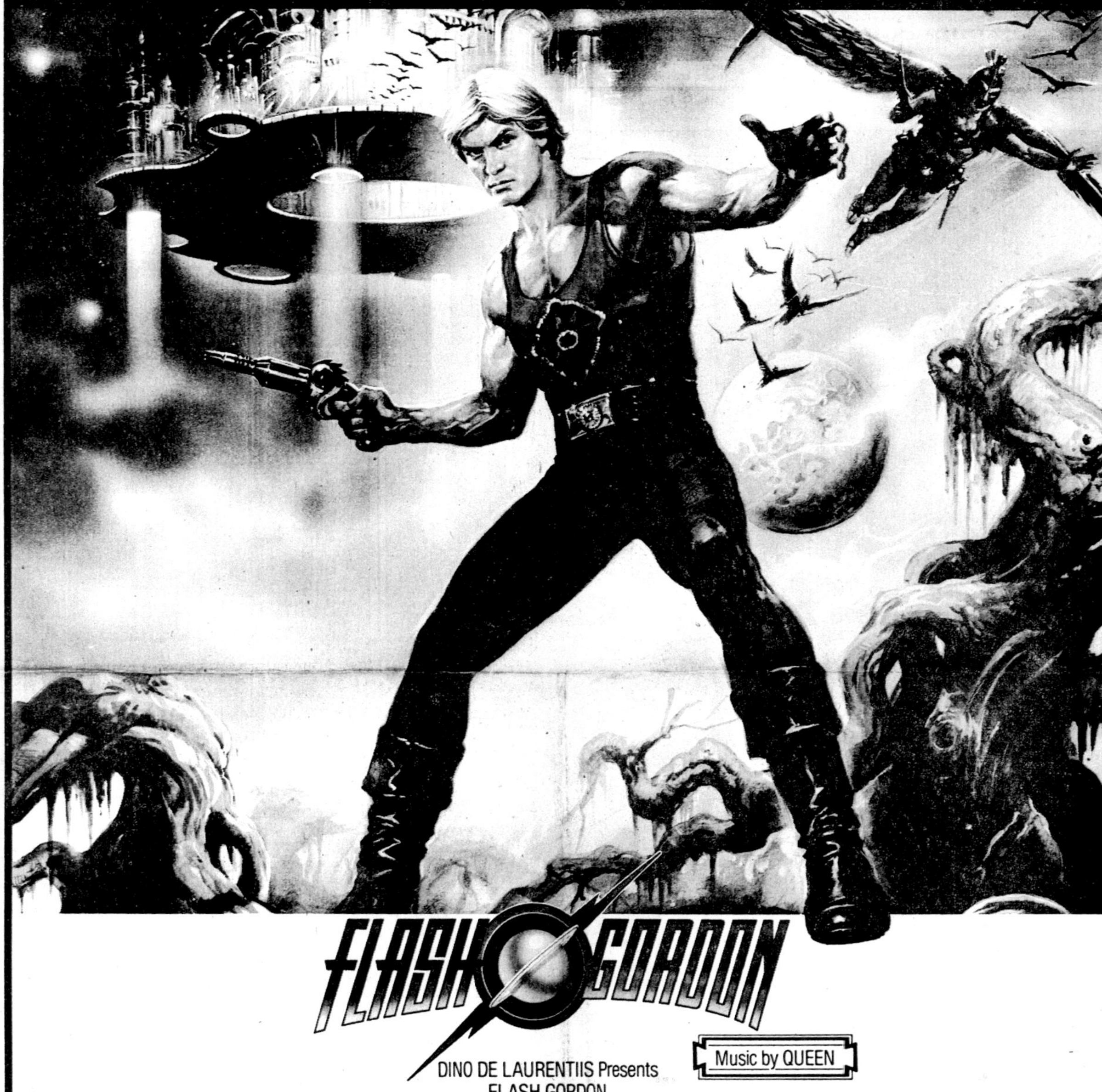

Music by QUEEN

DINO DE LAURENTIIS Presents
FLASH GORDON

SAM J. JONES ★ MELODY ANDERSON ★ ORNELLA MUTI ★ MAX VON SYDOW ★ TOPOL ★ TIMOTHY DALTON
MARIANGELA MELATO as Kala ★ BRIAN BLESSED ★ PETER WYNGARDE ★ Screenplay by LORENZO SEMPLE, JR.

DOLBY STEREO ★ IN SELECTED THEATRES — Produced by DINO DE LAURENTIIS ★ Directed by MIKE HODGES Filmed in TODD-AO®

Read the Novel from Jove Books

A UNIVERSAL RELEASE

PG PARENTAL GUIDANCE SUGGESTED — SOME MATERIAL MAY NOT BE SUITABLE FOR CHILDREN

NOW PLAYING at Universal Blue Ribbon Theatres Everywhere

MANHATTAN

- ★ RKO 86TH ST. 1 — ★ 86TH ST. & LEX. AVE. 289-8900 — 1, 3, 5, 7, 9, 11:10
- ★ GEMINI 1 — 2ND AVE. AT 64TH ST. 832-1670 — 12, 2:10, 4:15, 6:25, 8:35, 10:40
- ★ RIVOLI — B'WAY & 49th ST. 247-1633 — 12, 2:15, 4:25, 6:35, 8:45, 11
- QUAD 3 & 4 — 13TH ST. W. OF 5TH AVE. 255-8800 — 2:10, 3:10, 4:10, 5:05, 6:05, 7:05, 8, 9,10, 11, 12
- ★ EASTSIDE CINEMA — 3RD AVE. AT 55TH ST. 755-3020 — 12:30, 2:35, 4:40, 6:45, 8:50, 10:55

BRONX

- ALLERTON 1 547-2444 12:30, 2:30, 4:30, 6:25, 8:20, 10:10
- CAPRI 367-0558 • CALL FOR SHOW TIMES
- INTERBORO 2 • CALL FOR SHOW TIMES
- REDSTONE'S WHITESTONE DI BLUE 828-3330 • CALL FOR SHOW TIMES

CONNECTICUT

- GREENWICH CINEMA GREENWICH 869-4030 7:10, 9:15
- WILTON CINEMA WILTON 762-5678 7:10, 9:15

BROOKLYN

- FLORIN/CREATIVE'S CANARSIE 2 251-0700 7, 9, 11
- DUFFIELD 855-3967 • CALL FOR SHOW TIMES
- GOLDEN'S ★ FORTWAY 1 238-4200 1:55, 3:55, 5:55, 7:55, 10
- RKO KENMORE 2 284-5700 • CALL FOR SHOW TIMES
- MARBORO 1 232-4000 • CALL FOR SHOW TIMES
- CENTURY'S NOSTRAND 252-6112 • CALL FOR SHOW TIMES
- GOLDEN'S ★ OCEANA 1 743-4333 2:05, 4:05, 6:05, 8:05, 10:05

QUEENS

- RKO ALDEN 2 JAMAICA 739-8678 • CALL FOR SHOW TIMES
- QUARTET 1 FLUSHING 359-6777 • CALL FOR SHOW TIMES
- JACKSON 2 JACKSON HGHTS 335-0242 • CALL FOR SHOW TIMES
- MIDWAY 1 FOREST HILLS 261-8572 • CALL FOR SHOW TIMES
- LIGHTSTONE'S UTOPIA FLUSHING 454-2323 6, 8, 10
- CROSS BAY TWIN 1 OZONE PARK 848-1738 • CALL FOR SHOW TIMES

NASSAU

- B.S. MOSS'S CENTRAL 1 CEDARHURST 569-0105 7, 9, 11
- HICKSVILLE 2 HICKSVILLE 931-0749 • CALL FOR SHOW TIMES
- LYNBROOK 2 LYNBROOK 593-1033 • CALL FOR SHOW TIMES
- MEADOWBROOK 1 EAST MEADOW 735-7552 • CALL FOR SHOW TIMES
- PLAYHOUSE GREAT NECK 482-0500 • CALL FOR SHOW TIMES
- ★ SUNRISE MALL 6 MASSAPEQUA 795-2244 • CALL FOR SHOW TIMES
- WESTBURY D.I. WESTBURY 334-3400 • CALL FOR SHOW TIMES

SUFFOLK

- ★ BABYLON BABYLON 669-0200 • CALL FOR SHOW TIMES
- EASTHAMPTON 1 EASTHAMPTON 324-0448 • CALL FOR SHOW TIMES
- PATCHOGUE PATCHOGUE 475-0600 • CALL FOR SHOW TIMES
- CENTURY'S ★ SHORE 1 HUNTINGTON 421-5200 • CALL FOR SHOW TIMES
- SMITHTOWN SMITHTOWN 265-1551 • CALL FOR SHOW TIMES
- BAYSHORE D.I. BAYSHORE 665-1111 • CALL FOR SHOW TIMES

WESTCHESTER

- ★ BRONXVILLE 2 BRONXVILLE 961-4030 • CALL FOR SHOW TIMES
- UA CINEMA 946-2820 WHITE PLAINS • CALL FOR SHOW TIMES
- ★ MAMARONECK 1 MAMARONECK 698-2200 • CALL FOR SHOW TIMES
- RKO PROCTORS 2 NEW ROCHELLE 632-1101 • CALL FOR SHOW TIMES
- LESSER'S TRIANGLE YORKTOWN HEIGHTS 245-7555 7, 9

STATEN ISLAND

- ISLAND 2 761-6666 NEW SPRINGVILLE • CALL FOR SHOW TIMES

UPSTATE

- CARMEL 1 CARMEL 225-6500 • CALL FOR SHOW TIMES
- UA CINEMA 304 NEW CITY 634-8200 • CALL FOR SHOW TIMES
- ATM FINE ARTS 2 DANBURY, CONN. 775-0070 7:10, 9:15
- C.A.T.E.'S HUDSON PLAZA 1 POUGHKEEPSIE 454-2080 7:20, 9:30
- READE'S ★ MAYFAIR 1 KINGSTON 336-5313 2, 4:35, 7:10, 9:15
- MOVIES FOUR 4 DUTCHESS MALL FISHKILL 896-7220 5, 7, 9
- PEARL RIVER PEARL RIVER 735-6500 • CALL FOR SHOW TIMES
- C.A.T.E.'S WINDSOR 2 NEW WINDSOR 565-7777 7:20, 9:30

* CR CINEMA RADIO The sound system for the hard of hearing

★ DOLBY STEREO

NEW JERSEY

- MUSIC MAKERS' ABBY 2 728-8886 WEST MILLFORD 7:15, 9:20
- TM ★ ALLWOOD 1 CLIFTON 778-9747 7, 9:15
- REDSTONE'S ★ AMBOY SIXPLEX 6 SAYREVILLE 721-3400 2:15, 5, 7:45, 10:10, 12:20
- NATHAN'S BERKELEY 464-8888 BERKELEY HGHTS 7:15, 9:30
- RKO BRANFORD 1 NEWARK 623-5236 • CALL FOR SHOW TIMES
- CINEMA 35 PARAMUS 845-5070 7:50, 10
- CINEMA SERVICE'S CLAIRIDGE 746-5564 MONTCLAIR 7:30, 9:30
- REDSTONE'S NEWARK D.I. NEWARK 624-2330 • CALL FOR SHOW TIMES
- COLONY 992-0800 LIVINGSTON • CALL FOR SHOW TIMES
- MUSIC MAKERS' COMMUNITY 2 EATONTOWN 542-4200 7:20, 9:35
- MUSIC MAKERS' DOVER 2 TOMS RIVER 244-5454 7:20, 9:30
- FOX HACKENSACK 488-8000 • CALL FOR SHOW TIMES
- H'WAY 1 FAIRLAWN 796-1717 • CALL FOR SHOW TIMES
- LOEW'S HARMON COVE 1 SECAUCUS 866-1000 • CALL FOR SHOW TIMES
- TURNPIKE 2 E. BRUNSWICK 257-5050 • CALL FOR SHOW TIMES
- WAYNE WAYNE 694-4136 • CALL FOR SHOW TIMES
- MUSIC MAKERS' INTERSTATE 1 RAMSEY 327-0153 7:15, 9:30
- WOODS' LINDEN 1 925-9787 LINDEN 7, 9:10
- NATHAN'S SPARTA 1 SPARTA 729-5710 7, 9
- MUSIC MAKERS' ★ MALL 3 477-6661 BRICKTOWN 7:20, 9:30
- MIDDLESEX MALL 1 S. PLAINFIELD 548-3100 • CALL FOR SHOW TIMES
- MIDDLETOWN SEVEN 1 MIDDLETOWN 671-1020 • CALL FOR SHOW TIMES
- RKO MILLBURN 1 MILLBURN 376-0800 • CALL FOR SHOW TIMES
- NATHAN'S WASHINGTON 1 WASHINGTON 689-0451 • CALL FOR SHOW TIMES
- GENERAL CINEMA'S MORRIS COUNTY MALL 1 HANOVER TOWNSHIP 539-7966 1, 3:10, 5:15, 7:20, 9:30
- MUSIC MAKERS' QUAD 3 FREEHOLD 462-0600 7:20, 9:35
- RIALTO 2 WESTFIELD 232-1288 • CALL FOR SHOW TIMES
- AMC'S ★ ROCKAWAY 6, 1 ROCKAWAY TOWNSHIP 328-0666 5, 7:30, 9:55
- SHOWBOAT 3 EDGEWATER 941-3660 • CALL FOR SHOW TIMES
- GENERAL CINEMA'S SOMMERVILLE CIRCLE 3 RARITAN 526-0101 • CALL FOR SHOW TIMES
- STATE 1 653-5200 JERSEY CITY • CALL FOR SHOW TIMES
- TRI-STATE'S TRI-STATE MATAMORAS 491-4131 7:15, 9:15

PLEASE CHECK DAILY AS SHOWTIMES ARE SUBJECT TO CHANGE

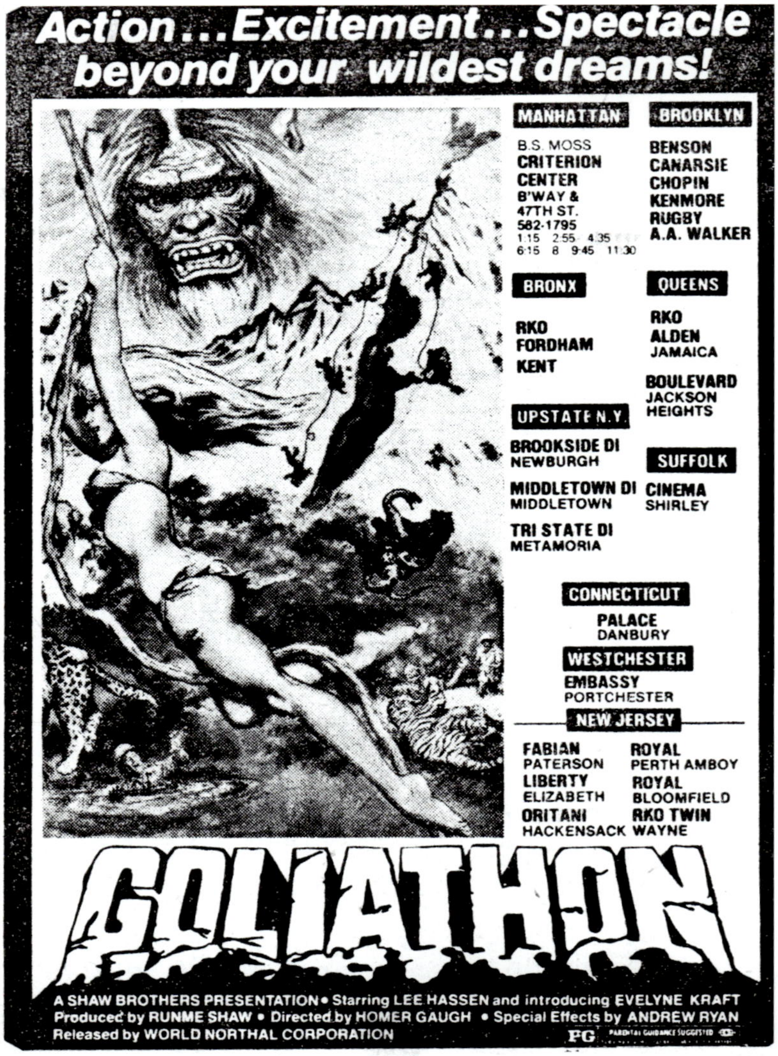

GOLIATHON

Distributor World Northal, whose stock in trade was martial arts flicks, unleashed a different kind of Asian action in the U.S. when it imported and retitled the Shaw Brothers' 1977 production *Mighty Peking Man.* A transparent, schlocky but still entertaining knockoff of the '76 *King Kong* remake, it was directed by one of the studio's busiest filmmakers, Ho Meng Hua (billed as "Homer Gaugh"), and stars Danny Lee, prior to his fame in John Woo action epics. The only review I could find for this release was by a Honolulu critic; although he seemed unfamiliar with the film at the time, he later noted that it had played as *Mighty Peking Man* in Cantonese at a local Chinese-language theater just a month before it turned up in this dubbed version.

"At no time do they call the ape Goliathon. They call him Peking Man presumably because he likes to peek through windows at the jungle girl. Movies like this can be fun if you're not expecting high art. ... Anyway, it's better than *Raise the Titanic*."

–Burl Burlingame, *Honolulu Star-Bulletin*

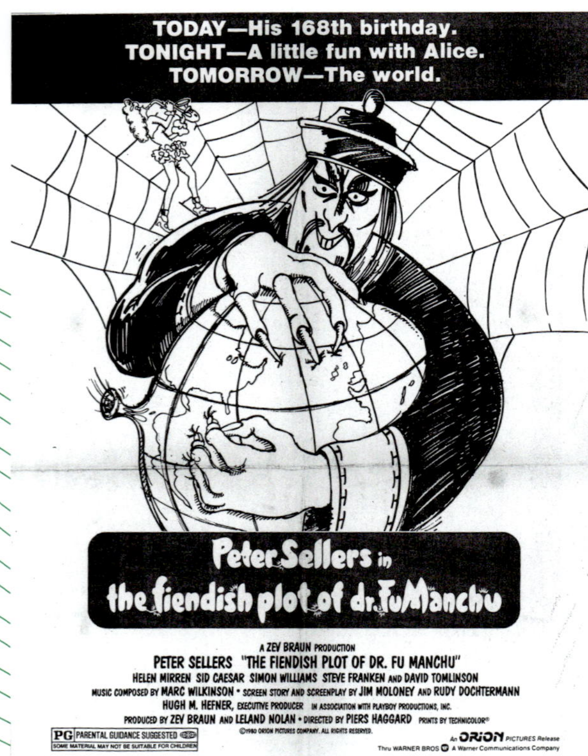

MAD MAX

A hit across the rest of the world, Australian filmmaker George Miller's high-octane futuristic smash-'em-up *Mad Max* didn't do as well in the States, where the heavy accents of the cast (led by a young Mel Gibson) were redubbed in "American." The altered voices weren't the issue with most critics, however; instead, they went after the movie for its metal- and flesh-rending violence. Only later, with the release of *Mad Max 2* (redubbed *The Road Warrior* in the U.S.), was Miller's debut feature reconsidered as a low-budget triumph.

"[L]ittle more than 90 minutes of brutal, high-speed car and motorcycle chases. ... Max [is] played by Mel Gibson, who looks like a thin Rex Reed."

–Gene Siskel, *Chicago Tribune*

"Gibson is exactly right for his role and at times even appears capable of acting. Some day, he's liable to get a part in a real movie, and then he might become a star."

–Henry Edgar, Newport News, VA *Daily Press*

> "...*Mad Max* is a disturbing cheapie that could only appeal to frustrated Hell's Angels rejects and people who think dead baby jokes are funny."
>
> **–MARYLYNN URICCHIO, *PITTSBURGH POST-GAZETTE***

"*Mad Max* is a road action picture of such awful, shallow predictability, populated by such uninviting and uninteresting people, that it is almost worth seeing as a textbook example of how not to make a film."

–Charles Champlin, *Los Angeles Times*

"*Mad Max* is ugly and incoherent, and aimed, probably accurately, at the most uncritical of moviegoers."

–Tom Buckley, *The New York Times*

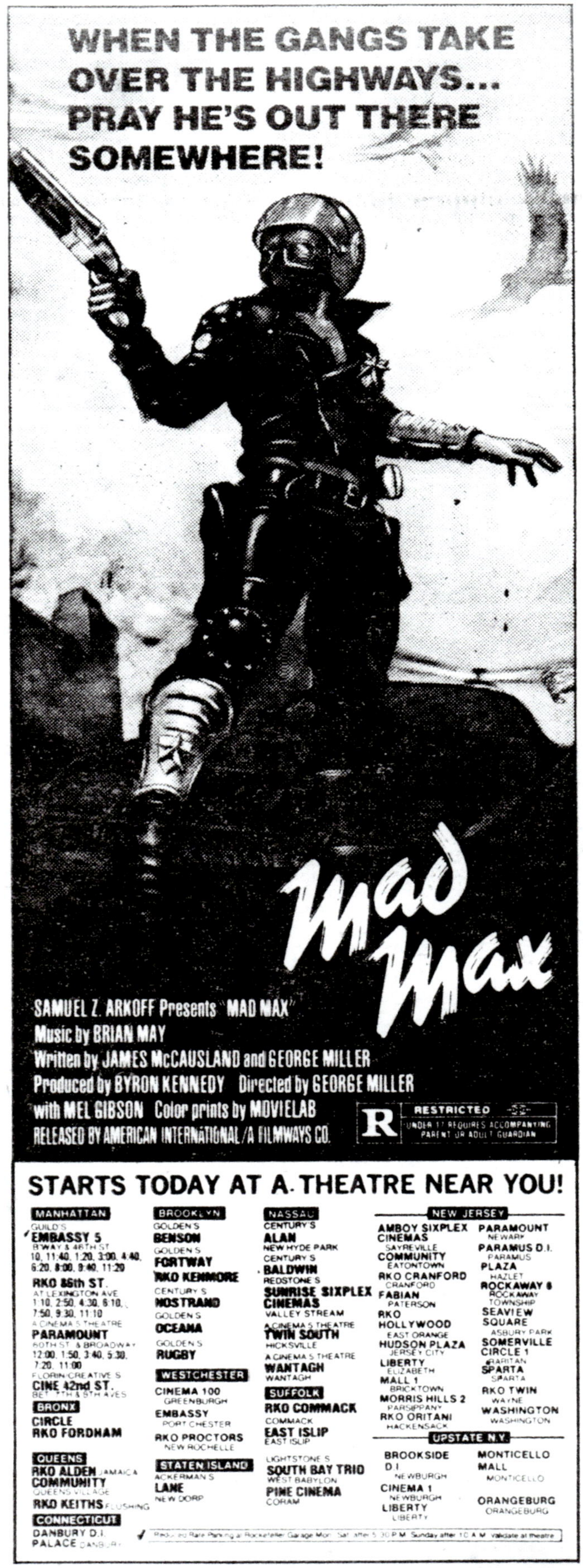

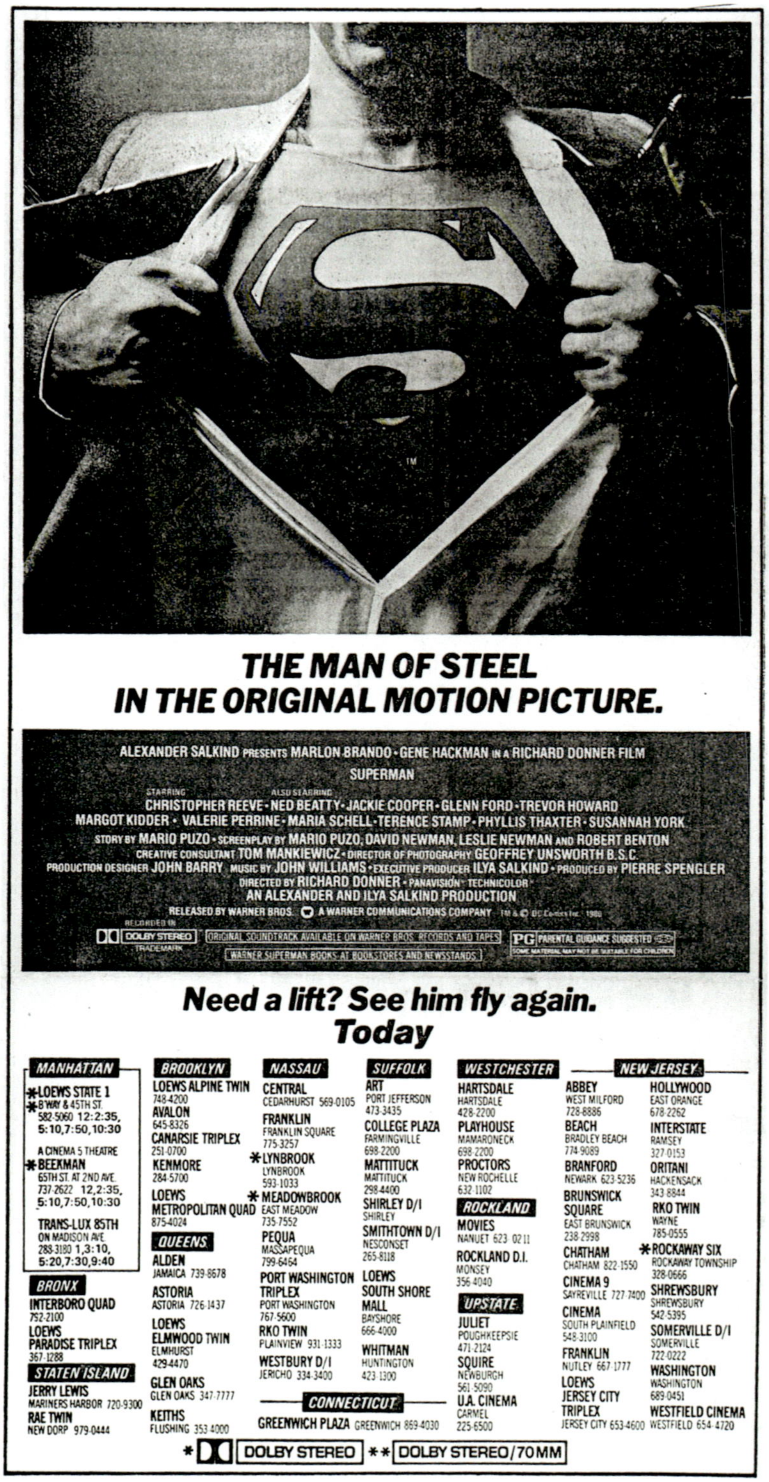

POPEYE

Following just one week on the heels of *Flash Gordon*, another comic-strip character, Popeye the Sailor Man, came to theaters in his first big-budget cinematic showcase. Paramount Pictures and Walt Disney Pictures joined forces on the project, which brought together an unusual creative team: director Robert Altman, satirical cartoonist Jules Feiffer as screenwriter, and Harry Nilsson writing the songs. Robin Williams, in his first leading movie role after becoming a TV star on *Mork and Mindy*, was a more obvious choice to play Popeye (under heavy makeup), and Shelley Duvall was even more so as Olive Oyl. All their combined efforts, and a sizable budget, couldn't rescue *Popeye* from becoming a box-office lightweight, however, and the critical response ran the gamut.

"This is what Hollywood constantly talks about making, but almost never does with any skill – a cartoon with real people in it. It's a perfect holiday film for the family, entirely faithful to the spirit and sensibility behind the original entertaining comic strip."

–Bruce McCabe, *The Boston Globe*

"Sitting through Robert Altman's *Popeye* is like having poison oak and not being able to scratch. This is a mean-spirited, joyless musical in which almost nothing happens."

–JOHN STARK, *SAN FRANCISCO EXAMINER*

"*Popeye* is…a flawed extravagance, but if you can survive its stumbling pace, its mumbling actors and its dreadful songs, you will eventually experience a charming, unique fantasy world quite unlike anything you've seen before."

–Rex Reed, New York *Daily News*

"Despite its style, technical polish and nostalgic value, *Popeye* is an even greater comic strip-to-film failure than the current *Flash Gordon*, which is at least true to its original action spirit. Feiffer's screenplay includes almost no action in the early going."

–Jack Mathews, *Detroit Free Press*

HAVES A HAPPY HOLIDAY WIT ME AN' OLIVE!

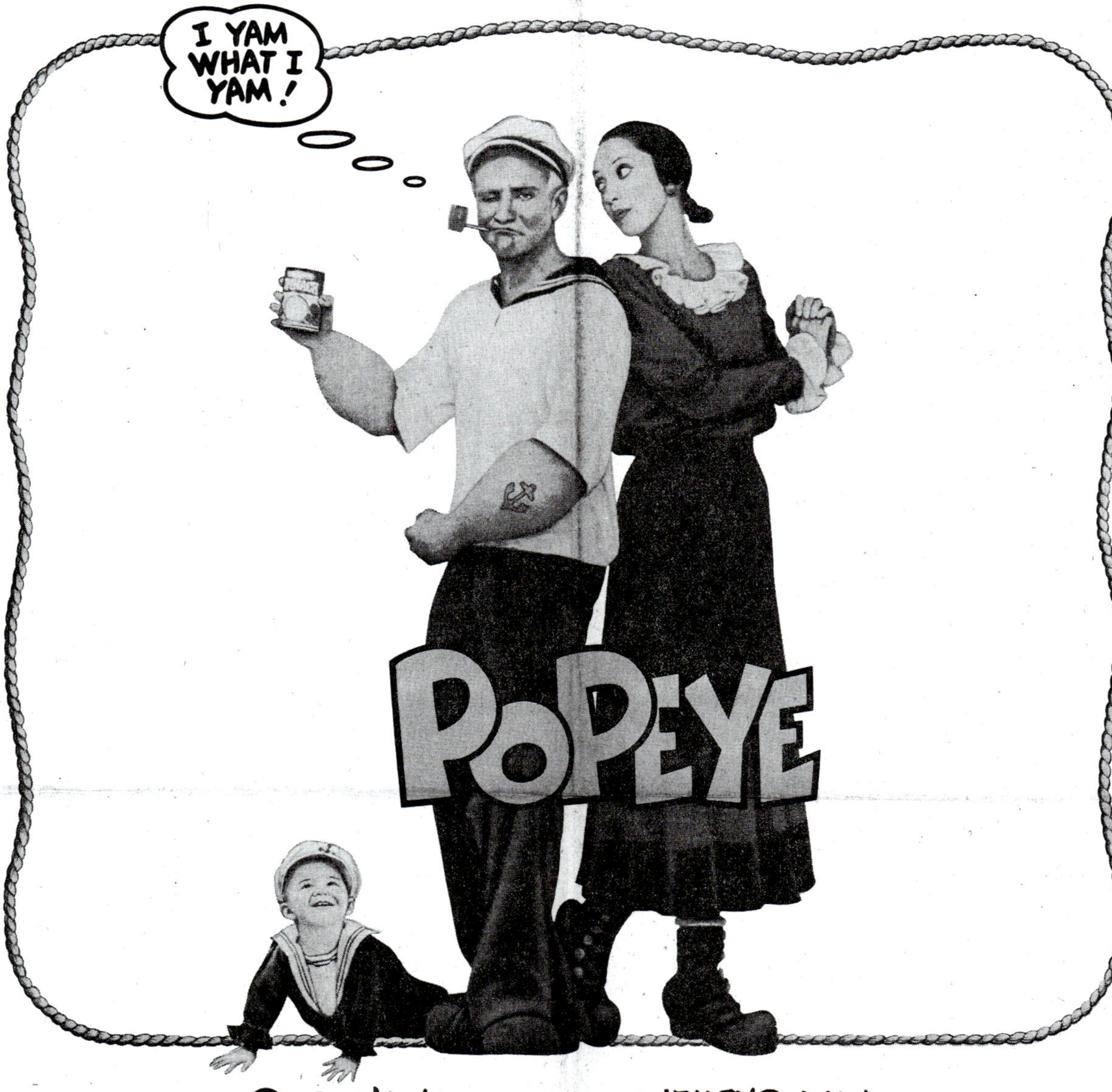

ROBIN WILLIAMS is POPEYE AND SHELLEY DUVALL is OLIVE OYL

PARAMOUNT PICTURES CORPORATION AND WALT DISNEY PRODUCTIONS PRESENT A ROBERT EVANS PRODUCTION A ROBERT ALTMAN FILM ROBIN WILLIAMS SHELLEY DUVALL POPEYE RAY WALSTON PAUL DOOLEY PAUL L. SMITH RICHARD LIBERTINI DONALD MOFFAT MUSIC & LYRICS BY HARRY NILSSON EXECUTIVE PRODUCER C. O. ERICKSON SCREENPLAY BY JULES FEIFFER PRODUCED BY ROBERT EVANS DIRECTED BY ROBERT ALTMAN READ THE AVON MOVIE NOVEL™ ORIGINAL SOUNDTRACK ALBUM FROM THE BOARDWALK ENTERTAINMENT CO.

PG PARENTAL GUIDANCE SUGGESTED
SOME MATERIAL MAY NOT BE SUITABLE FOR CHILDREN

A PARAMOUNT PICTURE

STARTS TODAY

MANHATTAN
LOEWS STATE 1 B'way & 45th St.
Fri, Sat, & Sun: 12, 2:10, 4:20, 6:30, 8:45, 11
LOEWS ORPHEUM 1 86th St. near 3rd Ave.
Fri, Sat, & Sun: 12, 2:10, 4:20, 6:30, 8:40, 10:50
Walter Reade's BAY CINEMA 32nd St. and 2nd Ave.
Fri: 12, 2:10, 4:20, 6:30, 8:40, 10:50
Sat: 12:10, 2:20, 4:30, 6:40, 8:50, 11
Sun: 1, 3:10, 5:20, 7:30, 9:40

BRONX
LOEWS AMERICAN TWIN
CITY CINEMA
DALE
LOEWS PARADISE QUAD

BROOKLYN
LOEWS GEORGETOWNE TWIN
RKO KENMORE
✓OCEANA 1
LOEWS ORIENTAL TWIN

NASSAU
Century's ALAN NEW HYDE PARK
RKO LAWRENCE LAWRENCE
LYNBROOK 1 LYNBROOK
THE MOVIES AT SUNRISE MALL MASSEPEQUA
LOEWS NASSAU QUAD LEVITTOWN
Century's ✓ROOSEVELT FIELD 2 GARDEN CITY

SUFFOLK
EAST HAMPTON EAST HAMPTON
ELWOOD ELWOOD
SOUTH BAY TRIO WEST BABYLON
LOEWS STONYBROOK TRIPLEX STONYBROOK
SUNWAVE 1 PATCHOGUE

QUEENS
BOULEVARD 1 JACKSON HEIGHTS
RKO KEITH FLUSHING
Century's MEADOWS 2 FRESH MEADOWS
✓LOEWS TRYLON FOREST HILLS

WESTCHESTER
CINEMA 22 BEDFORD VILLAGE
HARTSDALE CINEMA 3 HARTSDALE
MOVIELAND YONKERS
RKO PROCTOR NEW ROCHELLE
RYE RIDGE PORTCHESTER
WESTCHESTER MALL TRIPLEX 2 PEEKSKILL

ROCKLAND
NANUET ROUTE 59

UPSTATE N.Y.
KINGSTON KINGSTON TRIPLEX
LIBERTY LIBERTY TRIPLEX 2
MONROE MONROE
NEWBURGH SQUIRE TWIN

STATEN ISLAND
AMBOY TWIN ELTINGVILLE
RAE TWIN NEW DORP

CONNECTICUT
STAMFORD PALACE

✓CR CINEMA RADIO The sound system for the hard-of-hearing.

NEW JERSEY
BLOOMFIELD RKO ROYAL
BRICKTOWN MALL
CLIFTON CLIFTON 1
EAST BRUNSWICK LOEWS ROUTE 18 TWIN
EDGEWATER SHOWBOAT 3
FRANKLIN TOWNSHIP RUTGERS PLAZA 1
FREEHOLD POND ROAD
JERSEY CITY LOEWS JERSEY CITY TRIPLEX
MIDDLETOWN CINEMA 1
NEWTON NEWTON TWIN
✓PARAMUS RKO ROUTE 4
PARSIPPANY MORRIS HILLS 1
RIDGEWOOD RKO WARNER
ROCKAWAY TOWNSHIP ROCKAWAY 6
SAYREVILLE AMBOY SIXPLEX CINEMAS 4
SECAUCUS LOEWS HARMON COVE QUAD
SHREWSBURY CINEMA 2
SUCCASUNNA CINEMA 10 # 1
TOMS RIVER OCEAN COUNTY MALL 2
TOTOWA TOTOWA 2
UNION RKO UNION
WATCHUNG BLUE STAR 3
WEST ORANGE ESSEX GREEN 2
WEST END MOVIES 1

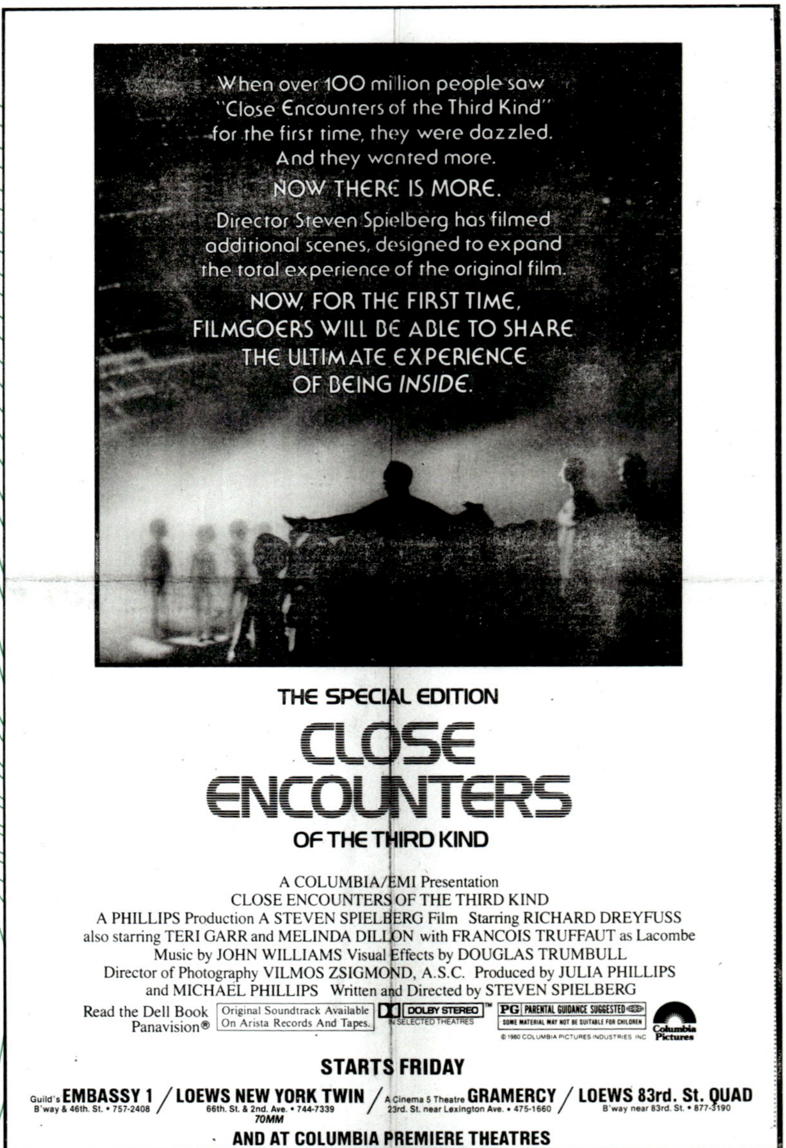

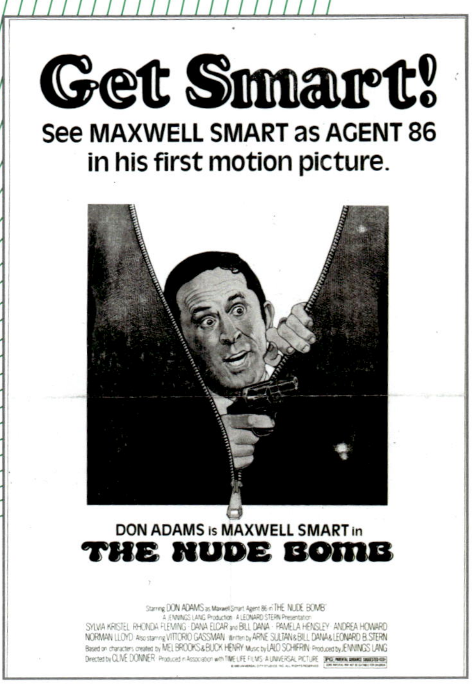

XANADU

Among other things, 1980 will be remembered as the year the screen musical reached its nadir. *Can't Stop the Music*, featuring Village People, put the final nail in the coffin of disco; Neil Diamond's *The Jazz Singer* did much better as an album than a movie; Cannon Films' extravagant *The Apple* barely got released at all; and *Xanadu*, a fantasy-tinged showcase for songs by ELO and star Olivia Newton-John (with veteran hoofer Gene Kelly in his last film role), had its critics' screenings cancelled at the last minute. Those reviewers who did venture out to cover this tale of a frustrated artist finding his magical, rollerskating muse were not, by and large, whistling a happy tune.

"To be sure, it's no *Singin' in the Rain*, but by golly it does have that classic's vibrant and charming star Gene Kelly and is a perfectly acceptable summer cooler that's been smoothly directed by Robert Greenwald."

–Kevin Thomas, *Los Angeles Times*

"So far, wherever it has played, the musical fantasy *Xanadu* with Olivia Newton-John has been laughed off the screen by critics calling it one of the year's worst films. But it's not that bad. It's more ridiculously naive than awful."

–Gene Siskel, *Chicago Tribune*

"Watching *Xanadu* is like watching instant kitsch. One ludicrous scene follows the next, and after a while, one doesn't know whether to laugh, cry or hiss. Or leave."

–ELEANOR RINGEL, *THE ATLANTA CONSTITUTION*

"The movie approaches desperation at times in its attempt to be all things to all audiences. ... There are times when *Xanadu* doesn't even feel like a movie fantasy, but like a shopping list of marketable pop images."

–Roger Ebert, *Chicago Sun-Times*

"In the end, *Xanadu* is a close cousin of the dismal *Sgt. Pepper's Lonely Hearts Club Band*, a film detested by critics everywhere, but adored by 11-year-old girls everywhere."

–Jon Marlowe, *The Miami News*

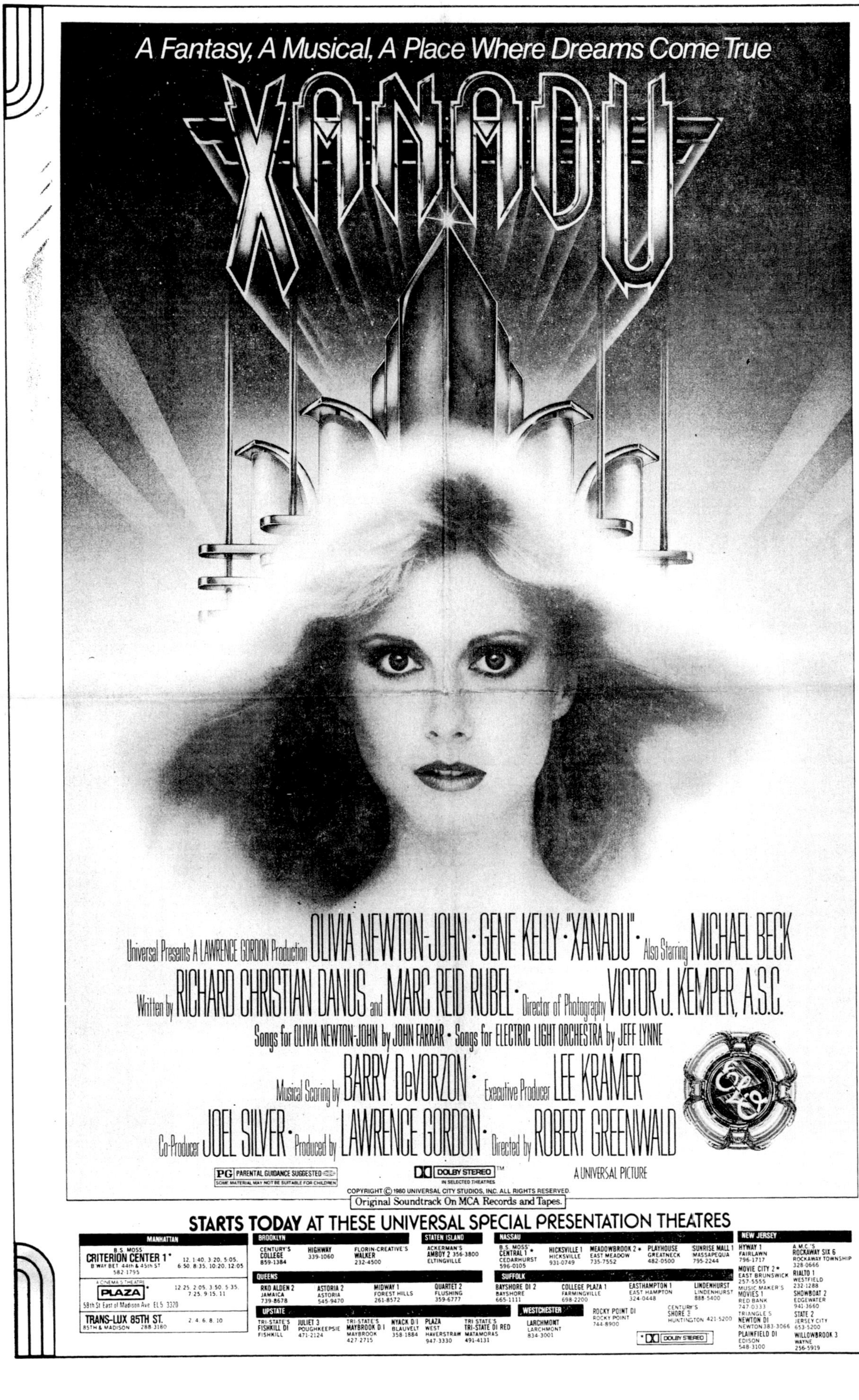
A Fantasy, A Musical, A Place Where Dreams Come True
XANADU
Universal Presents A LAWRENCE GORDON Production OLIVIA NEWTON-JOHN · GENE KELLY "XANADU" · Also Starring MICHAEL BECK
Written by RICHARD CHRISTIAN DANUS and MARC REID RUBEL · Director of Photography VICTOR J. KEMPER, A.S.C.
Songs for OLIVIA NEWTON-JOHN by JOHN FARRAR · Songs for ELECTRIC LIGHT ORCHESTRA by JEFF LYNNE
Musical Scoring by BARRY DeVORZON · Executive Producer LEE KRAMER
Co-Producer JOEL SILVER · Produced by LAWRENCE GORDON · Directed by ROBERT GREENWALD
PG PARENTAL GUIDANCE SUGGESTED
SOME MATERIAL MAY NOT BE SUITABLE FOR CHILDREN
DOLBY STEREO™
IN SELECTED THEATRES
A UNIVERSAL PICTURE
COPYRIGHT © 1980 UNIVERSAL CITY STUDIOS, INC. ALL RIGHTS RESERVED.
Original Soundtrack On MCA Records and Tapes.
STARTS TODAY AT THESE UNIVERSAL SPECIAL PRESENTATION THEATRES
MANHATTAN
B.S. MOSS CRITERION CENTER 1* B'WAY BET. 44th & 45th ST 582-1795 12, 1:40, 3:20, 5:05, 6:50, 8:35, 10:20, 12:05
A CINEMA 5 THEATRE PLAZA* 58th St East of Madison Ave EL5-3320 12:25, 2:05, 3:50, 5:35, 7:25, 9:15, 11
TRANS-LUX 85TH ST. 85TH & MADISON 288-3180 2, 4, 6, 8, 10
BROOKLYN
CENTURY'S COLLEGE 859-1384
HIGHWAY 339-1060
FLORIN-CREATIVE'S WALKER 232-4500
STATEN ISLAND
ACKERMAN'S AMBOY 2 356-3800 ELTINGVILLE
NASSAU
B.S. MOSS' CENTRAL 1* CEDARHURST 596-0105
HICKSVILLE 1 HICKSVILLE 931-0749
MEADOWBROOK 2* EAST MEADOW 735-7552
PLAYHOUSE GREATNECK 482-0500
SUNRISE MALL 1 MASSAPEQUA 795-2244
QUEENS
RKO ALDEN 2 JAMAICA 739-8678
ASTORIA 2 ASTORIA 545-9470
MIDWAY 1 FOREST HILLS 261-8572
QUARTET 2 FLUSHING 359-6777
SUFFOLK
BAYSHORE DI 2 BAYSHORE 665-1111
COLLEGE PLAZA 1 FARMINGVILLE 698-2200
EASTHAMPTON 1 EAST HAMPTON 324-0448
LINDENHURST LINDENHURST 888-5400
ROCKY POINT DI ROCKY POINT 744-8900
CENTURY'S SHORE 3 HUNTINGTON 421-5200
UPSTATE
TRI-STATE'S FISHKILL DI FISHKILL
JULIET 3 POUGHKEEPSIE 471-2124
TRI-STATE'S MAYBROOK D.I MAYBROOK 427-2715
NYACK D/I BLAUVELT 358-1884
PLAZA WEST HAVERSTRAW 947-3330
TRI STATE'S TRI-STATE DI RED MATAMORAS 491-4131
WESTCHESTER
LARCHMONT LARCHMONT 834-3001
NEW JERSEY
HYWAY 1 FAIRLAWN 796-1717
MOVIE CITY 2* EAST BRUNSWICK 257-5555
MUSIC MAKER'S MOVIES 1 RED BANK 747-0333
TRIANGLE'S NEWTON DI NEWTON 383-3066
PLAINFIELD DI EDISON 548-3100
A.M.C.'S ROCKAWAY SIX 6 ROCKAWAY TOWNSHIP 328-0666
RIALTO 1 WESTFIELD 232-1288
SHOWBOAT 2 EDGEWATER 941-3660
STATE 2 JERSEY CITY 653-5200
WILLOWBROOK 3 WAYNE 256-5919
* DOLBY STEREO

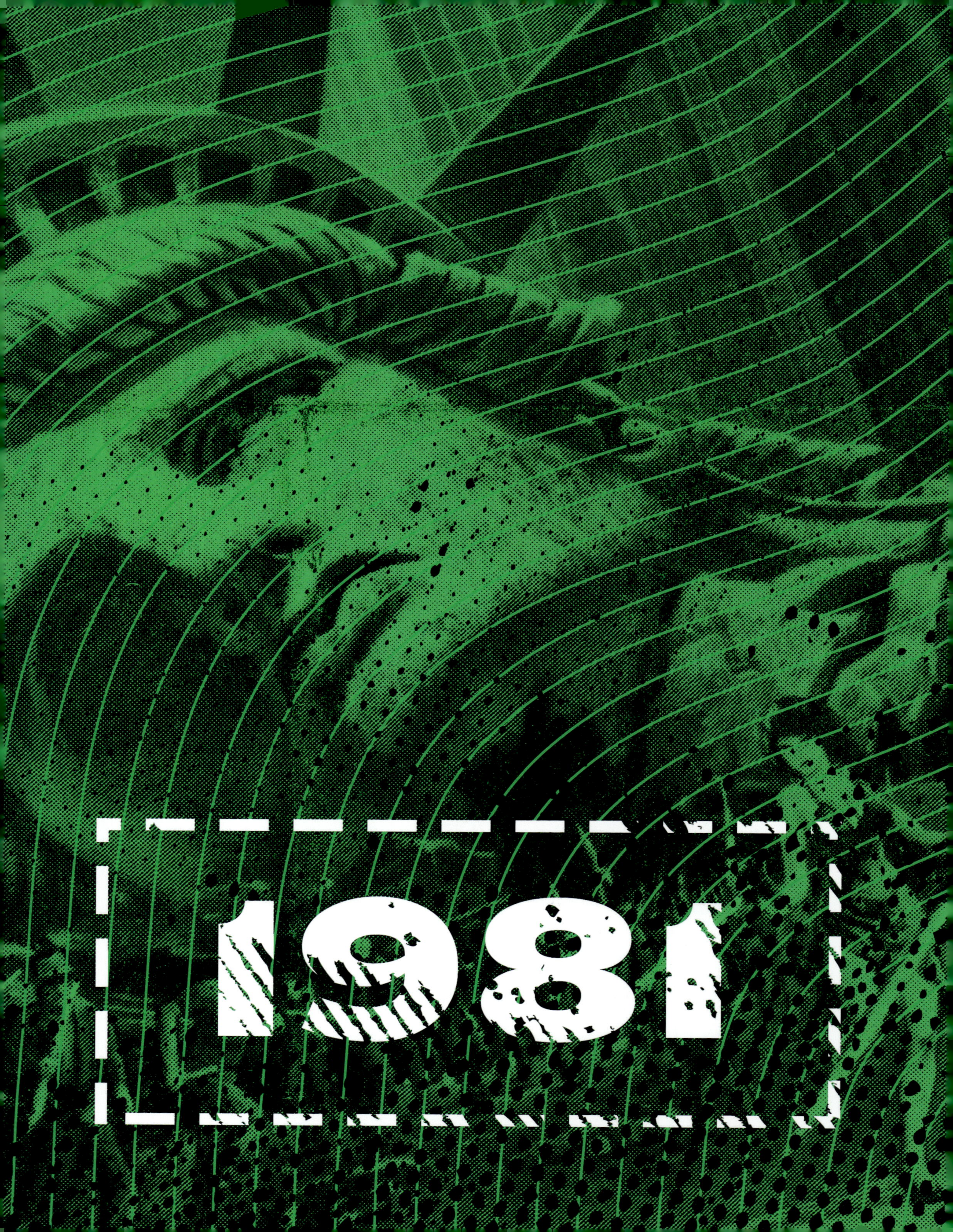
1981

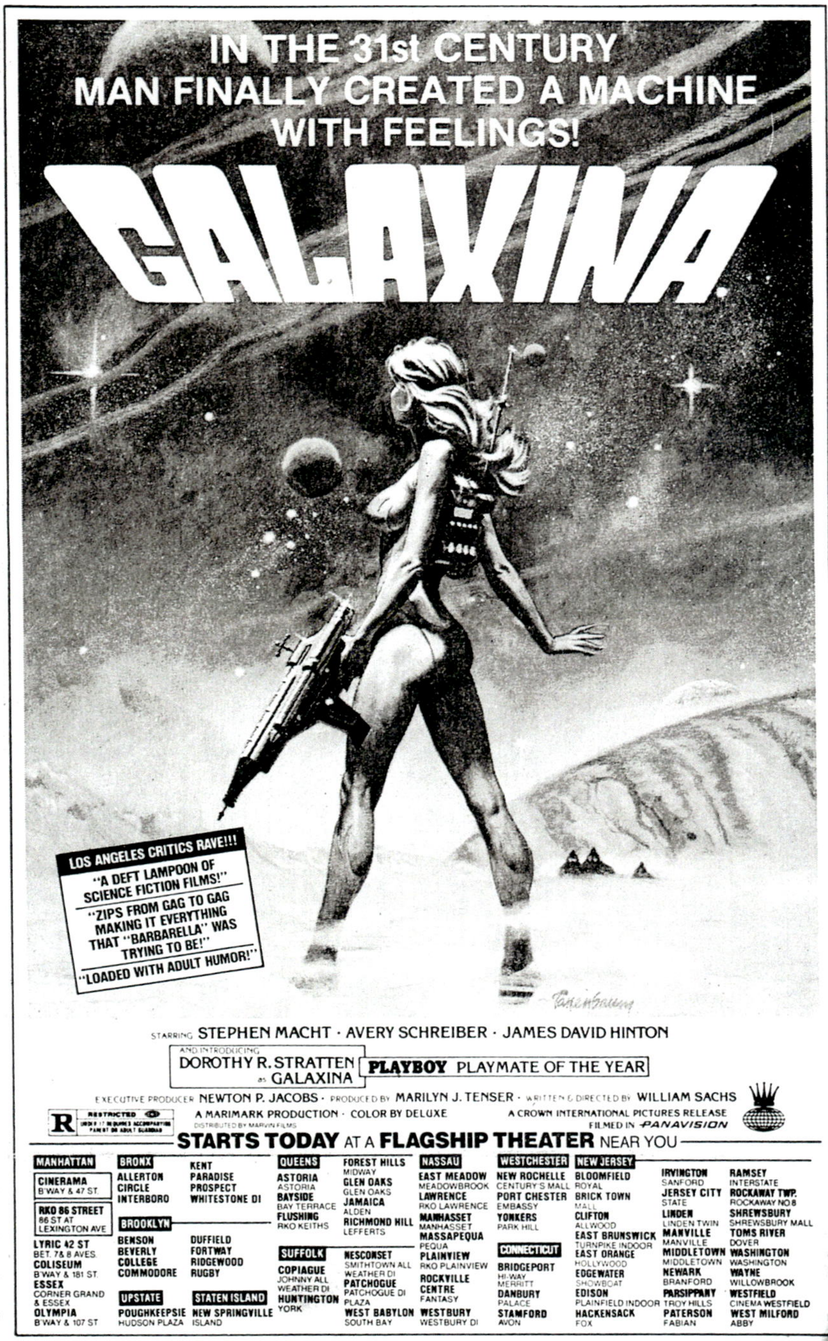

IN THE 31st CENTURY
MAN FINALLY CREATED A MACHINE
WITH FEELINGS!
GALAXINA
LOS ANGELES CRITICS RAVE!!!
"A DEFT LAMPOON OF SCIENCE FICTION FILMS!"
"ZIPS FROM GAG TO GAG MAKING IT EVERYTHING THAT "BARBARELLA" WAS TRYING TO BE!"
"LOADED WITH ADULT HUMOR!"
STARRING STEPHEN MACHT · AVERY SCHREIBER · JAMES DAVID HINTON
AND INTRODUCING DOROTHY R. STRATTEN AS GALAXINA
PLAYBOY PLAYMATE OF THE YEAR
EXECUTIVE PRODUCER NEWTON P. JACOBS · PRODUCED BY MARILYN J. TENSER · WRITTEN & DIRECTED BY WILLIAM SACHS
A MARIMARK PRODUCTION · COLOR BY DELUXE
A CROWN INTERNATIONAL PICTURES RELEASE
FILMED IN PANAVISION
STARTS TODAY AT A FLAGSHIP THEATER NEAR YOU
MANHATTAN
CINERAMA B'WAY & 47 ST.
RKO 86 STREET 86 ST AT LEXINGTON AVE
LYRIC 42 ST BET. 7& 8 AVES.
COLISEUM B'WAY & 181 ST.
ESSEX CORNER GRAND & ESSEX
OLYMPIA B'WAY & 107 ST
BRONX
ALLERTON
CIRCLE
INTERBORO
KENT
PARADISE
PROSPECT
WHITESTONE DI
BROOKLYN
BENSON
BEVERLY
COLLEGE
COMMODORE
DUFFIELD
FORTWAY
RIDGEWOOD
RUGBY
UPSTATE
POUGHKEEPSIE HUDSON PLAZA
STATEN ISLAND
NEW SPRINGVILLE ISLAND
QUEENS
ASTORIA ASTORIA
BAYSIDE BAY TERRACE
FLUSHING RKO KEITHS
FOREST HILLS MIDWAY
GLEN OAKS GLEN OAKS
JAMAICA ALDEN
RICHMOND HILL LEFFERTS
SUFFOLK
COPIAGUE JOHNNY ALL WEATHER DI
HUNTINGTON YORK
NESCONSET SMITHTOWN ALL WEATHER DI
PATCHOGUE PATCHOGUE DI
PLAZA
WEST BABYLON SOUTH BAY
NASSAU
EAST MEADOW MEADOWBROOK
LAWRENCE RKO LAWRENCE
MANHASSET MANHASSET
MASSAPEQUA PEQUA
PLAINVIEW RKO PLAINVIEW
ROCKVILLE CENTRE FANTASY
WESTBURY WESTBURY DI
WESTCHESTER
NEW ROCHELLE CENTURY'S MALL
PORT CHESTER EMBASSY
YONKERS PARK HILL
CONNECTICUT
BRIDGEPORT HI-WAY MERRITT
DANBURY PALACE
STAMFORD AVON
NEW JERSEY
BLOOMFIELD ROYAL
BRICK TOWN MALL
CLIFTON ALLWOOD
EAST BRUNSWICK TURNPIKE INDOOR
EAST ORANGE HOLLYWOOD
EDGEWATER SHOWBOAT
EDISON PLAINFIELD INDOOR
HACKENSACK FOX
IRVINGTON SANFORD
JERSEY CITY STATE
LINDEN LINDEN TWIN
MANVILLE MANVILLE
MIDDLETOWN MIDDLETOWN
NEWARK BRANFORD
PARSIPPANY TROY HILLS
PATERSON FABIAN
RAMSEY INTERSTATE
ROCKAWAY TWP. ROCKAWAY NO 8
SHREWSBURY SHREWSBURY MALL
TOMS RIVER DOVER
WASHINGTON WASHINGTON
WAYNE WILLOWBROOK
WESTFIELD CINEMA WESTFIELD
WEST MILFORD ABBY

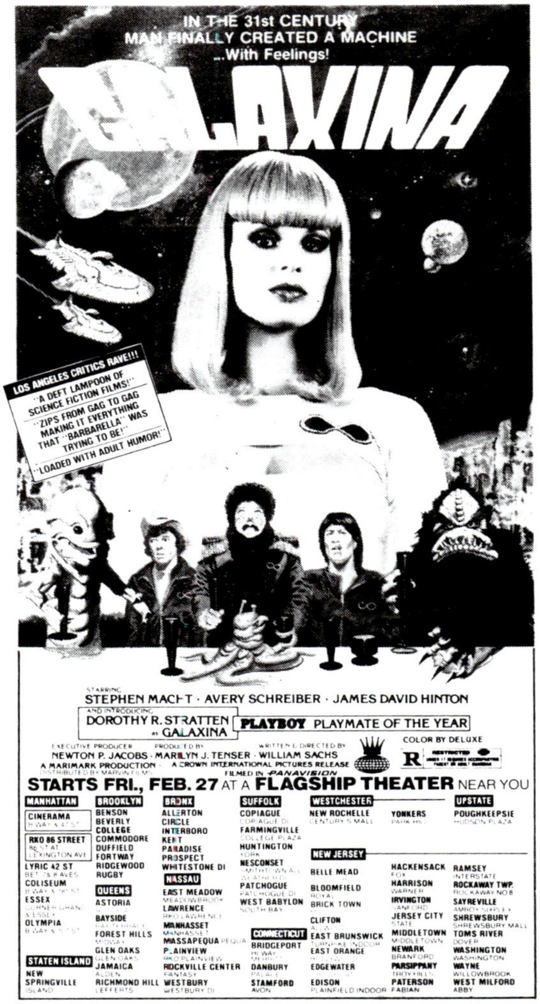

IN THE 31st CENTURY
MAN FINALLY CREATED A MACHINE
...With Feelings!
GALAXINA
LOS ANGELES CRITICS RAVE!!!
"A DEFT LAMPOON OF SCIENCE FICTION FILMS!"
"ZIPS FROM GAG TO GAG MAKING IT EVERYTHING THAT "BARBARELLA" WAS TRYING TO BE!"
"LOADED WITH ADULT HUMOR!"
STARRING STEPHEN MACHT · AVERY SCHREIBER · JAMES DAVID HINTON
AND INTRODUCING DOROTHY R. STRATTEN AS GALAXINA
PLAYBOY PLAYMATE OF THE YEAR
EXECUTIVE PRODUCER NEWTON P. JACOBS · PRODUCED BY MARILYN J. TENSER · WRITTEN & DIRECTED BY WILLIAM SACHS
A MARIMARK PRODUCTION · A CROWN INTERNATIONAL PICTURES RELEASE
COLOR BY DELUXE
FILMED IN PANAVISION
STARTS FRI., FEB. 27 AT A FLAGSHIP THEATER NEAR YOU

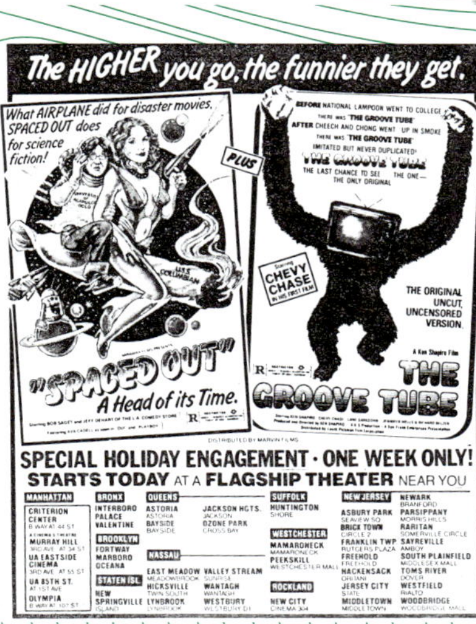

The HIGHER you go, the funnier they get.
What AIRPLANE did for disaster movies, SPACED OUT does for science fiction!
PLUS
"SPACED OUT"
A Head of its Time.
THE GROOVE TUBE
THE ORIGINAL UNCUT, UNCENSORED VERSION
CHEVY CHASE
SPECIAL HOLIDAY ENGAGEMENT · ONE WEEK ONLY!
STARTS TODAY AT A FLAGSHIP THEATER NEAR YOU

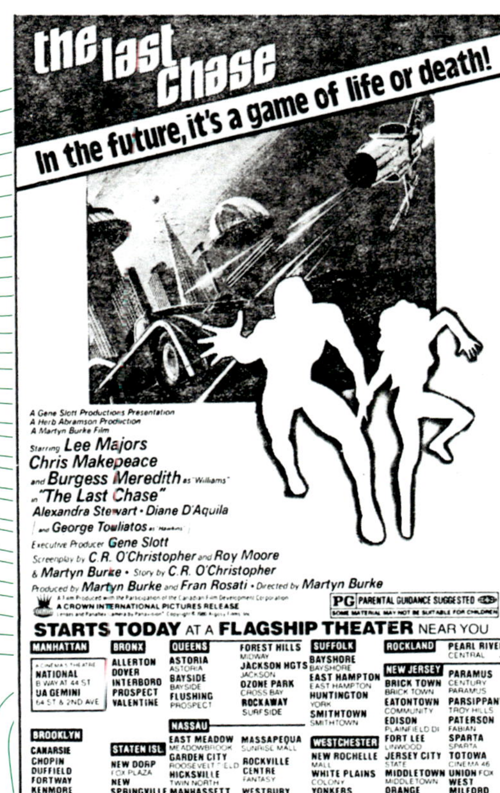

the last chase
In the future, it's a game of life or death!
A Gene Slott Productions Presentation
A Herb Abramson Production
A Martyn Burke Film
Starring Lee Majors
Chris Makepeace
and Burgess Meredith as "Williams"
in "The Last Chase"
Alexandra Stewart · Diane D'Aquila
and George Touliatos
Executive Producer Gene Slott
Screenplay by C.R. O'Christopher and Roy Moore
& Martyn Burke · Story by C.R. O'Christopher
Produced by Martyn Burke and Fran Rosati · Directed by Martyn Burke
A CROWN INTERNATIONAL PICTURES RELEASE
PG PARENTAL GUIDANCE SUGGESTED
STARTS TODAY AT A FLAGSHIP THEATER NEAR YOU

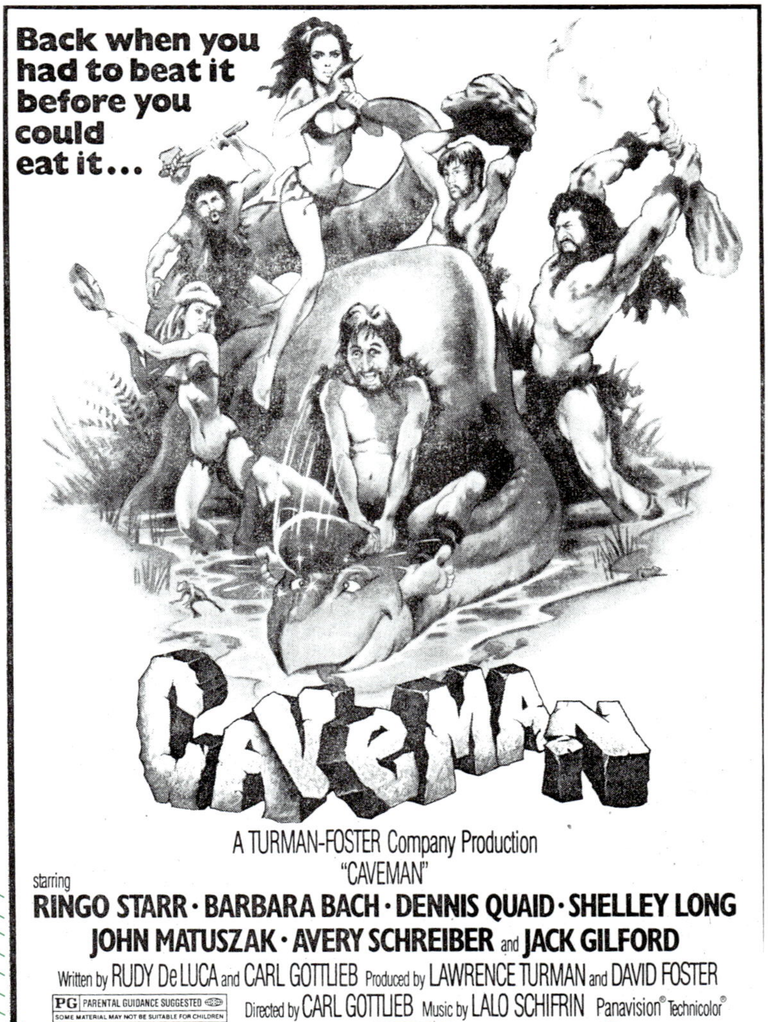

CAVEMAN

A prehistoric slapstick comedy starring Ringo Starr and featuring an array of stop-motion dinosaurs should have been catnip to young audiences, especially with animation supervised by David Allen (*Equinox*, *Laserblast*) and Jim Danforth (*When Dinosaurs Ruled the Earth*, *7 Faces of Dr. Lao*). When moviegoers didn't initially turn out in great numbers, United Artists tried an alternate, more cartoony campaign, then reopened the movie in an upscale Manhattan movie house and attempted to take advantage of the many positive reviews. None of it really took and the box office remained modest, but there was a happy ending for Starr and female lead Barbara Bach, who married the following year.

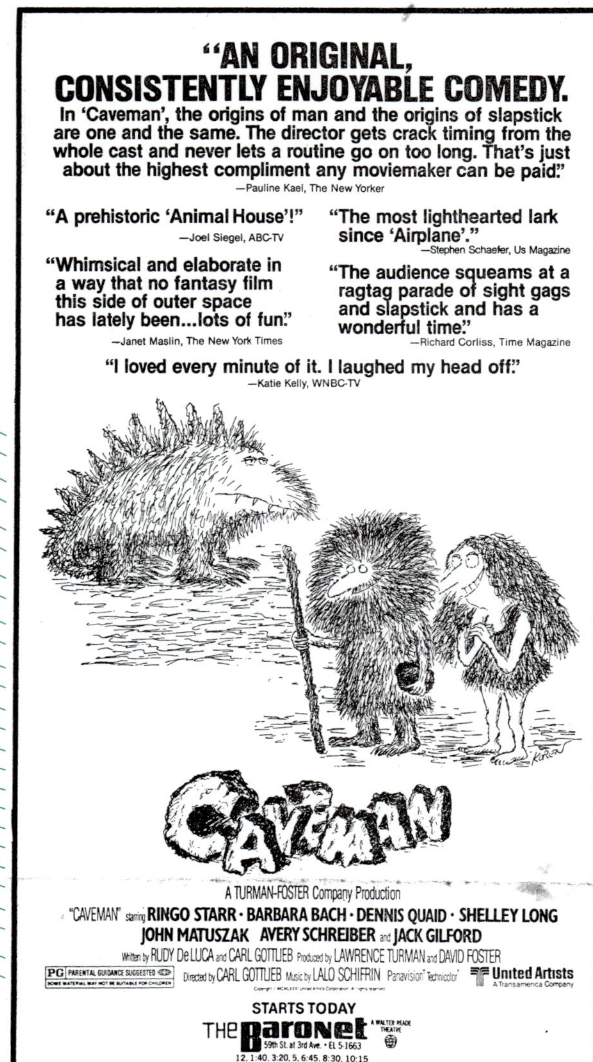

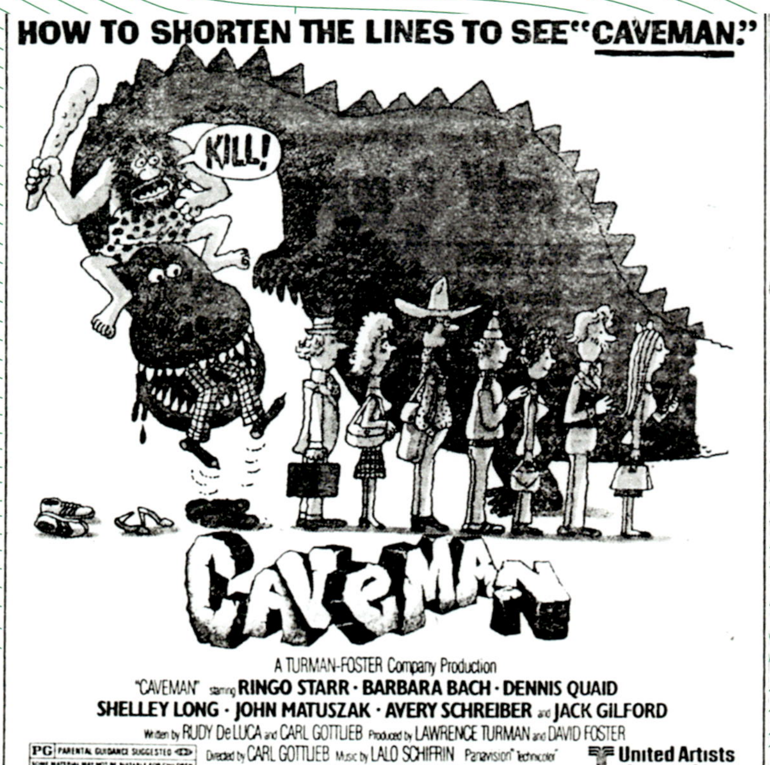

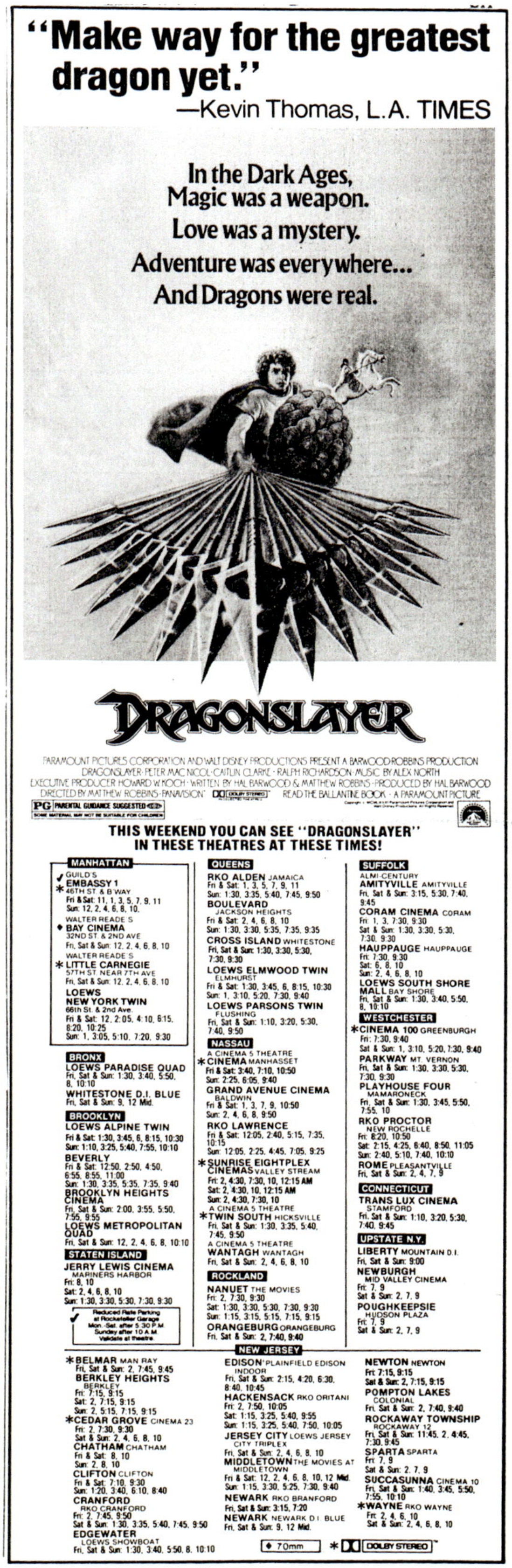
"Make way for the greatest dragon yet."
—Kevin Thomas, L.A. TIMES
In the Dark Ages,
Magic was a weapon.
Love was a mystery.
Adventure was everywhere...
And Dragons were real.
DRAGONSLAYER
PARAMOUNT PICTURES CORPORATION AND WALT DISNEY PRODUCTIONS PRESENT A BARWOOD ROBBINS PRODUCTION
DRAGONSLAYER · PETER MAC NICOL · CAITLIN CLARKE · RALPH RICHARDSON · MUSIC BY ALEX NORTH
EXECUTIVE PRODUCER HOWARD W. KOCH · WRITTEN BY HAL BARWOOD & MATTHEW ROBBINS · PRODUCED BY HAL BARWOOD
DIRECTED BY MATTHEW ROBBINS · PANAVISION · DOLBY STEREO · READ THE BALLANTINE BOOK · A PARAMOUNT PICTURE
PG PARENTAL GUIDANCE SUGGESTED
SOME MATERIAL MAY NOT BE SUITABLE FOR CHILDREN
THIS WEEKEND YOU CAN SEE "DRAGONSLAYER" IN THESE THEATRES AT THESE TIMES!
MANHATTAN
✓ GUILD'S ✱ EMBASSY 1 46TH ST. & B'WAY
Fri & Sat: 11, 1, 3, 5, 7, 9, 11
Sun: 12, 2, 4, 6, 8, 10.
WALTER READE'S ♦ BAY CINEMA 32ND ST. & 2ND AVE
Fri, Sat & Sun: 12, 2, 4, 6, 8, 10
WALTER READE'S ✱ LITTLE CARNEGIE 57TH ST. NEAR 7TH AVE
Fri, Sat & Sun: 12, 2, 4, 6, 8, 10
LOEWS NEW YORK TWIN 66th St. & 2nd Ave.
Fri & Sat: 12, 2:05, 4:10, 6:15, 8:20, 10:25
Sun: 1, 3:05, 5:10, 7:20, 9:30
BRONX
LOEWS PARADISE QUAD
Fri, Sat & Sun: 1:30, 3:40, 5:50, 8, 10:10
WHITESTONE D.I. BLUE
Fri, Sat & Sun: 9, 12 Mid.
BROOKLYN
LOEWS ALPINE TWIN
Fri & Sat: 1:30, 3:45, 6, 8:15, 10:30
Sun: 1:10, 3:25, 5:40, 7:55, 10:10
BEVERLY
Fri & Sat: 12:50, 2:50, 4:50, 6:55, 8:55, 11:00
Sun: 1:30, 3:35, 5:35, 7:35, 9:40
BROOKLYN HEIGHTS CINEMA
Fri, Sat & Sun: 2:00, 3:55, 5:50, 7:55, 9:55
LOEWS METROPOLITAN QUAD
Fri, Sat & Sun: 12, 2, 4, 6, 8, 10:10
STATEN ISLAND
JERRY LEWIS CINEMA MARINERS HARBOR
Fri: 8, 10
Sat: 2, 4, 6, 8, 10
Sun: 1:30, 3:30, 5:30, 7:30, 9:30
✓ Reduced Rate Parking at Rockefeller Garage Mon.-Sat. after 5:30 P.M. Sunday after 10 A.M. Validate at theatre.
QUEENS
RKO ALDEN JAMAICA
Fri & Sat: 1, 3, 5, 7, 9, 11
Sun: 1:30, 3:35, 5:40, 7:45, 9:50
BOULEVARD JACKSON HEIGHTS
Fri & Sat: 2, 4, 6, 8, 10
Sun: 1:30, 3:30, 5:35, 7:35, 9:35
CROSS ISLAND WHITESTONE
Fri, Sat & Sun: 1:30, 3:30, 5:30, 7:30, 9:30
LOEWS ELMWOOD TWIN ELMHURST
Fri & Sat: 1:30, 3:45, 6, 8:15, 10:30
Sun: 1, 3:10, 5:20, 7:30, 9:40
LOEWS PARSONS TWIN FLUSHING
Fri, Sat & Sun: 1:10, 3:20, 5:30, 7:40, 9:50
NASSAU
A CINEMA 5 THEATRE ✱ CINEMA MANHASSET
Fri & Sat: 3:40, 7:10, 10:50
Sun: 2:25, 6:05, 9:40
GRAND AVENUE CINEMA BALDWIN
Fri & Sat: 1, 3, 7, 9, 10:50
Sun: 2, 4, 6, 8, 9:50
RKO LAWRENCE
Fri & Sat: 12:05, 2:40, 5:15, 7:35, 10:15
Sun: 12:05, 2:25, 4:45, 7:05, 9:25
✱ SUNRISE EIGHTPLEX CINEMAS VALLEY STREAM
Fri: 2, 4:30, 7:30, 10, 12:15 AM
Sat: 2, 4:30, 10, 12:15 AM
Sun: 2, 4:30, 7:30, 10
A CINEMA 5 THEATRE ✱ TWIN SOUTH HICKSVILLE
Fri, Sat & Sun: 1:30, 3:35, 5:40, 7:45, 9:50
A CINEMA 5 THEATRE WANTAGH WANTAGH
Fri, Sat & Sun: 2, 4, 6, 8, 10
ROCKLAND
NANUET THE MOVIES
Fri: 2, 7:30, 9:30
Sat: 1:30, 3:30, 5:30, 7:30, 9:30
Sun: 1:15, 3:15, 5:15, 7:15, 9:15
ORANGEBURG ORANGEBURG
Fri, Sat & Sun: 2, 7:40, 9:40
SUFFOLK
ALMI-CENTURY AMITYVILLE AMITYVILLE
Fri, Sat & Sun: 3:15, 5:30, 7:40, 9:45
CORAM CINEMA CORAM
Fri: 1, 3, 7:30, 9:30
Sat & Sun: 1:30, 3:30, 5:30, 7:30, 9:30
HAUPPAUGE HAUPPAUGE
Fri: 7:30, 9:30
Sat: 6, 8, 10
Sun: 2, 4, 6, 8, 10
LOEWS SOUTH SHORE MALL BAY SHORE
Fri, Sat & Sun: 1:30, 3:40, 5:50, 8, 10:10
WESTCHESTER
✱ CINEMA 100 GREENBURGH
Fri: 7:30, 9:40
Sat & Sun: 1, 3:10, 5:20, 7:30, 9:40
PARKWAY MT. VERNON
Fri, Sat & Sun: 1:30, 3:30, 5:30, 7:30, 9:30
PLAYHOUSE FOUR MAMARONECK
Fri, Sat & Sun: 1:30, 3:45, 5:50, 7:55, 10
RKO PROCTOR NEW ROCHELLE
Fri: 8:20, 10:50
Sat: 2:15, 4:25, 6:40, 8:50, 11:05
Sun: 2:40, 5:10, 7:40, 10:10
ROME PLEASANTVILLE
Fri, Sat & Sun: 2, 4, 7, 9
CONNECTICUT
TRANS LUX CINEMA STAMFORD
Fri, Sat & Sun: 1:10, 3:20, 5:30, 7:40, 9:45
UPSTATE N.Y.
LIBERTY MOUNTAIN D.I.
Fri, Sat & Sun: 9:00
NEWBURGH MID VALLEY CINEMA
Fri: 7, 9
Sat & Sun: 2, 7, 9
POUGHKEEPSIE HUDSON PLAZA
Fri: 7, 9
Sat & Sun: 2, 7, 9
NEW JERSEY
✱ BELMAR MAN RAY
Fri, Sat & Sun: 2, 7:45, 9:45
BERKLEY HEIGHTS BERKLEY
Fri: 7:15, 9:15
Sat: 2, 7:15, 9:15
Sun: 2, 5:15, 7:15, 9:15
✱ CEDAR GROVE CINEMA 23
Fri: 2, 7:30, 9:30
Sat & Sun: 2, 4, 6, 8, 10
CHATHAM CHATHAM
Fri & Sat: 8, 10
Sun: 2, 8, 10
CLIFTON CLIFTON
Fri & Sat: 7:10, 9:30
Sun: 1:20, 3:40, 6:10, 8:40
CRANFORD RKO CRANFORD
Fri: 2, 7:45, 9:50
Sat & Sun: 1:30, 3:35, 5:40, 7:45, 9:50
EDGEWATER LOEWS SHOWBOAT
Fri, Sat & Sun: 1:30, 3:40, 5:50, 8, 10:10
EDISON PLAINFIELD EDISON INDOOR
Fri, Sat & Sun: 2:15, 4:20, 6:30, 8:40, 10:45
HACKENSACK RKO ORITANI
Fri: 2, 7:50, 10:05
Sat: 1:15, 3:25, 5:40, 9:55
Sun: 1:15, 3:25, 5:40, 7:50, 10:05
JERSEY CITY LOEWS JERSEY CITY TRIPLEX
Fri, Sat & Sun: 2, 4, 6, 8, 10
MIDDLETOWN THE MOVIES AT MIDDLETOWN
Fri & Sat: 12, 2, 4, 6, 8, 10, 12 Mid.
Sun: 1:15, 3:30, 5:25, 7:30, 9:40
NEWARK RKO BRANFORD
Fri, Sat & Sun: 3:15, 7:20
NEWARK NEWARK D.I. BLUE
Fri, Sat & Sun: 9, 12 Mid.
NEWTON NEWTON
Fri: 7:15, 9:15
Sat & Sun: 2, 7:15, 9:15
POMPTON LAKES COLONIAL
Fri, Sat & Sun: 2, 7:40, 9:40
ROCKAWAY TOWNSHIP ROCKAWAY 12
Fri, Sat & Sun: 11:45, 2, 4:45, 7:30, 9:45
SPARTA SPARTA
Fri: 7, 9
Sat & Sun: 2, 7, 9
SUCCASUNNA CINEMA 10
Fri, Sat & Sun: 1:40, 3:45, 5:50, 7:55, 10:10
✱ WAYNE RKO WAYNE
Fri: 2, 4, 6, 10
Sat & Sun: 2, 4, 6, 8, 10
♦ 70mm ✱ DOLBY STEREO

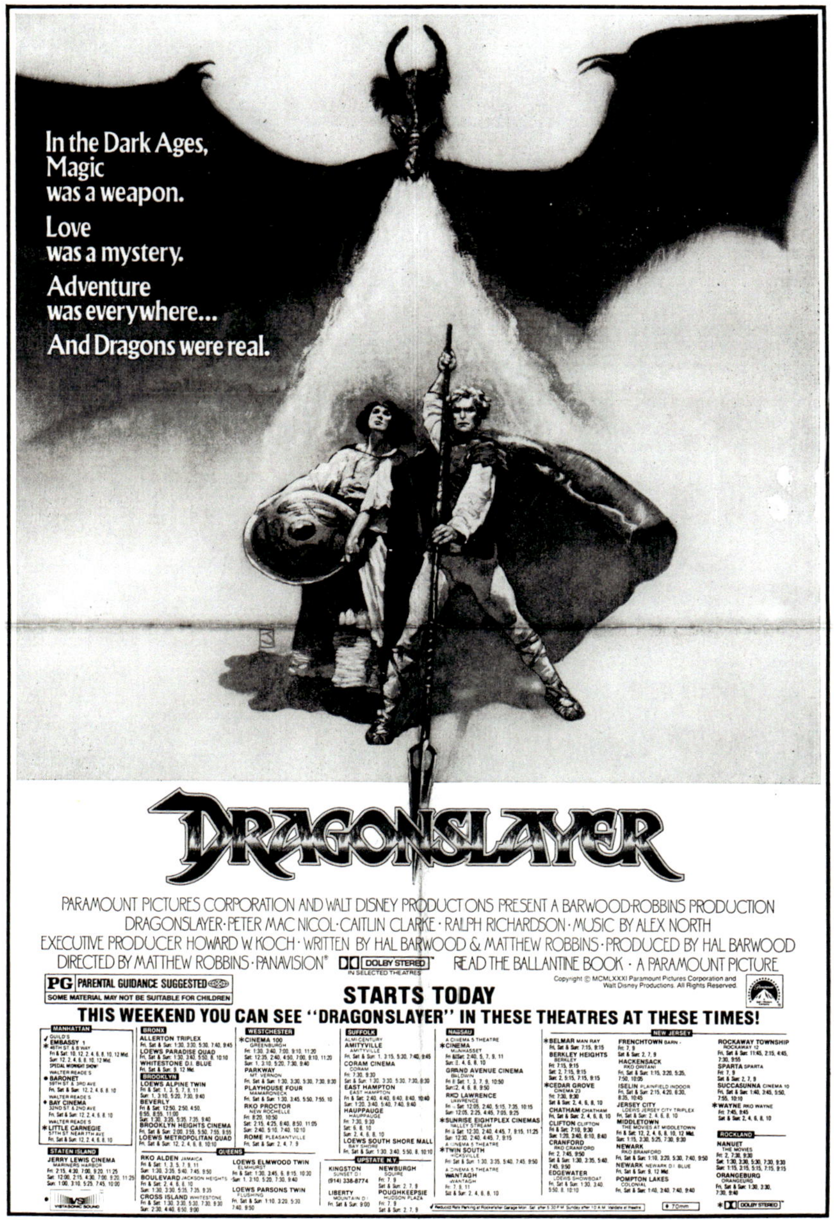
In the Dark Ages,
Magic was a weapon.
Love was a mystery.
Adventure was everywhere...
And Dragons were real.
DRAGONSLAYER
PARAMOUNT PICTURES CORPORATION AND WALT DISNEY PRODUCTIONS PRESENT A BARWOOD-ROBBINS PRODUCTION
DRAGONSLAYER · PETER MAC NICOL · CAITLIN CLARKE · RALPH RICHARDSON · MUSIC BY ALEX NORTH
EXECUTIVE PRODUCER HOWARD W. KOCH · WRITTEN BY HAL BARWOOD & MATTHEW ROBBINS · PRODUCED BY HAL BARWOOD
DIRECTED BY MATTHEW ROBBINS · PANAVISION · DOLBY STEREO IN SELECTED THEATRES · READ THE BALLANTINE BOOK · A PARAMOUNT PICTURE
PG PARENTAL GUIDANCE SUGGESTED
SOME MATERIAL MAY NOT BE SUITABLE FOR CHILDREN
Copyright © MCMLXXXI Paramount Pictures Corporation and Walt Disney Productions. All Rights Reserved.
STARTS TODAY
THIS WEEKEND YOU CAN SEE "DRAGONSLAYER" IN THESE THEATRES AT THESE TIMES!

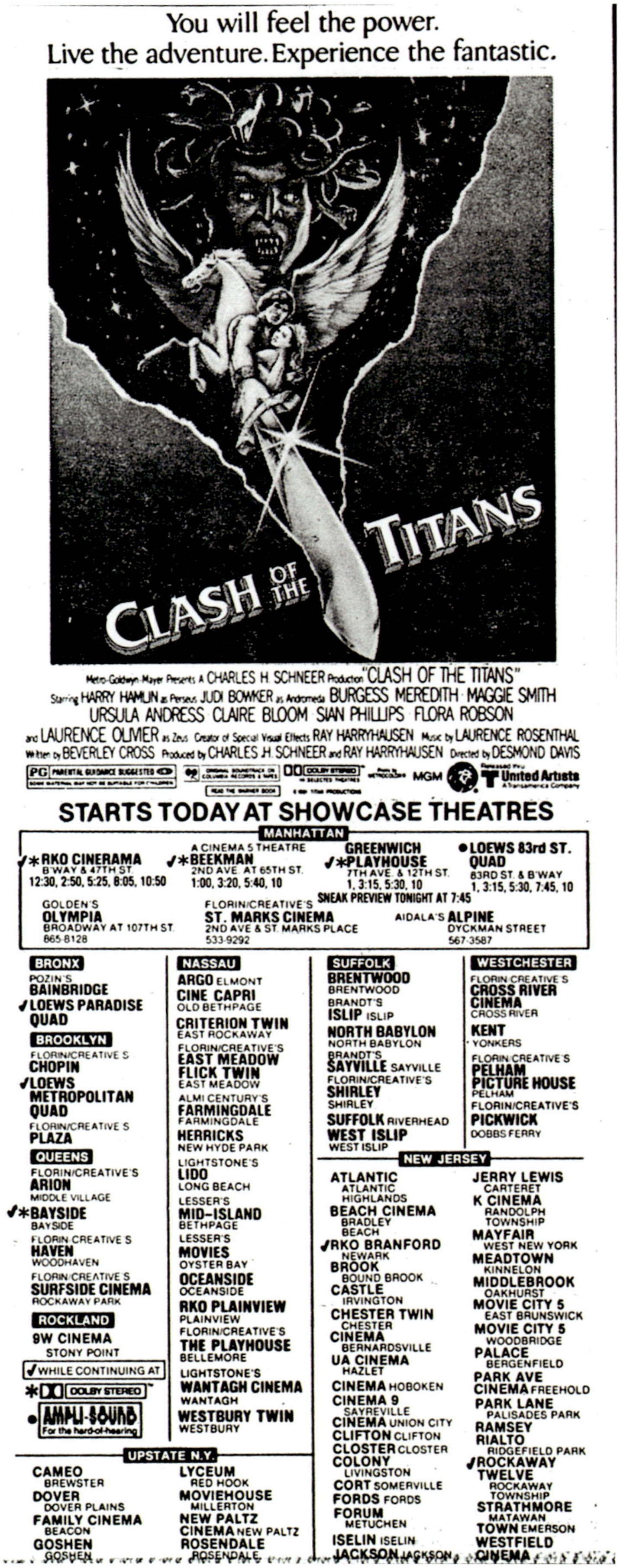

CLASH OF THE TITANS

Following their collaboration on three *Sinbad* movies and many other mythological and monstrous adventures, producer Charles H. Schneer and stop-motion maestro Ray Harryhausen took on the legend of Perseus, Andromeda, and the Kraken. With a gallery of major stars (led by Laurence Olivier) portraying the gods on Mount Olympus, and newcomer Harry Hamlin as Perseus, *Clash* opened in the thick of a season of films boasting more modern effects techniques (including *Dragonslayer*, with its computer-assisted "go-motion" animation). While it was a modest hit amidst all the competition, the changing times prevented Harryhausen and Schneer from finding backing for a follow-up feature called *Force of the Trojans*, and *Clash* would be their final production.

"*Clash of the Titans* is a grand and glorious romantic adventure, filled with grave heroes, beautiful heroines, fearsome monsters, and awe-inspiring duels to the death."

–Roger Ebert, *Chicago Sun-Times*

"*Clash* is…a gift – a smashing grab-bag of Greek gods, heroes and mythical creatures that asks nothing more of movie-goers than they sit back and enjoy the ride."

–Eleanor Ringel, *The Atlanta Constitution*

"Hamlin is *Clash of the Titans'* weakest link, an unexpressive actor who looks like a chiseled hero but doesn't much act like one. … That's not to say there's not a lot of fun in this Good Gods vs. the Bad Gods tale. Most of the pleasure to be taken comes in the form of the special effects provided by Ray Harryhausen."

–TERRY LAWSON, DAYTON, OH *JOURNAL HERALD*

"Beverley Cross' script suggests that she never read Edith Hamilton's *Mythology* [*note: Cross was a man*]…and Desmond Davis' direction recalls the poor integration of live action and special effects of *The Seventh Voyage of Sinbad*."

–Michael Blowen, *The Boston Globe*

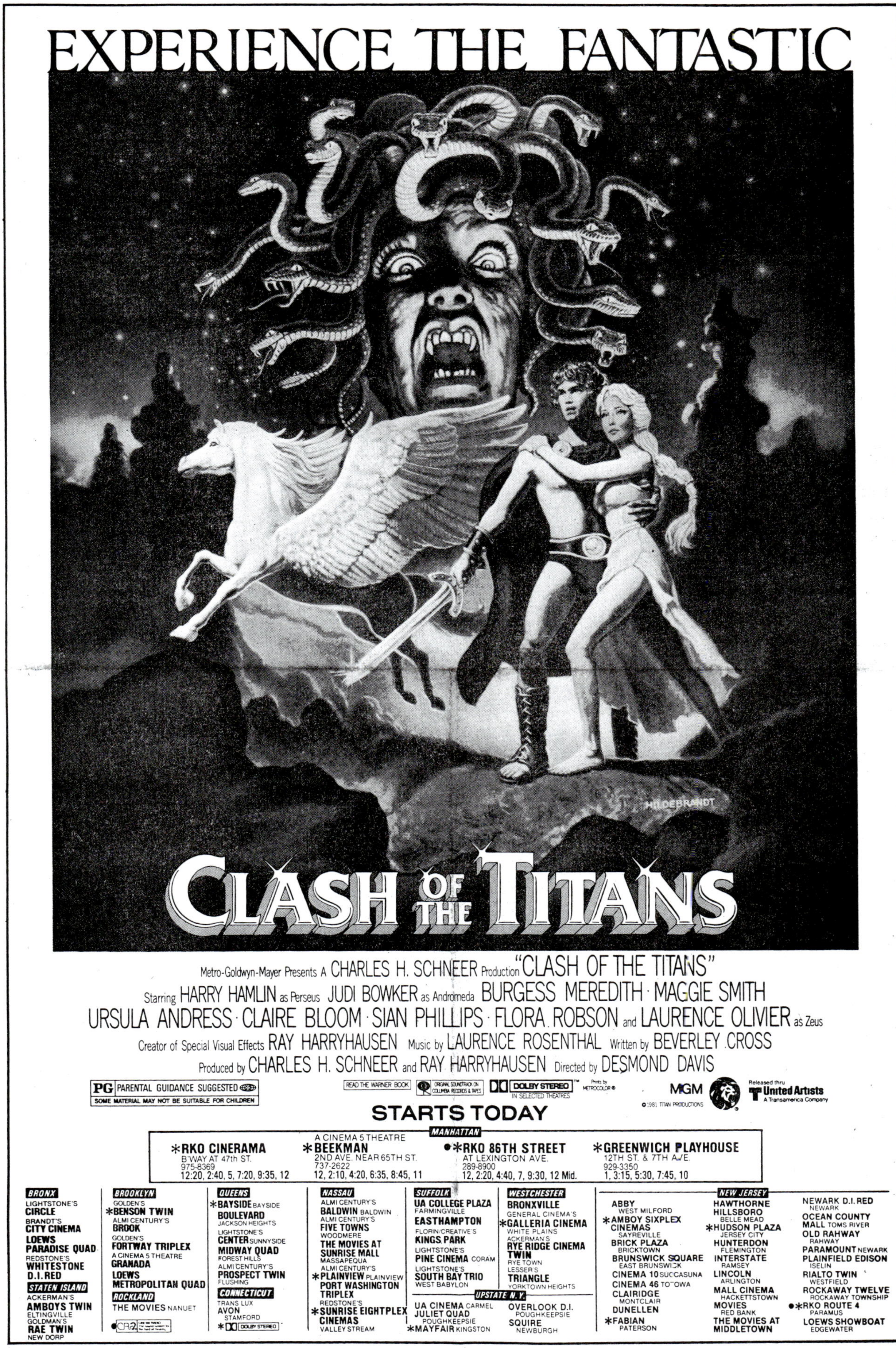

EXPERIENCE THE FANTASTIC
HILDEBRANDT
CLASH OF THE TITANS
Metro-Goldwyn-Mayer Presents A CHARLES H. SCHNEER Production "CLASH OF THE TITANS"
Starring HARRY HAMLIN as Perseus JUDI BOWKER as Andromeda BURGESS MEREDITH · MAGGIE SMITH
URSULA ANDRESS · CLAIRE BLOOM · SIAN PHILLIPS · FLORA ROBSON and LAURENCE OLIVIER as Zeus
Creator of Special Visual Effects RAY HARRYHAUSEN Music by LAURENCE ROSENTHAL Written by BEVERLEY CROSS
Produced by CHARLES H. SCHNEER and RAY HARRYHAUSEN Directed by DESMOND DAVIS
PG PARENTAL GUIDANCE SUGGESTED
SOME MATERIAL MAY NOT BE SUITABLE FOR CHILDREN
READ THE WARNER BOOK
ORIGINAL SOUNDTRACK ON COLUMBIA RECORDS & TAPES
DOLBY STEREO™ IN SELECTED THEATRES
Prints by METROCOLOR®
MGM
© 1981 TITAN PRODUCTIONS
Released thru United Artists A Transamerica Company
STARTS TODAY
MANHATTAN
*RKO CINERAMA B'WAY AT 47th ST. 975-8369 12:20, 2:40, 5, 7:20, 9:35, 12
A CINEMA 5 THEATRE *BEEKMAN 2ND AVE. NEAR 65TH ST. 737-2622 12, 2:10, 4:20, 6:35, 8:45, 11
•*RKO 86TH STREET AT LEXINGTON AVE. 289-8900 12, 2:20, 4:40, 7, 9:30, 12 Mid.
*GREENWICH PLAYHOUSE 12TH ST. & 7TH AVE. 929-3350 1, 3:15, 5:30, 7:45, 10
BRONX
LIGHTSTONE'S CIRCLE
BRANDT'S CITY CINEMA
LOEWS PARADISE QUAD
REDSTONE'S WHITESTONE D.I.RED
STATEN ISLAND
ACKERMAN'S AMBOYS TWIN ELTINGVILLE
GOLDMAN'S RAE TWIN NEW DORP
BROOKLYN
GOLDEN'S *BENSON TWIN
ALMI CENTURY'S BROOK
GOLDEN'S FORTWAY TRIPLEX
A CINEMA 5 THEATRE GRANADA
LOEWS METROPOLITAN QUAD
ROCKLAND
THE MOVIES NANUET
•CR2
QUEENS
*BAYSIDE BAYSIDE
BOULEVARD JACKSON HEIGHTS
LIGHTSTONE'S CENTER SUNNYSIDE
MIDWAY QUAD FOREST HILLS
ALMI CENTURY'S PROSPECT TWIN FLUSHING
CONNECTICUT
TRANS LUX AVON STAMFORD
* DOLBY STEREO
NASSAU
ALMI CENTURY'S BALDWIN BALDWIN
ALMI CENTURY'S FIVE TOWNS WOODMERE
THE MOVIES AT SUNRISE MALL MASSAPEQUA
ALMI CENTURY'S *PLAINVIEW PLAINVIEW
PORT WASHINGTON TRIPLEX
REDSTONE'S *SUNRISE EIGHTPLEX CINEMAS VALLEY STREAM
SUFFOLK
UA COLLEGE PLAZA FARMINGVILLE
EASTHAMPTON
FLORIN/CREATIVE'S KINGS PARK
LIGHTSTONE'S PINE CINEMA CORAM
LIGHTSTONE'S SOUTH BAY TRIO WEST BABYLON
WESTCHESTER
BRONXVILLE
GENERAL CINEMA'S *GALLERIA CINEMA WHITE PLAINS
ACKERMAN'S RYE RIDGE CINEMA TWIN RYE TOWN
LESSER'S TRIANGLE YORKTOWN HEIGHTS
UPSTATE N.Y.
UA CINEMA CARMEL
JULIET QUAD POUGHKEEPSIE
*MAYFAIR KINGSTON
OVERLOOK D.I. POUGHKEEPSIE
SQUIRE NEWBURGH
NEW JERSEY
ABBY WEST MILFORD
*AMBOY SIXPLEX CINEMAS SAYREVILLE
BRICK PLAZA BRICKTOWN
BRUNSWICK SQUARE EAST BRUNSWICK
CINEMA 10 SUCCASUNA
CINEMA 46 TOTOWA
CLAIRIDGE MONTCLAIR
DUNELLEN
*FABIAN PATERSON
HAWTHORNE
HILLSBORO BELLE MEAD
*HUDSON PLAZA JERSEY CITY
HUNTERDON FLEMINGTON
INTERSTATE RAMSEY
LINCOLN ARLINGTON
MALL CINEMA HACKETTSTOWN
MOVIES RED BANK
THE MOVIES AT MIDDLETOWN
NEWARK D.I. RED NEWARK
OCEAN COUNTY MALL TOMS RIVER
OLD RAHWAY RAHWAY
PARAMOUNT NEWARK
PLAINFIELD EDISON ISELIN
RIALTO TWIN WESTFIELD
ROCKAWAY TWELVE ROCKAWAY TOWNSHIP
•*RKO ROUTE 4 PARAMUS
LOEWS SHOWBOAT EDGEWATER

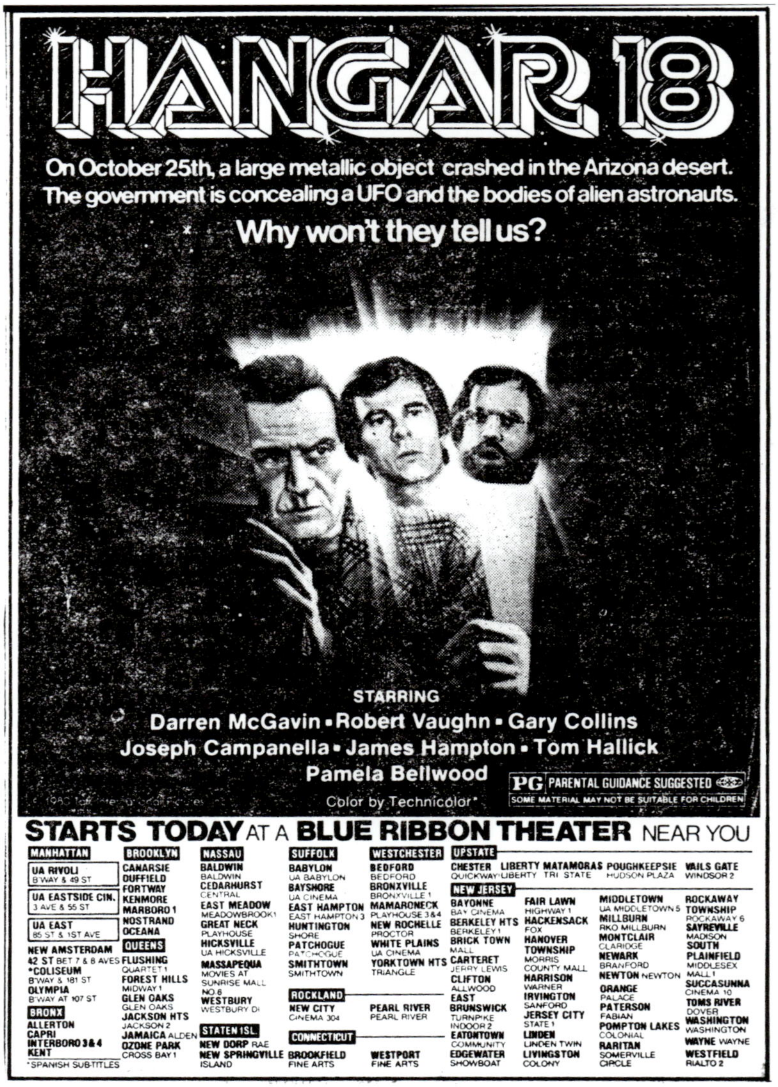

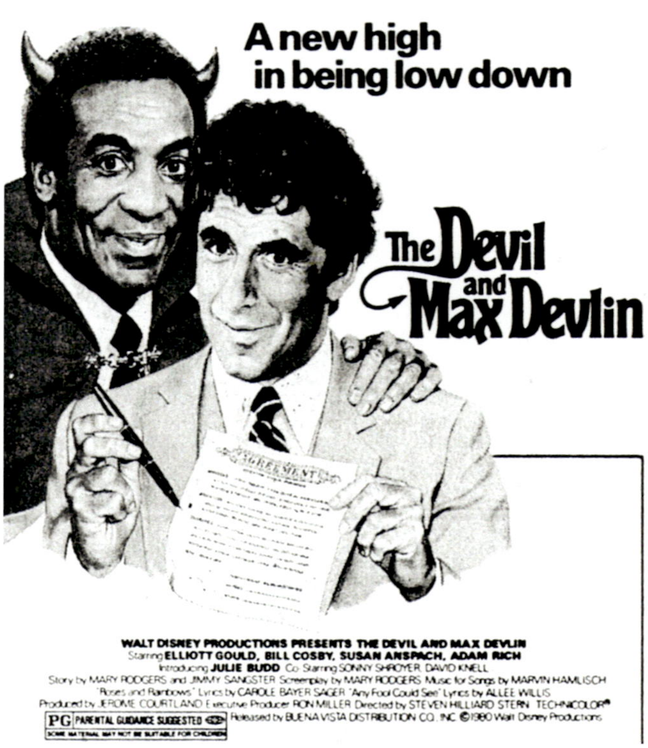

HEARTBEEPS

Today, *Heartbeeps* is likely best remembered as the movie that vied with *An American Werewolf in London* for the first competitive Academy Award for makeup. Stan Winston's prosthetics, which transform stars Andy Kaufman and Bernadette Peters into robots who fall in love and flee their servitude to humans, are indeed impressive. Reviewers largely found little else to praise about the movie, though.

"...*Heartbeeps* is packed with good, clean morality and enough bite to make it an entertaining children's film. ... [It] doesn't really succeed, but its sweet-tempered attempt makes it hard to find too much fault."

–Marylynn Uricchio, *Pittsburgh Post-Gazette*

"Unfortunately, these two [stars] are struggling mightily with a concept and a script that just aren't worth all the effort. It sounds clever and interesting when you describe it, but it doesn't play that way."

–David Goetz, Louisville, KY *Courier-Journal*

"Not only can you see the wheels turn in the plot machinery behind *Heartbeeps*, you hear them get clogged up in wretched dialogue. ... Since [the stars are] supposed to act stiff and mechanical, you can't really tell if they're acting or not."

–WAYMAN WONG, *SAN FRANCISCO EXAMINER*

"*Heartbeeps* is so silly and incompetently written that kids will probably scoff at its plot. And they're apt to remain cold to the film's rather lifeless characters."

–Greg Tozian, *The Tampa Tribune*

"*Heartbeeps*...is a three-minute television sketch stretched to last nearly 90 unbearable minutes. ... [It] was written by John Hill and directed by Allan Arkush...neither of whom show evidence of having much sense of humor."

–Vincent Canby, *The New York Times*

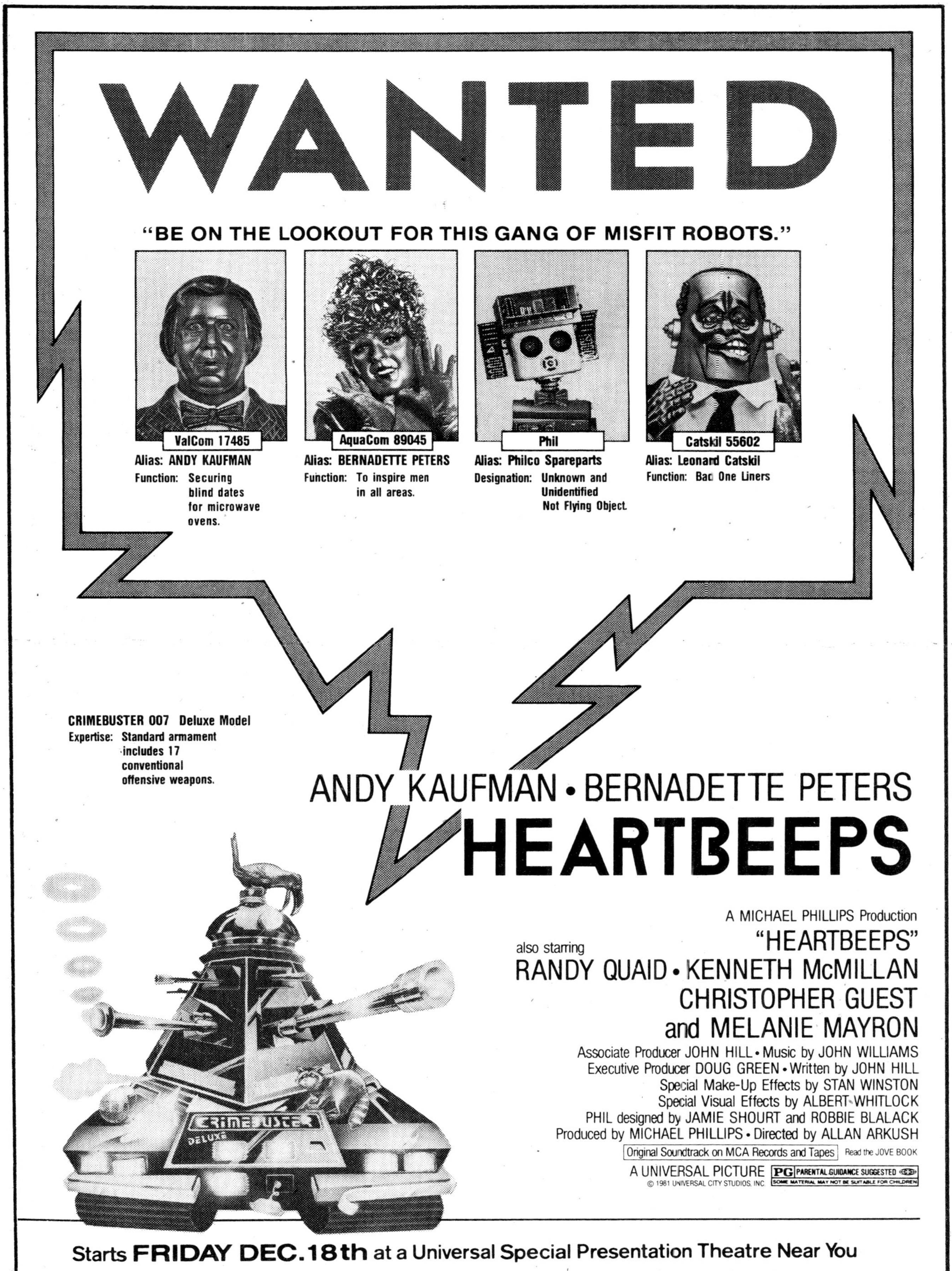
WANTED
"BE ON THE LOOKOUT FOR THIS GANG OF MISFIT ROBOTS."
ValCom 17485
Alias: ANDY KAUFMAN
Function: Securing blind dates for microwave ovens.
AquaCom 89045
Alias: BERNADETTE PETERS
Function: To inspire men in all areas.
Phil
Alias: Philco Spareparts
Designation: Unknown and Unidentified Not Flying Object.
Catskil 55602
Alias: Leonard Catskil
Function: Bad One Liners
CRIMEBUSTER 007 Deluxe Model
Expertise: Standard armament includes 17 conventional offensive weapons.
CRIMEBUSTER
DELUXE
ANDY KAUFMAN • BERNADETTE PETERS
HEARTBEEPS
A MICHAEL PHILLIPS Production
also starring
"HEARTBEEPS"
RANDY QUAID • KENNETH McMILLAN
CHRISTOPHER GUEST
and MELANIE MAYRON
Associate Producer JOHN HILL • Music by JOHN WILLIAMS
Executive Producer DOUG GREEN • Written by JOHN HILL
Special Make-Up Effects by STAN WINSTON
Special Visual Effects by ALBERT WHITLOCK
PHIL designed by JAMIE SHOURT and ROBBIE BLALACK
Produced by MICHAEL PHILLIPS • Directed by ALLAN ARKUSH
Original Soundtrack on MCA Records and Tapes
Read the JOVE BOOK
A UNIVERSAL PICTURE
PG PARENTAL GUIDANCE SUGGESTED
SOME MATERIAL MAY NOT BE SUITABLE FOR CHILDREN
© 1981 UNIVERSAL CITY STUDIOS, INC.
Starts FRIDAY DEC.18th at a Universal Special Presentation Theatre Near You

Indiana Jones—the new hero from the creators of JAWS and STAR WARS.

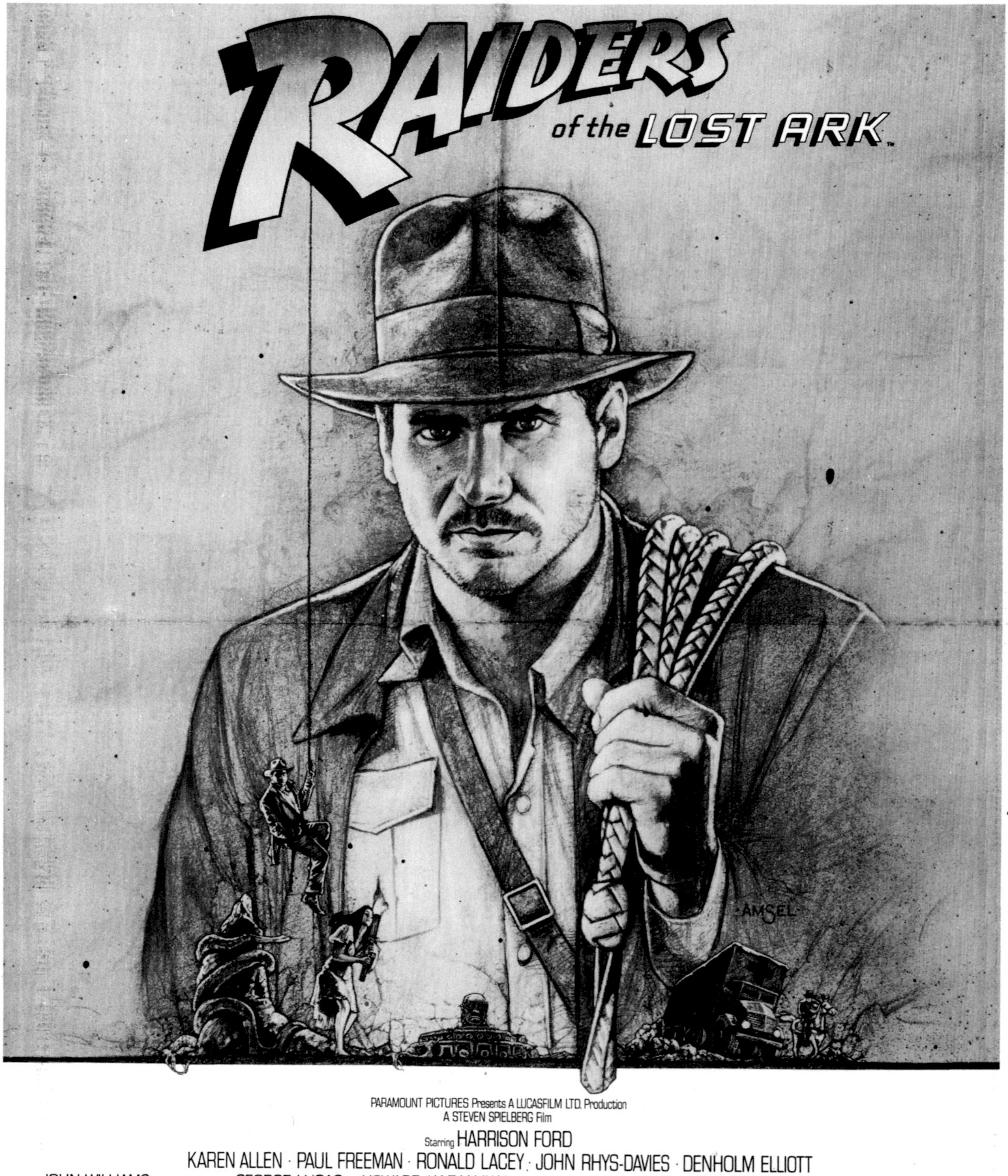

PARAMOUNT PICTURES Presents A LUCASFILM LTD. Production
A STEVEN SPIELBERG Film

Starring HARRISON FORD

KAREN ALLEN · PAUL FREEMAN · RONALD LACEY · JOHN RHYS-DAVIES · DENHOLM ELLIOTT

Music by JOHN WILLIAMS · Executive Producers GEORGE LUCAS and HOWARD KAZANJIAN · Screenplay by LAWRENCE KASDAN · Story by GEORGE LUCAS and PHILIP KAUFMAN

Produced by FRANK MARSHALL · Directed by STEVEN SPIELBERG Filmed in Panavision® DOLBY STEREO IN SELECTED THEATRES NOVELIZATION FROM BALLANTINE BOOKS ORIGINAL SOUNDTRACK ON COLUMBIA RECORDS & TAPES

PG PARENTAL GUIDANCE SUGGESTED
SOME MATERIAL MAY NOT BE SUITABLE FOR CHILDREN

A PARAMOUNT PICTURE

STARTS FRIDAY

✓*LOEWS ASTOR PLAZA
Broadway at 44th St. 869-8340

Walter Reade's
✓CORONET
3rd Ave. near 59th St. 355-1663

✓*LOEWS ORPHEUM
86th St. Near 3rd Ave. 289-4607

✓*LOEWS 34th ST. SHOWPLACE
34th Street bet. 2nd & 3rd Avenues 532-5544

* 70mm Six-Track

AND AT A THEATRE NEAR YOU

✓ DOLBY STEREO

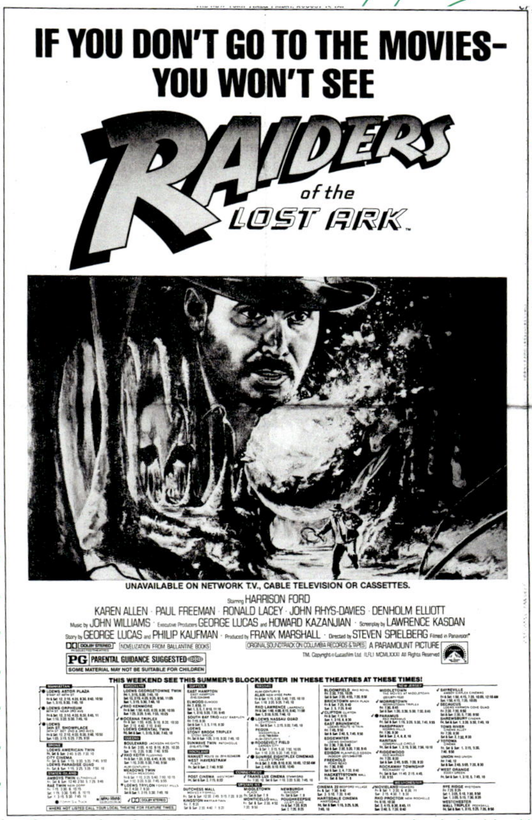
IF YOU DON'T GO TO THE MOVIES-
YOU WON'T SEE
RAIDERS
of the
LOST ARK
UNAVAILABLE ON NETWORK T.V., CABLE TELEVISION OR CASSETTES.
THIS WEEKEND SEE THIS SUMMER'S BLOCKBUSTER IN THESE THEATRES AT THESE TIMES!

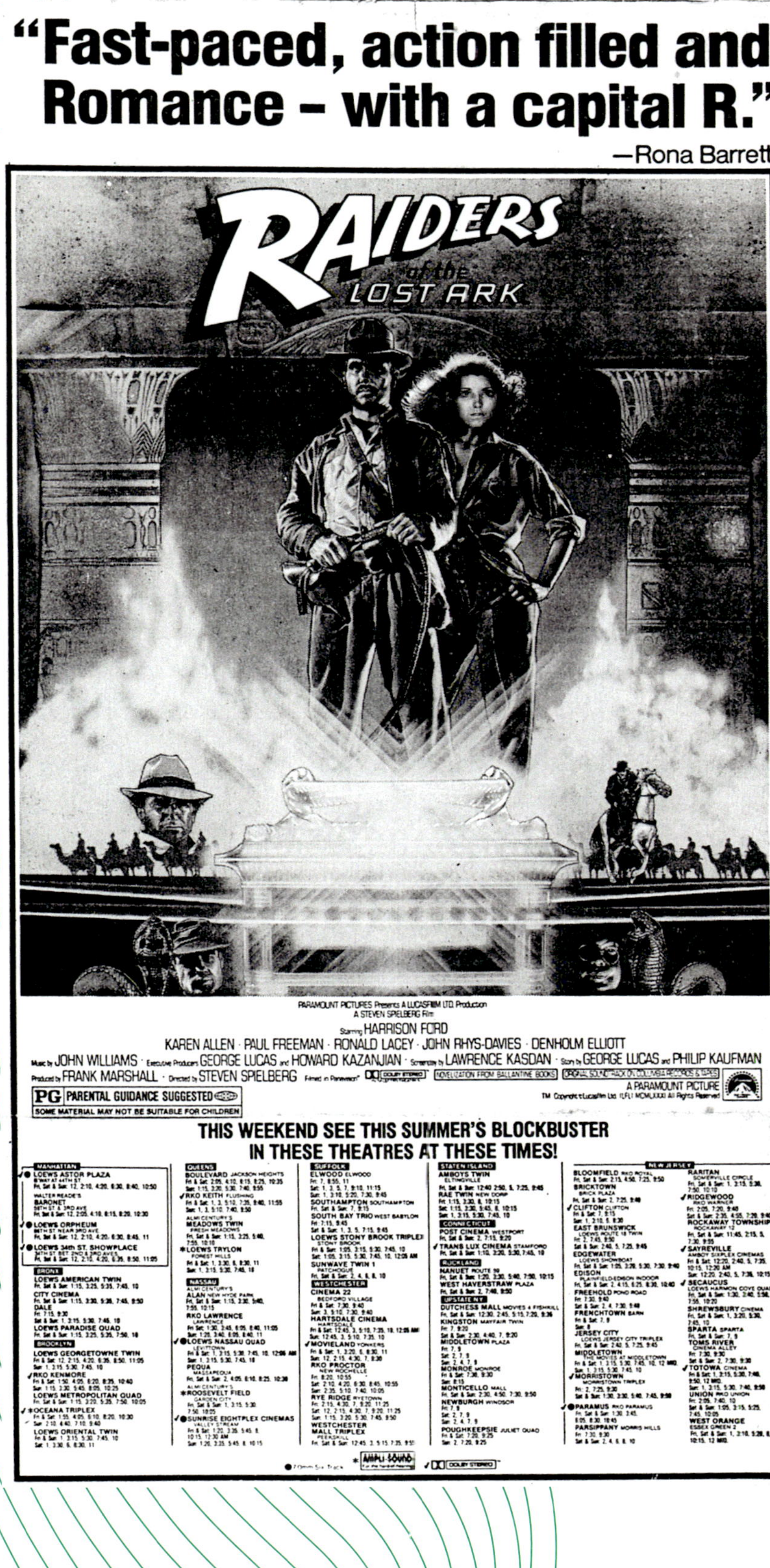
"Fast-paced, action filled and Romance – with a capital R."
—Rona Barrett
RAIDERS
of the
LOST ARK
PARAMOUNT PICTURES Presents A LUCASFILM LTD. Production
A STEVEN SPIELBERG Film
Starring HARRISON FORD
KAREN ALLEN · PAUL FREEMAN · RONALD LACEY · JOHN RHYS-DAVIES · DENHOLM ELLIOTT
Music by JOHN WILLIAMS · Executive Producers GEORGE LUCAS and HOWARD KAZANJIAN · Screenplay by LAWRENCE KASDAN · Story by GEORGE LUCAS and PHILIP KAUFMAN
Produced by FRANK MARSHALL · Directed by STEVEN SPIELBERG
PG PARENTAL GUIDANCE SUGGESTED
SOME MATERIAL MAY NOT BE SUITABLE FOR CHILDREN
A PARAMOUNT PICTURE
THIS WEEKEND SEE THIS SUMMER'S BLOCKBUSTER
IN THESE THEATRES AT THESE TIMES!

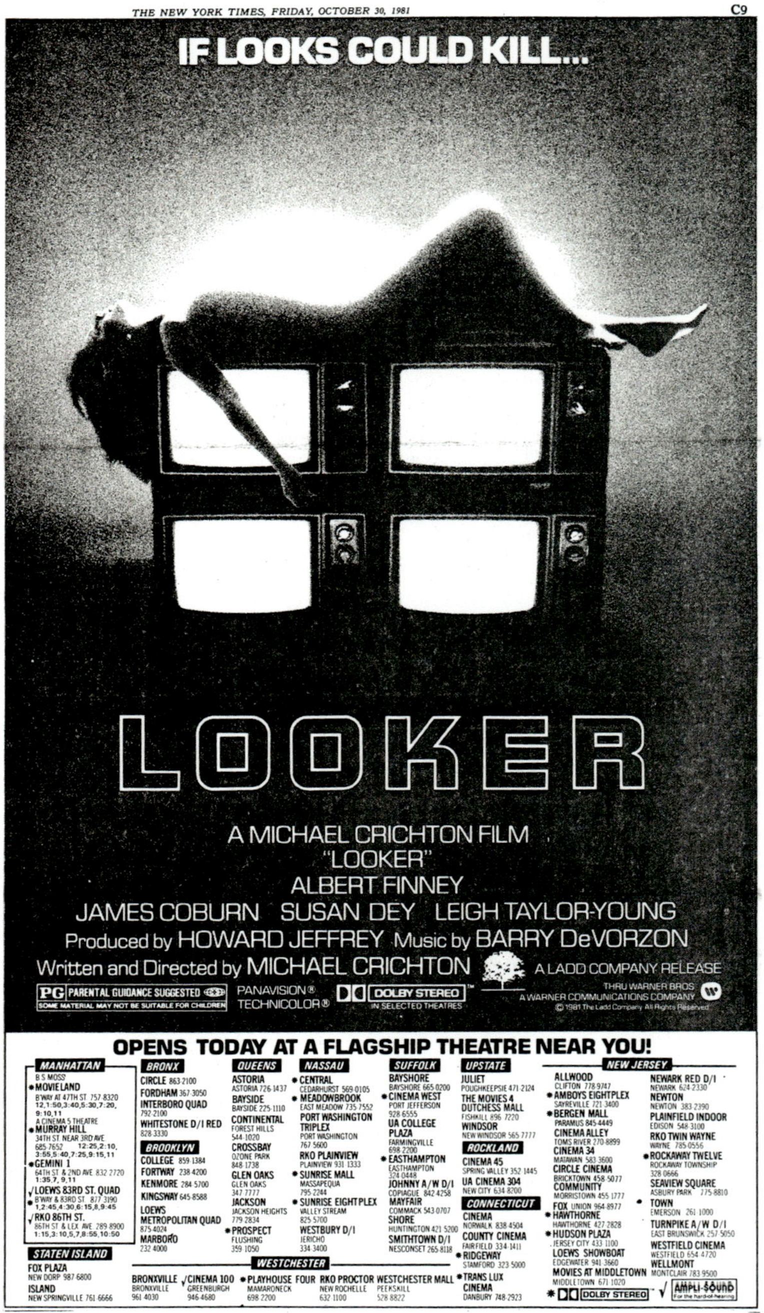

HEAVY METAL

In 1972, Ralph Bakshi's *Fritz the Cat* became the first animated feature to land an X rating, signaling that the days when cartoons were just kid stuff were over. Nine years later, producer Ivan Reitman reteamed with his *Meatballs* and *Stripes* scripters Daniel Goldberg and Len Blum to create a feature based on the *Heavy Metal* comics magazine and its groundbreaking graphic mix of sci-fi and sexy content. Directed by Gerald Potterton (though the segments within the film have their own directors), who had been an animator on the Beatles classic *Yellow Submarine*, this hard-R fantasy was one of those movies your parents wouldn't let you see back in the day, and reviewers responded with both enthusiasm and contempt.

"*Heavy Metal* has been animated with great verve, and scored very well. ... Superhuman fierceness is at the root of this kind of fantasy, but there are also enough sympathetic touches to make the material involving."

–Janet Maslin, *The New York Times*

"The film is full of grand adventures, including space flights, sword battles, sex scenes, and shootouts. And save for its consistently sexist treatment of women as objects of lust, *Heavy Metal* is an enormous amount of fun."

–Gene Siskel, *Chicago Tribune*

"Somehow a great deal of the charm leaked out on the way to the movie house, but all of the sadism stayed put. And then some. It's the most expensive adolescent fantasy revenge fulfillment wet dream ever to slither onto a screen."

–SHEILA BENSON, *LOS ANGELES TIMES*

"The artists are hardly descendants of Disney, Lantz and Fleischer—but they're not even successors to the more contemporary styles of Mad Magazine, R. Crumb or Ralph Bakshi. What they are is misogynist, paranoid, silly and grossly inept."

–Rob Baker, New York *Daily News*

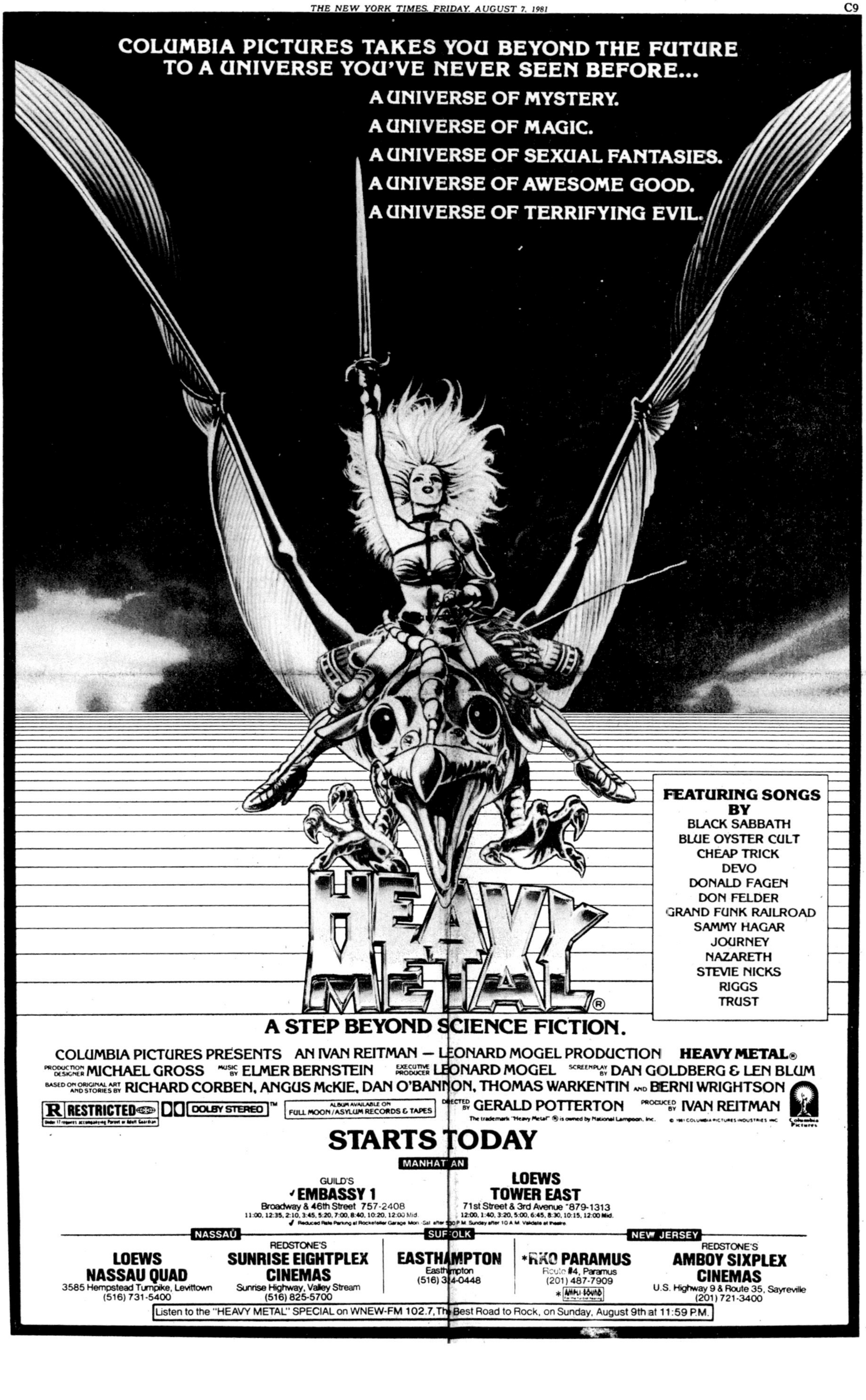
THE NEW YORK TIMES, FRIDAY, AUGUST 7, 1981
C9
COLUMBIA PICTURES TAKES YOU BEYOND THE FUTURE
TO A UNIVERSE YOU'VE NEVER SEEN BEFORE...
A UNIVERSE OF MYSTERY.
A UNIVERSE OF MAGIC.
A UNIVERSE OF SEXUAL FANTASIES.
A UNIVERSE OF AWESOME GOOD.
A UNIVERSE OF TERRIFYING EVIL.
FEATURING SONGS BY
BLACK SABBATH
BLUE OYSTER CULT
CHEAP TRICK
DEVO
DONALD FAGEN
DON FELDER
GRAND FUNK RAILROAD
SAMMY HAGAR
JOURNEY
NAZARETH
STEVIE NICKS
RIGGS
TRUST
HEAVY METAL®
A STEP BEYOND SCIENCE FICTION.
COLUMBIA PICTURES PRESENTS AN IVAN REITMAN — LEONARD MOGEL PRODUCTION HEAVY METAL®
PRODUCTION DESIGNER MICHAEL GROSS MUSIC BY ELMER BERNSTEIN EXECUTIVE PRODUCER LEONARD MOGEL SCREENPLAY BY DAN GOLDBERG & LEN BLUM
BASED ON ORIGINAL ART AND STORIES BY RICHARD CORBEN, ANGUS McKIE, DAN O'BANNON, THOMAS WARKENTIN AND BERNI WRIGHTSON
R RESTRICTED
Under 17 requires accompanying Parent or Adult Guardian
DOLBY STEREO™
ALBUM AVAILABLE ON FULL MOON/ASYLUM RECORDS & TAPES
DIRECTED BY GERALD POTTERTON PRODUCED BY IVAN REITMAN
The trademark "Heavy Metal" ® is owned by National Lampoon, Inc.
© 1981 COLUMBIA PICTURES INDUSTRIES INC
Columbia Pictures
STARTS TODAY
MANHATTAN
GUILD'S
✓EMBASSY 1
Broadway & 46th Street 757-2408
11:00, 12:35, 2:10, 3:45, 5:20, 7:00, 8:40, 10:20, 12:00 Mid.
LOEWS
TOWER EAST
71st Street & 3rd Avenue 879-1313
12:00, 1:40, 3:20, 5:00, 6:45, 8:30, 10:15, 12:00 Mid.
✓ Reduced Rate Parking at Rockefeller Garage Mon.-Sat. after 5:30 P.M. Sunday after 10 A.M. Validate at theatre.
NASSAU
LOEWS
NASSAU QUAD
3585 Hempstead Turnpike, Levittown
(516) 731-5400
REDSTONE'S
SUNRISE EIGHTPLEX
CINEMAS
Sunrise Highway, Valley Stream
(516) 825-5700
SUFFOLK
EASTHAMPTON
Easthampton
(516) 324-0448
NEW JERSEY
*RKO PARAMUS
Route #4, Paramus
(201) 487-7909
* AMPLI-SOUND
REDSTONE'S
AMBOY SIXPLEX
CINEMAS
U.S. Highway 9 & Route 35, Sayreville
(201) 721-3400
Listen to the "HEAVY METAL" SPECIAL on WNEW-FM 102.7, The Best Road to Rock, on Sunday, August 9th at 11:59 P.M.

16 D THE NEW YORK TIMES, SUNDAY, JULY 26, 1981
ONE OF THE BEST THINGS THAT EVER HAPPENED
IS ABOUT TO HAPPEN AGAIN.
THE EMPIRE STRIKES BACK
Starring
MARK HAMILL · HARRISON FORD · CARRIE FISHER
BILLY DEE WILLIAMS · ANTHONY DANIELS
Co-starring DAVID PROWSE KENNY BAKER PETER MAYHEW FRANK OZ
Directed by IRVIN KERSHNER Produced by GARY KURTZ
Screenplay by LEIGH BRACKETT and LAWRENCE KASDAN Story by GEORGE LUCAS
Executive Producer GEORGE LUCAS Music by JOHN WILLIAMS
DOLBY STEREO IN SELECTED THEATRES
ORIGINAL SOUNDTRACK ON RSO RECORDS
PG PARENTAL GUIDANCE SUGGESTED
SOME MATERIAL MAY NOT BE SUITABLE FOR CHILDREN
NOVELIZATION FROM BALLANTINE BOOKS
SPECIAL LIMITED ENGAGEMENT STARTS FRIDAY
B. S. MOSS
* CRITERION CENTER
B'WAY BET. 44TH & 45TH STS. 582-1795
*GEMINI 2
2ND AVE. AT 64TH ST. 832-2720
AND A SPECIALLY SELECTED THEATRE NEAR YOU
* in 70mm & DOLBY STEREO

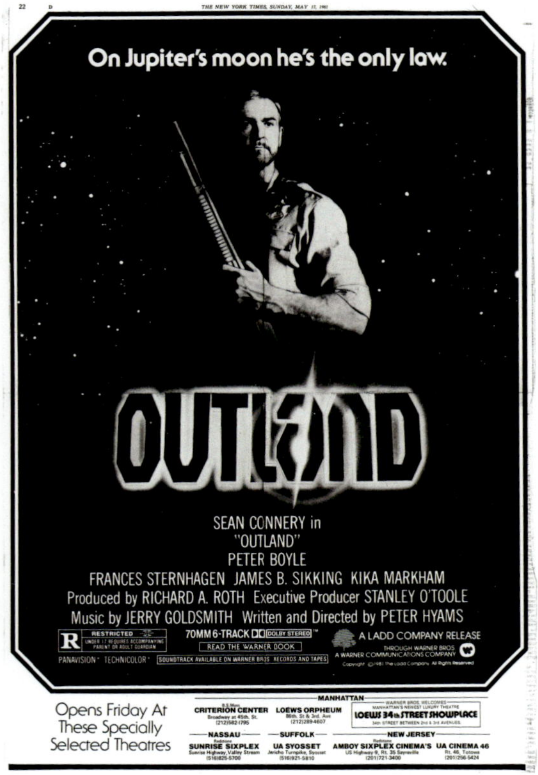
On Jupiter's moon he's the only law.
OUTLAND
SEAN CONNERY in
"OUTLAND"
PETER BOYLE
FRANCES STERNHAGEN JAMES B. SIKKING KIKA MARKHAM
Produced by RICHARD A. ROTH Executive Producer STANLEY O'TOOLE
Music by JERRY GOLDSMITH Written and Directed by PETER HYAMS
R RESTRICTED UNDER 17 REQUIRES ACCOMPANYING PARENT OR ADULT GUARDIAN
70MM 6-TRACK DOLBY STEREO
READ THE WARNER BOOK
A LADD COMPANY RELEASE
THROUGH WARNER BROS
A WARNER COMMUNICATIONS COMPANY
PANAVISION TECHNICOLOR
SOUNDTRACK AVAILABLE ON WARNER BROS RECORDS AND TAPES
Opens Friday At These Specially Selected Theatres
MANHATTAN
CRITERION CENTER
LOEWS ORPHEUM
LOEWS 34th STREET SHOWPLACE
NASSAU
SUNRISE SIXPLEX
SUFFOLK
UA SYOSSET
NEW JERSEY
AMBOY SIXPLEX CINEMA'S
UA CINEMA 46

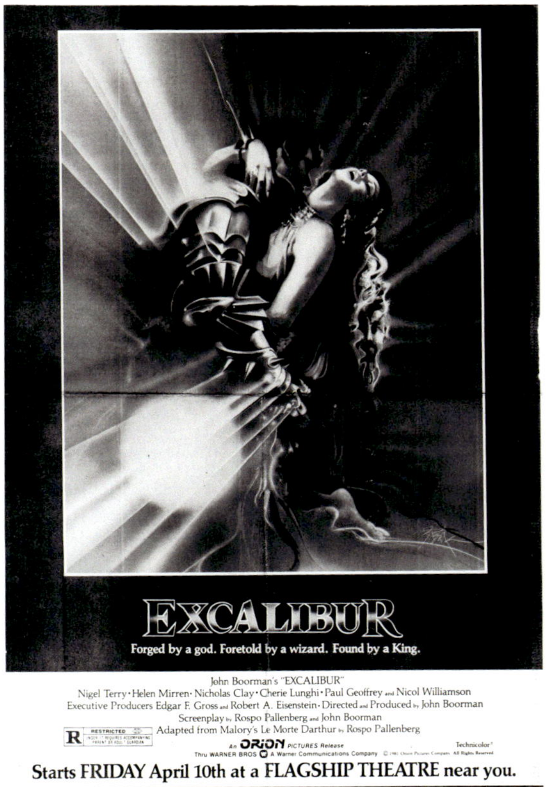
EXCALIBUR
Forged by a god. Foretold by a wizard. Found by a King.
John Boorman's "EXCALIBUR"
Nigel Terry • Helen Mirren • Nicholas Clay • Cherie Lunghi • Paul Geoffrey and Nicol Williamson
Executive Producers Edgar F. Gross and Robert A. Eisenstein • Directed and Produced by John Boorman
Screenplay by Rospo Pallenberg and John Boorman
Adapted from Malory's Le Morte Darthur by Rospo Pallenberg
R RESTRICTED
An ORION PICTURES Release
Thru WARNER BROS A Warner Communications Company
Technicolor
Starts FRIDAY April 10th at a FLAGSHIP THEATRE near you.

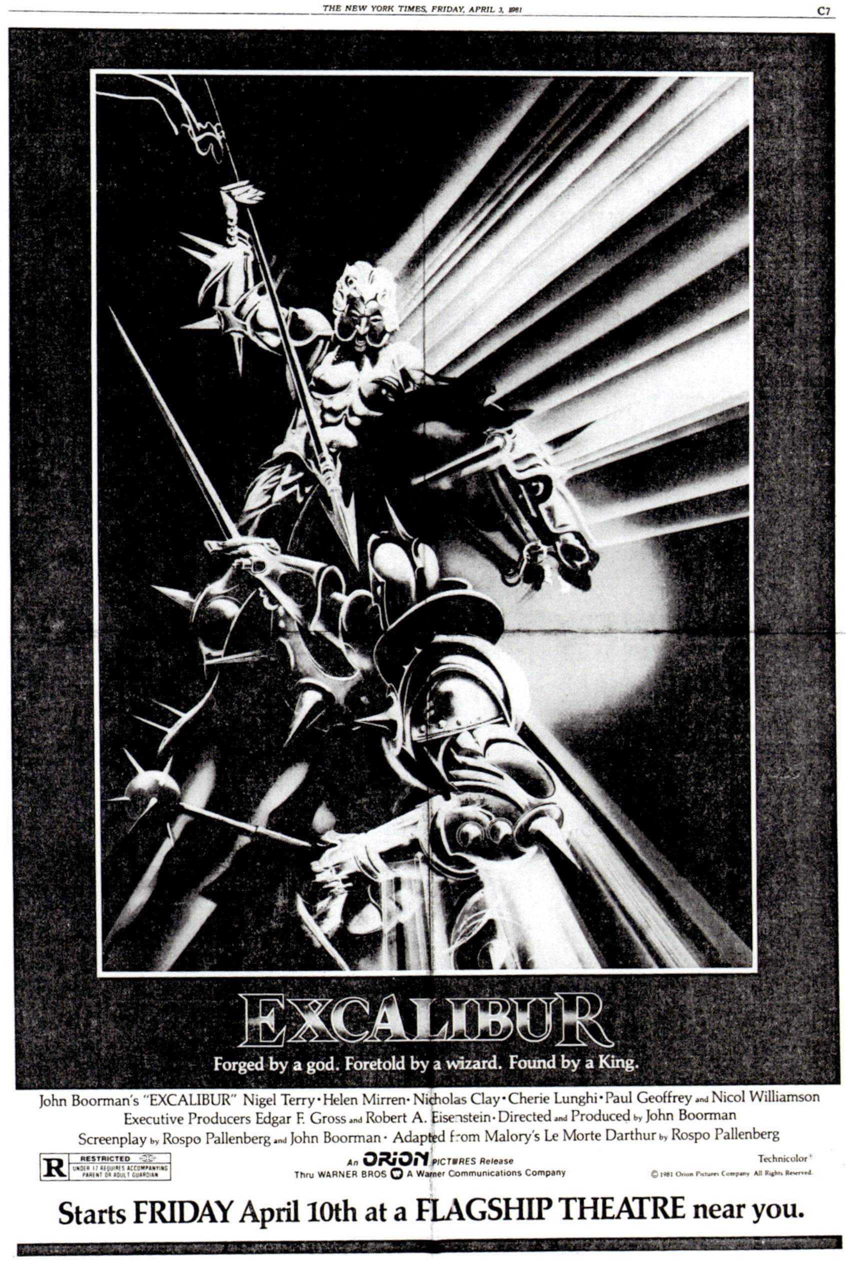
THE NEW YORK TIMES, FRIDAY, APRIL 3, 1981
C7
EXCALIBUR
Forged by a god. Foretold by a wizard. Found by a King.
John Boorman's "EXCALIBUR" Nigel Terry • Helen Mirren • Nicholas Clay • Cherie Lunghi • Paul Geoffrey and Nicol Williamson
Executive Producers Edgar F. Gross and Robert A. Eisenstein • Directed and Produced by John Boorman
Screenplay by Rospo Pallenberg and John Boorman • Adapted from Malory's Le Morte Darthur by Rospo Pallenberg
R RESTRICTED UNDER 17 REQUIRES ACCOMPANYING PARENT OR ADULT GUARDIAN
An ORION PICTURES Release
Thru WARNER BROS A Warner Communications Company
Technicolor
© 1981 Orion Pictures Company All Rights Reserved
Starts FRIDAY April 10th at a FLAGSHIP THEATRE near you.

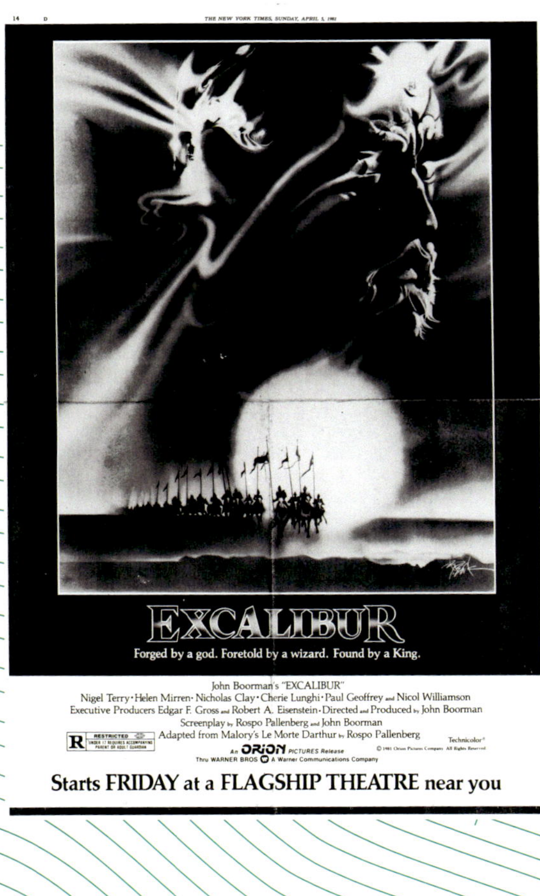
EXCALIBUR
Forged by a god. Foretold by a wizard. Found by a King.
John Boorman's "EXCALIBUR"
Nigel Terry • Helen Mirren • Nicholas Clay • Cherie Lunghi • Paul Geoffrey and Nicol Williamson
Executive Producers Edgar F. Gross and Robert A. Eisenstein • Directed and Produced by John Boorman
Screenplay by Rospo Pallenberg and John Boorman
Adapted from Malory's Le Morte Darthur by Rospo Pallenberg
R RESTRICTED
An ORION PICTURES Release
Thru WARNER BROS A Warner Communications Company
Technicolor
Starts FRIDAY at a FLAGSHIP THEATRE near you

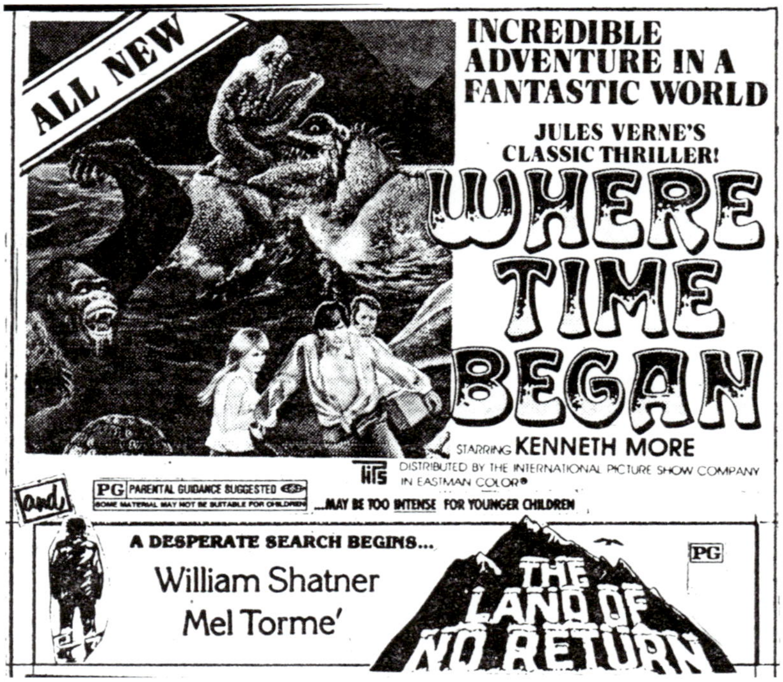

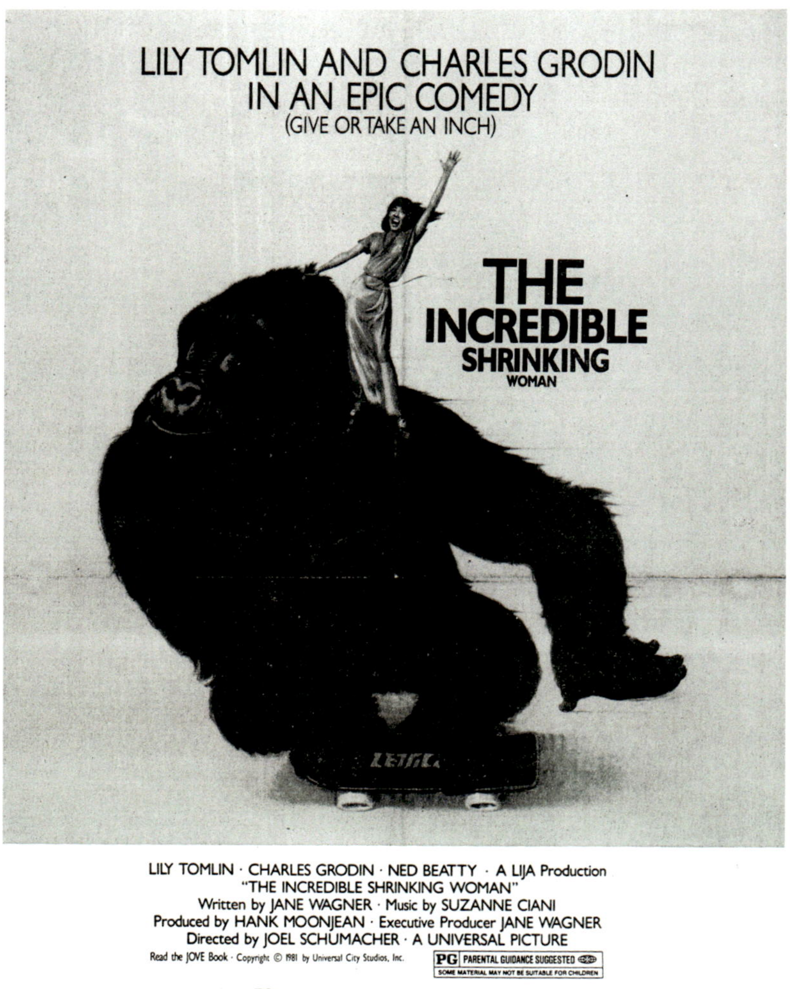

TIME BANDITS

After co-directing *Monty Python's Meaning of Life* and *Life of Brian* with Terry Jones (and guiding the medieval spoof *Jabberwocky* solo), Terry Gilliam and co-scripter Michael Palin embarked on this very odd fantasy, in which a gang of little people take a British schoolboy on a jaunt through assorted eras, encountering colorful characters played by everyone from fellow Pythonite John Cleese to Sean Connery to Shelley Duvall. It veers from knockabout comedy to surprisingly dark childhood-nightmare territory, to the point where even some critics who liked it weren't sure how much of it was supposed to be funny. Audiences responded, though, making *Time Bandits* a sleeper hit for American distributor Avco Embassy, which had heretofore specialized in horror fare.

"Terry Gilliam's *Time Bandits* is a joy to behold. It's an ingenious, witty, giggly, quirky, unpredictable, musical, occasionally farcical, occasionally suspenseful, and occasionally riotous adventure story."

–Bruce McCabe, *The Boston Globe*

"It's a sort of fractured fairy tale that combines elements of myth, the land of Oz, *Star Wars*, assorted rude noises and bumbling characters into a mirthful stew that's funny, scary and yet thoughtful at the same time."

–GEORGE POWELL,
SAN FRANCISCO EXAMINER

"*Time Bandits* is the kind of movie I might have enjoyed as a child. It contains a couple of chunks of good humor, a bunch of gee-whiz special effects, and plenty of dull patches that would allow for repeated trips to the candy counter."

–Gene Siskel, *Chicago Tribune*

"[S]omething of a disappointment despite its mouth-watering cast and whimsical premise. It doesn't exactly steal your time but it verges on wasting it."

–Eleanor Ringel, *The Atlanta Constitution*

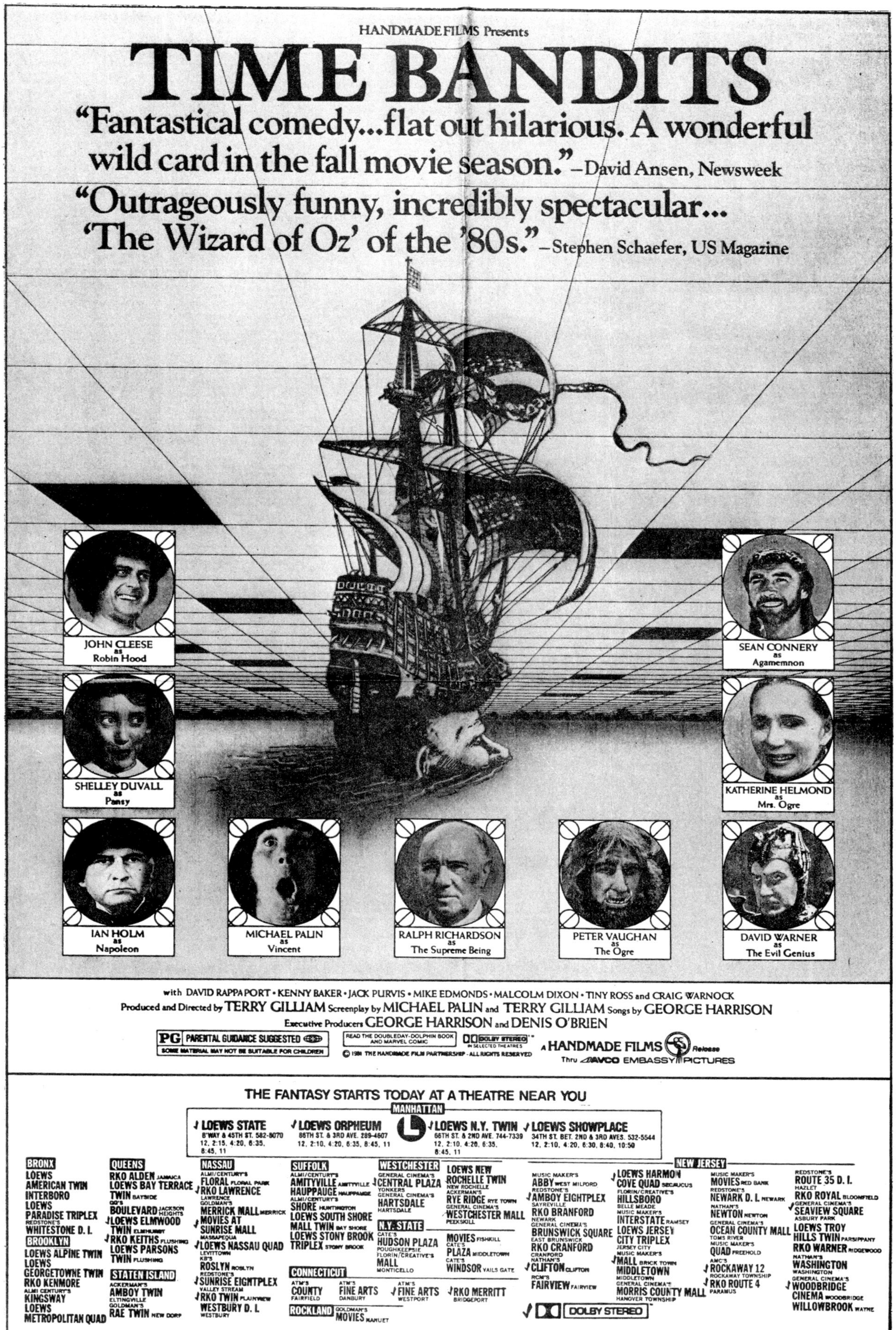

HANDMADE FILMS Presents
TIME BANDITS
"Fantastical comedy...flat out hilarious. A wonderful wild card in the fall movie season." –David Ansen, Newsweek
"Outrageously funny, incredibly spectacular... 'The Wizard of Oz' of the '80s." –Stephen Schaefer, US Magazine
JOHN CLEESE as Robin Hood
SEAN CONNERY as Agamemnon
SHELLEY DUVALL as Pansy
KATHERINE HELMOND as Mrs. Ogre
IAN HOLM as Napoleon
MICHAEL PALIN as Vincent
RALPH RICHARDSON as The Supreme Being
PETER VAUGHAN as The Ogre
DAVID WARNER as The Evil Genius
with DAVID RAPPAPORT • KENNY BAKER • JACK PURVIS • MIKE EDMONDS • MALCOLM DIXON • TINY ROSS and CRAIG WARNOCK
Produced and Directed by TERRY GILLIAM Screenplay by MICHAEL PALIN and TERRY GILLIAM Songs by GEORGE HARRISON
Executive Producers GEORGE HARRISON and DENIS O'BRIEN
PG PARENTAL GUIDANCE SUGGESTED
SOME MATERIAL MAY NOT BE SUITABLE FOR CHILDREN
READ THE DOUBLEDAY-DOLPHIN BOOK AND MARVEL COMIC
© 1981 THE HANDMADE FILM PARTNERSHIP - ALL RIGHTS RESERVED
DOLBY STEREO IN SELECTED THEATRES
A HANDMADE FILMS Release
Thru AVCO EMBASSY PICTURES
THE FANTASY STARTS TODAY AT A THEATRE NEAR YOU
MANHATTAN
LOEWS STATE B'WAY & 45TH ST. 582-5070 12, 2:15, 4:20, 6:35, 8:45, 11
LOEWS ORPHEUM 86TH ST. & 3RD AVE. 289-4607 12, 2:10, 4:20, 6:35, 8:45, 11
LOEWS N.Y. TWIN 66TH ST. & 2ND AVE. 744-7339 12, 2:10, 4:20, 6:35, 8:45, 11
LOEWS SHOWPLACE 34TH ST. BET. 2ND & 3RD AVES. 532-5544 12, 2:10, 4:20, 6:30, 8:40, 10:50
BRONX
LOEWS AMERICAN TWIN
INTERBORO
LOEWS PARADISE TRIPLEX
REDSTONE'S WHITESTONE D. I.
BROOKLYN
LOEWS ALPINE TWIN
LOEWS GEORGETOWNE TWIN
RKO KENMORE
ALMI CENTURY'S KINGSWAY
LOEWS METROPOLITAN QUAD
QUEENS
RKO ALDEN JAMAICA
LOEWS BAY TERRACE TWIN BAYSIDE
QQ'S BOULEVARD JACKSON HEIGHTS
LOEWS ELMWOOD TWIN ELMHURST
RKO KEITHS FLUSHING
LOEWS PARSONS TWIN FLUSHING
STATEN ISLAND
ACKERMAN'S AMBOY TWIN ELTINGVILLE
GOLDMAN'S RAE TWIN NEW DORP
NASSAU
ALMI/CENTURY'S FLORAL FLORAL PARK
RKO LAWRENCE LAWRENCE
GOLDMAN'S MERRICK MALL MERRICK
MOVIES AT SUNRISE MALL MASSAPEQUA
LOEWS NASSAU QUAD LEVITTOWN
KB'S ROSLYN ROSLYN
REDSTONE'S SUNRISE EIGHTPLEX VALLEY STREAM
RKO TWIN PLAINVIEW
WESTBURY D. I. WESTBURY
SUFFOLK
ALMI/CENTURY'S AMITYVILLE AMITYVILLE
HAUPPAUGE HAUPPAUGE
ALMI/CENTURY'S SHORE HUNTINGTON
LOEWS SOUTH SHORE MALL TWIN BAY SHORE
LOEWS STONY BROOK TRIPLEX STONY BROOK
CONNECTICUT
ATM'S COUNTY FAIRFIELD
ATM'S FINE ARTS DANBURY
ATM'S FINE ARTS WESTPORT
RKO MERRITT BRIDGEPORT
ROCKLAND
GOLDMAN'S MOVIES NANUET
WESTCHESTER
GENERAL CINEMA'S CENTRAL PLAZA YONKERS
GENERAL CINEMA'S HARTSDALE HARTSDALE
LOEWS NEW ROCHELLE TWIN NEW ROCHELLE
ACKERMAN'S RYE RIDGE RYE TOWN
GENERAL CINEMA'S WESTCHESTER MALL PEEKSKILL
N.Y. STATE
CATE'S HUDSON PLAZA POUGHKEEPSIE
FLORIN/CREATIVE'S MALL MONTICELLO
MOVIES FISHKILL
CATE'S PLAZA MIDDLETOWN
CATE'S WINDSOR VAILS GATE
NEW JERSEY
MUSIC MAKER'S ABBY WEST MILFORD
REDSTONE'S AMBOY EIGHTPLEX SAYREVILLE
RKO BRANFORD NEWARK
GENERAL CINEMA'S BRUNSWICK SQUARE EAST BRUNSWICK
RKO CRANFORD CRANFORD
NATHAN'S CLIFTON CLIFTON
RCM'S FAIRVIEW FAIRVIEW
LOEWS HARMON COVE QUAD SECAUCUS
FLORIN/CREATIVE'S HILLSBORO BELLE MEADE
MUSIC MAKER'S INTERSTATE RAMSEY
LOEWS JERSEY CITY TRIPLEX JERSEY CITY
MUSIC MAKER'S MALL BRICK TOWN
MIDDLETOWN MIDDLETOWN
GENERAL CINEMA'S MORRIS COUNTY MALL HANOVER TOWNSHIP
MUSIC MAKER'S MOVIES RED BANK
REDSTONE'S NEWARK D. I. NEWARK
NATHAN'S NEWTON NEWTON
GENERAL CINEMA'S OCEAN COUNTY MALL TOMS RIVER
MUSIC MAKER'S QUAD FREEHOLD
AMC'S ROCKAWAY 12 ROCKAWAY TOWNSHIP
RKO ROUTE 4 PARAMUS
REDSTONE'S ROUTE 35 D. I. HAZLET
RKO ROYAL BLOOMFIELD
GENERAL CINEMA'S SEAVIEW SQUARE ASBURY PARK
LOEWS TROY HILLS TWIN PARSIPPANY
RKO WARNER RIDGEWOOD
NATHAN'S WASHINGTON WASHINGTON
GENERAL CINEMA'S WOODBRIDGE CINEMA WOODBRIDGE
WILLOWBROOK WAYNE
DOLBY STEREO

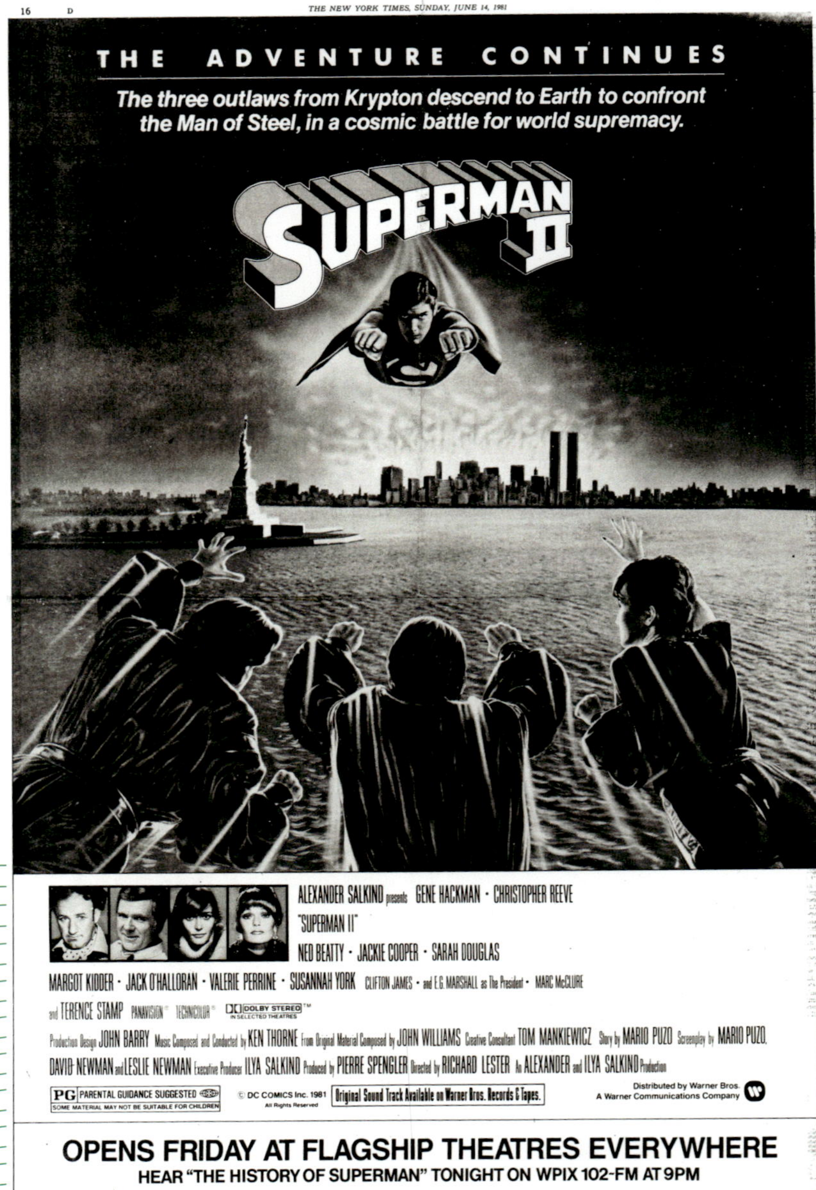
16 D
THE NEW YORK TIMES, SUNDAY, JUNE 14, 1981
THE ADVENTURE CONTINUES
The three outlaws from Krypton descend to Earth to confront the Man of Steel, in a cosmic battle for world supremacy.
SUPERMAN II
ALEXANDER SALKIND presents GENE HACKMAN · CHRISTOPHER REEVE
"SUPERMAN II"
NED BEATTY · JACKIE COOPER · SARAH DOUGLAS
MARGOT KIDDER · JACK O'HALLORAN · VALERIE PERRINE · SUSANNAH YORK CLIFTON JAMES · and E.G. MARSHALL as The President · MARC McCLURE
and TERENCE STAMP PANAVISION® TECHNICOLOR® DOLBY STEREO™ IN SELECTED THEATRES
Production Design JOHN BARRY Music Composed and Conducted by KEN THORNE From Original Material Composed by JOHN WILLIAMS Creative Consultant TOM MANKIEWICZ Story by MARIO PUZO Screenplay by MARIO PUZO, DAVID NEWMAN and LESLIE NEWMAN Executive Producer ILYA SALKIND Produced by PIERRE SPENGLER Directed by RICHARD LESTER An ALEXANDER and ILYA SALKIND Production
PG PARENTAL GUIDANCE SUGGESTED
SOME MATERIAL MAY NOT BE SUITABLE FOR CHILDREN
© DC COMICS Inc. 1981
All Rights Reserved
Original Sound Track Available on Warner Bros. Records & Tapes.
Distributed by Warner Bros.
A Warner Communications Company
OPENS FRIDAY AT FLAGSHIP THEATRES EVERYWHERE
HEAR "THE HISTORY OF SUPERMAN" TONIGHT ON WPIX 102-FM AT 9PM

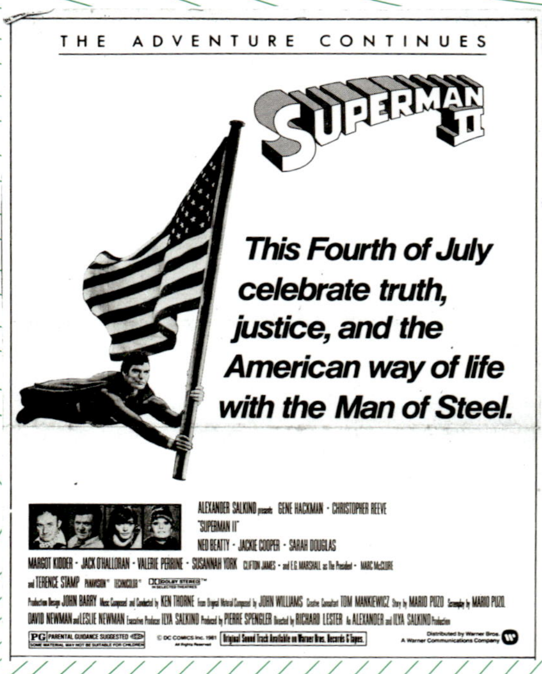
THE ADVENTURE CONTINUES
SUPERMAN II
This Fourth of July celebrate truth, justice, and the American way of life with the Man of Steel.
ALEXANDER SALKIND presents GENE HACKMAN · CHRISTOPHER REEVE
"SUPERMAN II"
NED BEATTY · JACKIE COOPER · SARAH DOUGLAS
MARGOT KIDDER · JACK O'HALLORAN · VALERIE PERRINE · SUSANNAH YORK CLIFTON JAMES · and E.G. MARSHALL as The President · MARC McCLURE
and TERENCE STAMP PANAVISION® TECHNICOLOR® DOLBY STEREO™ IN SELECTED THEATRES
Production Design JOHN BARRY Music Composed and Conducted by KEN THORNE From Original Material Composed by JOHN WILLIAMS Creative Consultant TOM MANKIEWICZ Story by MARIO PUZO Screenplay by MARIO PUZO, DAVID NEWMAN and LESLIE NEWMAN Executive Producer ILYA SALKIND Produced by PIERRE SPENGLER Directed by RICHARD LESTER An ALEXANDER and ILYA SALKIND Production
PG PARENTAL GUIDANCE SUGGESTED
SOME MATERIAL MAY NOT BE SUITABLE FOR CHILDREN
© DC COMICS Inc. 1981
All Rights Reserved
Original Sound Track Available on Warner Bros. Records & Tapes.
Distributed by Warner Bros.
A Warner Communications Company

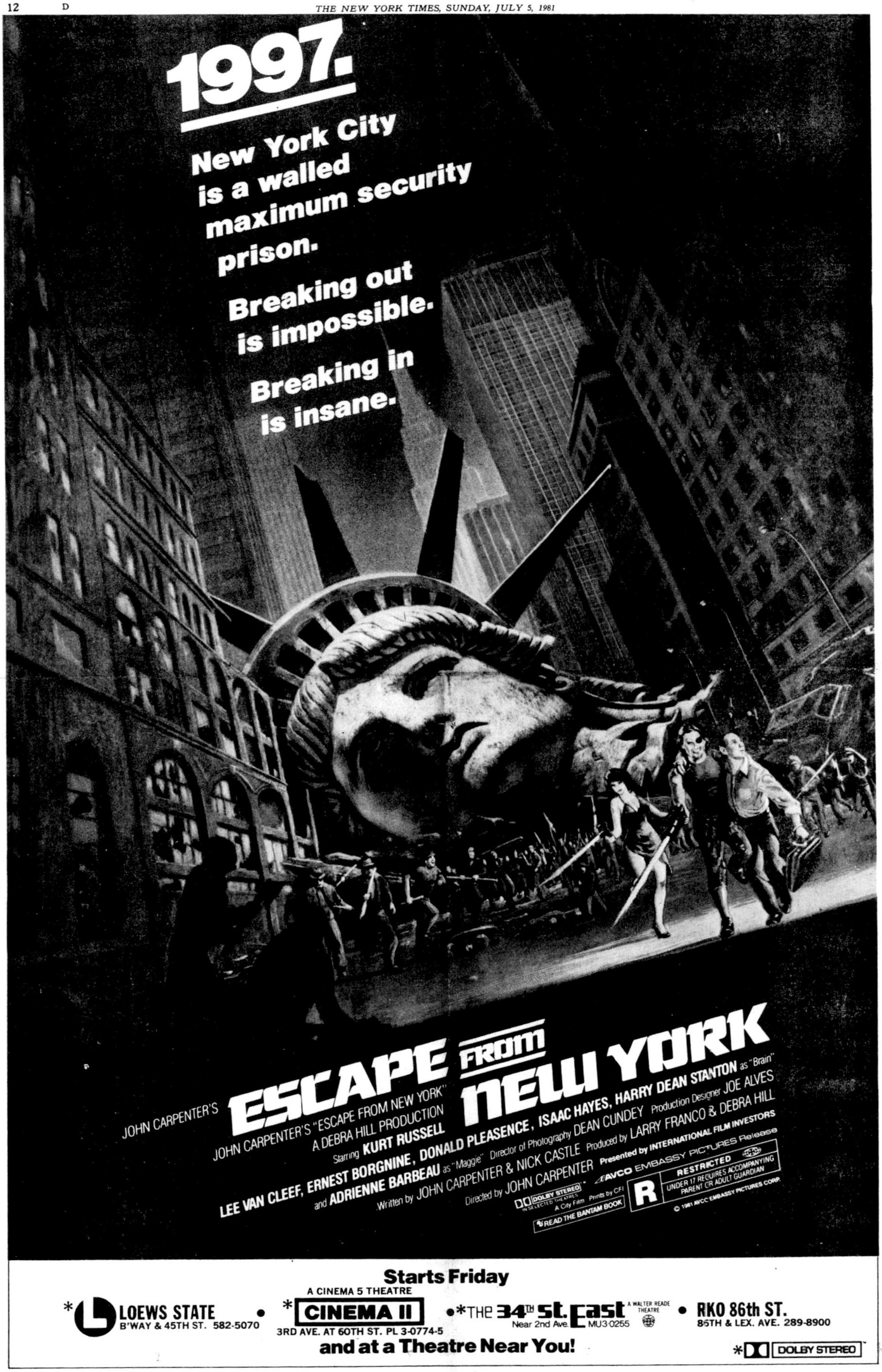
1997.
New York City is a walled maximum security prison.
Breaking out is impossible.
Breaking in is insane.
JOHN CARPENTER'S
ESCAPE FROM NEW YORK
JOHN CARPENTER'S "ESCAPE FROM NEW YORK"
A DEBRA HILL PRODUCTION
Starring KURT RUSSELL
LEE VAN CLEEF, ERNEST BORGNINE, DONALD PLEASENCE, ISAAC HAYES, HARRY DEAN STANTON as "Brain"
and ADRIENNE BARBEAU as "Maggie" Director of Photography DEAN CUNDEY Production Designer JOE ALVES
Written by JOHN CARPENTER & NICK CASTLE Produced by LARRY FRANCO & DEBRA HILL
Directed by JOHN CARPENTER Presented by INTERNATIONAL FILM INVESTORS
AVCO EMBASSY PICTURES Release
DOLBY STEREO IN SELECTED THEATRES
A City Film Prints by CFI
READ THE BANTAM BOOK
R RESTRICTED UNDER 17 REQUIRES ACCOMPANYING PARENT OR ADULT GUARDIAN
© 1981 AVCO EMBASSY PICTURES CORP.
Starts Friday
*LOEWS STATE B'WAY & 45TH ST. 582-5070
A CINEMA 5 THEATRE *CINEMA II 3RD AVE. AT 60TH ST. PL 3-0774-5
*THE 34TH St. East Near 2nd Ave. MU3-0255 A WALTER READE THEATRE
RKO 86th ST. 86TH & LEX. AVE. 289-8900
and at a Theatre Near You!
*DOLBY STEREO

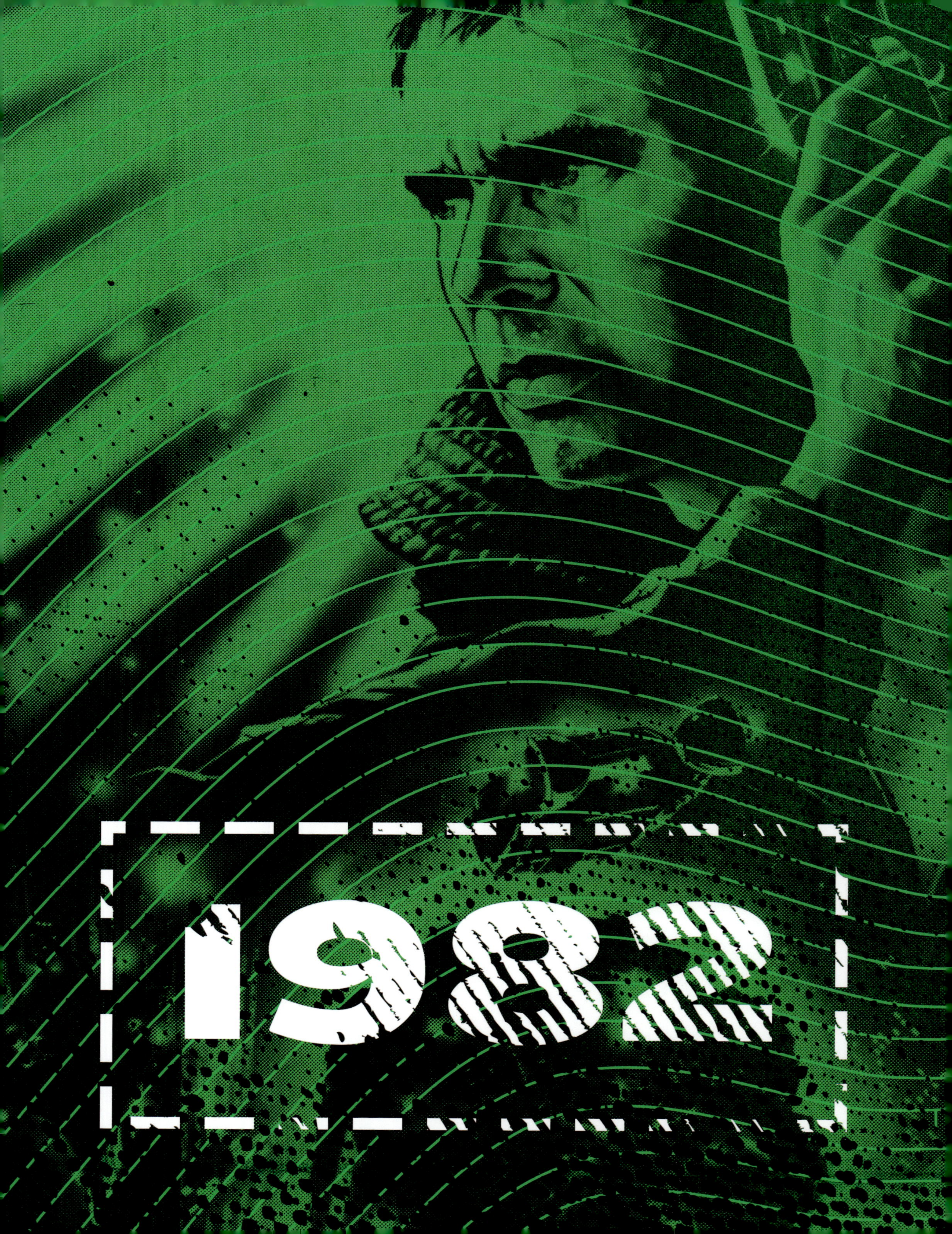
1982

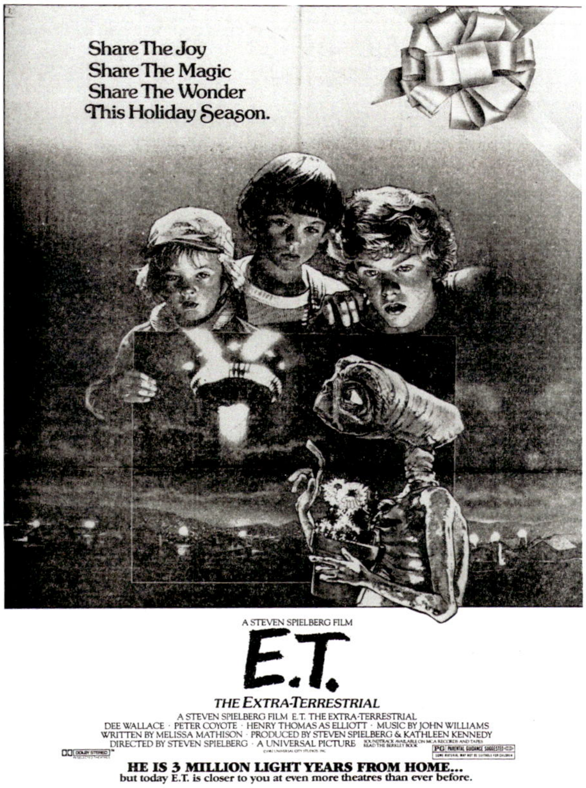
Share The Joy
Share The Magic
Share The Wonder
This Holiday Season.
A STEVEN SPIELBERG FILM
E.T.
THE EXTRA-TERRESTRIAL
A STEVEN SPIELBERG FILM E.T. THE EXTRA-TERRESTRIAL
DEE WALLACE · PETER COYOTE · HENRY THOMAS AS ELLIOTT · MUSIC BY JOHN WILLIAMS
WRITTEN BY MELISSA MATHISON · PRODUCED BY STEVEN SPIELBERG & KATHLEEN KENNEDY
DIRECTED BY STEVEN SPIELBERG · A UNIVERSAL PICTURE
HE IS 3 MILLION LIGHT YEARS FROM HOME...
but today E.T. is closer to you at even more theatres than ever before.

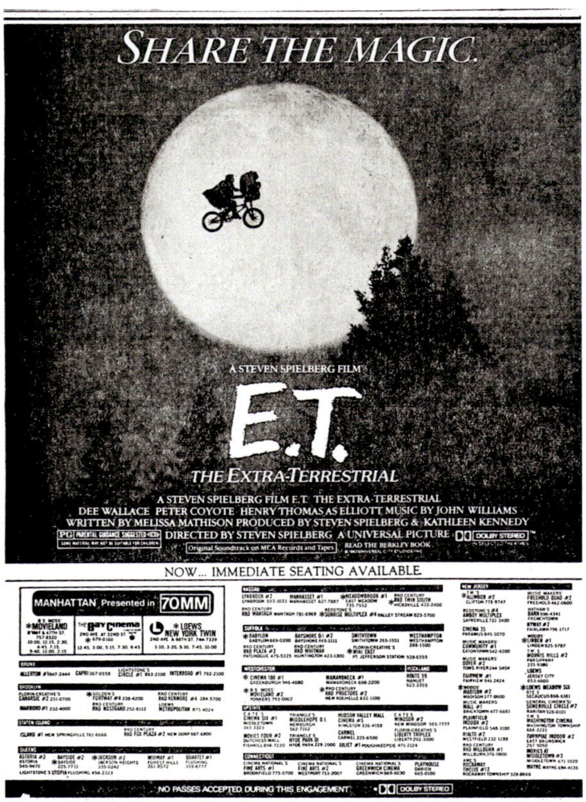
SHARE THE MAGIC.
A STEVEN SPIELBERG FILM
E.T.
THE EXTRA-TERRESTRIAL
A STEVEN SPIELBERG FILM E.T. THE EXTRA-TERRESTRIAL
DEE WALLACE PETER COYOTE HENRY THOMAS AS ELLIOTT MUSIC BY JOHN WILLIAMS
WRITTEN BY MELISSA MATHISON PRODUCED BY STEVEN SPIELBERG & KATHLEEN KENNEDY
DIRECTED BY STEVEN SPIELBERG A UNIVERSAL PICTURE
Original Soundtrack on MCA Records and Tapes
READ THE BERKLEY BOOK
NOW... IMMEDIATE SEATING AVAILABLE.
MANHATTAN Presented in 70MM
NO PASSES ACCEPTED DURING THIS ENGAGEMENT

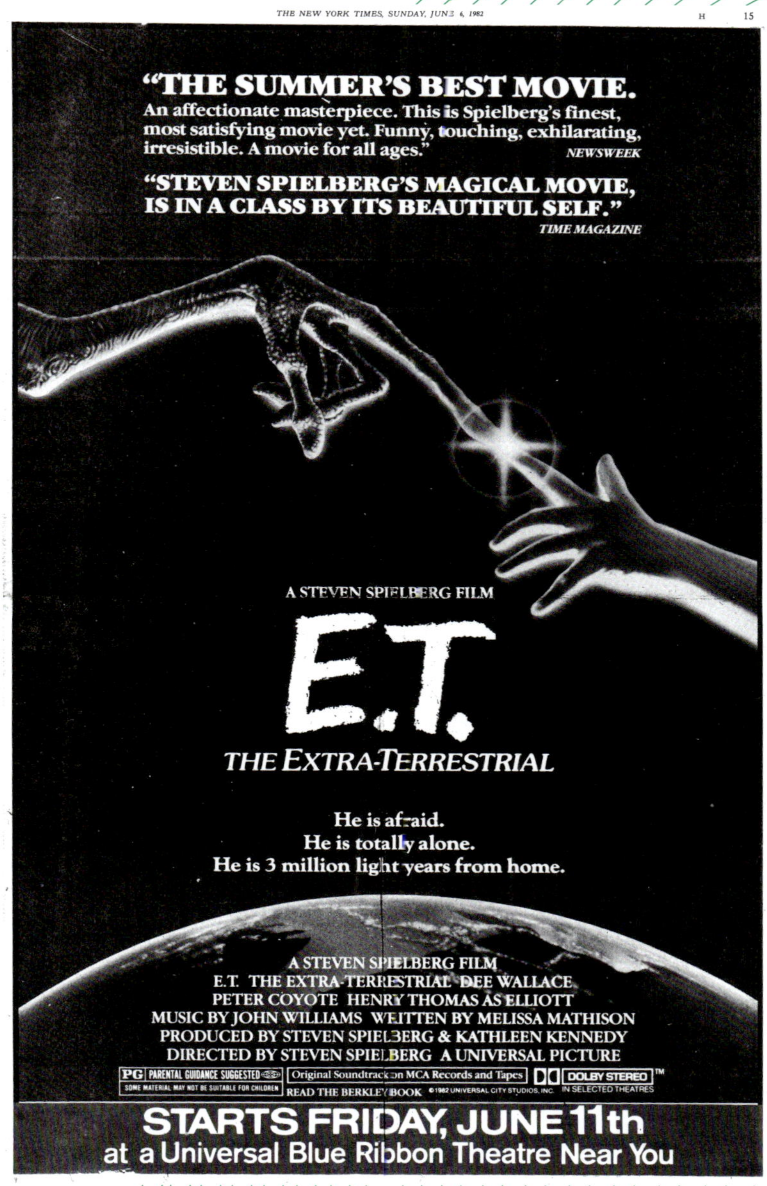
THE NEW YORK TIMES, SUNDAY, JUNE 6, 1982
"THE SUMMER'S BEST MOVIE.
An affectionate masterpiece. This is Spielberg's finest, most satisfying movie yet. Funny, touching, exhilarating, irresistible. A movie for all ages."
NEWSWEEK
"STEVEN SPIELBERG'S MAGICAL MOVIE, IS IN A CLASS BY ITS BEAUTIFUL SELF."
TIME MAGAZINE
A STEVEN SPIELBERG FILM
E.T.
THE EXTRA-TERRESTRIAL
He is afraid.
He is totally alone.
He is 3 million light years from home.
A STEVEN SPIELBERG FILM
E.T. THE EXTRA-TERRESTRIAL DEE WALLACE
PETER COYOTE HENRY THOMAS AS ELLIOTT
MUSIC BY JOHN WILLIAMS WRITTEN BY MELISSA MATHISON
PRODUCED BY STEVEN SPIELBERG & KATHLEEN KENNEDY
DIRECTED BY STEVEN SPIELBERG A UNIVERSAL PICTURE
PG PARENTAL GUIDANCE SUGGESTED
SOME MATERIAL MAY NOT BE SUITABLE FOR CHILDREN
Original Soundtrack on MCA Records and Tapes
DOLBY STEREO
IN SELECTED THEATRES
READ THE BERKLEY BOOK
©1982 UNIVERSAL CITY STUDIOS, INC.
STARTS FRIDAY, JUNE 11th
at a Universal Blue Ribbon Theatre Near You

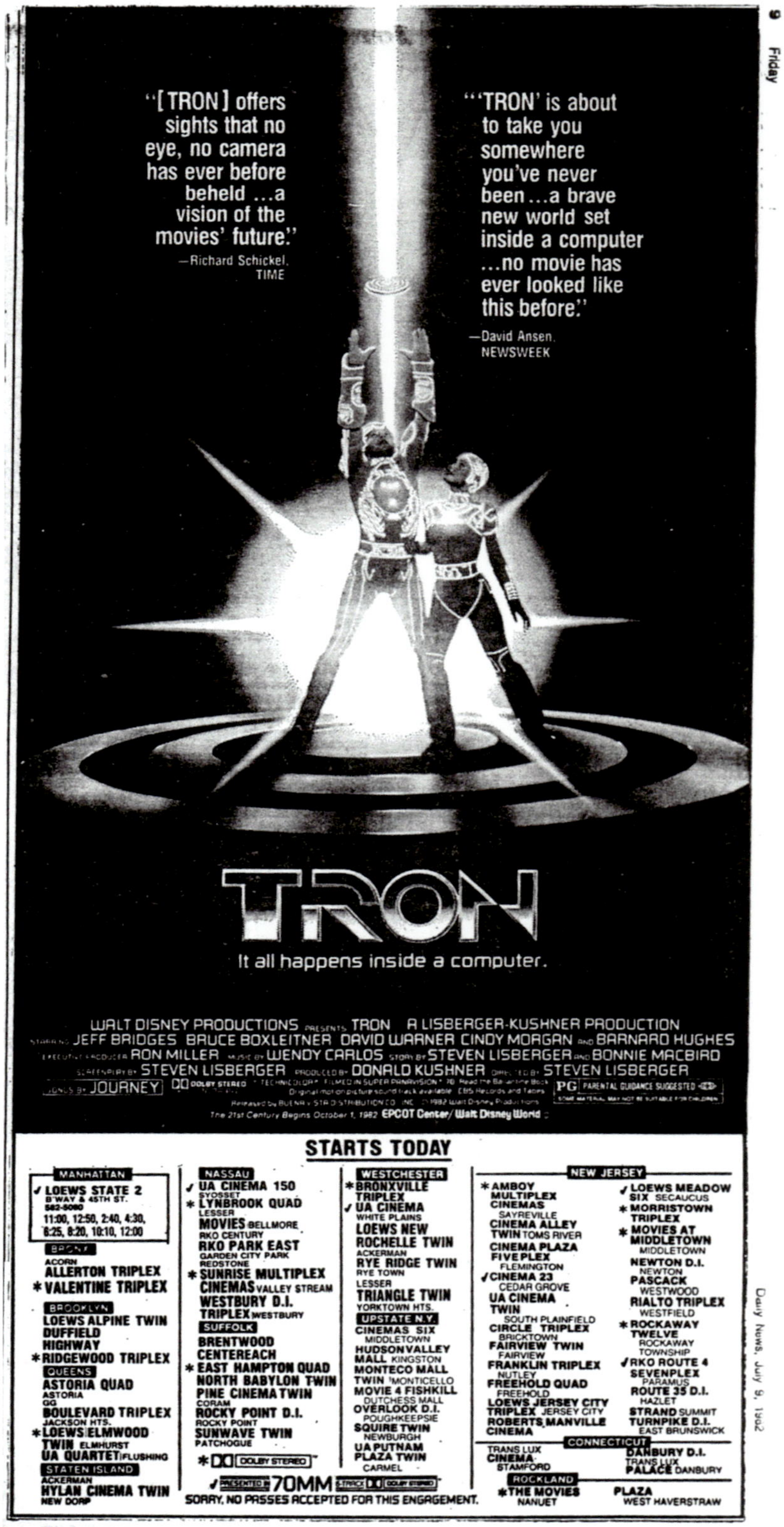

BLADE RUNNER

Ridley Scott's venture into the future (i.e., 2019, the year these words are being written) is among the poster children for '80s movies that were dismissed in large part by critics, only to find classic status later. (John Carpenter's *The Thing*, an even more extreme example, opened the same day.) The consensus was that Scott's focus on rain-drenched neon-noir visuals and atmosphere overwhelmed the story about Harrison's Ford's "blade runner" character hunting down renegade "replicants"; nonetheless, a few reviewers appreciated the film even at the time.

"For a change, it's nice to be able to credit the writers in a big-budget Hollywood film as strongly as the special effects people and the production designers. This is a thinking moviegoer's entertainment, one with more than a little consideration for the direction of mankind."

–Candice Russell, *Fort Lauderdale News*

"Through his ability to work with designers in creating densely textured worlds that pull us into their vortices, Scott endows old stories with new meanings and new terrors."

–Malcolm L. Johnson, *Hartford Courant*

"Despite all the splendid creations of architecture, vehicle, robot, and Harrison Ford itself, the picture is really nothing more than that basic battle between Good and Evil, which the movies are now offering wholesale. ... The kids may be able to swallow this stuff without gagging."

–ARCHER WINSTEN, *NEW YORK POST*

"[S]o much care has been lavished on this bizarre and very convincing vision of urban America in 2019 that what the film looks like has taken precedence over what happens in it. ... The problem is that Scott has forgotten some of the basics of telling a story."

–Desmond Ryan, *The Philadelphia Inquirer*

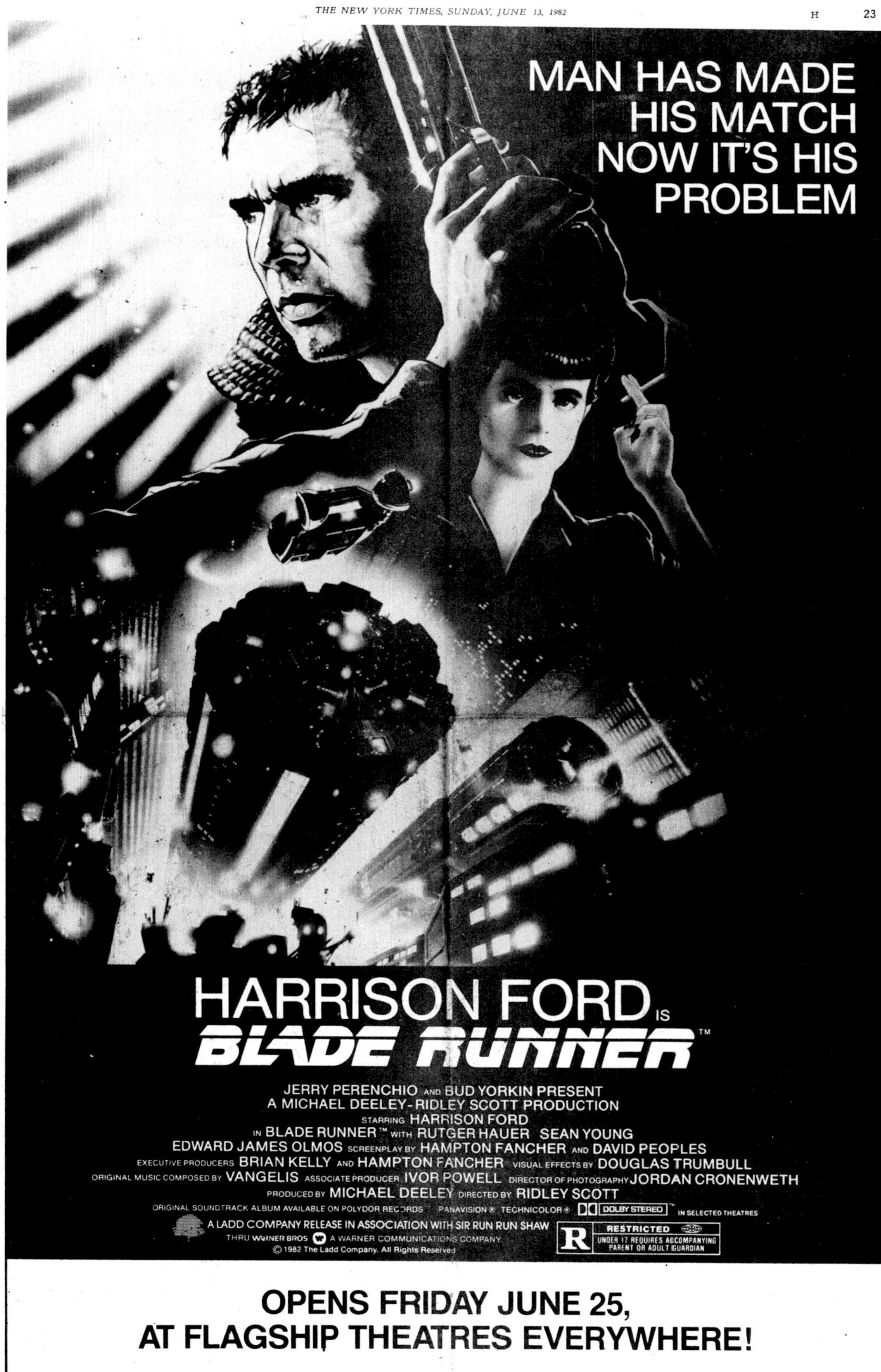
THE NEW YORK TIMES, SUNDAY, JUNE 13, 1982
H 23
MAN HAS MADE HIS MATCH NOW IT'S HIS PROBLEM
HARRISON FORD IS
BLADE RUNNER™
JERRY PERENCHIO AND BUD YORKIN PRESENT
A MICHAEL DEELEY-RIDLEY SCOTT PRODUCTION
STARRING HARRISON FORD
IN BLADE RUNNER™ WITH RUTGER HAUER SEAN YOUNG
EDWARD JAMES OLMOS SCREENPLAY BY HAMPTON FANCHER AND DAVID PEOPLES
EXECUTIVE PRODUCERS BRIAN KELLY AND HAMPTON FANCHER VISUAL EFFECTS BY DOUGLAS TRUMBULL
ORIGINAL MUSIC COMPOSED BY VANGELIS ASSOCIATE PRODUCER IVOR POWELL DIRECTOR OF PHOTOGRAPHY JORDAN CRONENWETH
PRODUCED BY MICHAEL DEELEY DIRECTED BY RIDLEY SCOTT
ORIGINAL SOUNDTRACK ALBUM AVAILABLE ON POLYDOR RECORDS PANAVISION® TECHNICOLOR® DOLBY STEREO™ IN SELECTED THEATRES
A LADD COMPANY RELEASE IN ASSOCIATION WITH SIR RUN RUN SHAW
THRU WARNER BROS A WARNER COMMUNICATIONS COMPANY
© 1982 The Ladd Company. All Rights Reserved
R RESTRICTED
UNDER 17 REQUIRES ACCOMPANYING PARENT OR ADULT GUARDIAN
OPENS FRIDAY JUNE 25,
AT FLAGSHIP THEATRES EVERYWHERE!

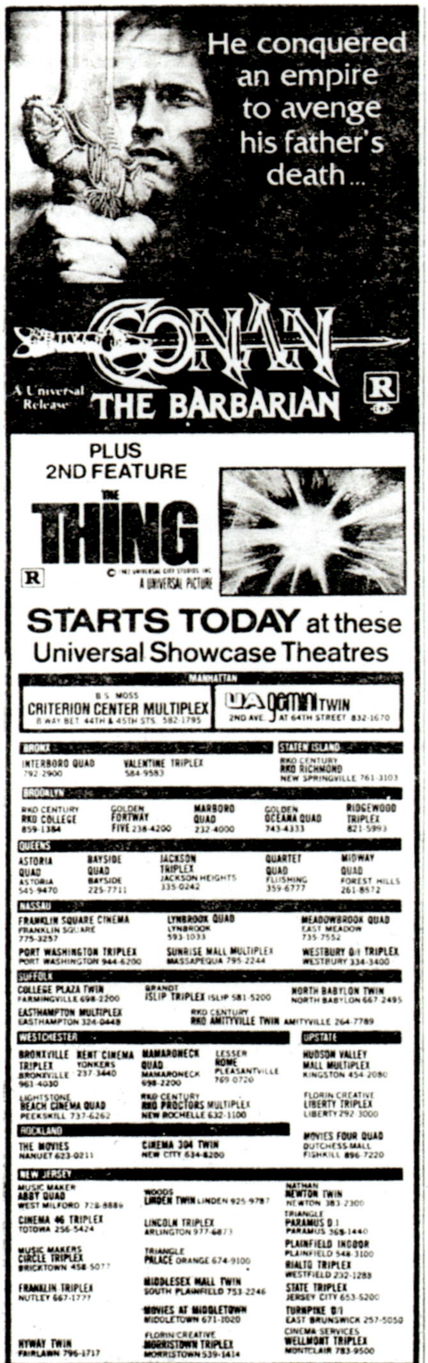

CONAN THE BARBARIAN

Early in 1982, Universal Pictures released ads trumpeting its genre lineup for the coming year, which ranged from the future blockbuster *E.T.* to the box-office disappointments *Cat People* and *The Thing*. Falling in between on the grosses scale was *Conan the Barbarian*, John Milius' epic featuring the prehistoric hero of Robert E. Howard's pulp stories, played by Arnold Schwarzenegger in his first leading role since his early turn (dubbed and renamed "Arnold Strong") in 1969's *Hercules in New York*. The movie became enough of a hit to launch Schwarzenegger as a bankable action star, though it wasn't until *The Terminator* two years later that one of his projects received widespread critical approval to match.

"With its prehistoric setting, *Conan the Barbarian* hasn't the scope of the outer-spacious *Star Wars* or the globe-girdling *Raiders*, but on its own terms it's just as much fun. ... *Conan* takes itself just seriously enough to be amusing and not so seriously as to be campy."

–Kevin Thomas, *Los Angeles Times*

"The film is knee-deep in blood and burdened with the crushing weight of director John Milius' excessive machismo and Arnold Schwarzenegger's acting. Its centerpiece is a giant, hydraulically operated snake. Unfortunately, similar mechanical aids to facial movement could not be installed in Schwarzenegger."

–DESMOND RYAN, *PHILADELPHIA INQUIRER*

"[A] titanic laugh riot full of grunts, growls and kidney stones based on the cartoons from the 1930s created by Robert Howard, a sickly crackpot who blew his brains out when he was 30, leaving behind enough idiot fodder for generations of violent sadists to drool over... How nuts like [Milius] keep getting the millions to waste on junk movies like *Conan the Barbarian* is just one of the unsolved mysteries that keeps the psychiatrists of Beverly Hills up to their tax deductible eyeballs in silver coke spoons and Japanese gardeners."

–Rex Reed, New York *Daily News*

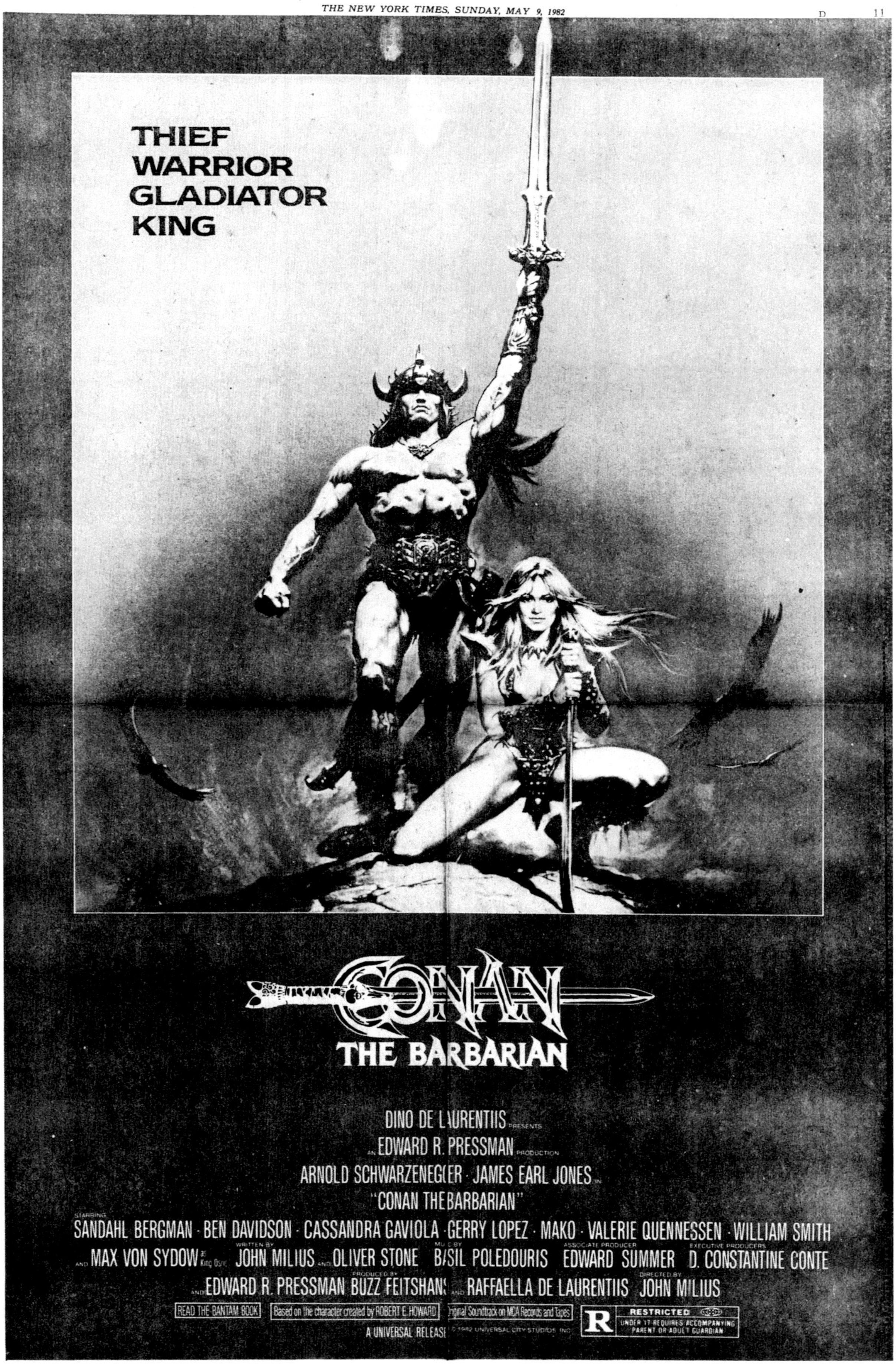
THE NEW YORK TIMES, SUNDAY, MAY 9, 1982
D 11
THIEF
WARRIOR
GLADIATOR
KING
CONAN
THE BARBARIAN
DINO DE LAURENTIIS PRESENTS
AN EDWARD R. PRESSMAN PRODUCTION
ARNOLD SCHWARZENEGGER · JAMES EARL JONES IN
"CONAN THE BARBARIAN"
STARRING
SANDAHL BERGMAN · BEN DAVIDSON · CASSANDRA GAVIOLA · GERRY LOPEZ · MAKO · VALERIE QUENNESSEN · WILLIAM SMITH
AND MAX VON SYDOW AS King Osric
WRITTEN BY JOHN MILIUS AND OLIVER STONE
MUSIC BY BASIL POLEDOURIS
ASSOCIATE PRODUCER EDWARD SUMMER
EXECUTIVE PRODUCERS D. CONSTANTINE CONTE AND EDWARD R. PRESSMAN
PRODUCED BY BUZZ FEITSHANS AND RAFFAELLA DE LAURENTIIS
DIRECTED BY JOHN MILIUS
READ THE BANTAM BOOK
Based on the character created by ROBERT E. HOWARD
Original Soundtrack on MCA Records and Tapes
A UNIVERSAL RELEASE © 1982 UNIVERSAL CITY STUDIOS, INC.
R
RESTRICTED
UNDER 17 REQUIRES ACCOMPANYING PARENT OR ADULT GUARDIAN

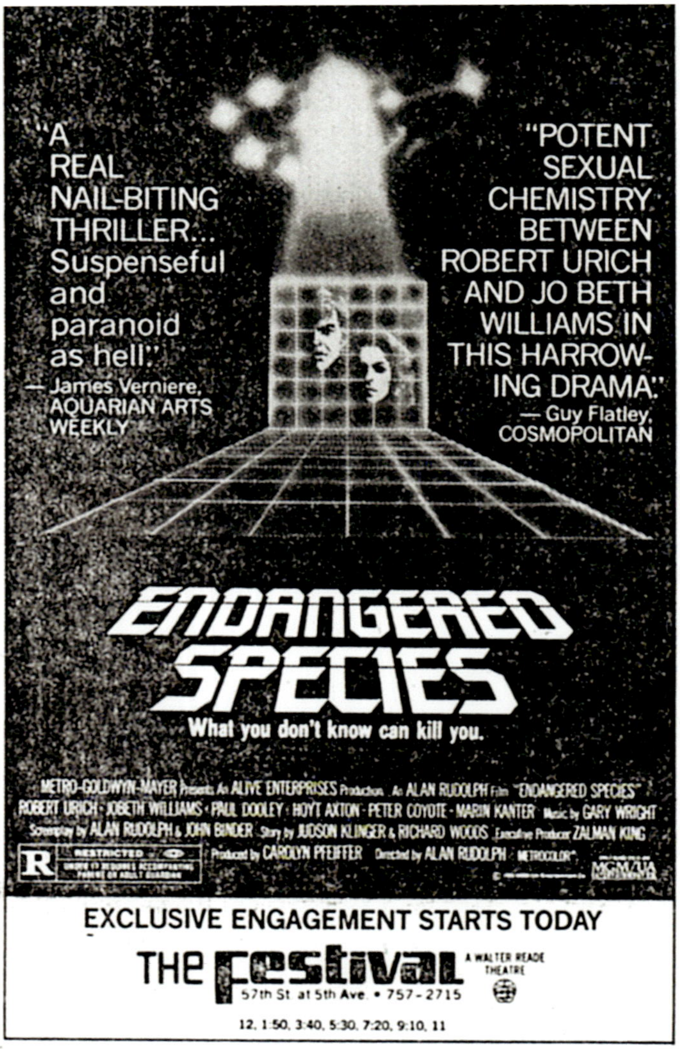

THE DARK CRYSTAL

Jim Henson spent a couple of decades delighting children on *Sesame Street* and *The Muppet Show* before he moved into scarier territory in his first non-Muppet feature, about an elf-like creature's epic quest through a dangerous, monster-filled realm in order to retrieve a missing piece of a magical crystal that can restore his world. Populated entirely by groundbreaking animatronic characters designed by noted illustrator Brian Froud, *The Dark Crystal* was Universal's big Christmas release. Though modestly successful, it was overshadowed by more adult-oriented offerings such as *Tootsie*, *48 HRS.*, and *The Verdict*. Mixed reviews didn't help.

"Unlike many screen fantasies, *The Dark Crystal* casts its spell from its very first frames and proceeds so briskly that it's over before you realize it. You're left with the feeling you have just awakened from a dream."

–Kevin Thomas, *Los Angeles Times*

"*The Dark Crystal* is filled with creatures big and small, funny and scary. Henson's creative mind is cleverly active and winsome, and his hairy, furry, slimy, fuzzy things... are delights to watch. The story itself isn't much, but then, it needn't be: This movie is for the eye."

–JACQUI TULLY, *ARIZONA DAILY STAR*

"Of course, good is going to triumph over evil in a fairy tale such as *The Dark Crystal*, but must we be told that is going to happen at least three times during the first hour of the picture?"

–Gene Siskel, *Chicago Tribune*

"Most surprising is the lack of either humor or wit. ... Miss Piggy would not be kind to *The Dark Crystal*, though I don't know if she would go so far as to sigh, 'Quel bore.'"

–Vincent Canby, *The New York Times*

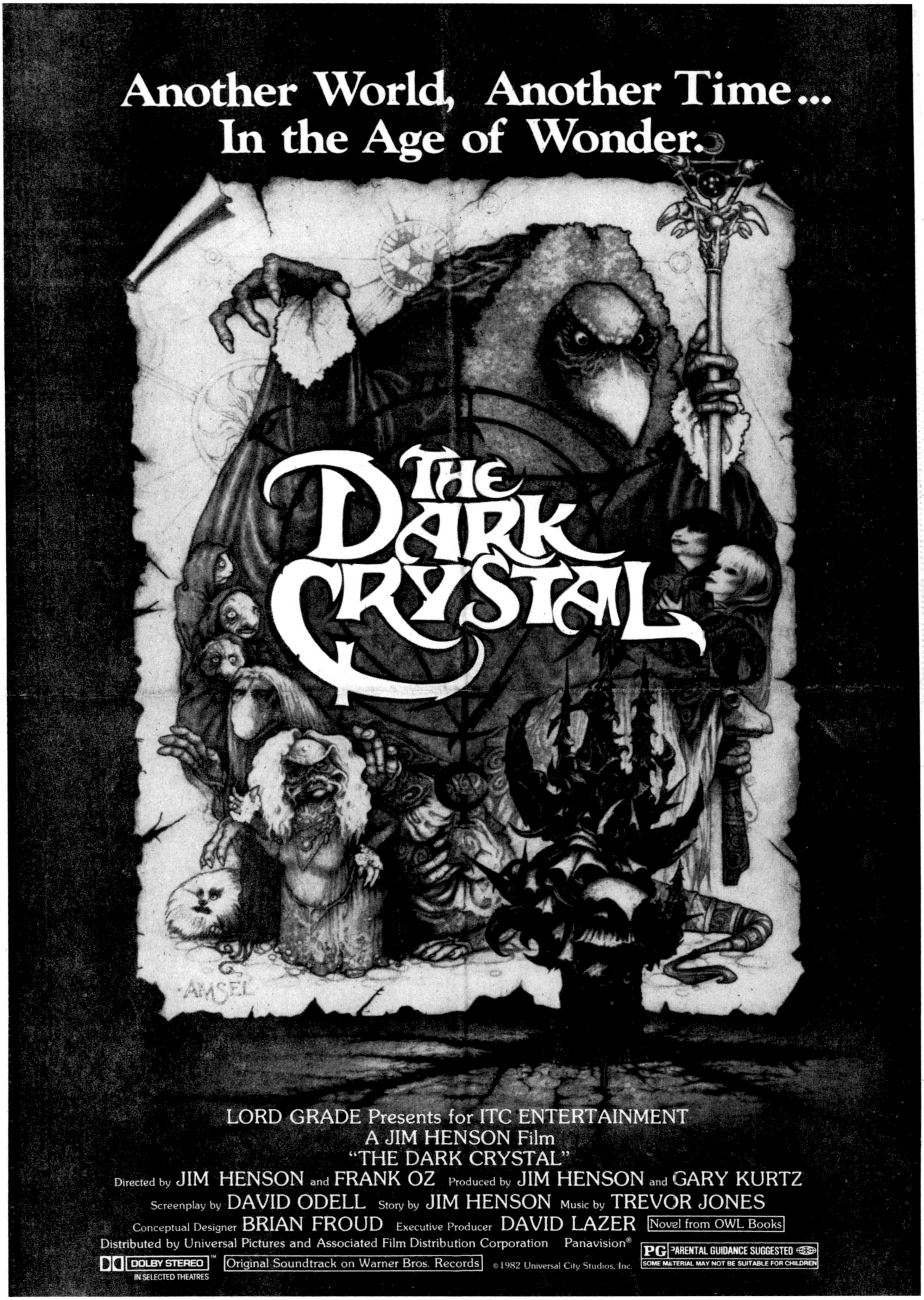
Another World, Another Time...
In the Age of Wonder.
THE DARK CRYSTAL
AMSEL
LORD GRADE Presents for ITC ENTERTAINMENT
A JIM HENSON Film
"THE DARK CRYSTAL"
Directed by JIM HENSON and FRANK OZ Produced by JIM HENSON and GARY KURTZ
Screenplay by DAVID ODELL Story by JIM HENSON Music by TREVOR JONES
Conceptual Designer BRIAN FROUD Executive Producer DAVID LAZER
Novel from OWL Books
Distributed by Universal Pictures and Associated Film Distribution Corporation Panavision®
PG PARENTAL GUIDANCE SUGGESTED
SOME MATERIAL MAY NOT BE SUITABLE FOR CHILDREN
DOLBY STEREO™
IN SELECTED THEATRES
Original Soundtrack on Warner Bros. Records
©1982 Universal City Studios, Inc.

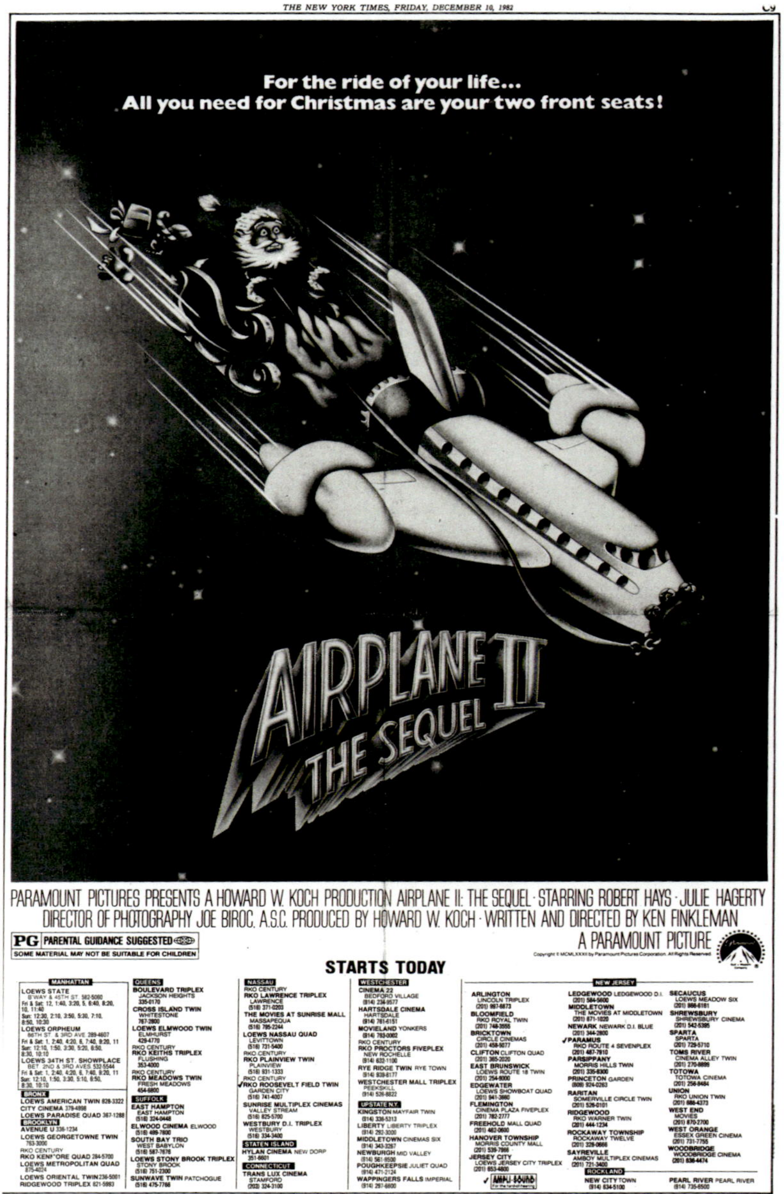

MEGAFORCE

With *Smokey and the Bandit*, stuntman-turned-director Hal Needham had the second-highest-grossing film of 1977 after *Star Wars*, but his own venture into science fiction with *Megaforce* carried none of the same magic. Needham had managed to defy bad reviews with his hit *The Cannonball Run*, but not this time; hero Barry Bostwick was no Burt Reynolds, and the film's highly touted Introvision visual effects looked like a megafarce on screen.

"Mr. Needham...has tried in *Megaforce* to combine down-home joviality with stunts, special effects, funny-looking futuristic jumpsuits and a great deal of hardware. The combination is original – just as a peanut butter and olive loaf sandwich might be – but it isn't any good."

–Janet Maslin, *The New York Times*

"It's hard to say when the thought struck: *Megaforce* may be the worst major motion picture even unleashed on an unsuspecting public."

–FRED ABEL, *ORLANDO SENTINEL*

"*Megaforce*, Hal Needham's new anti-Castro fantasy, has all the power of an assault with colored ping pong balls."

–Malcolm L. Johnson, *Hartford Courant*

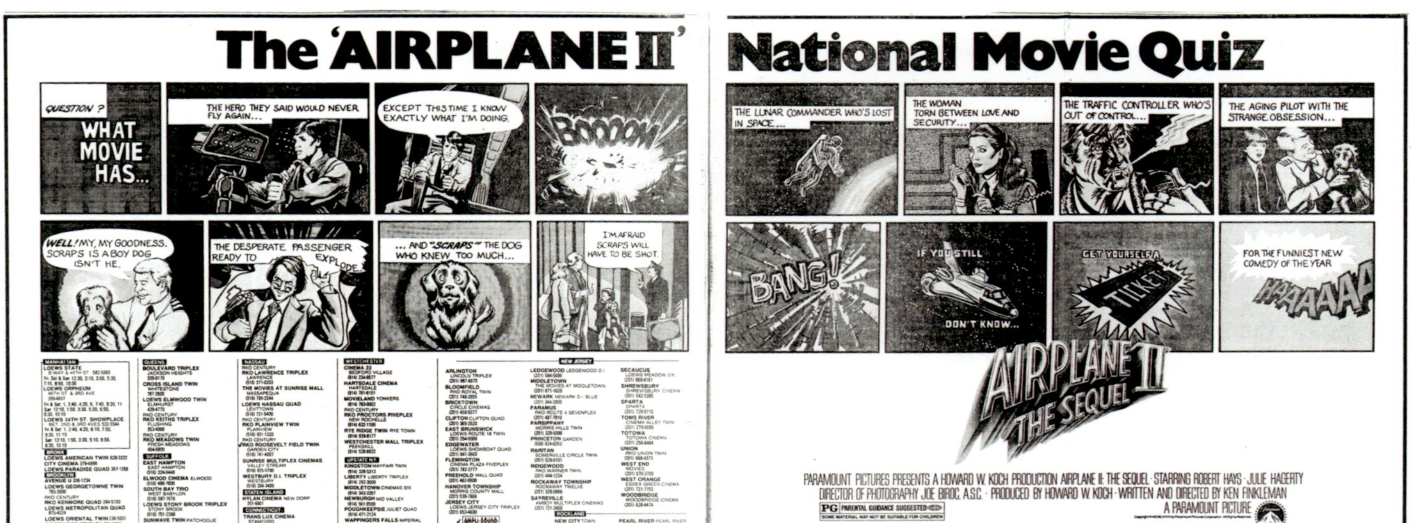

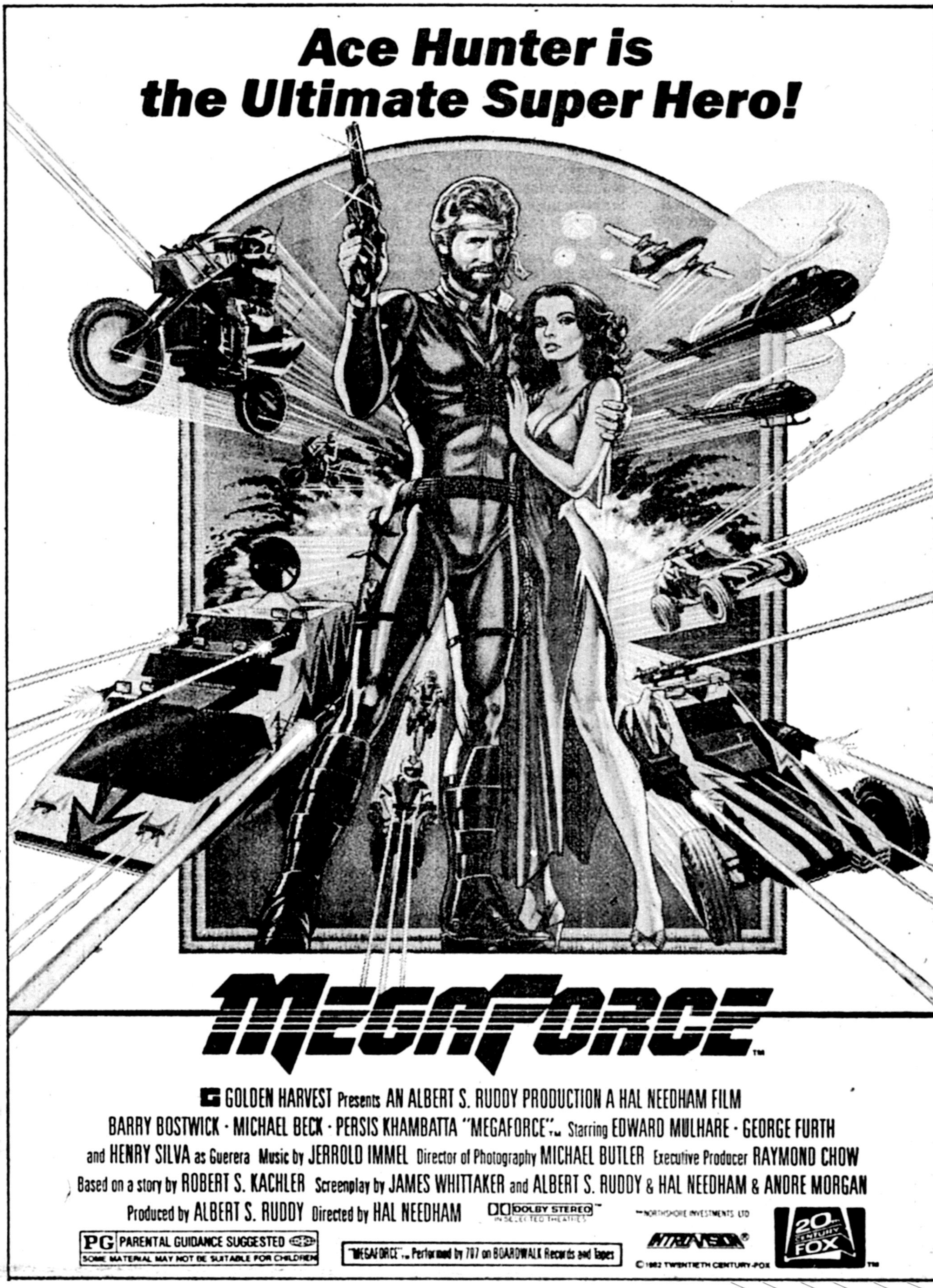

Ace Hunter is
the Ultimate Super Hero!
MEGAFORCE™
GOLDEN HARVEST Presents AN ALBERT S. RUDDY PRODUCTION A HAL NEEDHAM FILM
BARRY BOSTWICK · MICHAEL BECK · PERSIS KHAMBATTA "MEGAFORCE"™ Starring EDWARD MULHARE · GEORGE FURTH
and HENRY SILVA as Guerera Music by JERROLD IMMEL Director of Photography MICHAEL BUTLER Executive Producer RAYMOND CHOW
Based on a story by ROBERT S. KACHLER Screenplay by JAMES WHITTAKER and ALBERT S. RUDDY & HAL NEEDHAM & ANDRE MORGAN
Produced by ALBERT S. RUDDY Directed by HAL NEEDHAM
DOLBY STEREO™
IN SELECTED THEATRES
PG PARENTAL GUIDANCE SUGGESTED
SOME MATERIAL MAY NOT BE SUITABLE FOR CHILDREN
"MEGAFORCE"™ Performed by 707 on BOARDWALK Records and Tapes
NORTHSHORE INVESTMENTS LTD
©1982 TWENTIETH CENTURY-FOX
20th CENTURY FOX

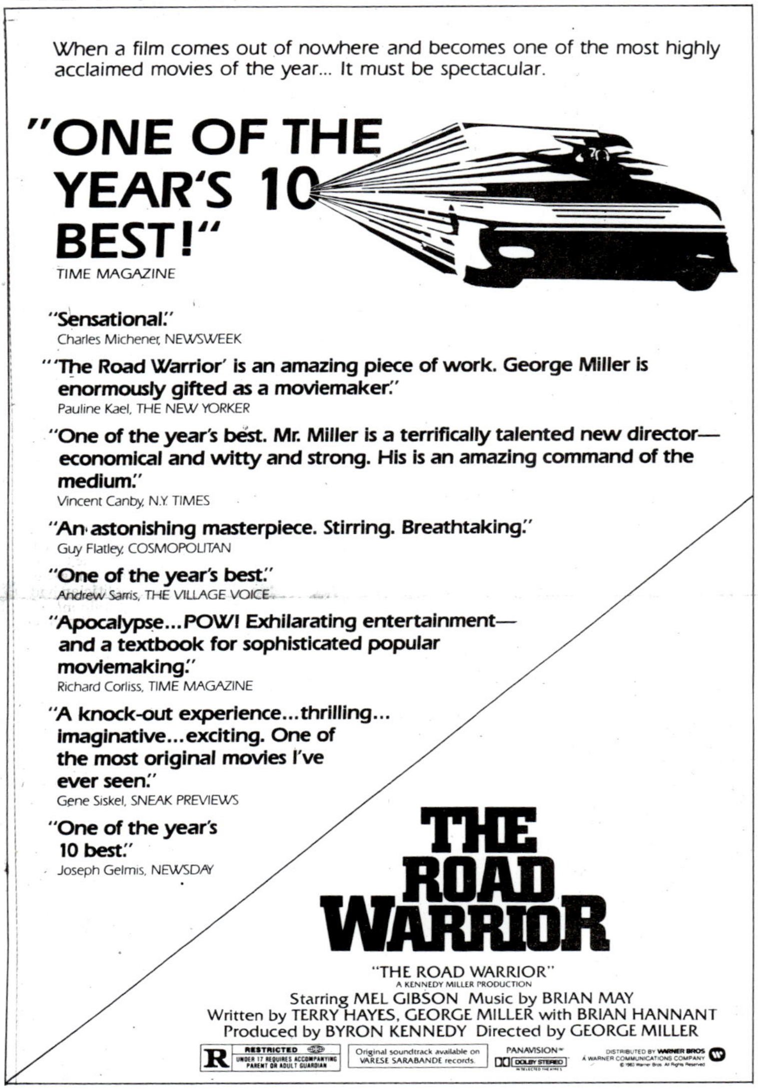

THE ROAD WARRIOR

What a difference a couple of years and a larger budget make. American critics might not have gotten the appeal of George Miller's original *Mad Max*, but a lot of them were far more impressed with his epic postapocalyptic sequel (known as *Mad Max 2* in the rest of the world), which tells a more contained story yet is bigger in every other sense. Though a few still objected to the violent content, and *The Road Warrior* was only a modest box-office hit, it became one of the genre's great trendsetters (resulting in scores of ripoffs) and launched Mel Gibson toward international stardom.

"...*The Road Warrior* is a superbly made action film that is in constant, deadly motion. Not one second is wasted on anything but thrills, chills, and a little comedy."

–Jon Marlowe, *The Miami News*

"The experience is frightening, sometimes disgusting, and (if the truth be told) exhilarating. This is very skillful filmmaking, and *The Road Warrior* is a movie like no other."

–Roger Ebert, *Chicago Sun-Times*

"Here is the decline and fall of Western civilization, signed, sealed and delivered in a movie both technically brilliant and morally bankrupt. You leave the theater feeling like you've been run over – and wondering why you enjoyed it."

–ELEANOR RINGEL, *THE ATLANTA CONSTITUTION*

"*The Road Warrior* is a flamboyant and exciting Australian film that is propelled by a bleak and self-renewing wit that lurks behind the motorcycle and car crashes."

–Desmond Ryan, *Philadelphia Inquirer*

"A fantasy-adventure of the near future, it has the skinniest of stories and a lush, full-throttle way of telling it. You wouldn't go to *The Road Warrior* for layered subtlety of character; you'd go for a smashing good time at the movies."

–Sheila Benson, *Los Angeles Times*

OPENS FRIDAY AT FLAGSHIP THEATRES EVERYWHERE!

"APOCALYPSE...POW! EXHILARATING ENTERTAINMENT."

–Richard Corliss, TIME MAGAZINE

"A sensational slam-bang end-of-the-world picture."

–Charles Michener, NEWSWEEK

"Enough supercharged excitement to fill a couple of movies. A final pursuit sequence as breathtaking as the big chase in 'Raiders of the Lost Ark.'"

–Bruce Williamson, PLAYBOY MAGAZINE

"An astonishing action masterpiece. Stirring. Breathtaking."

–Guy Flatley, COSMOPOLITAN

"A smashing good time at the movies...A sizzler... George Miller and company have pulled off a winner."

–Sheila Benson, LOS ANGELES TIMES

"'The Road Warrior' literally is action: a series of spectacular chases, stunts, crashes, battles and rescues."

–Stephen Schaefer, US MAGAZINE

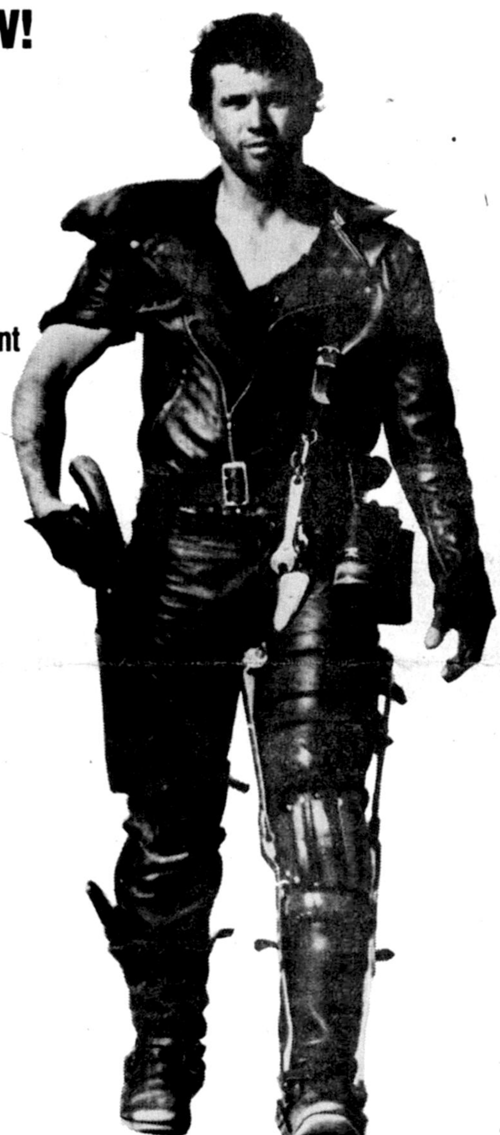

THE ROAD WARRIOR

"THE ROAD WARRIOR"

A KENNEDY MILLER PRODUCTION

Starring MEL GIBSON Music by BRIAN MAY

Written by TERRY HAYES, GEORGE MILLER with BRIAN HANNANT

Produced by BYRON KENNEDY Directed by GEORGE MILLER

R RESTRICTED UNDER 17 REQUIRES ACCOMPANYING PARENT OR ADULT GUARDIAN

Original soundtrack available on VARESE SARABANDE records

PANAVISION® DOLBY STEREO

WARNER BROS

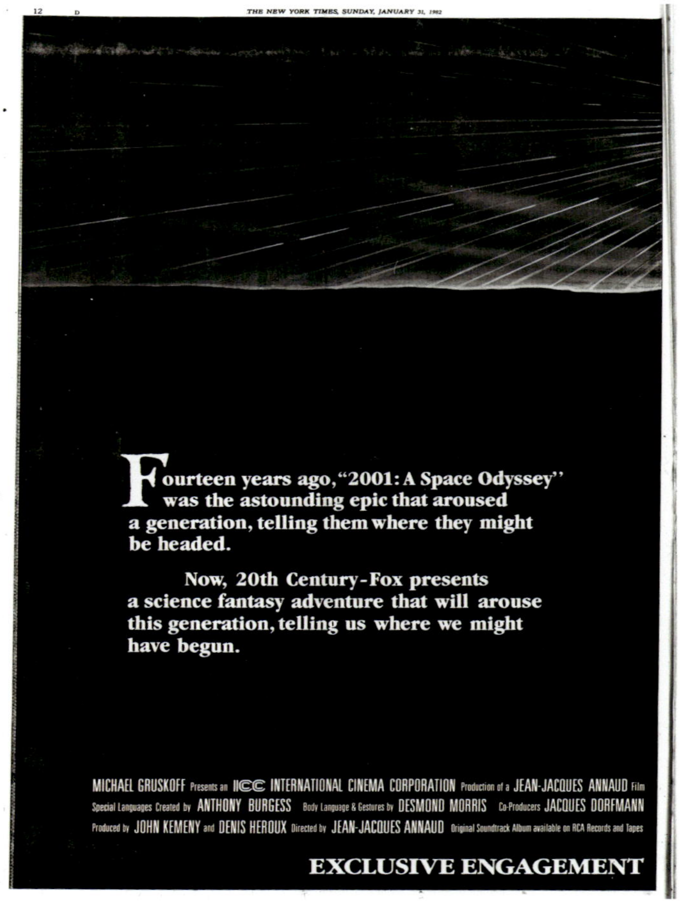

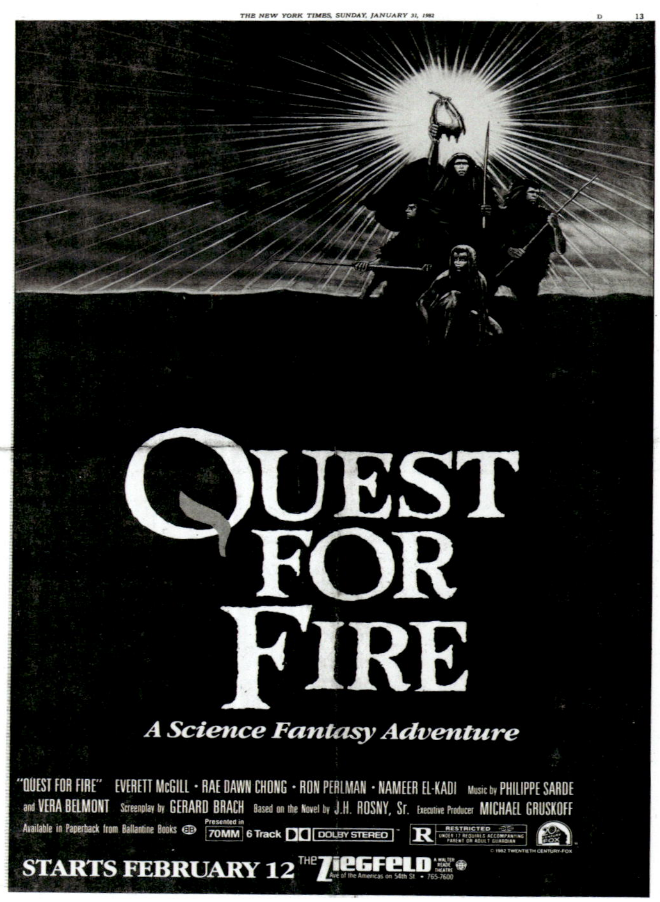

STAR TREK II: THE WRATH OF KHAN

When *Star Trek: The Motion Picture* opened in 1979 to disappointing reviews and box office below expectations, many fans lamented that the brain trust behind the *Enterprise* had blown their shot at a big-screen adventure. Three years later, with a much lower budget and without the creative oversight of series creator Gene Roddenberry, Paramount won back the fans' enthusiasm with a sequel revisiting one of the show's most vivid villains. In a genre-crowded summer, *The Wrath of Khan* held its own and ensured *Star Trek's* survival as a cinematic franchise. It remains one of its most critically acclaimed entries.

"The lessons [of the original] have been learned well. ... *Star Trek II: The Wrath of Khan* is a rousingly entertaining and totally satisfying film."

–George Anderson, *Pittsburgh Post-Gazette*

"Amazing grace is what director Nicholas Meyer...has brought to this movie, and what a difference it makes. ... There's a neatness and precision in Meyer's filmmaking; he's perfect for sci-fi fantasy because he understands that such stuff works only if it adheres to its own inner logic."

–Eleanor Ringel, *The Atlanta Constitution*

"I don't much care if the battles aren't that amazing, because the story doesn't depend on them. It's about a sacrifice made by Spock, and it draws on the sentiment and audience identification developed over the years by the TV series."

–ROGER EBERT, *CHICAGO SUN-TIMES*

"[A] brisk, handsomely designed film in which its hardware, sturdy as it is, never overwhelms its humanity. However, *Star Trek II* is not likely to attract many new fans – it requires too much familiarity with the TV series."

–Kevin Thomas, *Los Angeles Times*

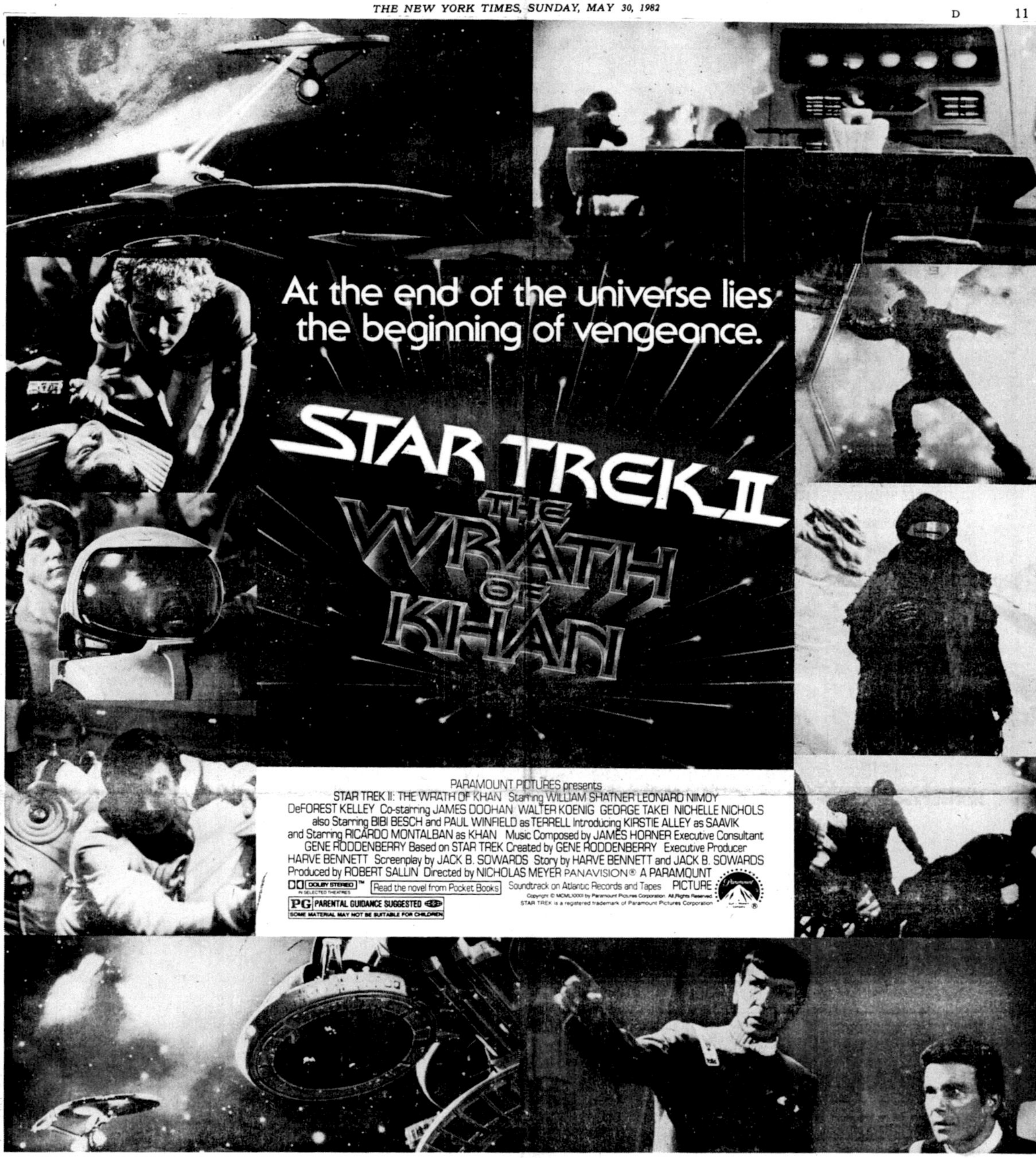

STARTS FRIDAY

70MM

SIX-TRACK DOLBY STEREO™ PRESENTATION

MANHATTAN

LOEWS STATE B'WAY & 45th ST 582-5070
LOEWS ORPHEUM 86th ST NR 3rd AVE 289-4607
LOEWS 34th ST. SHOWPLACE BETWEEN 2nd & 3rd AVES 532-5544

NASSAU

LOEWS NASSAU QUAD LEVITTOWN
SUNRISE MULTIPLEX CINEMAS VALLEY STREAM

NEW JERSEY

✓PARAMUS RKO ROUTE 4 SEVENPLEX

BRONX

LOEWS AMERICAN TWIN
CITY CINEMA
LOEWS PARADISE QUAD
WHITESTONE D.I.

BROOKLYN

AVENUE U
LOEWS GEORGETOWNE TWIN
RKO CENTURY RKO KENMORE QUAD
LOEWS METROPOLITAN QUAD
LOEWS ORIENTAL TWIN

NASSAU

RKO CENTURY RKO FLORAL FLORAL PARK
RKO CENTURY RKO LAWRENCE TRIPLEX
THE MOVIES AT SUNRISE MALL #1 MASSAPEQUA
* THE MOVIES AT SUNRISE MALL #2 MASSAPEQUA
RKO CENTURY
✓ RKO ROOSEVELT FIELD TWIN GARDEN CITY
WESTBURY D.I. TRIPLEX JERICHO

SUFFOLK

BAY SHORE SUNRISE D.I. BAY SHORE
* EAST HAMPTON EAST HAMPTON
* ELWOOD CINEMA ELWOOD
SOUTH BAY TRIO WEST BABYLON
LOEWS STONY BROOK TRIPLEX
SUNWAVE TWIN PATCHOGUE

QUEENS

BOULEVARD TRIPLEX JACKSON
CROSS ISLAND TWIN WHITESTONE
* LOEWS ELMWOOD TWIN ELMHURST
RKO CENTURY RKO KEITHS TRIPLEX FLUSHING
RKO CENTURY RKO MEADOWS TWIN FRESH MEADOWS

STATEN ISLAND

LANE NEW DORP

ROCKLAND

NEW CITY TOWN
ORANGEBURG 303 D.I.
PEARL RIVER CENTRAL

WESTCHESTER

CINEMA 22 BEDFORD VILLAGE
HARTSDALE CINEMA HARTSDALE
* MOVIELAND YONKERS
RKO CENTURY RKO PROCTORS FIVEPLEX NEW ROCHELLE
RYE RIDGE TWIN RYE TOWN
WESTCHESTER MALL TRIPLEX PEEKSKILL

UPSTATE N.Y.

CARMEL UA CINEMA
* HYDE PARK ROOSEVELT
KINGSTON MAYFAIR TWIN
LIBERTY LIBERTY TRIPLEX
MIDDLETOWN CINEMAS SIX
NEWBURGH SQUIRE
WARWICK WARWICK D.I.

* DOLBY STEREO™

NEW JERSEY

BLOOMFIELD RKO ROYAL TWIN
* BRICKTOWN MALL
* CLIFTON CLIFTON TWIN
EAST BRUNSWICK LOEWS ROUTE 18 TWIN
EDGEWATER LOEWS SHOWBOAT QUAD
FRANKLIN TOWNSHIP RUTGERS PLAZA
FLEMINGTON CINEMA PLAZA #3 #4
FREEHOLD MALL QUAD
HAZLET PLAZA
JERSEY CITY LOEWS JERSEY CITY TRIPLEX
* MORRISTOWN MORRISTOWN TRIPLEX CINEMAS
PARSIPPANY MORRIS HILLS TWIN
RARITAN SOMERVILLE CIRCLE TWIN
ROCKAWAY TOWNSHIP ROCKAWAY TWELVE
* RIDGEWOOD RKO WARNER TWIN
* SAYERVILLE AMBOY MULTIPLEX CINEMAS
* SECAUCUS LOEWS HARMON COVE QUAD
SHEWSBURY SHREWSBURY
TOMS RIVER DOVER
* TOTOWA TOTOWA
UNION RKO FOX TWIN
* WEST END MOVIES
* WEST ORANGE ESSEX GREEN
WOODBRIDGE WOODBRIDGE

CONNECTICUT

POST CINEMA WESTPORT
* TRANS LUX LANDMARK SQUARE STAMFORD

✓ AMPLI-SOUND For the hard-of-hearing

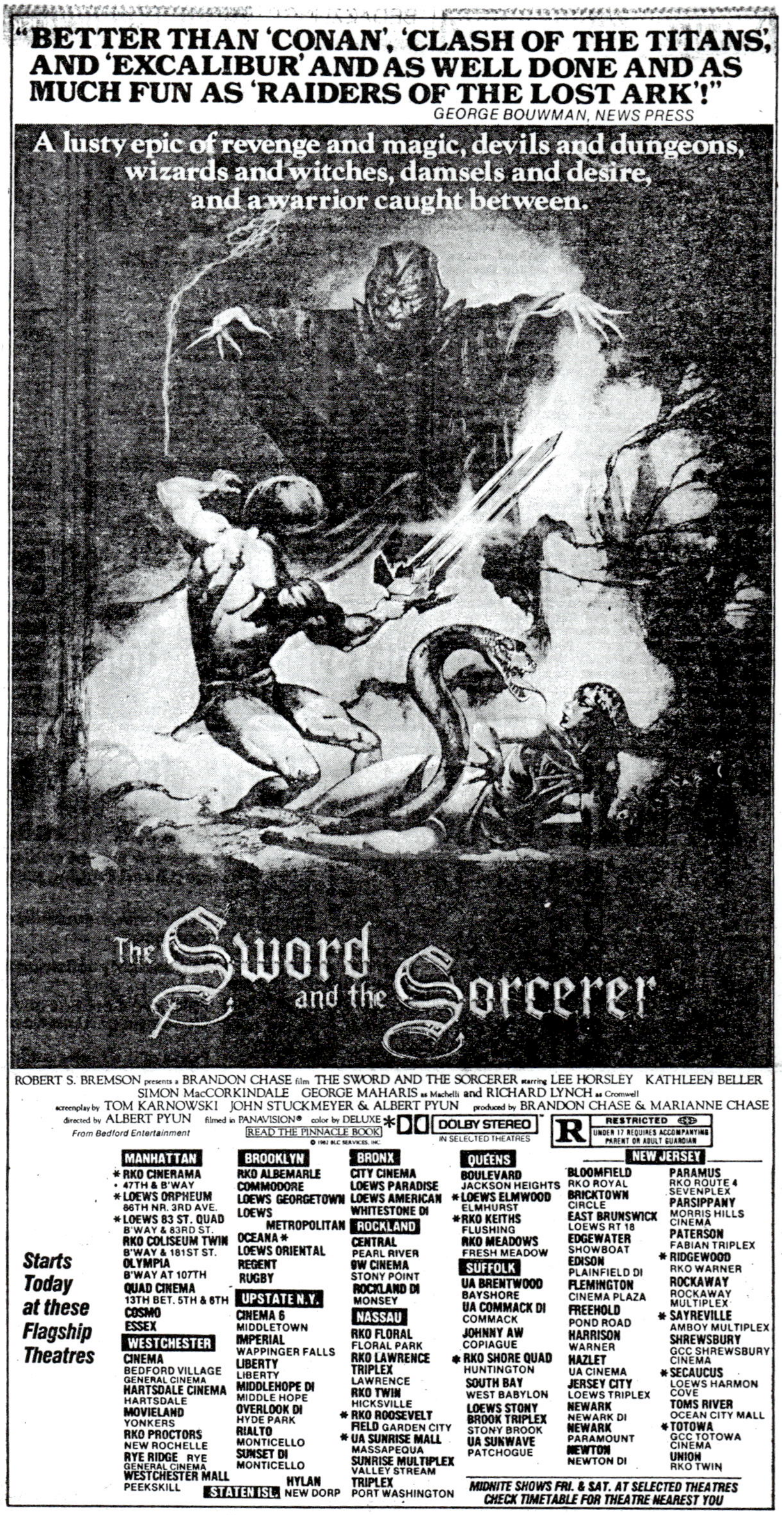

THE SWORD AND THE SORCERER

Conan the Barbarian was supposed to be the major hardcore fantasy-adventure event of summer 1982 – and so it was, yet right behind it was a scrappy independent from first-time director Albert Pyun. Producer/distributor Group 1, which had previously specialized in horror cheapies such as *The Giant Spider Invasion* and *Mansion of the Doomed* before taking a big step up with *Alligator*, hit paydirt with *The Sword and the Sorcerer*, a bloody and largely critically reviled film that nonetheless wound up outgrossing *Tron*, *Blade Runner* and many other much more expensive and highly touted features. Group 1 appears to have taken the money and run, getting out of the business of filmmaking (aside from the 1994 women-directed anthology *Erotique*, featuring an early appearance by Bryan Cranston) and releasing. (In 1986, the company made an ultimately unsuccessful foray into the VHS vending machine market.) Pyun kept on making films in various genres, but none came close to achieving *Sword*'s success.

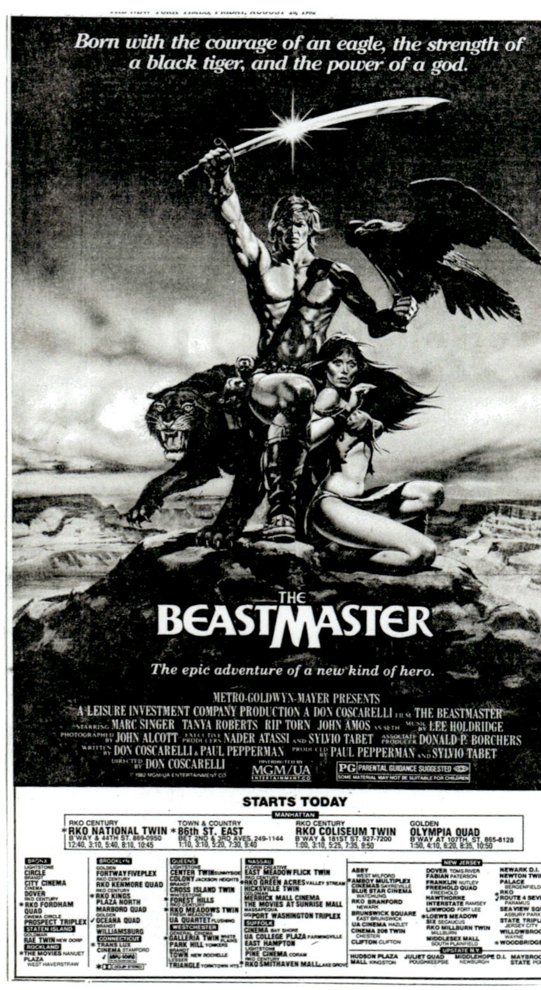

ZAPPED!

Originally conceived as *The Wiz Kid* and intended to occupy a PG-rated middle ground between Disney fare and R-rated raunch, this telekinesis-themed comedy toplining future *Charles in Charge* stars Scott Baio and William Aames wound up falling squarely in the latter camp. No doubt this surprised actress Heather Thomas, who told columnist Marilyn Beck in January '82, "I understand they're going to get rid of the boob jokes, and that they're going to make the film PG." After refusing to do nudity during the shoot, Thomas was incensed to find that a body double had been hired to provide her character with topless scenes, and filed a complaint with the Screen Actors Guild, resulting in a disclaimer being placed in the end credits. She wasn't the only one to find *Zapped!* exploitative, either.

"Director Robert J. Rosenthal and his co-screenwriter Bruce Rubin have a genuine feeling for kids and capture some of the twinges of being different. However, the material is inherently mediocre in its attempt to combine Walt Disney-type fare with T&A titillation."

–Linda Gross, *Los Angeles Times*

"It wouldn't matter that it's not funny to adults if it were funny to kids. But kids old enough to see it legally, or even old enough to know how to sneak in, will quickly recognize that everything here is executed about as deftly as walruses jump rope."

–DAVID HINCKLEY, NEW YORK *DAILY NEWS*

"The gags – both visual and verbal – are painfully trite, and the acting is forced at best. Even the special effects are clumsy."

–Josephine Marcotty, Minneapolis, MN *Star Tribune*

"*Zapped!*...is a half-baked, rather retarded parody of *Carrie* and a number of other films that, using the awesome power of their ignorance, drove telekinesis into the ground."

–Vincent Canby, *The New York Times*

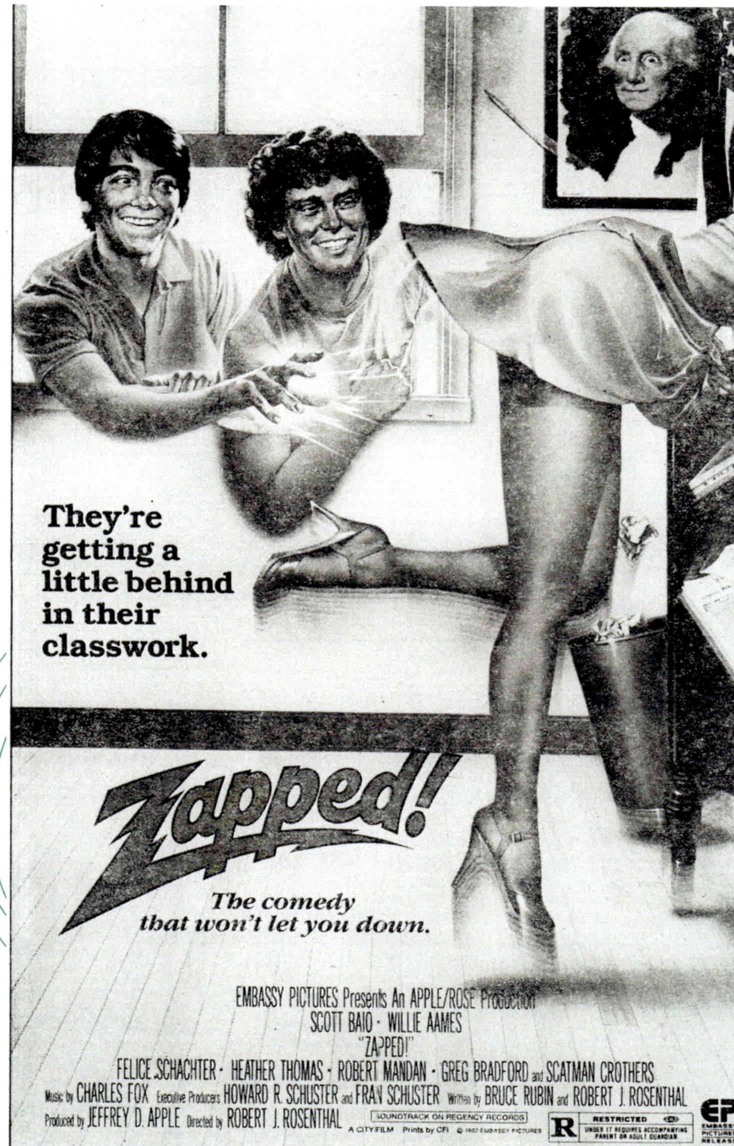

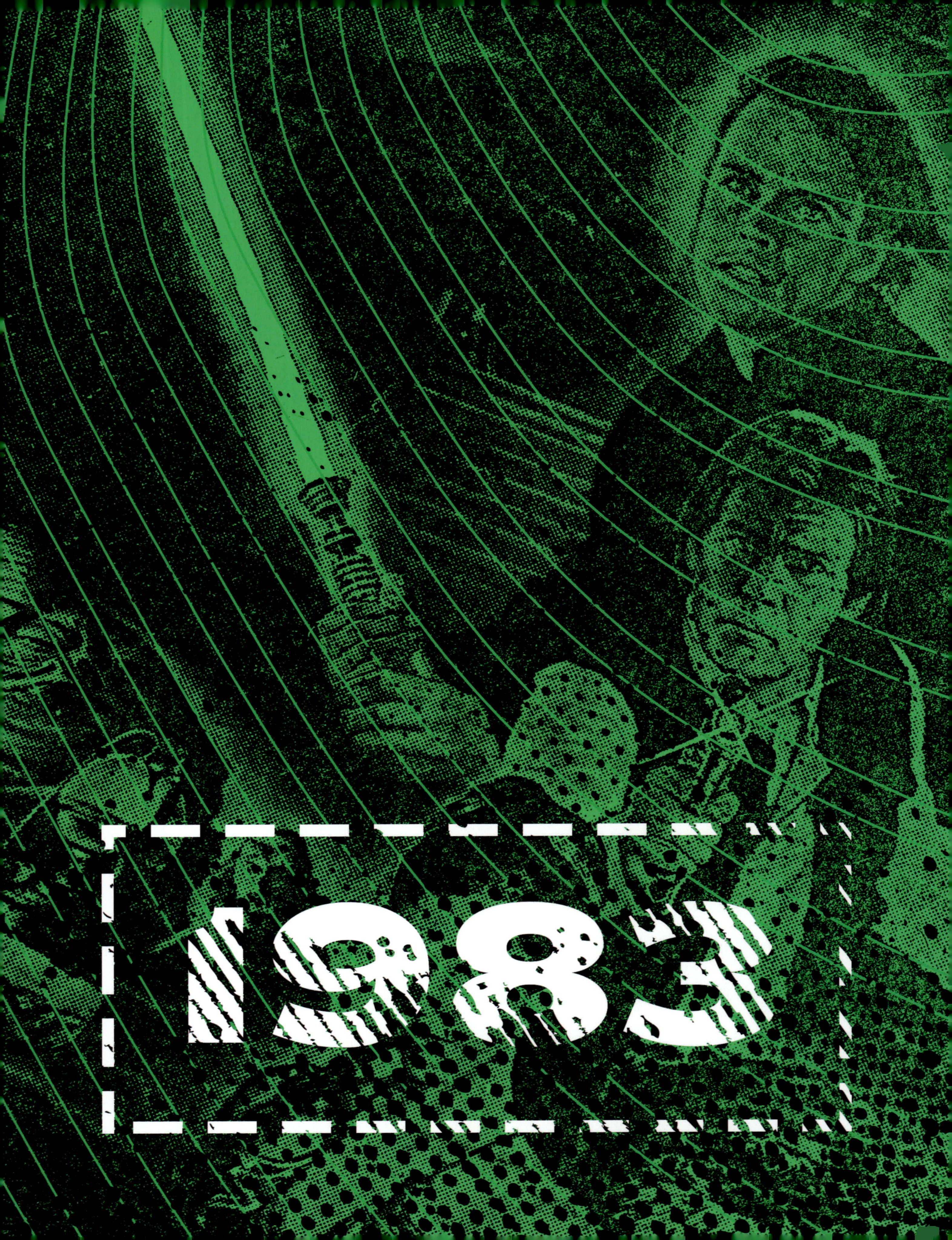
1983

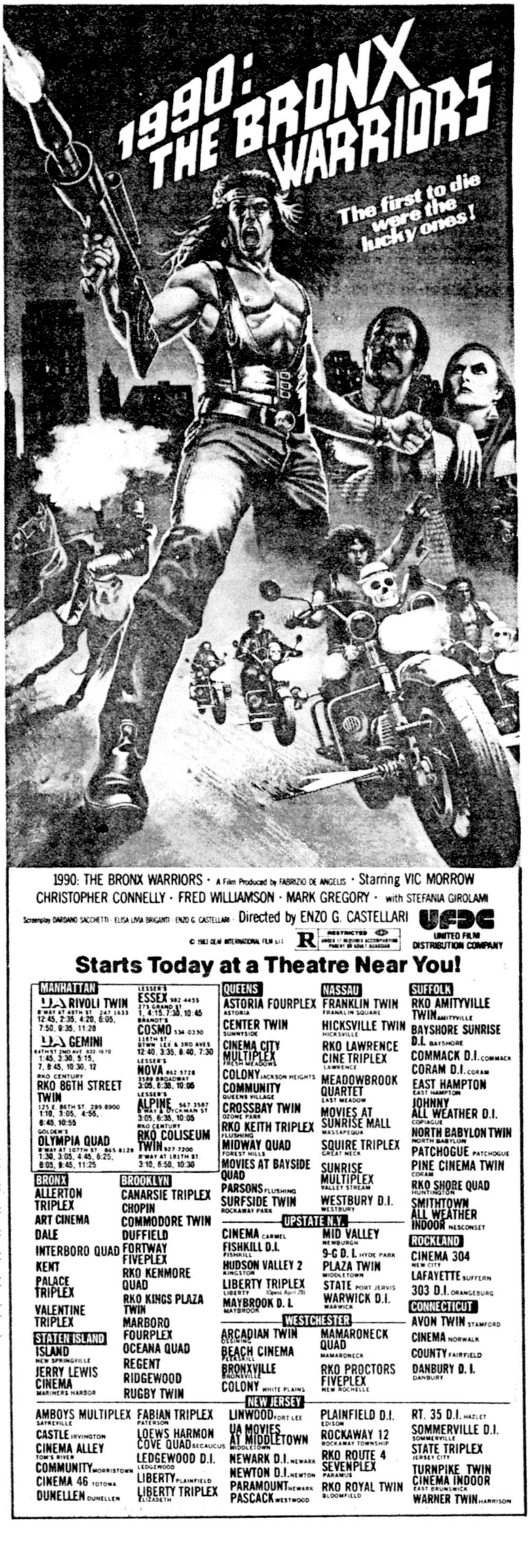
1990: THE BRONX WARRIORS
The first to die were the lucky ones!
1990: THE BRONX WARRIORS · A Film Produced by FABRIZIO DE ANGELIS · Starring VIC MORROW
CHRISTOPHER CONNELLY · FRED WILLIAMSON · MARK GREGORY · with STEFANIA GIROLAMI
Screenplay DARDANO SACCHETTI · ELISA LIVIA BRIGANTI · ENZO G. CASTELLARI · Directed by ENZO G. CASTELLARI
UFDC
UNITED FILM DISTRIBUTION COMPANY
R RESTRICTED
Starts Today at a Theatre Near You!
MANHATTAN
UA RIVOLI TWIN B'WAY AT 49TH ST 247-1633 12:45, 2:35, 4:20, 6:05, 7:50, 9:35, 11:20
UA GEMINI 64TH ST 2ND AVE 832-1670 1:45, 3:30, 5:15, 7, 8:45, 10:30, 12
RKO CENTURY RKO 86TH STREET TWIN 125 E. 86TH ST. 289-8900 1:10, 3:05, 4:55, 6:45, 10:55
GOLDEN'S OLYMPIA QUAD B'WAY AT 107TH ST 865-8128 1:30, 3:05, 4:45, 6:25, 8:05, 9:45, 11:25
LESSER'S ESSEX 982-4455 275 GRAND ST 1, 4:15, 7:30, 10:45
BRANDT'S COSMO 534-0330 116TH ST BTWN LEX & 3RD AVES 12:40, 3:35, 6:40, 7:30
LESSER'S NOVA 862-5728 3589 BROADWAY 3:05, 6:35, 10:06
LESSER'S ALPINE 567-3587 B'WAY & DYCKMAN ST 3:05, 6:35, 10:05
RKO CENTURY RKO COLISEUM TWIN 927-7200 B'WAY AT 181TH ST. 3:10, 6:50, 10:30
BRONX
ALLERTON TRIPLEX
ART CINEMA
DALE
INTERBORO QUAD
KENT
PALACE TRIPLEX
VALENTINE TRIPLEX
STATEN ISLAND
ISLAND NEW SPRINGVILLE
JERRY LEWIS CINEMA MARINERS HARBOR
BROOKLYN
CANARSIE TRIPLEX
CHOPIN
COMMODORE TWIN
DUFFIELD
FORTWAY FIVEPLEX
RKO KENMORE QUAD
RKO KINGS PLAZA TWIN
MARBORO FOURPLEX
OCEANA QUAD
REGENT
RIDGEWOOD
RUGBY TWIN
QUEENS
ASTORIA FOURPLEX ASTORIA
CENTER TWIN SUNNYSIDE
CINEMA CITY MULTIPLEX FRESH MEADOWS
COLONY JACKSON HEIGHTS
COMMUNITY QUEENS VILLAGE
CROSSBAY TWIN OZONE PARK
RKO KEITH TRIPLEX FLUSHING
MIDWAY QUAD FOREST HILLS
MOVIES AT BAYSIDE QUAD
PARSONS FLUSHING
SURFSIDE TWIN ROCKAWAY PARK
NASSAU
FRANKLIN TWIN FRANKLIN SQUARE
HICKSVILLE TWIN HICKSVILLE
RKO LAWRENCE CINE TRIPLEX LAWRENCE
MEADOWBROOK QUARTET EAST MEADOW
MOVIES AT SUNRISE MALL MASSAPEQUA
SQUIRE TRIPLEX GREAT NECK
SUNRISE MULTIPLEX VALLEY STREAM
WESTBURY D.I. WESTBURY
UPSTATE N.Y.
CINEMA CARMEL
FISHKILL D.I. FISHKILL
HUDSON VALLEY 2 KINGSTON
LIBERTY TRIPLEX LIBERTY (Opens April 29)
MAYBROOK D. I. MAYBROOK
MID VALLEY NEWBURGH
9-G D. I. HYDE PARK
PLAZA TWIN MIDDLETOWN
STATE PORT JERVIS
WARWICK D.I. WARWICK
WESTCHESTER
ARCADIAN TWIN OSSINING
BEACH CINEMA PEEKSKILL
BRONXVILLE BRONXVILLE
COLONY WHITE PLAINS
MAMARONECK QUAD MAMARONECK
RKO PROCTORS FIVEPLEX NEW ROCHELLE
SUFFOLK
RKO AMITYVILLE TWIN AMITYVILLE
BAYSHORE SUNRISE D.I. BAYSHORE
COMMACK D.I. COMMACK
CORAM D.I. CORAM
EAST HAMPTON EAST HAMPTON
JOHNNY ALL WEATHER D.I. COPIAGUE
NORTH BABYLON TWIN NORTH BABYLON
PATCHOGUE PATCHOGUE
PINE CINEMA TWIN CORAM
RKO SHORE QUAD HUNTINGTON
SMITHTOWN ALL WEATHER INDOOR NESCONSET
ROCKLAND
CINEMA 304 NEW CITY
LAFAYETTE SUFFERN
303 D.I. ORANGEBURG
CONNECTICUT
AVON TWIN STAMFORD
CINEMA NORWALK
COUNTY FAIRFIELD
DANBURY D. I. DANBURY
NEW JERSEY
AMBOYS MULTIPLEX SAYREVILLE
CASTLE IRVINGTON
CINEMA ALLEY TOM'S RIVER
COMMUNITY MORRISTOWN
CINEMA 46 TOTOWA
DUNELLEN DUNELLEN
FABIAN TRIPLEX PATERSON
LOEWS HARMON COVE QUAD SECAUCUS
LEDGEWOOD D.I. LEDGEWOOD
LIBERTY PLAINFIELD
LIBERTY TRIPLEX ELIZABETH
LINWOOD FORT LEE
UA MOVIES AT MIDDLETOWN MIDDLETOWN
NEWARK D.I. NEWARK
NEWTON D.I. NEWTON
PARAMOUNT NEWARK
PASCACK WESTWOOD
PLAINFIELD D.I. EDISON
ROCKAWAY 12 ROCKAWAY TOWNSHIP
RKO ROUTE 4 SEVENPLEX PARAMUS
RKO ROYAL TWIN BLOOMFIELD
RT. 35 D.I. HAZLET
SOMMERVILLE D.I. SOMMERVILLE
STATE TRIPLEX JERSEY CITY
TURNPIKE TWIN CINEMA INDOOR EAST BRUNSWICK
WARNER TWIN HARRISON

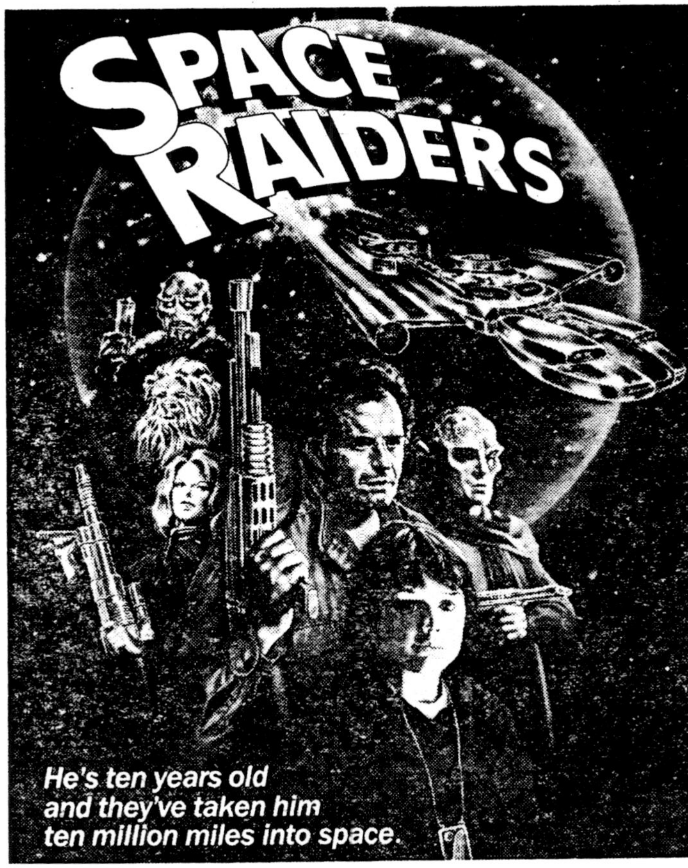
SPACE RAIDERS
He's ten years old
and they've taken him
ten million miles into space.

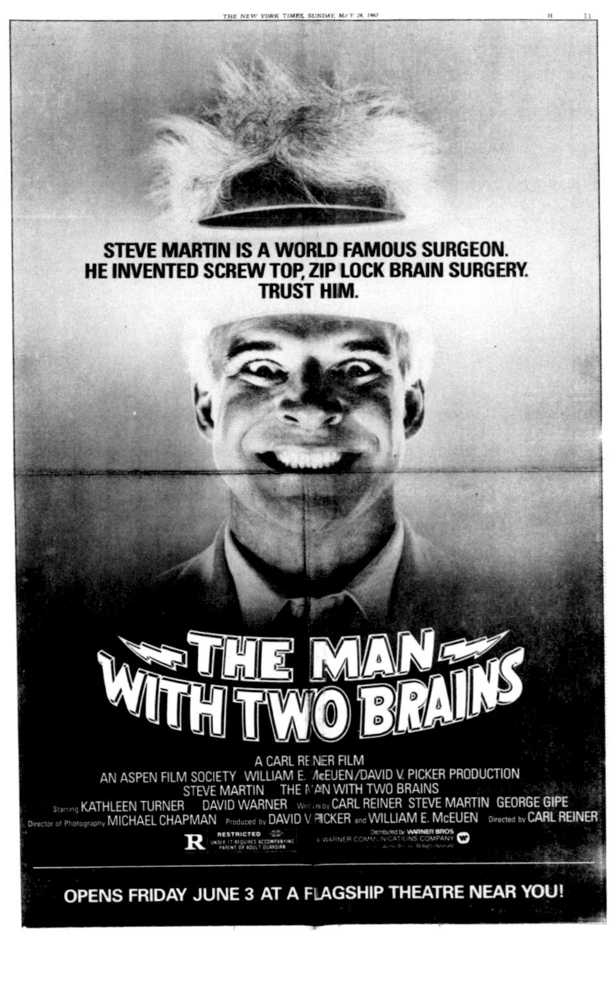
THE NEW YORK TIMES, SUNDAY, MAY 29, 1983
STEVE MARTIN IS A WORLD FAMOUS SURGEON.
HE INVENTED SCREW TOP, ZIP LOCK BRAIN SURGERY.
TRUST HIM.
THE MAN WITH TWO BRAINS
A CARL REINER FILM
AN ASPEN FILM SOCIETY WILLIAM E. McEUEN/DAVID V. PICKER PRODUCTION
STEVE MARTIN THE MAN WITH TWO BRAINS
Starring KATHLEEN TURNER DAVID WARNER Written by CARL REINER STEVE MARTIN GEORGE GIPE
Director of Photography MICHAEL CHAPMAN Produced by DAVID V. PICKER and WILLIAM E. McEUEN Directed by CARL REINER
R RESTRICTED
Distributed by WARNER BROS
A WARNER COMMUNICATIONS COMPANY
OPENS FRIDAY JUNE 3 AT A FLAGSHIP THEATRE NEAR YOU!

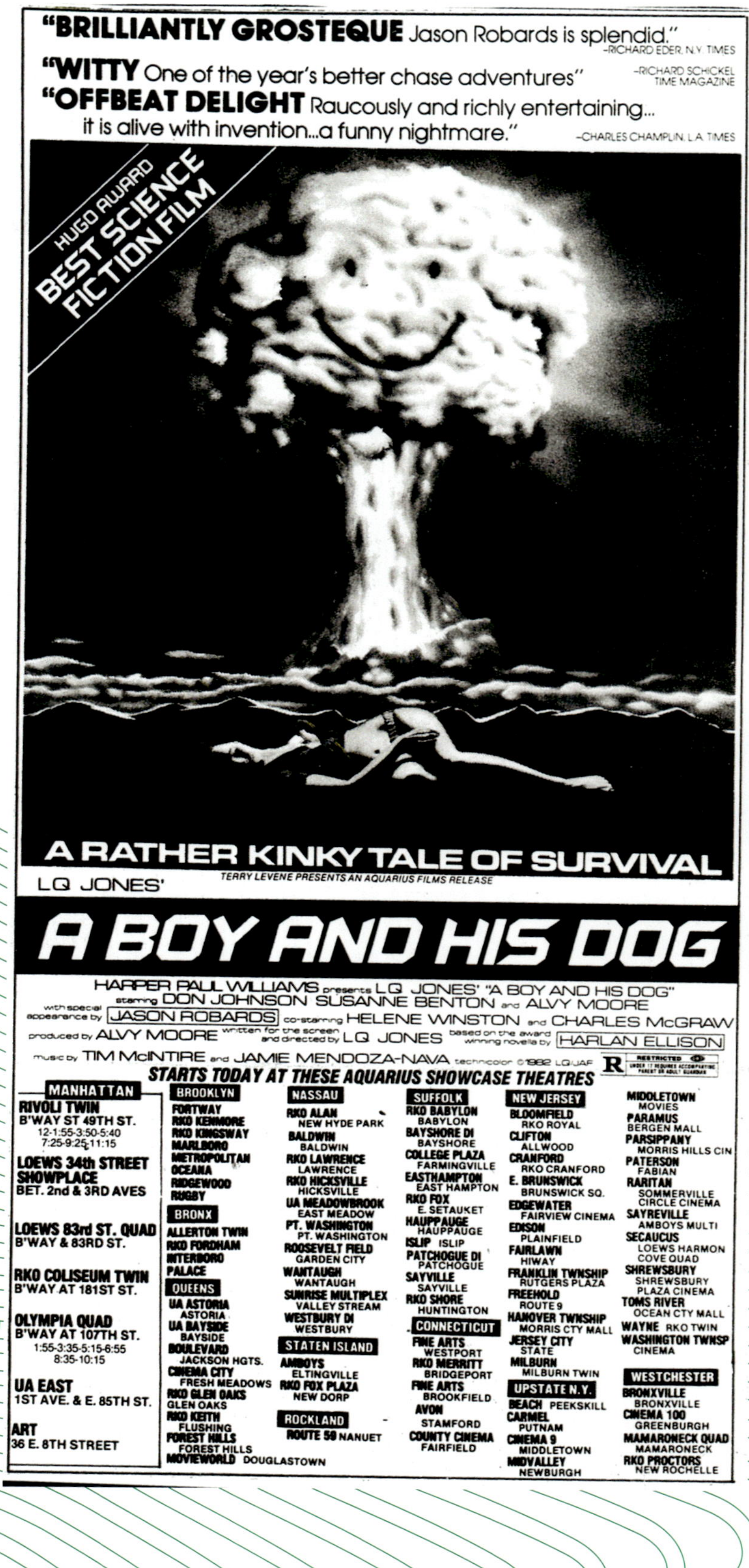

A BOY AND HIS DOG

If only they had waited another year or so to reissue actor-turned-director L.Q. Jones' satirical postapocalyptic saga (first released in 1975), they could have cashed in on lead actor Don Johnson's newfound stardom in TV's *Miami Vice*, which premiered in 1984. As it stood, the additional theatrical exposure helped the movie build the cult following it still enjoys today. I wasn't one of those devotees at the time, though; I recall talking a couple of friends into seeing "Vincent Dawn"/ Bruno Mattei's *Night of the Zombies* instead of *Boy and His Dog*, and they probably still haven't forgiven me.

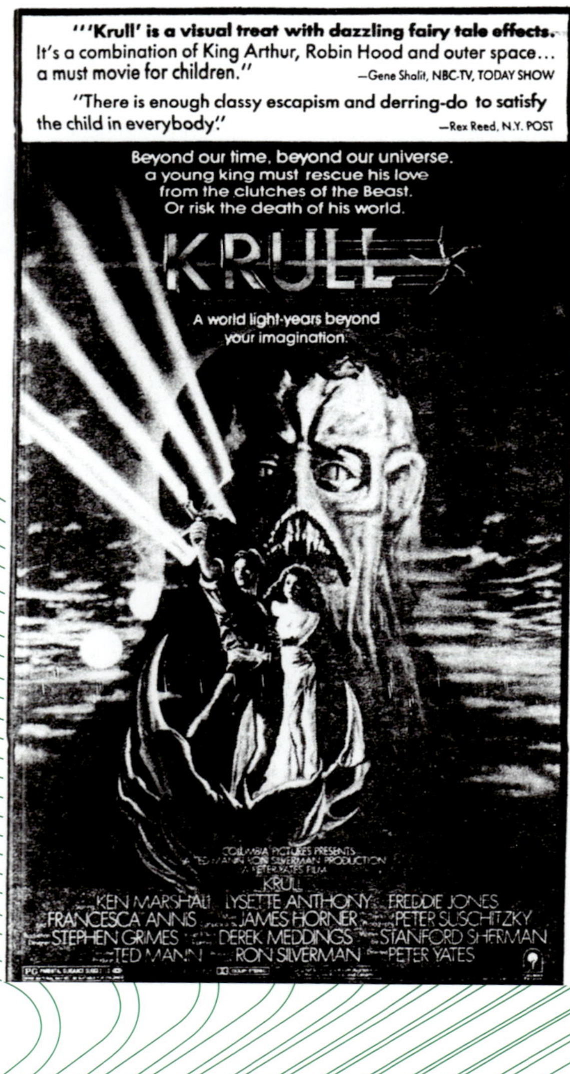

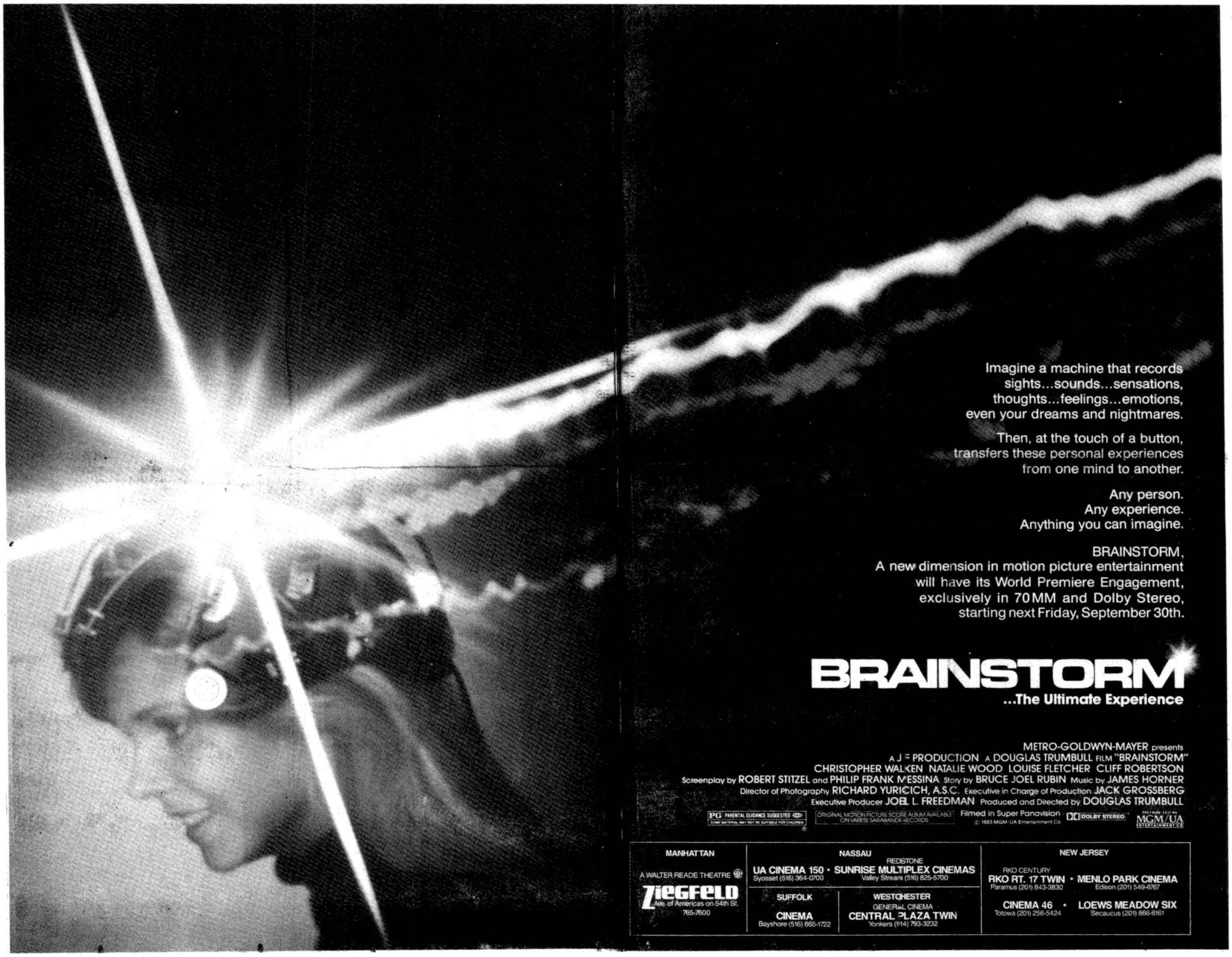
Imagine a machine that records
sights...sounds...sensations,
thoughts...feelings...emotions,
even your dreams and nightmares.
Then, at the touch of a button,
transfers these personal experiences
from one mind to another.
Any person.
Any experience.
Anything you can imagine.
BRAINSTORM,
A new dimension in motion picture entertainment
will have its World Premiere Engagement,
exclusively in 70MM and Dolby Stereo,
starting next Friday, September 30th.
BRAINSTORM
...The Ultimate Experience
METRO-GOLDWYN-MAYER presents
A DOUGLAS TRUMBULL FILM "BRAINSTORM"
CHRISTOPHER WALKEN NATALIE WOOD LOUISE FLETCHER CLIFF ROBERTSON
Screenplay by ROBERT STITZEL and PHILIP FRANK MESSINA Story by BRUCE JOEL RUBIN Music by JAMES HORNER
Director of Photography RICHARD YURICICH, A.S.C. Executive in Charge of Production JACK GROSSBERG
Executive Producer JOEL L. FREEDMAN Produced and Directed by DOUGLAS TRUMBULL
PG PARENTAL GUIDANCE SUGGESTED
ORIGINAL MOTION PICTURE SCORE ALBUM AVAILABLE ON VARESE SARABANDE RECORDS
Filmed in Super Panavision
© 1983 MGM/UA Entertainment Co.
DOLBY STEREO
MGM/UA
MANHATTAN
A WALTER READE THEATRE
ZIEGFELD
Ave. of Americas on 54th St.
765-7600
NASSAU
UA CINEMA 150 • REDSTONE SUNRISE MULTIPLEX CINEMAS
Syosset (516) 364-0700
Valley Stream (516) 825-5700
SUFFOLK
CINEMA
Bayshore (516) 665-1722
WESTCHESTER
GENERAL CINEMA
CENTRAL PLAZA TWIN
Yonkers (914) 793-3232
NEW JERSEY
RKO CENTURY
RKO RT. 17 TWIN • MENLO PARK CINEMA
Paramus (201) 843-3830
Edison (201) 549-6767
CINEMA 46 • LOEWS MEADOW SIX
Totowa (201) 256-5424
Secaucus (201) 866-6161

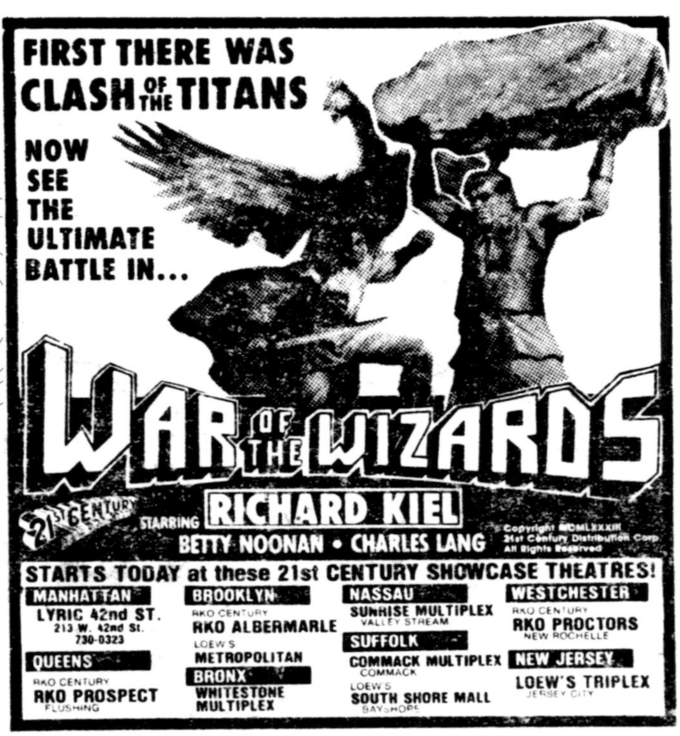
FIRST THERE WAS
CLASH OF THE TITANS
NOW SEE THE ULTIMATE BATTLE IN...
WAR OF THE WIZARDS
21st CENTURY
STARRING RICHARD KIEL
BETTY NOONAN • CHARLES LANG
Copyright MCMLXXXIII
21st Century Distribution Corp.
All Rights Reserved
STARTS TODAY at these 21st CENTURY SHOWCASE THEATRES!
MANHATTAN
LYRIC 42nd ST.
213 W. 42nd St.
730-0323
QUEENS
RKO CENTURY
RKO PROSPECT
FLUSHING
BROOKLYN
RKO CENTURY
RKO ALBERMARLE
LOEW'S
METROPOLITAN
BRONX
WHITESTONE MULTIPLEX
NASSAU
SUNRISE MULTIPLEX
VALLEY STREAM
SUFFOLK
COMMACK MULTIPLEX
COMMACK
LOEW'S
SOUTH SHORE MALL
BAYSHORE
WESTCHESTER
RKO CENTURY
RKO PROCTORS
NEW ROCHELLE
NEW JERSEY
LOEW'S TRIPLEX
JERSEY CITY

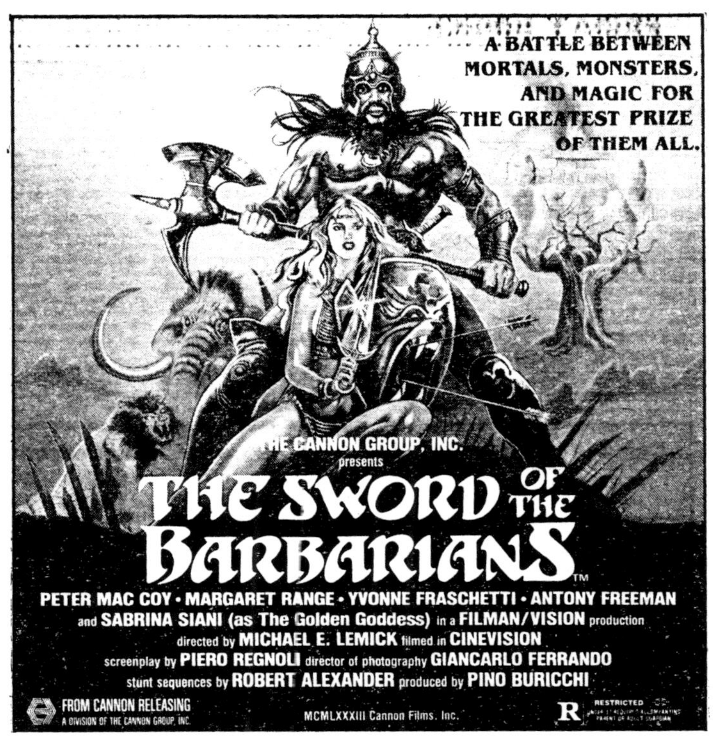
A BATTLE BETWEEN
MORTALS, MONSTERS,
AND MAGIC FOR
THE GREATEST PRIZE
OF THEM ALL.
THE CANNON GROUP, INC.
presents
THE SWORD OF THE BARBARIANS
PETER MAC COY • MARGARET RANGE • YVONNE FRASCHETTI • ANTONY FREEMAN
and SABRINA SIANI (as The Golden Goddess) in a FILMAN/VISION production
directed by MICHAEL E. LEMICK filmed in CINEVISION
screenplay by PIERO REGNOLI director of photography GIANCARLO FERRANDO
stunt sequences by ROBERT ALEXANDER produced by PINO BURICCHI
FROM CANNON RELEASING
A DIVISION OF THE CANNON GROUP, INC.
MCMLXXXIII Cannon Films, Inc.
R RESTRICTED

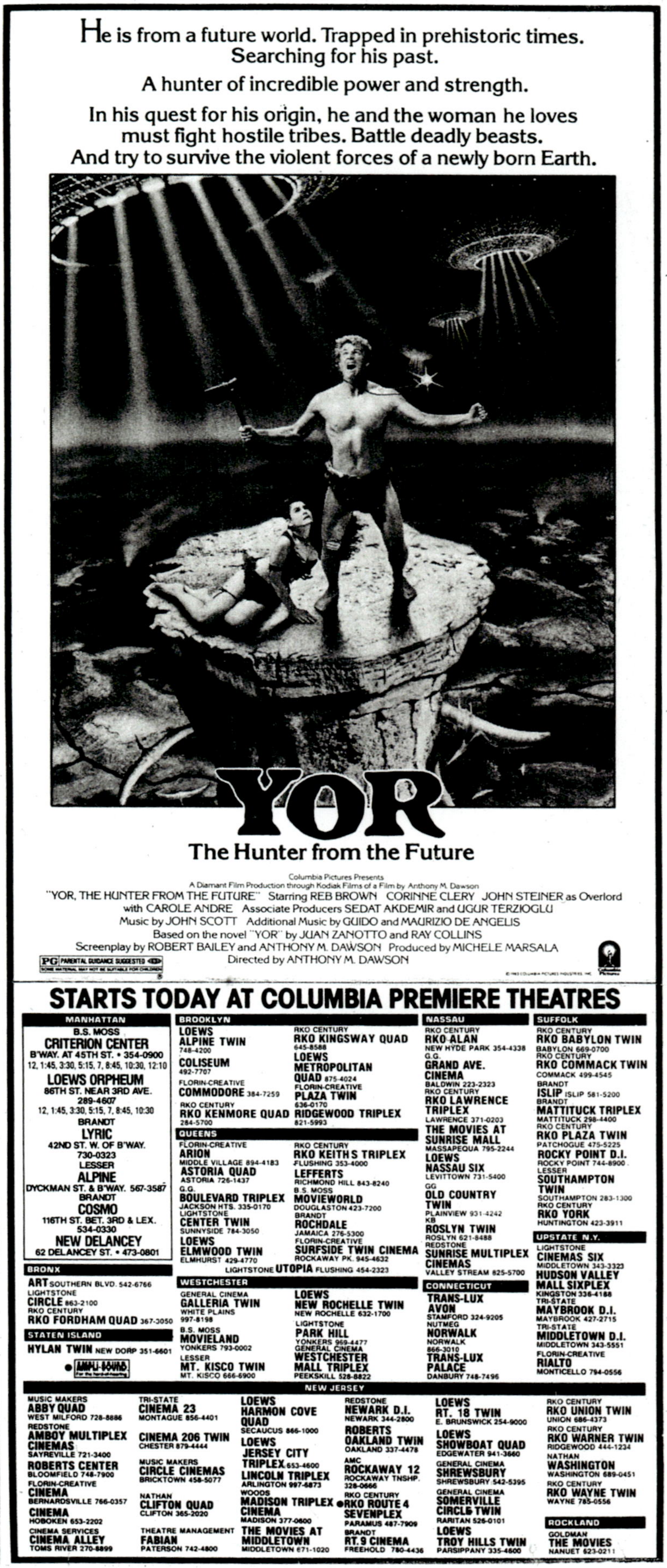

HERCULES & YOR, HUNTER FROM THE FUTURE

Arguably, 1983 is the last year two movies as tacky as this pair of Italian imports were released by major studios. MGM/UA and Cannon's *Hercules*, an attempt to do for Lou Ferrigno what *Conan* did for Arnold Schwarzenegger, and Columbia's *Yor*, a condensation of a four-part TV miniseries, were essentially revivals of the '60s *peplum* (sword and sandal) movies garnished with not-exactly-state-of-the-art special effects. The directors of both took their traditional pseudonyms – *Hercules*' Luigi Cozzi as "Lewis Coates," and *Yor*'s Antonio Margheriti as "Anthony M. Dawson" – and the reviews were pretty much what you'd expect. Samples for *Hercules* are below; for *Yor*, I will simply provide a headline for one that I recall, from a paper I sadly can't remember: "Up Yor's."

"Director-writer Lewis Coates is to be congratulated on having left no myth un-dug, nor modern studio facilities untapped in this encyclopedic assembly of everything calculated to impress the meagerly educated."

–Archer Winsten, *New York Post*

"[Ferrigno's] voice is obviously dubbed by someone who would be better suited to selling rich Corinthian leather than talking to the Gods. So we watch Ferrigno as Hercules at an emotional distance, wondering mostly whether the veins in his chest and arms are going to burst."

–GENE SISKEL, *CHICAGO TRIBUNE*

"*Hercules* travels to outer space, encounters laser beams, separates Europe from Africa (I swear!), wrestles with some of the worst dialogue that has ever been written for the screen and boasts special effects which are just laughable."

–Hank Gallo, New York *Daily News*

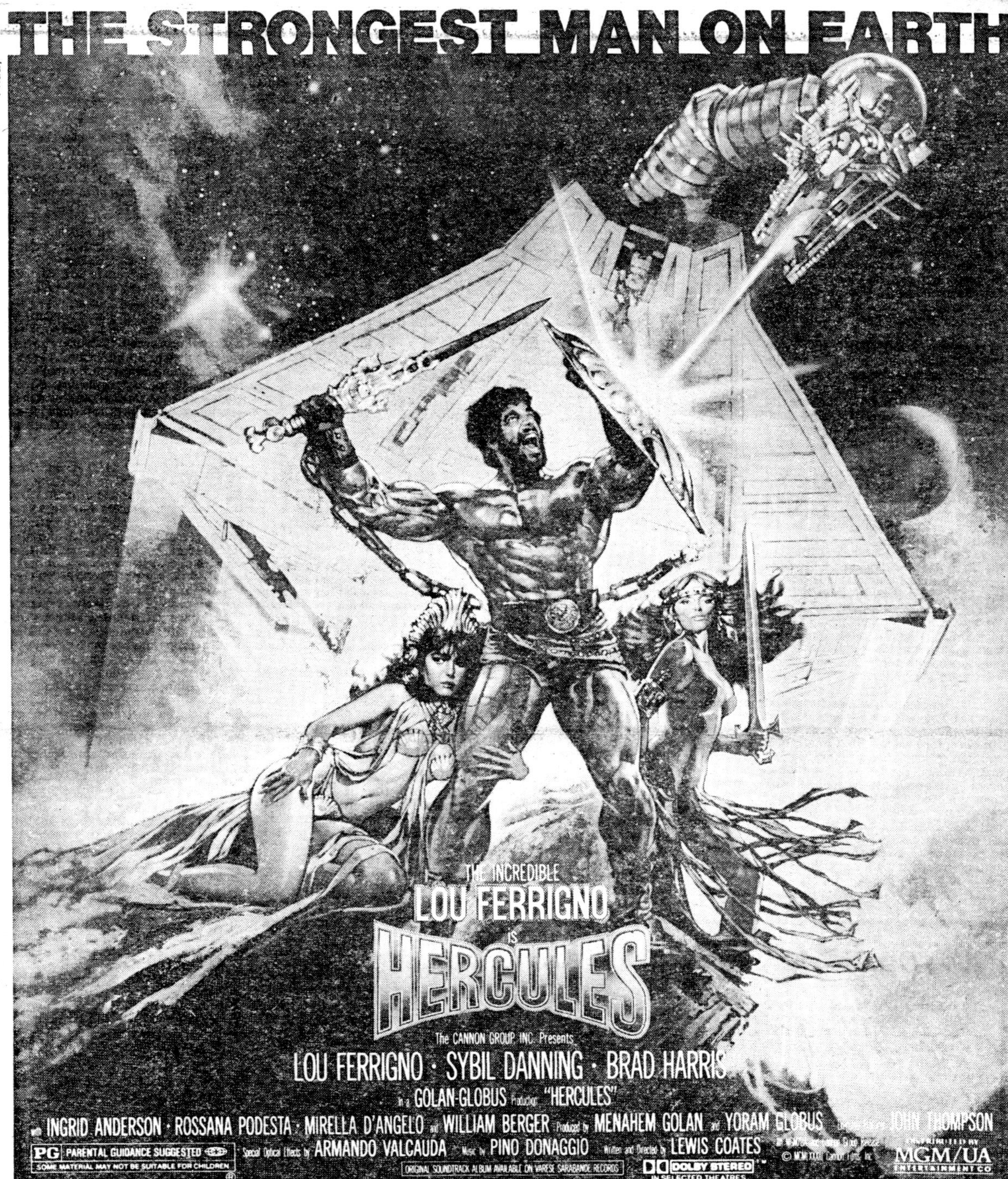

STARTS TODAY

MANHATTAN

RKO CENTURY
RKO WARNER TWIN
B'WAY & 47TH ST. 975-8366
12, 2:20, 4:45, 7:10, 9:35, 12 MID.

A CINEMA 5 THEATRE
MANHATTAN TWIN
59TH ST. E. OF 3RD AVE. 935-6420
1, 3, 5, 7, 9, 11

RKO CENTURY
✓ **RKO 86TH STREET TWIN**
86TH ST. & LEX. AVE. 289-8900
1, 3:10, 5:25, 7:40, 10, 12 MID.

(Spanish subtitles)
ASTRAL
181 ST. & AUDUBON AVE. 928-1060

LESSER
ESSEX
ESSEX & GRAND ST. 982-4455

BRONX

LIGHTSTONE **CIRCLE**
BRANDT **CITY CINEMA**
CINEMA **DOVER**
RKO CENTURY **RKO FORDHAM QUAD**
LESSER **KENT**
CINEMA CIRCLE **PROSPECT TRIPLEX**

STATEN ISLAND

RKO CENTURY **RKO RICHMOND** NEW SPRINGVILLE

CONNECTICUT

TRANS LUX AVON STAMFORD

ROCKLAND

THE MOVIES NANUET
9W CINEMA STONY POINT

BROOKLYN

FLORIN CREATIVE **CANARSIE TRIPLEX**
COMMODORE
DUFFIELD
GOLDEN **FORTWAY FIVEPLEX**
HIGHWAY
RKO CENTURY **RKO KINGSWAY QUAD**
RIDGEWOOD TRIPLEX
GOLDEN **RUGBY TWIN**

UPSTATE N.Y.

MAYFAIR KINGSTON
MIDDLEHOPE D.I. NEWBURGH
MOUNTAIN D.I. LIBERTY
NEW PALTZ CINEMA NEW PALTZ
PLAZA MIDDLETOWN
RIALTO MONTICELLO

QUEENS

BAYSIDE QUAD BAYSIDE
COLONY JACKSON HEIGHTS
FOREST HILLS FOREST HILLS
RKO CENTURY **RKO MEADOWS TWIN** FRESH MEADOWS
PLAZA (Spanish subtitles) CORONA
FLORIN CREATIVE **SURFSIDE TWIN CINEMA** ROCKAWAY PK.

NASSAU

RKO CENTURY **RKO BALDWIN**
G & W **FRANKLIN** FRANKLIN SQUARE
RKO CENTURY **RKO GREEN ACRES** VALLEY STREAM
MANHASSET TRIPLEX
THE MOVIES AT SUNRISE MALL MASSAPEQUA
✓ **SYOSSET** SYOSSET
WESTBURY D.I. TRIPLEX WESTBURY

WESTCHESTER

GENERAL CINEMA **ARCADIAN TWIN** OSSINING
LESSER **BEACH CINEMA TRIPLEX** PEEKSKILL
GENERAL CINEMA **CENTRAL PLAZA TWIN** YONKERS
PLAYHOUSE FOUR MAMARONECK
RKO CENTURY **RKO PROCTORS FIVEPLEX** NEW ROCHELLE

SUFFOLK

UA **COLLEGE PLAZA TWIN** FARMINGVILLE
COPIAGUE A/W D.I. COPIAGUE
RKO CENTURY **RKO MALL** SMITH HAVEN
PINE CINEMA CORAM
BRANDT **SAYVILLE TRIPLEX** SAYVILLE
SHIRLEY D.I. SHIRLEY
LESSER **SOUTHAMPTON TWIN** SOUTHAMPTON

✓ AMPLI-SOUND For the hard-of-hearing

NEW JERSEY

AMBOY MULTIPLEX CINEMAS SAYREVILLE
BELLEVUE UPPER MONTCLAIR
BLUE STAR WATCHUNG
BRUNSWICK SQUARE EAST BRUNSWICK
CIRCLE CINEMAS BRICKTOWN
CLIFTON QUAD CLIFTON
FABIAN PATERSON
LOEWS HARMON COVE QUAD SECAUCUS
LINWOOD FORT LEE
MADISON MADISON
RKO MILLBURN TWIN MILLBURN
THE MOVIES AT MIDDLETOWN MIDDLETOWN
NEWARK D.I. NEWARK
NEWTON D.I. NEWTON
OCEAN COUNTY MALL TOMS RIVER
PALACE BERGENFIELD
PARAMOUNT NEWARK
ROCKAWAY TWELVE ROCKAWAY TOWNSHIP
ROUTE 9 CINEMA FREEHOLD
✓ **RKO ROUTE 4 SEVENPLEX** PARAMUS
ROUTE 35 D.I. HAZLET
SHREWSBURY PLAZA NEW SHREWSBURY
SOMERVILLE D.I. SOMERVILLE
STATE TRIPLEX JERSEY CITY
WASHINGTON WASHINGTON
WOODBRIDGE WOODBRIDGE
RKO WAYNE TWIN WAYNE

Daily News, August 26, 1983

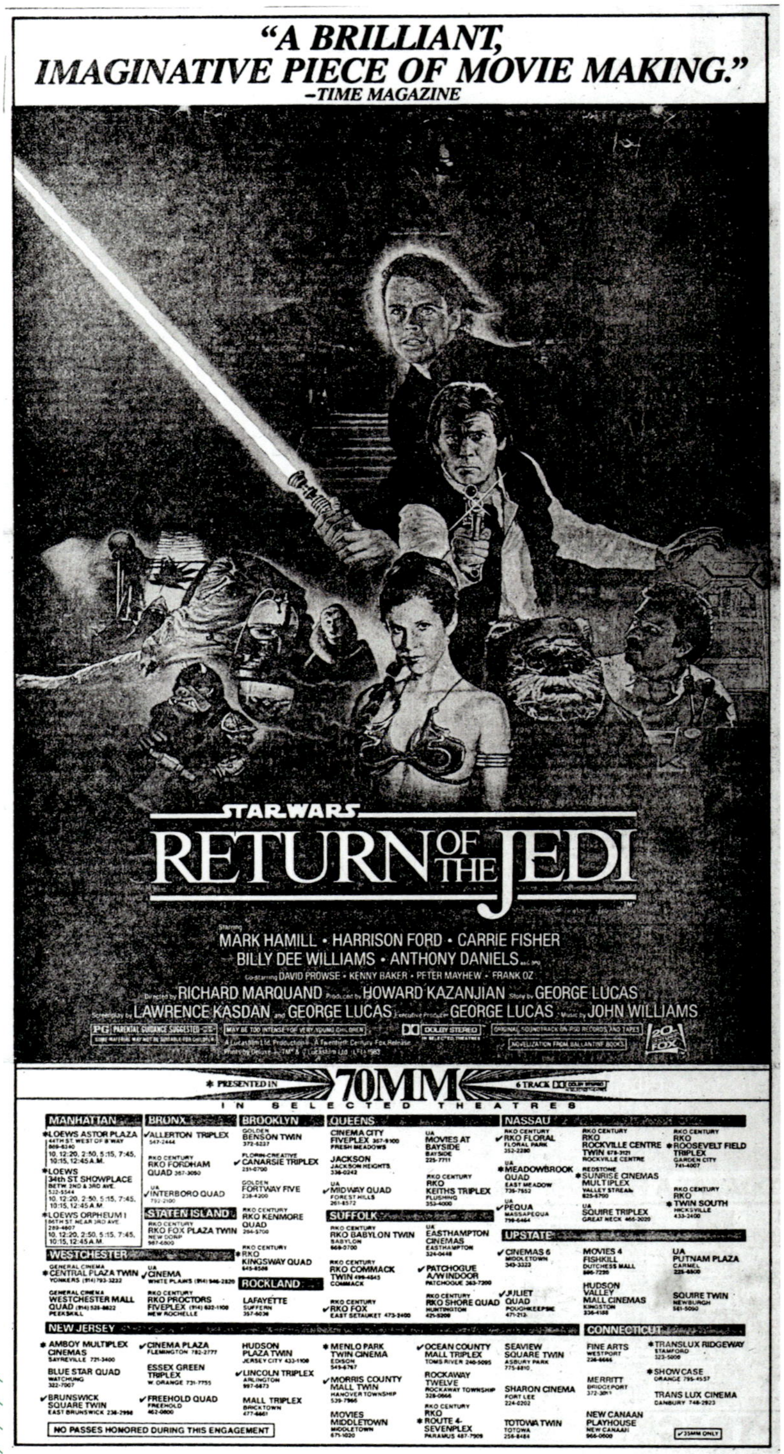

RETURN OF THE JEDI

Apparently, Rex Reed forgot that he had raved about *The Empire Strikes Back* three years before, because when he addressed *Jedi*, he wrote that *Empire* "proved that the whole idea was running out of steam." Not everyone agreed that *Jedi* represented a downward trend for the *Star Wars* saga, though there were definitely more doubters than there were for the previous two films.

"*Return of the Jedi*...is the best one yet. The script, performances and special effects are clearly superior to both *Star Wars* and *The Empire Strikes Back*."

–Michael Blowen, *The Boston Globe*

"The movie is a complete entertainment, a feast for the eyes and a delight for the fancy. It's a little amazing how Lucas and his associates keep topping themselves."

–Roger Ebert, *Chicago Sun-Times*

"Let's hear it for avarice and greed, and the security money can bring. But let's not pretend we're watching art. Richard Marquand, who directed with George Lucas' instructions, is certainly not pretending. He's given *Return of the Jedi* all of the style of a Saturday kiddie matinee serial."

-REX REED,
NEW YORK POST

"*Return of the Jedi* is a childlike delight. It's the best video game around. And for the professional moviegoers, it is particularly enjoyable to watch every facet of filmmaking at its best."

–Gene Siskel, *Chicago Tribune*

"Despite its pyrotechnical wizardry, *Return of the Jedi* lacks vision and a stamp of originality... There's not a genuinely intimate or natural moment in the whole two hours."

–John Stark, *San Francisco Examiner*

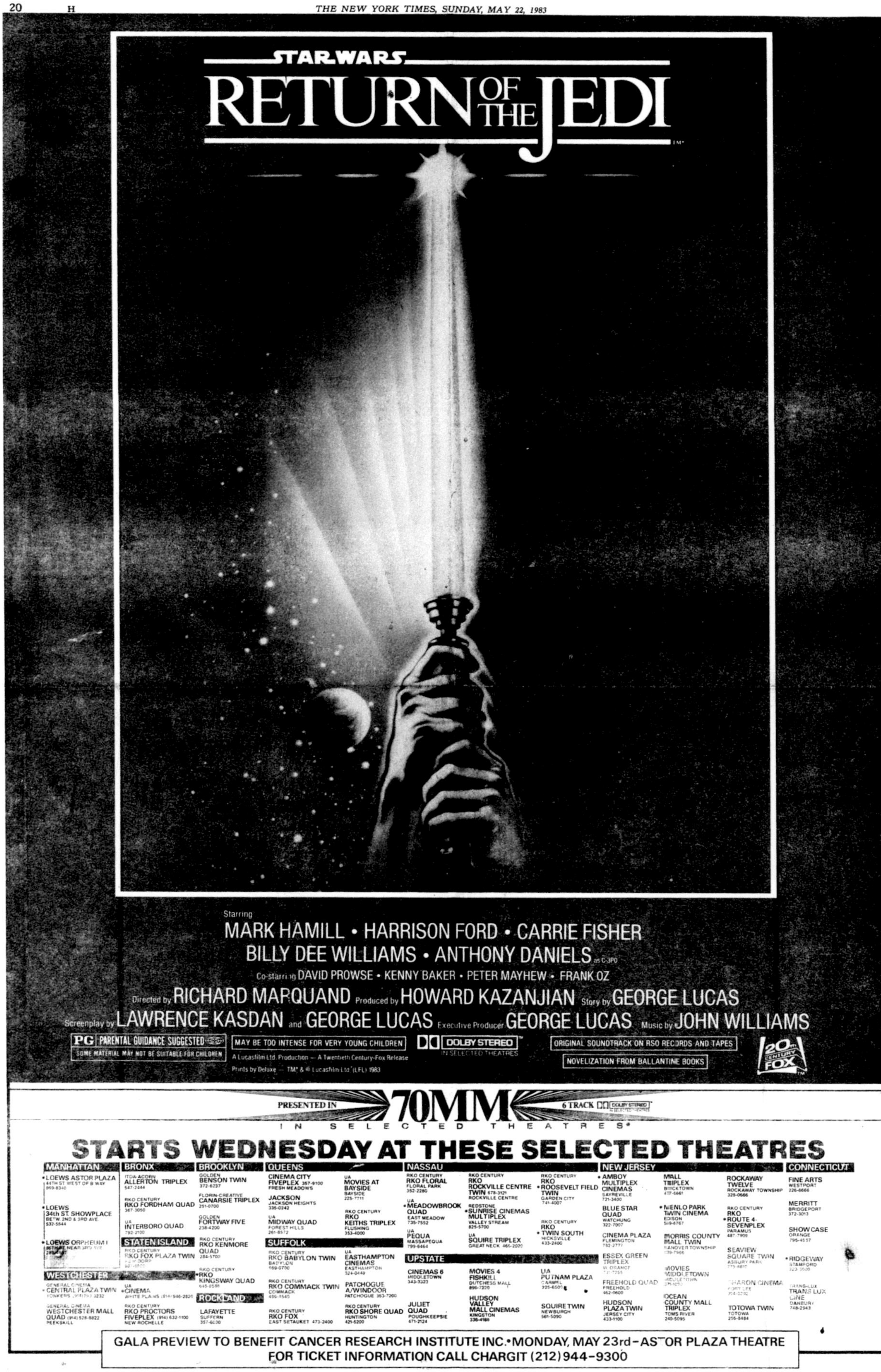
STAR WARS
RETURN OF THE JEDI
Starring
MARK HAMILL • HARRISON FORD • CARRIE FISHER
BILLY DEE WILLIAMS • ANTHONY DANIELS as C-3PO
Co-starring DAVID PROWSE • KENNY BAKER • PETER MAYHEW • FRANK OZ
Directed by RICHARD MARQUAND Produced by HOWARD KAZANJIAN Story by GEORGE LUCAS
Screenplay by LAWRENCE KASDAN and GEORGE LUCAS Executive Producer GEORGE LUCAS Music by JOHN WILLIAMS
PG PARENTAL GUIDANCE SUGGESTED
SOME MATERIAL MAY NOT BE SUITABLE FOR CHILDREN
MAY BE TOO INTENSE FOR VERY YOUNG CHILDREN
DOLBY STEREO
IN SELECTED THEATRES
A Lucasfilm Ltd. Production — A Twentieth Century-Fox Release
Prints by Deluxe — TM & © Lucasfilm Ltd. (LFL) 1983
ORIGINAL SOUNDTRACK ON RSO RECORDS AND TAPES
NOVELIZATION FROM BALLANTINE BOOKS
20th CENTURY FOX
PRESENTED IN 70MM 6 TRACK DOLBY STEREO
IN SELECTED THEATRES*
STARTS WEDNESDAY AT THESE SELECTED THEATRES
MANHATTAN
•LOEWS ASTOR PLAZA 44TH ST. WEST OF B'WAY
•LOEWS 34th ST. SHOWPLACE BETW. 2ND & 3RD AVE. 532-5544
•LOEWS ORPHEUM I
BRONX
ALLERTON TRIPLEX 547-2444
RKO FORDHAM QUAD
INTERBORO QUAD 792-2100
STATEN ISLAND
RKO FOX PLAZA TWIN
BROOKLYN
BENSON TWIN 372-6237
CANARSIE TRIPLEX 251-0700
FORTWAY FIVE 238-4200
RKO KENMORE QUAD 284-5700
•RKO KINGSWAY QUAD
ROCKLAND
LAFAYETTE SUFFERN 357-6030
WESTCHESTER
•CENTRAL PLAZA TWIN YONKERS
•CINEMA WHITE PLAINS
WESTCHESTER MALL QUAD PEEKSKILL
RKO PROCTORS FIVEPLEX (914) 632-1100 NEW ROCHELLE
QUEENS
CINEMA CITY FIVEPLEX 357-9100 FRESH MEADOWS
JACKSON JACKSON HEIGHTS
MIDWAY QUAD FOREST HILLS
MOVIES AT BAYSIDE BAYSIDE 225-7711
RKO KEITHS TRIPLEX FLUSHING 353-4000
SUFFOLK
RKO BABYLON TWIN BABYLON
RKO COMMACK TWIN COMMACK
RKO FOX EAST SETAUKET 473-2400
EASTHAMPTON CINEMAS
PATCHOGUE A/WINDOOR PATCHOGUE
RKO SHORE QUAD HUNTINGTON
NASSAU
RKO FLORAL FLORAL PARK 352-2280
•MEADOWBROOK QUAD EAST MEADOW 735-7552
PEQUA MASSAPEQUA 799-6464
RKO ROCKVILLE CENTRE TWIN ROCKVILLE CENTRE
•SUNRISE CINEMAS MULTIPLEX VALLEY STREAM 825-5700
SQUIRE TRIPLEX GREAT NECK
•RKO ROOSEVELT FIELD TWIN GARDEN CITY 741-4007
•RKO TWIN SOUTH HICKSVILLE 433-2400
UPSTATE
CINEMAS 6 MIDDLETOWN 343-3323
JULIET QUAD POUGHKEEPSIE 471-2124
MOVIES 4 FISHKILL DUTCHESS MALL
HUDSON VALLEY MALL CINEMAS KINGSTON
PUTNAM PLAZA CARMEL
SQUIRE TWIN NEWBURGH 561-5090
NEW JERSEY
•AMBOY MULTIPLEX CINEMAS SAYREVILLE 721-3400
BLUE STAR QUAD WATCHUNG 322-7007
CINEMA PLAZA FLEMINGTON
ESSEX GREEN TRIPLEX
FREEHOLD QUAD FREEHOLD 462-0600
HUDSON PLAZA TWIN JERSEY CITY 433-1100
MALL TRIPLEX
•MENLO PARK TWIN CINEMA EDISON
MORRIS COUNTY MALL TWIN
MOVIES MIDDLETOWN
OCEAN COUNTY MALL TRIPLEX TOMS RIVER 240-5095
ROCKAWAY TWELVE ROCKAWAY TOWNSHIP
•RKO ROUTE 4 SEVENPLEX PARAMUS
SEAVIEW SQUARE TWIN ASBURY PARK
SHARON CINEMA FORT LEE
TOTOWA TWIN TOTOWA 256-8484
CONNECTICUT
FINE ARTS WESTPORT 226-6666
MERRITT BRIDGEPORT 372-3013
SHOW CASE ORANGE
•RIDGEWAY STAMFORD
TRANS LUX CINE DANBURY 748-2943
GALA PREVIEW TO BENEFIT CANCER RESEARCH INSTITUTE INC.•MONDAY, MAY 23rd–ASTOR PLAZA THEATRE
FOR TICKET INFORMATION CALL CHARGIT (212) 944-9300

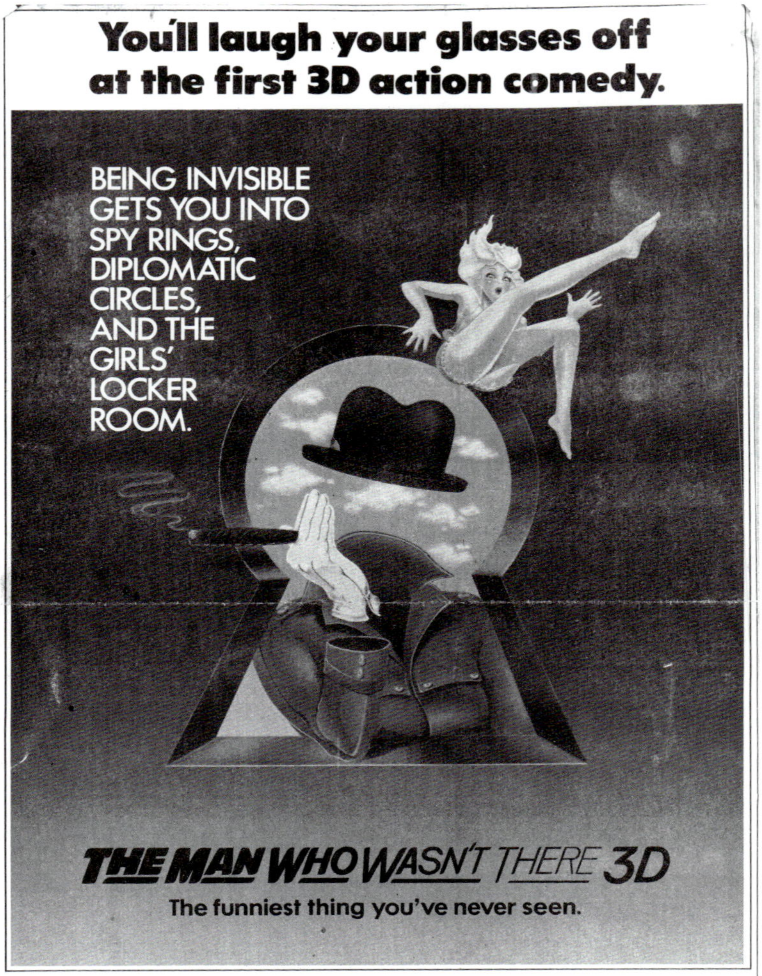

SPACEHUNTER/ METALSTORM/ TREASURE OF THE FOUR CROWNS/ THE MAN WHO WASN'T THERE

After the surprise success of the dimensional cheapie Western *Comin' at Ya* in 1981 and the big grosses of the following year's *Friday the 13th Part III*, 3D became the gimmick of choice, as this quartet of '83 releases demonstrates. However, the only film to ride it to decent box office that year was *Jaws 3-D*. *Spacehunter*, confounding Columbia's promises of longevity, was forgotten by the end of the summer; *Metalstorm* (which Universal piggybacked into theaters following *Jaws 3-D*) and *Treasure of the Four Crowns* performed like the schlock items they were; and *The Man Who Wasn't There*, an invisibility comedy from *Friday III* producer Frank Mancuso Jr., vanished from theaters within a couple of weeks. It failed to capitalize on the more salacious possibilities of its central idea – see the ad for *School Spirit* in the 1985 section for further study.

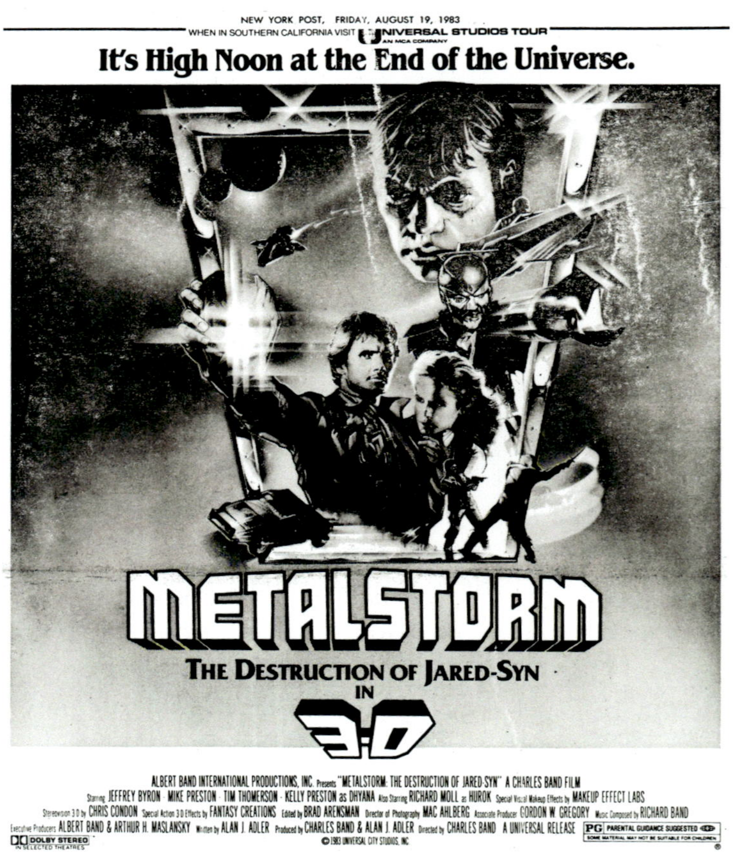

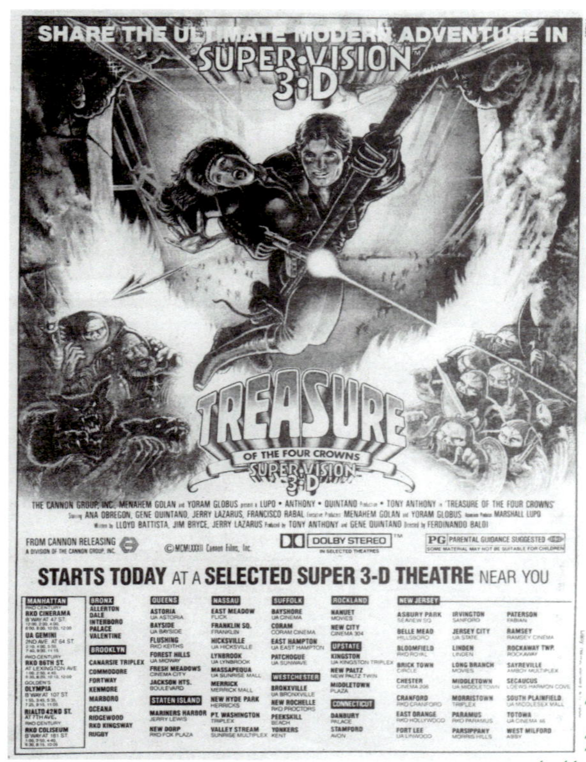

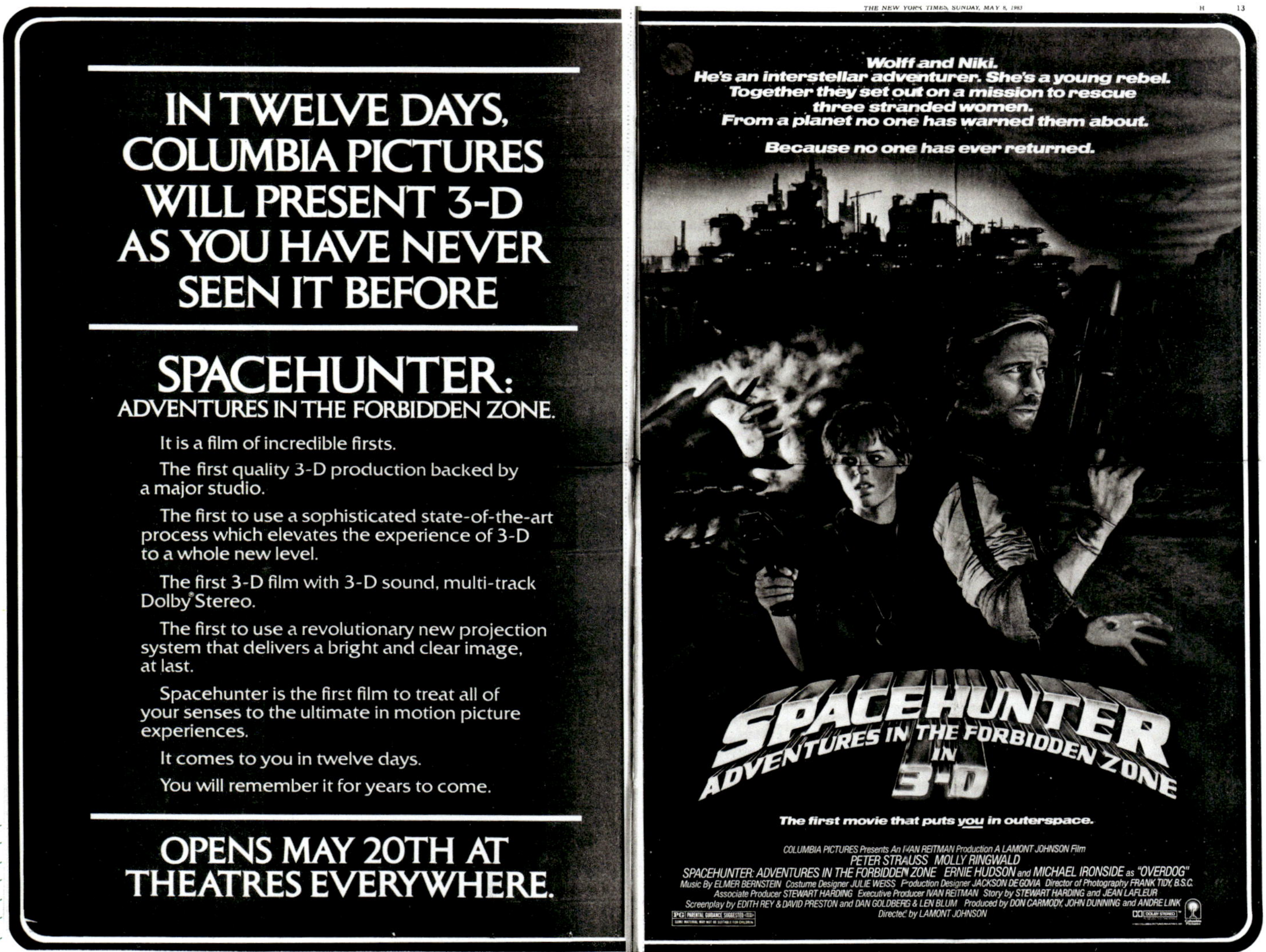

THE NEW YORK TIMES, SUNDAY, MAY 8, 1983
IN TWELVE DAYS, COLUMBIA PICTURES WILL PRESENT 3-D AS YOU HAVE NEVER SEEN IT BEFORE
SPACEHUNTER: ADVENTURES IN THE FORBIDDEN ZONE.
It is a film of incredible firsts.
The first quality 3-D production backed by a major studio.
The first to use a sophisticated state-of-the-art process which elevates the experience of 3-D to a whole new level.
The first 3-D film with 3-D sound, multi-track Dolby® Stereo.
The first to use a revolutionary new projection system that delivers a bright and clear image, at last.
Spacehunter is the first film to treat all of your senses to the ultimate in motion picture experiences.
It comes to you in twelve days.
You will remember it for years to come.
OPENS MAY 20TH AT THEATRES EVERYWHERE.
Wolff and Niki.
He's an interstellar adventurer. She's a young rebel.
Together they set out on a mission to rescue three stranded women.
From a planet no one has warned them about.
Because no one has ever returned.
SPACEHUNTER ADVENTURES IN THE FORBIDDEN ZONE IN 3-D
The first movie that puts you in outerspace.
COLUMBIA PICTURES Presents An IVAN REITMAN Production A LAMONT JOHNSON Film
PETER STRAUSS MOLLY RINGWALD
SPACEHUNTER: ADVENTURES IN THE FORBIDDEN ZONE ERNIE HUDSON and MICHAEL IRONSIDE as "OVERDOG"
Music By ELMER BERNSTEIN Costume Designer JULIE WEISS Production Designer JACKSON DE GOVIA Director of Photography FRANK TIDY, B.S.C.
Associate Producer STEWART HARDING Executive Producer IVAN REITMAN Story by STEWART HARDING and JEAN LAFLEUR
Screenplay by EDITH REY & DAVID PRESTON and DAN GOLDBERG & LEN BLUM Produced by DON CARMODY, JOHN DUNNING and ANDRE LINK
Directed by LAMONT JOHNSON
PG PARENTAL GUIDANCE SUGGESTED
DOLBY STEREO

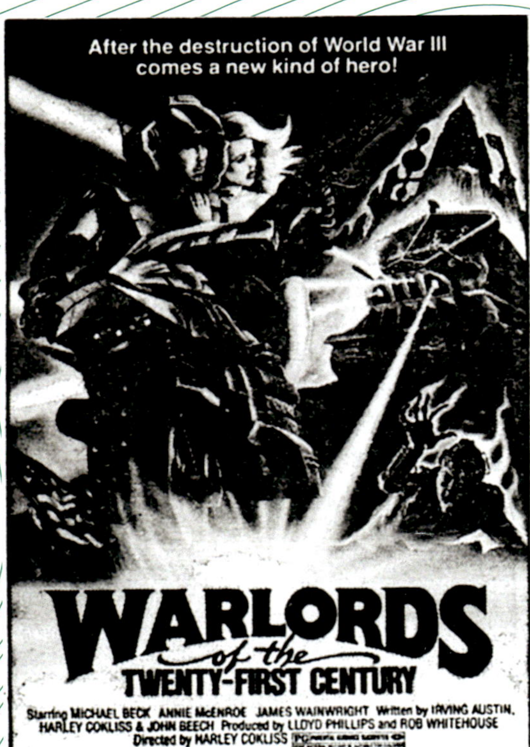

After the destruction of World War III comes a new kind of hero!
WARLORDS of the TWENTY-FIRST CENTURY
Starring MICHAEL BECK ANNIE McENROE JAMES WAINWRIGHT Written by IRVING AUSTIN, HARLEY COKLISS & JOHN BEECH Produced by LLOYD PHILLIPS and ROB WHITEHOUSE
Directed by HARLEY COKLISS

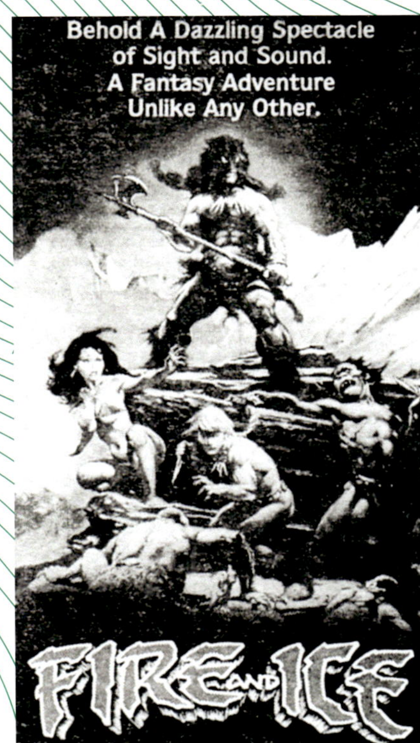

Behold A Dazzling Spectacle of Sight and Sound.
A Fantasy Adventure Unlike Any Other.
FIRE AND ICE

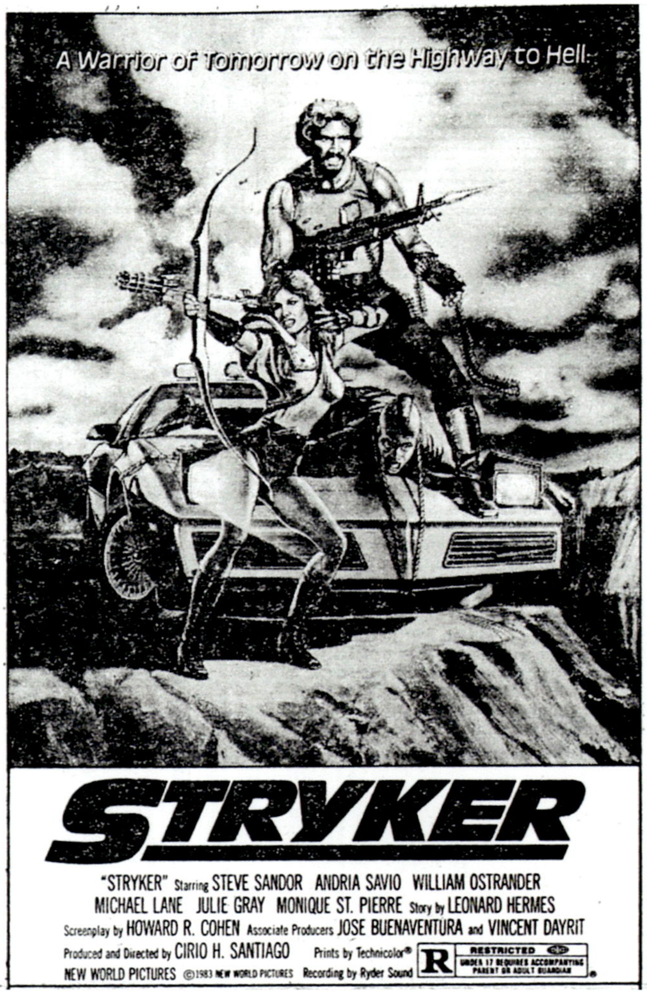

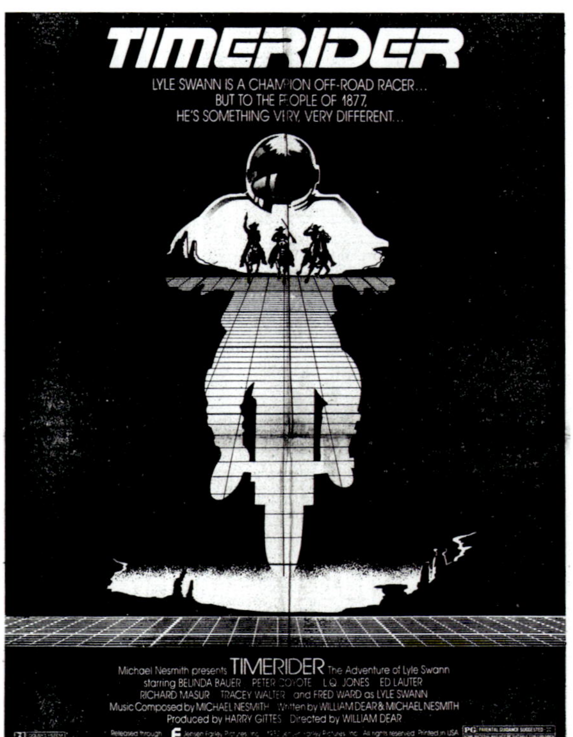

SUPERMAN III

After *Return of the Jedi*, this was the most-awaited threequel of summer '83. After all, what could be better than a follow-up to the highly praised hits *Superman* and *Superman II* with the added comic genius of Richard Pryor? Well, *Superman III* was one of the first lessons of my youth that a much-anticipated big-ticket flick could fall far short of expectations. I walked in certain that the critics, who were pretty much unanimous in their disappointment, had to be wrong about this one, and walked out feeling that, sadly, they were right.

"The separate elements of *Superman III* are very well executed, but they don't mesh together very well. ... The screenplay has some moments of genuine wit and gives the characters some very pressing contemporary problems."

–Desmond Ryan, *Philadelphia Inquirer*

"Despite superb performances from [Christopher] Reeve, [Richard] Pryor, and [Robert] Vaughn, *Superman* dies. Not from kryptonite, but from directorial neglect. ... The S on [Superman's] chest stands for stale."

–Michael Blowen, *The Boston Globe*

"*Superman III* is for people who prefer Roger Moore in *Moonraker* to Sean Connery in *Goldfinger*."

–ELEANOR RINGEL, *THE ATLANTA CONSTITUTION*

"Disjointed and dispirited, *Superman III* is a mediocre to downright crummy movie for the most part. I can only guess that its creators' feverish attempt to make it seem timely by infusing the plot with computer technology is the key to why the thing is so disarrayed."

–Peter Stack, *San Francisco Chronicle*

"[O]f all the summer trash we're drowning in, *Superman III* is the stupidest and the trashiest. They've taken the old Superman comics as far as the idea will go, run out of steam, and now turned the whole thing into a mindless farce."

–Rex Reed, *New York Post*

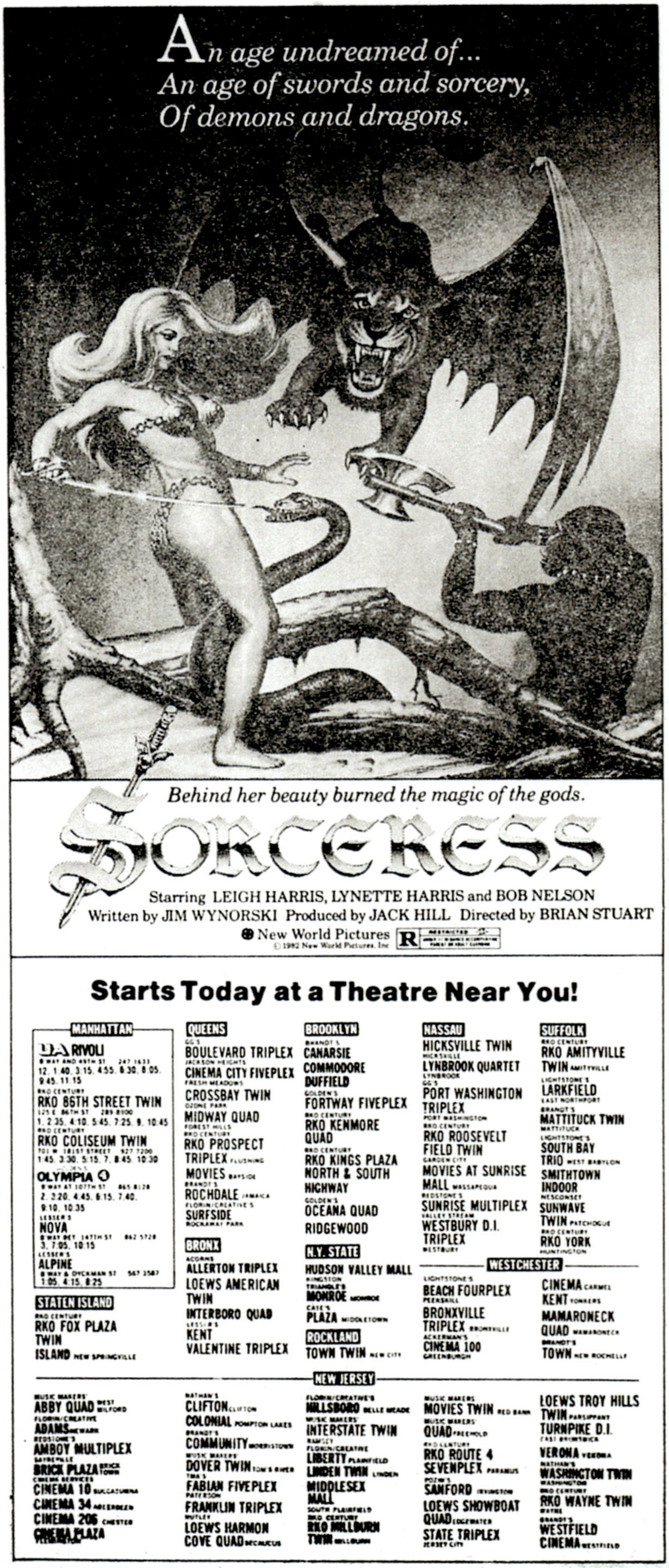

TWILIGHT ZONE: THE MOVIE

When it comes to anthology features, opinions usually vary widely about which segment is the best. Not so for this feature revival of Rod Serling's classic TV series, in which the reactions fell into two camps: those who felt John Landis and Steven Spielberg's initial pair of segments were lackluster and Joe Dante and George Miller's entries were much better, and those who thought only Miller's truly delivered the goods. A few singled out Landis' funny prologue with Dan Aykroyd and Albert Brooks for praise, and then there were those who couldn't help bringing up the tragic deaths of Vic Morrow and two child actors during production.

"Spielberg, who produced the whole project, perhaps sensed that he and Landis had the weakest results, since he assembles the stories in an ascending order of excitement. *Twilight Zone* starts slow, almost grinds to a halt, and then has a fast comeback."

–Roger Ebert, *Chicago Sun-Times*

"It's a shame that the entire movie isn't as funny or as frightening as the prologue. ... After that... it's pretty much straight downhill for the first two episodes and then straight back uphill for the last two."

–Gene Siskel, *Chicago Tribune*

"A lot of money and several lives might have been saved if the producers had just rereleased the original programs. Of the four stories, the last, directed by George Miller, is tops, meaning that it's pretty good."

–VINCENT CANBY, *THE NEW YORK TIMES*

"The first half, particularly, is a bit of a snooze. But the overall effect is an enticing bit of crafty weirdness and witty mayhem. It's even got two or three 'wow' scenes."

–Rick Lyman, *Philadelphia Inquirer*

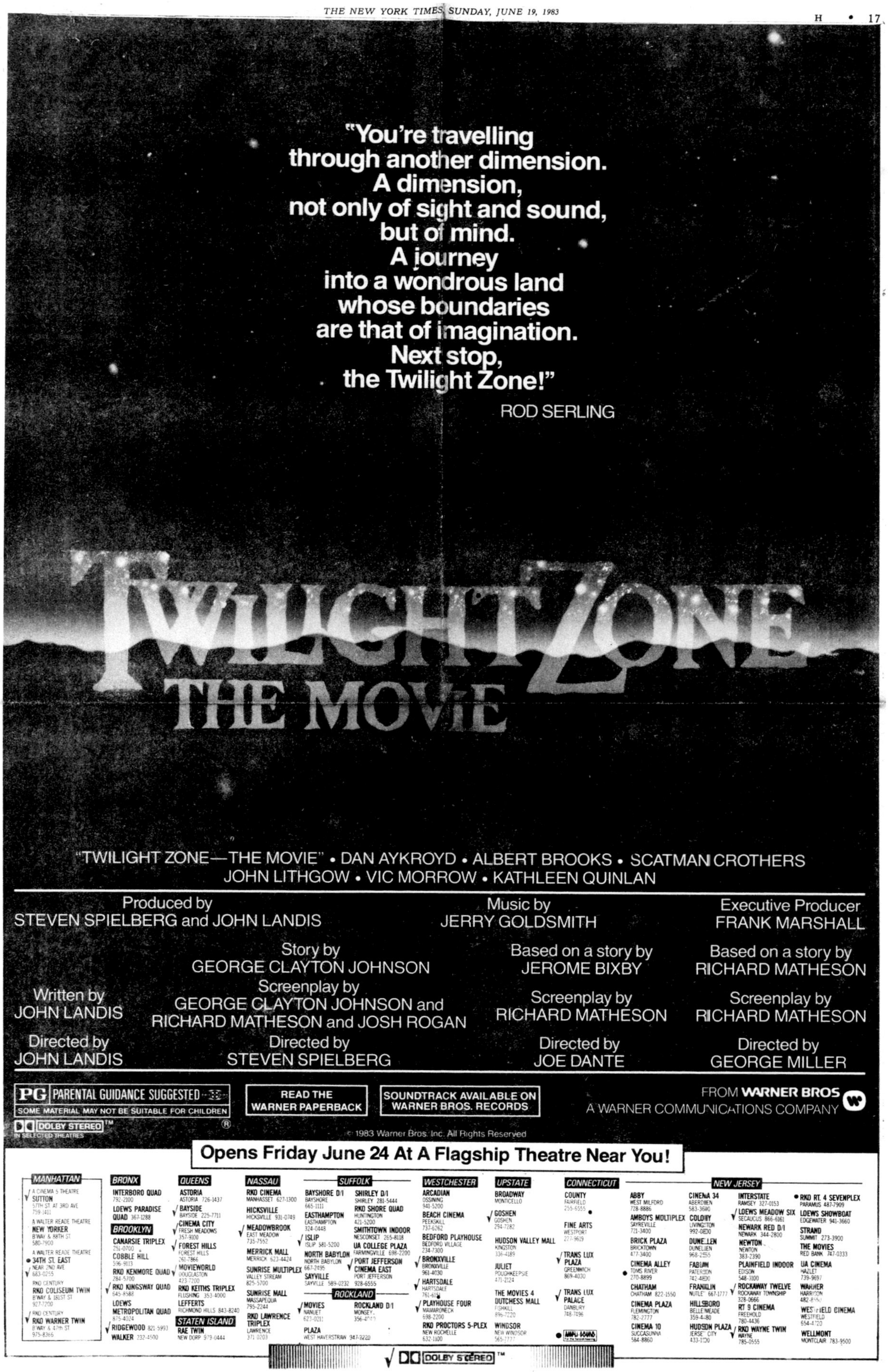
THE NEW YORK TIMES, SUNDAY, JUNE 19, 1983
H • 17
"You're travelling through another dimension. A dimension, not only of sight and sound, but of mind. A journey into a wondrous land whose boundaries are that of imagination. Next stop, the Twilight Zone!"
ROD SERLING
TWILIGHT ZONE
THE MOVIE
"TWILIGHT ZONE—THE MOVIE" • DAN AYKROYD • ALBERT BROOKS • SCATMAN CROTHERS
JOHN LITHGOW • VIC MORROW • KATHLEEN QUINLAN
Produced by STEVEN SPIELBERG and JOHN LANDIS
Music by JERRY GOLDSMITH
Executive Producer FRANK MARSHALL
Written by JOHN LANDIS
Directed by JOHN LANDIS
Story by GEORGE CLAYTON JOHNSON
Screenplay by GEORGE CLAYTON JOHNSON and RICHARD MATHESON and JOSH ROGAN
Directed by STEVEN SPIELBERG
Based on a story by JEROME BIXBY
Screenplay by RICHARD MATHESON
Directed by JOE DANTE
Based on a story by RICHARD MATHESON
Screenplay by RICHARD MATHESON
Directed by GEORGE MILLER
PG PARENTAL GUIDANCE SUGGESTED
SOME MATERIAL MAY NOT BE SUITABLE FOR CHILDREN
DOLBY STEREO™ IN SELECTED THEATRES
READ THE WARNER PAPERBACK
SOUNDTRACK AVAILABLE ON WARNER BROS. RECORDS
FROM WARNER BROS
A WARNER COMMUNICATIONS COMPANY
© 1983 Warner Bros. Inc. All Rights Reserved
Opens Friday June 24 At A Flagship Theatre Near You!
MANHATTAN
√ A CINEMA 5 THEATRE SUTTON 57TH ST. AT 3RD AVE 759-1411
A WALTER READE THEATRE NEW YORKER B'WAY & 88TH ST 580-7900
A WALTER READE THEATRE • 34TH ST. EAST NEAR 2ND AVE 683-0255
RKO CENTURY RKO COLISEUM TWIN B'WAY & 181ST ST 927-7200
√ RKO CENTURY RKO WARNER TWIN B'WAY & 47th ST 975-8366
BRONX
INTERBORO QUAD 792-2100
LOEWS PARADISE QUAD 367-1288
BROOKLYN
CANARSIE TRIPLEX 251-0700
COBBLE HILL 596-9113
RKO KENMORE QUAD 284-5700
√ RKO KINGSWAY QUAD 645-8588
LOEWS METROPOLITAN QUAD 875-4024
√ RIDGEWOOD 821-5993
WALKER 232-4500
QUEENS
ASTORIA ASTORIA 726-1437
√ BAYSIDE BAYSIDE 225-7711
√ CINEMA CITY FRESH MEADOWS 357-9100
√ FOREST HILLS FOREST HILLS 261-7866
√ MOVIEWORLD DOUGLASTON 423-7200
RKO KEITHS TRIPLEX FLUSHING 353-4000
LEFFERTS RICHMOND HILLS 843-8240
STATEN ISLAND
RAE TWIN NEW DORP 979-0444
NASSAU
RKO CINEMA MANHASSET 627-1300
HICKSVILLE HICKSVILLE 931-0749
√ MEADOWBROOK EAST MEADOW 735-7552
MERRICK MALL MERRICK 623-4424
SUNRISE MULTIPLEX VALLEY STREAM 825-5700
SUNRISE MALL MASSAPEQUA 795-2244
RKO LAWRENCE TRIPLEX LAWRENCE 371 0203
SUFFOLK
BAYSHORE D/I BAYSHORE 665-1111
EASTHAMPTON EASTHAMPTON 324-0448
√ ISLIP ISLIP 581-5200
NORTH BABYLON NORTH BABYLON 667-2495
SAYVILLE SAYVILLE 589-0232
SHIRLEY D/I SHIRLEY 281-5444
RKO SHORE QUAD HUNTINGTON 421-5200
SMITHTOWN INDOOR NESCONSET 265-8118
UA COLLEGE PLAZA FARMINGVILLE 698-2200
√ PORT JEFFERSON CINEMA EAST PORT JEFFERSON 928-6555
ROCKLAND
√ MOVIES NANUET 623-0211
PLAZA WEST HAVERSTRAW 947-3220
ROCKLAND D/I MONSEY
WESTCHESTER
ARCADIAN OSSINING 941-5200
BEACH CINEMA PEEKSKILL 737-6262
BEDFORD PLAYHOUSE BEDFORD VILLAGE 234-7300
√ BRONXVILLE BRONXVILLE 961-4030
√ HARTSDALE HARTSDALE
√ PLAYHOUSE FOUR MAMARONECK 698-2200
RKO PROCTORS 5-PLEX NEW ROCHELLE 632-1100
UPSTATE
BROADWAY MONTICELLO
√ GOSHEN GOSHEN 294-7282
HUDSON VALLEY MALL KINGSTON 336-4189
JULIET POUGHKEEPSIE 471-2124
THE MOVIES 4 DUTCHESS MALL FISHKILL 896-7220
WINDSOR NEW WINDSOR
CONNECTICUT
COUNTY FAIRFIELD 255-6555
FINE ARTS WESTPORT 227-9619
√ TRANS LUX PLAZA GREENWICH 869-4030
√ TRANS LUX PALACE DANBURY 748-7496
NEW JERSEY
ABBY WEST MILFORD 728-8886
AMBOYS MULTIPLEX SAYREVILLE 721-3400
BRICK PLAZA BRICKTOWN 477-3400
• CINEMA ALLEY TOMS RIVER 270-8899
CHATHAM CHATHAM 822-1550
CINEMA PLAZA FLEMINGTON 782-2777
CINEMA 10 SUCCASUNNA 584-8860
CINEMA 34 ABERDEEN
COLONY LIVINGSTON
DUNELLEN DUNELLEN
FABIAN PATERSON
FRANKLIN NUTLEY 667-1777
HILLSBORO BELLE MEADE
HUDSON PLAZA JERSEY CITY
INTERSTATE RAMSEY 327-0153
√ LOEWS MEADOW SIX SECAUCUS 866-6161
NEWARK RED D/I NEWARK 344-2800
NEWTON NEWTON 383-2390
PLAINFIELD INDOOR EDISON 548-3100
√ ROCKAWAY TWELVE ROCKAWAY TOWNSHIP 328-0666
RT 9 CINEMA FREEHOLD 780-4436
√ RKO WAYNE TWIN WAYNE 785-0555
• RKO RT. 4 SEVENPLEX PARAMUS 487-7909
LOEWS SHOWBOAT EDGEWATER 941-3660
STRAND SUMMIT 273-3900
THE MOVIES RED BANK 747-0333
UA CINEMA HAZLET 739-9697
WARNER HARRISON
WESTFIELD CINEMA WESTFIELD
WELLMONT MONTCLAIR 783-9500
√ DOLBY STEREO™

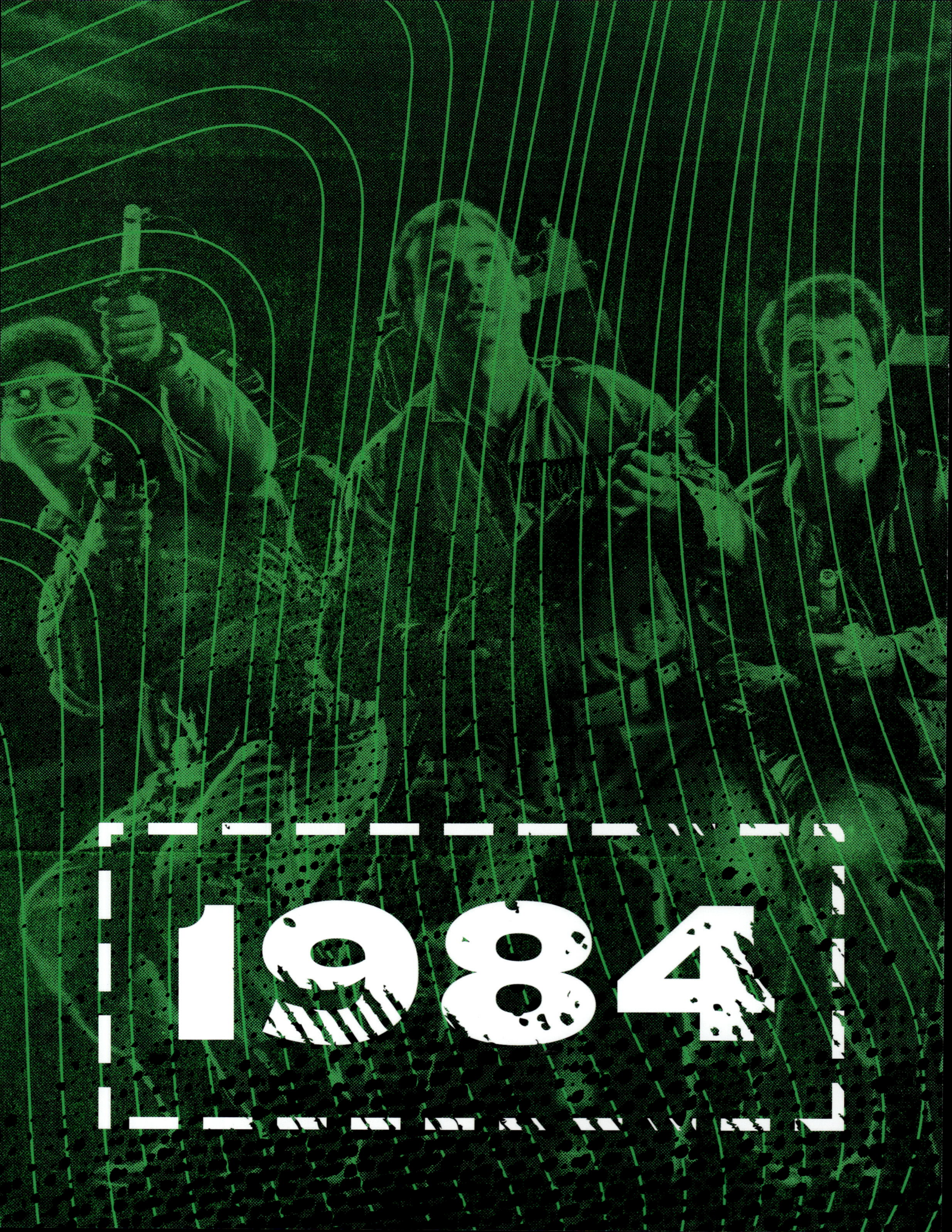
1984

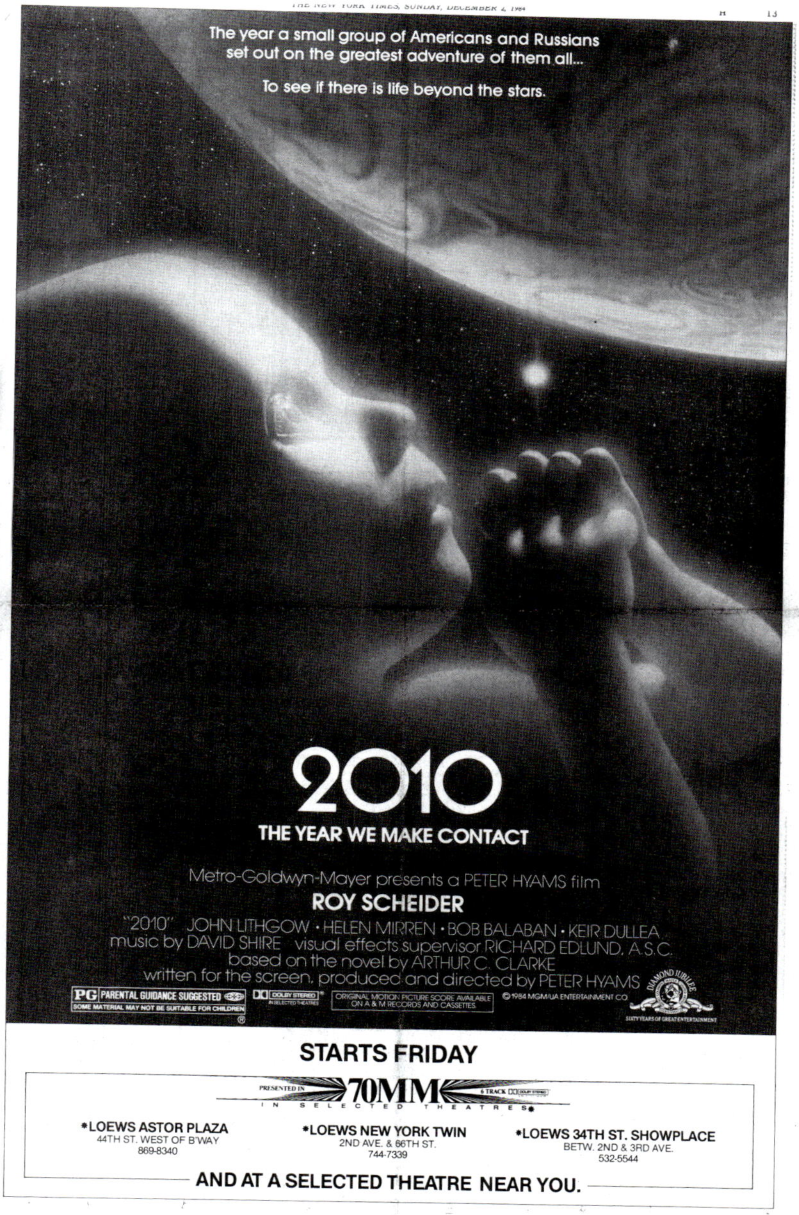

The year a small group of Americans and Russians set out on the greatest adventure of them all...
To see if there is life beyond the stars.
2010
THE YEAR WE MAKE CONTACT
Metro-Goldwyn-Mayer presents a PETER HYAMS film
ROY SCHEIDER
"2010" JOHN LITHGOW · HELEN MIRREN · BOB BALABAN · KEIR DULLEA
music by DAVID SHIRE visual effects supervisor RICHARD EDLUND, A.S.C.
based on the novel by ARTHUR C. CLARKE
written for the screen, produced and directed by PETER HYAMS
PG PARENTAL GUIDANCE SUGGESTED
SOME MATERIAL MAY NOT BE SUITABLE FOR CHILDREN
ORIGINAL MOTION PICTURE SCORE AVAILABLE ON A & M RECORDS AND CASSETTES
© 1984 MGM/UA ENTERTAINMENT CO.
STARTS FRIDAY
70MM
IN SELECTED THEATRES
•LOEWS ASTOR PLAZA
44TH ST. WEST OF B'WAY
869-8340
•LOEWS NEW YORK TWIN
2ND AVE. & 86TH ST.
744-7339
•LOEWS 34TH ST. SHOWPLACE
BETW. 2ND & 3RD AVE.
532-5544
AND AT A SELECTED THEATRE NEAR YOU.

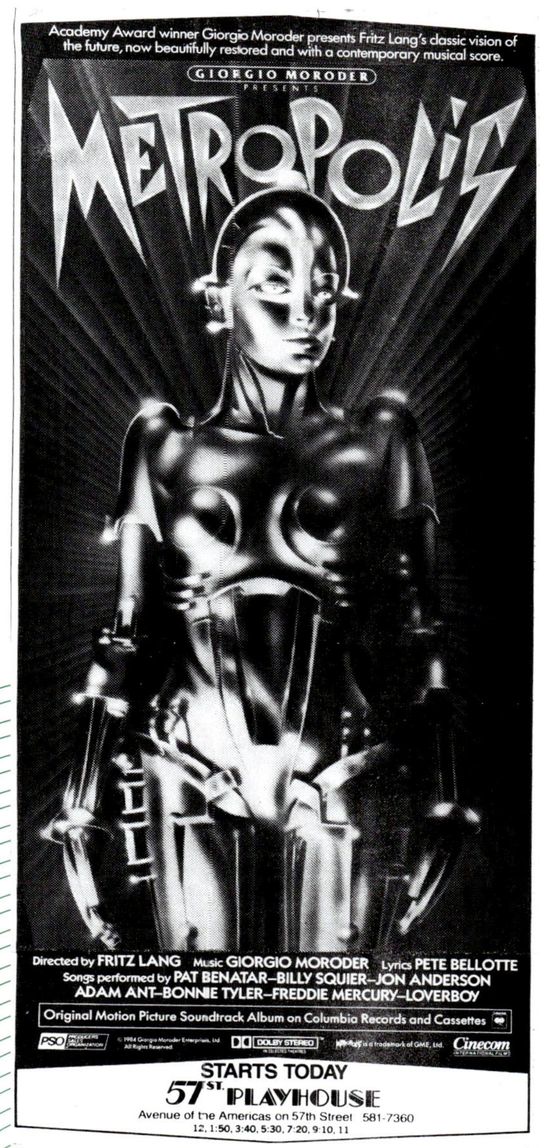

Academy Award winner Giorgio Moroder presents Fritz Lang's classic vision of the future, now beautifully restored and with a contemporary musical score.
GIORGIO MORODER
PRESENTS
METROPOLIS
Directed by FRITZ LANG Music GIORGIO MORODER Lyrics PETE BELLOTTE
Songs performed by PAT BENATAR–BILLY SQUIER–JON ANDERSON
ADAM ANT–BONNIE TYLER–FREDDIE MERCURY–LOVERBOY
Original Motion Picture Soundtrack Album on Columbia Records and Cassettes
Cinecom
STARTS TODAY
57ST PLAYHOUSE
Avenue of the Americas on 57th Street 581-7360
12, 1:50, 3:40, 5:30, 7:20, 9:10, 11

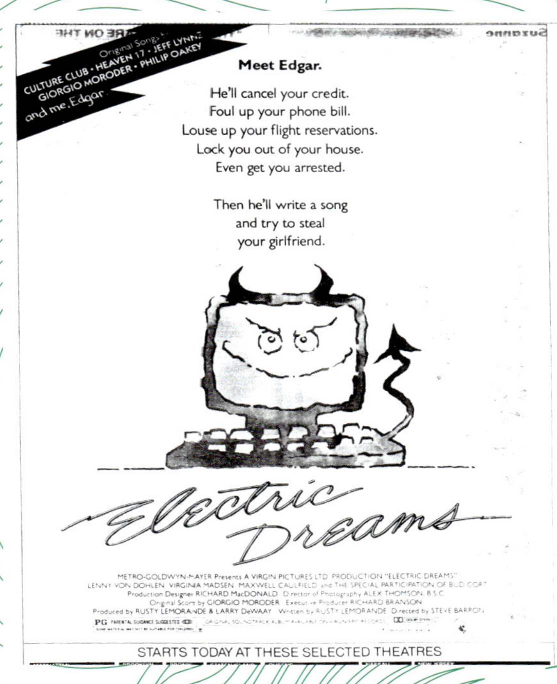

Original Songs
CULTURE CLUB · HEAVEN 17 · JEFF LYNNE
GIORGIO MORODER · PHILIP OAKEY
and me, Edgar
Meet Edgar.
He'll cancel your credit.
Foul up your phone bill.
Louse up your flight reservations.
Lock you out of your house.
Even get you arrested.
Then he'll write a song
and try to steal
your girlfriend.
Electric Dreams
STARTS TODAY AT THESE SELECTED THEATRES

12 H THE NEW YORK TIMES, SUNDAY, SEPTEMBER 30, 1984

Eight Things You Should Know Before Seeing BUCKAROO BANZAI

1. Aliens from Planet 10 are divided between Red Lectroids and Black Lectroids (the good guys).
2. Black Lectroids hate Red Lectroids and may have to blow up our world to get rid of them.
3. Buckaroo Banzai stands between you, the President (his buddy), nuclear disaster and having a nice day.
4. Buckaroo's sidekicks, the Hong Kong Cavaliers, are tougher than the N. Y. Jets.
5. Penny Priddy's twin sister was once Buckaroo's wife.
6. Lord John Whorfin (alias Dr. Lizardo) needs Buckaroo's Oscillation Overthruster to get back to the 8th Dimension.
7. Orson Welles' 1938 "War of the Worlds" broadcast was not a hoax.
8. If Buckaroo wins, we all win. If he doesn't...

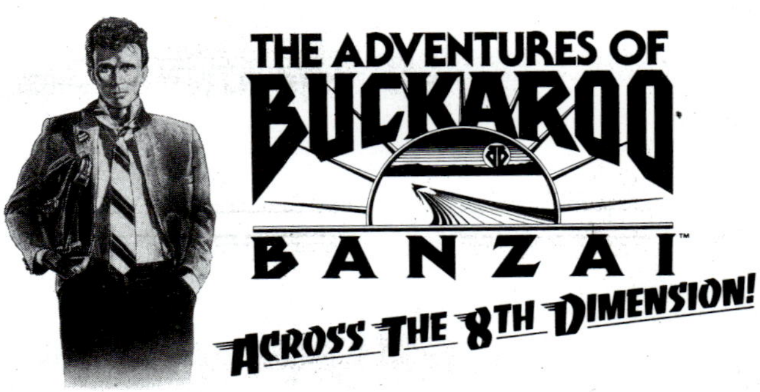

SHERWOOD PRODUCTIONS PRESENTS A SIDNEY BECKERMAN PRODUCTION
THE ADVENTURES OF BUCKAROO BANZAI
Starring PETER WELLER JOHN LITHGOW ELLEN BARKIN Also starring JEFF GOLDBLUM CHRISTOPHER LLOYD
Executive Producer SIDNEY BECKERMAN Produced by NEIL CANTON AND W. D. RICHTER
Written by EARL MAC RAUCH Directed by W. D. RICHTER

SHERWOOD PRODUCTIONS INC PG PARENTAL GUIDANCE SUGGESTED SOME MATERIAL MAY NOT BE SUITABLE FOR CHILDREN DOLBY STEREO IN SELECTED THEATRES Now in Paperback from POCKET BOOKS

TM 1984 Sherwood Productions, Inc. © 1984 Twentieth Century Fox

STARTS FRIDAY
AT A SPECIALLY SELECTED THEATER NEAR YOU

DUNE & THE ADVENTURES OF BUCKAROO BANZAI

As science fiction films, David Lynch's adaptation of Frank Herbert's classic novel and W.D. Richter's oddball comedy are as different as can be, with one exception: both introduce audiences to such unusual arrays of characters, settings and incidents, the distributors felt potential audiences needed a bit of education beforehand. So Universal provided *Dune* terminology sheets to be given out at theaters, while 20th Century Fox put the helpful hints right in the ads. Neither helped their respective movies achieve financial success, though both have many admirers now. *Dune* also suffered the handicap of some of the year's most hostile critical notices.

"Several of the characters in *Dune* are psychic, which puts them in the unique position of being able to understand what goes on in the movie. The plot of *Dune* is perilously overloaded, as is virtually everything else about it."

–Janet Maslin, *The New York Times*

"[I]f you can imagine a 500-page book in which every other page of text has been deleted and replaced by a terrific illustration, you have a fair idea of the discontinuity in the narrative."

–Joseph Gelmis, New York *Newsday*

"Throughout the film, characters make reference to the members of the Guild who, after sniffing spice, can travel through space without moving – an apt description of the movie."

–MICHAEL BLOWEN, *THE BOSTON GLOBE*

"Based on a cult book that served as a Bible for dopers in the '60s, *Dune* is like a drug manual for zombies. The movie is on a freaked-out trip, too, but I dare anyone whose brain isn't already fried to tell me exactly what the trip is all about."

–Rex Reed, *New York Post*

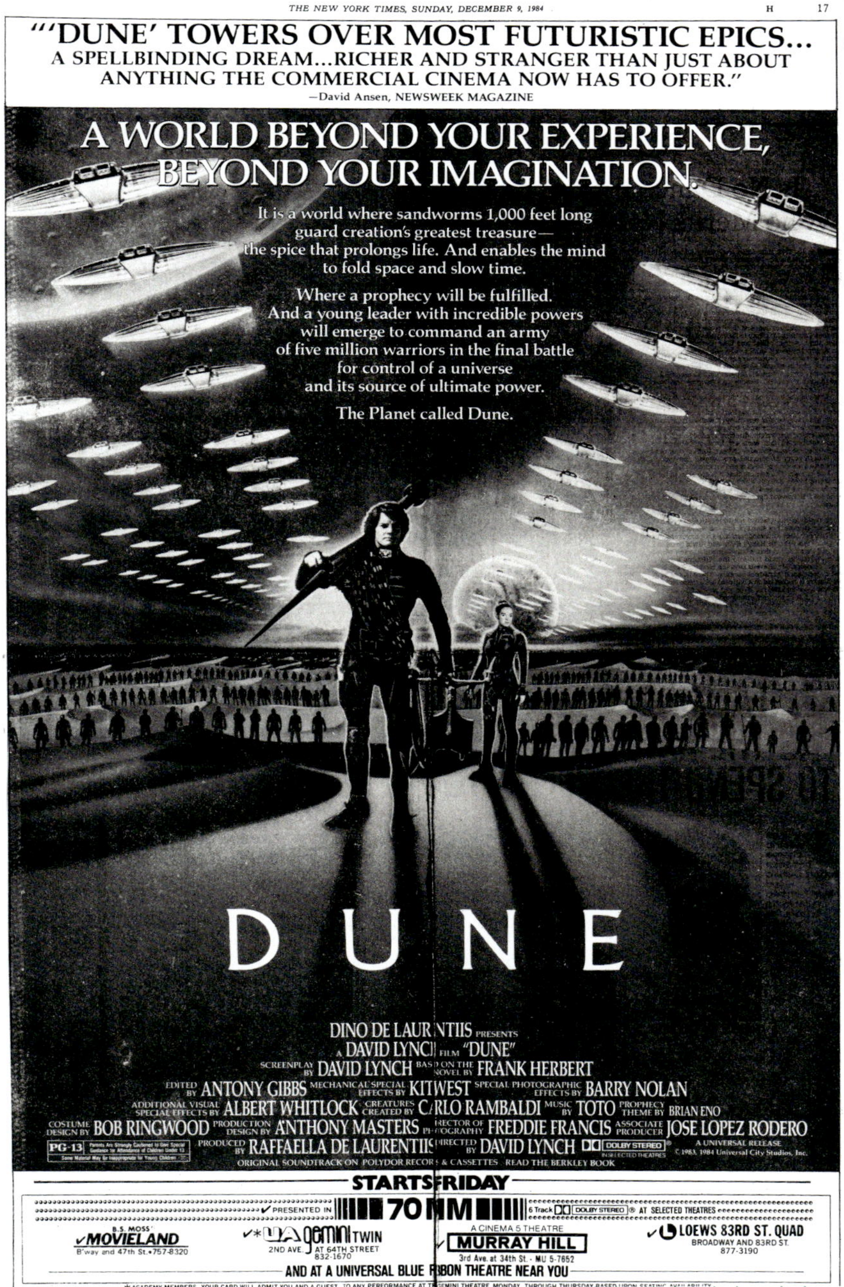

DUNE
TERMINOLOGY

ARRAKEEN (Ar-ra-keen): the capitol of the planet Arrakis, known as DUNE.

ARRAKIS (Ar-rak-is): the desert planet known as DUNE.

ATREIDES (A-tray-i-deez): ruling House of the planet Caladan. The Atreides family currently comprises Duke Leto, his formal concubine the Lady Jessica, and their son Paul.

BENE GESSERIT (Be-na Jess-er-it): the ancient school of mental and physical training established primarily for female students. The program had as its object the breeding, over generations, of a person they called the "Kwisatz Haderach," a term signifying "one who can be in many places at once." Specifically, their selective breeding program aimed at producing a human with mental powers permitting him to understand and use higher-order dimensions, including that of prescience.

CALADAN (Ca-la-dan): the lush green home planet of House Atreides.

CARRYALL (Car-ry-all): the aerial transport of Arrakis, used to carry, place and pick up large spice mining and refining equipment.

CRYSKNIFE (Kris-knife): the sacred knife of the Fremen on Arrakis. It is made from the teeth of dead sandworms.

FREMEN (Freh-men): the free tribes of Arrakis, desert dwellers.

FREMKIT (Frem-kit): desert survival kit of Fremen manufacture.

GIEDI PRIME (Gee-dee Prime): the home planet of House Harkonnen.

GOM JABBAR (Gom Jab-bar): a poison needle tipped with meta-cyanide used by the Bene Gesserit.

GUILD (Gild): the Spacing Guild, to which belong the Spacing Guild Navigators, able to traverse — and thus unite — the Known Universe by "folding space." The Navigators have achieved this power by having ingested Spice Melange over generations, an ingestion which has also mutated them physically.

HARVESTER: a large spice mining machine, often called a "crawler" because of buglike body on independent tracks. Used on Arrakis, known as Dune.

HUNTER-SEEKER: a sliver of suspensor-buoyed metal guided as a weapon by a near-by control console or individual; a common assassination device.

IMPERIAL CONDITIONING: a development of the Suk Medical Schools: the highest conditioning against taking human life. Initiates are marked by a diamond tattoo on the forehead.

KAITAIN (Ky-tane): home planet of the Padishah Emperor Shaddam IV.

KANLY: formal feud or vendetta under the rules of the Great Convention; originally designed to protect innocent bystanders.

KWISATZ HADERACH (Kwis-ats Ha-de-rack): the one for whom the Bene Gesserit wait, and at whose production their selective breeding program is aimed. He will be able to "bridge time and space," "to be in many places at once." In a sense, a male Bene Gesserit whose mental powers would be beyond any yet known.

MAKER HOOKS: the hooks used for capturing, mounting, and steering a sandworm of Arrakis.

MELANGE (May-lahnj): the "spice of spices," the crop for which Arrakis is the unique source. The spice, noted for its geriatric qualities, is of greatest importance in empowering the Guild Navigators with the ability to "fold space," thus uniting the Universe under the Emperor.

MENTAT (Men-tat): that class of Imperial citizens trained for supreme accomplishments of logic; known as "human computers."

MUAD DIB (Moo-ad-deeb): the name Paul Atreides chose to be known by, publicly, among the Fremen. He took it from the mouse shadow on Arrakis' second moon. The creature is admired by the Fremen for its ability to survive in the open desert.

ORNITHOPTER (Or-ni-thopter): small aircraft capable of sustained wing-beat flight in the manner of birds.

REVEREND MOTHER: originally, a leader of the Bene Gesserit, one who has transformed an "illuminating poison" within her body, raising herself to a higher state of awareness. Title adopted by Fremen for their own religious leaders who accomplished a similar illumination.

SANDCRAWLER: general term for machinery designed to operate on Arrakis surface in collecting spice melange.

SANDWORM (known as Shai-Hulud): Sandworm of Arrakis. Sandworms grow to enormous length. Some are 1500 feet long and 125 feet high; they live to great age, unless drowned in water, which is poisonous to them.

SAPHO (Sa-foe): high energy liquid extracted from roots. Commonly used by Mentats who claim it amplifies mental powers. Users develop ruby stains on mouth and lips.

SARDAUKAR (Sar-da-kar): the soldier-fanatics of the Padishah Emperor. They are men from an environmental background of such ferocity that it killed six out of thirteen persons before the age of eleven. Their military training emphasized ruthlessness and a near-suicidal disregard for personal safety.

SHAI-HULUD (Shy-Hoo-lood): another name for the sandworm of Arrakis.

SIETCH (Seetch): Fremen term designating any cave warren inhabited by one of their tribal communities. The term means "place of assembly in time of danger."

STILLSUIT: body-enclosing garment invented on Arrakis and used by the Fremen. Its fabric is a micro-sandwich which catches and filters moisture from body wastes. The reclaimed moisture is made available by tube from catchpockets in the suit. On Arrakis, water is life.

SUSPENSOR BELT: worn by the Baron Harkonnen, who is so grossly fat that he cannot walk. Within limits, it nullifies gravity, permitting the Baron to float through the air.

THUMPER: short stake with clapper at one end. Its purpose is to be driven into the sand and set "thumping" to summon the sandworm, or to distract the worm from a specific target, such as a group of Fremen or a sandcrawler.

TRUTHSAYER: a Reverend Mother qualified to enter truthtrance and detect insincerity or falsehood.

USUL (You-sul): the secret name chosen by Paul for his life among the Fremen. It means "the base of the pillar."

VOICE: a technique originated by the Bene Gesserit which permits an adept to control others merely by selected tone shadings of the voice.

WATER OF LIFE: the liquid exhalation of a sandworm produced at the moment of its death from drowning, which is changed by a Fremen Reverend Mother to become the narcotic which increases awareness. Since it is, before changing, a poison, only those worthy of becoming Reverend Mothers among the Fremen survive it.

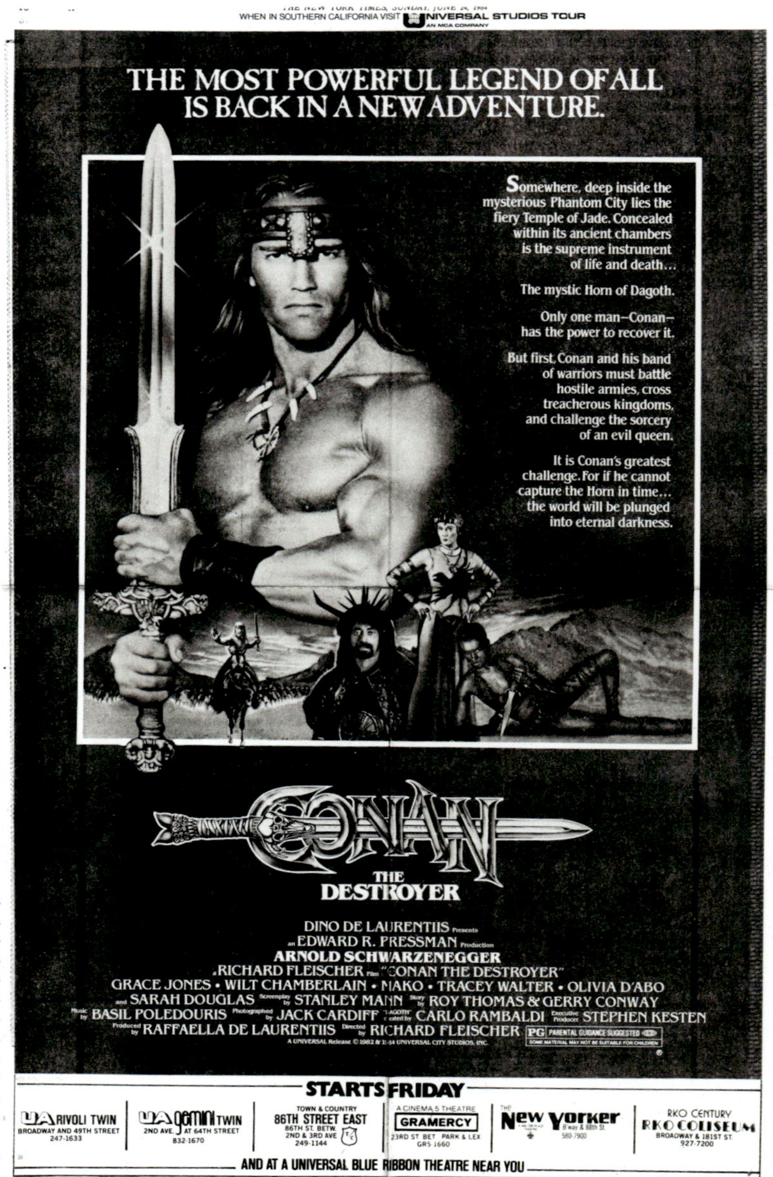

CONAN THE DESTROYER, THE LAST STARFIGHTER & ICEMAN

At a certain point in the mid-'80s, Universal Pictures apparently decided that the best way to grab potential audiences' attention with its publicity material was to give them lots to read on it. Thus, pithy taglines were replaced with short essays evidently intended to keep people looking at the poster or newspaper ad long enough to make them feel invested in a visit to the theater. The sequel to *Conan the Barbarian*, Nick Castle's sleeper about a video-game whiz recruited for real space battle, and the story of a caveman unfrozen in modern times are three examples; see *Dune* for another.

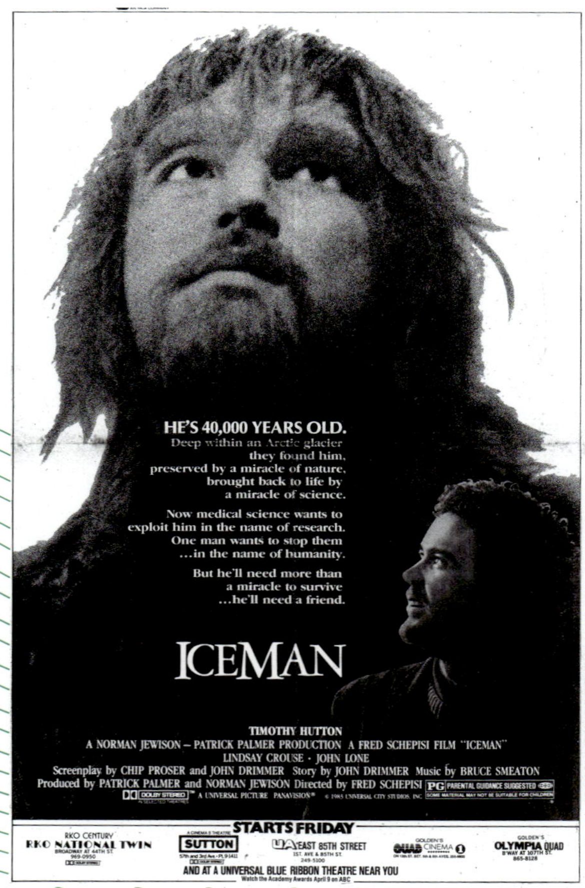

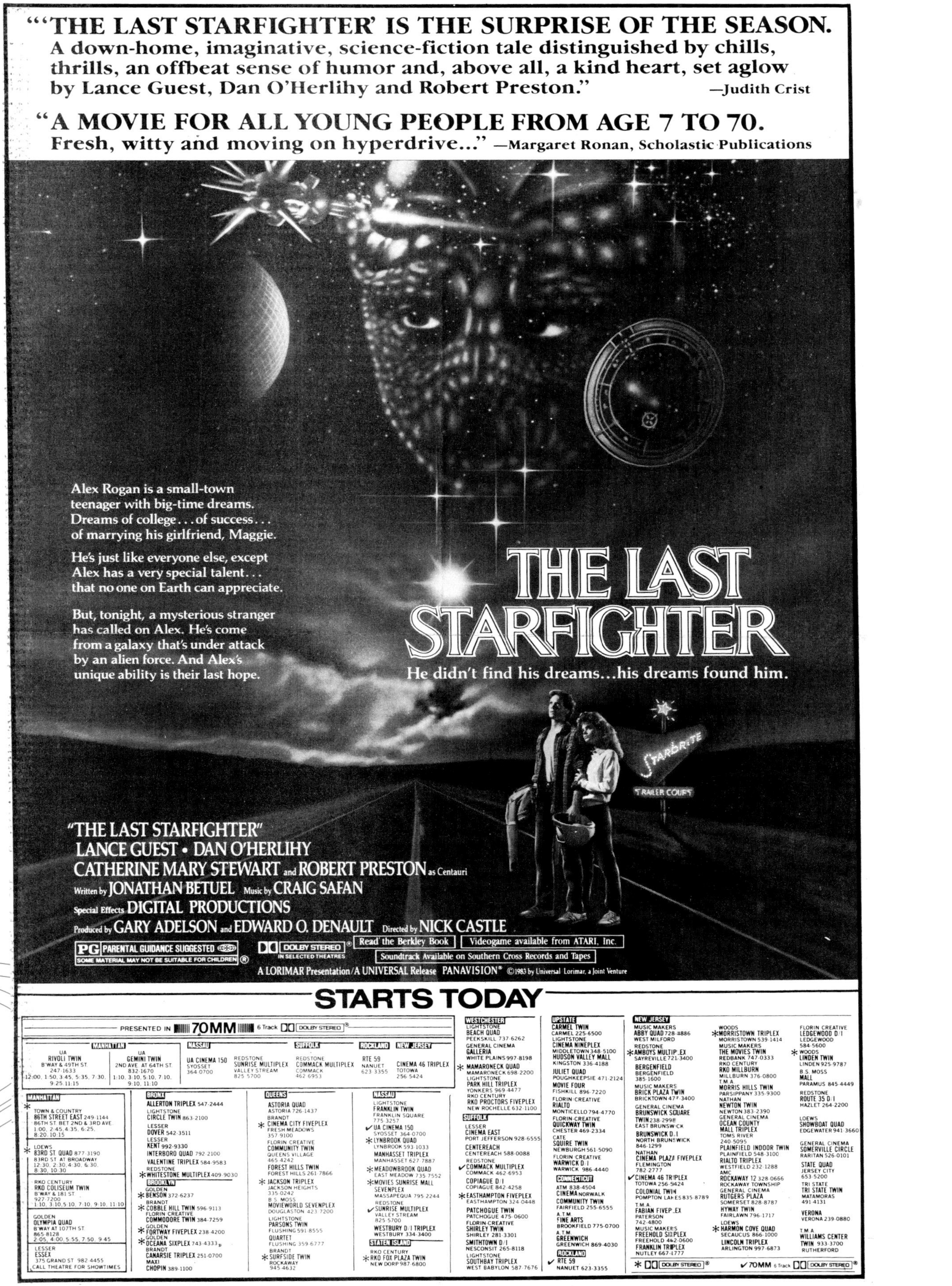
"'THE LAST STARFIGHTER' IS THE SURPRISE OF THE SEASON.
A down-home, imaginative, science-fiction tale distinguished by chills, thrills, an offbeat sense of humor and, above all, a kind heart, set aglow by Lance Guest, Dan O'Herlihy and Robert Preston." —Judith Crist
"A MOVIE FOR ALL YOUNG PEOPLE FROM AGE 7 TO 70.
Fresh, witty and moving on hyperdrive..." —Margaret Ronan, Scholastic Publications
Alex Rogan is a small-town teenager with big-time dreams. Dreams of college... of success... of marrying his girlfriend, Maggie.
He's just like everyone else, except Alex has a very special talent... that no one on Earth can appreciate.
But, tonight, a mysterious stranger has called on Alex. He's come from a galaxy that's under attack by an alien force. And Alex's unique ability is their last hope.
THE LAST STARFIGHTER
He didn't find his dreams...his dreams found him.
STARBRITE
TRAILER COURT
"THE LAST STARFIGHTER"
LANCE GUEST • DAN O'HERLIHY
CATHERINE MARY STEWART and ROBERT PRESTON as Centauri
Written by JONATHAN BETUEL Music by CRAIG SAFAN
Special Effects DIGITAL PRODUCTIONS
Produced by GARY ADELSON and EDWARD O. DENAULT Directed by NICK CASTLE
PG PARENTAL GUIDANCE SUGGESTED SOME MATERIAL MAY NOT BE SUITABLE FOR CHILDREN ®
DOLBY STEREO ® IN SELECTED THEATRES
Read the Berkley Book
Videogame available from ATARI, Inc.
Soundtrack Available on Southern Cross Records and Tapes
A LORIMAR Presentation/A UNIVERSAL Release PANAVISION® ©1983 by Universal Lorimar, a Joint Venture
STARTS TODAY
PRESENTED IN 70MM 6 Track DOLBY STEREO ®
MANHATTAN
UA RIVOLI TWIN B'WAY & 49TH ST. 247-1633 12:00, 1:50, 3:45, 5:35, 7:30, 9:25, 11:15
UA GEMINI TWIN 2ND AVE. AT 64TH ST. 832-1670 1:10, 3:10, 5:10, 7:10, 9:10, 11:10
NASSAU
UA CINEMA 150 SYOSSET 364-0700
REDSTONE SUNRISE MULTIPLEX VALLEY STREAM 825-5700
SUFFOLK
REDSTONE COMMACK MULTIPLEX COMMACK 462-6953
ROCKLAND
RTE 59 NANUET 623-3355
NEW JERSEY
CINEMA 46 TRIPLEX TOTOWA 256-5424
MANHATTAN
* TOWN & COUNTRY 86TH STREET EAST 249-1144 86TH ST. BET 2ND & 3RD AVE. 1:00, 2:45, 4:35, 6:25, 8:20, 10:15
* LOEWS 83RD ST. QUAD 877-3190 83RD ST. AT BROADWAY 12:30, 2:30, 4:30, 6:30, 8:30, 10:30
RKO CENTURY RKO COLISEUM TWIN B'WAY & 181 ST. 927-7200 1:10, 3:10, 5:10, 7:10, 9:10, 11:10
GOLDEN OLYMPIA QUAD B'WAY AT 107TH ST. 865-8128 2:05, 4:00, 5:55, 7:50, 9:45
LESSER ESSEX 375 GRAND ST. 982-4455 CALL THEATRE FOR SHOWTIMES
BRONX
ALLERTON TRIPLEX 547-2444
LIGHTSTONE CIRCLE TWIN 863-2100
LESSER DOVER 542-3511
LESSER KENT 992-9330
INTERBORO QUAD 792-2100
VALENTINE TRIPLEX 584-9583
REDSTONE *WHITESTONE MULTIPLEX 409-9030
BROOKLYN
GOLDEN *BENSON 372-6237
BRANDT *COBBLE HILL TWIN 596-9113
FLORIN CREATIVE COMMODORE TWIN 384-7259
GOLDEN *FORTWAY FIVEPLEX 238-4200
GOLDEN *OCEANA SIXPLEX 743-4333
BRANDT CANARSIE TRIPLEX 251-0700
MAXI CHOPIN 389-1100
QUEENS
ASTORIA QUAD ASTORIA 726-1437
BRANDT *CINEMA CITY FIVEPLEX FRESH MEADOWS 357-9100
FLORIN CREATIVE COMMUNITY TWIN QUEENS VILLAGE 465-4242
FOREST HILLS TWIN FOREST HILLS 261-7866
*JACKSON TRIPLEX JACKSON HEIGHTS 335-0242
B.S. MOSS MOVIEWORLD SEVENPLEX DOUGLASTON 423-7200
LIGHTSTONE PARSONS TWIN FLUSHING 591-8555
QUARTET FLUSHING 359-6777
BRANDT *SURFSIDE TWIN ROCKAWAY 945-4632
NASSAU
LIGHTSTONE FRANKLIN TWIN FRANKLIN SQUARE 775-3257
✓UA CINEMA 150 SYOSSET 364-0700
*LYNBROOK QUAD LYNBROOK 593-1033
MANHASSET TRIPLEX MANHASSET 627-7887
*MEADOWBROOK QUAD EAST MEADOW 735-7552
*MOVIES SUNRISE MALL SEVENPLEX MASSAPEQUA 795-2244
REDSTONE ✓SUNRISE MULTIPLEX VALLEY STREAM 825-5700
WESTBURY D/I TRIPLEX WESTBURY 334-3400
STATEN ISLAND
RKO CENTURY *RKO FOX PLAZA TWIN NEW DORP 987-6800
WESTCHESTER
LIGHTSTONE BEACH QUAD PEEKSKILL 737-6262
GENERAL CINEMA GALLERIA WHITE PLAINS 997-8198
*MAMARONECK QUAD MAMARONECK 698-2200
LIGHTSTONE PARK HILL TRIPLEX YONKERS 969-4477
RKO CENTURY RKO PROCTORS FIVEPLEX NEW ROCHELLE 632-1100
SUFFOLK
LESSER CINEMA EAST PORT JEFFERSON 928-6555
CENTEREACH CENTEREACH 588-0088
REDSTONE ✓COMMACK MULTIPLEX COMMACK 462-6953
COPIAGUE D/I COPIAGUE 842-4258
*EASTHAMPTON FIVEPLEX EASTHAMPTON 324-0448
PATCHOGUE TWIN PATCHOGUE 475-0600
FLORIN-CREATIVE SHIRLEY TWIN SHIRLEY 281-3301
SMITHTOWN D/I NESCONSIT 265-8118
LIGHTSTONE SOUTHBAY TRIPLEX WEST BABYLON 587-7676
UPSTATE
CARMEL TWIN CARMEL 225-6500
LIGHTSTONE CINEMA NINEPLEX MIDDLETOWN 348-5100
HUDSON VALLEY MALL KINGSTON 336-4188
JULIET QUAD POUGHKEEPSIE 471-2124
MOVIE FOUR FISHKILL 896-7220
FLORIN/CREATIVE RIALTO MONTICELLO 794-4770
FLORIN-CREATIVE QUICKWAY TWIN CHESTER 469-2334
CATE SQUIRE TWIN NEWBURGH 561-5090
FLORIN/CREATIVE WARWICK D/I WARWICK 986-4440
CONNECTICUT
ATM 838-4504 CINEMA NORWALK
COMMUNITY TWIN FAIRFIELD 255-6555
A.T.M. FINE ARTS BROOKFIELD 775-0700
A.T.M. GREENWICH GREENWICH 869-4030
ROCKLAND
✓RTE 59 NANUET 623-3355
NEW JERSEY
MUSIC MAKERS ABBY QUAD 728-4886 WEST MILFORD
REDSTONE *AMBOYS MULTIPLEX SAYREVILLE 721-3400
BERGENFIELD BERGENFIELD 385-1600
MUSIC MAKERS BRICK PLAZA TWIN BRICKTOWN 477-3400
GENERAL CINEMA BRUNSWICK SQUARE TWIN 238-2998 EAST BRUNSWICK
BRUNSWICK D.I NORTH BRUNSWICK 846-1299
NATHAN CINEMA PLAZA FIVEPLEX FLEMINGTON 782-2777
✓CINEMA 46 TRIPLEX TOTOWA 256-5424
COLONIAL TWIN POMPTON LAKES 835-8789
T.M.A. FABIAN FIVEPLEX PATERSON 742-4800
MUSIC MAKERS FREEHOLD SIXPLEX FREEHOLD 462-0600
FRANKLIN TRIPLEX NUTLEY 667-4777
WOODS *MORRISTOWN TRIPLEX MORRISTOWN 539-1414
MUSIC MAKERS THE MOVIES TWIN REDBANK 747-0333
RKO CENTURY RKO MILLBURN MILLBURN 376-0800
T.M.A. MORRIS HILLS TWIN PARSIPPANY 335-9300
NATHAN NEWTON TWIN NEWTON 383-2390
GENERAL CINEMA OCEAN COUNTY MALL TRIPLEX TOMS RIVER 240-5095
PLAINFIELD INDOOR TWIN PLAINFIELD 548-3100
RIALTO TRIPLEX WESTFIELD 232-1288
AMC ROCKAWAY 12 328-0666 ROCKAWAY TOWNSHIP
GENERAL CINEMA RUTGERS PLAZA SOMERSET 828-8787
HYWAY TWIN FAIRLAWN 796-1717
LOEWS *HARMON COVE QUAD SECAUCUS 866-1000
LINCOLN TRIPLEX ARLINGTON 997-6873
FLORIN CREATIVE LEDGEWOOD D/I LEDGEWOOD 584-5600
*WOODS LINDEN TWIN LINDEN 925-9787
B.S. MOSS MALL PARAMUS 845-4449
REDSTONE ROUTE 35 D/I HAZLET 264-2200
LOEWS SHOWBOAT QUAD EDGEWATER 941-3660
GENERAL CINEMA SOMERVILLE CIRCLE RARITAN 526-0101
STATE QUAD JERSEY CITY 653-5200
TRI STATE TRI STATE TWIN MATAMORAS 491-4131
VERONA VERONA 239-0880
T.M.A. WILLIAMS CENTER TWIN 933-3700 RUTHERFORD
* DOLBY STEREO ®
✓70MM 6 Track DOLBY STEREO ®

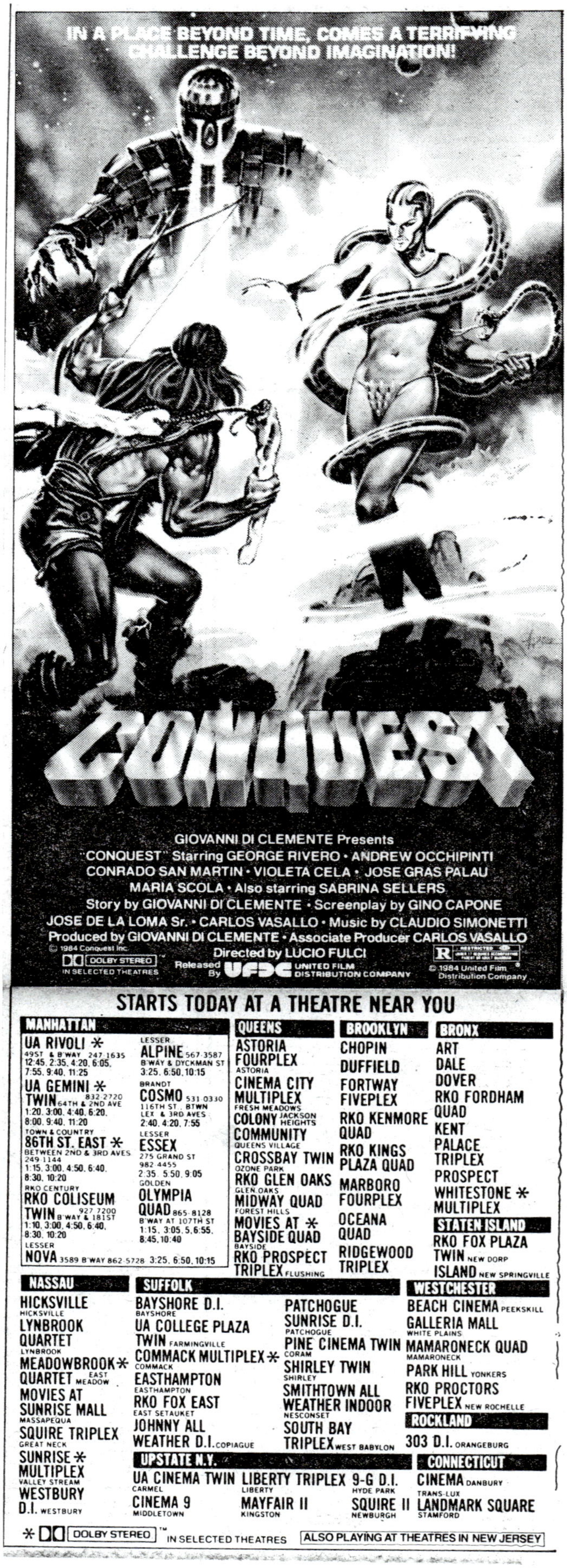

GHOSTBUSTERS

Director Ivan Reitman and star Bill Murray established their anarchic comedic cred with the low-budget *Meatballs* and the bigger *Stripes* before tackling the tricky mix of laughs and big-scale special effects with *Ghostbusters*. They and co-stars Dan Aykroyd, Harold Ramis (these two also scripted), Sigourney Weaver, Rick Moranis, Annie Potts, and Ernie Hudson, along with the army of technicians, got it just right, and *Ghostbusters* became the highest-grossing comedy of all time. Not all the critics were impressed, but many of those who were cool on the movie nonetheless warmed to Murray's hip humor.

"[The leads are] funny, but they're not afraid to reveal that they're also quick-witted and intelligent; their dialogue puts nice little spins on American clichés, and it uses understatement, irony, in-jokes, vast cynicism, and cheerful goofiness. Rarely has a movie this expensive provided so many quotable lines."

–Roger Ebert, *Chicago Sun-Times*

"True silliness is a delicious state, not easy to enter and slippery to maintain. ... And with *Ghostbusters*... the maniacal trio of Bill Murray, Dan Aykroyd, and Harold Ramis pass into a state of pure silliness bordering on the divine, never once wavering."

–SHEILA BENSON, *LOS ANGELES TIMES*

"Yes, the script is poorly structured. Sure, the direction is weak and the camerawork boxy. But when Murray's on screen, you're entranced. The rest of the picture seems to vanish."

–Jay Boyar, *Orlando Sentinel*

"[H]owever good an idea it may have been to unleash Mr. Murray in an *Exorcist*-like setting, this film hasn't gotten very far past the idea stage. Its jokes, characters, and story line are as wispy as the ghosts themselves, and a good deal less substantial."

–Janet Maslin, *The New York Times*

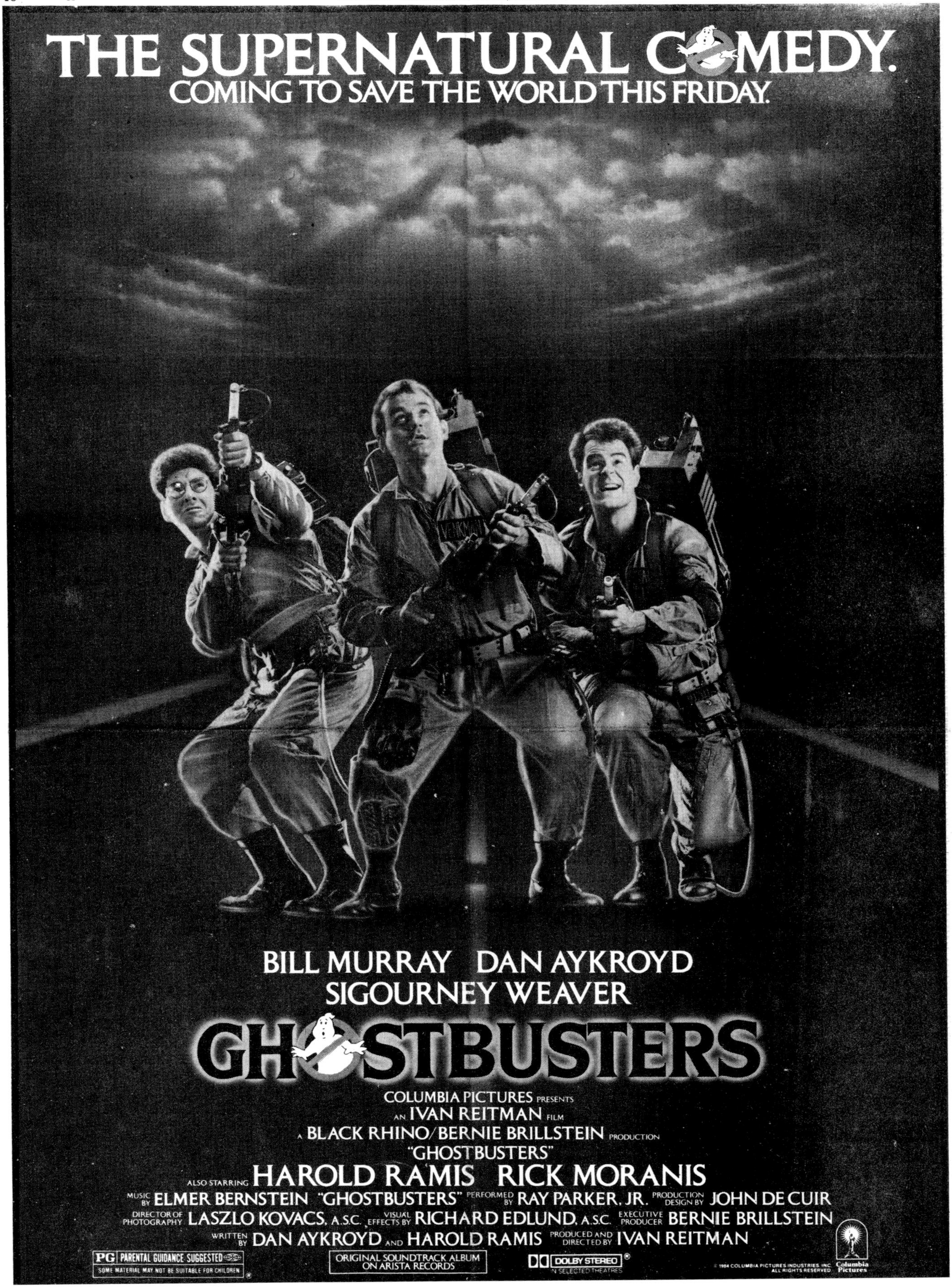
THE SUPERNATURAL COMEDY.
COMING TO SAVE THE WORLD THIS FRIDAY.
BILL MURRAY DAN AYKROYD
SIGOURNEY WEAVER
GHOSTBUSTERS
COLUMBIA PICTURES PRESENTS
AN IVAN REITMAN FILM
A BLACK RHINO/BERNIE BRILLSTEIN PRODUCTION
"GHOSTBUSTERS"
ALSO STARRING HAROLD RAMIS RICK MORANIS
MUSIC BY ELMER BERNSTEIN "GHOSTBUSTERS" PERFORMED BY RAY PARKER, JR. PRODUCTION DESIGN BY JOHN DE CUIR
DIRECTOR OF PHOTOGRAPHY LASZLO KOVACS, A.S.C. VISUAL EFFECTS BY RICHARD EDLUND, A.S.C. EXECUTIVE PRODUCER BERNIE BRILLSTEIN
WRITTEN BY DAN AYKROYD AND HAROLD RAMIS PRODUCED AND DIRECTED BY IVAN REITMAN
PG PARENTAL GUIDANCE SUGGESTED
SOME MATERIAL MAY NOT BE SUITABLE FOR CHILDREN
ORIGINAL SOUNDTRACK ALBUM ON ARISTA RECORDS
DOLBY STEREO
IN SELECTED THEATRES
© 1984 COLUMBIA PICTURES INDUSTRIES, INC. ALL RIGHTS RESERVED
Columbia Pictures

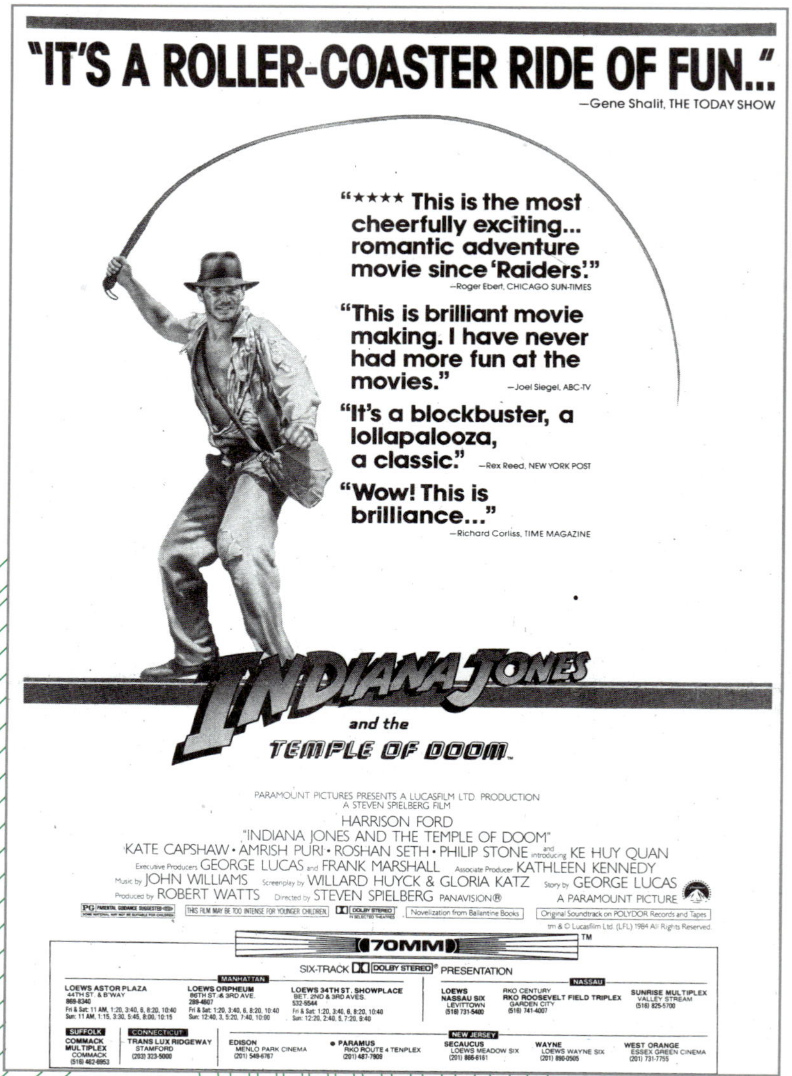

INDIANA JONES AND THE TEMPLE OF DOOM

There were two ways newspaper pundits addressed Steven Spielberg's sequel to his unanimously lauded *Raiders of the Lost Ark*: in terms of how it lived up to its predecessor (the jury was mixed in that respect), and regarding its violent content. Almost every review noted that Spielberg went over the top with the mayhem and gross-outs, and many felt he took them too far, especially for a PG-rated film aimed at young audiences. Joe Dante's *Gremlins* attracted similar scrutiny the same summer, with the result that by July, the new PG-13 rating was in place. The first film to be given that tag (though the second to be released, after *Red Dawn*), was *Dreamscape*, co-starring *Temple of Doom* heroine Kate Capshaw.

"*Indiana Jones* is too shapeless to be the fun that *Raiders* is, but shape may be beside the point. Old-time, 15-part movie serials didn't have shape. They just went on and on and on, which is what *Indiana Jones* does with humor and technical invention."

–Vincent Canby, *The New York Times*

"[W]hat we have is an endurance test of breakneck action – wall-to-wall, mind-contracting, and finally numbing. ... Someone has misread the voltage on state-of-the-art effects, and they're going to have to scrape youngsters out from under the seats like old chewing gum with this one."

–SHEILA BENSON, *LOS ANGELES TIMES*

"This is that rare bird that is practically unheard of in movie history – a sequel that is even better than the original. It's unpretentious and totally entertaining. It even has the courage to poke fun at itself."

–Rex Reed, *New York Post*

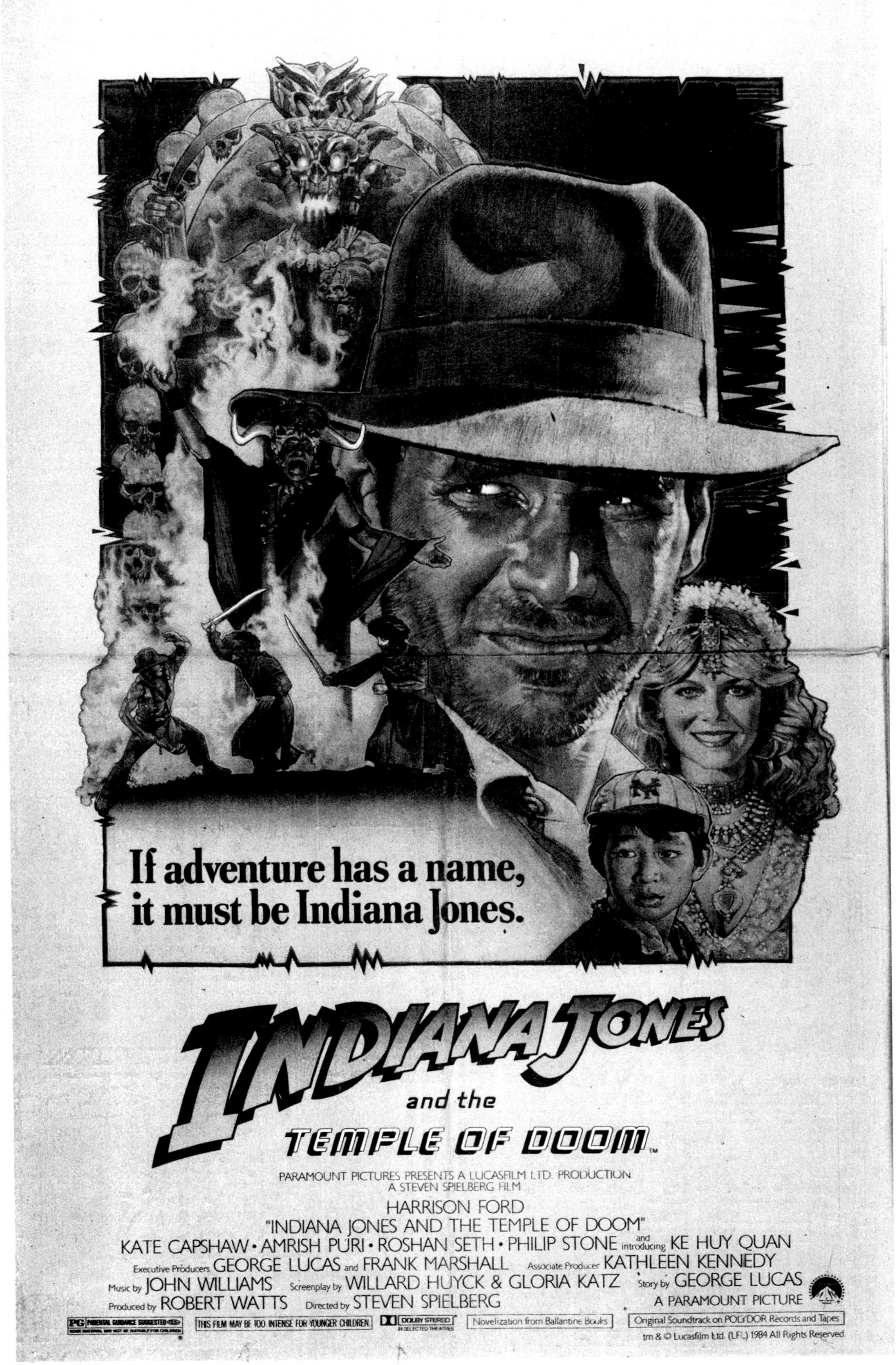
If adventure has a name,
it must be Indiana Jones.
INDIANA JONES
and the
TEMPLE OF DOOM™
PARAMOUNT PICTURES PRESENTS A LUCASFILM LTD. PRODUCTION
A STEVEN SPIELBERG FILM
HARRISON FORD
"INDIANA JONES AND THE TEMPLE OF DOOM"
KATE CAPSHAW • AMRISH PURI • ROSHAN SETH • PHILIP STONE and introducing KE HUY QUAN
Executive Producers GEORGE LUCAS and FRANK MARSHALL Associate Producer KATHLEEN KENNEDY
Music by JOHN WILLIAMS Screenplay by WILLARD HUYCK & GLORIA KATZ Story by GEORGE LUCAS
Produced by ROBERT WATTS Directed by STEVEN SPIELBERG
A PARAMOUNT PICTURE
PG PARENTAL GUIDANCE SUGGESTED
THIS FILM MAY BE TOO INTENSE FOR YOUNGER CHILDREN.
DOLBY STEREO IN SELECTED THEATRES
Novelization from Ballantine Books
Original Soundtrack on POLYDOR Records and Tapes
tm & © Lucasfilm Ltd. (LFL) 1984 All Rights Reserved

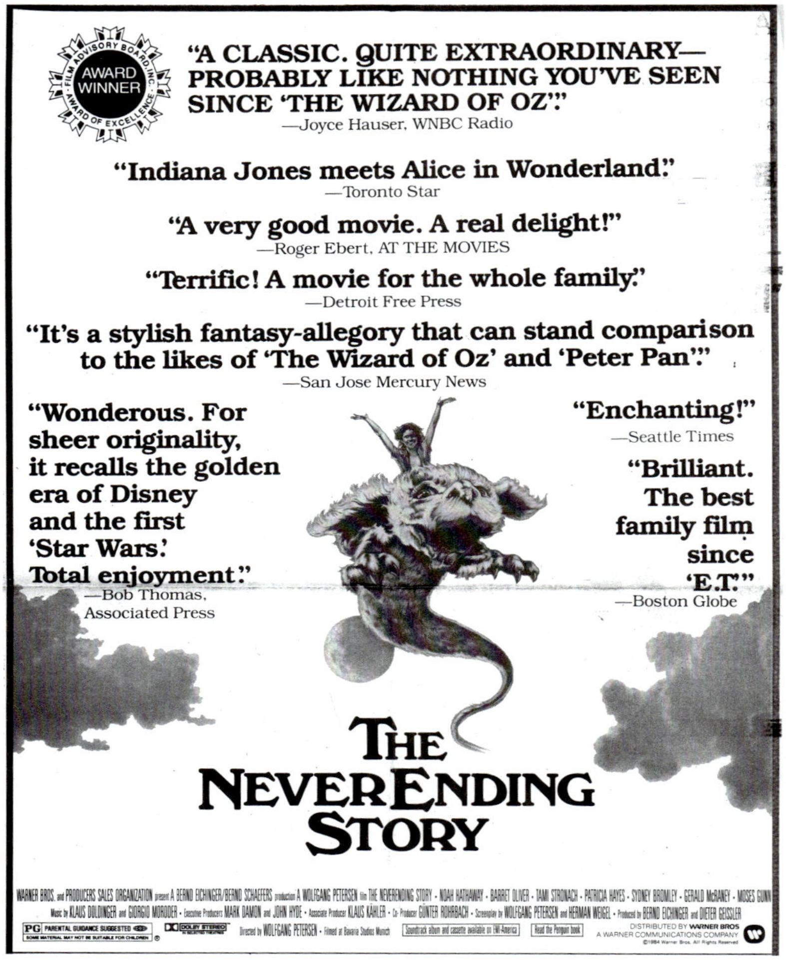

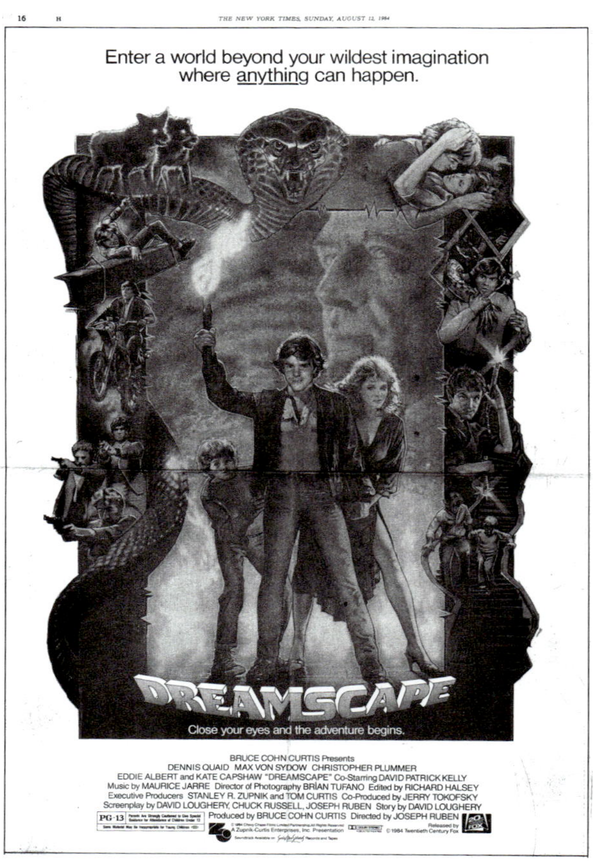

THE NEVERENDING STORY

With controversy swirling around the violence and scariness of *Indiana Jones and the Temple of Doom* and *Gremlins*, Wolfgang Petersen's heartstring-tugging adaptation of German author Michael Ende's novel was marketed in summer '84 as a "non-violent fantasy film." With that quality, and a storyline centered on the importance of reading and using one's imagination, *The NeverEnding Story* was something any respectable critic seeking to recommend a movie for families had to approve of, right? Not in all cases, as it turned out.

"This is an exceptionally handsome production. Furthermore, its message, that childhood fantasies are irreplaceable and important, has a timeless appeal. There is no risk that this movie will go out of style."

–Scott Cain, *The Atlanta Constitution*

"When the movie is not sounding like The Pre-Teenager's Guide to Existentialism, it's simply a series of resolutely unexciting encounters between Atreyu and the creatures that alternately help and hinder his mission...[including] a dragon with white fur and feathers that suggests an impractical bath mat."

–VINCENT CANBY,
THE NEW YORK TIMES

"*The NeverEnding Story* should delight youngsters. Beautifully photographed and visually impressive, it is made with intelligence, care and respect for its young audience."

–Marylynn Uricchio, *Pittsburgh Post-Gazette*

"[T]here is this thing in our midst, designed for children with little or no taste and alarmingly low IQ's. It is called *The NeverEnding Story*... It is worse than Girl Scout cookies."

–Rex Reed, *New York Post*

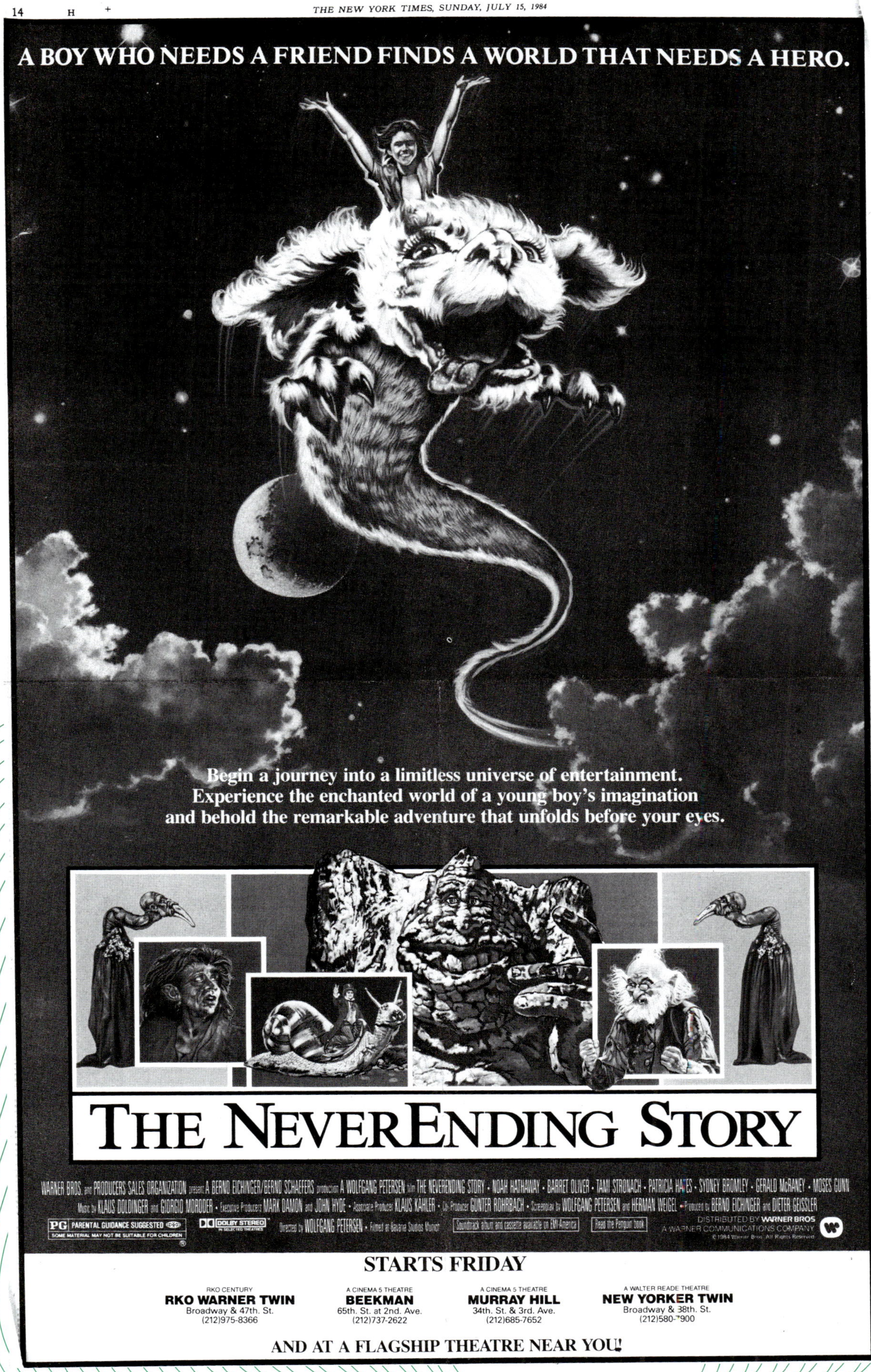
14 H + THE NEW YORK TIMES, SUNDAY, JULY 15, 1984
A BOY WHO NEEDS A FRIEND FINDS A WORLD THAT NEEDS A HERO.
Begin a journey into a limitless universe of entertainment.
Experience the enchanted world of a young boy's imagination
and behold the remarkable adventure that unfolds before your eyes.
THE NEVERENDING STORY
WARNER BROS. and PRODUCERS SALES ORGANIZATION present A BERND EICHINGER/BERND SCHAEFERS production A WOLFGANG PETERSEN film THE NEVERENDING STORY · NOAH HATHAWAY · BARRET OLIVER · TAMI STRONACH · PATRICIA HAYES · SYDNEY BROMLEY · GERALD McRANEY · MOSES GUNN
Music by KLAUS DOLDINGER and GIORGIO MORODER · Executive Producers MARK DAMON and JOHN HYDE · Associate Producer KLAUS KAHLER · Co-Producer GUNTER ROHRBACH · Screenplay by WOLFGANG PETERSEN and HERMAN WEIGEL · Produced by BERND EICHINGER and DIETER GEISSLER
PG PARENTAL GUIDANCE SUGGESTED
SOME MATERIAL MAY NOT BE SUITABLE FOR CHILDREN
DOLBY STEREO
IN SELECTED THEATRES
Directed by WOLFGANG PETERSEN · Filmed at Bavaria Studios Munich
Soundtrack album and cassette available on EMI-America
Read the Penguin book
DISTRIBUTED BY WARNER BROS
A WARNER COMMUNICATIONS COMPANY
© 1984 Warner Bros. All Rights Reserved
STARTS FRIDAY
RKO CENTURY
RKO WARNER TWIN
Broadway & 47th. St.
(212)975-8366
A CINEMA 5 THEATRE
BEEKMAN
65th. St. at 2nd. Ave.
(212)737-2622
A CINEMA 5 THEATRE
MURRAY HILL
34th. St. & 3rd. Ave.
(212)685-7652
A WALTER READE THEATRE
NEW YORKER TWIN
Broadway & 38th. St.
(212)580-7900
AND AT A FLAGSHIP THEATRE NEAR YOU!

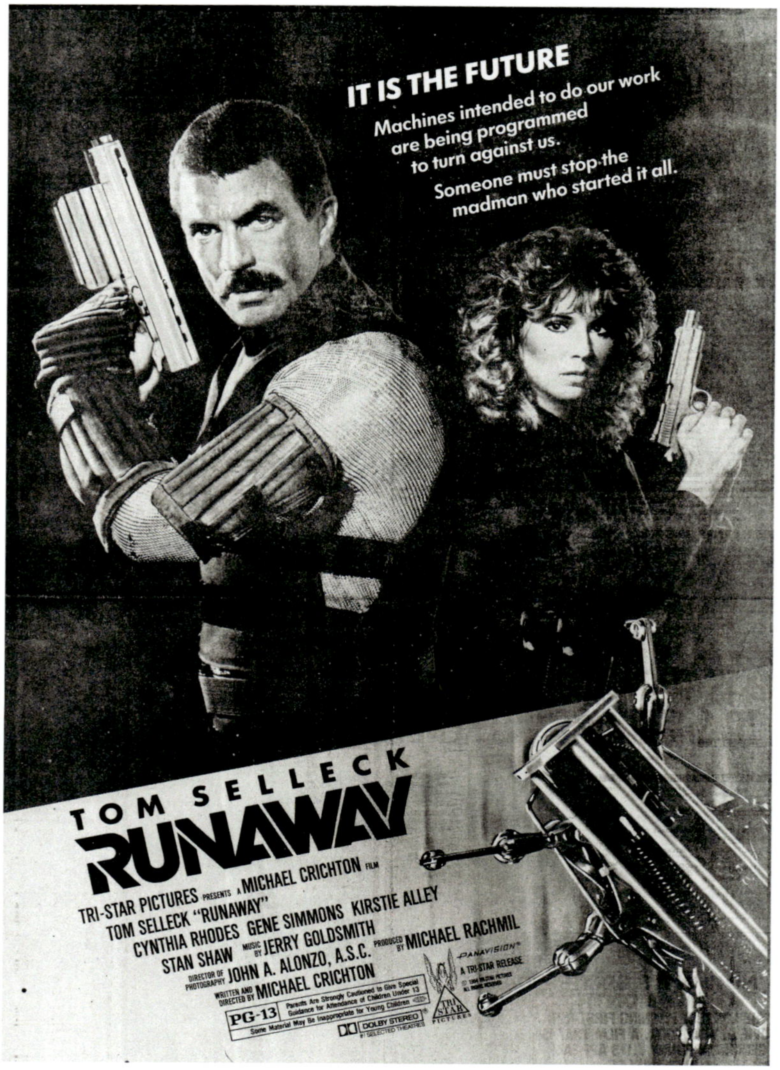

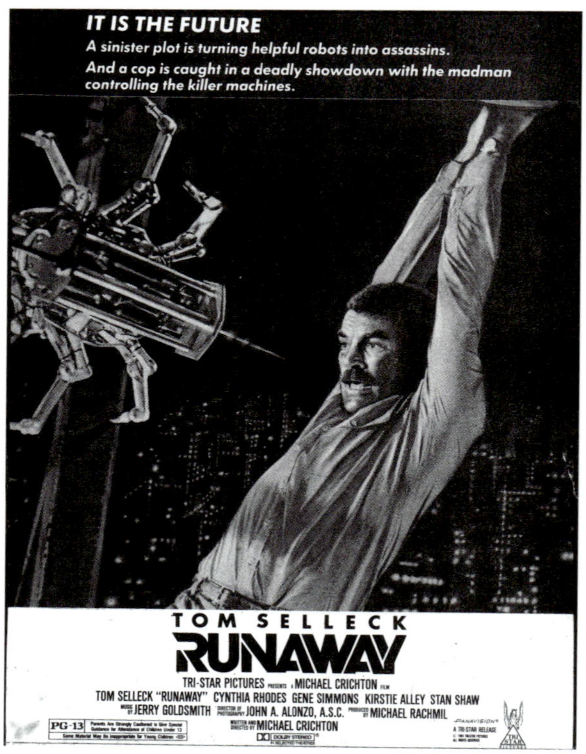

STAR TREK III: THE SEARCH FOR SPOCK

Conventional wisdom among *Star Trek* fans long contended that the even-numbered films are far superior to the odd-numbered ones. That wasn't quite fair in the case of *Star Trek III*, which found Leonard Nimoy making an assured debut in the director's chair but had the disadvantage of coming out between two of the most beloved entries, and being more subdued than the action-packed *II* and the comedic *IV*. Nevertheless, it rallied more critical support than either the first or fifth films.

"*Star Trek III*, in its unabashed, deliberate squareness in all aspects...comes out strongly for the old-fashion virtues of loyalty, bravery and sacrifice."

–Kevin Thomas, *Los Angeles Times*

"*Star Trek III* strikes a middle ground between character and action. It's solid entertainment that only breaks faith with a too-abrupt ending that leaves us wanting for – you guessed it – *Star Trek IV*."

–Gene Siskel, *Chicago Tribune*

"Wonder of wonders, it does the logical thing, combining the best elements of the television series and enhancing them – instead of drowning them out – with big-screen impact and effects."

–MICHAEL MCLEOD, *THE CINCINNATI ENQUIRER*

"It's strict catnip for Trekkers, excitement-plus for young sci-fi addicts, and ho-hum for those who have seen it once, twice, and more."

–Archer Winsten, *New York Post*

"*Star Trek III* is once again another cheap looking made-for-TV Enterprise-episode blown up to big-screen size."

–Jon Marlowe, *The Miami News*

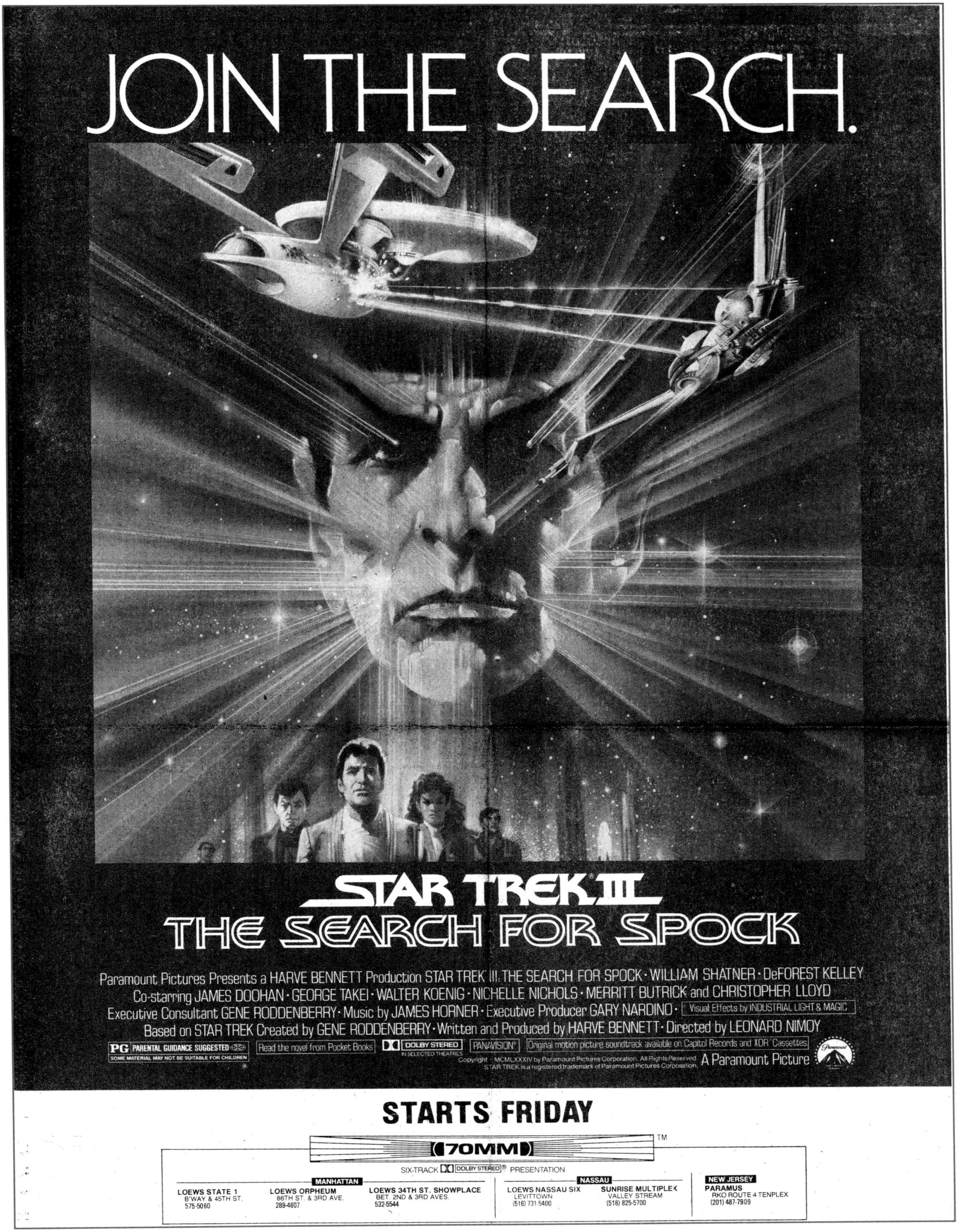
JOIN THE SEARCH.
STAR TREK III
THE SEARCH FOR SPOCK
Paramount Pictures Presents a HARVE BENNETT Production STAR TREK III: THE SEARCH FOR SPOCK · WILLIAM SHATNER · DeFOREST KELLEY
Co-starring JAMES DOOHAN · GEORGE TAKEI · WALTER KOENIG · NICHELLE NICHOLS · MERRITT BUTRICK and CHRISTOPHER LLOYD
Executive Consultant GENE RODDENBERRY · Music by JAMES HORNER · Executive Producer GARY NARDINO · Visual Effects by INDUSTRIAL LIGHT & MAGIC
Based on STAR TREK Created by GENE RODDENBERRY · Written and Produced by HARVE BENNETT · Directed by LEONARD NIMOY
PG PARENTAL GUIDANCE SUGGESTED
SOME MATERIAL MAY NOT BE SUITABLE FOR CHILDREN
Read the novel from Pocket Books
DOLBY STEREO
IN SELECTED THEATRES
PANAVISION®
Original motion picture soundtrack available on Capitol Records and XDR Cassettes.
Copyright © MCMLXXXIV by Paramount Pictures Corporation. All Rights Reserved.
STAR TREK is a registered trademark of Paramount Pictures Corporation.
A Paramount Picture
STARTS FRIDAY
70MM TM
SIX-TRACK DOLBY STEREO® PRESENTATION
MANHATTAN
LOEWS STATE 1
B'WAY & 45TH ST.
575-5060
LOEWS ORPHEUM
86TH ST. & 3RD AVE.
289-4607
LOEWS 34TH ST. SHOWPLACE
BET. 2ND & 3RD AVES.
532-5544
NASSAU
LOEWS NASSAU SIX
LEVITTOWN
(516) 731-5400
SUNRISE MULTIPLEX
VALLEY STREAM
(516) 825-5700
NEW JERSEY
PARAMUS
RKO ROUTE 4 TENPLEX
(201) 487-7909

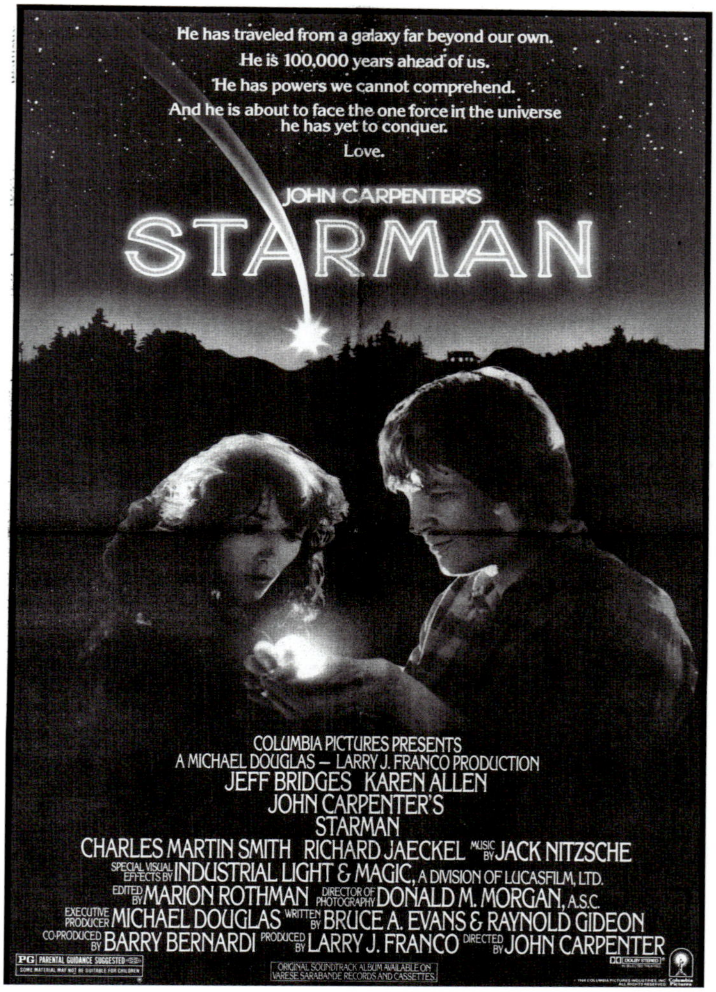

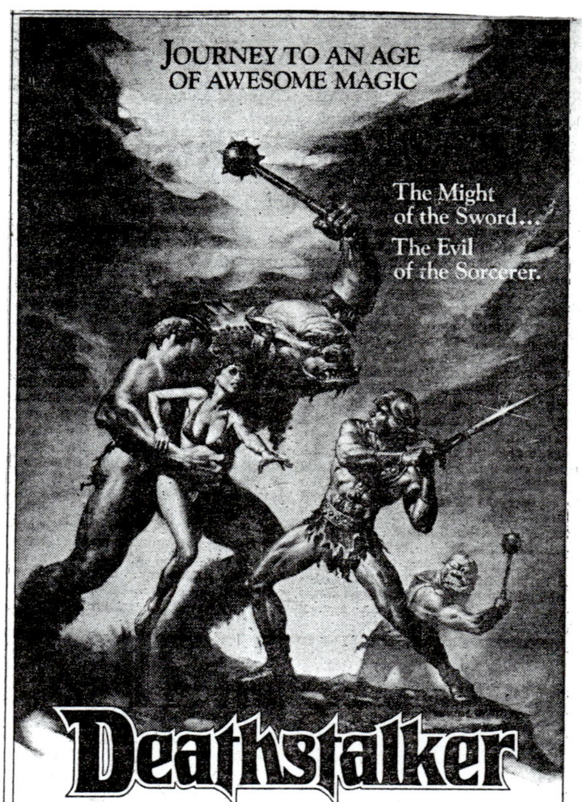

SUPERGIRL

When *Superman III* put some tarnish on the Man of Steel, rights holders Alexander and Ilya Salkind decided to ground him and give another Kryptonian, Kara Zor-El (a.k.a. Supergirl), her own film. Just as in the first *Superman*, an unknown, Helen Slater, was selected for the lead, and Jeannot Szwarc, who had previously guided Christopher Reeve through *Somewhere in Time*, and helmed *Jaws 2*, got the directing job. A dispute over the release date led Warner Bros., which put out the three *Superman* movies, to drop *Supergirl*, which wound up with TriStar. It was anything but super at the box office or with critics – though Slater's career survived.

"*Supergirl* is not quite in the same class as *Superman* or *Superman II*. But it's lively escapist fun – especially if you enjoy seeing a woman do a superman's job."

–Kathleen Carroll, New York *Daily News*

"Because of Supergirl's secondary status, her stories have often benefited from an ingratiating small-time feeling. I was pleased to discover that the new *Supergirl* movie captures this quality, but I kept wishing it had been used to better advantage."

–Jay Boyar, *Orlando Sentinel*

"Slater is the best thing in the film. She shares with Christopher Reeve the ability to wear a funny costume and not look ridiculous. We look at her and we see *Supergirl*. We look around her and we see the results of a gag-writer's convention."

–ROGER EBERT, *CHICAGO SUN-TIMES*

"[Slater's] presence bleaches the sets, the costumes and the colorful antics of her co-stars, making them as wispy and drab as her tinted all-American hair."

–Phil Bronstein, *San Francisco Examiner*

"All an audience expects from this overwrought comic-book concoction is a few laughs, a decent plot and a few engaging action scenes. No such luck."

–Michael Blowen, *The Boston Globe*

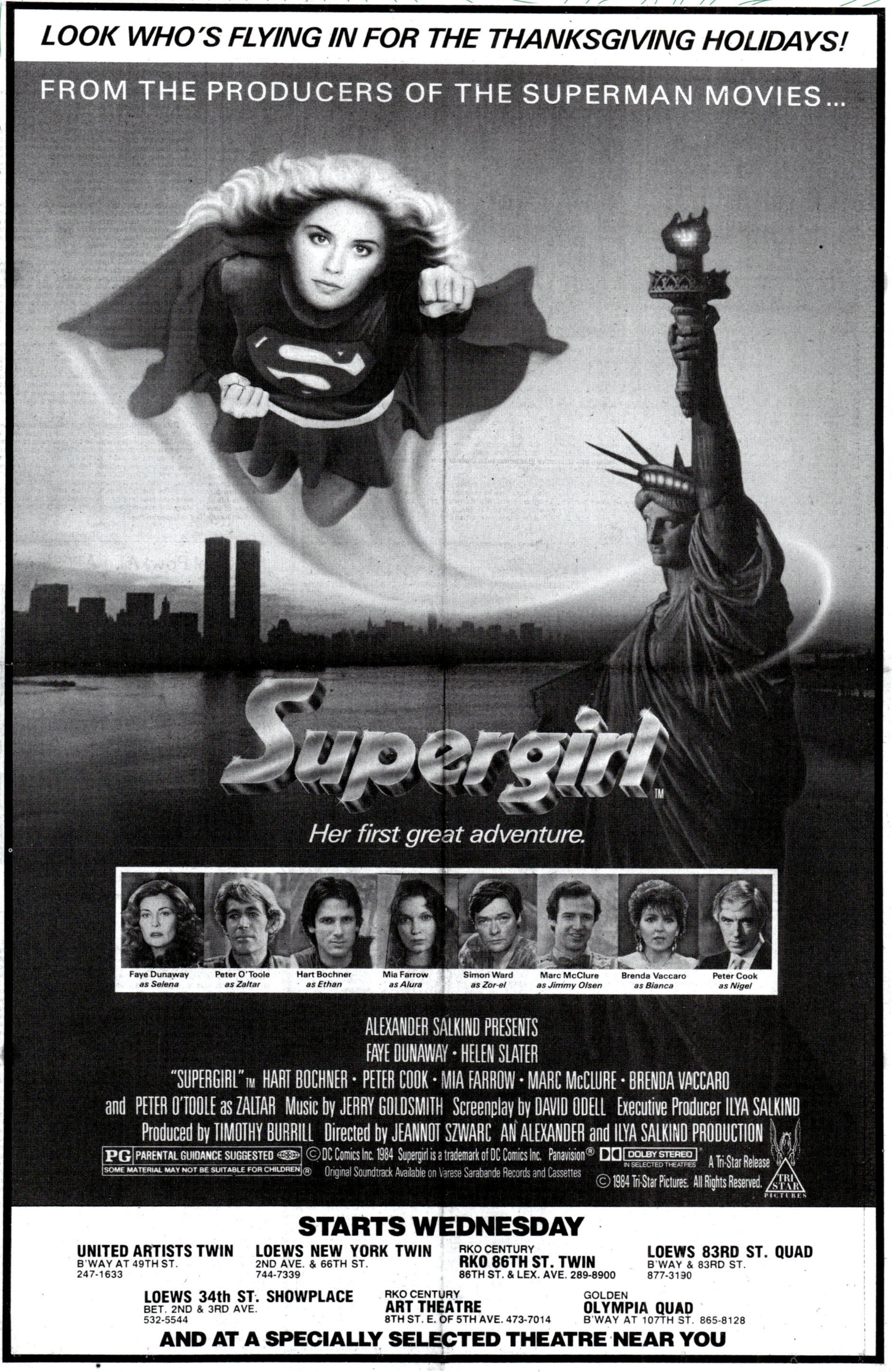

LOOK WHO'S FLYING IN FOR THE THANKSGIVING HOLIDAYS!
FROM THE PRODUCERS OF THE SUPERMAN MOVIES...
Supergirl™
Her first great adventure.
Faye Dunaway as Selena
Peter O'Toole as Zaltar
Hart Bochner as Ethan
Mia Farrow as Alura
Simon Ward as Zor-el
Marc McClure as Jimmy Olsen
Brenda Vaccaro as Bianca
Peter Cook as Nigel
ALEXANDER SALKIND PRESENTS
FAYE DUNAWAY · HELEN SLATER
"SUPERGIRL"™ HART BOCHNER · PETER COOK · MIA FARROW · MARC McCLURE · BRENDA VACCARO
and PETER O'TOOLE as ZALTAR Music by JERRY GOLDSMITH Screenplay by DAVID ODELL Executive Producer ILYA SALKIND
Produced by TIMOTHY BURRILL Directed by JEANNOT SZWARC AN ALEXANDER and ILYA SALKIND PRODUCTION
PG PARENTAL GUIDANCE SUGGESTED
SOME MATERIAL MAY NOT BE SUITABLE FOR CHILDREN
© DC Comics Inc. 1984 Supergirl is a trademark of DC Comics Inc. Panavision®
DOLBY STEREO IN SELECTED THEATRES
A Tri-Star Release
Original Soundtrack Available on Varese Sarabande Records and Cassettes
© 1984 Tri-Star Pictures. All Rights Reserved.
TRI STAR PICTURES
STARTS WEDNESDAY
UNITED ARTISTS TWIN
B'WAY AT 49TH ST.
247-1633
LOEWS NEW YORK TWIN
2ND AVE. & 66TH ST.
744-7339
RKO CENTURY
RKO 86TH ST. TWIN
86TH ST. & LEX. AVE. 289-8900
LOEWS 83RD ST. QUAD
B'WAY & 83RD ST.
877-3190
LOEWS 34th ST. SHOWPLACE
BET. 2ND & 3RD AVE.
532-5544
RKO CENTURY
ART THEATRE
8TH ST. E. OF 5TH AVE. 473-7014
GOLDEN
OLYMPIA QUAD
B'WAY AT 107TH ST. 865-8128
AND AT A SPECIALLY SELECTED THEATRE NEAR YOU

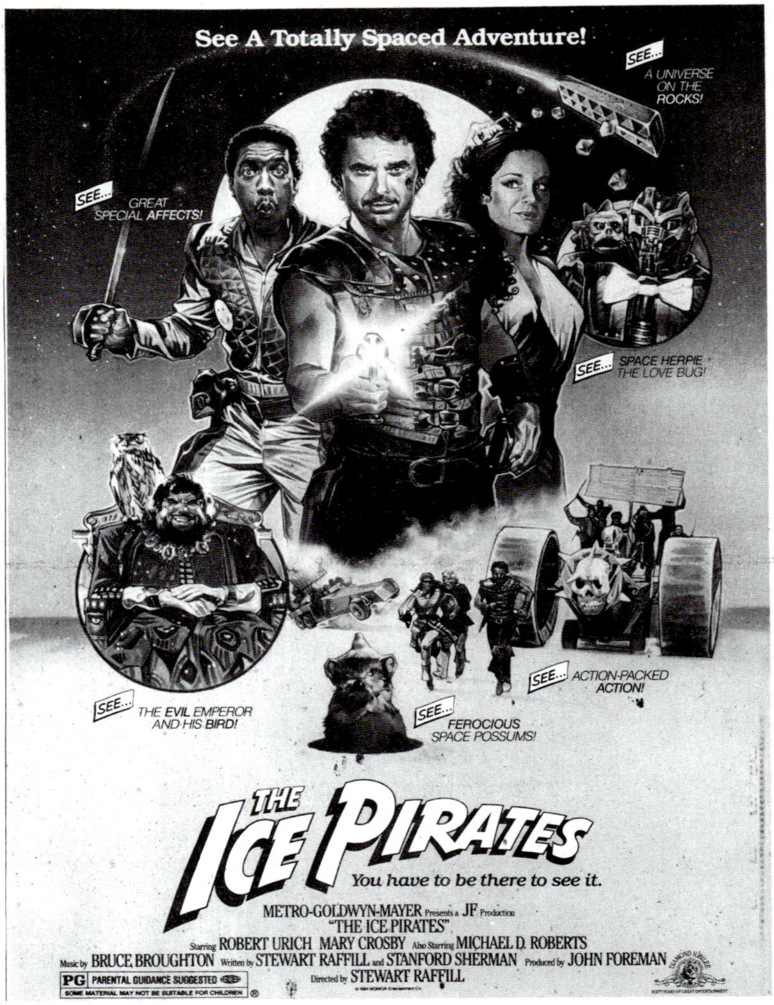

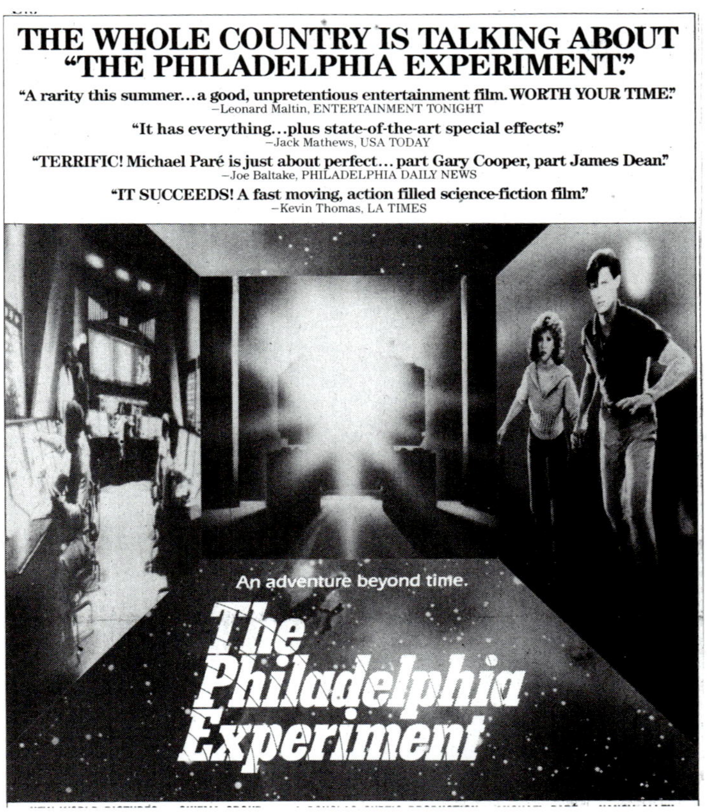

THE TERMINATOR

It sounded, at the time, like a joke: Arnold Schwarzenegger playing a robot – what appropriate casting! But the actor, along with director James Cameron, had the last laugh when *The Terminator* became the sleeper hit of 1984. Orion only pre-screened the movie at the last minute, and got the benefit of the best reviews for a Schwarzenegger vehicle thus far.

"It's the kind of slam-bang B movie that's almost disappeared from Hollywood, loaded with fuel-injected chase scenes, clever special effects, and even a welcome dose of sly humor."

–Patrick Goldstein, *Los Angeles Times*

"*The Terminator*...is the best non-stop, no-nonsense, bone-crunching, blood-letting action movie since *The Road Warrior*. Director-writer James Cameron...seems a specialist to this particular manner born."

–ALLAN ULRICH, *SAN FRANCISCO EXAMINER*

"Forget that the premise is silly and the acting second-rate because director James Cameron has the action formula down pat. ... The best aspect of *The Terminator* is its sense of humor."

–Michael Blowen, *The Boston Globe*

"*The Terminator*...is a B-movie with flair. Much of it, as directed by James Cameron (*Piranha II*), has suspense and personality, and only the obligatory mayhem becomes dull."

–Janet Maslin, *The New York Times*

"Unfortunately, a lot of the sardonic humor plays as if it's unintentional. Much of the movie is trite, if not outright stolen material. ... But this is a stylish thriller, a B-movie that should please Schwarzenegger fans."

–Sid Smith, *Chicago Tribune*

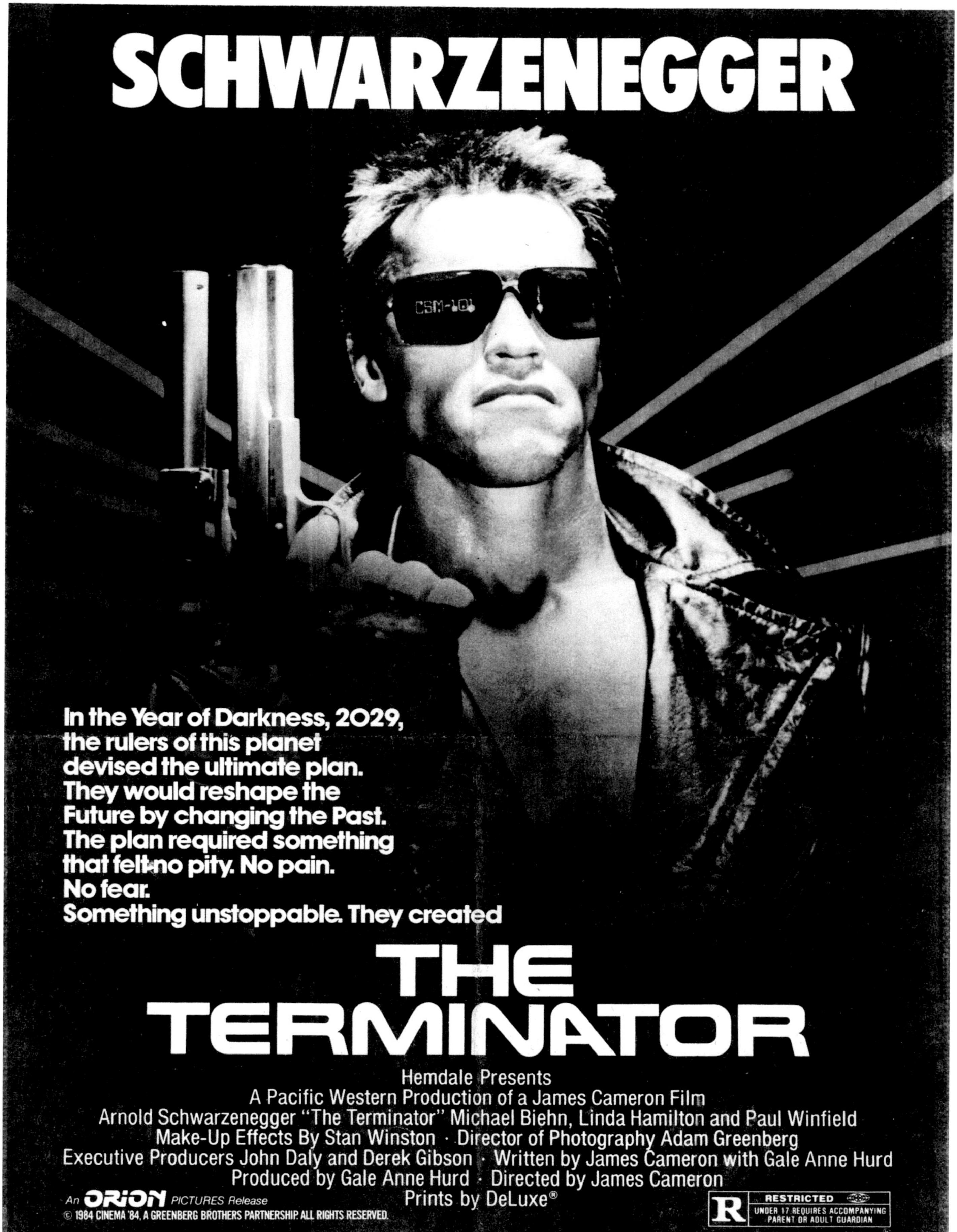
SCHWARZENEGGER
In the Year of Darkness, 2029,
the rulers of this planet
devised the ultimate plan.
They would reshape the
Future by changing the Past.
The plan required something
that felt no pity. No pain.
No fear.
Something unstoppable. They created
THE TERMINATOR
Hemdale Presents
A Pacific Western Production of a James Cameron Film
Arnold Schwarzenegger "The Terminator" Michael Biehn, Linda Hamilton and Paul Winfield
Make-Up Effects By Stan Winston · Director of Photography Adam Greenberg
Executive Producers John Daly and Derek Gibson · Written by James Cameron with Gale Anne Hurd
Produced by Gale Anne Hurd · Directed by James Cameron
Prints by DeLuxe®
An ORION PICTURES Release
© 1984 CINEMA '84, A GREENBERG BROTHERS PARTNERSHIP. ALL RIGHTS RESERVED.
R RESTRICTED
UNDER 17 REQUIRES ACCOMPANYING PARENT OR ADULT GUARDIAN

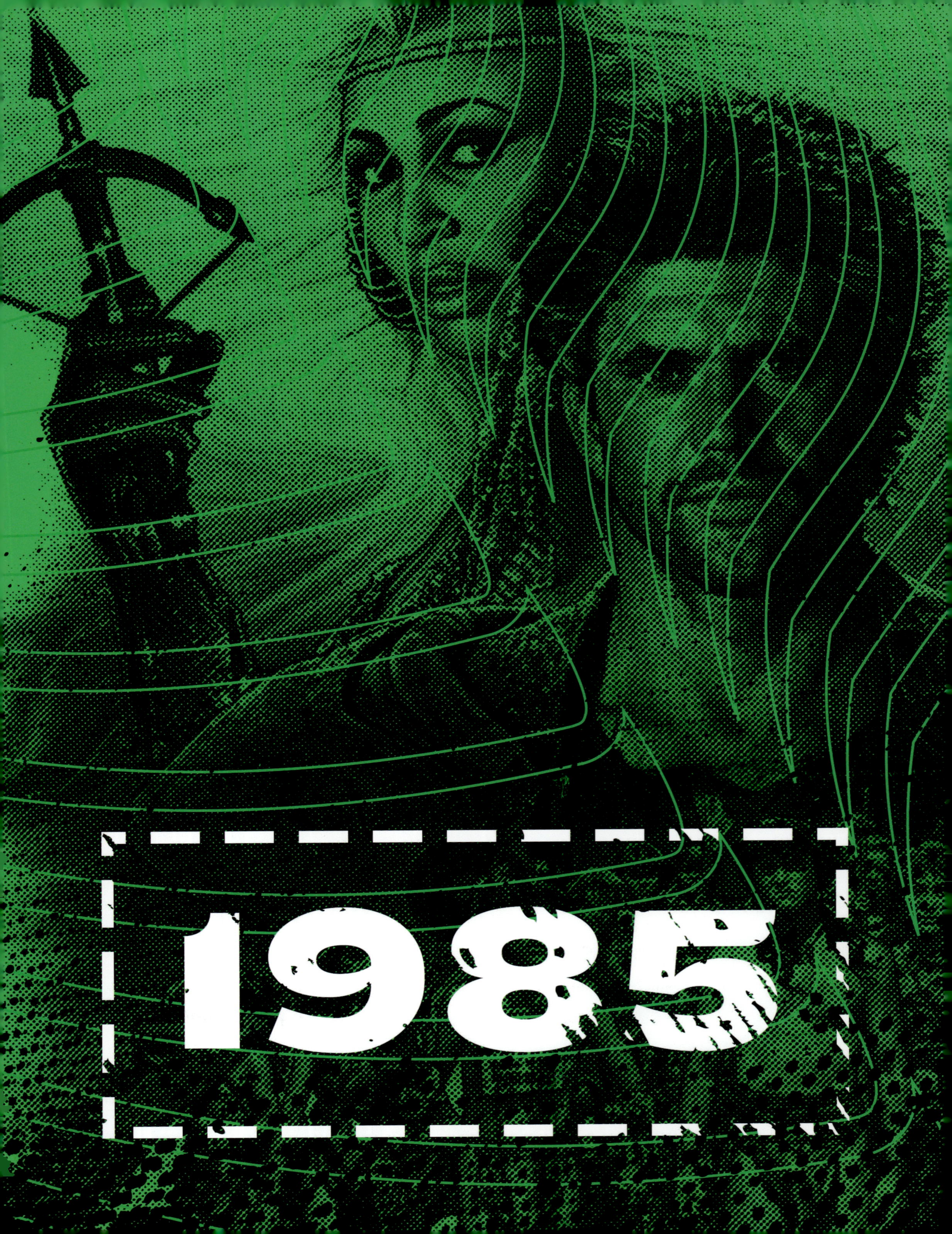
1985

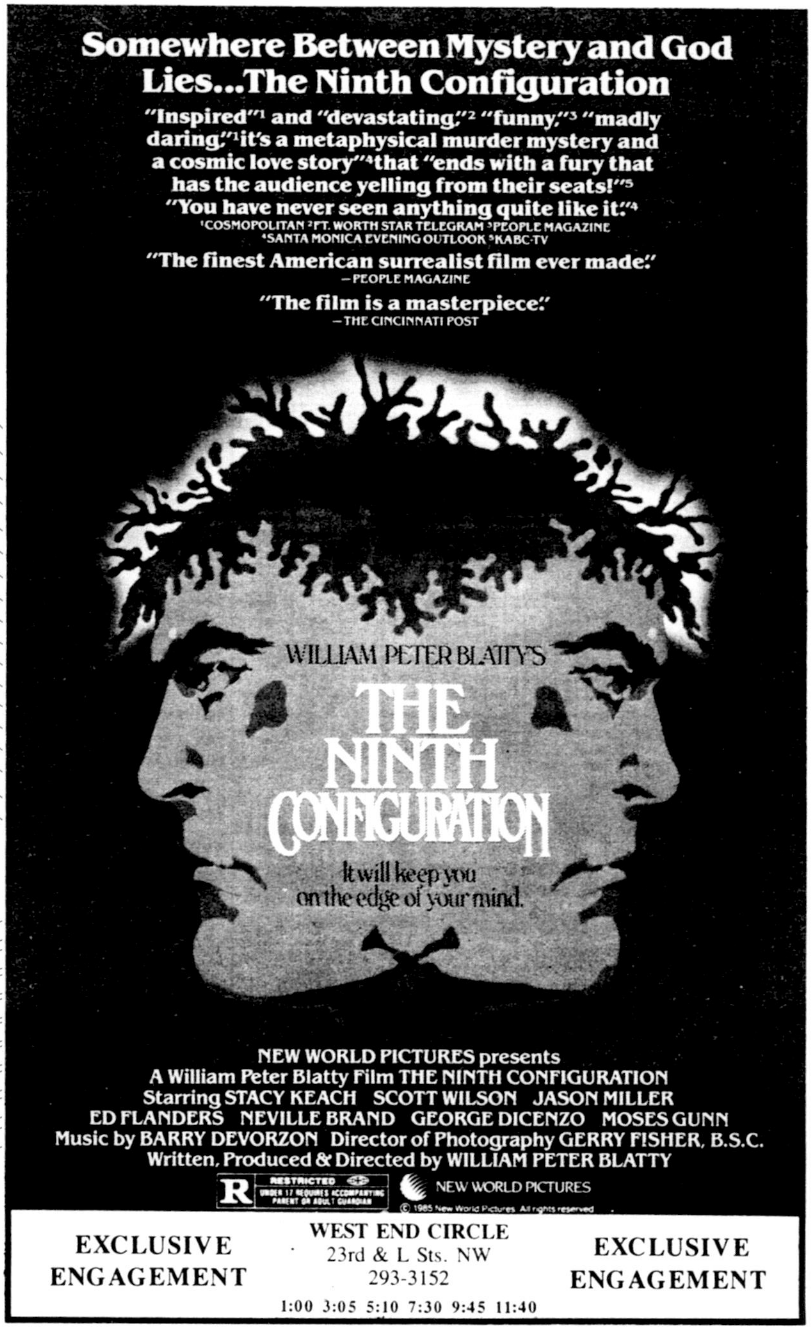

Somewhere Between Mystery and God Lies...The Ninth Configuration
"Inspired"1 and "devastating,"2 "funny,"3 "madly daring,"1 it's a metaphysical murder mystery and a cosmic love story"4 that "ends with a fury that has the audience yelling from their seats!"5
"You have never seen anything quite like it."4
1COSMOPOLITAN 2FT. WORTH STAR TELEGRAM 3PEOPLE MAGAZINE 4SANTA MONICA EVENING OUTLOOK 5KABC-TV
"The finest American surrealist film ever made." —PEOPLE MAGAZINE
"The film is a masterpiece." —THE CINCINNATI POST
WILLIAM PETER BLATTY'S
THE NINTH CONFIGURATION
It will keep you on the edge of your mind.
NEW WORLD PICTURES presents
A William Peter Blatty Film THE NINTH CONFIGURATION
Starring STACY KEACH SCOTT WILSON JASON MILLER
ED FLANDERS NEVILLE BRAND GEORGE DICENZO MOSES GUNN
Music by BARRY DEVORZON Director of Photography GERRY FISHER, B.S.C.
Written, Produced & Directed by WILLIAM PETER BLATTY
R RESTRICTED UNDER 17 REQUIRES ACCOMPANYING PARENT OR ADULT GUARDIAN
NEW WORLD PICTURES
© 1985 New World Pictures All rights reserved
EXCLUSIVE ENGAGEMENT
WEST END CIRCLE
23rd & L Sts. NW
293-3152
EXCLUSIVE ENGAGEMENT
1:00 3:05 5:10 7:30 9:45 11:40

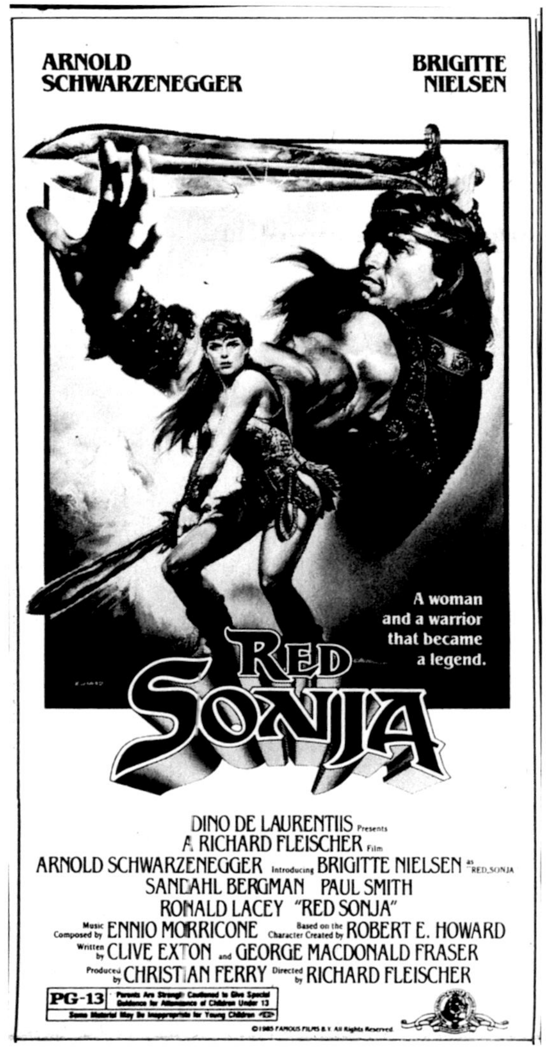

ARNOLD SCHWARZENEGGER
BRIGITTE NIELSEN
A woman and a warrior that became a legend.
RED SONJA
DINO DE LAURENTIIS Presents
A RICHARD FLEISCHER Film
ARNOLD SCHWARZENEGGER Introducing BRIGITTE NIELSEN as RED SONJA
SANDAHL BERGMAN PAUL SMITH
RONALD LACEY "RED SONJA"
Music Composed by ENNIO MORRICONE Based on the Character Created by ROBERT E. HOWARD
Written by CLIVE EXTON and GEORGE MACDONALD FRASER
Produced by CHRISTIAN FERRY Directed by RICHARD FLEISCHER
PG-13
©1985 FAMOUS FILMS B.V. All Rights Reserved

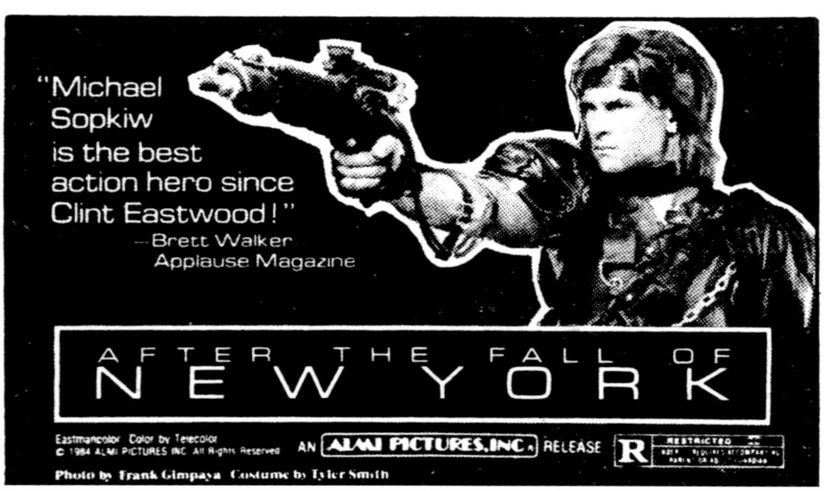

"Michael Sopkiw is the best action hero since Clint Eastwood!"
—Brett Walker Applause Magazine
AFTER THE FALL OF NEW YORK
Eastmancolor Color by Telecolor
© 1984 ALMI PICTURES INC. All Rights Reserved
AN ALMI PICTURES, INC. RELEASE
R RESTRICTED
Photo by Frank Gimpaya Costume by Tyler Smith

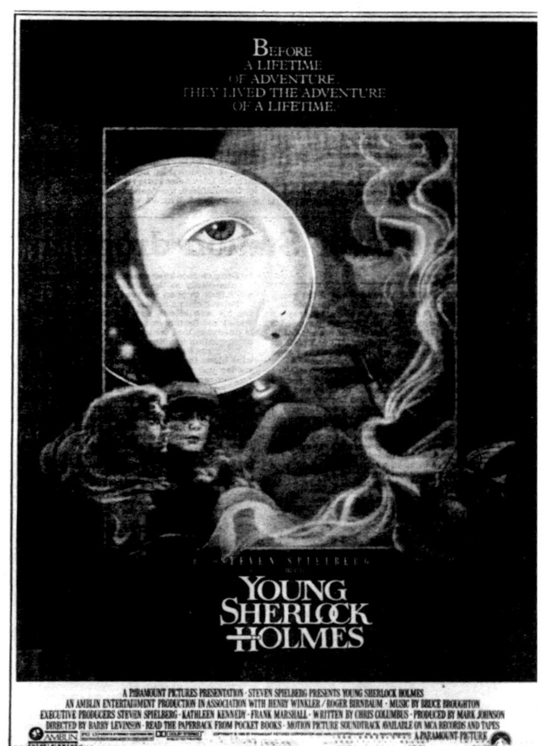

BEFORE A LIFETIME OF ADVENTURE, THEY LIVED THE ADVENTURE OF A LIFETIME.
YOUNG SHERLOCK HOLMES
A PARAMOUNT PICTURES PRESENTATION · STEVEN SPIELBERG PRESENTS YOUNG SHERLOCK HOLMES
AN AMBLIN ENTERTAINMENT PRODUCTION IN ASSOCIATION WITH HENRY WINKLER / ROGER BIRNBAUM · MUSIC BY BRUCE BROUGHTON
EXECUTIVE PRODUCERS STEVEN SPIELBERG · KATHLEEN KENNEDY · FRANK MARSHALL · WRITTEN BY CHRIS COLUMBUS · PRODUCED BY MARK JOHNSON
DIRECTED BY BARRY LEVINSON · READ THE PAPERBACK FROM POCKET BOOKS · MOTION PICTURE SOUNDTRACK AVAILABLE ON MCA RECORDS AND TAPES
AMBLIN
A PARAMOUNT PICTURE

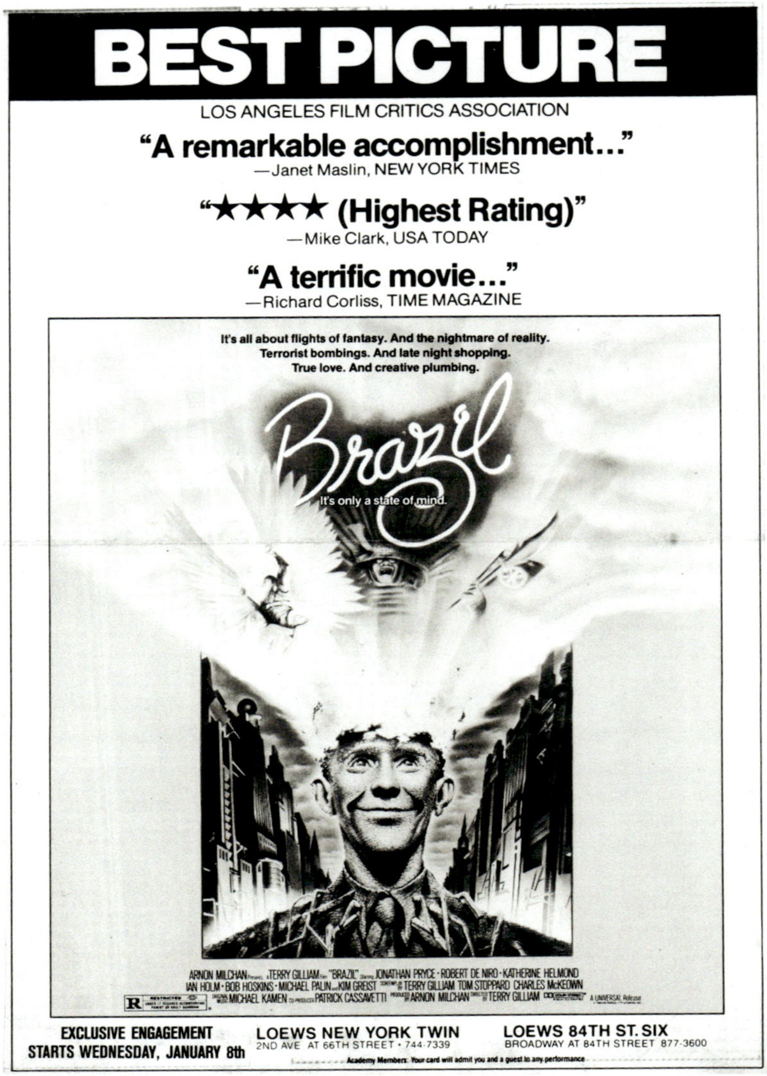

BRAZIL

Terry Gilliam's galvanizing vision of a dystopian society actually made its theatrical debut in December 1984. The director had been waging a long battle with Universal and its chairman, Sid Sheinberg, to have his cut of the movie released, with his bleak ending intact. He even took out a full-page ad in *Variety* asking simply, "Dear Sid Sheinberg, When are you going to release my film 'Brazil'?" At an impasse, Gilliam secretly screened the movie for the Los Angeles Film Critics Association, which responded by awarding it Best Picture, Best Director, and Best Screenplay in mid-December '84. Sheinberg had little choice but to concede, and Universal hurriedly booked one-week Oscar-qualifying runs for *Brazil* in New York (where I was fortunate enough to catch it with a sold-out crowd) and Los Angeles before the year was out. The Academy only nominated it in two categories, Best Screenplay and Best Production Design, and it won neither, but the true victory was Gilliam seeing his vision making it to release in '85.

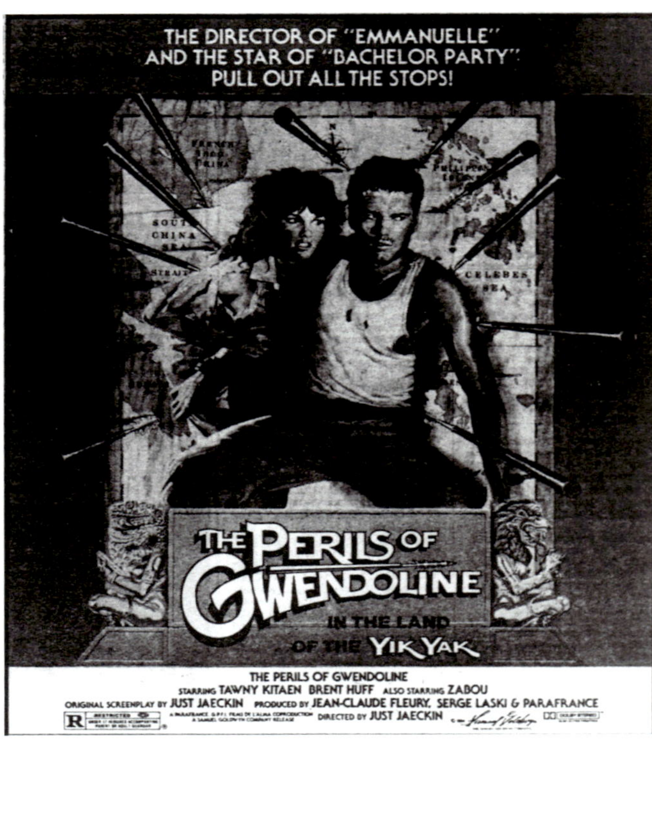

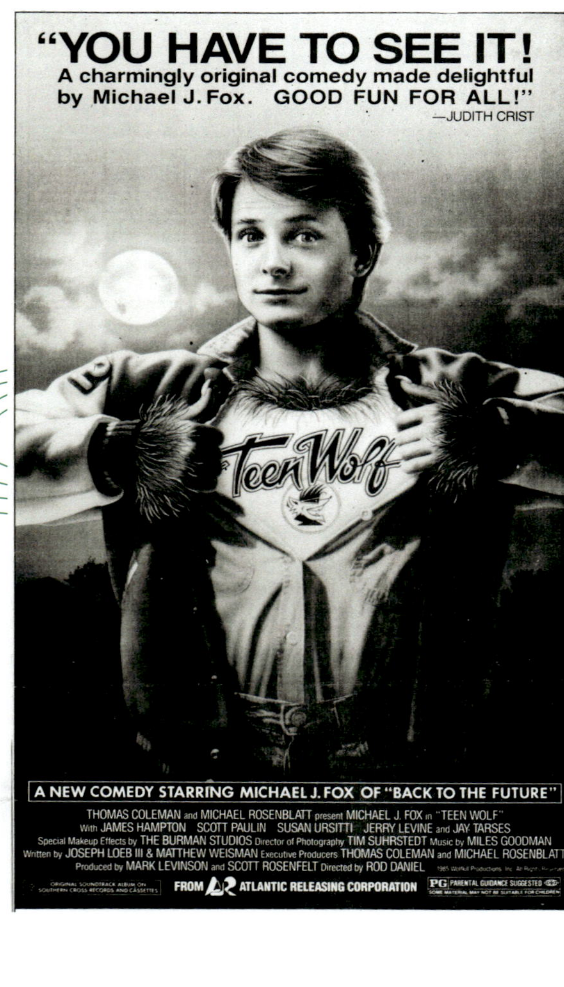

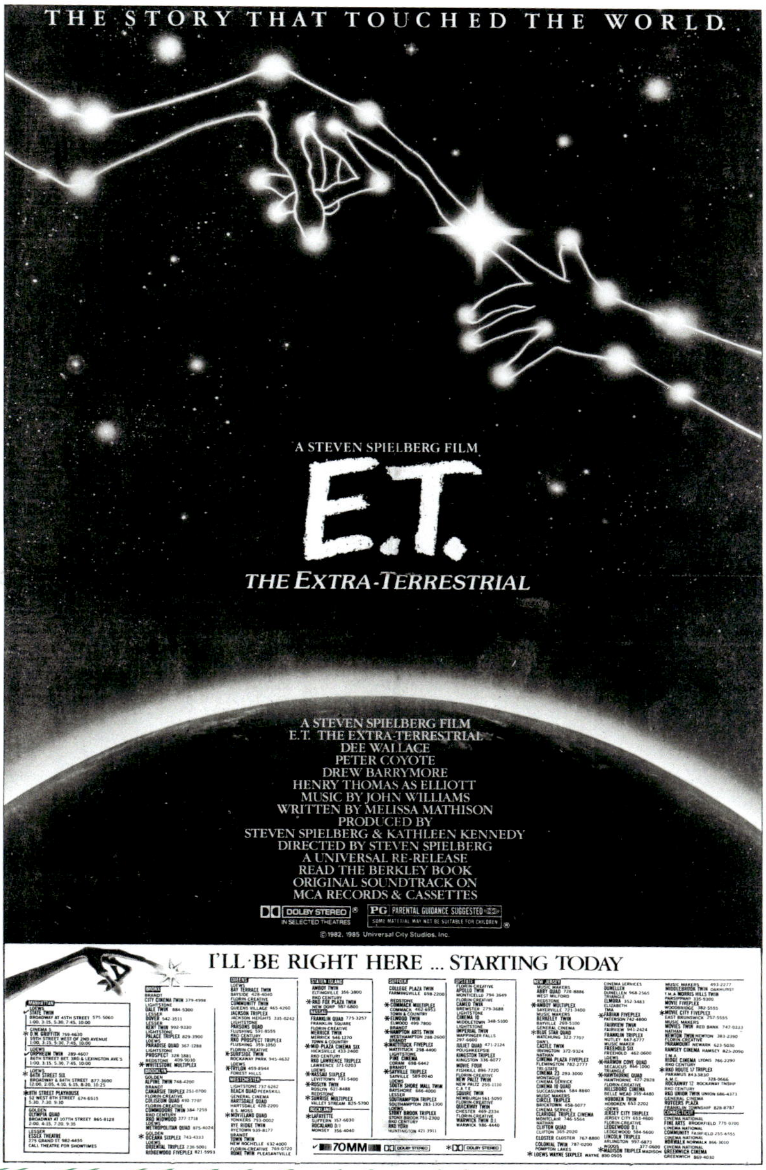
THE STORY THAT TOUCHED THE WORLD.
A STEVEN SPIELBERG FILM
E.T.
THE EXTRA-TERRESTRIAL
A STEVEN SPIELBERG FILM
E.T. THE EXTRA-TERRESTRIAL
DEE WALLACE
PETER COYOTE
DREW BARRYMORE
HENRY THOMAS AS ELLIOTT
MUSIC BY JOHN WILLIAMS
WRITTEN BY MELISSA MATHISON
PRODUCED BY
STEVEN SPIELBERG & KATHLEEN KENNEDY
DIRECTED BY STEVEN SPIELBERG
A UNIVERSAL RE-RELEASE
READ THE BERKLEY BOOK
ORIGINAL SOUNDTRACK ON
MCA RECORDS & CASSETTES
DOLBY STEREO IN SELECTED THEATRES
PG PARENTAL GUIDANCE SUGGESTED
©1982, 1985 Universal City Studios, Inc.
I'LL BE RIGHT HERE ... STARTING TODAY
70MM

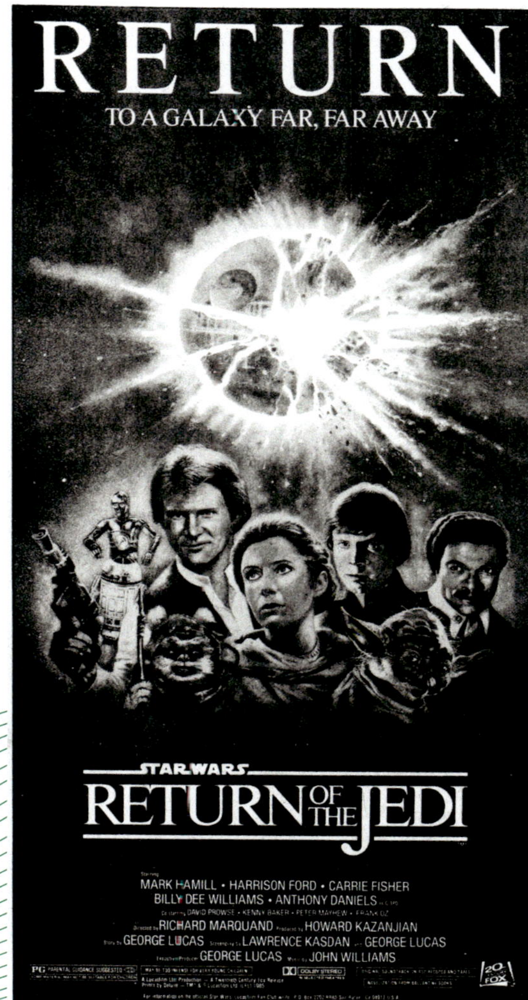
RETURN
TO A GALAXY FAR, FAR AWAY
STAR WARS
RETURN OF THE JEDI
MARK HAMILL • HARRISON FORD • CARRIE FISHER
BILLY DEE WILLIAMS • ANTHONY DANIELS
RICHARD MARQUAND
HOWARD KAZANJIAN
GEORGE LUCAS
LAWRENCE KASDAN
GEORGE LUCAS
GEORGE LUCAS
JOHN WILLIAMS
PG
DOLBY STEREO
20th FOX

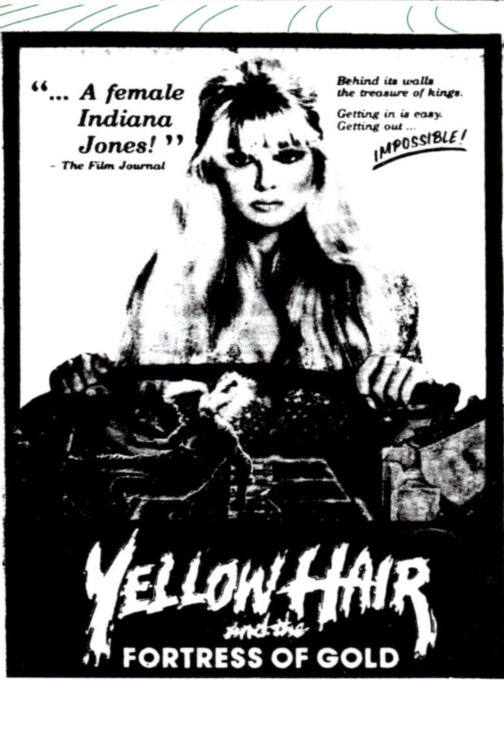
"... A female Indiana Jones!"
- The Film Journal
Behind its walls the treasure of kings.
Getting in is easy. Getting out ...
IMPOSSIBLE!
YELLOW HAIR
and the
FORTRESS OF GOLD

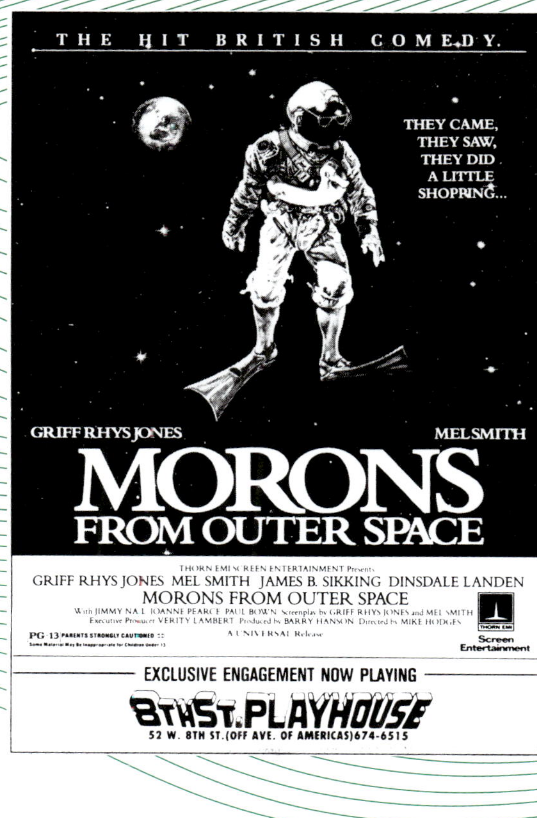
THE HIT BRITISH COMEDY.
THEY CAME, THEY SAW, THEY DID A LITTLE SHOPPING...
GRIFF RHYS JONES
MEL SMITH
MORONS
FROM OUTER SPACE
THORN EMI SCREEN ENTERTAINMENT Presents
GRIFF RHYS JONES MEL SMITH JAMES B. SIKKING DINSDALE LANDEN
MORONS FROM OUTER SPACE
With JIMMY NAIL JOANNE PEARCE PAUL BOWN Screenplay by GRIFF RHYS JONES and MEL SMITH
Executive Producer VERITY LAMBERT Produced by BARRY HANSON Directed by MIKE HODGES
A UNIVERSAL Release
PG-13 PARENTS STRONGLY CAUTIONED
THORN EMI Screen Entertainment
EXCLUSIVE ENGAGEMENT NOW PLAYING
8TH ST. PLAYHOUSE
52 W. 8TH ST. (OFF AVE. OF AMERICAS) 674-6515

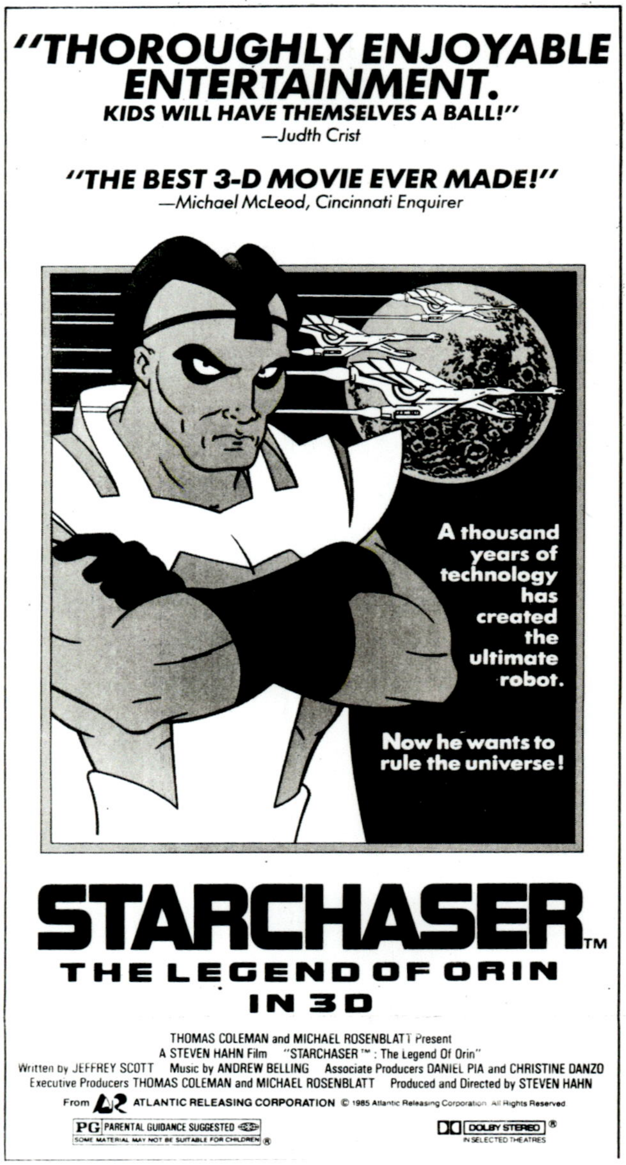

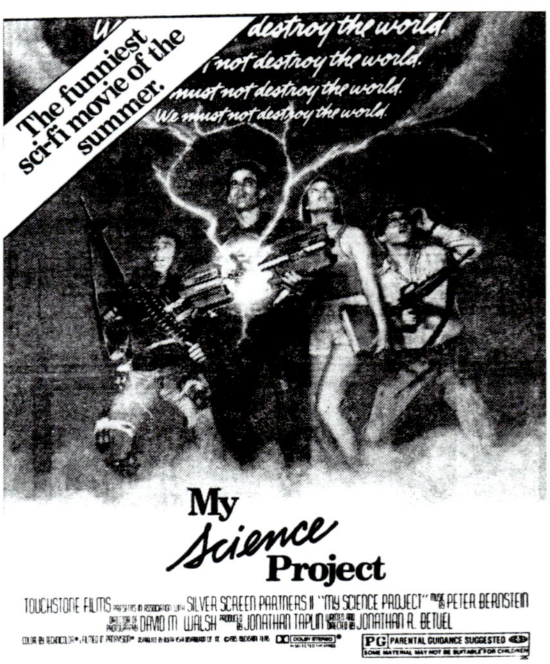

COCOON

Science fiction, in the big-studio scheme of things, is largely seen as a young people's genre. So could such a movie cast with actors past retirement age be a contender? The answer, when it came to *Cocoon*, was a resounding yes. In between the teen exploits of *The Goonies* and *Back to the Future* came Ron Howard's exploration of mortality in the guise of an alien-visitor drama, which charmed audiences and critics in equal measure.

"*Cocoon* is one of the sweetest, gentlest science-fiction movies I've seen, a hymn to the notion that aliens might come from outer space and yet still be almost as corny and impulsive as we are."

–Roger Ebert, *Chicago Sun-Times*

"If Spielberg doesn't watch it, Howard is going to become the new king of the feel-good movie. ... *Cocoon*, Howard's second film, is as winning as *Splash*, his first." [*Actually,* Splash *was his third and* Cocoon *was his fourth, after 1977's* Grand Theft Auto *and 1982's* Night Shift.]

–Jay Carr, *The Boston Globe*

"*Cocoon*...is a sly and salty bit of wish fulfillment that, by its tremendous close, has its entire audience wishing along with it. The combined energy it generates is probably enough to raise the Titanic."

–SHEILA BENSON, *LOS ANGELES TIMES*

"*Cocoon* has a built-in frailty that is magnified as the story progresses: Its conception of old age, though wonderfully sympathetic, is filtered through, and limited by, the eyes of the young. ... Don Ameche, Hume Cronyn, and Wilford Brimley make a marvelous trio."

–Janet Maslin, *The New York Times*

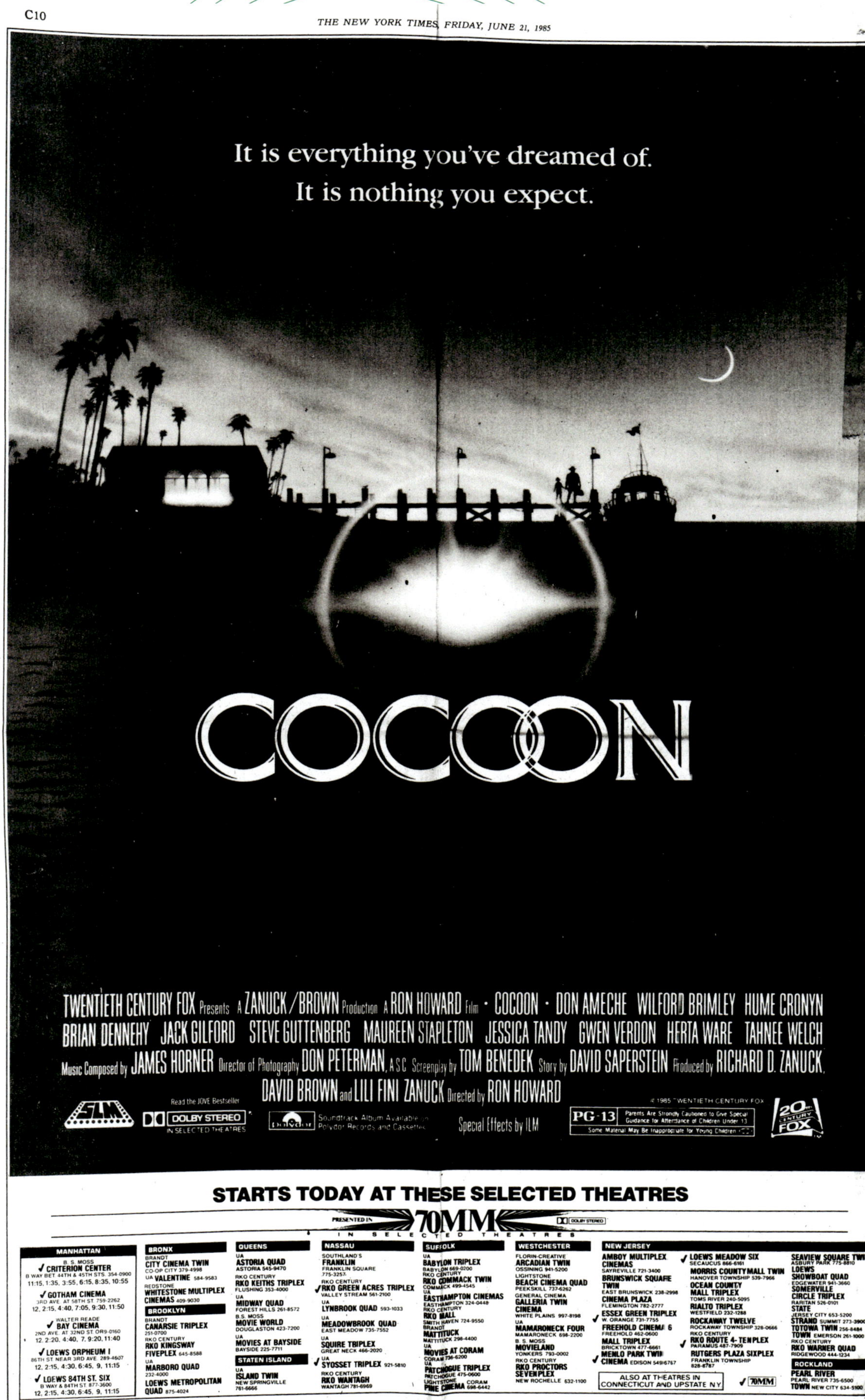
C10 THE NEW YORK TIMES, FRIDAY, JUNE 21, 1985

It is everything you've dreamed of.
It is nothing you expect.

COCOON

TWENTIETH CENTURY FOX Presents A ZANUCK/BROWN Production A RON HOWARD Film · COCOON · DON AMECHE WILFORD BRIMLEY HUME CRONYN BRIAN DENNEHY JACK GILFORD STEVE GUTTENBERG MAUREEN STAPLETON JESSICA TANDY GWEN VERDON HERTA WARE TAHNEE WELCH Music Composed by JAMES HORNER Director of Photography DON PETERMAN, A.S.C. Screenplay by TOM BENEDEK Story by DAVID SAPERSTEIN Produced by RICHARD D. ZANUCK, DAVID BROWN and LILI FINI ZANUCK Directed by RON HOWARD

Read the JOVE Bestseller

DOLBY STEREO IN SELECTED THEATRES

Soundtrack Album Available on Polydor Records and Cassettes

Special Effects by ILM

© 1985 TWENTIETH CENTURY FOX

PG-13 Parents Are Strongly Cautioned to Give Special Guidance for Attendance of Children Under 13. Some Material May Be Inappropriate for Young Children

STARTS TODAY AT THESE SELECTED THEATRES

PRESENTED IN 70MM IN SELECTED THEATRES — DOLBY STEREO

MANHATTAN

B. S. MOSS
✓ CRITERION CENTER
B'WAY BET. 44TH & 45TH STS. 354-0900
11:15, 1:35, 3:55, 6:15, 8:35, 10:55

✓ GOTHAM CINEMA
3RD AVE. AT 58TH ST. 759-2262
12, 2:15, 4:40, 7:05, 9:30, 11:50

WALTER READE
✓ BAY CINEMA
2ND AVE. AT 32ND ST. OR9-0160
12, 2:20, 4:40, 7, 9:20, 11:40

✓ LOEWS ORPHEUM I
86TH ST. NEAR 3RD AVE. 289-4607
12, 2:15, 4:30, 6:45, 9, 11:15

✓ LOEWS 84TH ST. SIX
B'WAY & 84TH ST. 877-3600
12, 2:15, 4:30, 6:45, 9, 11:15

BRONX

BRANDT CITY CINEMA TWIN CO-OP CITY 379-4998
UA VALENTINE 584-9583
REDSTONE WHITESTONE MULTIPLEX CINEMAS 409-9030

BROOKLYN

BRANDT CANARSIE TRIPLEX 251-0700
RKO CENTURY RKO KINGSWAY FIVEPLEX 645-8588
UA MARBORO QUAD 232-4000
LOEWS METROPOLITAN QUAD 875-4024

QUEENS

UA ASTORIA QUAD ASTORIA 545-9470
RKO CENTURY RKO KEITHS TRIPLEX FLUSHING 353-4000
UA MIDWAY QUAD FOREST HILLS 261-8572
B.S. MOSS MOVIE WORLD DOUGLASTON 423-7200
UA MOVIES AT BAYSIDE BAYSIDE 225-7711

STATEN ISLAND

UA ISLAND TWIN NEW SPRINGVILLE 761-6666

NASSAU

SOUTHLAND'S FRANKLIN FRANKLIN SQUARE 775-3257
RKO CENTURY ✓ RKO GREEN ACRES TRIPLEX VALLEY STREAM 561-2100
UA LYNBROOK QUAD 593-1033
UA MEADOWBROOK QUAD EAST MEADOW 735-7552
UA SQUIRE TRIPLEX GREAT NECK 466-2020
✓ UA SYOSSET TRIPLEX 921-5810
RKO CENTURY RKO WANTAGH WANTAGH 781-6969

SUFFOLK

UA BABYLON TRIPLEX BABYLON 669-0200
RKO CENTURY RKO COMMACK TWIN COMMACK 499-4545
UA EASTHAMPTON CINEMAS EASTHAMPTON 324-0448
RKO CENTURY RKO MALL SMITH HAVEN 724-9550
BRANDT MATTITUCK MATTITUCK 298-4400
UA MOVIES AT CORAM CORAM 736-6200
UA PATCHOGUE TRIPLEX PATCHOGUE 475-0600
LIGHTSTONE PINE CINEMA CORAM 698-6442

WESTCHESTER

FLORIN-CREATIVE ARCADIAN TWIN OSSINING 941-5200
LIGHTSTONE BEACH CINEMA QUAD PEEKSKILL 737-6262
GENERAL CINEMA GALLERIA TWIN CINEMA WHITE PLAINS 997-8198
UA MAMARONECK FOUR MAMARONECK 698-2200
B. S. MOSS MOVIELAND YONKERS 793-0002
RKO CENTURY RKO PROCTORS SEVENPLEX NEW ROCHELLE 632-1100

NEW JERSEY

AMBOY MULTIPLEX CINEMAS SAYREVILLE 721-3400
BRUNSWICK SQUARE TWIN EAST BRUNSWICK 238-2998
CINEMA PLAZA FLEMINGTON 782-2777
✓ ESSEX GREEN TRIPLEX W. ORANGE 731-7755
FREEHOLD CINEMA 6 FREEHOLD 462-0600
MALL TRIPLEX BRICKTOWN 477-6661
✓ MENLO PARK TWIN CINEMA EDISON 549-6767
✓ LOEWS MEADOW SIX SECAUCUS 866-6161
MORRIS COUNTY MALL TWIN HANOVER TOWNSHIP 539-7966
OCEAN COUNTY MALL TRIPLEX TOMS RIVER 240-5095
RIALTO TRIPLEX WESTFIELD 232-1288
ROCKAWAY TWELVE ROCKAWAY TOWNSHIP 328-0666
RKO CENTURY ✓ RKO ROUTE 4-TENPLEX PARAMUS 487-7909
RUTGERS PLAZA SIXPLEX FRANKLIN TOWNSHIP 828-8787
SEAVIEW SQUARE TWIN ASBURY PARK 775-8810
LOEWS SHOWBOAT QUAD EDGEWATER 941-3660
SOMERVILLE CIRCLE TRIPLEX RARITAN 526-0101
STATE JERSEY CITY 653-5200
STRAND SUMMIT 273-3900
TOTOWA TWIN 256-8484
TOWN EMERSON 261-1000
RKO CENTURY RKO WARNER QUAD RIDGEWOOD 444-1234

ROCKLAND

PEARL RIVER PEARL RIVER 735-6500
TOWN NEW CITY 634-5100

ALSO AT THEATRES IN CONNECTICUT AND UPSTATE N.Y.

✓ 70MM

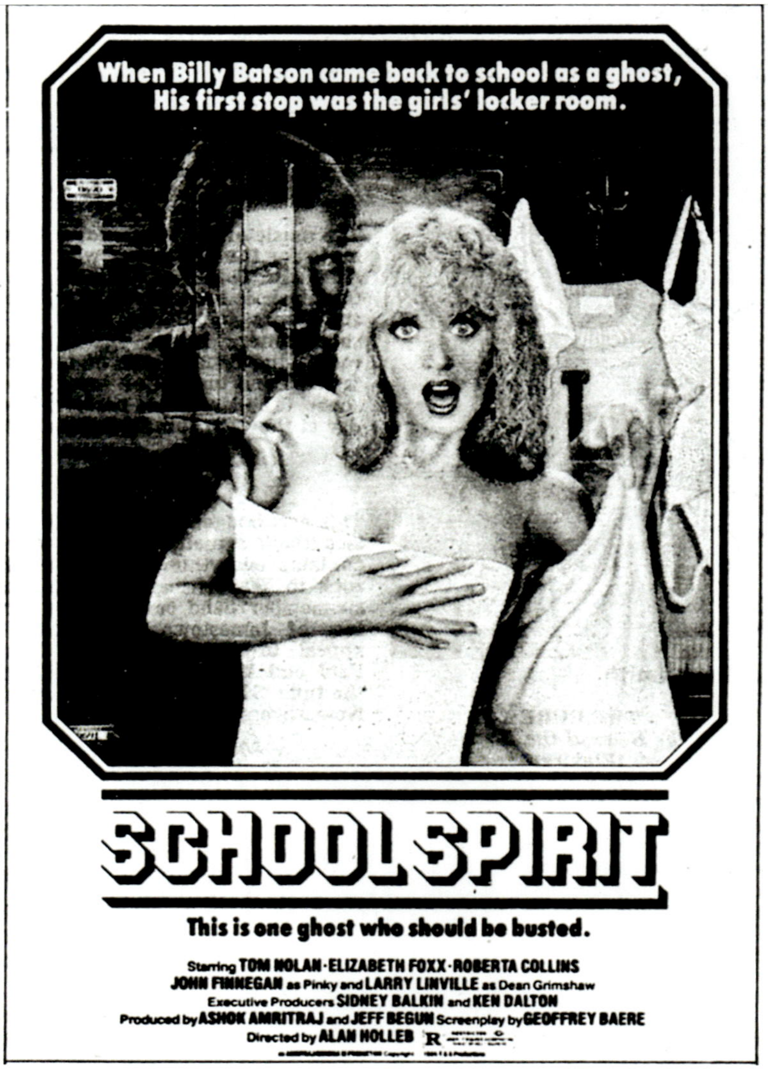

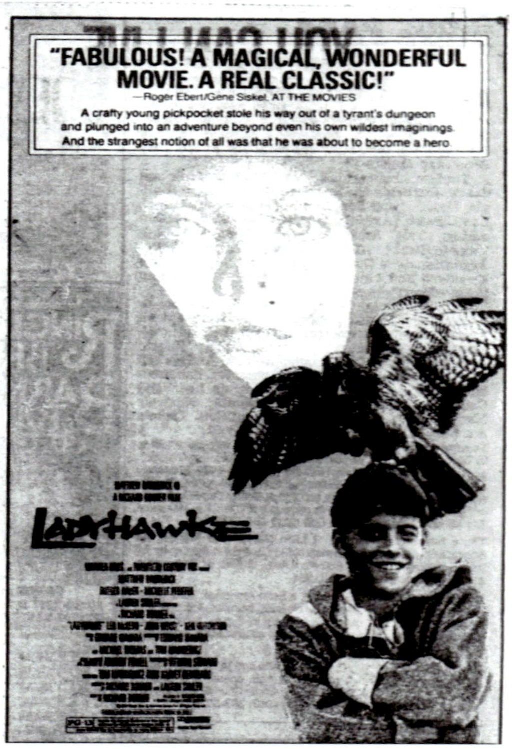

EXPLORERS

A year after hitting it big with *Gremlins*, director Joe Dante was back with another subversive genre piece. Just as his monster mash tore picture-postcard Christmas-film standards to shreds, *Explorers* turned the sense-of-wonder children's space fantasy into a snarky shaggy-dog story. Its three youthful protagonists (including a young Ethan Hawke) cobble together a homemade spacecraft and head into the stars – where the aliens they meet turn out not to be awe-inspiring beings, but goofballs hooked on Earth's pop culture. This time, unfortunately, neither audiences nor most critics got the joke.

"*Explorers*...is bubble-thin, but it glides by gracefully on the charm of its three young heroes and their vividly envisioned adventure in space. It's also a truly gentle film, one of the precious few that actually is suitable for children."

–Kevin Thomas, *Los Angeles Times*

"Of all the Spielberg-inspired fantasy films afoot at the moment, Joe Dante's *Explorers* is by far the most eccentric. It's charmingly odd at some moments, just plain goofy at others."

–Janet Maslin, *The New York Times*

"In one bizarre sense, it's nice to see such a total mess as *Explorers* appear. Maybe this will finally be the one to make Hollywood wake up and realize that's it. No more. We've tapped every single angle of this friendly-alien film genre dry."

–JON MARLOWE, *THE MIAMI NEWS*

"Even in the movie's final third – when *Explorers* changes from Spielberg-inspired teen fantasy to something deranged and absurdist, something right up Dante's alley – the snail's pace undercuts the fun."

–Rick Lyman, *Philadelphia Inquirer*

"In the stampede of mind-numbing summer children's pictures, I think it is safe to predict that nothing will turn up that is more boring, uninspired, or sub-mental than *Explorers*."

–Rex Reed, *New York Post*

FROM THE DIRECTOR OF 'GREMLINS.'

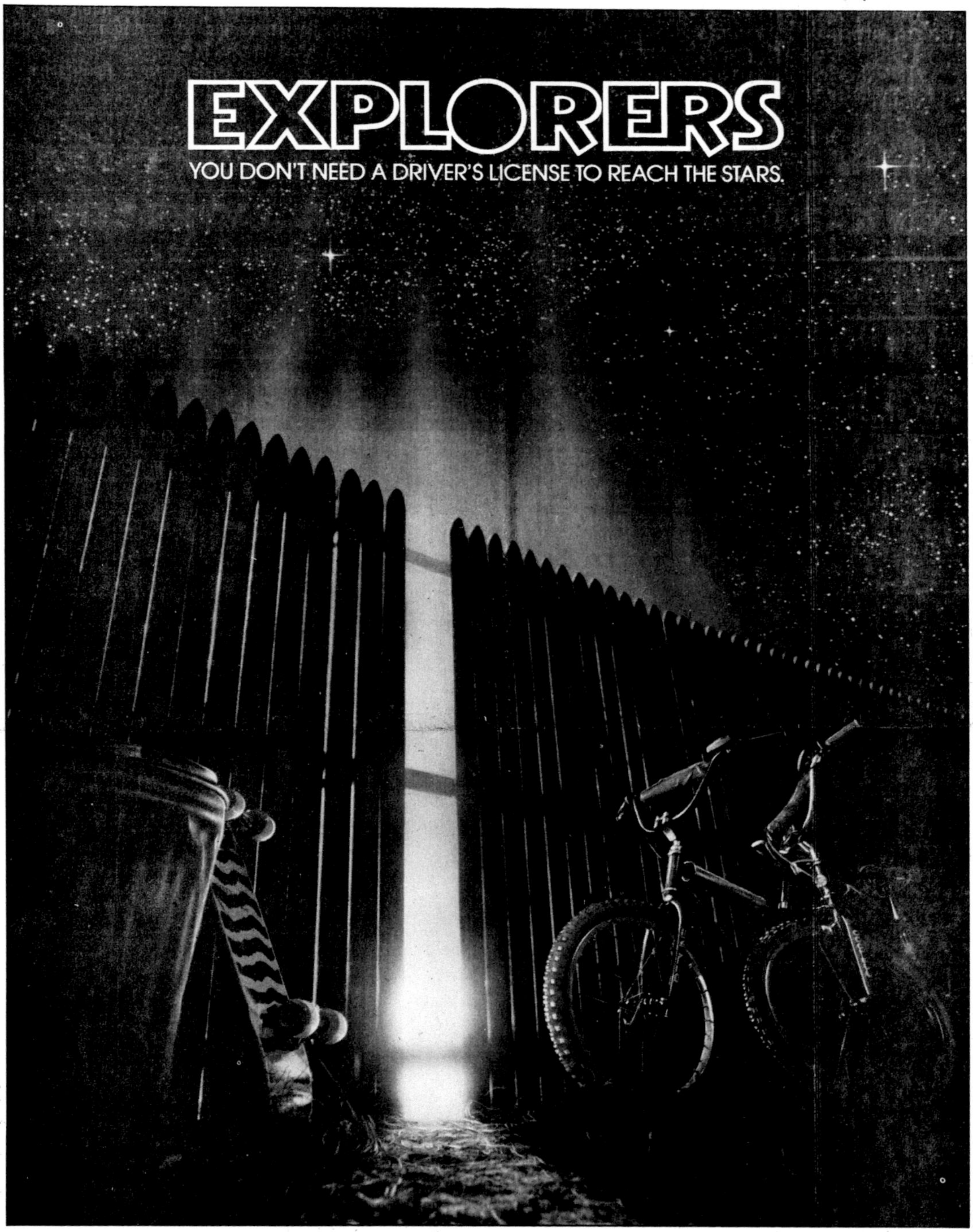

The adventure begins in your own back yard.

PARAMOUNT PICTURES PRESENTS AN EDWARD S. FELDMAN PRODUCTION · EXPLORERS
ETHAN HAWKE · RIVER PHOENIX · JASON PRESSON · MUSIC BY JERRY GOLDSMITH
PRODUCTION DESIGNED BY ROBERT F. BOYLE · DIRECTOR OF PHOTOGRAPHY JOHN HORA
EXECUTIVE PRODUCER MICHAEL FINNELL · WRITTEN BY ERIC LUKE
PRODUCED BY EDWARD S. FELDMAN AND DAVID BOMBYK · DIRECTED BY JOE DANTE
VISUAL EFFECTS BY INDUSTRIAL LIGHT & MAGIC · SPECIAL MAKE-UP EFFECTS BY ROB BOTTIN
MOTION PICTURE SOUNDTRACK ALBUM ON MCA RECORDS & TAPES.
READ THE PAPERBACK FROM POCKET BOOKS A PARAMOUNT PICTURE

PG PARENTAL GUIDANCE SUGGESTED
SOME MATERIAL MAY NOT BE SUITABLE FOR CHILDREN

DOLBY STEREO® IN SELECTED THEATRES

STARTS FRIDAY, JULY 12TH, AT A THEATRE NEAR YOU

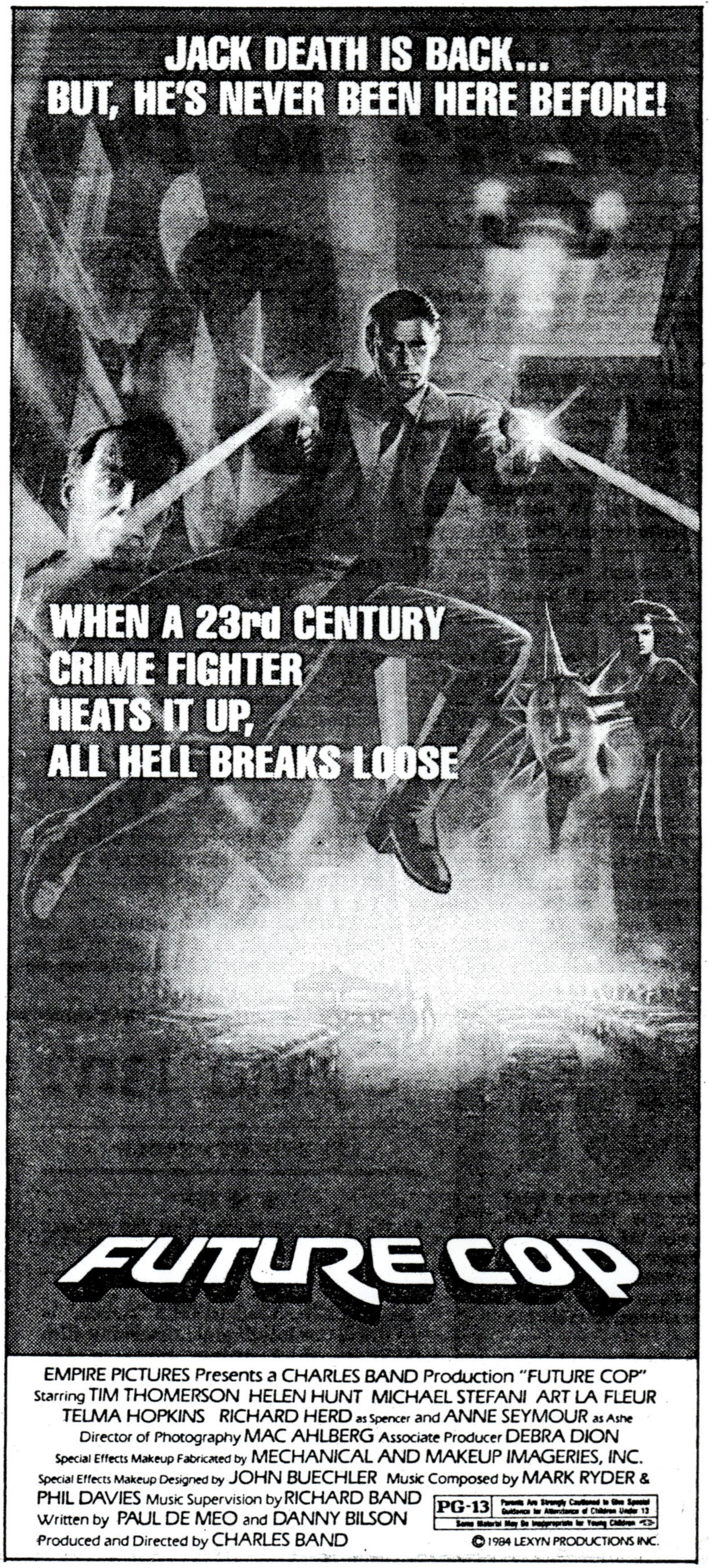

FUTURE COP

Charles Band's sci-fi actioner starring Tim Thomerson as time-tripping law enforcement officer Jack Deth was filmed as *Trancers*, after the psychically altered killers pursued by our hero. Yet, when it came time to release the movie, Band evidently felt that term was too obscure, so it was rechristened *Future Cop* when his Empire Pictures sent it to theaters in that city and others in the Eastern part of the U.S. in summer '85. When the movie later opened in California and other Western states, as well as Canada, *Trancers* was the title again, as it was on the subsequent video releases.

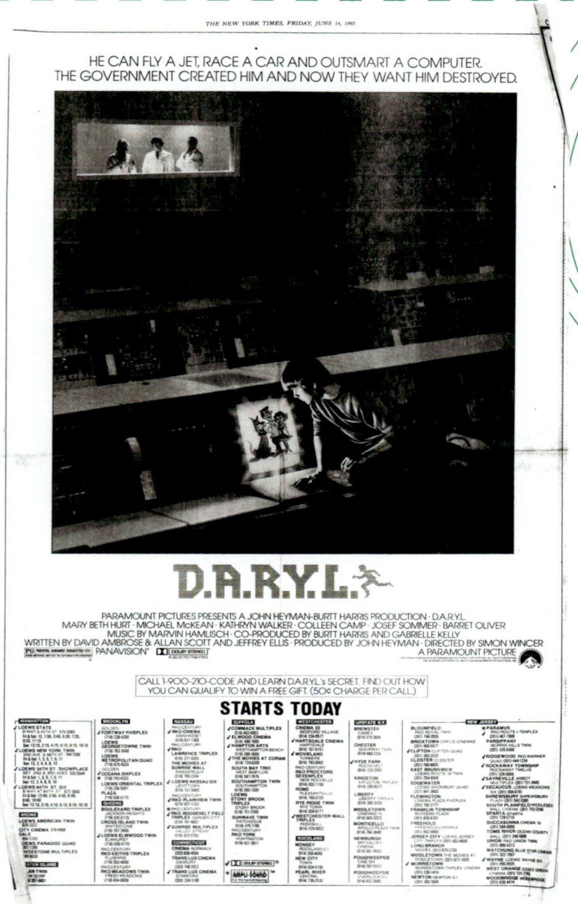

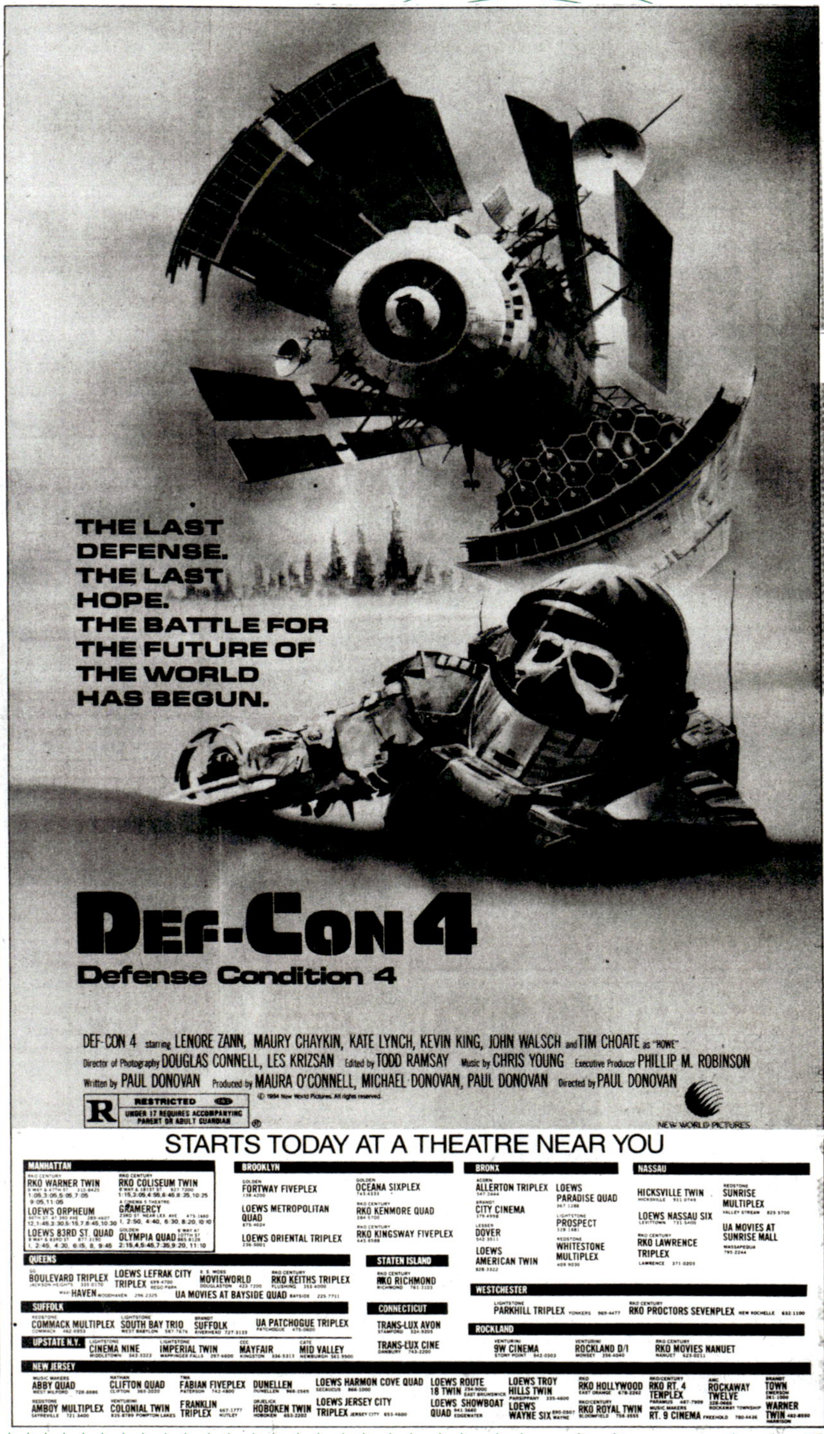
THE LAST DEFENSE. THE LAST HOPE. THE BATTLE FOR THE FUTURE OF THE WORLD HAS BEGUN.
DEF-CON 4
Defense Condition 4
DEF-CON 4 starring LENORE ZANN, MAURY CHAYKIN, KATE LYNCH, KEVIN KING, JOHN WALSCH and TIM CHOATE as "HOWE"
Director of Photography DOUGLAS CONNELL, LES KRIZSAN Edited by TODD RAMSAY Music by CHRIS YOUNG Executive Producer PHILLIP M. ROBINSON
Written by PAUL DONOVAN Produced by MAURA O'CONNELL, MICHAEL DONOVAN, PAUL DONOVAN Directed by PAUL DONOVAN
R RESTRICTED UNDER 17 REQUIRES ACCOMPANYING PARENT OR ADULT GUARDIAN
NEW WORLD PICTURES
STARTS TODAY AT A THEATRE NEAR YOU
MANHATTAN
BROOKLYN
BRONX
NASSAU
QUEENS
STATEN ISLAND
WESTCHESTER
SUFFOLK
CONNECTICUT
ROCKLAND
UPSTATE N.Y.
NEW JERSEY

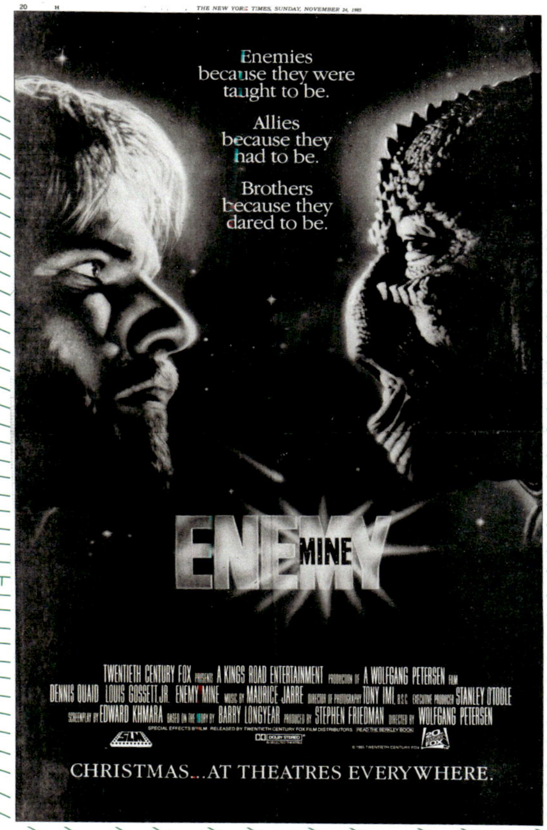
THE NEW YORK TIMES, SUNDAY, NOVEMBER 24, 1985
Enemies because they were taught to be.
Allies because they had to be.
Brothers because they dared to be.
ENEMY MINE
TWENTIETH CENTURY FOX presents A KINGS ROAD ENTERTAINMENT production of A WOLFGANG PETERSEN film
DENNIS QUAID LOUIS GOSSETT, JR. ENEMY MINE music by MAURICE JARRE director of photography TONY IMI B.S.C. executive producer STANLEY O'TOOLE
screenplay by EDWARD KHMARA based on the story by BARRY LONGYEAR produced by STEPHEN FRIEDMAN directed by WOLFGANG PETERSEN
CHRISTMAS...AT THEATRES EVERYWHERE.

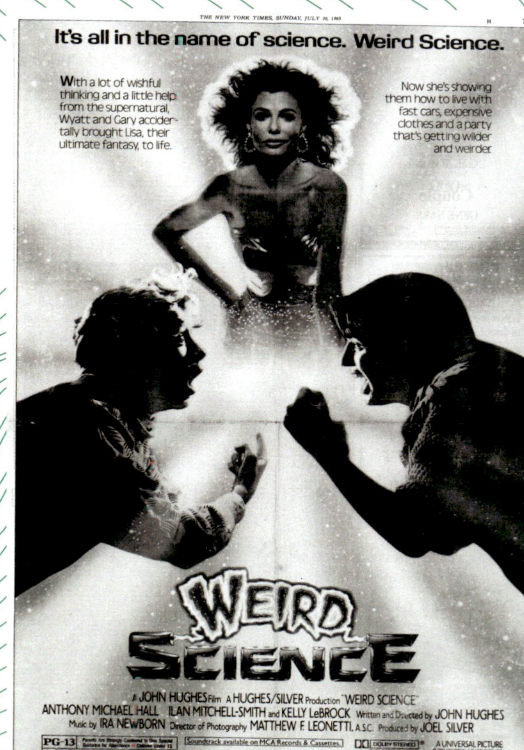
THE NEW YORK TIMES, SUNDAY, JULY 28, 1985
It's all in the name of science. Weird Science.
With a lot of wishful thinking and a little help from the supernatural, Wyatt and Gary accidentally brought Lisa, their ultimate fantasy, to life.
Now she's showing them how to live with fast cars, expensive clothes and a party that's getting wilder and weirder.
WEIRD SCIENCE
A JOHN HUGHES Film A HUGHES/SILVER Production "WEIRD SCIENCE"
ANTHONY MICHAEL HALL ILAN MITCHELL-SMITH and KELLY LeBROCK Written and Directed by JOHN HUGHES
Music by IRA NEWBORN Director of Photography MATTHEW F. LEONETTI, A.S.C. Produced by JOEL SILVER
PG-13
Soundtrack available on MCA Records & Cassettes.
A UNIVERSAL PICTURE

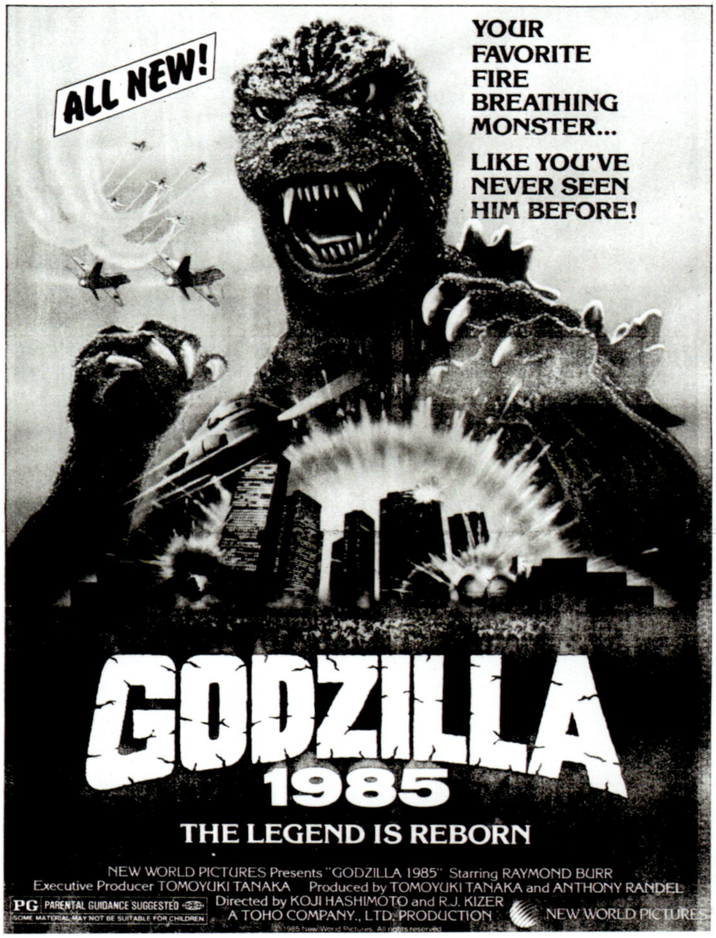

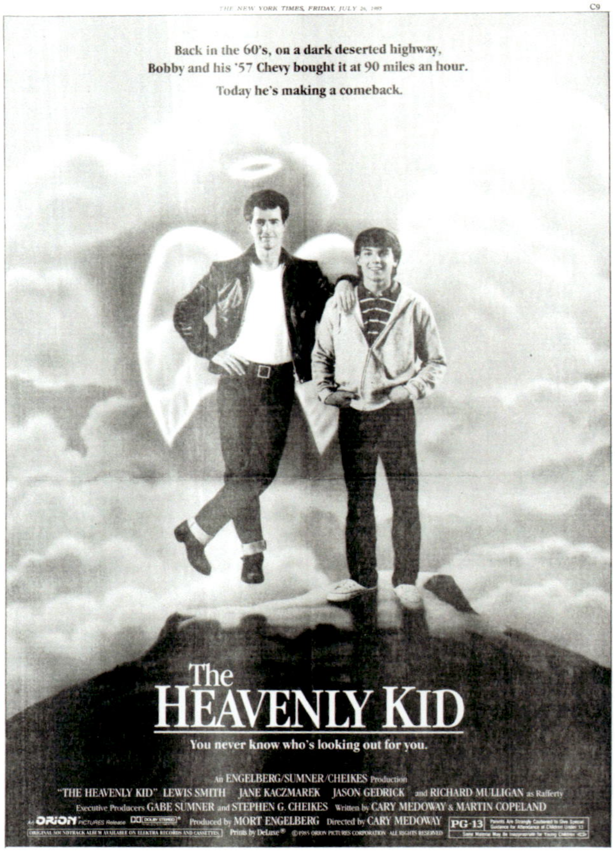

MAD MAX BEYOND THUNDERDOME

If you ask fans of the *Mad Max* series today what the best installment is, it's likely the great majority will say *The Road Warrior*. Then they'll add that *Beyond Thunderdome* has great opening and closing acts, with a knockout titular setpiece and Tina Turner lending fiery support to Mel Gibson, but gets a little sluggish around the middle. Yet when the last part of the trilogy first opened, many critics judged it equal, if not superior, to its predecessor.

"It's not supposed to happen this way. Sequels are not supposed to be better than the movies that inspired them. The third movie in a series isn't supposed to create a world more complex, more visionary and more entertaining than the first two."

–Roger Ebert, *Chicago Sun-Times*

"*Mad Max Beyond Thunderdome*...is the most visually spectacular installment by far, with a few innovations – most notably the one of the title – that are far more elaborate than anything George Miller...has attempted before."

–Janet Maslin, *The New York Times*

"With its violence, punk fashion and sense of humor in overdrive, *Mad Max Beyond Thunderdome* is what high-grade pro football is to other sports. It grabs your attention and screams, 'Watch me!'"

–Gene Siskel, *Chicago Tribune*

"In the end the crazy images and unthinkable brutality creates and communicates a unique, crude poetry that is both primitive and beautiful."

–REX REED, *NEW YORK POST*

"[Turner] isn't a particularly convincing actress, but her warmly amused attitude is fun. Otherwise, *Mad Max Beyond Thunderdome*...is a grim movie that no amount of action can make palatable."

–George Anderson, *Pittsburgh Post-Gazette*

"AN INCREDIBLE, EXCITING AND ORIGINAL ACTION EPIC

that I think is one of the best films of the year."

— Roger Ebert, "AT THE MOVIES"

"Max is madder, tougher and better than ever!"

— Pat Collins, CBS MORNING NEWS, CBS-TV

"A series of films that just keep getting better and better -- 'Mad Max Beyond Thunderdome' is great."

— Gene Siskel, "AT THE MOVIES"

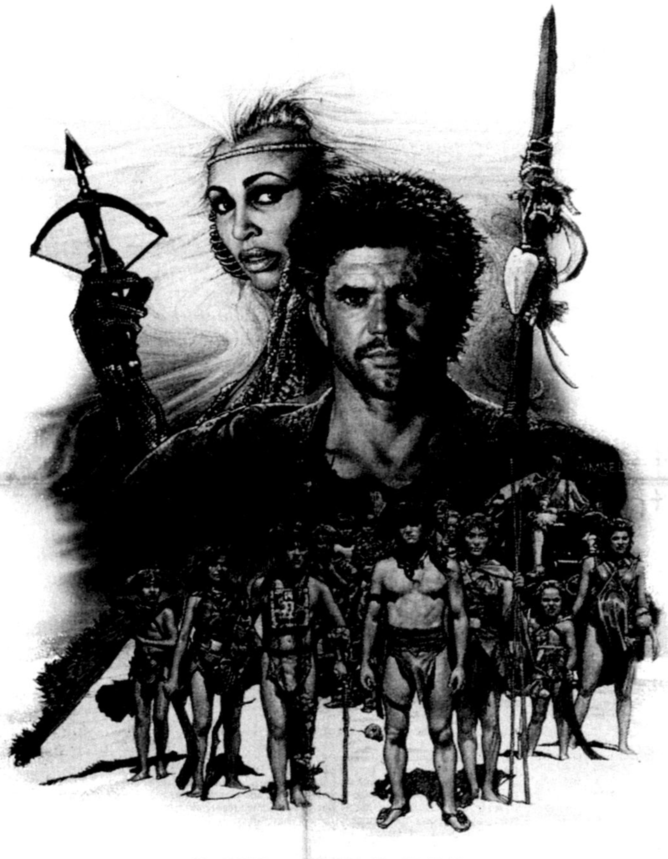

MEL GIBSON IS

MAD MAX BEYOND THUNDERDOME

Starring **TINA TURNER**

KENNEDY MILLER Presents
MEL GIBSON TINA TURNER "MAD MAX BEYOND THUNDERDOME"
Music by MAURICE JARRE Director of Photography DEAN SEMLER A.C.S. Written by TERRY HAYES & GEORGE MILLER
Co-Produced by DOUG MITCHELL and TERRY HAYES Produced by GEORGE MILLER Directed by GEORGE MILLER and GEORGE OGILVIE

PG-13 Parents Are Strongly Cautioned to Give Special Guidance for Attendance of Children Under 13 Some Material May Be Inappropriate for Young Children

ORIGINAL SOUNDTRACK ALBUM ON CAPITOL RECORDS AND TAPES

DOLBY STEREO® IN SELECTED THEATRES

READ THE WARNER PAPERBACK

DISTRIBUTED BY WARNER BROS. A WARNER COMMUNICATIONS COMPANY

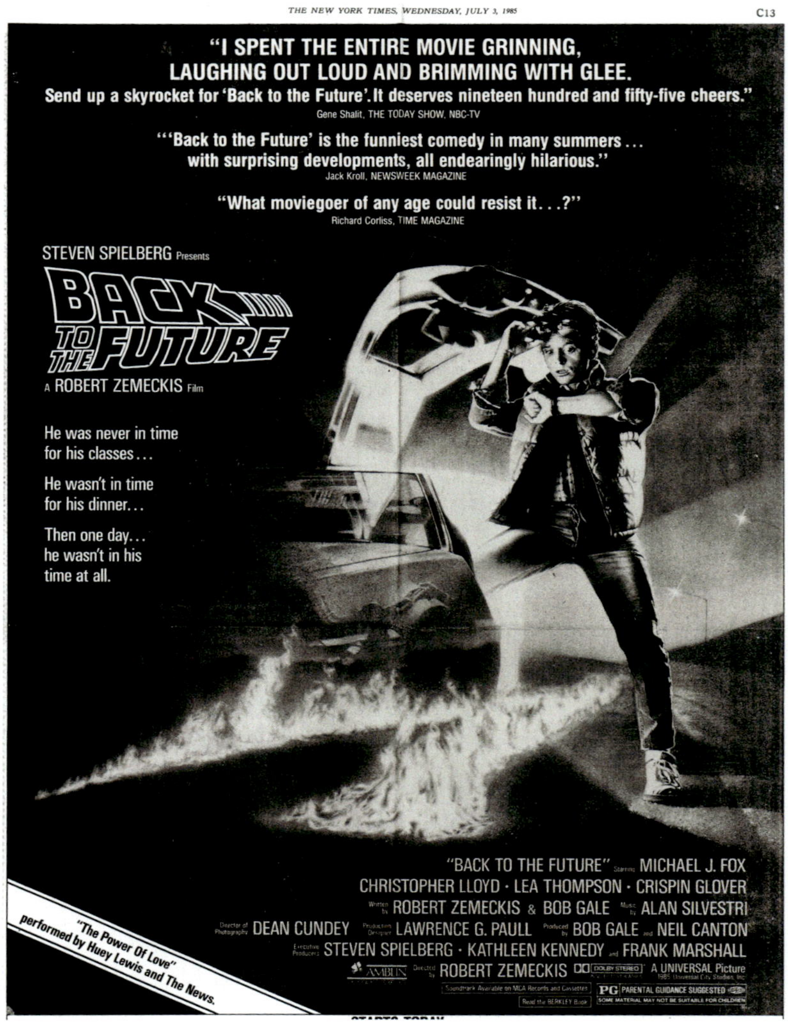

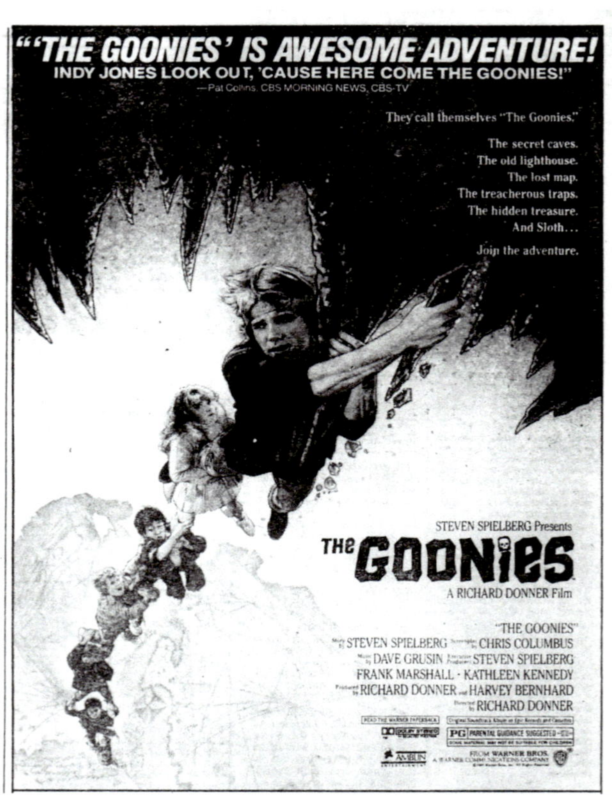

RETURN TO OZ

It's one thing to sequelize a recent success, but Walt Disney Pictures was letting itself in for it when it tackled a long-after-the-fact follow-up to arguably the most beloved fantasy film of all time. Director Walter Murch and his team promised greater fidelity to the source material – L. Frank Baum's books *The Marvelous Land of Oz* and *Ozma of Oz* – but few felt the result, which took an intentionally darker tone, lived up to the wonder and charm of its predecessor.

"Unlike most children's films, this one never stoops to condescension. It respects the intelligence of its audience while providing fresh thrills to keep even the most fidgety moppet awake and glued to the screen."

–Rex Reed, *New York Post*

"[T]hese vistas and characters are not only breathtakingly faithful to the original spirit of Oz, they are beautiful on their own. Yet *Return to Oz* doesn't soar when it so clearly should."

–Sheila Benson, *Los Angeles Times*

"Murch's attempt to capture the harsh, surreal flavor of the Baum stories in a way that doesn't violate memories of the Judy Garland classic is an enormously daring undertaking – and he nearly pulls it off. ... Despite its strengths, however, Disney's $28 million spectacular is uneven and frequently rather cold."

–Rick Lyman, *The Philadelphia Inquirer*

"*Return to Oz* is so lacking in wit and warmth it should leave the audience feeling as emotionally detached as the stone residents of the Emerald City."

–KATHLEEN CARROLL, NEW YORK *DAILY NEWS*

"*Return to* Oz...is the work of ingenious technicians who seem either not to know what gave the original film its magic, or not to care."

–Janet Maslin, *The New York Times*

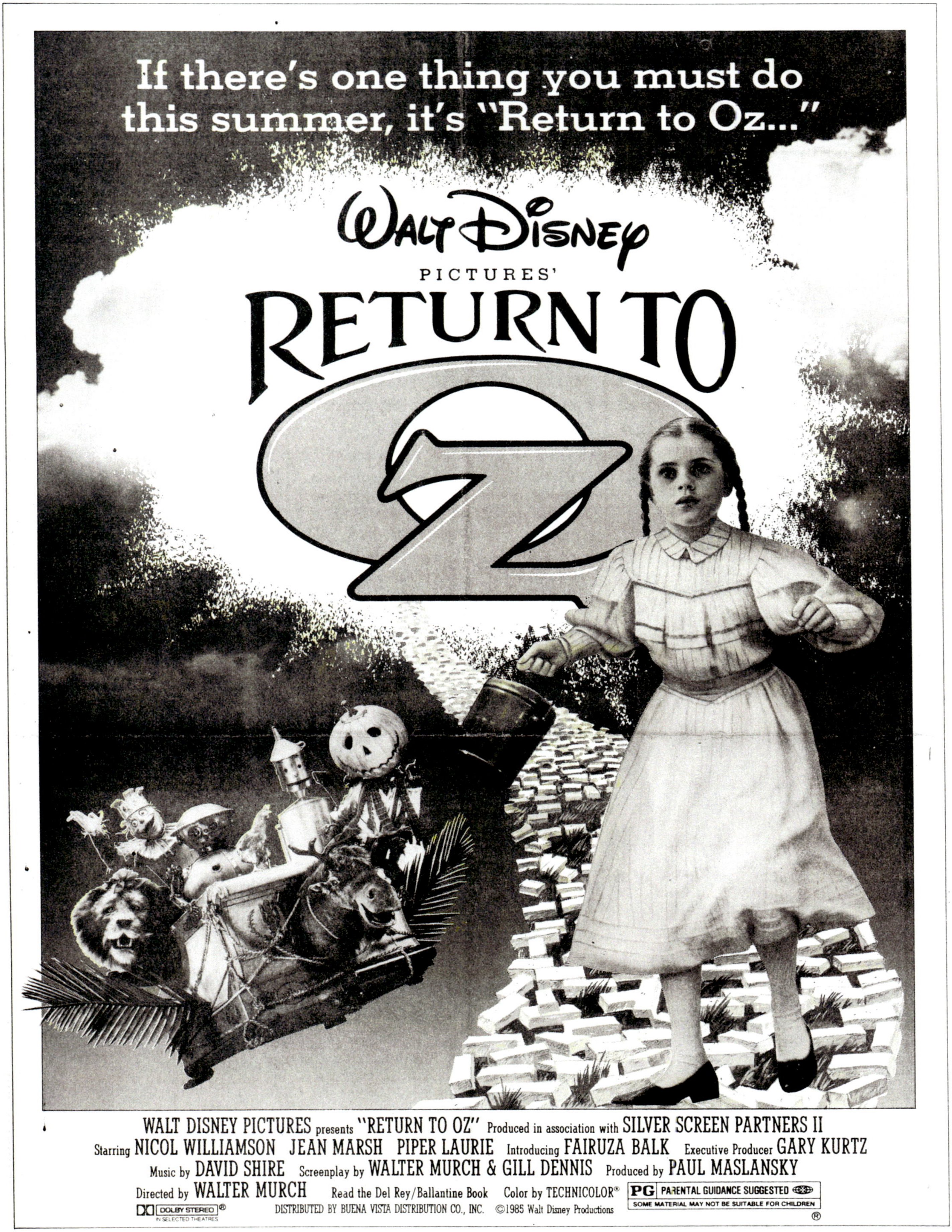
If there's one thing you must do this summer, it's "Return to Oz..."
Walt Disney
PICTURES'
RETURN TO OZ
WALT DISNEY PICTURES presents "RETURN TO OZ" Produced in association with SILVER SCREEN PARTNERS II
Starring NICOL WILLIAMSON JEAN MARSH PIPER LAURIE Introducing FAIRUZA BALK Executive Producer GARY KURTZ
Music by DAVID SHIRE Screenplay by WALTER MURCH & GILL DENNIS Produced by PAUL MASLANSKY
Directed by WALTER MURCH Read the Del Rey/Ballantine Book Color by TECHNICOLOR®
PG PARENTAL GUIDANCE SUGGESTED
SOME MATERIAL MAY NOT BE SUITABLE FOR CHILDREN
DOLBY STEREO®
IN SELECTED THEATRES
DISTRIBUTED BY BUENA VISTA DISTRIBUTION CO., INC. ©1985 Walt Disney Productions

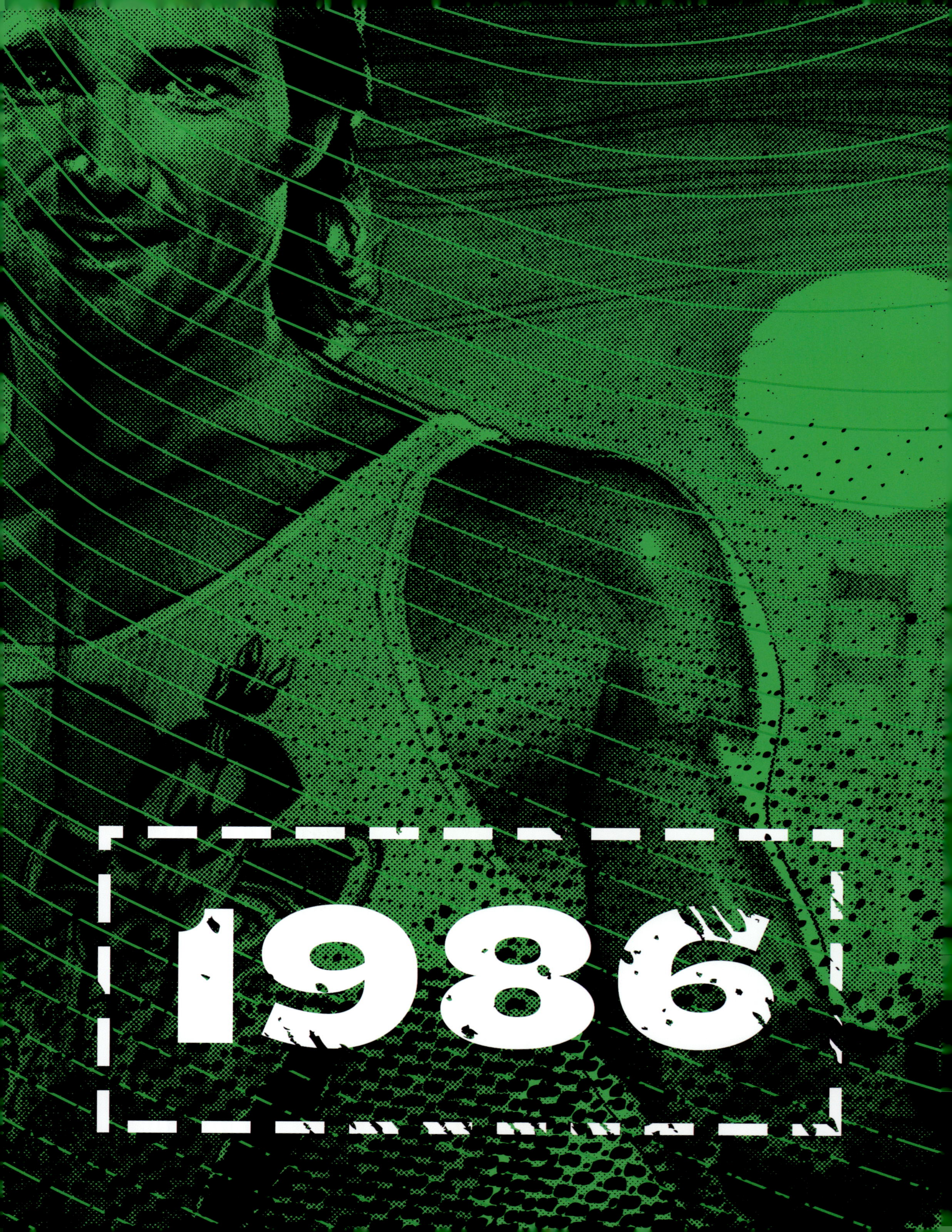
1986

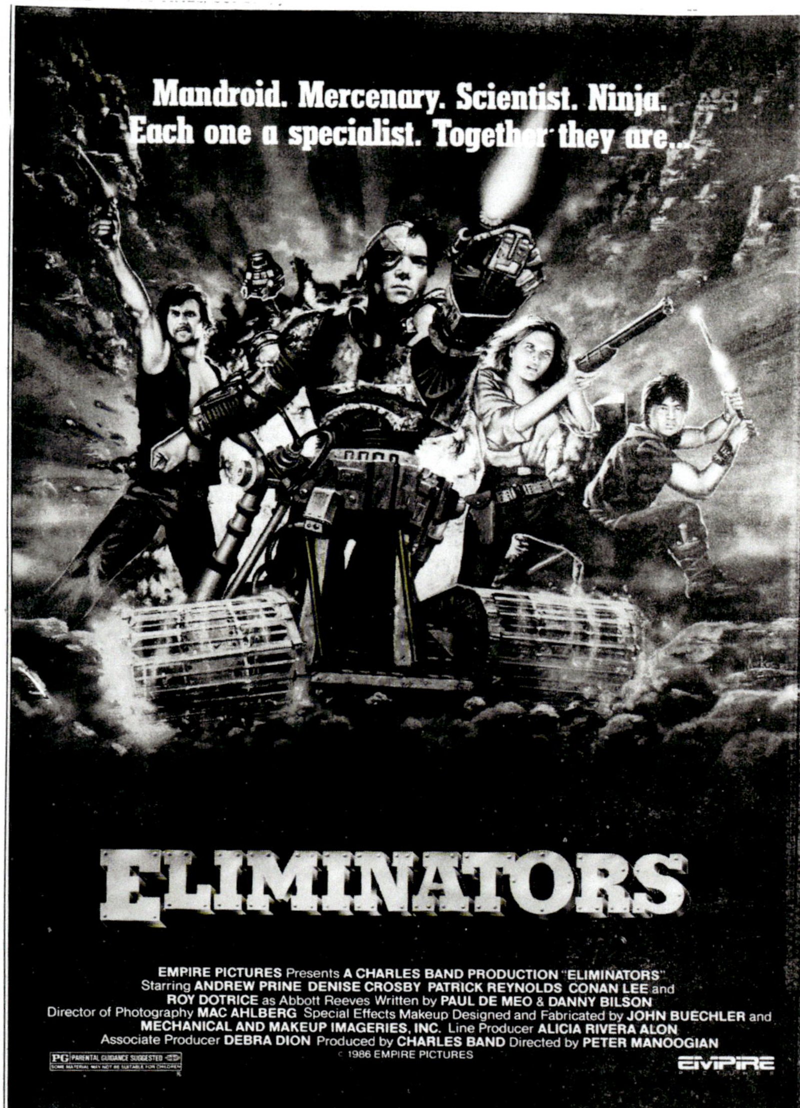

Mandroid. Mercenary. Scientist. Ninja.
Each one a specialist. Together they are...
ELIMINATORS
EMPIRE PICTURES Presents A CHARLES BAND PRODUCTION "ELIMINATORS"
Starring ANDREW PRINE DENISE CROSBY PATRICK REYNOLDS CONAN LEE and
ROY DOTRICE as Abbott Reeves Written by PAUL DE MEO & DANNY BILSON
Director of Photography MAC AHLBERG Special Effects Makeup Designed and Fabricated by JOHN BUECHLER and
MECHANICAL AND MAKEUP IMAGERIES, INC. Line Producer ALICIA RIVERA ALON
Associate Producer DEBRA DION Produced by CHARLES BAND Directed by PETER MANOOGIAN
PG PARENTAL GUIDANCE SUGGESTED
SOME MATERIAL MAY NOT BE SUITABLE FOR CHILDREN
© 1986 EMPIRE PICTURES
EMPIRE

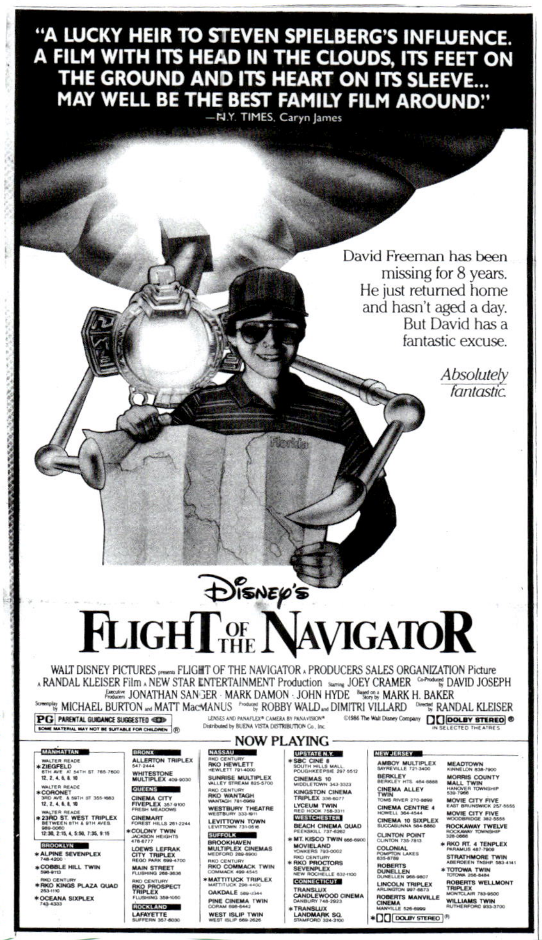

"A LUCKY HEIR TO STEVEN SPIELBERG'S INFLUENCE.
A FILM WITH ITS HEAD IN THE CLOUDS, ITS FEET ON
THE GROUND AND ITS HEART ON ITS SLEEVE...
MAY WELL BE THE BEST FAMILY FILM AROUND."
—N.Y. TIMES, Caryn James
David Freeman has been missing for 8 years. He just returned home and hasn't aged a day. But David has a fantastic excuse.
Absolutely fantastic.
Disney's
FLIGHT OF THE NAVIGATOR
WALT DISNEY PICTURES presents FLIGHT OF THE NAVIGATOR A PRODUCERS SALES ORGANIZATION Picture
A RANDAL KLEISER Film A NEW STAR ENTERTAINMENT Production Starring JOEY CRAMER Co-Produced by DAVID JOSEPH
Executive Producers JONATHAN SANGER · MARK DAMON · JOHN HYDE Based on a Story by MARK H. BAKER
Screenplay by MICHAEL BURTON and MATT MacMANUS Produced by ROBBY WALD and DIMITRI VILLARD Directed by RANDAL KLEISER
PG PARENTAL GUIDANCE SUGGESTED
SOME MATERIAL MAY NOT BE SUITABLE FOR CHILDREN
LENSES AND PANAFLEX® CAMERA BY PANAVISION®
Distributed by BUENA VISTA DISTRIBUTION Co., Inc.
©1986 The Walt Disney Company
DOLBY STEREO IN SELECTED THEATRES
NOW PLAYING

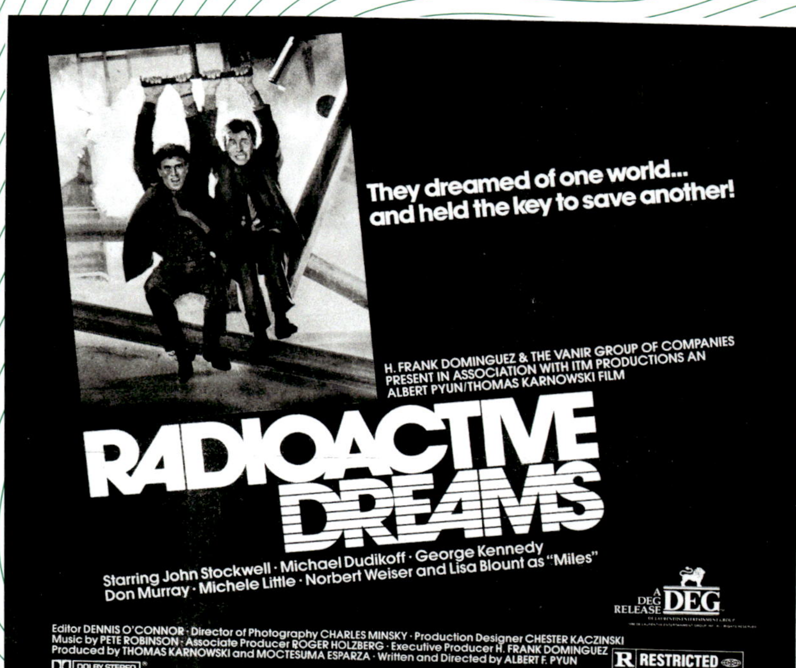

They dreamed of one world...
and held the key to save another!
H. FRANK DOMINGUEZ & THE VANIR GROUP OF COMPANIES
PRESENT IN ASSOCIATION WITH ITM PRODUCTIONS AN
ALBERT PYUN/THOMAS KARNOWSKI FILM
RADIOACTIVE DREAMS
Starring John Stockwell · Michael Dudikoff · George Kennedy
Don Murray · Michele Little · Norbert Weiser and Lisa Blount as "Miles"
A DEG RELEASE DEG
Editor DENNIS O'CONNOR · Director of Photography CHARLES MINSKY · Production Designer CHESTER KACZINSKI
Music by PETE ROBINSON · Associate Producer ROGER HOLZBERG · Executive Producer H. FRANK DOMINGUEZ
Produced by THOMAS KARNOWSKI and MOCTESUMA ESPARZA · Written and Directed by ALBERT F. PYUN
DOLBY STEREO IN SELECTED THEATRES
R RESTRICTED

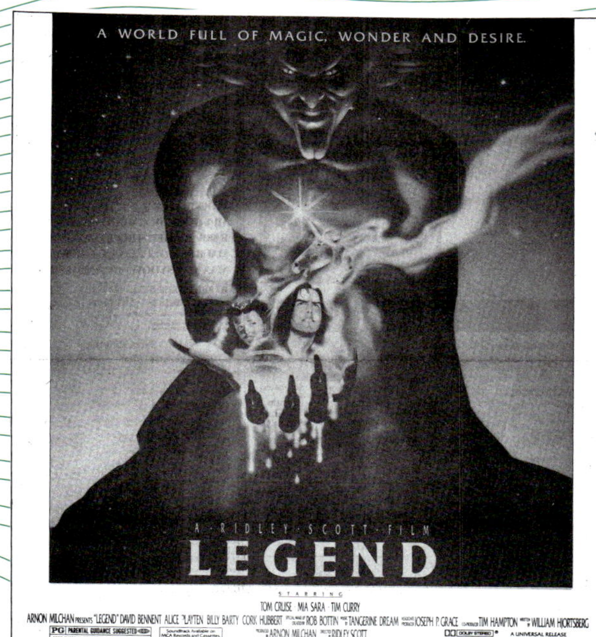

A WORLD FULL OF MAGIC, WONDER AND DESIRE.
A RIDLEY SCOTT FILM
LEGEND
STARRING
TOM CRUISE · MIA SARA · TIM CURRY
ARNON MILCHAN PRESENTS "LEGEND" DAVID BENNENT ALICE PLAYTEN BILLY BARTY CORK HUBBERT ROB BOTTIN TANGERINE DREAM JOSEPH P. GRACE TIM HAMPTON WILLIAM HJORTSBERG
PG PARENTAL GUIDANCE SUGGESTED
SOME MATERIAL MAY NOT BE SUITABLE FOR CHILDREN
Soundtrack Available on MCA Records and Cassettes.
ARNON MILCHAN RIDLEY SCOTT
DOLBY STEREO
A UNIVERSAL RELEASE

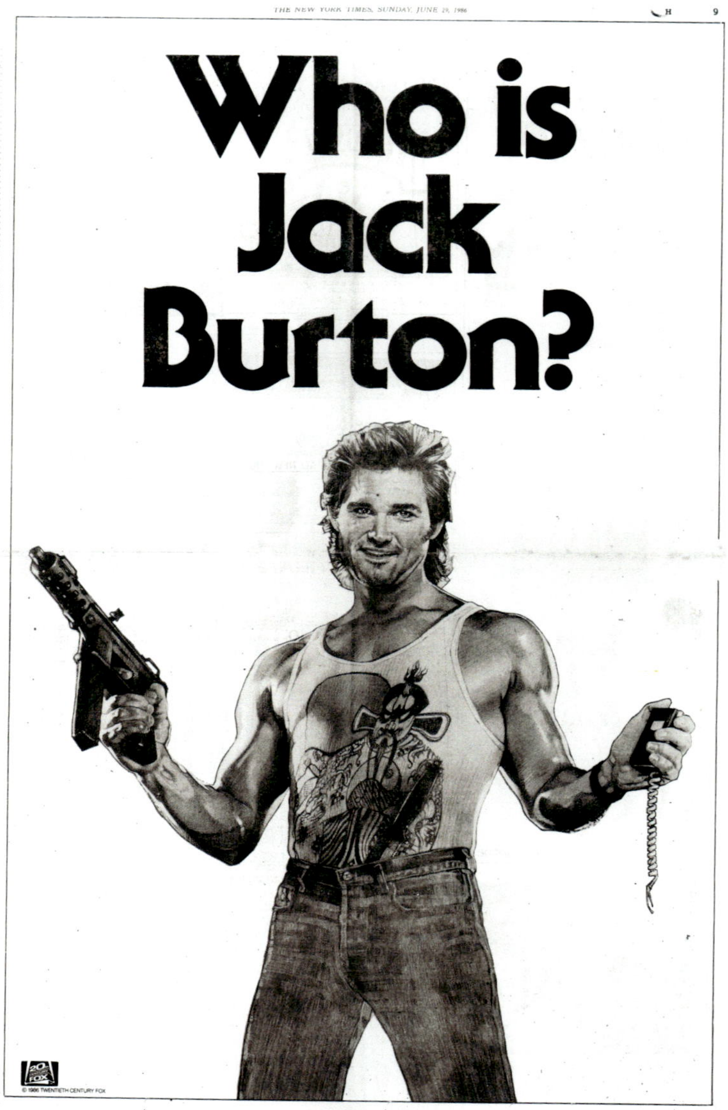

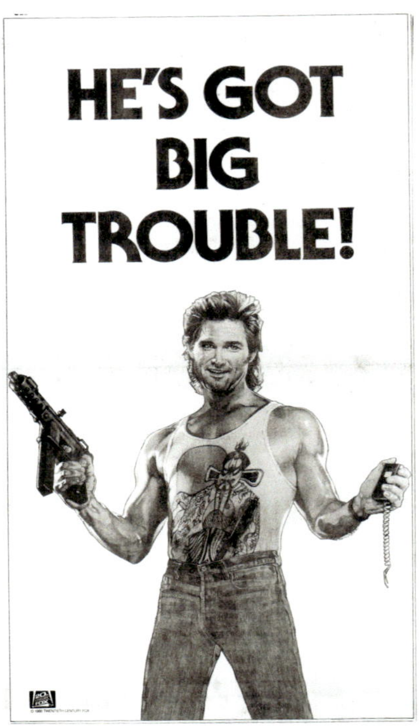

BIG TROUBLE IN LITTLE CHINA

Never mind *The Matrix* and *Charlie's Angels* – the first big-studio action epic to immerse itself in the tropes of Asian genre cinema was John Carpenter's wild descent into a supernatural world beneath San Francisco's Chinatown. Having rebounded from the critical slings and arrows hurled at *The Thing* with the modestly successful *Christine* and the critically beloved *Starman*, Carpenter unfortunately saw his latest team-up with Kurt Russell largely derided by critics who had no idea about his influences, didn't get what he was after, and apparently only wised up later. As with *The Thing*, Carpenter would only find appreciation for *Big Trouble* in the years following its release.

"What matters is the stunts and the spirit, and this latest set of exotic exploits of an indomitable hero (Kurt Russell) and a spunky heroine (Kim Cattrall) gives good value. ... In kidding the flavorsome proceedings even as he gets the juice out of them, the director, John Carpenter, is conspicuously with it."

–Walter Goodman, *The New York Times*

"Though the film does contain a few minutes of patented Carpenter camera magic, it is unable to sustain either story or character. For all its flash and color, it is a dull film—an artless dig in the Spielberg garden."

–Rick Kogan, *Chicago Tribune*

"In the press kit, the movie is described as a 'mystical action-adventure-comedy-kung-fu-monster-ghost story.' Actually, it's none of the above. It's just another movie that can't make up its 6-year-old mind."

–MICHAEL BLOWEN, *THE BOSTON GLOBE*

"*Big Trouble in Little China* is a try at mock-Oriental movie magic that goes leaden about a third of the way through – and finally detonates into great, whomping fireballs of overcalculated, underinspired absurdity."

–Michael Wilmington, *Los Angeles Times*

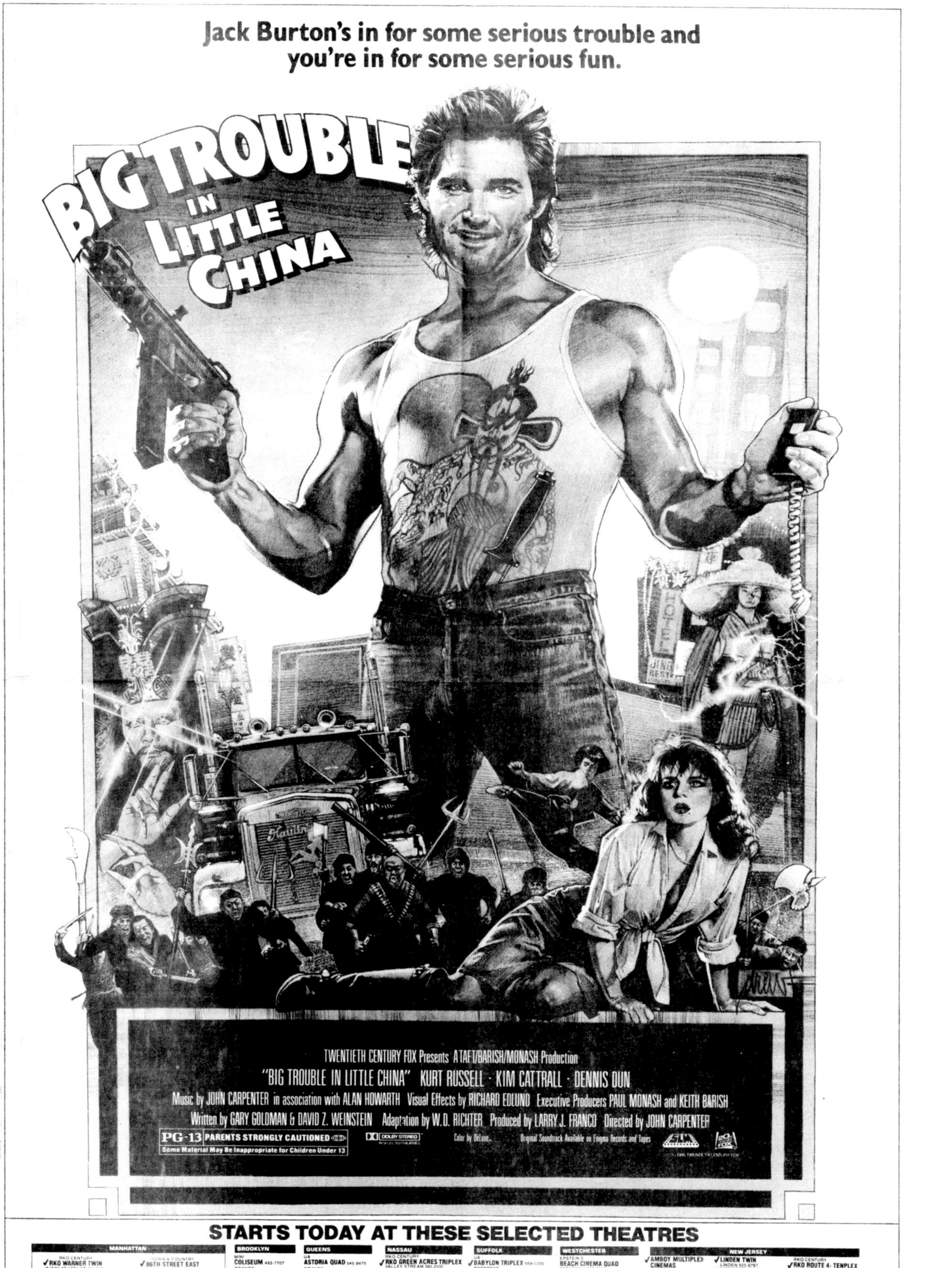

Jack Burton's in for some serious trouble and
you're in for some serious fun.
BIG TROUBLE IN LITTLE CHINA
TWENTIETH CENTURY FOX Presents A TAFT/BARISH/MONASH Production
"BIG TROUBLE IN LITTLE CHINA" KURT RUSSELL · KIM CATTRALL · DENNIS DUN
Music by JOHN CARPENTER in association with ALAN HOWARTH Visual Effects by RICHARD EDLUND Executive Producers PAUL MONASH and KEITH BARISH
Written by GARY GOLDMAN & DAVID Z. WEINSTEIN Adaptation by W.D. RICHTER Produced by LARRY J. FRANCO Directed by JOHN CARPENTER
PG-13 PARENTS STRONGLY CAUTIONED
Some Material May Be Inappropriate for Children Under 13
DOLBY STEREO
Color by DeLuxe.
Original Soundtrack Available on Enigma Records and Tapes
STARTS TODAY AT THESE SELECTED THEATRES
MANHATTAN
RKO CENTURY ✓RKO WARNER TWIN B'WAY AT 47TH ST 315-8425 12, 1, 2, 3, 4, 5, 6, 7, 8, 9, 10
TOWN & COUNTRY ✓86TH STREET EAST BETW. 2ND & 3RD AVE 249-1144 1, 2:45, 4:35, 6:25, 8:20, 10:15
AN RKO CINEMA 5 THEATRE ✓PLAZA 58TH ST E. OF MADISON 355-3320 12, 2, 4, 6, 8, 10, 12 MID.
B.S. MOSS ✓MOVIELAND 8TH STREET TRIPLEX 8TH ST & UNIVERSITY PLACE 477-6600 1:10, 3:10, 5:10, 7:10, 9:10, 11:10
LESSER NOVA B'WAY AND 147TH ST 862-5728 5:15, 9:20
RKO CENTURY RKO COLISEUM TWIN B'WAY AND 181ST ST 927-7200 1:15, 3:15, 5:15, 7:15, 9:10
BRONX
MINI CINEMA CENTRE 292-3893
UA INTERBORO QUAD 792-2100
LESSER KENT 992-9330
EPSTEIN'S PALACE TWIN 829-3900
✓UA VALENTINE 584-9583
REDSTONE ✓WHITESTONE MULTIPLEX CINEMAS 409-9030
BROOKLYN
MINI COLISEUM 492-7707
BRANDT COMMODORE 384-7259
RKO CENTURY ✓RKO KENMORE QUAD 284-5700
RKO CENTURY ✓RKO KINGS PLAZA QUAD 253-1111
UA MARBORO QUAD 232-4000
✓LOEWS METROPOLITAN QUAD 875-4024
✓RIDGEWOOD 821-5993
QUEENS
UA ASTORIA QUAD 545-9470
BRANDT ✓CINEMA CITY FIVEPLEX FRESH MEADOWS 357-9100
COLONY JACKSON HEIGHTS 478-8777
UA MIDWAY QUAD FOREST HILLS 261-8572
B.S. MOSS ✓MOVIE WORLD DOUGLASTON 423-7200
UA ✓MOVIES AT BAYSIDE BAYSIDE 225-7711
RKO CENTURY ✓RKO PROSPECT TRIPLEX FLUSHING 359-1050
ALSO AT THEATRES IN UPSTATE N.Y.
NASSAU
RKO CENTURY ✓RKO GREEN ACRES TRIPLEX VALLEY STREAM 561-2100
UA ✓MANHASSET TRIPLEX 627-7887
✓UA MEADOWBROOK QUAD EAST MEADOW 735-7552
✓UA MOVIES AT SUNRISE MALL MASSAPEQUA 795-2244
TOWN & COUNTRY ✓MID-PLAZA CINEMA 6 HICKSVILLE 433-2400
STUDIO ONE LYNBROOK 599-1444
CONNECTICUT
HIWAY CINEMA BRIDGEPORT 378-0014
✓TRANSLUX CINE DANBURY 743-2200
✓TRANSLUX PLAZA CINEMA GREENWICH 869-4030
SUFFOLK
UA ✓BABYLON TRIPLEX 669-0200
REDSTONE ✓BROOKHAVEN MULTIPLEX CINEMAS MEDFORD 289-8900
REDSTONE ✓COMMACK MULTIPLEX CINEMAS COMMACK 462-6953
UA ✓EASTHAMPTON CINEMAS EASTHAMPTON 324-0448
RKO CENTURY ✓RKO MALL SMITH HAVEN 724-9550
BRANDT ✓MATTITUCK 298-4400
UA MOVIES AT CORAM 736-6200
UA ✓PATCHOGUE TRIPLEX 475-0600
UA ROCKY POINT D.I. 744-8900
WESTCHESTER
EPSTEIN'S BEACH CINEMA QUAD PEEKSKILL 737-6262
GENERAL CINEMA ✓HARTSDALE CINEMA QUAD HARTSDALE 761-6151
UA ✓MAMARONECK FOUR 698-2200
B.S. MOSS ✓MOVIELAND YONKERS 793-0002
UA ✓THE MOVIES AT JEFFERSON VALLEY 245-0220
RKO CENTURY ✓RKO PROCTORS SEVENPLEX NEW ROCHELLE 632-1100
STATEN ISLAND
UA ISLAND TWIN NEW SPRINGVILLE 761-6666
✓ DOLBY STEREO ®
NEW JERSEY
✓AMBOY MULTIPLEX CINEMAS SAYREVILLE 721-3400
✓BRUNSWICK SQUARE TWIN EAST BRUNSWICK 238-2998
CINEMA UNION CITY 865-5600
✓CINEMA 23 CEDAR GROVE 239-1462
✓CINEMA CENTRE BRICKTOWN 477-6661
CLINTON POINT CLINTON 735-7813
✓ESSEX GREEN TRIPLEX W. ORANGE 731-7755
✓FABIAN FIVEPLEX PATERSON 742-4800
✓LINDEN TWIN LINDEN 925-6787
✓LINWOOD TWIN FORT LEE 944-6900
✓MENLO PARK TWIN CINEMA EDISON 549-6767
✓MORRIS COUNTY MALL TWIN 539-7966 HANOVER TOWNSHIP
✓MOVIES MIDDLETOWN MIDDLETOWN 671-1020
✓PASCACK WESTWOOD 664-3200
RIALTO TRIPLEX WESTFIELD 232-1288
✓ROCKAWAY TWELVE ROCKAWAY TOWNSHIP 328-0666
ROUTE 9 CINEMAS FREEHOLD 780-4436
RKO CENTURY ✓RKO ROUTE 4- TENPLEX PARAMUS 487-7909
SHREWSBURY TRIPLEX SHREWSBURY 542-5395
SOMERVILLE CIRCLE TRIPLEX RARITAN 526-0101
✓TOTOWA TWIN TOTOWA 256-8484
RKO CENTURY ✓RKO WARNER QUAD RIDGEWOOD 444-1234
ROCKLAND
ROUTE 59 NANUET 623-3355
303 D.I. ORANGEBURG 359-2021
WATCH THE "BIG TROUBLE IN LITTLE CHINA" "NIGHT FLIGHT" SPECIAL MIDNITE, JULY 4TH ON THE USA NETWORK.

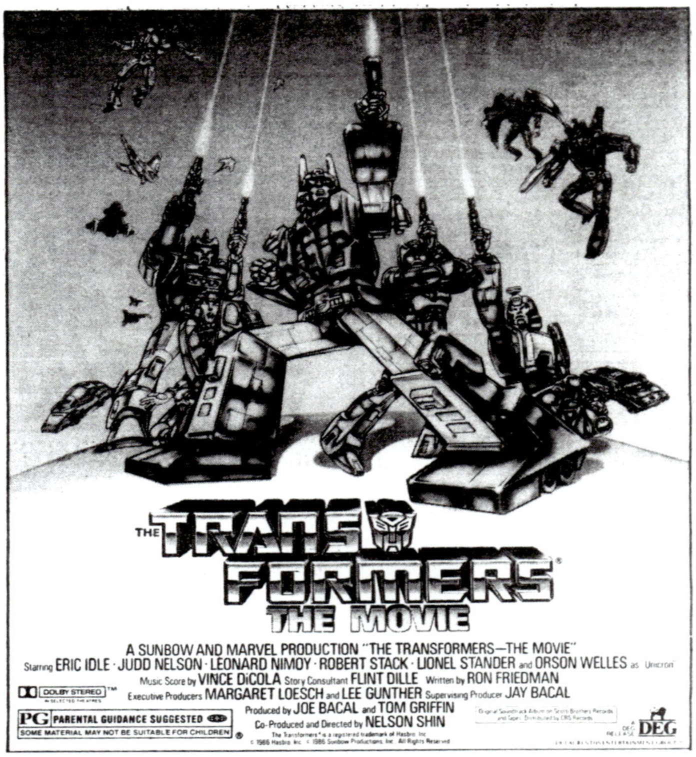

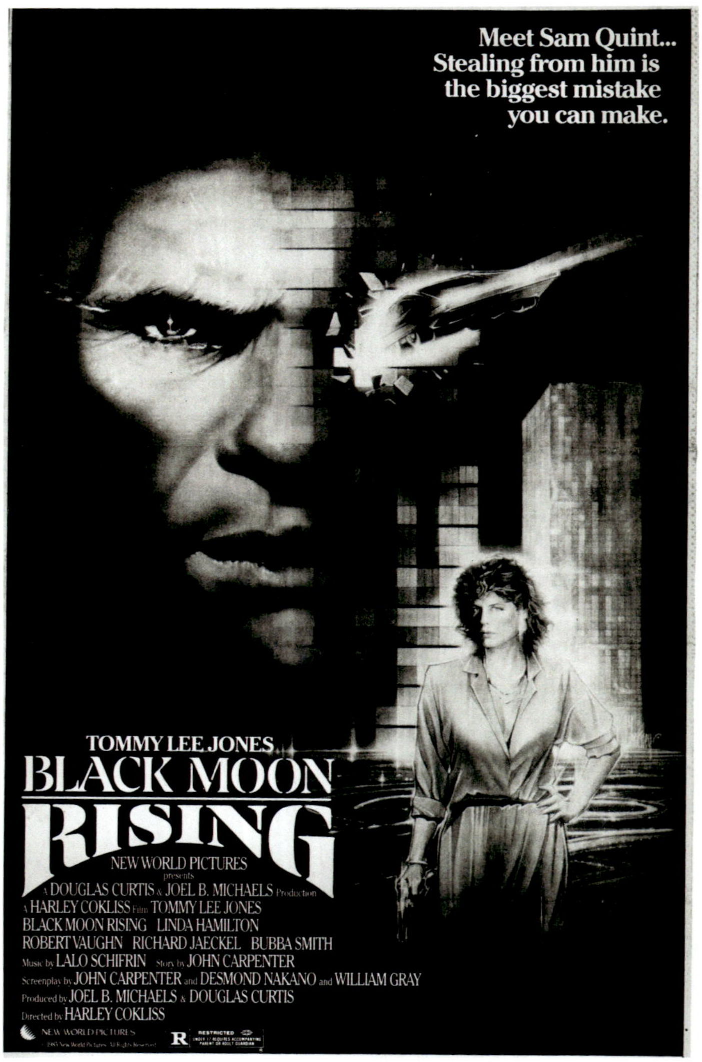

HIGHLANDER

There can be only one? Well, not really, since *Highlander* – the Chistopher Lambert vehicle about immortal, sword-wielding Scotsmen – wound up spawning sequels, multiple TV series and more. Anyone at the time it first opened would have found that immortality unlikely, however, given the soft box office and savage reviews.

"The combination of sight and sound is often thrilling. ... But the plot brewed up by Gregory Widen is just too hard to swallow."

–Malcolm L. Johnson, *Hartford Courant*

"Since none of the characters makes sense even on the movie's own terms, *Highlander* keeps on exploding for almost two hours, with nothing at stake."

–Walter Goodman, *The New York Times*

"It could well be another three centuries before anyone can again muster the timeless stupidity found in *Highlander*."

–DESMOND RYAN, *PHILADELPHIA INQUIRER*

"'He's a Highlander, by God, and the last sound he hears won't be that of a wailing woman.' Feminists may shudder to hear this line, but they should be brave: The last sound the makers of *Highlander* will hear is that of a groaning audience."

–Michael Sragow, *San Francisco Examiner*

"About halfway through...*Highlander*, one character talks about how it was the custom during ancient times to throw babies into a pit of hungry dogs. Well, there were more than a few times during this hyperviolent film in which I felt as if I were a baby being thrown to a dog of a movie."

–Gene Siskel, *Chicago Tribune*

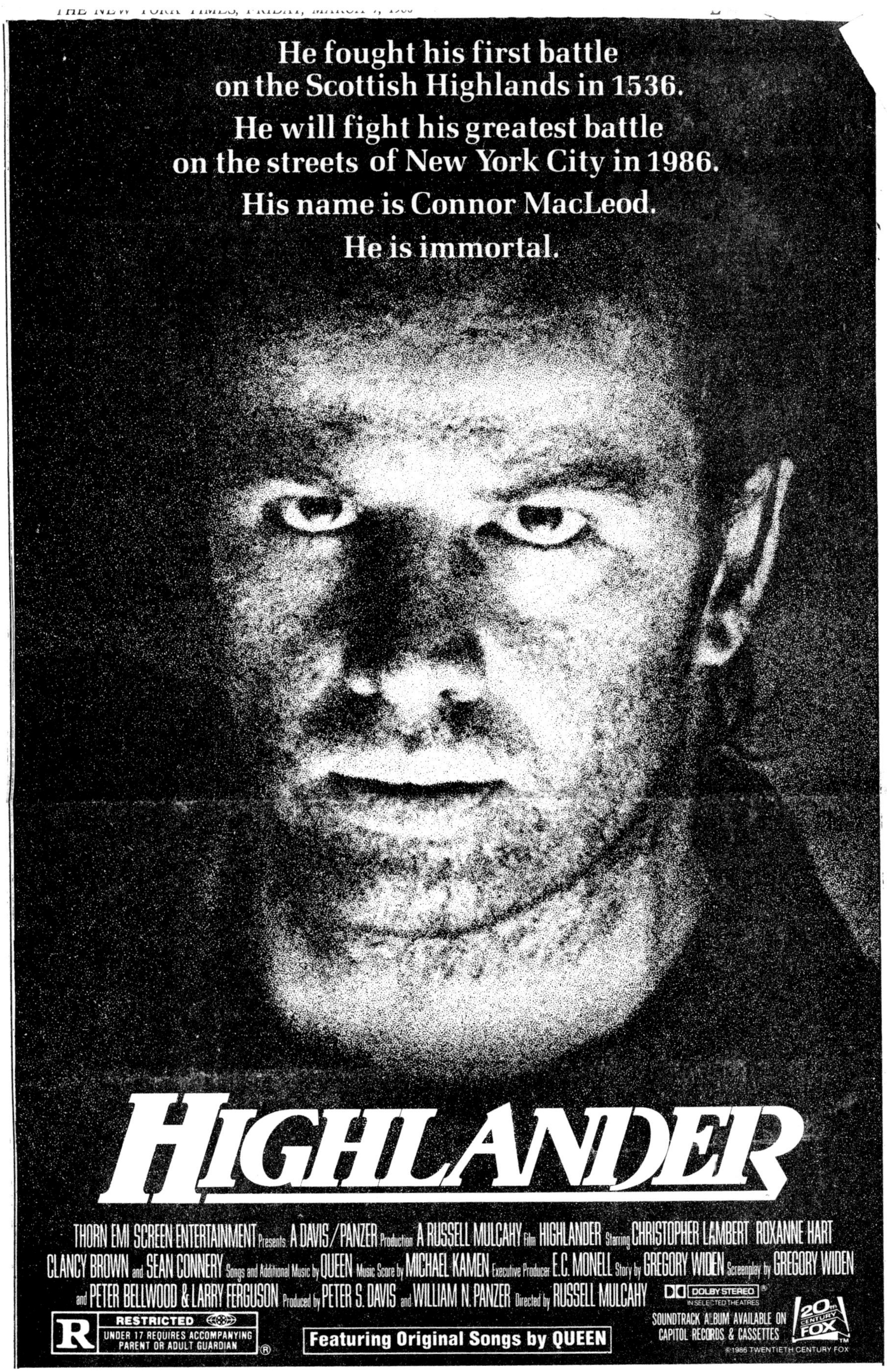
He fought his first battle
on the Scottish Highlands in 1536.
He will fight his greatest battle
on the streets of New York City in 1986.
His name is Connor MacLeod.
He is immortal.
HIGHLANDER
THORN EMI SCREEN ENTERTAINMENT Presents A DAVIS/PANZER Production A RUSSELL MULCAHY Film HIGHLANDER Starring CHRISTOPHER LAMBERT ROXANNE HART CLANCY BROWN and SEAN CONNERY Songs and Additional Music by QUEEN Music Score by MICHAEL KAMEN Executive Producer E.C. MONELL Story by GREGORY WIDEN Screenplay by GREGORY WIDEN and PETER BELLWOOD & LARRY FERGUSON Produced by PETER S. DAVIS and WILLIAM N. PANZER Directed by RUSSELL MULCAHY
DOLBY STEREO IN SELECTED THEATRES
R RESTRICTED UNDER 17 REQUIRES ACCOMPANYING PARENT OR ADULT GUARDIAN
Featuring Original Songs by QUEEN
SOUNDTRACK ALBUM AVAILABLE ON CAPITOL RECORDS & CASSETTES
20th CENTURY FOX
©1986 TWENTIETH CENTURY FOX

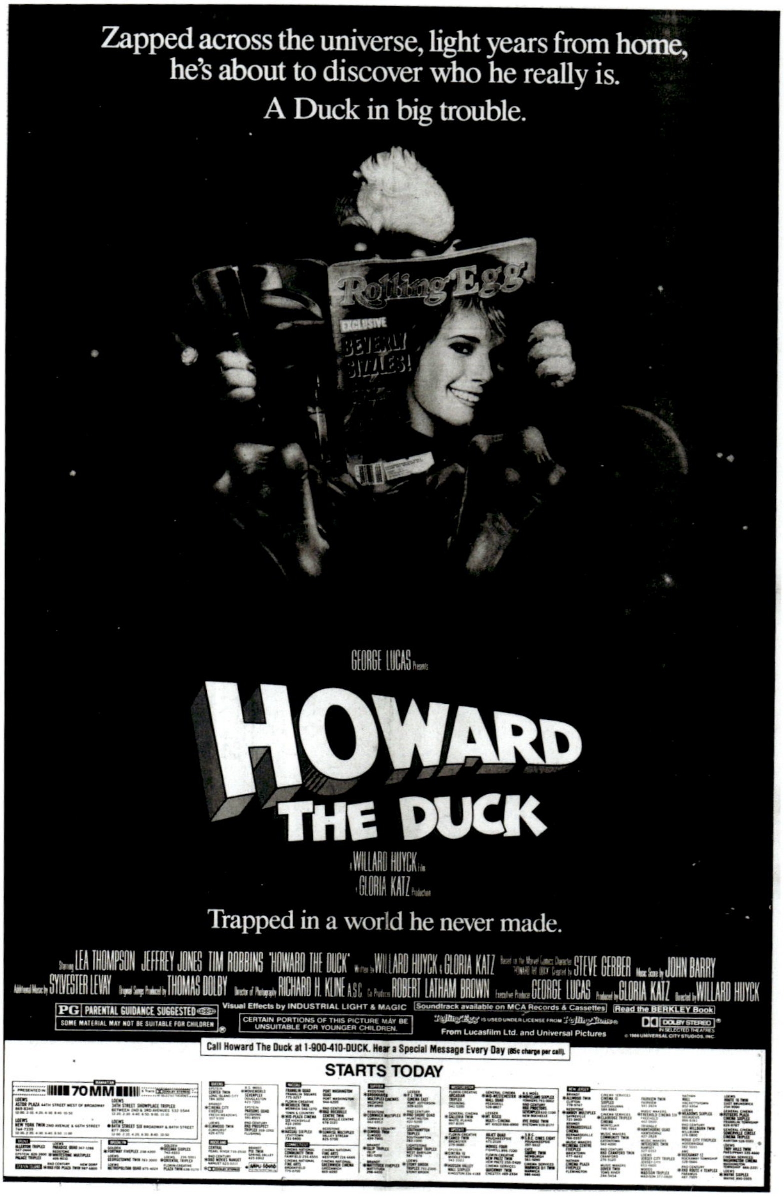

HOWARD THE DUCK

If any film in this book is synonymous with cinematic disaster, it's probably producer George Lucas' unfortunate attempt to give Steve Gerber's sarcastic Marvel Comics character a flashy screen showcase. Like pretty much every '80s movie that got trashed at the time of release, *Howard the Duck* now has a flock of followers who insist it has been underappreciated – though it took a while to find a reviewer who harbored that opinion in '86.

"...*Howard the Duck* isn't as bad as you've probably heard. It is fairly entertaining, if insistently on the juvenile level, and the special effects are more than just ducky."

–Ron Cowan, Salem, OR *Statesman-Journal*

"The surprise is that Howard turns out to be dispensable in his own movie. *Howard the Duck* begins as a mild satire about a duck who fell to earth, but midway through, the star is upstaged by horrifying demons and dazzling light shows."

–Caryn James, *The New York Times*

"Howard is about as lovable as a dishwasher. The movie depends on Howard's irresistibility, yet there's nothing in the character to respond to."

–Dave Kehr, *Chicago Tribune*

"'Hope,' wrote Emily Dickinson, 'is the thing with feathers.' Obviously, she hadn't seen *Howard the Duck*. ... [It's] like a crash course in What's Wrong with American Movies."

–STEPHEN HUNTER, *THE BALTIMORE SUN*

"This leaden duck movie drives you so daffy that, at one screening, a distinguished colleague stood up and turned to the audience in the manner of a college professor. 'Any questions?' he asked."

–Kathleen Carroll, New York *Daily News*

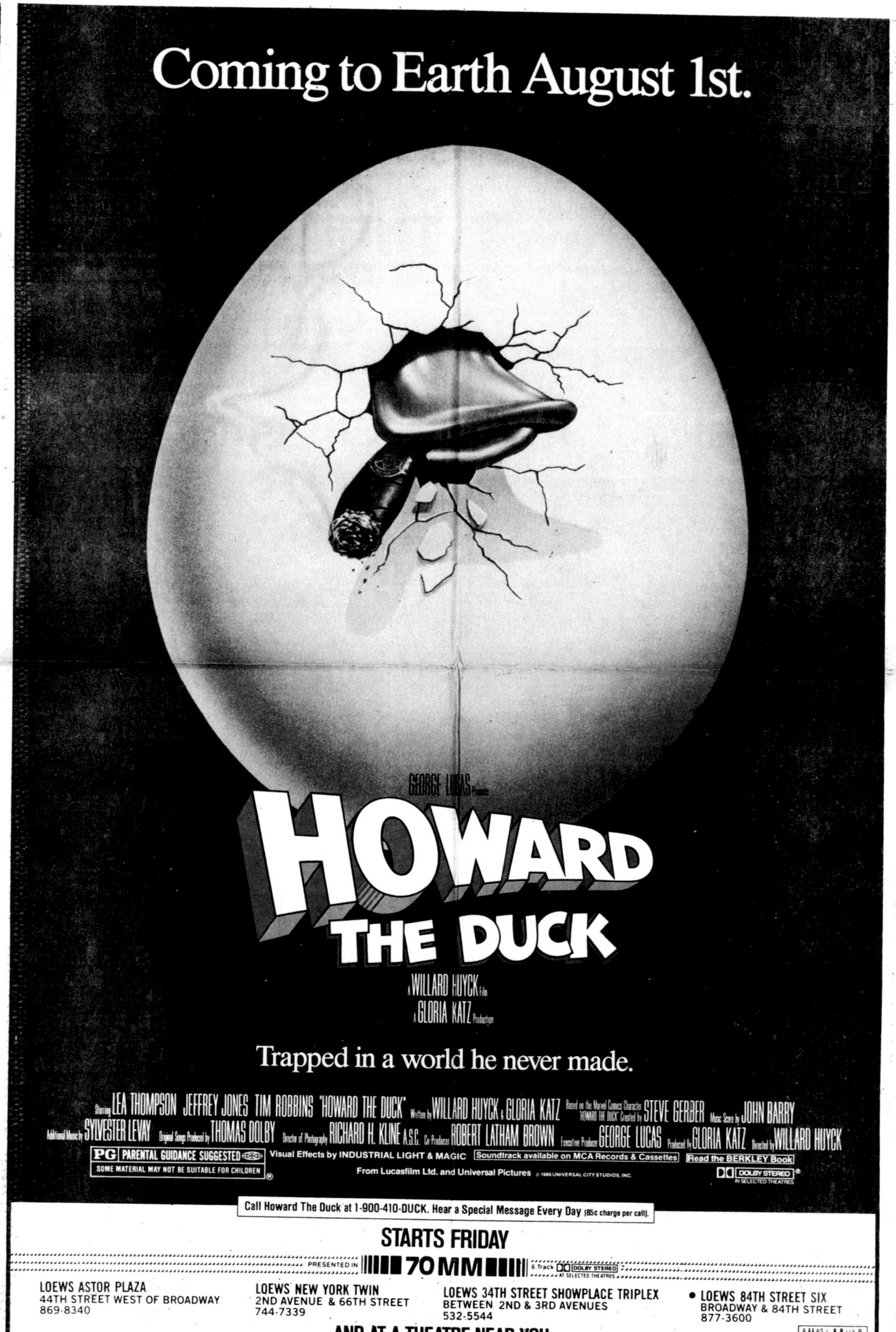
Coming to Earth August 1st.
GEORGE LUCAS Presents
HOWARD THE DUCK
A WILLARD HUYCK Film
A GLORIA KATZ Production
Trapped in a world he never made.
Starring LEA THOMPSON JEFFREY JONES TIM ROBBINS "HOWARD THE DUCK" Written by WILLARD HUYCK & GLORIA KATZ Based on the Marvel Comics Character "HOWARD THE DUCK" Created by STEVE GERBER Music Score by JOHN BARRY
Additional Music by SYLVESTER LEVAY Original Songs Produced by THOMAS DOLBY Director of Photography RICHARD H. KLINE A.S.C. Co-Producer ROBERT LATHAM BROWN Executive Producer GEORGE LUCAS Produced by GLORIA KATZ Directed by WILLARD HUYCK
PG PARENTAL GUIDANCE SUGGESTED
SOME MATERIAL MAY NOT BE SUITABLE FOR CHILDREN
Visual Effects by INDUSTRIAL LIGHT & MAGIC
Soundtrack available on MCA Records & Cassettes
Read the BERKLEY Book
From Lucasfilm Ltd. and Universal Pictures © 1986 UNIVERSAL CITY STUDIOS, INC.
DOLBY STEREO IN SELECTED THEATRES
Call Howard The Duck at 1-900-410-DUCK. Hear a Special Message Every Day (85c charge per call).
STARTS FRIDAY
PRESENTED IN 70MM
6 Track DOLBY STEREO AT SELECTED THEATRES
LOEWS ASTOR PLAZA
44TH STREET WEST OF BROADWAY
869-8340
LOEWS NEW YORK TWIN
2ND AVENUE & 66TH STREET
744-7339
LOEWS 34TH STREET SHOWPLACE TRIPLEX
BETWEEN 2ND & 3RD AVENUES
532-5544
• LOEWS 84TH STREET SIX
BROADWAY & 84TH STREET
877-3600
AND AT A THEATRE NEAR YOU
• AMPLI-SOUND For the hard-of-hearing

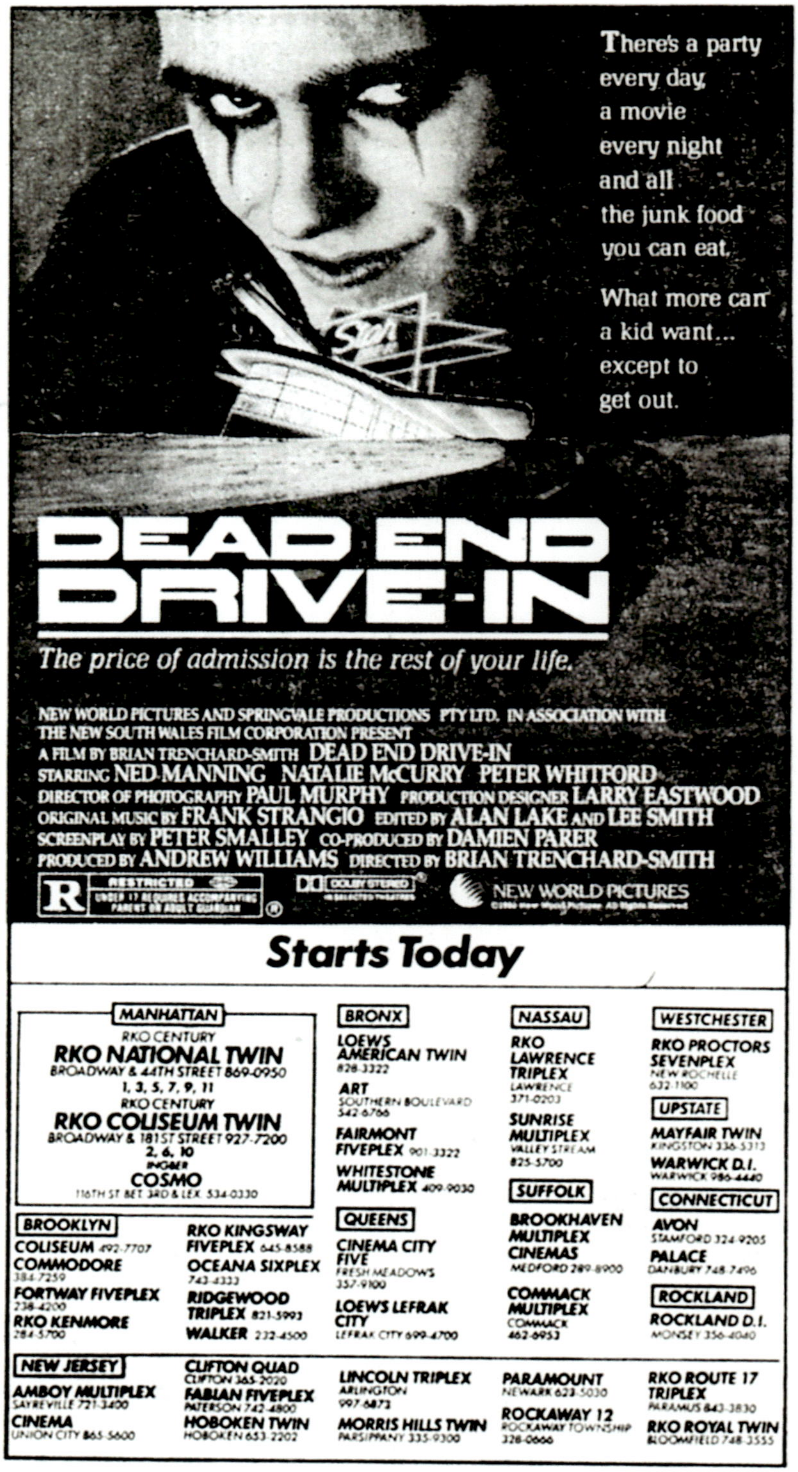

LABYRINTH

Two of the majordomos of screen fantasy, Jim Henson and George Lucas, got together for this excursion into a world of animatronic beings, bringing along an otherworldly human, David Bowie, to play the villain. For this teenage viewer, the main appeal was seeing Jennifer Connelly again – who knew she'd have such a career after *Creepers*? Just as with Henson's *The Dark Crystal*, not all critics were beguiled with the characters, living or puppeteered.

"Jim Henson's *Labyrinth* would be an amazing movie if only for the advances it represents in the technology of the cinema and for its rich execution of an imaginative fantasy. But what really sets it apart is the risks it takes."

–Desmond Ryan, *Philadelphia Inquirer*

"[A]n extravagant homage to juvenile literature and storytelling, a blend of Maurice Sendak and Oz and *Lord of the Rings* all served up with eye-boggling technology."

–Robert Garrett, *The Boston Globe*

"It has been said many times before in this space that the sight of a baby in peril is one of the sleaziest gimmicks a film can employ to gain our attention, but Henson does it."

–GENE SISKEL, *CHICAGO TRIBUNE*

"Without a strong plot line to pull us through, all movies like this run the danger of becoming just a series of incidents. There's no structure to the order of the adventures. Sarah does this, she does that, she's almost killed here, almost trapped there, until at last nothing much matters."

–Roger Ebert, *Chicago Sun-Times*

"Unfortunately, it's a pretty trying trip, with less humor, less wit and fewer flashes of great imagery than you might imagine from this crowd. This in spite of miracles of puppetry and, in one case, computer graphics."

–Sheila Benson, *Los Angeles Times*

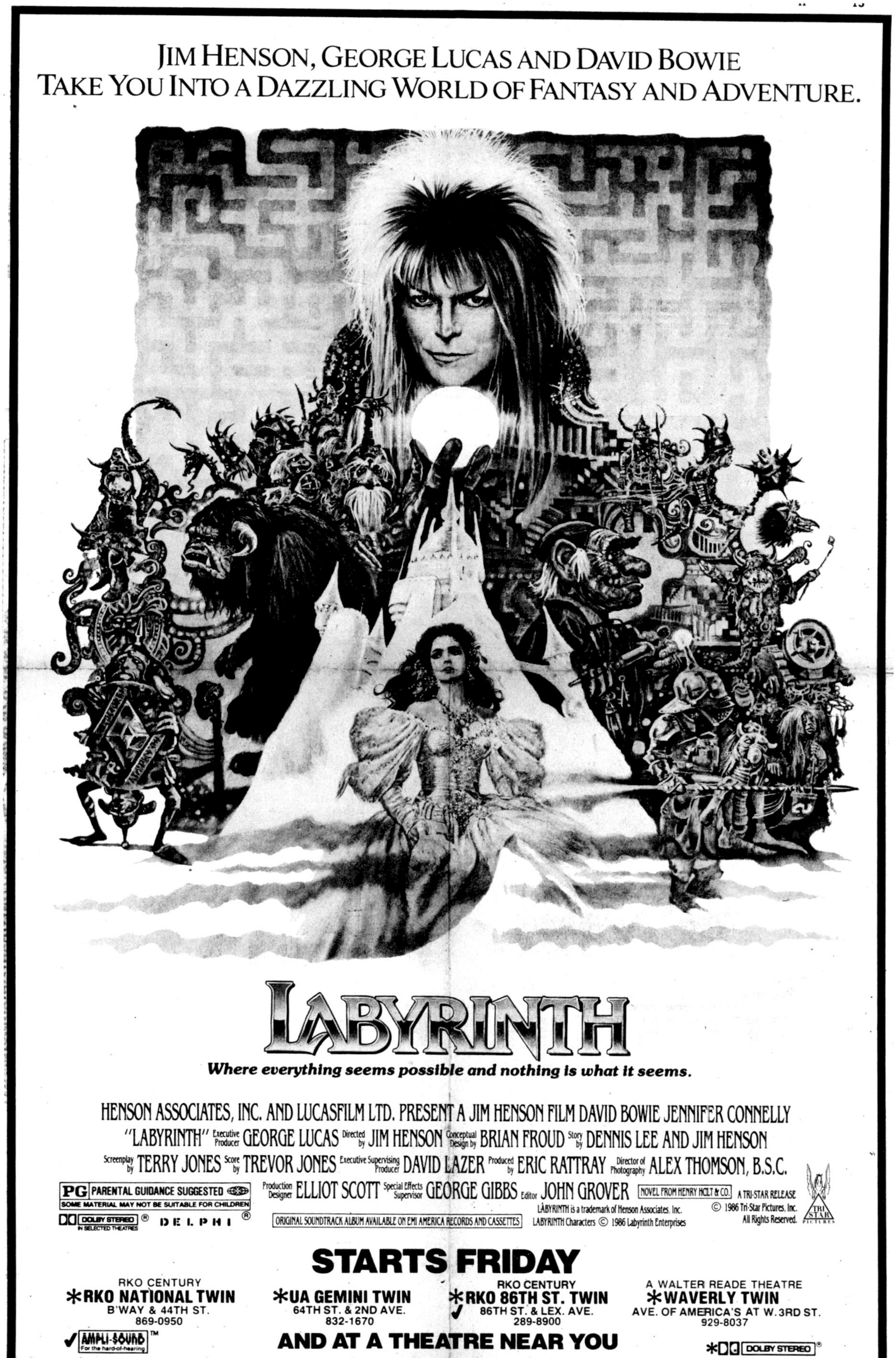
JIM HENSON, GEORGE LUCAS AND DAVID BOWIE
TAKE YOU INTO A DAZZLING WORLD OF FANTASY AND ADVENTURE.
LABYRINTH
Where everything seems possible and nothing is what it seems.
HENSON ASSOCIATES, INC. AND LUCASFILM LTD. PRESENT A JIM HENSON FILM DAVID BOWIE JENNIFER CONNELLY
"LABYRINTH" Executive Producer GEORGE LUCAS Directed by JIM HENSON Conceptual Design by BRIAN FROUD Story by DENNIS LEE AND JIM HENSON
Screenplay by TERRY JONES Score by TREVOR JONES Executive Supervising Producer DAVID LAZER Produced by ERIC RATTRAY Director of Photography ALEX THOMSON, B.S.C.
Production Designer ELLIOT SCOTT Special Effects Supervisor GEORGE GIBBS Editor JOHN GROVER
NOVEL FROM HENRY HOLT & CO.
A TRI-STAR RELEASE
PG PARENTAL GUIDANCE SUGGESTED
SOME MATERIAL MAY NOT BE SUITABLE FOR CHILDREN
DOLBY STEREO ® IN SELECTED THEATRES
DELPHI ®
ORIGINAL SOUNDTRACK ALBUM AVAILABLE ON EMI AMERICA RECORDS AND CASSETTES
LABYRINTH is a trademark of Henson Associates, Inc.
LABYRINTH Characters © 1986 Labyrinth Enterprises
© 1986 Tri-Star Pictures, Inc. All Rights Reserved.
TRI STAR PICTURES
STARTS FRIDAY
RKO CENTURY
*RKO NATIONAL TWIN
B'WAY & 44TH ST.
869-0950
*UA GEMINI TWIN
64TH ST. & 2ND AVE.
832-1670
RKO CENTURY
*RKO 86TH ST. TWIN
✓ 86TH ST. & LEX. AVE.
289-8900
A WALTER READE THEATRE
*WAVERLY TWIN
AVE. OF AMERICA'S AT W. 3RD ST.
929-8037
✓ AMPLI-SOUND™ For the hard-of-hearing
AND AT A THEATRE NEAR YOU
* DOLBY STEREO ®

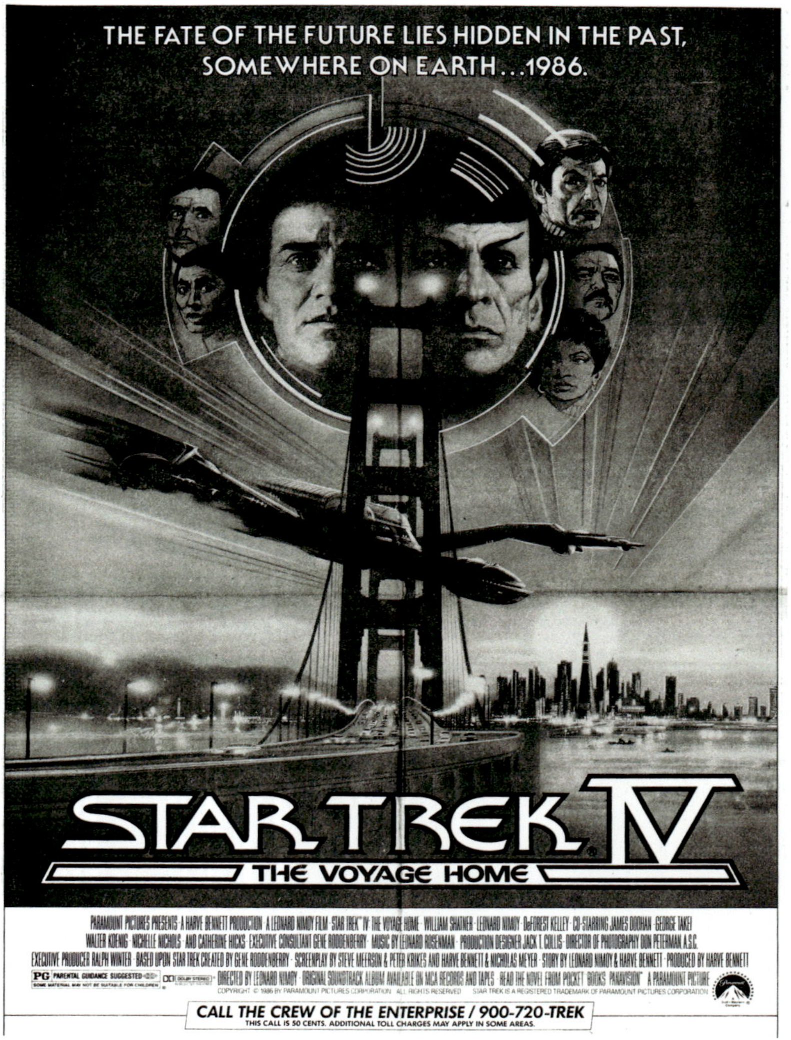

STAR TREK IV: THE VOYAGE HOME

Eddie Murphy in a *Star Trek* film? It could have happened, as a role was written for him in an early draft of *Star Trek IV*. Fortunately, Murphy decided to do *The Golden Child* instead (fortunate for everyone except those who saw *The Golden Child*, that is), but *Star Trek IV* retained a more humorous bent than its predecessors, as Kirk, Spock and other crew members make their way through 1986 San Francisco on an Earth-saving mission. That helped the film win the best reviews and the strongest box office of the franchise.

"This is easily the most absurd of the *Star Trek* stories – and yet, oddly enough, it is also the best, the funniest and the most enjoyable in simple human terms."

–Roger Ebert, *Chicago Sun-Times*

"Funny, sweet and stirring, *Star Trek IV: The Voyage Home* has got to be, in every sense, the family movie of the year."

–MICHAEL SRAGOW, *SAN FRANCISCO EXAMINER*

"It has an irresistibly sure touch, an easy command of its audience. It hits the right buttons, strikes the right chords, plays with our expectations with the right blend of savvy, guile, and imagination."

–Michael Wilmington, *Los Angeles Times*

"Nimoy, who directed the third *Star Trek* movie as though it were a funeral march, shows he has learned a thing or two. The pace is much better this time around, and the humor is timed to perfection."

–Jim DeBrosse, *The Cincinnati Enquirer*

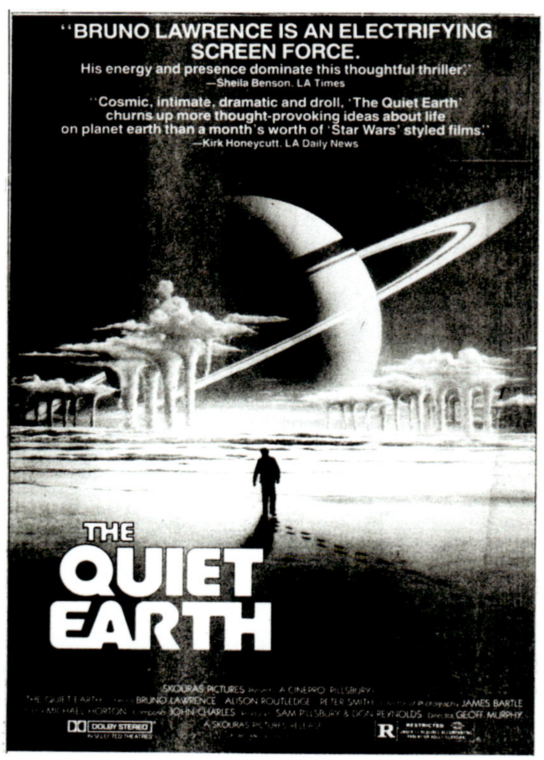

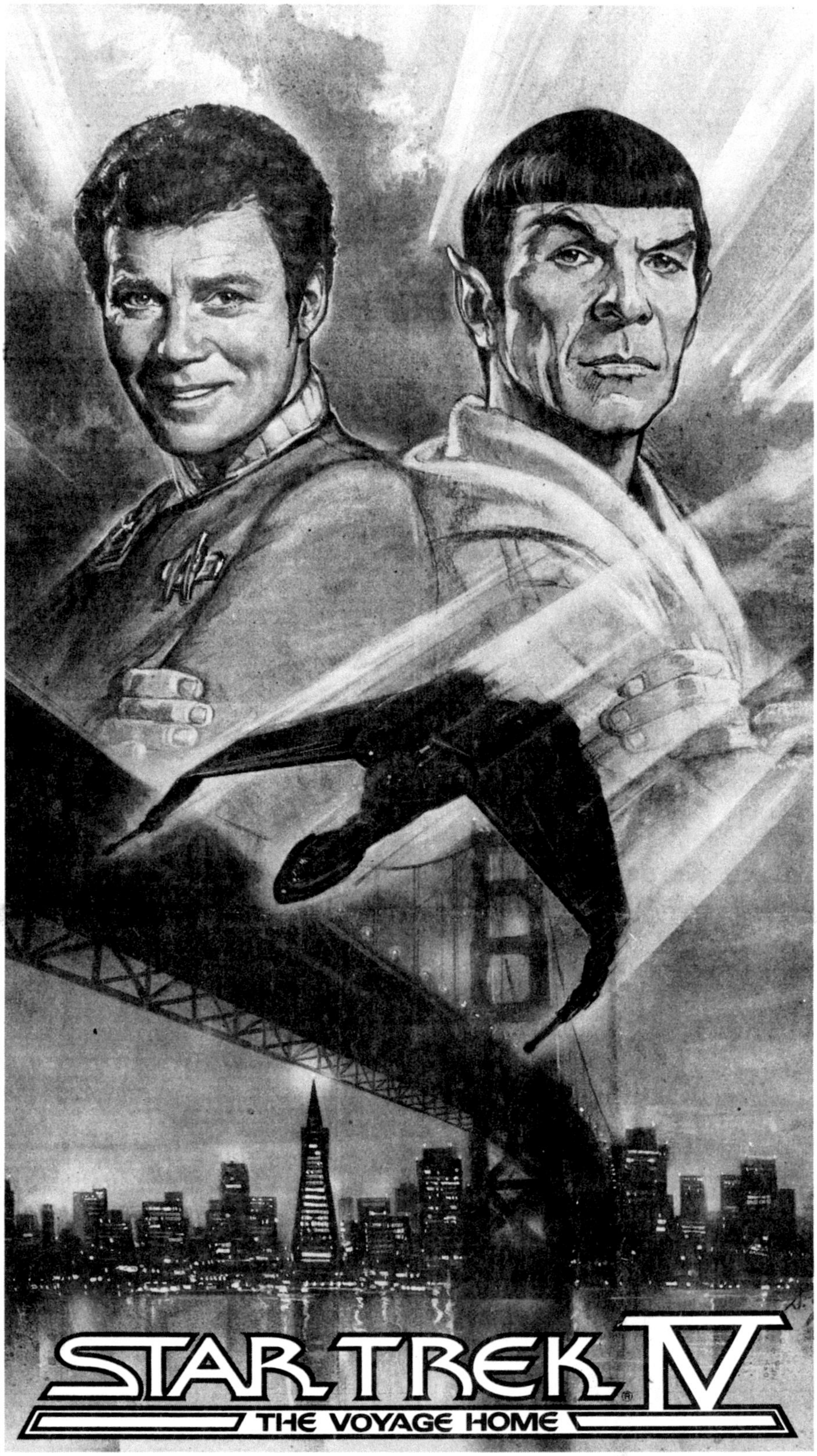

WALTER KOENIG · NICHELLE NICHOLS · AND CATHERINE HICKS · EXECUTIVE CONSULTANT GENE RODDENBERRY · MUSIC BY LEONARD ROSENMAN · PRODUCTION DESIGNER JACK T. COLLIS · DIRECTOR OF PHOTOGRAPHY DON PETERMAN A.S.C. LEONARD NIMOY & HARVE BENNETT · PRODUCED BY HARVE BENNETT · DIRECTED BY LEONARD NIMOY

DOLBY STEREO® IN SELECTED THEATRES

A PARAMOUNT PICTURE

"This is **the holiday film of 1986**... the film I've been waiting for all year. It's everything I wanted and more... the best. A total 10."
Susan Granger, WMCA RADIO

"**I loved it.** I haven't had such a good time at the movies all year. It's the best..."
Katie Kelly, ENTERTAINMENT TONIGHT

"**Ideal holiday entertainment**... A high spirited... comedy with dazzling special effects."
James Verniere, BOSTON HERALD

"A **soaring** success."
Rona Barrett, MUTUAL RADIO NETWORK

"...A genuine **holiday treat**."
Michael Wilmington, LOS ANGELES TIMES

"Large, **lavish... entertainment**."
Janet Maslin, NEW YORK TIMES

"What makes 'Star Trek IV' better than its predecessors is its **marvelous sense of humor**."
Michael Blowen, BOSTON GLOBE

"'Star Trek IV' is **the best**..."
Richard Freedman, STAR LEDGER

"'Star Trek IV' is **irresistible**."
Deborah J. Kunk, LOS ANGELES HERALD-EXAMINER

"**Best** of the Trekker spectaculars to date."
Judith Crist, WOR-TV

"'Star Trek IV: The Voyage Home' should easily cruise past the other likely holiday hits at warp speed... filmmaking that's **masterful**."
Jack Curry, USA TODAY

"...You don't have to be a Trekkie to enjoy "**Star Trek IV**.""
Joseph Gelmis, NEWSDAY

"**The best** of the 'Star Trek' movies."
Barbara Phillips, WALL STREET JOURNAL

"...May be the **best** film of the Christmas season."
Mick Martin, THE SACRAMENTO UNION

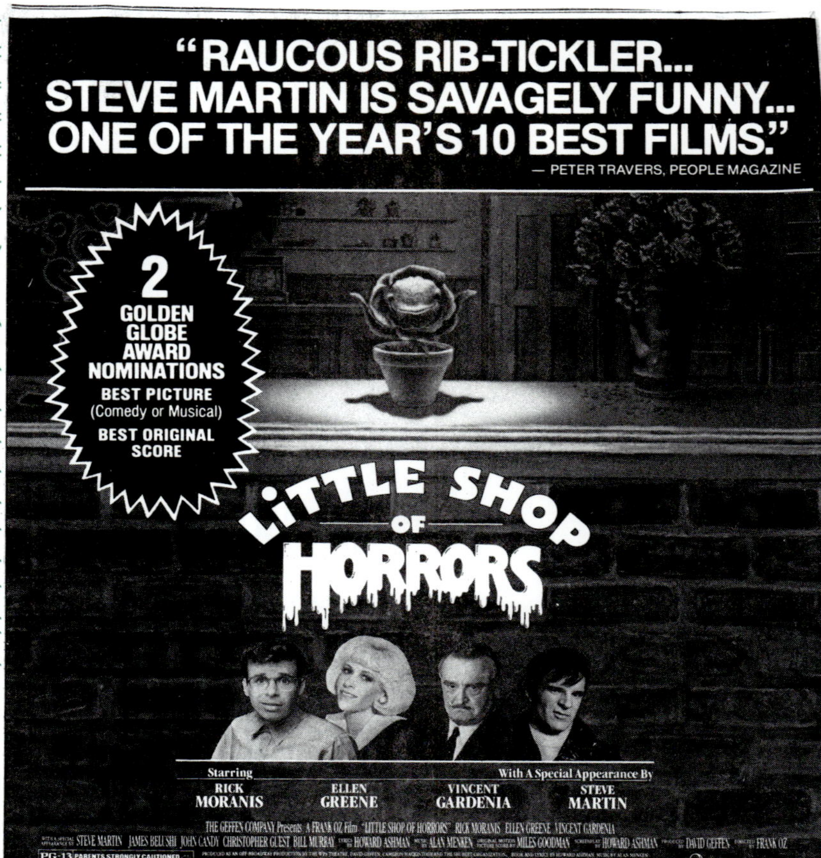

"RAUCOUS RIB-TICKLER...
STEVE MARTIN IS SAVAGELY FUNNY...
ONE OF THE YEAR'S 10 BEST FILMS."
— PETER TRAVERS, PEOPLE MAGAZINE
2 GOLDEN GLOBE AWARD NOMINATIONS
BEST PICTURE (Comedy or Musical)
BEST ORIGINAL SCORE
LITTLE SHOP OF HORRORS
Starring
RICK MORANIS
ELLEN GREENE
VINCENT GARDENIA
With A Special Appearance By
STEVE MARTIN
THE GEFFEN COMPANY Presents A FRANK OZ Film "LITTLE SHOP OF HORRORS" RICK MORANIS ELLEN GREENE VINCENT GARDENIA
STEVE MARTIN JAMES BELUSHI JOHN CANDY CHRISTOPHER GUEST BILL MURRAY HOWARD ASHMAN ALAN MENKEN MILES GOODMAN HOWARD ASHMAN DAVID GEFFEN FRANK OZ
PG-13 PARENTS STRONGLY CAUTIONED

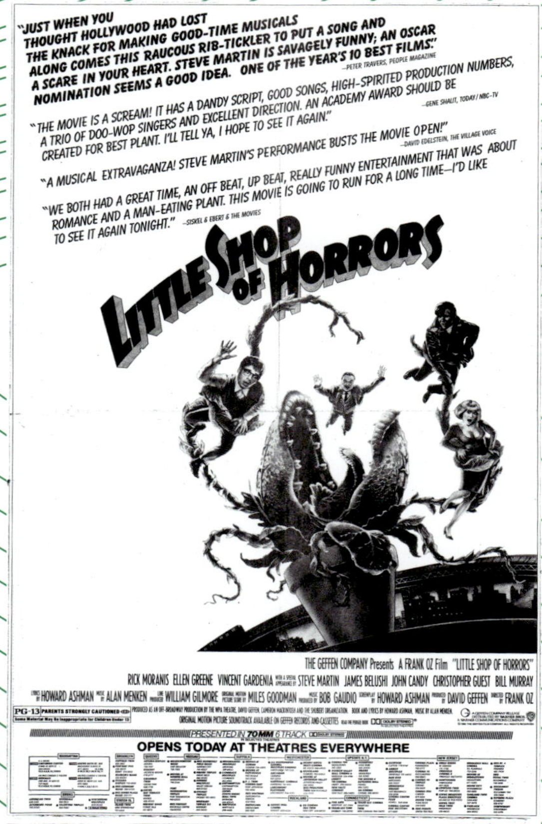

"JUST WHEN YOU THOUGHT HOLLYWOOD HAD LOST THE KNACK FOR MAKING GOOD-TIME MUSICALS ALONG COMES THIS RAUCOUS RIB-TICKLER TO PUT A SONG AND A SCARE IN YOUR HEART. STEVE MARTIN IS SAVAGELY FUNNY; AN OSCAR NOMINATION SEEMS A GOOD IDEA. ONE OF THE YEAR'S 10 BEST FILMS." —PETER TRAVERS, PEOPLE MAGAZINE
"THE MOVIE IS A SCREAM! IT HAS A DANDY SCRIPT, GOOD SONGS, HIGH-SPIRITED PRODUCTION NUMBERS, A TRIO OF DOO-WOP SINGERS AND EXCELLENT DIRECTION. AN ACADEMY AWARD SHOULD BE CREATED FOR BEST PLANT. I'LL TELL YA, I HOPE TO SEE IT AGAIN." —GENE SHALIT, TODAY/NBC-TV
"A MUSICAL EXTRAVAGANZA! STEVE MARTIN'S PERFORMANCE BUSTS THE MOVIE OPEN!" —DAVID EDELSTEIN, THE VILLAGE VOICE
"WE BOTH HAD A GREAT TIME, AN OFF BEAT, UP BEAT, REALLY FUNNY ENTERTAINMENT THAT WAS ABOUT ROMANCE AND A MAN-EATING PLANT. THIS MOVIE IS GOING TO RUN FOR A LONG TIME—I'D LIKE TO SEE IT AGAIN TONIGHT." —SISKEL & EBERT & THE MOVIES
LITTLE SHOP OF HORRORS
THE GEFFEN COMPANY Presents A FRANK OZ Film "LITTLE SHOP OF HORRORS"
RICK MORANIS ELLEN GREENE VINCENT GARDENIA STEVE MARTIN JAMES BELUSHI JOHN CANDY CHRISTOPHER GUEST BILL MURRAY
HOWARD ASHMAN ALAN MENKEN WILLIAM GILMORE MILES GOODMAN BOB GAUDIO HOWARD ASHMAN DAVID GEFFEN FRANK OZ
PG-13 PARENTS STRONGLY CAUTIONED
PRODUCED AS AN OFF-BROADWAY PRODUCTION BY THE WPA THEATRE, DAVID GEFFEN, CAMERON MACKINTOSH AND THE SHUBERT ORGANIZATION. BOOK AND LYRICS BY HOWARD ASHMAN, MUSIC BY ALAN MENKEN.
ORIGINAL MOTION PICTURE SOUNDTRACK AVAILABLE ON GEFFEN RECORDS AND CASSETTES
PRESENTED IN 70MM 6 TRACK
OPENS TODAY AT THEATRES EVERYWHERE

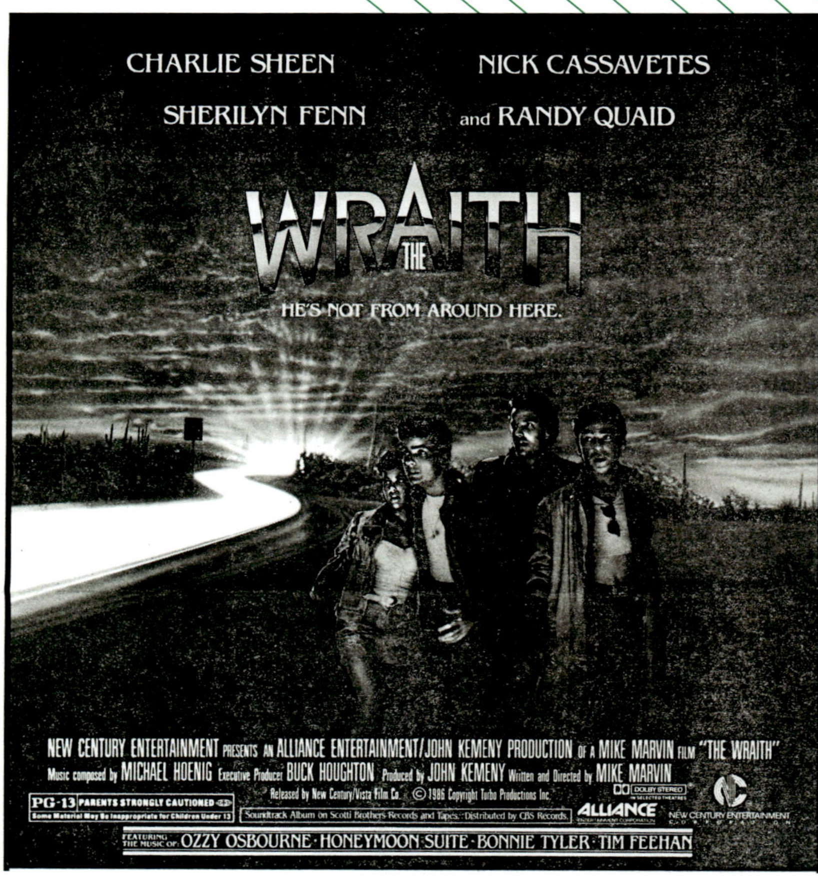

CHARLIE SHEEN
NICK CASSAVETES
SHERILYN FENN
and RANDY QUAID
THE WRAITH
HE'S NOT FROM AROUND HERE.
NEW CENTURY ENTERTAINMENT PRESENTS AN ALLIANCE ENTERTAINMENT/JOHN KEMENY PRODUCTION OF A MIKE MARVIN FILM "THE WRAITH"
Music composed by MICHAEL HOENIG Executive Producer BUCK HOUGHTON Produced by JOHN KEMENY Written and Directed by MIKE MARVIN
Released by New Century/Vista Film Co. © 1986 Copyright Turbo Productions Inc.
PG-13 PARENTS STRONGLY CAUTIONED
Some Material May Be Inappropriate for Children Under 13
Soundtrack Album on Scotti Brothers Records and Tapes. Distributed by CBS Records.
ALLIANCE
NEW CENTURY ENTERTAINMENT
FEATURING THE MUSIC OF: OZZY OSBOURNE · HONEYMOON SUITE · BONNIE TYLER · TIM FEEHAN

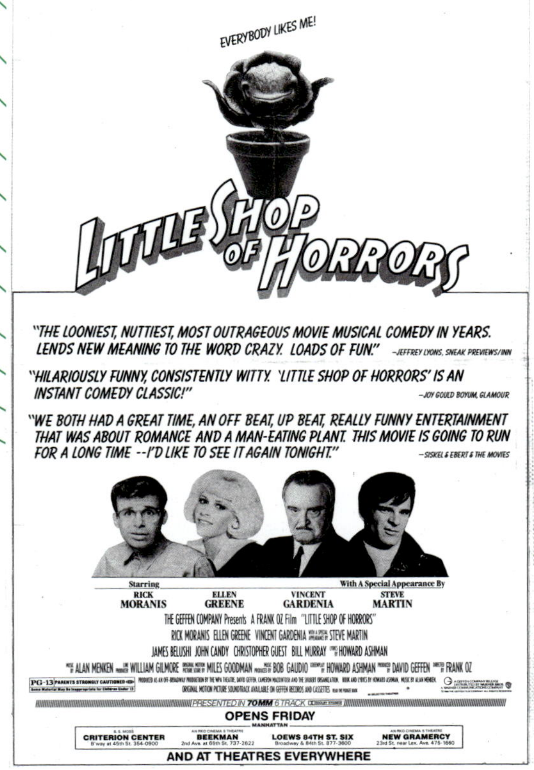

EVERYBODY LIKES ME!
LITTLE SHOP OF HORRORS
"THE LOONIEST, NUTTIEST, MOST OUTRAGEOUS MOVIE MUSICAL COMEDY IN YEARS. LENDS NEW MEANING TO THE WORD CRAZY. LOADS OF FUN." —JEFFREY LYONS, SNEAK PREVIEWS/INN
"HILARIOUSLY FUNNY, CONSISTENTLY WITTY. 'LITTLE SHOP OF HORRORS' IS AN INSTANT COMEDY CLASSIC!" —JOY GOULD BOYUM, GLAMOUR
"WE BOTH HAD A GREAT TIME, AN OFF BEAT, UP BEAT, REALLY FUNNY ENTERTAINMENT THAT WAS ABOUT ROMANCE AND A MAN-EATING PLANT. THIS MOVIE IS GOING TO RUN FOR A LONG TIME --I'D LIKE TO SEE IT AGAIN TONIGHT." —SISKEL & EBERT & THE MOVIES
Starring
RICK MORANIS
ELLEN GREENE
VINCENT GARDENIA
With A Special Appearance By
STEVE MARTIN
THE GEFFEN COMPANY Presents A FRANK OZ Film "LITTLE SHOP OF HORRORS"
RICK MORANIS ELLEN GREENE VINCENT GARDENIA STEVE MARTIN
JAMES BELUSHI JOHN CANDY CHRISTOPHER GUEST BILL MURRAY HOWARD ASHMAN
ALAN MENKEN WILLIAM GILMORE MILES GOODMAN BOB GAUDIO HOWARD ASHMAN DAVID GEFFEN FRANK OZ
PG-13 PARENTS STRONGLY CAUTIONED
PRODUCED AS AN OFF-BROADWAY PRODUCTION BY THE WPA THEATRE, DAVID GEFFEN, CAMERON MACKINTOSH AND THE SHUBERT ORGANIZATION. BOOK AND LYRICS BY HOWARD ASHMAN, MUSIC BY ALAN MENKEN.
ORIGINAL MOTION PICTURE SOUNDTRACK AVAILABLE ON GEFFEN RECORDS AND CASSETTES
PRESENTED IN 70MM 6 TRACK
OPENS FRIDAY
MANHATTAN
CRITERION CENTER B'way at 45th St. 354-0900
BEEKMAN 2nd Ave. at 65th St. 737-2622
LOEWS 84TH ST. SIX Broadway & 84th St. 877-3600
NEW GRAMERCY 23rd St. near Lex. Ave. 475-1660
AND AT THEATRES EVERYWHERE

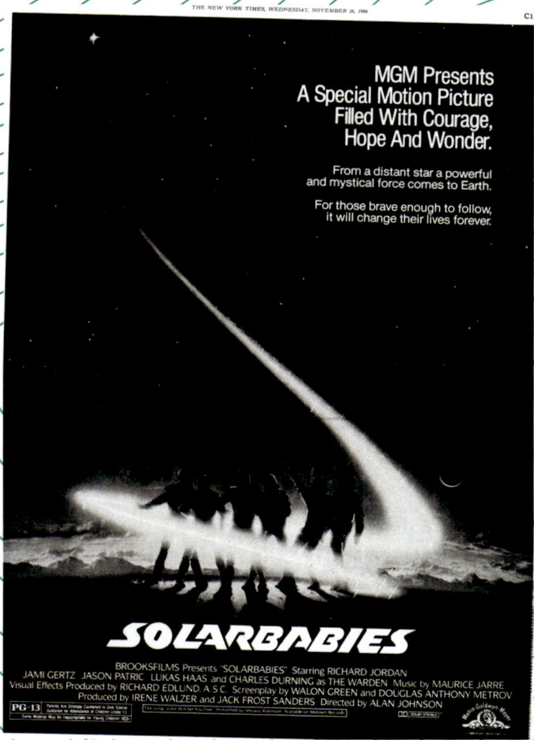
THE NEW YORK TIMES, WEDNESDAY, NOVEMBER 26, 1986
MGM Presents
A Special Motion Picture
Filled With Courage,
Hope And Wonder.
From a distant star a powerful
and mystical force comes to Earth.
For those brave enough to follow,
it will change their lives forever.
SOLARBABIES
BROOKSFILMS Presents "SOLARBABIES" Starring RICHARD JORDAN
JAMI GERTZ JASON PATRIC LUKAS HAAS and CHARLES DURNING as THE WARDEN Music by MAURICE JARRE
Visual Effects Produced by RICHARD EDLUND, A.S.C. Screenplay by WALON GREEN and DOUGLAS ANTHONY METROV
Produced by IRENE WALZER and JACK FROST SANDERS Directed by ALAN JOHNSON
PG-13

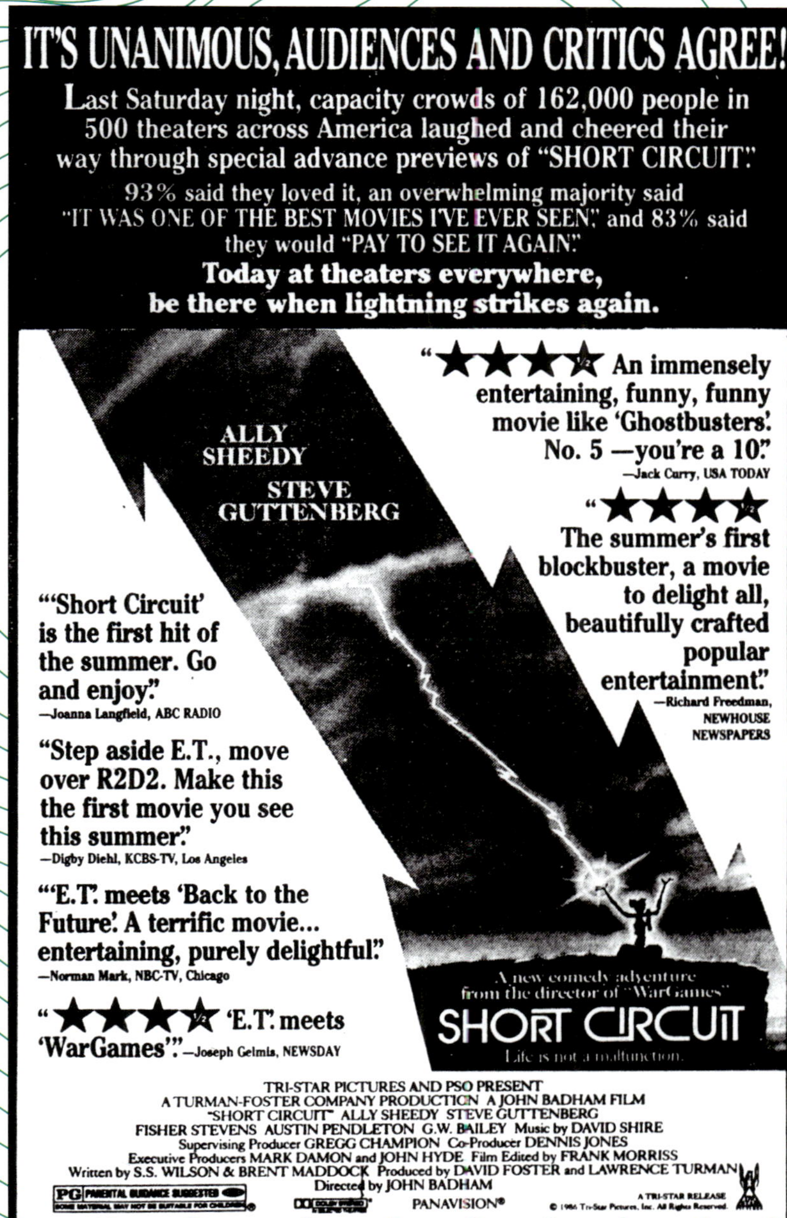
IT'S UNANIMOUS, AUDIENCES AND CRITICS AGREE!
Last Saturday night, capacity crowds of 162,000 people in 500 theaters across America laughed and cheered their way through special advance previews of "SHORT CIRCUIT."
93% said they loved it, an overwhelming majority said "IT WAS ONE OF THE BEST MOVIES I'VE EVER SEEN," and 83% said they would "PAY TO SEE IT AGAIN."
Today at theaters everywhere, be there when lightning strikes again.
ALLY SHEEDY
STEVE GUTTENBERG
"★★★★½ An immensely entertaining, funny, funny movie like 'Ghostbusters.' No. 5 —you're a 10." —Jack Curry, USA TODAY
"★★★★½ The summer's first blockbuster, a movie to delight all, beautifully crafted popular entertainment." —Richard Freedman, NEWHOUSE NEWSPAPERS
"'Short Circuit' is the first hit of the summer. Go and enjoy." —Joanna Langfield, ABC RADIO
"Step aside E.T., move over R2D2. Make this the first movie you see this summer." —Digby Diehl, KCBS-TV, Los Angeles
"'E.T.' meets 'Back to the Future.' A terrific movie... entertaining, purely delightful." —Norman Mark, NBC-TV, Chicago
"★★★½ 'E.T.' meets 'WarGames'." —Joseph Gelmis, NEWSDAY
A new comedy adventure from the director of "WarGames"
SHORT CIRCUIT
Life is not a malfunction.
TRI-STAR PICTURES AND PSO PRESENT
A TURMAN-FOSTER COMPANY PRODUCTION A JOHN BADHAM FILM
"SHORT CIRCUIT" ALLY SHEEDY STEVE GUTTENBERG
FISHER STEVENS AUSTIN PENDLETON G.W. BAILEY Music by DAVID SHIRE
Supervising Producer GREGG CHAMPION Co-Producer DENNIS JONES
Executive Producers MARK DAMON and JOHN HYDE Film Edited by FRANK MORRISS
Written by S.S. WILSON & BRENT MADDOCK Produced by DAVID FOSTER and LAWRENCE TURMAN
Directed by JOHN BADHAM
PG PARENTAL GUIDANCE SUGGESTED
PANAVISION®
A TRI-STAR RELEASE
© 1986 Tri-Star Pictures, Inc. All Rights Reserved.

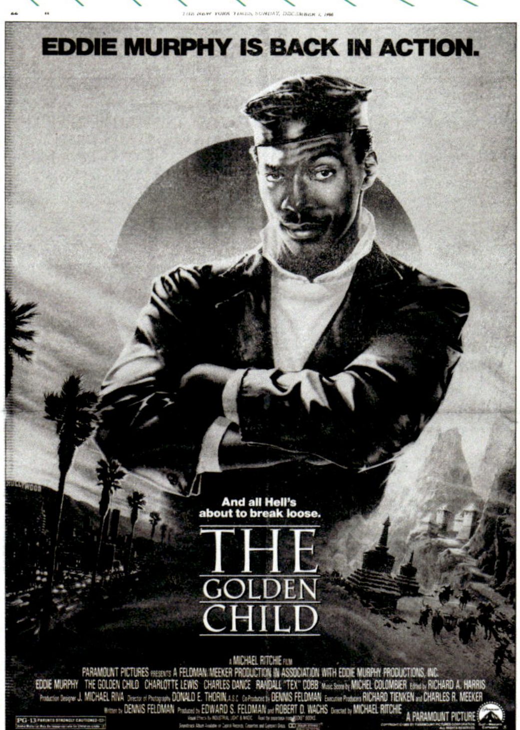
EDDIE MURPHY IS BACK IN ACTION.
And all Hell's about to break loose.
THE GOLDEN CHILD
A MICHAEL RITCHIE FILM
PARAMOUNT PICTURES PRESENTS A FELDMAN/MEEKER PRODUCTION IN ASSOCIATION WITH EDDIE MURPHY PRODUCTIONS, INC.
EDDIE MURPHY THE GOLDEN CHILD CHARLOTTE LEWIS CHARLES DANCE RANDALL "TEX" COBB Music Score by MICHEL COLOMBIER Edited by RICHARD A. HARRIS
Production Designer J. MICHAEL RIVA Director of Photography DONALD E. THORIN, A.S.C. Co-Produced by DENNIS FELDMAN Executive Producers RICHARD TIENKEN and CHARLES R. MEEKER
Written by DENNIS FELDMAN Produced by EDWARD S. FELDMAN and ROBERT D. WACHS Directed by MICHAEL RITCHIE
A PARAMOUNT PICTURE
PG-13

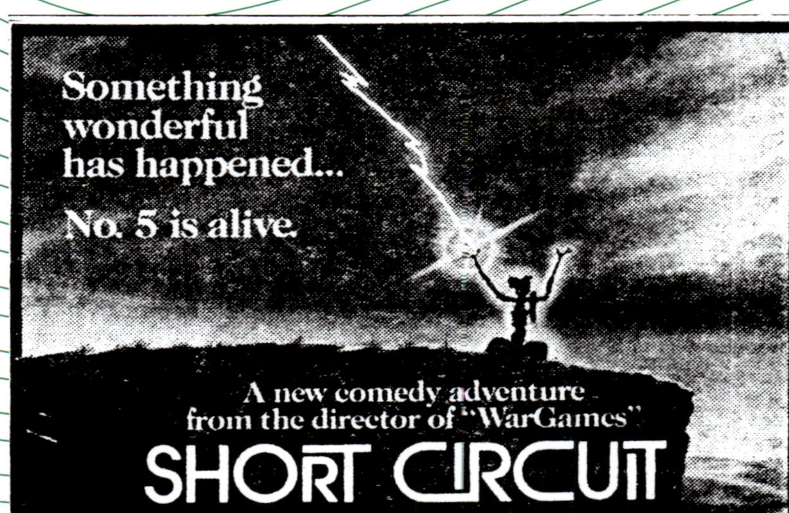
Something wonderful has happened...
No. 5 is alive.
A new comedy adventure from the director of "WarGames"
SHORT CIRCUIT

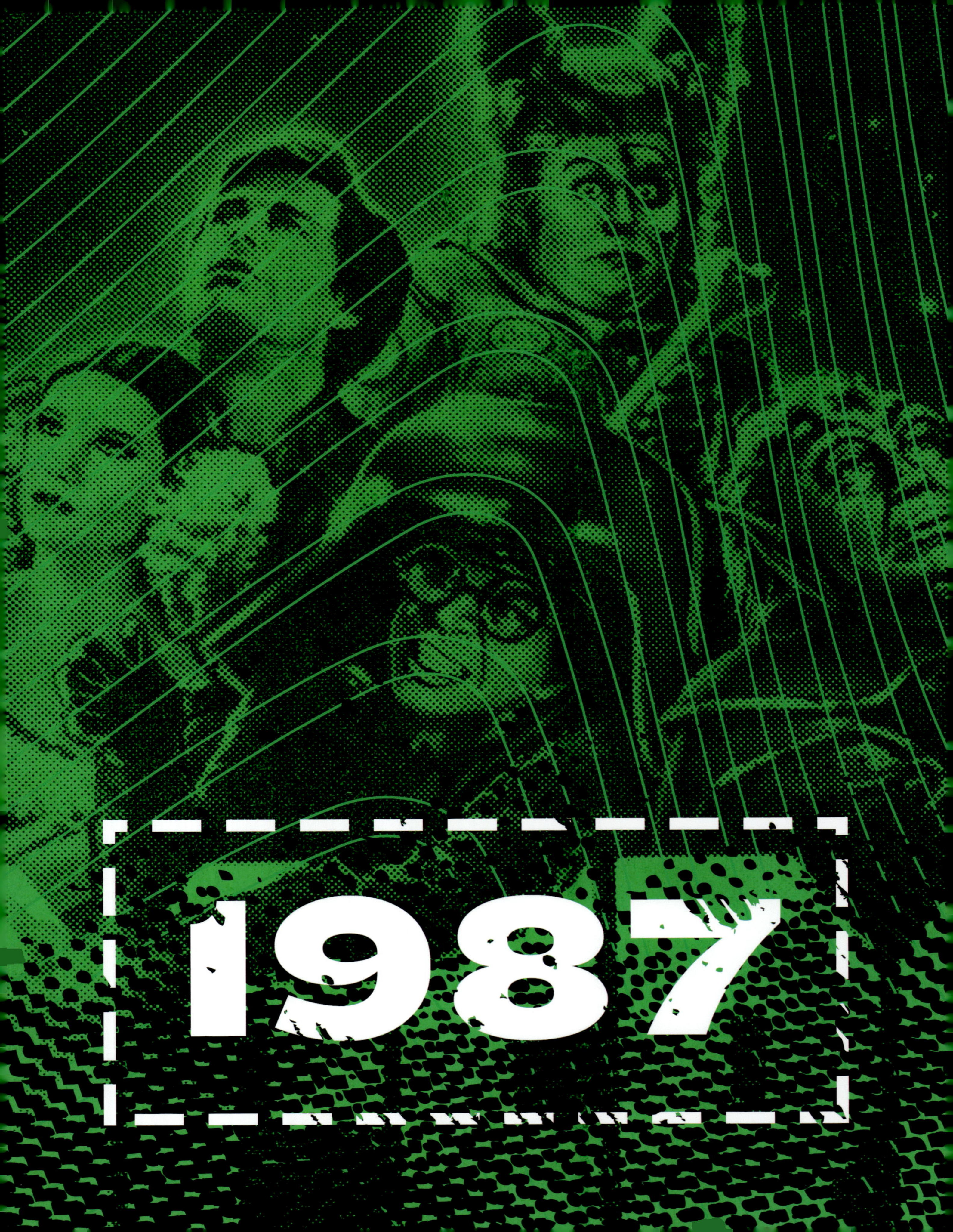
1987

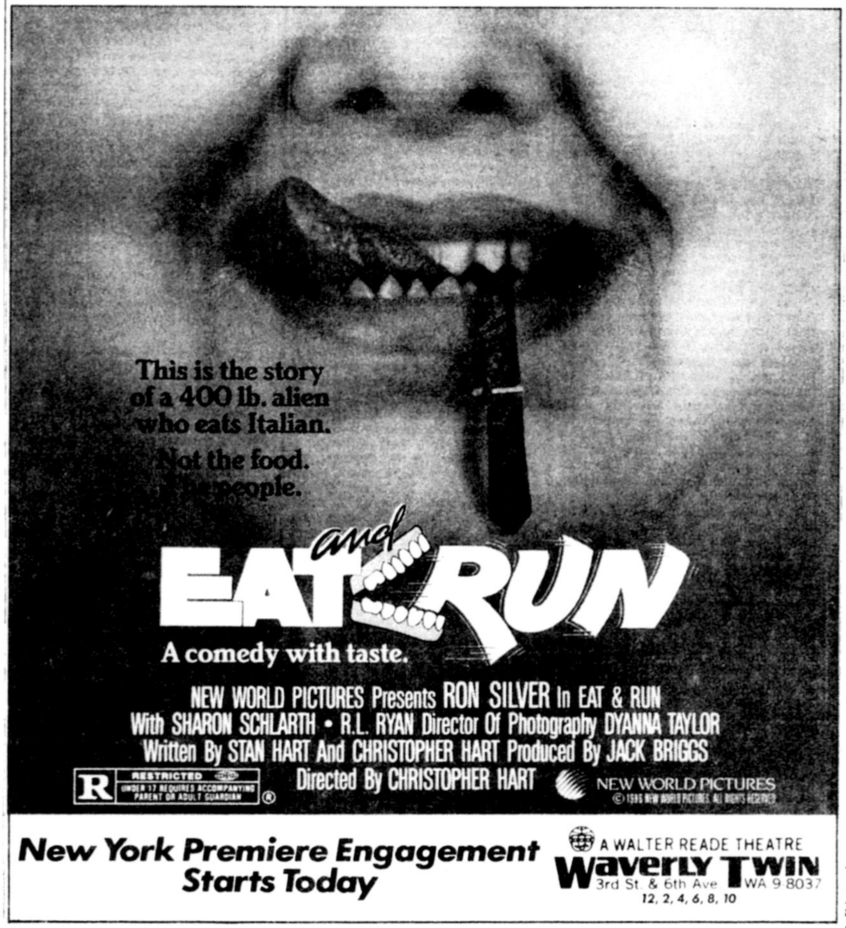

This is the story of a 400 lb. alien who eats Italian.
Not the food. The people.
EAT and RUN
A comedy with taste.
NEW WORLD PICTURES Presents RON SILVER In EAT & RUN
With SHARON SCHLARTH • R.L. RYAN Director Of Photography DYANNA TAYLOR
Written By STAN HART And CHRISTOPHER HART Produced By JACK BRIGGS
Directed By CHRISTOPHER HART
R RESTRICTED UNDER 17 REQUIRES ACCOMPANYING PARENT OR ADULT GUARDIAN
NEW WORLD PICTURES
New York Premiere Engagement
Starts Today
A WALTER READE THEATRE
Waverly TWIN
3rd St. & 6th Ave WA 9-8037
12, 2, 4, 6, 8, 10

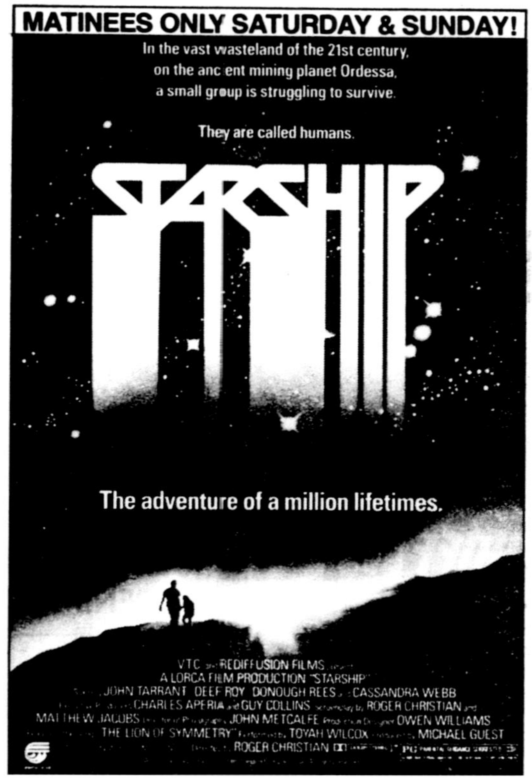

MATINEES ONLY SATURDAY & SUNDAY!
In the vast wasteland of the 21st century, on the ancient mining planet Ordessa, a small group is struggling to survive.
They are called humans.
STARSHIP
The adventure of a million lifetimes.
VTC REDIFFUSION FILMS
A LORCA FILM PRODUCTION "STARSHIP"
JOHN TARRANT DEEP ROY DONOUGH REES CASSANDRA WEBB
CHARLES APERIA GUY COLLINS ROGER CHRISTIAN
MATTHEW JACOBS JOHN METCALFE OWEN WILLIAMS
THE LION OF SYMMETRY TOYAH WILCOX MICHAEL GUEST
ROGER CHRISTIAN

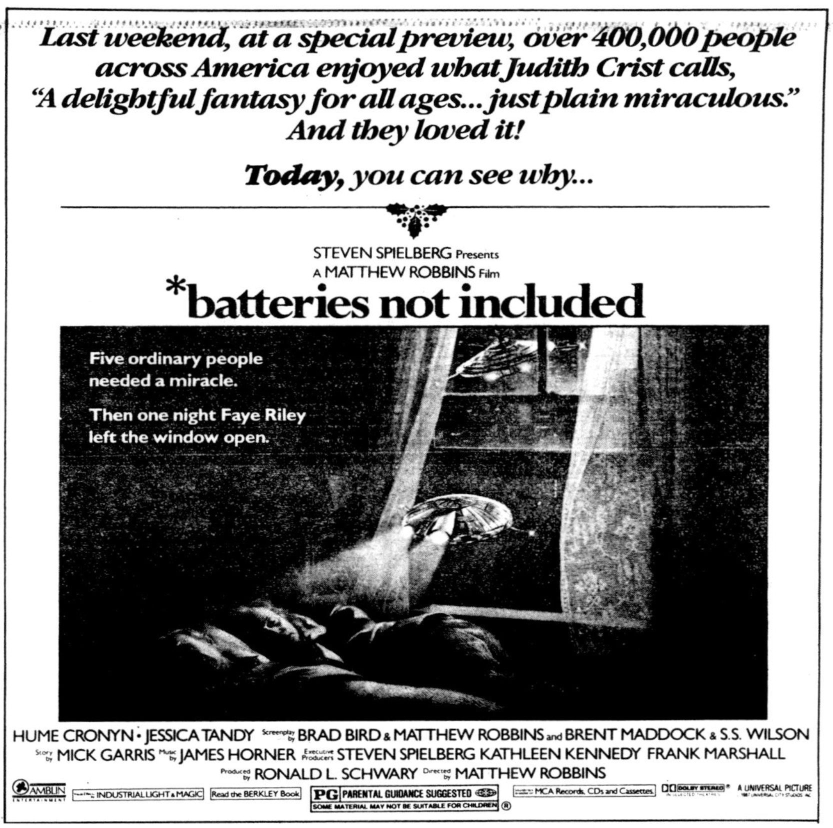

Last weekend, at a special preview, over 400,000 people across America enjoyed what Judith Crist calls,
"A delightful fantasy for all ages... just plain miraculous."
And they loved it!
Today, you can see why...
STEVEN SPIELBERG Presents
A MATTHEW ROBBINS Film
*batteries not included
Five ordinary people needed a miracle.
Then one night Faye Riley left the window open.
HUME CRONYN • JESSICA TANDY Screenplay by BRAD BIRD & MATTHEW ROBBINS and BRENT MADDOCK & S.S. WILSON
Story by MICK GARRIS Music by JAMES HORNER Executive Producers STEVEN SPIELBERG KATHLEEN KENNEDY FRANK MARSHALL
Produced by RONALD L. SCHWARY Directed by MATTHEW ROBBINS
AMBLIN ENTERTAINMENT
INDUSTRIAL LIGHT & MAGIC
Read the BERKLEY Book
PG PARENTAL GUIDANCE SUGGESTED
SOME MATERIAL MAY NOT BE SUITABLE FOR CHILDREN
MCA Records, CDs and Cassettes
DOLBY STEREO
A UNIVERSAL PICTURE

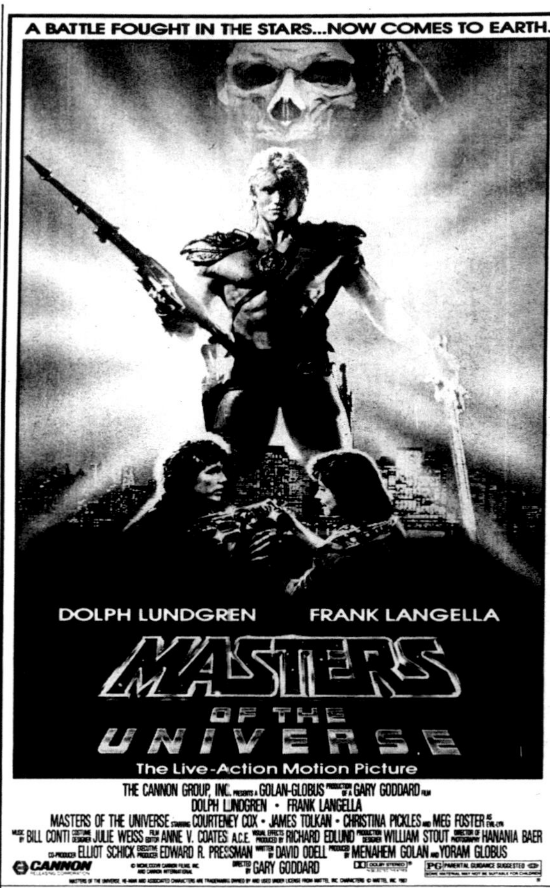

A BATTLE FOUGHT IN THE STARS...NOW COMES TO EARTH.
DOLPH LUNDGREN
FRANK LANGELLA
MASTERS OF THE UNIVERSE
The Live-Action Motion Picture
THE CANNON GROUP, INC. presents a GOLAN-GLOBUS production of a GARY GODDARD film
DOLPH LUNDGREN • FRANK LANGELLA
MASTERS OF THE UNIVERSE starring COURTENEY COX • JAMES TOLKAN • CHRISTINA PICKLES and MEG FOSTER
Music by BILL CONTI Costume Designer JULIE WEISS Film Editor ANNE V. COATES A.C.E. Visual Effects Produced by RICHARD EDLUND Production Designer WILLIAM STOUT Director of Photography HANANIA BAER
Co-Producer ELLIOT SCHICK Executive Producer EDWARD R. PRESSMAN Written by DAVID ODELL Produced by MENAHEM GOLAN and YORAM GLOBUS
Directed by GARY GODDARD
CANNON
PG PARENTAL GUIDANCE SUGGESTED

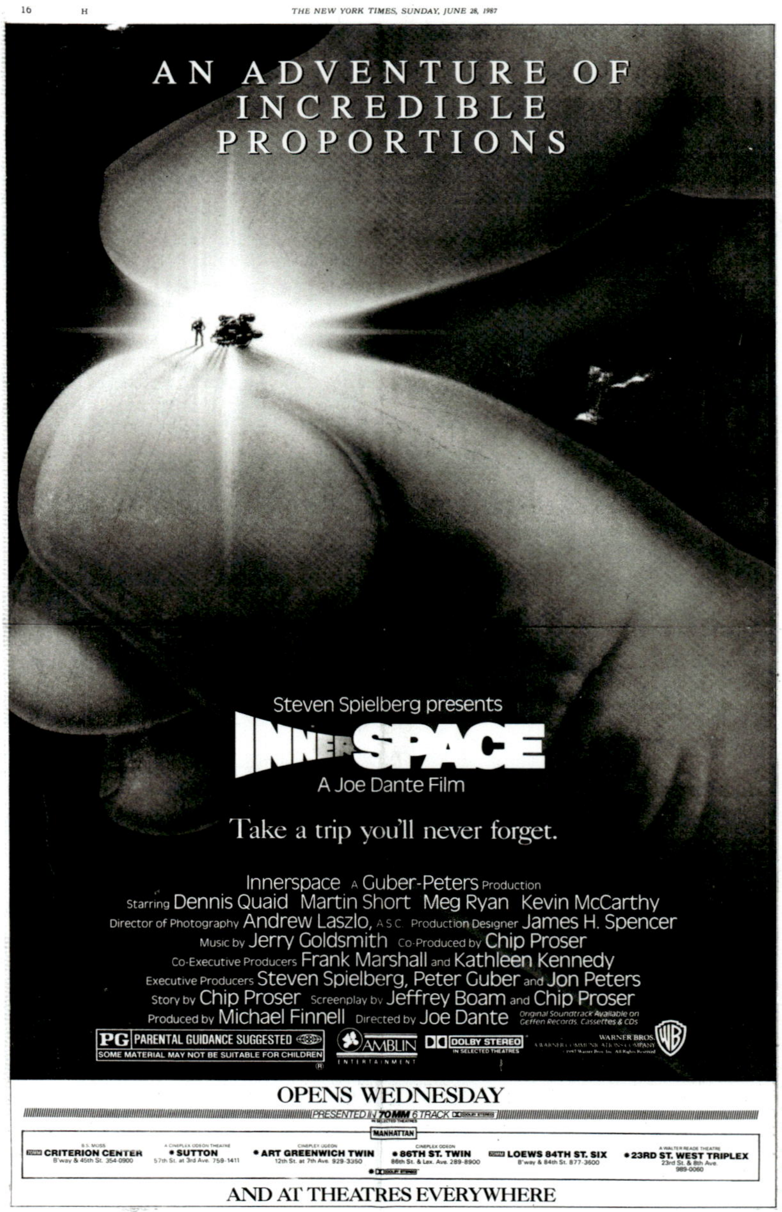

INNERSPACE

Once again, Joe Dante delivered a genre piece with a humorous bent, this time via a sort-of remake of *Fantastic Voyage*, in which a miniaturized Dennis Quaid travels through the body of hypochondriac Martin Short. Initially, Warner Bros. chose to emphasize the fantastic side of the voyage, yet even with the Steven Spielberg imprimatur attached, the initial box-office grosses were well below expectations (it finished just below the second week of *Spaceballs*). The studio quickly revised the campaign to put the emphasis on its appealing trio of stars (rounded out by Meg Ryan), but it didn't help, and *Innerspace* would only find its audience on, appropriately enough, the smaller format of home video.

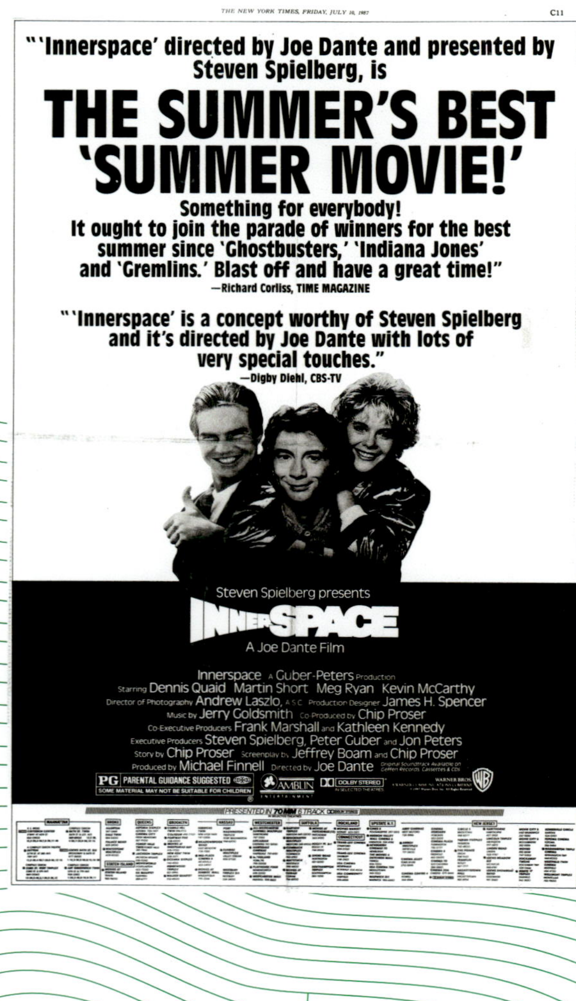

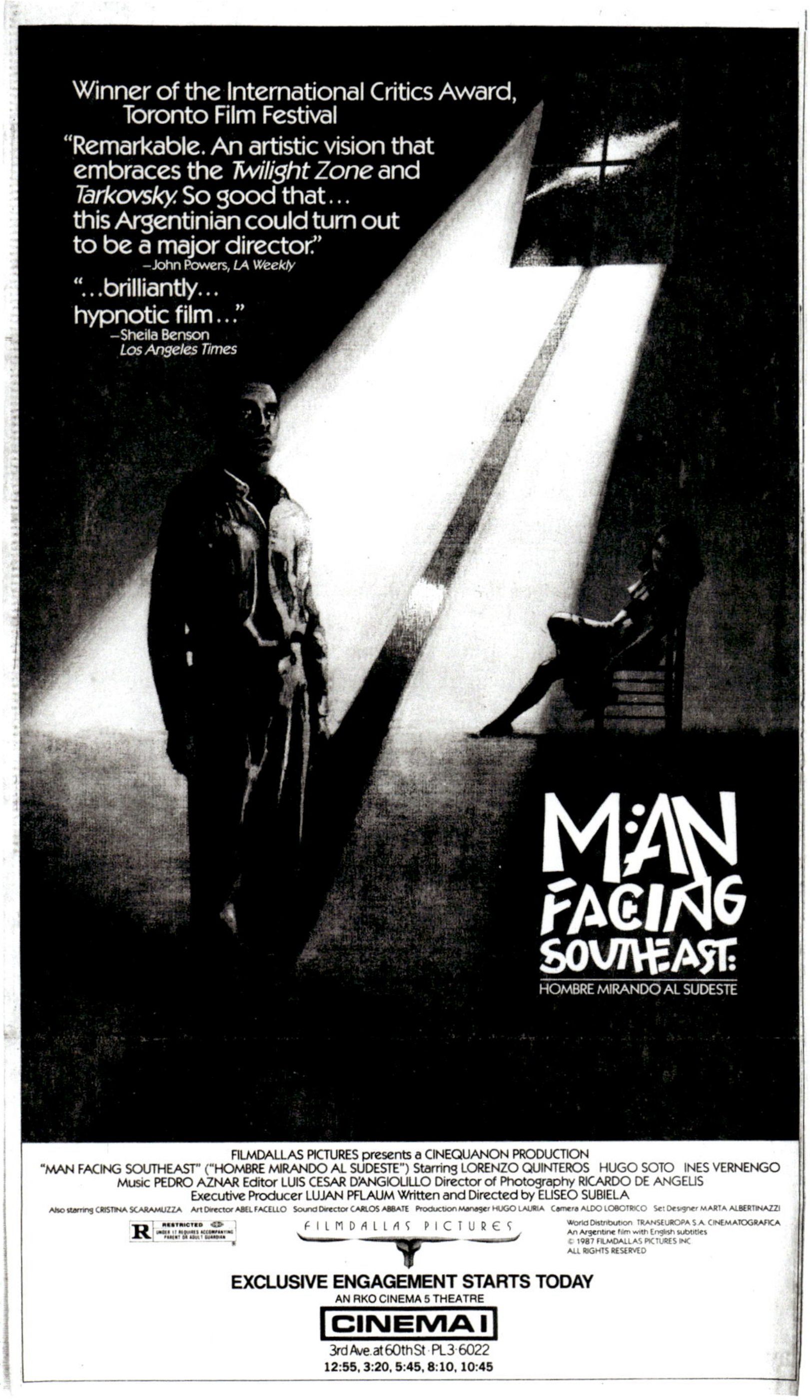

Winner of the International Critics Award, Toronto Film Festival
"Remarkable. An artistic vision that embraces the *Twilight Zone* and *Tarkovsky.* So good that… this Argentinian could turn out to be a major director."
–John Powers, *LA Weekly*
"…brilliantly… hypnotic film…"
–Sheila Benson *Los Angeles Times*
MAN FACING SOUTHEAST
HOMBRE MIRANDO AL SUDESTE
FILMDALLAS PICTURES presents a CINEQUANON PRODUCTION
"MAN FACING SOUTHEAST" ("HOMBRE MIRANDO AL SUDESTE") Starring LORENZO QUINTEROS HUGO SOTO INES VERNENGO
Music PEDRO AZNAR Editor LUIS CESAR D'ANGIOLILLO Director of Photography RICARDO DE ANGELIS
Executive Producer LUJAN PFLAUM Written and Directed by ELISEO SUBIELA
Also starring CRISTINA SCARAMUZZA Art Director ABEL FACELLO Sound Director CARLOS ABBATE Production Manager HUGO LAURIA Camera ALDO LOBOTRICO Set Designer MARTA ALBERTINAZZI
R RESTRICTED
FILMDALLAS PICTURES
World Distribution: TRANSEUROPA S.A. CINEMATOGRAFICA
An Argentine film with English subtitles
© 1987 FILMDALLAS PICTURES INC
ALL RIGHTS RESERVED
EXCLUSIVE ENGAGEMENT STARTS TODAY
AN RKO CINEMA 5 THEATRE
CINEMA I
3rd Ave. at 60th St · PL3·6022
12:55, 3:20, 5:45, 8:10, 10:45

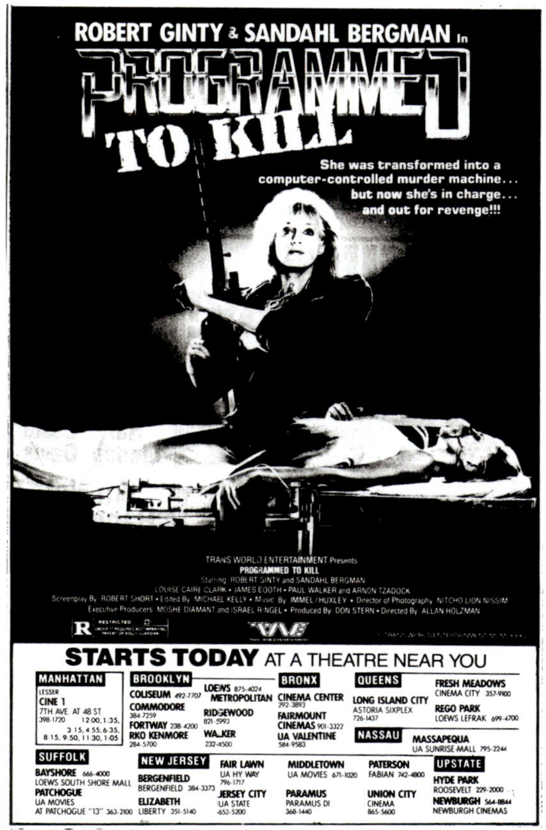

ROBERT GINTY & SANDAHL BERGMAN in
PROGRAMMED TO KILL
She was transformed into a computer-controlled murder machine... but now she's in charge... and out for revenge!!!
TRANS WORLD ENTERTAINMENT Presents
PROGRAMMED TO KILL
Starring ROBERT GINTY and SANDAHL BERGMAN
LOUISE CAIRE CLARK • JAMES BOOTH • PAUL WALKER and ARNON TZADOCK
Screenplay By ROBERT SHORT • Edited By MICHAEL KELLY • Music By IMMEL / HUXLEY • Director of Photography NITCHO LION NISSIM
Executive Producers MOSHE DIAMANT and ISRAEL RINGEL • Produced By: DON STERN • Directed By ALLAN HOLZMAN
R RESTRICTED
STARTS TODAY AT A THEATRE NEAR YOU
MANHATTAN
LESSER CINE 1 7TH AVE. AT 48 ST 398-1720 12:00, 1:35, 3:15, 4:55, 6:35, 8:15, 9:50, 11:30, 1:05
BROOKLYN
COLISEUM 492-7707
COMMODORE 384-7259
FORTWAY 238-4200
RKO KENMORE 284-5700
LOEWS 875-4024 METROPOLITAN
RIDGEWOOD 821-5993
WALKER 232-4500
BRONX
CINEMA CENTER 292-3893
FAIRMOUNT CINEMAS 901-3322
UA VALENTINE 584-9583
QUEENS
LONG ISLAND CITY ASTORIA SIXPLEX 726-1437
FRESH MEADOWS CINEMA CITY 357-9100
REGO PARK LOEWS LEFRAK 699-4700
NASSAU
MASSAPEQUA UA SUNRISE MALL 795-2244
SUFFOLK
BAYSHORE 666-4000 LOEWS SOUTH SHORE MALL
PATCHOGUE UA MOVIES AT PATCHOGUE "13" 363-2100
NEW JERSEY
BERGENFIELD BERGENFIELD 384-3373
ELIZABETH LIBERTY 351-5140
FAIR LAWN UA HY WAY 796-1717
JERSEY CITY UA STATE 653-5200
MIDDLETOWN UA MOVIES 671-1020
PARAMUS PARAMUS DI 368-1440
PATERSON FABIAN 742-4800
UNION CITY CINEMA 865-5600
UPSTATE
HYDE PARK ROOSEVELT 229-2000
NEWBURGH 564-8844 NEWBURGH CINEMAS

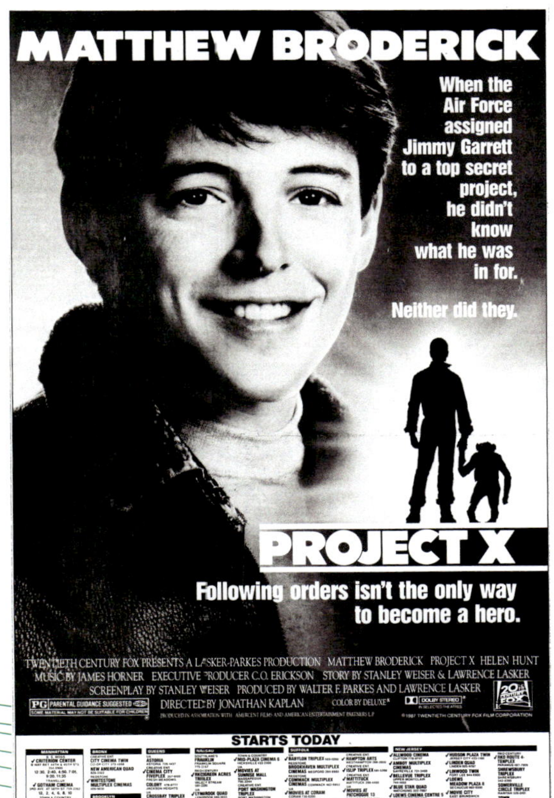

MATTHEW BRODERICK
When the Air Force assigned Jimmy Garrett to a top secret project, he didn't know what he was in for.
Neither did they.
PROJECT X
Following orders isn't the only way to become a hero.
TWENTIETH CENTURY FOX PRESENTS A LASKER-PARKES PRODUCTION MATTHEW BRODERICK PROJECT X HELEN HUNT
MUSIC BY JAMES HORNER EXECUTIVE PRODUCER C.O. ERICKSON STORY BY STANLEY WEISER & LAWRENCE LASKER
SCREENPLAY BY STANLEY WEISER PRODUCED BY WALTER F. PARKES AND LAWRENCE LASKER
PG PARENTAL GUIDANCE SUGGESTED
DIRECTED BY JONATHAN KAPLAN
COLOR BY DELUXE
DOLBY STEREO
20th CENTURY FOX
© 1987 TWENTIETH CENTURY FOX FILM CORPORATION
STARTS TODAY

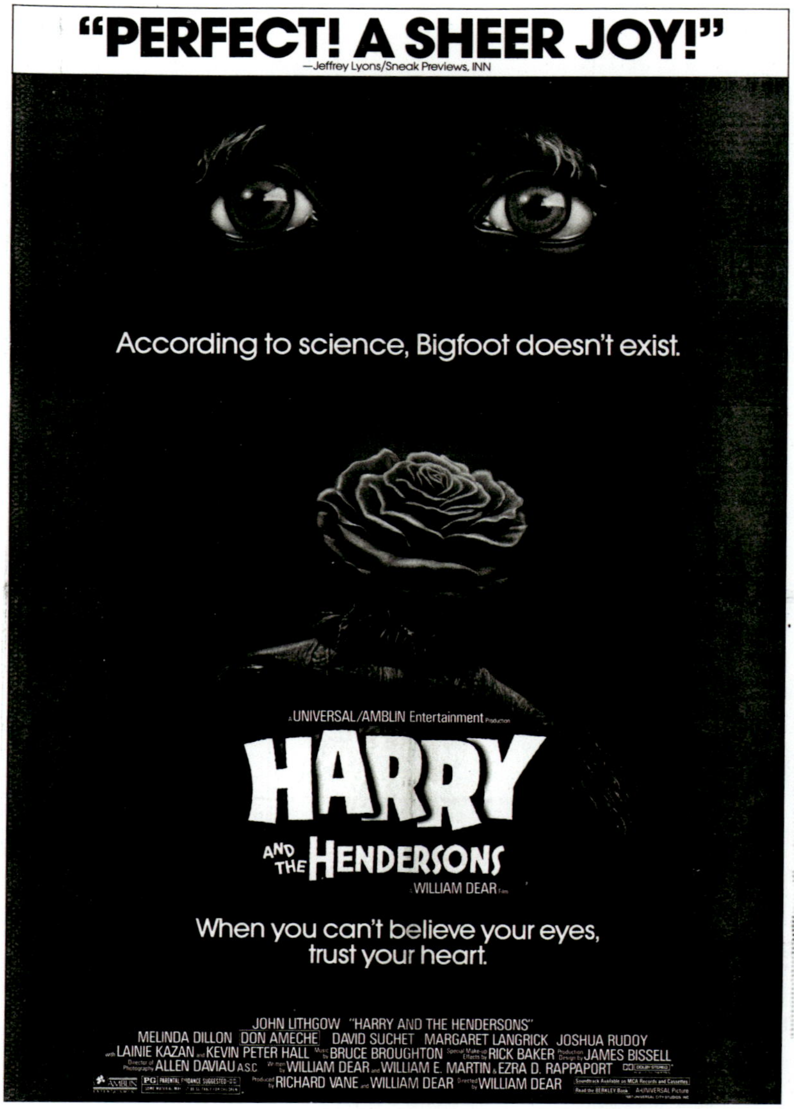

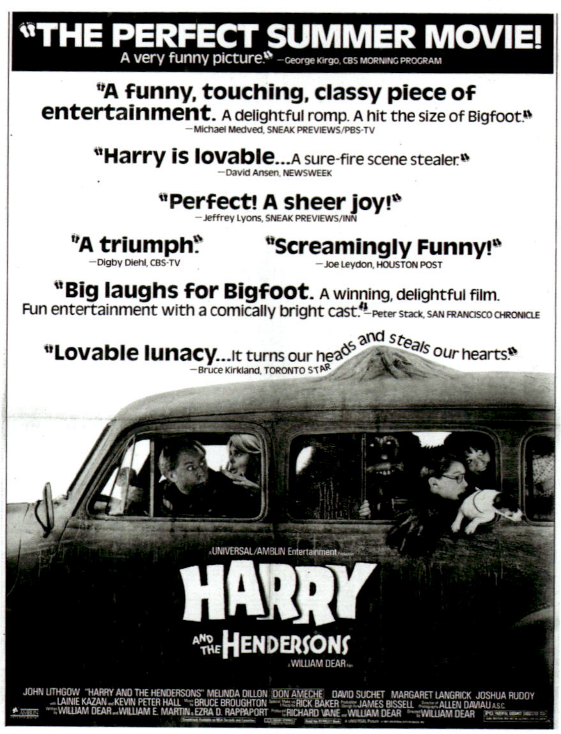

THE PRINCESS BRIDE

Directors from *Superman II*'s Richard Lester to French New Wave icon Francois Truffaut had tried to turn William Goldman's literary homage to the power of love and storytelling into a film since the early '70s. Rob Reiner finally pulled it off, with a screenplay by Goldman himself and a perfect cast. The reviews were warm, some of them stellar. So why wasn't it a bigger hit in theaters, leaving it to become beloved via video? It's... inconceivable!

"William Goldman adapted his own book for the screen, and packed it with word-play, sword-play, and scenes that work even better on film than on the page."

–Jami Bernard, *New York Post*

"I love *The Princess Bride*. It's one of the best movies of the year. It appeals to the child in me and to the middle-aged man I have become."

–JOSEPH GELMIS, NEW YORK *NEWSDAY*

"...*The Princess Bride* has sweetness and sincerity on its side, and when it comes to fairy tales, those are major assets. It also has a delightful cast and a cheery, earnest style that turns out to be ever more disarming as the film moves along."

–Janet Maslin, *The New York Times*

"The humor of *The Princess Bride* is its most distinctive feature, but Reiner doesn't lose sight of such basic values as action, adventure, and romance."

–Jay Boyar, *Orlando Sentinel*

"...I wish *The Princess Bride* had a bit more tang and flavor. But despite a certain flatness, it's the kind of movie that parents will relish taking their children to on the grounds that they themselves will also be entertained."

–Jay Carr, *The Boston Globe*

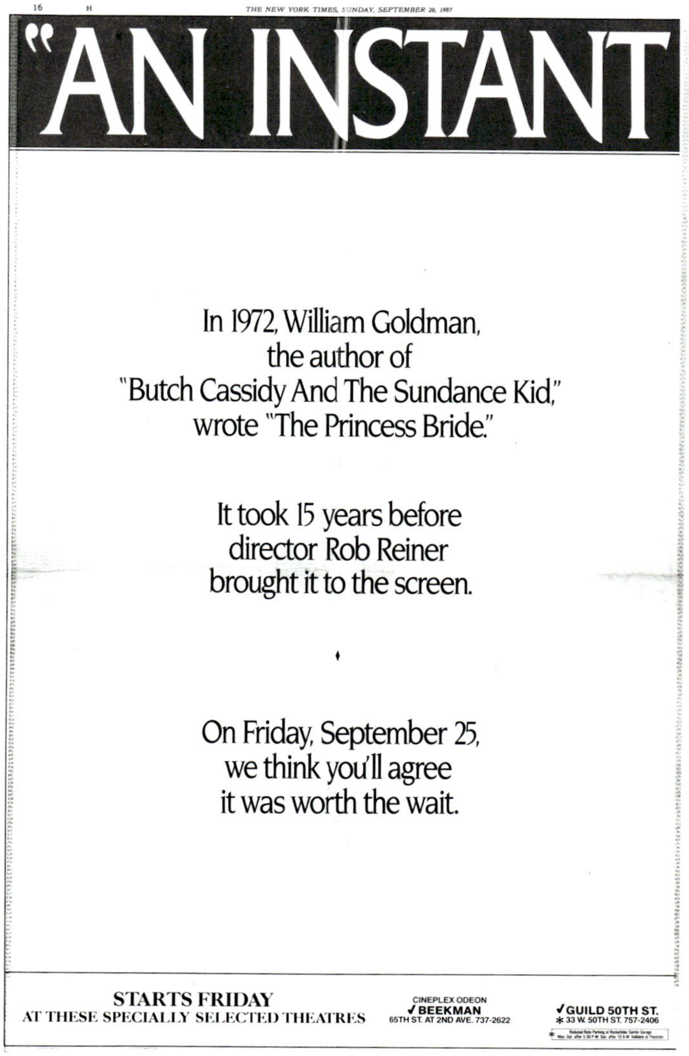
16 H
THE NEW YORK TIMES, SUNDAY, SEPTEMBER 20, 1987
"AN INSTANT
In 1972, William Goldman,
the author of
"Butch Cassidy And The Sundance Kid,"
wrote "The Princess Bride."
It took 15 years before
director Rob Reiner
brought it to the screen.
On Friday, September 25,
we think you'll agree
it was worth the wait.
STARTS FRIDAY
AT THESE SPECIALLY SELECTED THEATRES
CINEPLEX ODEON
✓BEEKMAN
65TH ST. AT 2ND AVE. 737-2622
✓GUILD 50TH ST.
33 W. 50TH ST. 757-2406

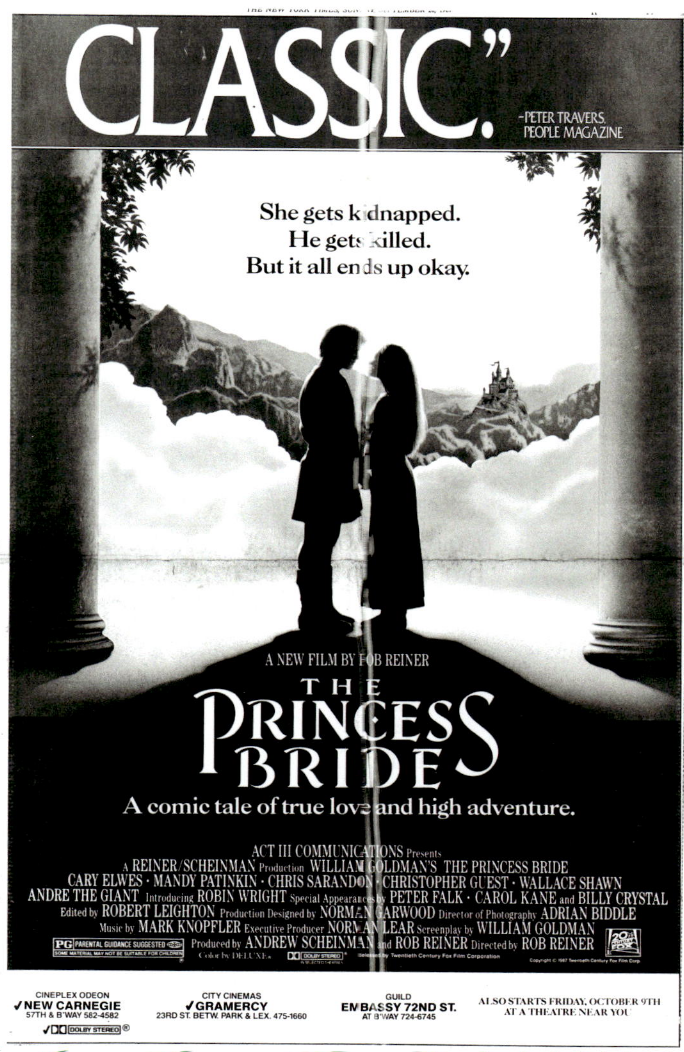
CLASSIC."
—PETER TRAVERS,
PEOPLE MAGAZINE
She gets kidnapped.
He gets killed.
But it all ends up okay.
A NEW FILM BY ROB REINER
THE
PRINCESS
BRIDE
A comic tale of true love and high adventure.
ACT III COMMUNICATIONS Presents
A REINER/SCHEINMAN Production WILLIAM GOLDMAN'S THE PRINCESS BRIDE
CARY ELWES · MANDY PATINKIN · CHRIS SARANDON · CHRISTOPHER GUEST · WALLACE SHAWN
ANDRE THE GIANT Introducing ROBIN WRIGHT Special Appearances by PETER FALK · CAROL KANE and BILLY CRYSTAL
Edited by ROBERT LEIGHTON Production Designed by NORMAN GARWOOD Director of Photography ADRIAN BIDDLE
Music by MARK KNOPFLER Executive Producer NORMAN LEAR Screenplay by WILLIAM GOLDMAN
PG PARENTAL GUIDANCE SUGGESTED
SOME MATERIAL MAY NOT BE SUITABLE FOR CHILDREN
Produced by ANDREW SCHEINMAN and ROB REINER Directed by ROB REINER
Color by DELUXE
DOLBY STEREO
Released by Twentieth Century Fox Film Corporation
Copyright © 1987 Twentieth Century Fox Film Corp.
CINEPLEX ODEON
✓NEW CARNEGIE
57TH & B'WAY 582-4582
✓DOLBY STEREO
CITY CINEMAS
✓GRAMERCY
23RD ST. BETW. PARK & LEX. 475-1660
GUILD
EMBASSY 72ND ST.
AT B'WAY 724-6745
ALSO STARTS FRIDAY, OCTOBER 9TH
AT A THEATRE NEAR YOU

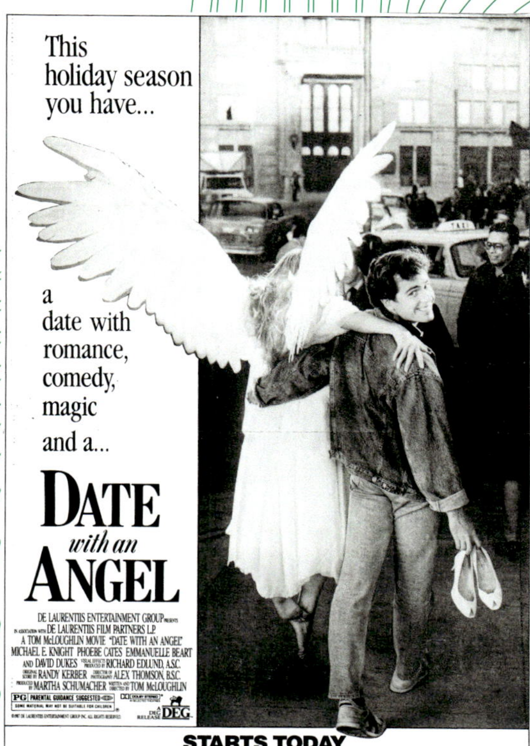
This
holiday season
you have...
a
date with
romance,
comedy,
magic
and a...
DATE
with an
ANGEL
DE LAURENTIIS ENTERTAINMENT GROUP PRESENTS
IN ASSOCIATION WITH DE LAURENTIIS FILM PARTNERS L.P.
A TOM McLOUGHLIN MOVIE "DATE WITH AN ANGEL"
MICHAEL E. KNIGHT PHOEBE CATES EMMANUELLE BEART
AND DAVID DUKES VISUAL EFFECTS PRODUCED BY RICHARD EDLUND, A.S.C.
ORIGINAL SCORE BY RANDY KERBER DIRECTOR OF PHOTOGRAPHY ALEX THOMSON, B.S.C.
PRODUCED BY MARTHA SCHUMACHER WRITTEN AND DIRECTED BY TOM McLOUGHLIN
PG PARENTAL GUIDANCE SUGGESTED
SOME MATERIAL MAY NOT BE SUITABLE FOR CHILDREN
A DEG RELEASE
DEG
STARTS TODAY

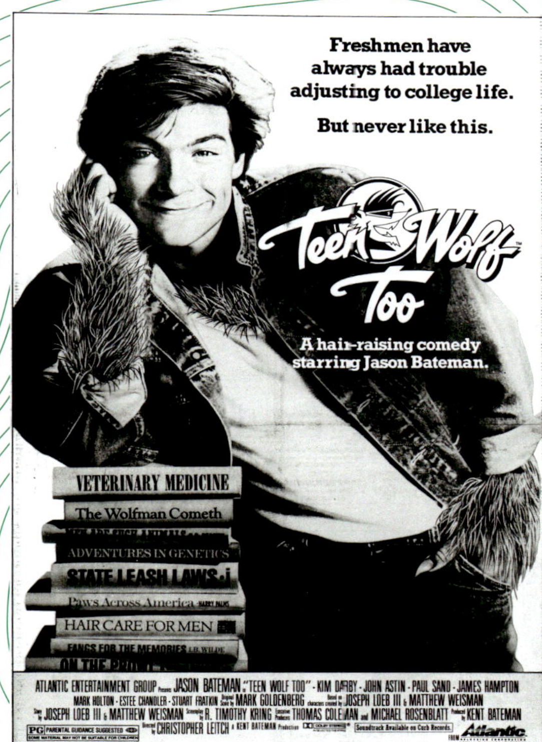
Freshmen have
always had trouble
adjusting to college life.
But never like this.
Teen Wolf
Too
A hair-raising comedy
starring Jason Bateman.
VETERINARY MEDICINE
The Wolfman Cometh
ADVENTURES IN GENETICS
STATE LEASH LAWS
Paws Across America
HAIR CARE FOR MEN
FANGS FOR THE MEMORIES
ATLANTIC ENTERTAINMENT GROUP Presents JASON BATEMAN in "TEEN WOLF TOO" · KIM DARBY · JOHN ASTIN · PAUL SAND · JAMES HAMPTON
MARK HOLTON · ESTEE CHANDLER · STUART FRATKIN Original Score by MARK GOLDENBERG characters created by JOSEPH LOEB III & MATTHEW WEISMAN
Story by JOSEPH LOEB III & MATTHEW WEISMAN Screenplay by R. TIMOTHY KRING Executive Producers THOMAS COLEMAN and MICHAEL ROSENBLATT Produced by KENT BATEMAN
PG PARENTAL GUIDANCE SUGGESTED
SOME MATERIAL MAY NOT BE SUITABLE FOR CHILDREN
Directed by CHRISTOPHER LEITCH A KENT BATEMAN Production
Soundtrack Available on Curb Records.
FROM Atlantic

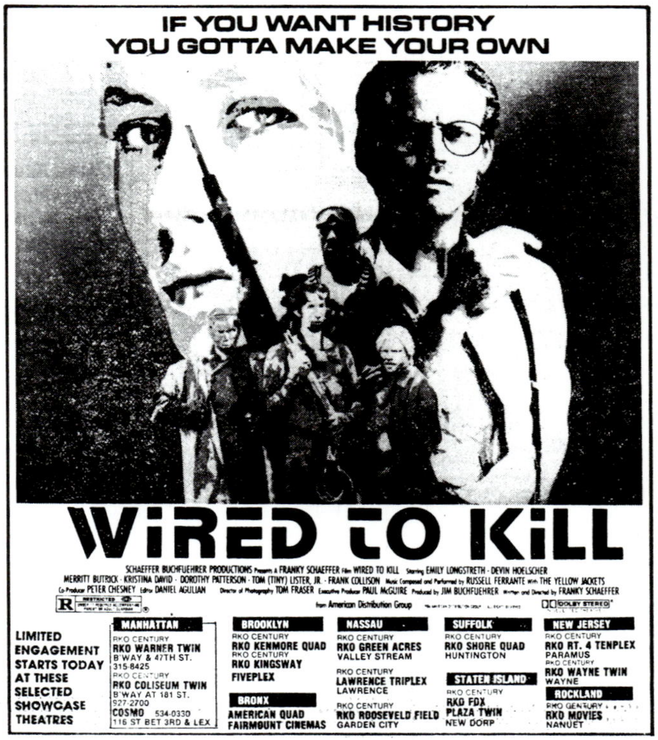

ROBOCOP

Like Orion's *The Terminator*, *RoboCop* – which used that film's music in its trailer – didn't seem like a film to take very seriously at first. Then critics, followed by audiences, saw it and turned it into a sleeper hit. Amidst the unexpectedly moving drama of Peter Weller's Murphy struggling to regain his humanity behind RoboCop's metal face, Edward Neumeier and Michael Miner's screenplay offered an abundance of wit and social commentary, while director Paul Verhoeven delivered hard-hitting, often gory action. Pretty much all the reviews noted the extreme level of bloodshed – though only a few found it a dealbreaker.

"[I]n its own perverse, ultra violent way, Verhoeven's new comic book/science fiction/super cop movie glistens with a ll the dark brilliance of the now almost legendary *Blade Runner*."

–Malcolm L. Johnson, *Hartford Courant*

"Despite a level of lurid violence that may offend many, this movie has a motor humming inside. It's been assembled with ferocious, gleeful expertise, crammed with humor, cynicism, and jolts of energy. In many ways, it's the best action movie of the year."

–Michael Wilmington, *Los Angeles Times*

"In *RoboCop*, Verhoeven delivers a twitchy, offbeat, utterly heartless science-fiction flick that gives a transfusion of battery acid and wit into sanitized summer-action fare. ... [T]his is science fiction from the wild side, and it's fun. In a gory way, that is."

–ROBERT S. CAUTHORN, *ARIZONA DAILY STAR*

"The gap between the toy-like level the movie operates on and the dangerous games it plays is queasy. *RoboCop* is not just a movie you feel guilty about the morning after; it's one you feel guilty about as soon as you exit the theater."

–Michael Sragow, *San Francisco Examiner*

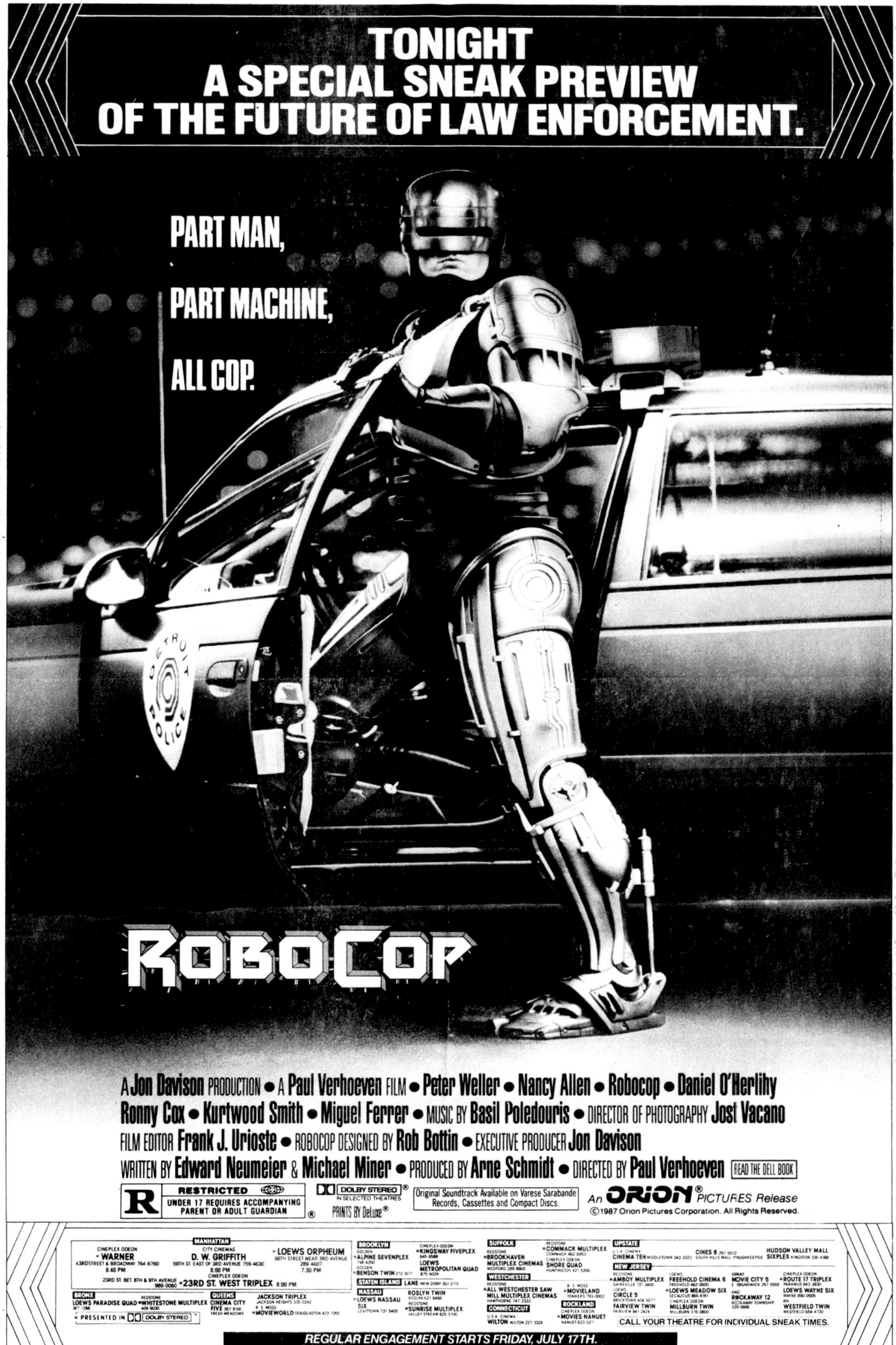
TONIGHT
A SPECIAL SNEAK PREVIEW
OF THE FUTURE OF LAW ENFORCEMENT.
PART MAN,
PART MACHINE,
ALL COP.
DETROIT POLICE
ROBOCOP
A Jon Davison PRODUCTION • A Paul Verhoeven FILM • Peter Weller • Nancy Allen • Robocop • Daniel O'Herlihy
Ronny Cox • Kurtwood Smith • Miguel Ferrer • MUSIC BY Basil Poledouris • DIRECTOR OF PHOTOGRAPHY Jost Vacano
FILM EDITOR Frank J. Urioste • ROBOCOP DESIGNED BY Rob Bottin • EXECUTIVE PRODUCER Jon Davison
WRITTEN BY Edward Neumeier & Michael Miner • PRODUCED BY Arne Schmidt • DIRECTED BY Paul Verhoeven
READ THE DELL BOOK
R RESTRICTED
UNDER 17 REQUIRES ACCOMPANYING PARENT OR ADULT GUARDIAN
DOLBY STEREO IN SELECTED THEATRES
PRINTS BY DeLuxe®
Original Soundtrack Available on Varese Sarabande Records, Cassettes and Compact Discs.
An ORION® PICTURES Release
©1987 Orion Pictures Corporation. All Rights Reserved.
MANHATTAN
CINEPLEX ODEON *WARNER 43RDSTREET & BROADWAY 764-6760 8:40 PM
CITY CINEMAS D. W. GRIFFITH 59TH ST. EAST OF 3RD AVENUE 759-4630 8:00 PM
*LOEWS ORPHEUM 86TH STREET NEAR 3RD AVENUE 289-4607 7:30 PM
CINEPLEX ODEON *23RD ST. WEST TRIPLEX 23RD ST. BET. 8TH & 9TH AVENUE 989-0060 8:00 PM
BRONX
LOEWS PARADISE QUAD 367-1288
REDSTONE *WHITESTONE MULTIPLEX 409-9030
QUEENS
CINEMA CITY FIVE 357-9100 FRESH MEADOWS
JACKSON TRIPLEX JACKSON HEIGHTS 335-0242
B. S. MOSS *MOVIEWORLD DOUGLASTON 423-7200
* PRESENTED IN DOLBY STEREO
BROOKLYN
GOLDEN *ALPINE SEVENPLEX 748-4200
GOLDEN *BENSON TWIN 372-1617
CINEPLEX ODEON *KINGSWAY FIVEPLEX 645-8588
LOEWS METROPOLITAN QUAD 875-4024
STATEN ISLAND
LANE NEW DORP 351-2110
NASSAU
*LOEWS NASSAU SIX LEVITTOWN 731-5400
ROSLYN TWIN ROSLYN 621-8488
REDSTONE *SUNRISE MULTIPLEX VALLEY STREAM 825-5700
SUFFOLK
REDSTONE *BROOKHAVEN MULTIPLEX CINEMAS MEDFORD 289-8900
REDSTONE *COMMACK MULTIPLEX COMMACK 462-6953
CINEPLEX ODEON SHORE QUAD HUNTINGTON 421-5200
WESTCHESTER
REDSTONE *ALL WESTCHESTER SAW MILL MULTIPLEX CINEMAS HAWTHORNE 747-2333
B. S. MOSS *MOVIELAND YONKERS 793-0002
CONNECTICUT
U.S.A. CINEMA WILTON WILTON 227-3324
ROCKLAND
CINEPLEX ODEON *MOVIES NANUET NANUET 623-0211
UPSTATE
U.S.A. CINEMA CINEMA TEN MIDDLETOWN 343-3323
CINES 8 297-5512 SOUTH HILLS MALL POUGHKEEPSIE
HUDSON VALLEY MALL SIXPLEX KINGSTON 336-4188
NEW JERSEY
REDSTONE *AMBOY MULTIPLEX SAYREVILLE 721-3400
LOEWS CIRCLE 5 BRICKTOWN 458-5077
FAIRVIEW TWIN FAIRVIEW 941-2424
LOEWS FREEHOLD CINEMA 6 FREEHOLD 462-0600
*LOEWS MEADOW SIX SECAUCUS 866-6161
CINEPLEX ODEON MILLBURN TWIN MILLBURN 376-0800
GRANT MOVIE CITY 5 E. BRUNSWICK 257-5555
AMC ROCKAWAY 12 ROCKAWAY TOWNSHIP 328-0666
CINEPLEX ODEON *ROUTE 17 TRIPLEX PARAMUS 843-3830
LOEWS WAYNE SIX WAYNE 890-0505
RH WESTFIELD TWIN WESTFIELD 654-4720
CALL YOUR THEATRE FOR INDIVIDUAL SNEAK TIMES.
REGULAR ENGAGEMENT STARTS FRIDAY, JULY 17TH.

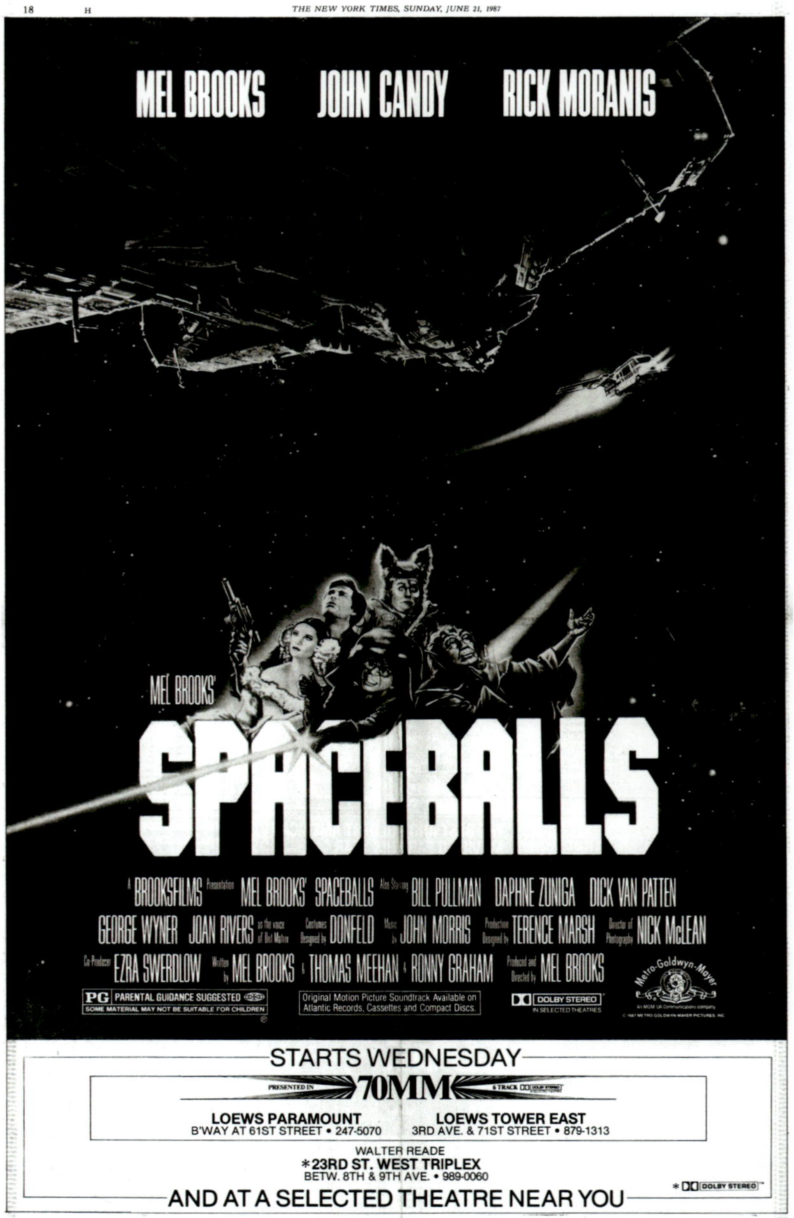

SPACEBALLS

Mel Brooks' previous spoofs had lampooned classic films and forms: westerns, Universal monsters, silent movies and Hitchcock thrillers. For his first feature in the six years since *History of the World, Pt. 1*, he went after a more recent target: *Star Wars*, along with other sci-fi favorites. When it comes to reviewing this kind of gagfest, it boils down to whether you laugh or you don't, and sure enough, when it came to *Spaceballs*, The Schwartz was with only some critics.

"*Spaceballs* is Mel Brooks' funniest movie since *Young Frankenstein*. ... [It] has the happy air of a comic enterprise that knows it's going right."

–Jay Carr, *The Boston Globe*

"Brooks, who has been off target more than he has been on over the past decade, has rediscovered his creative juices for this often-hilarious film."

–Jack Garner, Gannett News Service

"[I]t's hardly a secret that Brooks will stop at nothing for a laugh. But even if the story line sags a bit, it's really a kick to watch Brooks playfully zap everything from *Aliens* to *Planet of the Apes*."

–Kathleen Carroll, New York *Daily News*

"[S]ince the gags are a little tacky... it seems wrong that the sets and effects aren't more tacky, too. *Spaceballs* might have been much funnier and more inventive on a much smaller budget."

–MICHAEL WILMINGTON, *LOS ANGELES TIMES*

"Fashion in humor is fickle, and changing tastes have left Mel Brooks' new comedy, *Spaceballs*, looking like a vaguely embarrassing souvenir of the early '70s. ... Brooks' own timing as a director doesn't seem up to its usual snuff."

–Dave Kehr, *Chicago Tribune*

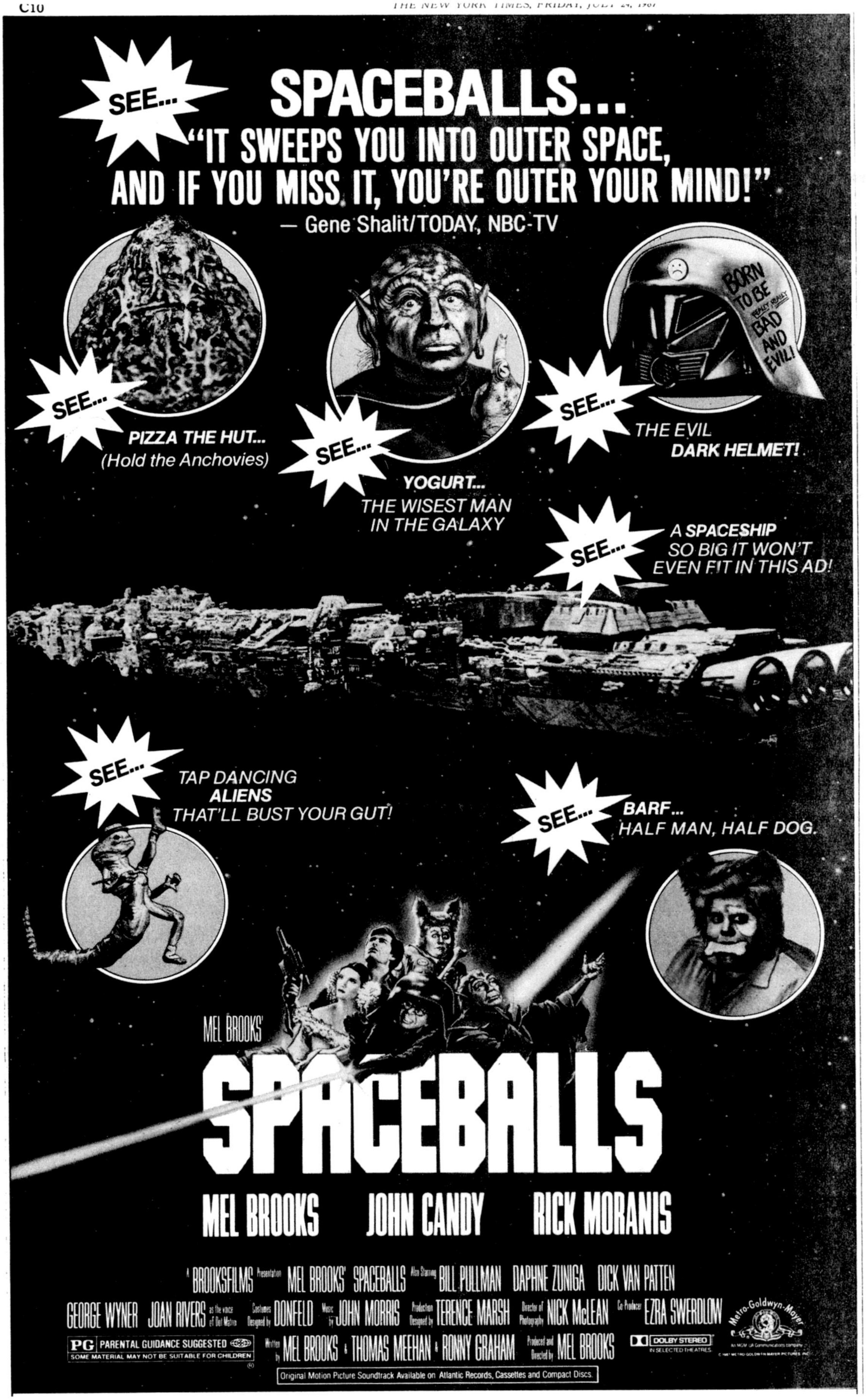
SEE...
SPACEBALLS...
"IT SWEEPS YOU INTO OUTER SPACE, AND IF YOU MISS IT, YOU'RE OUTER YOUR MIND!"
— Gene Shalit/TODAY, NBC-TV
BORN TO BE BAD AND EVIL!
SEE...
PIZZA THE HUT...
(Hold the Anchovies)
SEE...
YOGURT...
THE WISEST MAN IN THE GALAXY
SEE...
THE EVIL DARK HELMET!
SEE...
A SPACESHIP SO BIG IT WON'T EVEN FIT IN THIS AD!
SEE...
TAP DANCING ALIENS THAT'LL BUST YOUR GUT!
SEE...
BARF... HALF MAN, HALF DOG.
MEL BROOKS'
SPACEBALLS
MEL BROOKS JOHN CANDY RICK MORANIS
A BROOKSFILMS Presentation MEL BROOKS' SPACEBALLS Also Starring BILL PULLMAN DAPHNE ZUNIGA DICK VAN PATTEN
GEORGE WYNER JOAN RIVERS as the voice of Dot Matrix Costumes Designed by DONFELD Music by JOHN MORRIS Production Designed by TERENCE MARSH Director of Photography NICK McLEAN Co-Producer EZRA SWERDLOW
PG PARENTAL GUIDANCE SUGGESTED
SOME MATERIAL MAY NOT BE SUITABLE FOR CHILDREN
Written by MEL BROOKS & THOMAS MEEHAN & RONNY GRAHAM Produced and Directed by MEL BROOKS
DOLBY STEREO
IN SELECTED THEATRES
Metro-Goldwyn-Mayer
Original Motion Picture Soundtrack Available on Atlantic Records, Cassettes and Compact Discs.

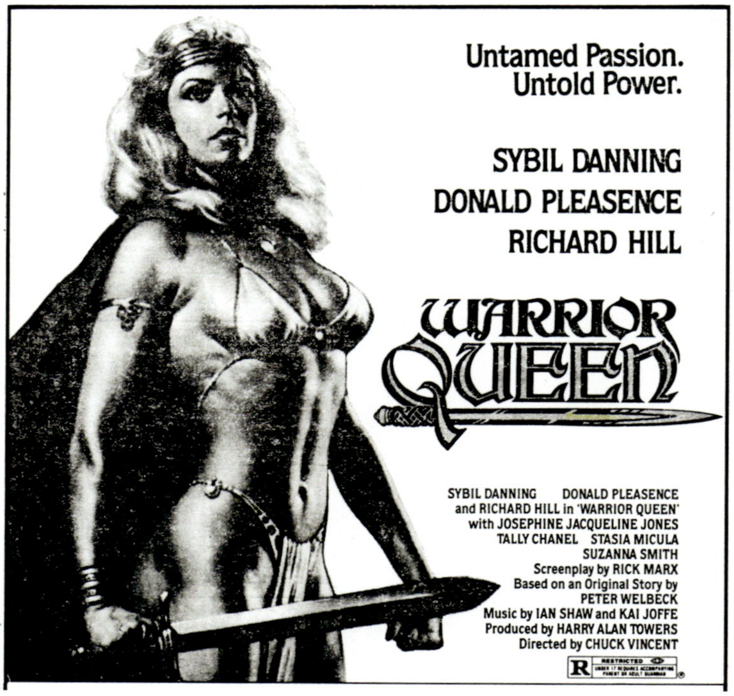

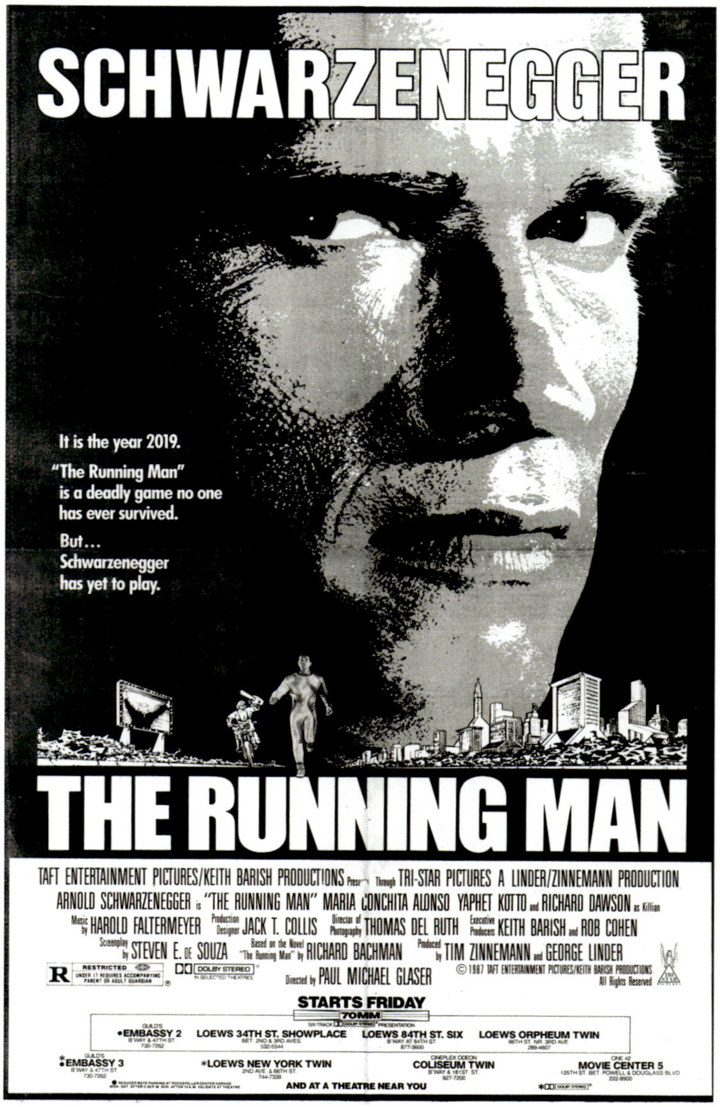

SUPERMAN IV: THE QUEST FOR PEACE

When the latest incarnation of a property as big as *Superman* opens with no critics' screenings, you know something's wrong. In fact, something was wrong from the moment the Salkinds signed over the rights to the franchise to the notorious schlockmeisters at Cannon Films, who cheaped out on *Superman IV*'s budget in general and the special effects in particular, and stymied Christopher Reeve's attempts to tell a relevant story about the Man of Steel fighting for disarmament. The critical response was not so much distressing as inevitable.

"The cast wears costumes that are swanky but very strange, and the dialogue is also unexpectedly funny at times. ... Threadbare as it's beginning to look, the Superman series hasn't lost its *raison d'etre*. There's life in the old boy yet."

–Janet Maslin, *The New York Times*

"It's a plane – it's a bird – it's a *turkey!!! Superman IV: The Quest for Peace* gets aloft with all the grace and intelligence of a 400-pound gobbler that's been lobotomized."

–ROGER FRISTOE, LOUISVILLE, KY *COURIER-JOURNAL*

"With 30 minutes lobbed [sic] out at the last moment, *Superman IV: The Quest for Peace* is only 85 minutes long and suffers from choppiness, but it is not the outright disaster that Hollywood gossips predicted."

–Scott Cain, *The Atlanta Constitution*

"*Superman IV: The Quest for* Peace...weighs in as a 90-pound weakling among superhero movies. It's not grating or offensive. It *is* tacky and skimpy."

–Michael Sragow, *San Francisco Examiner*

"*Superman IV* is a pathetic appendage to the series, a dull, shoddy film. ... The signs of budget slashing are everywhere, from the frequent recourse to stock footage to the shaky flying sequences, so poorly matted that they would shame the hero of a Republic serial."

–Dave Kehr, *Chicago Tribune*

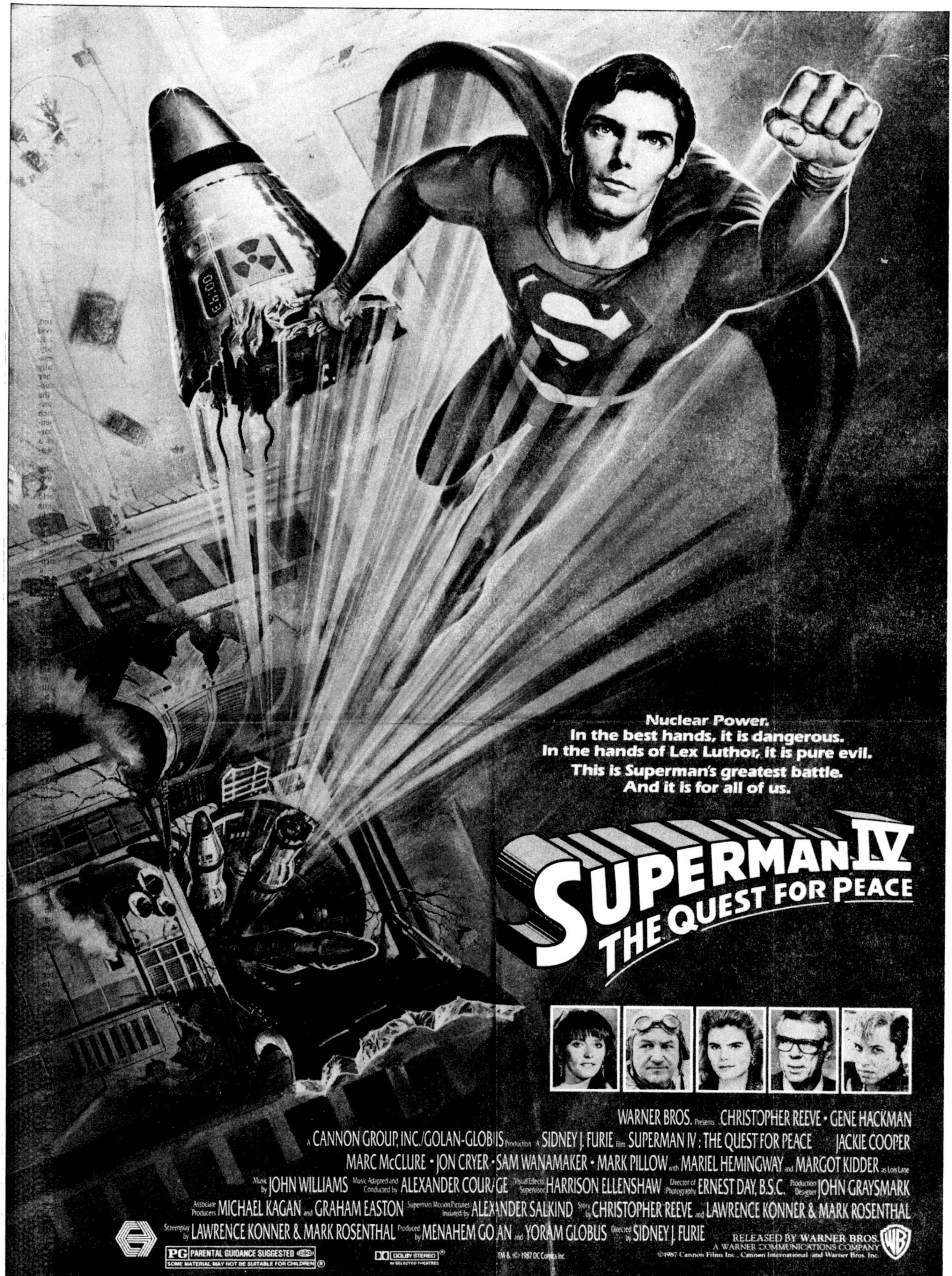
Nuclear Power.
In the best hands, it is dangerous.
In the hands of Lex Luthor, it is pure evil.
This is Superman's greatest battle.
And it is for all of us.
SUPERMAN IV
THE QUEST FOR PEACE
WARNER BROS. Presents CHRISTOPHER REEVE • GENE HACKMAN
A CANNON GROUP, INC./GOLAN-GLOBUS Production A SIDNEY J. FURIE Film SUPERMAN IV : THE QUEST FOR PEACE JACKIE COOPER
MARC McCLURE • JON CRYER • SAM WANAMAKER • MARK PILLOW with MARIEL HEMINGWAY and MARGOT KIDDER as Lois Lane
Music by JOHN WILLIAMS Music Adapted and Conducted by ALEXANDER COURAGE Visual Effects Supervisor HARRISON ELLENSHAW Director of Photography ERNEST DAY, B.S.C. Production Designer JOHN GRAYSMARK
Associate Producers MICHAEL KAGAN and GRAHAM EASTON Superman Motion Pictures Initiated by ALEXANDER SALKIND Story by CHRISTOPHER REEVE and LAWRENCE KONNER & MARK ROSENTHAL
Screenplay by LAWRENCE KONNER & MARK ROSENTHAL Produced by MENAHEM GOLAN and YORAM GLOBUS Directed by SIDNEY J. FURIE
PG PARENTAL GUIDANCE SUGGESTED
SOME MATERIAL MAY NOT BE SUITABLE FOR CHILDREN
DOLBY STEREO
IN SELECTED THEATRES
TM & © 1987 DC Comics Inc.
RELEASED BY WARNER BROS.
A WARNER COMMUNICATIONS COMPANY
©1987 Cannon Films Inc., Cannon International and Warner Bros. Inc.

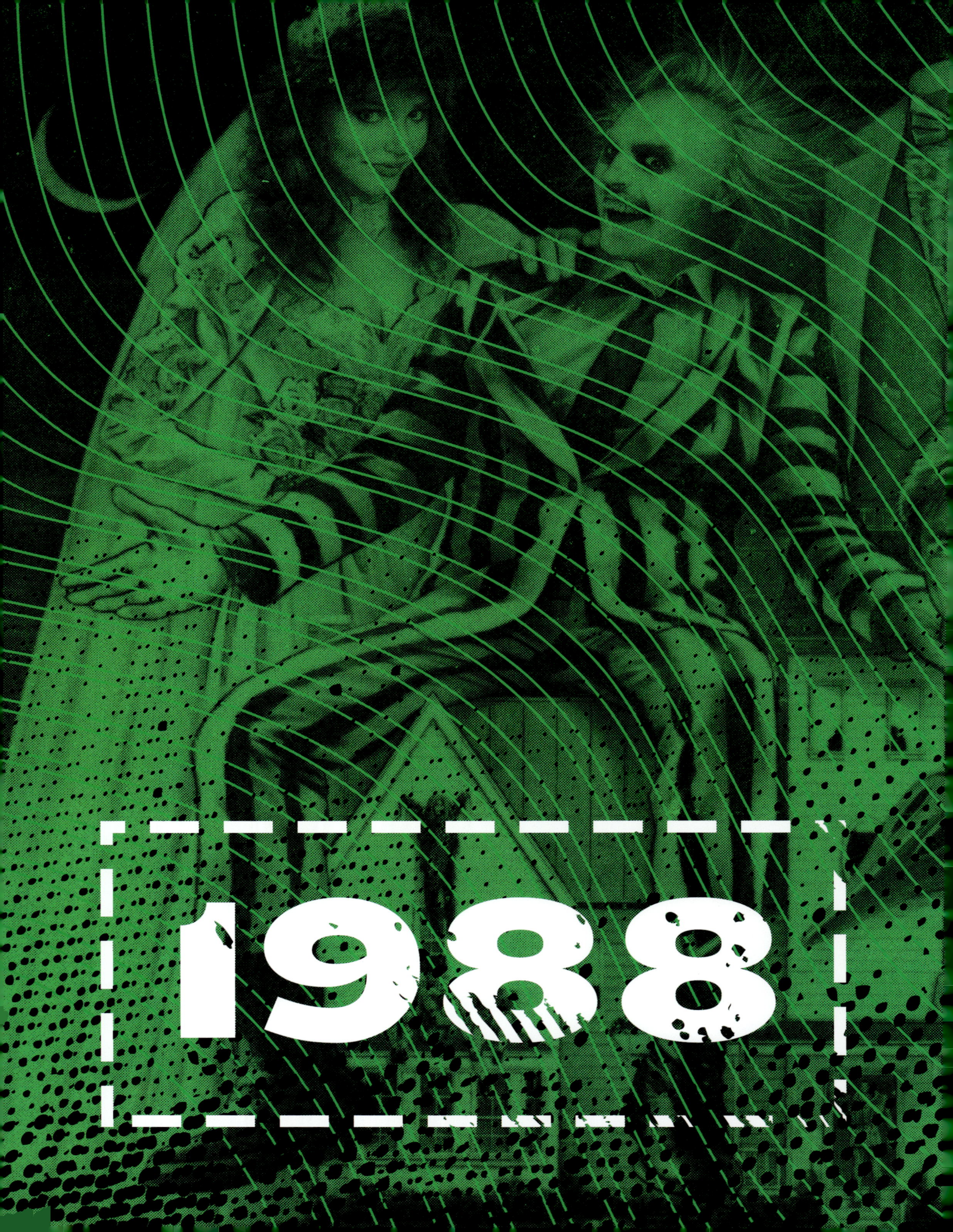
1988

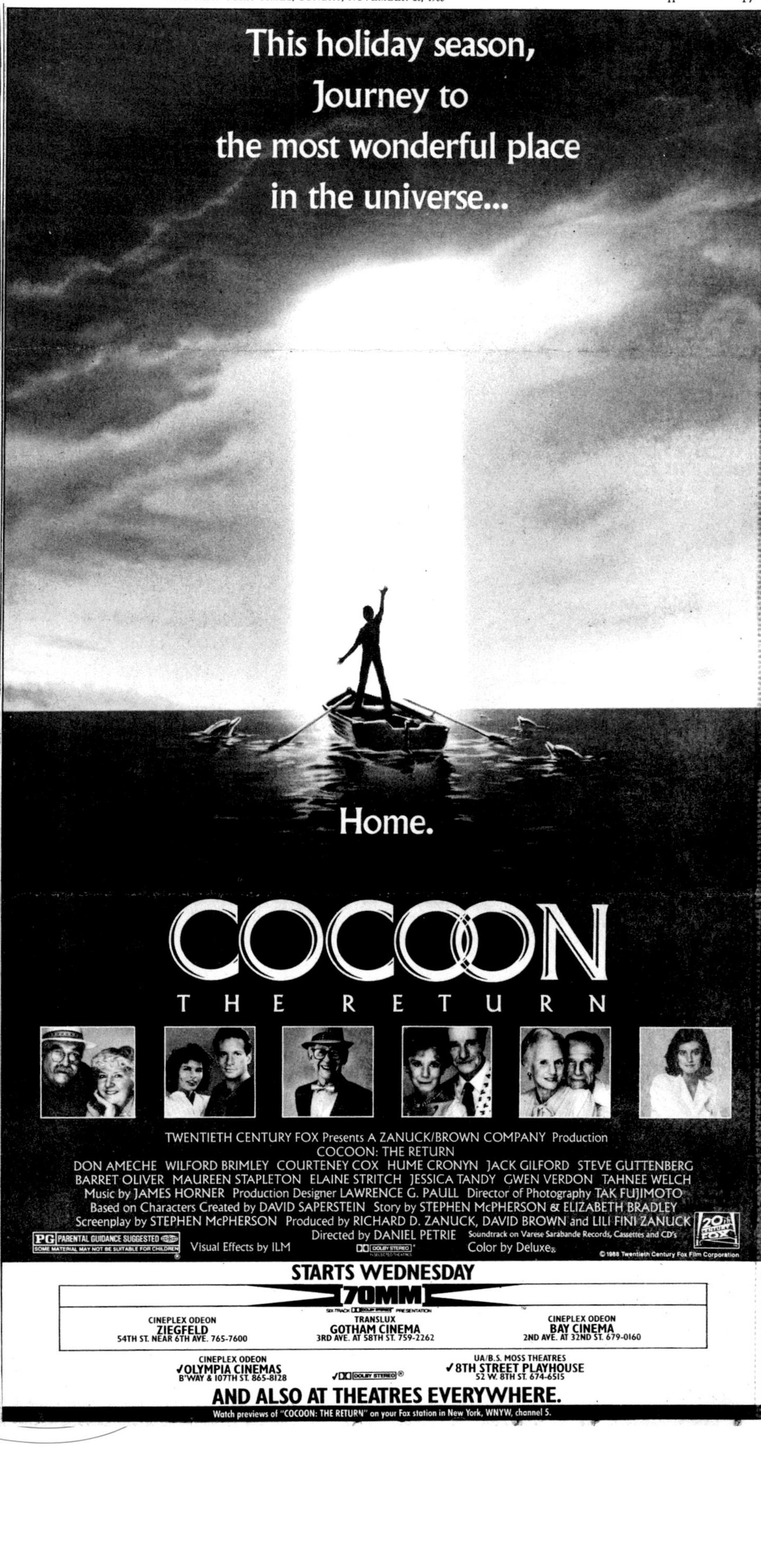
This holiday season,
Journey to
the most wonderful place
in the universe...
Home.
COCOON
THE RETURN
TWENTIETH CENTURY FOX Presents A ZANUCK/BROWN COMPANY Production
COCOON: THE RETURN
DON AMECHE WILFORD BRIMLEY COURTENEY COX HUME CRONYN JACK GILFORD STEVE GUTTENBERG
BARRET OLIVER MAUREEN STAPLETON ELAINE STRITCH JESSICA TANDY GWEN VERDON TAHNEE WELCH
Music by JAMES HORNER Production Designer LAWRENCE G. PAULL Director of Photography TAK FUJIMOTO
Based on Characters Created by DAVID SAPERSTEIN Story by STEPHEN McPHERSON & ELIZABETH BRADLEY
Screenplay by STEPHEN McPHERSON Produced by RICHARD D. ZANUCK, DAVID BROWN and LILI FINI ZANUCK
Directed by DANIEL PETRIE
Soundtrack on Varese Sarabande Records, Cassettes and CD's
PG PARENTAL GUIDANCE SUGGESTED
SOME MATERIAL MAY NOT BE SUITABLE FOR CHILDREN
Visual Effects by ILM
Color by Deluxe
© 1988 Twentieth Century Fox Film Corporation
STARTS WEDNESDAY
70MM
CINEPLEX ODEON ZIEGFELD 54TH ST. NEAR 6TH AVE. 765-7600
TRANSLUX GOTHAM CINEMA 3RD AVE. AT 58TH ST. 759-2262
CINEPLEX ODEON BAY CINEMA 2ND AVE. AT 32ND ST. 679-0160
CINEPLEX ODEON ✓OLYMPIA CINEMAS B'WAY & 107TH ST. 865-8128
UA/B.S. MOSS THEATRES ✓8TH STREET PLAYHOUSE 52 W. 8TH ST. 674-6515
AND ALSO AT THEATRES EVERYWHERE.
Watch previews of "COCOON: THE RETURN" on your Fox station in New York, WNYW, channel 5.

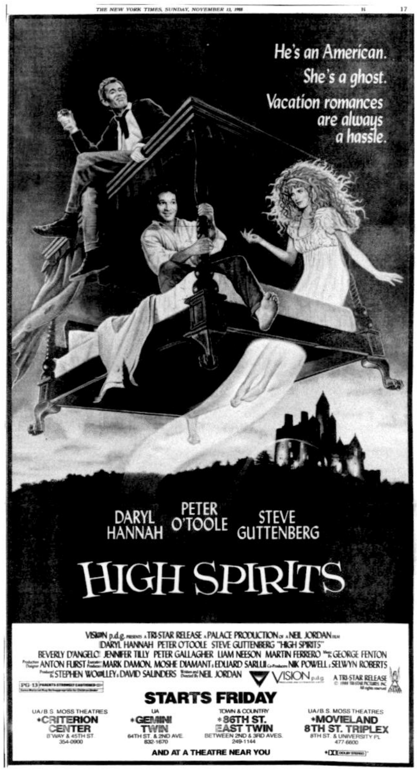
He's an American.
She's a ghost.
Vacation romances
are always
a hassle.
DARYL HANNAH
PETER O'TOOLE
STEVE GUTTENBERG
HIGH SPIRITS
VISION p.d.g. presents a TRI-STAR RELEASE a PALACE PRODUCTION of a NEIL JORDAN film
DARYL HANNAH PETER O'TOOLE STEVE GUTTENBERG "HIGH SPIRITS"
BEVERLY D'ANGELO JENNIFER TILLY PETER GALLAGHER LIAM NEESON MARTIN FERRERO Music by GEORGE FENTON
Production Designer ANTON FURST Executive Producers MARK DAMON, MOSHE DIAMANT & EDUARD SARLUI Co-Producers NIK POWELL & SELWYN ROBERTS
Produced by STEPHEN WOOLLEY & DAVID SAUNDERS Written and Directed by NEIL JORDAN
A TRI-STAR RELEASE
STARTS FRIDAY
UA/B.S. MOSS THEATRES +CRITERION CENTER B'WAY & 45TH ST. 354-0900
UA +GEMINI TWIN 64TH ST. & 2ND AVE. 832-1670
TOWN & COUNTRY +86TH ST. EAST TWIN BETWEEN 2ND & 3RD AVES. 249-1144
UA/B.S. MOSS THEATRES +MOVIELAND 8TH ST. TRIPLEX 8TH ST. & UNIVERSITY PL. 477-6600
AND AT A THEATRE NEAR YOU

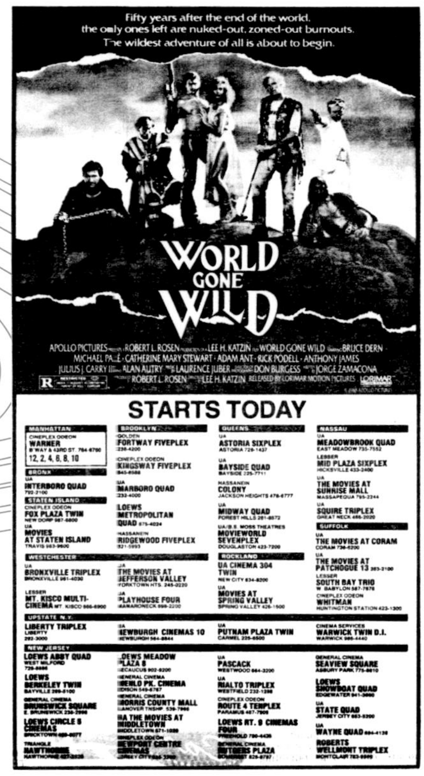
Fifty years after the end of the world,
the only ones left are nuked-out, zoned-out burnouts.
The wildest adventure of all is about to begin.
WORLD GONE WILD
APOLLO PICTURES presents a ROBERT L. ROSEN production of a LEE H. KATZIN film WORLD GONE WILD starring BRUCE DERN
MICHAEL PARÉ · CATHERINE MARY STEWART · ADAM ANT · RICK PODELL · ANTHONY JAMES
JULIUS J. CARRY III · ALAN AUTRY Music by LAURENCE JUBER Director of Photography DON BURGESS Written by JORGE ZAMACONA
Produced by ROBERT L. ROSEN Directed by LEE H. KATZIN RELEASED BY LORIMAR MOTION PICTURES LORIMAR
STARTS TODAY
MANHATTAN
CINEPLEX ODEON WARNER B'WAY & 43RD ST. 764-6760 12, 2, 4, 6, 8, 10
BRONX
UA INTERBORO QUAD 792-2100
STATEN ISLAND
CINEPLEX ODEON FOX PLAZA TWIN NEW DORP 987-6800
UA MOVIES AT STATEN ISLAND TRAVIS 983-9600
BROOKLYN
GOLDEN FORTWAY FIVEPLEX 238-4200
CINEPLEX ODEON KINGSWAY FIVEPLEX 645-8588
UA MARBORO QUAD 232-4000
LOEWS METROPOLITAN QUAD 875-4024
HASSANEIN RIDGEWOOD FIVEPLEX 821-5993
QUEENS
UA ASTORIA SIXPLEX ASTORIA 726-1437
UA BAYSIDE QUAD BAYSIDE 225-7711
HASSANEIN COLONY JACKSON HEIGHTS 478-6777
UA MIDWAY QUAD FOREST HILLS 261-8572
UA/B.S. MOSS THEATRES MOVIEWORLD SEVENPLEX DOUGLASTON 423-7200
NASSAU
UA MEADOWBROOK QUAD EAST MEADOW 735-7552
LESSER MID PLAZA SIXPLEX HICKSVILLE 433-2400
UA THE MOVIES AT SUNRISE MALL MASSAPEQUA 795-2244
UA SQUIRE TRIPLEX GREAT NECK 466-2020
SUFFOLK
UA THE MOVIES AT CORAM CORAM 736-6200
UA THE MOVIES AT PATCHOGUE 13 363-2100
LESSER SOUTH BAY TRIO W. BABYLON 587-7676
CINEPLEX ODEON WHITMAN HUNTINGTON STATION 423-1300
WESTCHESTER
UA BRONXVILLE TRIPLEX BRONXVILLE 961-4030
LESSER MT. KISCO MULTI-CINEMA MT. KISCO 666-6900
UA THE MOVIES AT JEFFERSON VALLEY YORKTOWN HTS. 245-0220
UA PLAYHOUSE FOUR MAMARONECK 698-2200
ROCKLAND
UA CINEMA 304 TWIN NEW CITY 634-8200
UA MOVIES AT SPRING VALLEY SPRING VALLEY 426-1500
UPSTATE N.Y.
LIBERTY TRIPLEX LIBERTY 292-3000
UA NEWBURGH CINEMAS 10 NEWBURGH 564-8844
UA PUTNAM PLAZA TWIN CARMEL 225-6500
CINEMA SERVICES WARWICK TWIN D.I. WARWICK 986-4440
NEW JERSEY
LOEWS ABBY QUAD WEST MILFORD
LOEWS BERKELEY TWIN BAYVILLE 269-5100
GENERAL CINEMA BRUNSWICK SQUARE E. BRUNSWICK
LOEWS CIRCLE 8 CINEMAS BRICKTOWN
TRIANGLE HAWTHORNE HAWTHORNE
LOEWS MEADOW PLAZA 8 SECAUCUS 902-9200
GENERAL CINEMA MENLO PK. CINEMA EDISON 549-6767
GENERAL CINEMA MORRIS COUNTY MALL HANOVER TWSHP.
UA THE MOVIES AT MIDDLETOWN MIDDLETOWN 671-1020
CINEPLEX ODEON NEWPORT CENTRE CINEMAS JERSEY CITY
UA PASCACK WESTWOOD 664-3200
UA RIALTO TRIPLEX WESTFIELD 232-1288
CINEPLEX ODEON ROUTE 4 TENPLEX PARAMUS 487-7909
LOEWS RT. 9 CINEMAS FOUR FREEHOLD 780-4436
GENERAL CINEMA RUTGERS PLAZA SOMERSET
GENERAL CINEMA SEAVIEW SQUARE ASBURY PARK 775-8810
LOEWS SHOWBOAT QUAD EDGEWATER 941-3660
UA STATE QUAD JERSEY CITY 653-5200
UA WAYNE QUAD 694-4136
ROBERTS WELLMONT TRIPLEX MONTCLAIR 783-9500

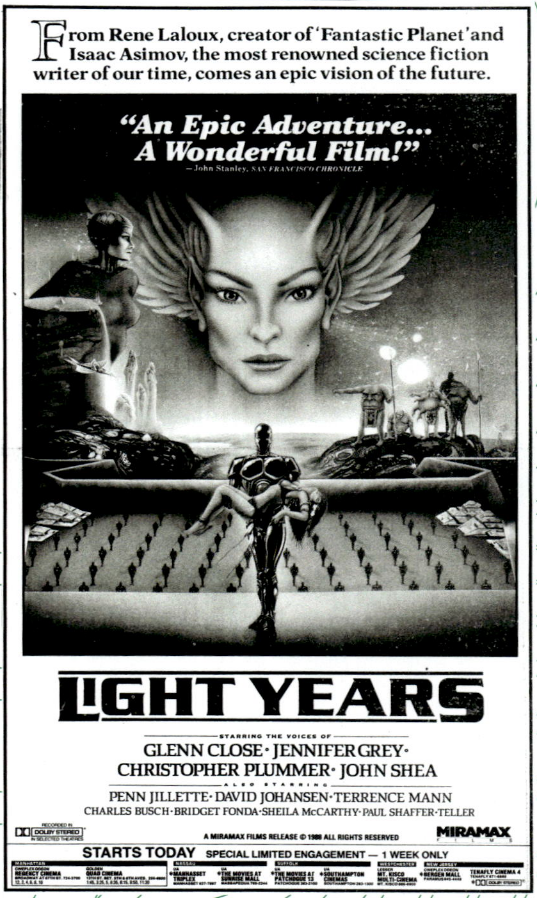
From Rene Laloux, creator of 'Fantastic Planet' and Isaac Asimov, the most renowned science fiction writer of our time, comes an epic vision of the future.
"An Epic Adventure... A Wonderful Film!"
— John Stanley, SAN FRANCISCO CHRONICLE
LIGHT YEARS
STARRING THE VOICES OF
GLENN CLOSE · JENNIFER GREY · CHRISTOPHER PLUMMER · JOHN SHEA
ALSO STARRING
PENN JILLETTE · DAVID JOHANSEN · TERRENCE MANN
CHARLES BUSCH · BRIDGET FONDA · SHEILA McCARTHY · PAUL SHAFFER · TELLER
DOLBY STEREO
A MIRAMAX FILMS RELEASE © 1988 ALL RIGHTS RESERVED
MIRAMAX FILMS
STARTS TODAY SPECIAL LIMITED ENGAGEMENT — 1 WEEK ONLY

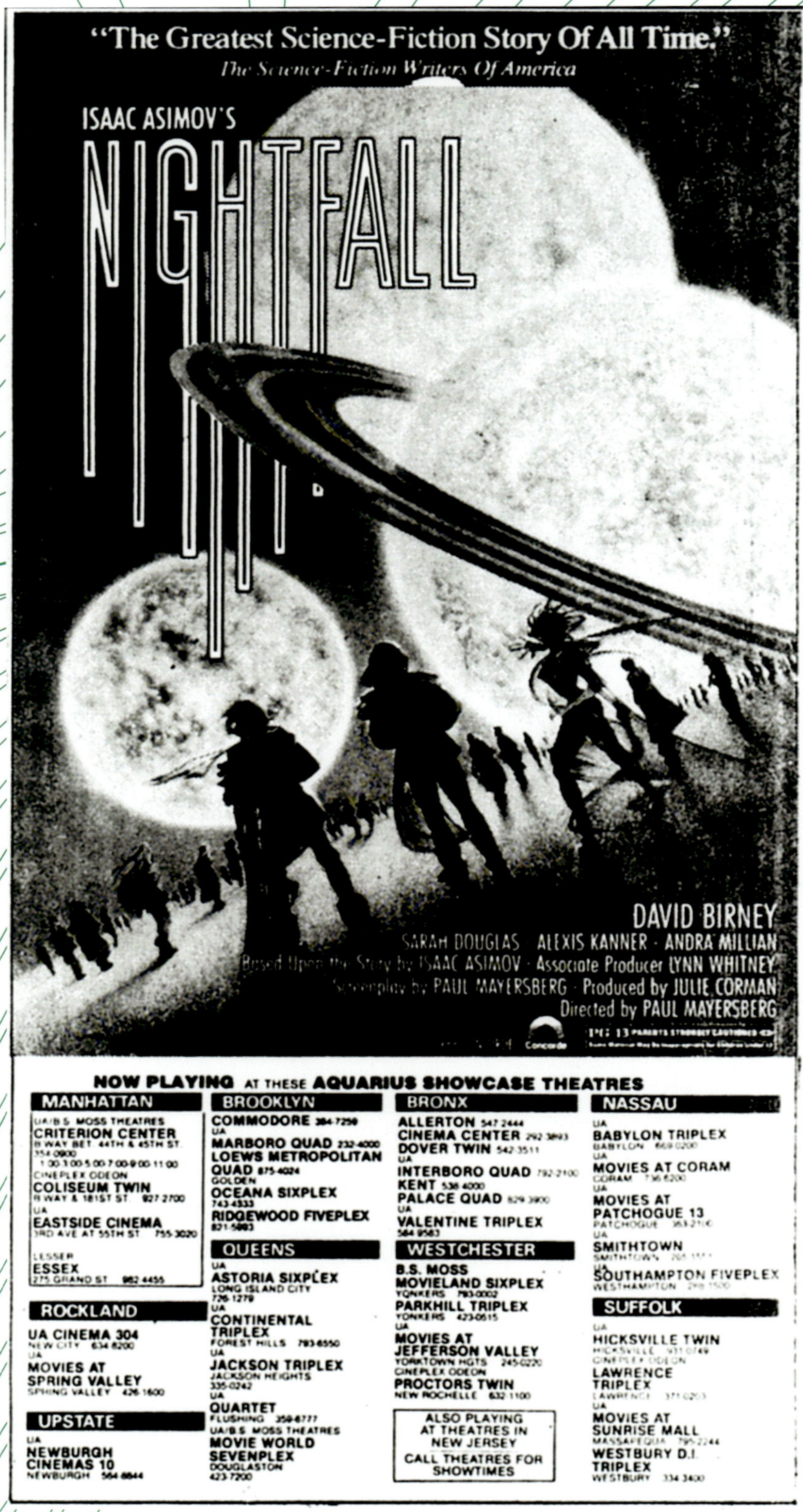
"The Greatest Science-Fiction Story Of All Time."
The Science-Fiction Writers Of America
ISAAC ASIMOV'S
NIGHTFALL
DAVID BIRNEY
SARAH DOUGLAS · ALEXIS KANNER · ANDRA MILLIAN
Based Upon the Story by ISAAC ASIMOV · Associate Producer LYNN WHITNEY
Screenplay by PAUL MAYERSBERG · Produced by JULIE CORMAN
Directed by PAUL MAYERSBERG
Concorde
PG 13
NOW PLAYING AT THESE AQUARIUS SHOWCASE THEATRES
MANHATTAN
UA/B.S. MOSS THEATRES
CRITERION CENTER
B'WAY BET. 44TH & 45TH ST.
354-0900
1:00-3:00-5:00-7:00-9:00-11:00
CINEPLEX ODEON
COLISEUM TWIN
B'WAY & 181ST ST. 927-2700
UA
EASTSIDE CINEMA
3RD AVE AT 55TH ST. 755-3020
LESSER
ESSEX
275 GRAND ST. 982-4455
ROCKLAND
UA CINEMA 304
NEW CITY 634-8200
UA
MOVIES AT SPRING VALLEY
SPRING VALLEY 426-1600
UPSTATE
UA
NEWBURGH CINEMAS 10
NEWBURGH 564-8844
BROOKLYN
COMMODORE 384-7259
UA
MARBORO QUAD 232-4000
LOEWS METROPOLITAN QUAD 875-4024
GOLDEN
OCEANA SIXPLEX
743-4333
RIDGEWOOD FIVEPLEX
821-5993
QUEENS
UA
ASTORIA SIXPLEX
LONG ISLAND CITY
726-1279
UA
CONTINENTAL TRIPLEX
FOREST HILLS 793-6550
UA
JACKSON TRIPLEX
JACKSON HEIGHTS
335-0242
UA
QUARTET
FLUSHING 359-6777
UA/B.S. MOSS THEATRES
MOVIE WORLD SEVENPLEX
DOUGLASTON
423-7200
BRONX
ALLERTON 547-2444
CINEMA CENTER 292-3893
DOVER TWIN 542-3511
UA
INTERBORO QUAD 792-2100
KENT 538-4000
PALACE QUAD 829-3900
UA
VALENTINE TRIPLEX
584-9583
WESTCHESTER
B.S. MOSS
MOVIELAND SIXPLEX
YONKERS 793-0002
PARKHILL TRIPLEX
YONKERS 423-0515
UA
MOVIES AT JEFFERSON VALLEY
YORKTOWN HGTS 245-0220
CINEPLEX ODEON
PROCTORS TWIN
NEW ROCHELLE 632-1100
ALSO PLAYING AT THEATRES IN NEW JERSEY
CALL THEATRES FOR SHOWTIMES
NASSAU
UA
BABYLON TRIPLEX
BABYLON 669-0200
UA
MOVIES AT CORAM
CORAM 736-6200
UA
MOVIES AT PATCHOGUE 13
PATCHOGUE 363-2100
UA
SMITHTOWN
SMITHTOWN
UA
SOUTHAMPTON FIVEPLEX
WESTHAMPTON 288-1500
SUFFOLK
UA
HICKSVILLE TWIN
HICKSVILLE 931-0749
CINEPLEX ODEON
LAWRENCE TRIPLEX
LAWRENCE 371-0203
UA
MOVIES AT SUNRISE MALL
MASSAPEQUA 795-2244
WESTBURY D.I. TRIPLEX
WESTBURY 334-3400

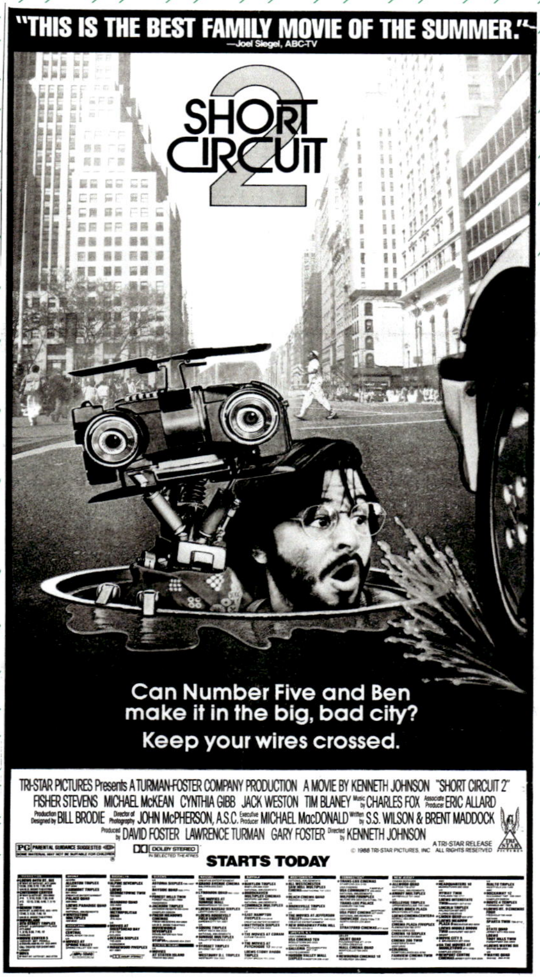
"THIS IS THE BEST FAMILY MOVIE OF THE SUMMER."
—Joel Siegel, ABC-TV
SHORT CIRCUIT 2
Can Number Five and Ben make it in the big, bad city?
Keep your wires crossed.
TRI-STAR PICTURES Presents A TURMAN-FOSTER COMPANY PRODUCTION A MOVIE BY KENNETH JOHNSON "SHORT CIRCUIT 2"
FISHER STEVENS MICHAEL McKEAN CYNTHIA GIBB JACK WESTON TIM BLANEY Music by CHARLES FOX Associate Producer ERIC ALLARD
Production Designed by BILL BRODIE Director of Photography JOHN McPHERSON, A.S.C. Executive Producer MICHAEL MacDONALD Written by S.S. WILSON & BRENT MADDOCK
Produced by DAVID FOSTER LAWRENCE TURMAN GARY FOSTER Directed by KENNETH JOHNSON
PG PARENTAL GUIDANCE SUGGESTED
DOLBY STEREO IN SELECTED THEATRES
A TRI-STAR RELEASE
© 1988 TRI-STAR PICTURES, INC. ALL RIGHTS RESERVED
STARTS TODAY

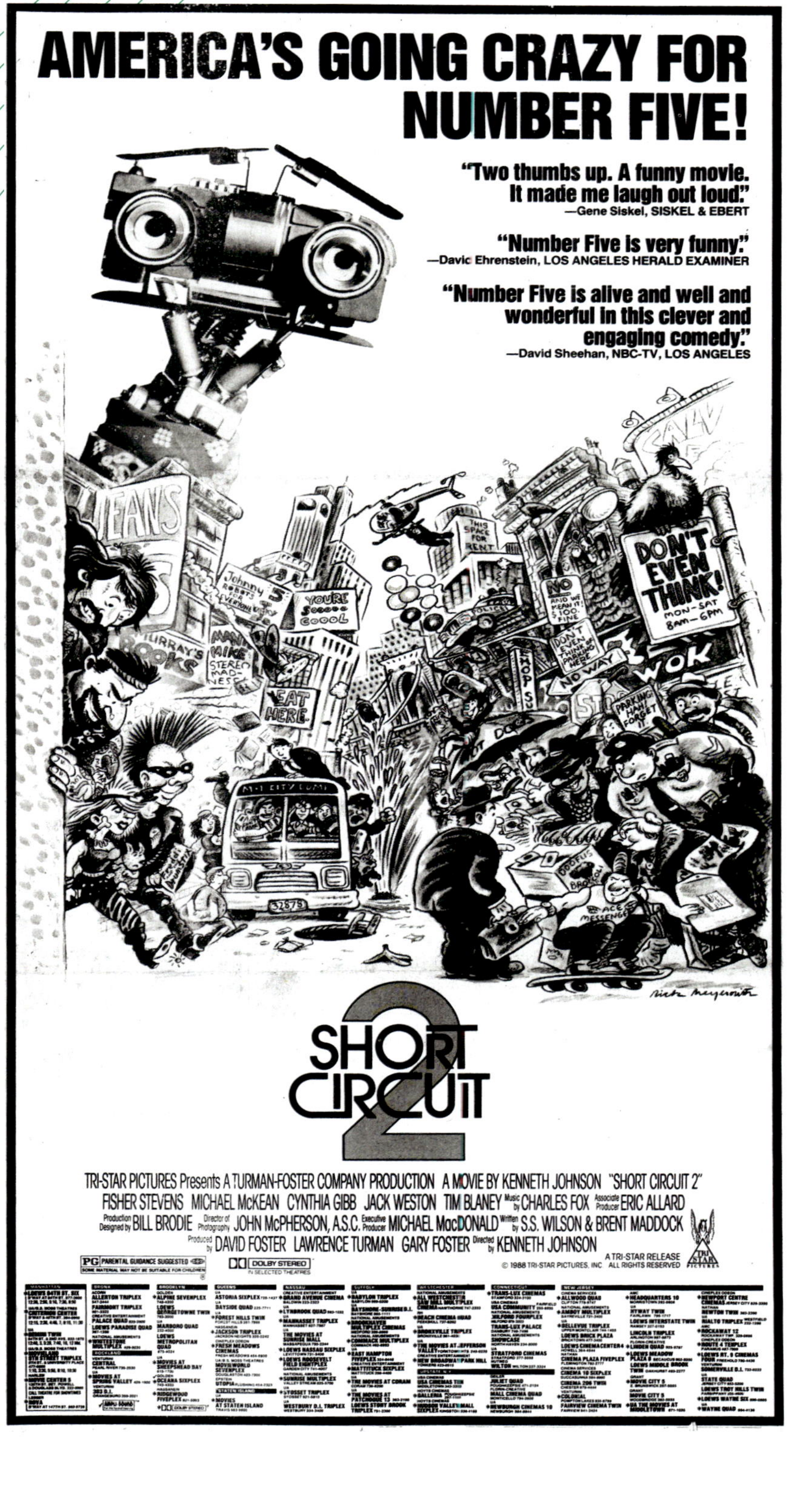
AMERICA'S GOING CRAZY FOR NUMBER FIVE!
"Two thumbs up. A funny movie. It made me laugh out loud."
—Gene Siskel, SISKEL & EBERT
"Number Five is very funny."
—David Ehrenstein, LOS ANGELES HERALD EXAMINER
"Number Five is alive and well and wonderful in this clever and engaging comedy."
—David Sheehan, NBC-TV, LOS ANGELES
SHORT CIRCUIT 2
TRI-STAR PICTURES Presents A TURMAN-FOSTER COMPANY PRODUCTION A MOVIE BY KENNETH JOHNSON "SHORT CIRCUIT 2"
FISHER STEVENS MICHAEL McKEAN CYNTHIA GIBB JACK WESTON TIM BLANEY Music by CHARLES FOX Associate Producer ERIC ALLARD
Production Designed by BILL BRODIE Director of Photography JOHN McPHERSON, A.S.C. Executive Producer MICHAEL MacDONALD Written by S.S. WILSON & BRENT MADDOCK
Produced by DAVID FOSTER LAWRENCE TURMAN GARY FOSTER Directed by KENNETH JOHNSON
PG PARENTAL GUIDANCE SUGGESTED
SOME MATERIAL MAY NOT BE SUITABLE FOR CHILDREN
DOLBY STEREO IN SELECTED THEATRES
A TRI-STAR RELEASE
© 1988 TRI-STAR PICTURES, INC. ALL RIGHTS RESERVED

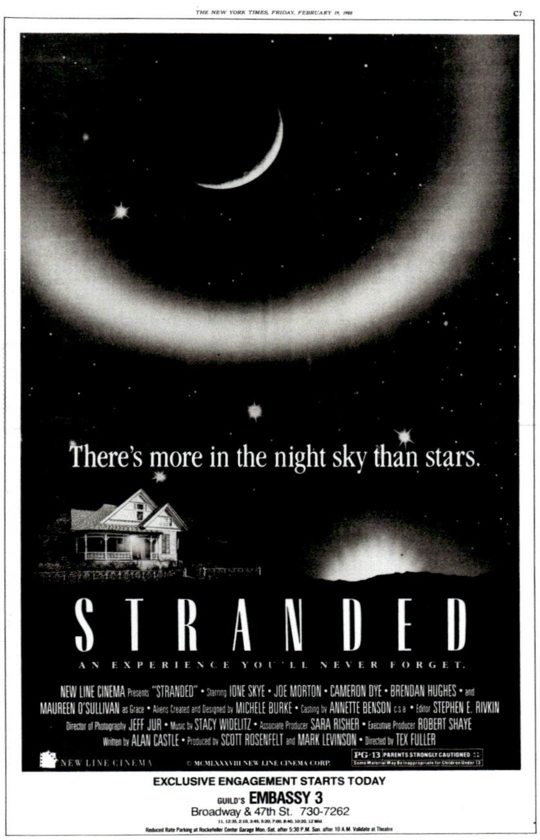
THE NEW YORK TIMES, FRIDAY, FEBRUARY 19, 1988 C7
There's more in the night sky than stars.
STRANDED
AN EXPERIENCE YOU'LL NEVER FORGET.
NEW LINE CINEMA Presents "STRANDED" • Starring IONE SKYE • JOE MORTON • CAMERON DYE • BRENDAN HUGHES • and MAUREEN O'SULLIVAN as Grace • Aliens Created and Designed by MICHELE BURKE • Casting by ANNETTE BENSON c.s.a. • Editor STEPHEN E. RIVKIN
Director of Photography JEFF JUR • Music by STACY WIDELITZ • Associate Producer SARA RISHER • Executive Producer ROBERT SHAYE
Written by ALAN CASTLE • Produced by SCOTT ROSENFELT and MARK LEVINSON • Directed by TEX FULLER
NEW LINE CINEMA
© MCMLXXXVIII NEW LINE CINEMA CORP.
PG-13 PARENTS STRONGLY CAUTIONED
EXCLUSIVE ENGAGEMENT STARTS TODAY
GUILD'S EMBASSY 3
Broadway & 47th St. 730-7262

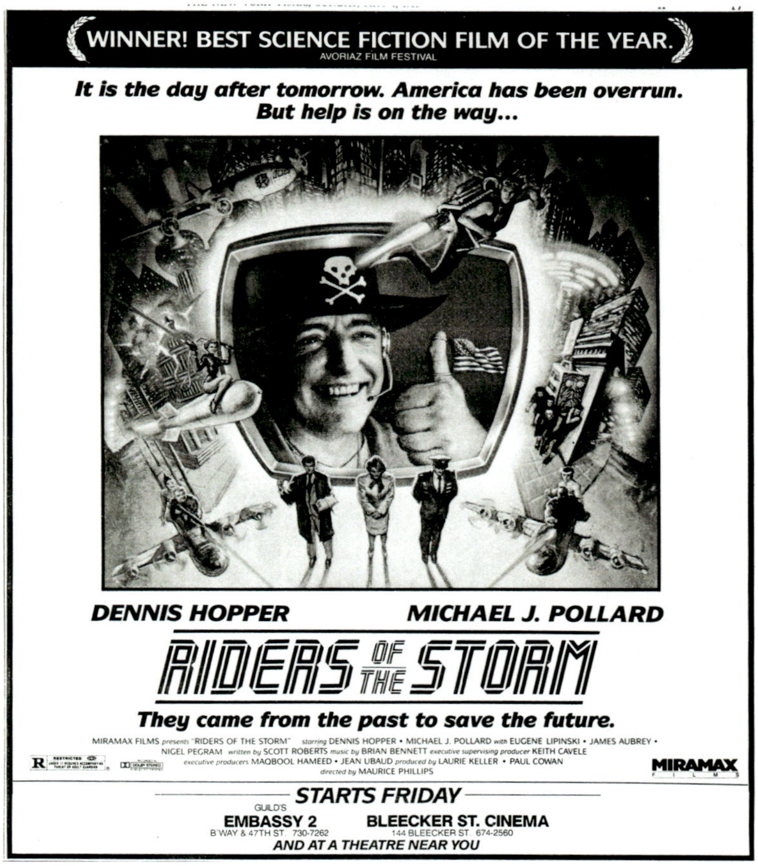

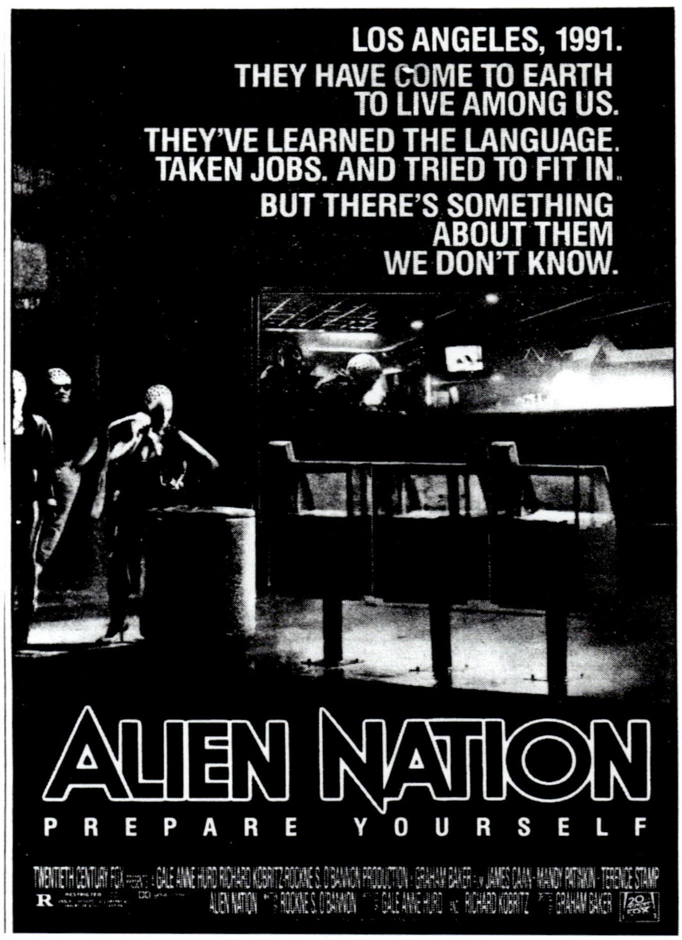

BEETLEJUICE

After scoring a sleeper with *Pee-wee's Big Adventure*, Tim Burton surprised again by delivering a full-scale hit with a film for which many had only predicted cult status. It turned out that this odd melange of horror, humor, surreal special effects and heart really was for all tastes, or at least those of a whole lot of moviegoers. For something this strange, predictably, the reviews were split between admiration and aversion.

"By the time this irresistible treat is over, it has created some of the funniest moments and most inspired visual humor and design we may expect to experience at the movies all year."

–Kevin Thomas, *Los Angeles Times*

"Burton doesn't bother with details but films only what makes him happy, and his self-enjoyment is infectious. For all the film's popped eyeballs and severed limbs, *Beetlejuice* retains an innocence that makes the grotesque humor very appealing."

–DAVE KEHR, *CHICAGO TRIBUNE*

"The film sometimes is too bizarre for its own good and takes a very long time to energize itself, but it's a rewarding experience for those whose tastes run to off-the-wall entertainment."

–Jack Garner, Gannett News Service

"[I]n this underwritten, overproduced effort, the action and yuks are in the décor. ... Why didn't Burton tell Keaton he shouldn't chew scenery, because the scenery is the movie's joke?"

–Carrie Rickey, *Philadelphia Inquirer*

"Mr. Burton, who seems to take his inspiration from toy stores and rock videos in equal measure, tries anything and everything for effect, and only occasionally manages something marginally funny."

–Janet Maslin, *The New York Times*

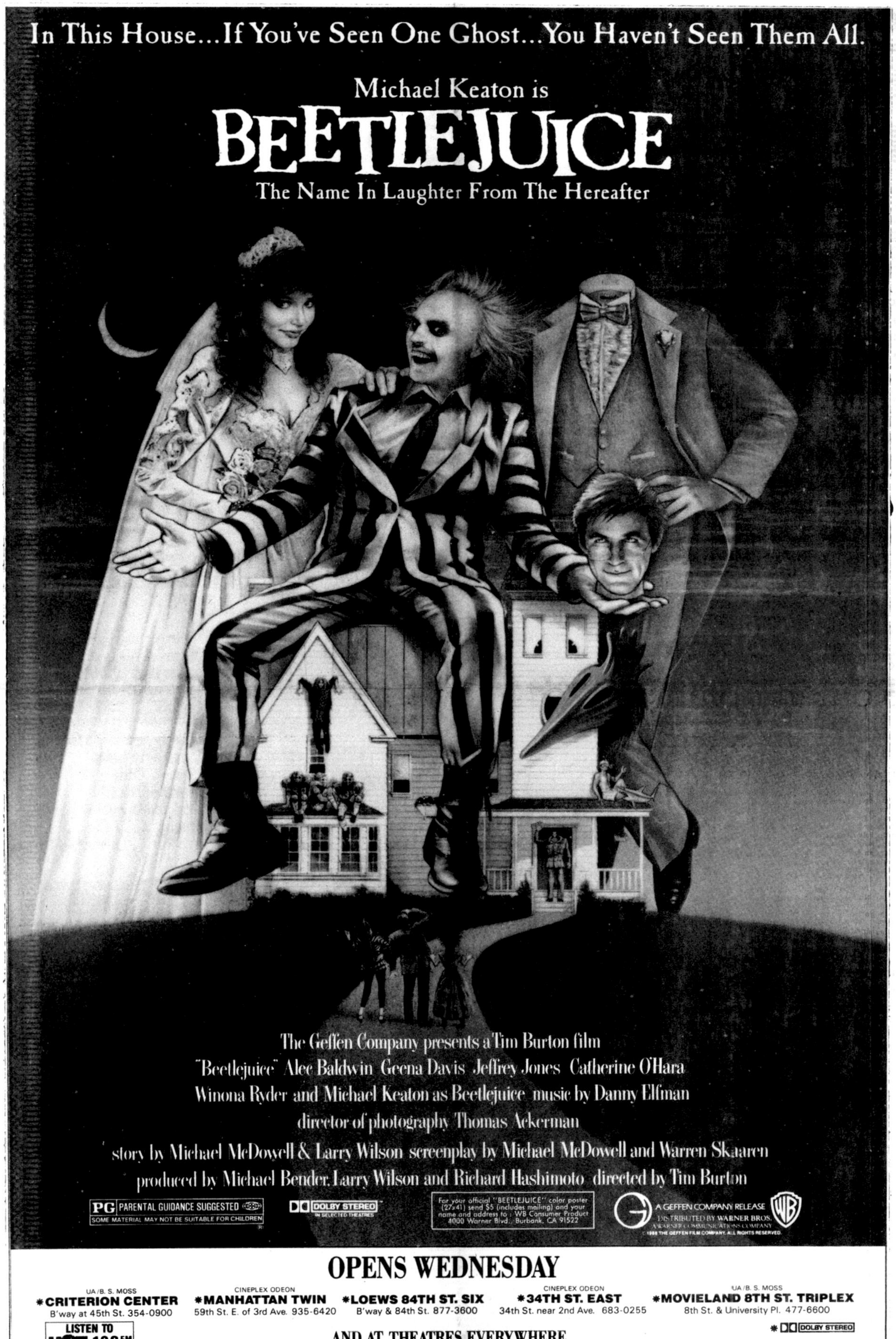

In This House...If You've Seen One Ghost...You Haven't Seen Them All.
Michael Keaton is
BEETLEJUICE
The Name In Laughter From The Hereafter
The Geffen Company presents a Tim Burton film
"Beetlejuice" Alec Baldwin Geena Davis Jeffrey Jones Catherine O'Hara
Winona Ryder and Michael Keaton as Beetlejuice music by Danny Elfman
director of photography Thomas Ackerman
story by Michael McDowell & Larry Wilson screenplay by Michael McDowell and Warren Skaaren
produced by Michael Bender, Larry Wilson and Richard Hashimoto directed by Tim Burton
PG PARENTAL GUIDANCE SUGGESTED
SOME MATERIAL MAY NOT BE SUITABLE FOR CHILDREN
DOLBY STEREO
IN SELECTED THEATRES
For your official "BEETLEJUICE" color poster (27x41) send $5 (includes mailing) and your name and address to: WB Consumer Product 4000 Warner Blvd., Burbank, CA 91522
A GEFFEN COMPANY RELEASE
DISTRIBUTED BY WARNER BROS.
A WARNER COMMUNICATIONS COMPANY
© 1988 THE GEFFEN FILM COMPANY. ALL RIGHTS RESERVED.
OPENS WEDNESDAY
UA/B. S. MOSS
*CRITERION CENTER
B'way at 45th St. 354-0900
CINEPLEX ODEON
*MANHATTAN TWIN
59th St. E. of 3rd Ave. 935-6420
*LOEWS 84TH ST. SIX
B'way & 84th St. 877-3600
CINEPLEX ODEON
*34TH ST. EAST
34th St. near 2nd Ave. 683-0255
UA/B. S. MOSS
*MOVIELAND 8TH ST. TRIPLEX
8th St. & University Pl. 477-6600
LISTEN TO
HOT 103FM
AND AT THEATRES EVERYWHERE
* DOLBY STEREO

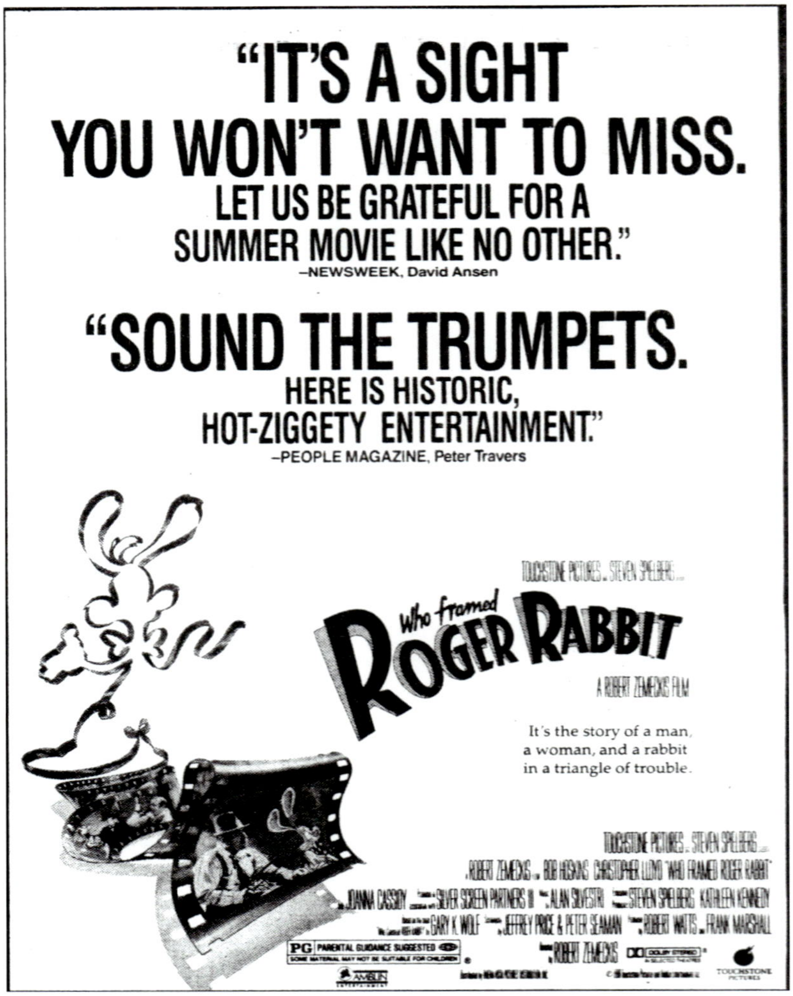

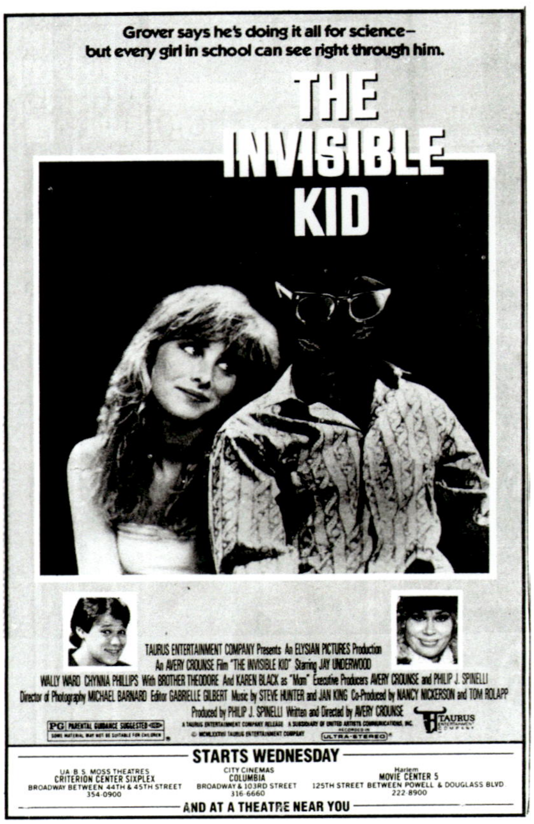

MAC AND ME

The behind-the-scenes details of this alien-on-Earth family flick should have drawn a bit of goodwill, as the wheelchair-bound young lead was cast with an acting newcomer, Jade Calegory, who actually had spina bifida and got around in such a vehicle, and a portion of the profits was intended to go to the Ronald McDonald House charity for critically ill children. However, critics could only respond to what they saw on the screen – including a scene in which the ailing extraterrestrial is revived with Coca-Cola, and an appearance by Mr. McDonald himself – and they all reacted pretty much the same way.

"There are some delightful moments in *MAC and Me*, but the movie, doing a yeoman job of borrowing from a familiar story – namely, *E.T.* – really doesn't break new ground."

–Bill Kaufman, New York *Newsday*

"With its cardboard family and familiar aliens, *MAC and Me* would seem like the generic version of *E.T.* if it were not so full of brand-name commercials."

–Caryn James, *The New York Times*

"Originality lies smothered under special sauce and wilting on a sesame seed bun in the science-fiction kiddie show, *MAC and Me*. ... It's an amazingly bald-faced copy of *E.T.* even though this is *E.T.* in a sticky wrapper, left under the heater two hours too long."

–MICHAEL WILMINGTON, *LOS ANGELES TIMES*

"How can producer R.J. Louis and director Stewart Raffill face themselves when they get up in the morning? And how can this team of brazen appropriators face *filmmeister* Steven Spielberg if their paths ever cross?"

–Steven Rea, *Philadelphia Inquirer*

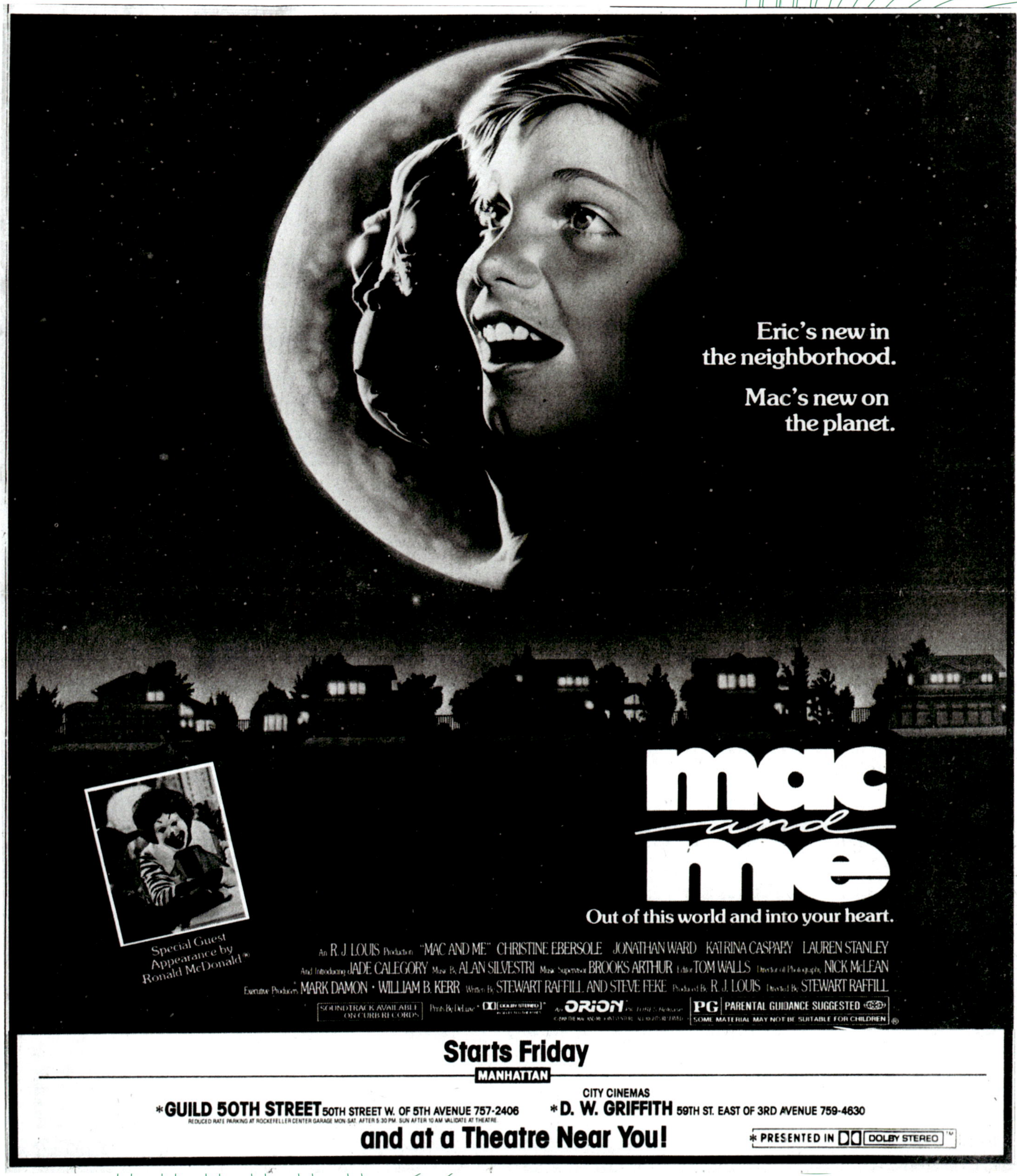

Eric's new in the neighborhood.
Mac's new on the planet.
mac and me
Out of this world and into your heart.
Special Guest Appearance by Ronald McDonald®
An R. J. LOUIS Production "MAC AND ME" CHRISTINE EBERSOLE JONATHAN WARD KATRINA CASPARY LAUREN STANLEY
And Introducing JADE CALEGORY Music By ALAN SILVESTRI Music Supervisor BROOKS ARTHUR Editor TOM WALLS Director of Photography NICK McLEAN
Executive Producers MARK DAMON · WILLIAM B. KERR Written By STEWART RAFFILL AND STEVE FEKE Produced By R. J. LOUIS Directed By STEWART RAFFILL
SOUNDTRACK AVAILABLE ON CURB RECORDS
Prints By DeLuxe®
DOLBY STEREO
An ORION Pictures Release
PG PARENTAL GUIDANCE SUGGESTED
SOME MATERIAL MAY NOT BE SUITABLE FOR CHILDREN
Starts Friday
MANHATTAN
*GUILD 50TH STREET 50TH STREET W. OF 5TH AVENUE 757-2406
REDUCED RATE PARKING AT ROCKEFELLER CENTER GARAGE MON-SAT. AFTER 5:30 PM. SUN AFTER 10 AM VALIDATE AT THEATRE
CITY CINEMAS
*D. W. GRIFFITH 59TH ST. EAST OF 3RD AVENUE 759-4630
and at a Theatre Near You!
* PRESENTED IN DOLBY STEREO ™

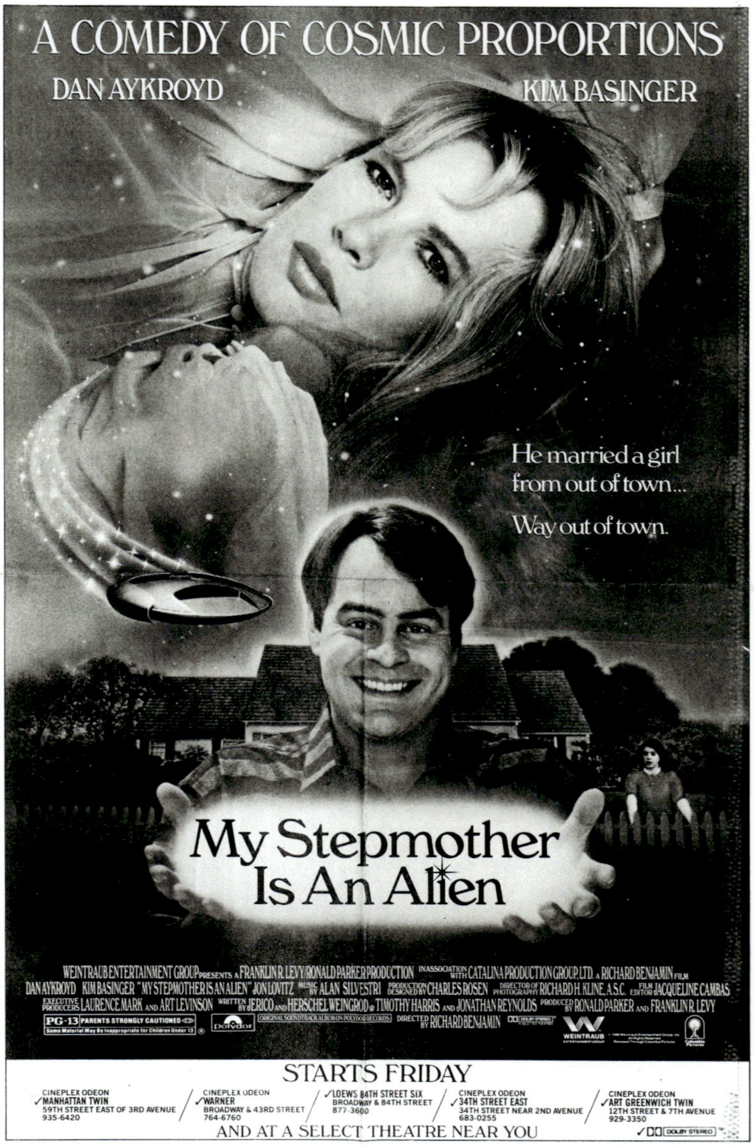

SCROOGED

There had never been a *Christmas Carol* adaptation quite like *Scrooged*, which placed Bill Murray among spirits more festive than the ones in *Ghostbusters*. The movie's attack on Christmas commercialism and television pandering won a few fans then and has gained quite a few more since, though most reviewers found the satire mixed awkwardly with sentiment as Murray's crass TV exec learns to embrace the holiday spirit.

"Though this is surely a minority opinion, I found much of *Scrooged* hilarious and wasn't much bothered by the sections that are saccharine or slow. *Scrooged* may have its problems, but it's also got a timely idea."

–Janet Maslin, *The New York Times* (Sunday edition)

"...*Scrooged* arrives just in time. We are all poised here, defenseless, about to be pelted by [Christmas] sugarplums and stomped by reindeer, and here comes a most welcome touch of 'bah-humbuggery' in a time of otherwise unalloyed sweetness."

–Mike McGrady, New York *Newsday*

"When they do insane riffs in the margins of Dickens, the picture comes to life. But this is a big-budget holiday blockbuster, and they pull their punches. It's not a solid Murray flick and it's not a decent Scrooge. It's humbug."

–DAVID EDELSTEIN, *NEW YORK POST*

"It was obviously intended as a comedy, but there is little comic about it, and indeed the movie's overriding emotions seem to be pain and anger. This entire production seems to be in dire need of visits from the ghosts of Christmas."

–Roger Ebert, *Chicago Sun-Times*

"[I]t is not a bad notion for a satiric comedy and this one begins well, but then veers entirely out of hand; it is as over-inflated as its own Ghost of Christmas Yet to Come and as funny as a mugging."

–Sheila Benson, *Los Angeles Times*

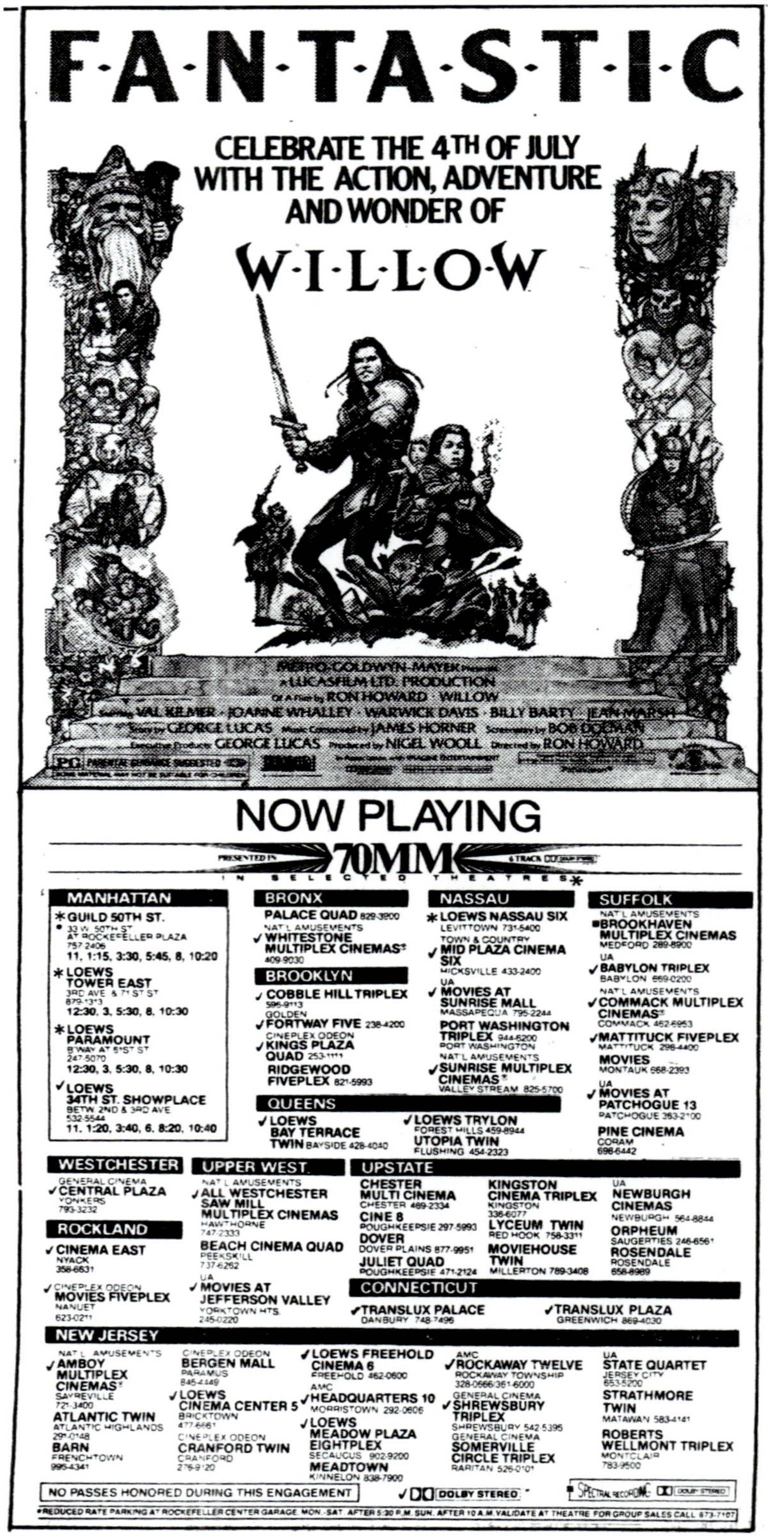

WILLOW

There was a lot riding on *Willow* for George Lucas, who may still have been licking his wounds two years after *Howard the Duck* became an infamous flop. Bringing director Ron Howard back to the realm of the fantastic after he scored with *Cocoon* could only be seen as an advantage. Yet *Willow* scored only marginally well with critics and at the box office. A widely syndicated interview by *The New York Times*' Aljean Harmetz following the film's release noted how Lucas was upset by what he described as "95 percent apoplectic" reviews, and they weren't *that* bad, but...

"Time-worn myths and legends get a zestful, entertaining reworking in *Willow*. ... [Howard and Lucas have] rejuvenated overly familiar material with memorable characters, strong emotions, and a striking visual sensibility."

–Jack Garner, Gannett News Service

"If it evaporates from memory with the airiness of a bubble bath, at least it leaves a friendly glow and a sense of a magical world lovingly evoked."

–Sheila Benson, *Los Angeles Times*

"Willow is long, long, long. It is also violent, violent, violent. The story has too many threads, too many scenes, too many characters whose names we can't pronounce, let alone remember."

–CHRIS CHASE, NEW YORK *DAILY NEWS*

"It's less a movie than a collection of morbid symptoms: a labored, arrhythmic narrative; a pathetic dependency on recycled themes and borrowed images; a sour, self-mocking humor that suggests the end is near."

–Dave Kehr, *Chicago Tribune*

"It's the kind of debacle that results from a chaotic and self-absorbed imagination operating under the delusion that it's simple and life-embracing."

–Michael Sragow, *San Francisco Examiner*

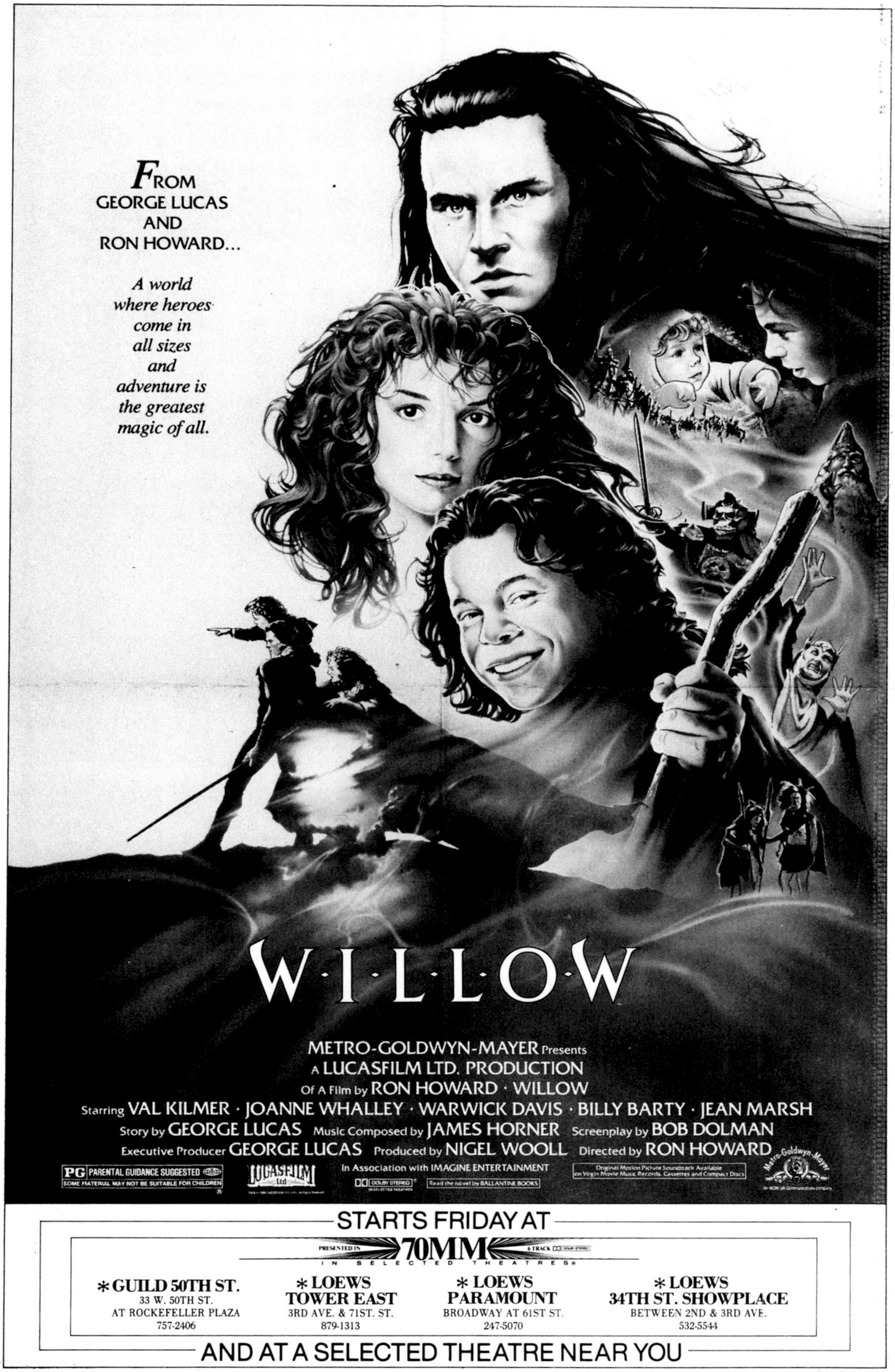

FROM
GEORGE LUCAS
AND
RON HOWARD...
A world
where heroes
come in
all sizes
and
adventure is
the greatest
magic of all.
W·I·L·L·O·W
METRO-GOLDWYN-MAYER Presents
A LUCASFILM LTD. PRODUCTION
Of A Film by RON HOWARD · WILLOW
Starring VAL KILMER · JOANNE WHALLEY · WARWICK DAVIS · BILLY BARTY · JEAN MARSH
Story by GEORGE LUCAS Music Composed by JAMES HORNER Screenplay by BOB DOLMAN
Executive Producer GEORGE LUCAS Produced by NIGEL WOOLL Directed by RON HOWARD
PG PARENTAL GUIDANCE SUGGESTED
SOME MATERIAL MAY NOT BE SUITABLE FOR CHILDREN
LUCASFILM Ltd
In Association with IMAGINE ENTERTAINMENT
DOLBY STEREO
Read the novel by BALLANTINE BOOKS
Original Motion Picture Soundtrack Available on Virgin Movie Music Records, Cassettes and Compact Discs
Metro-Goldwyn-Mayer
STARTS FRIDAY AT
PRESENTED IN 70MM 6 TRACK
IN SELECTED THEATRES*
*GUILD 50TH ST.
33 W. 50TH ST.
AT ROCKEFELLER PLAZA
757-2406
*LOEWS
TOWER EAST
3RD AVE. & 71ST. ST.
879-1313
*LOEWS
PARAMOUNT
BROADWAY AT 61ST ST.
247-5070
*LOEWS
34TH ST. SHOWPLACE
BETWEEN 2ND & 3RD AVE.
532-5544
AND AT A SELECTED THEATRE NEAR YOU

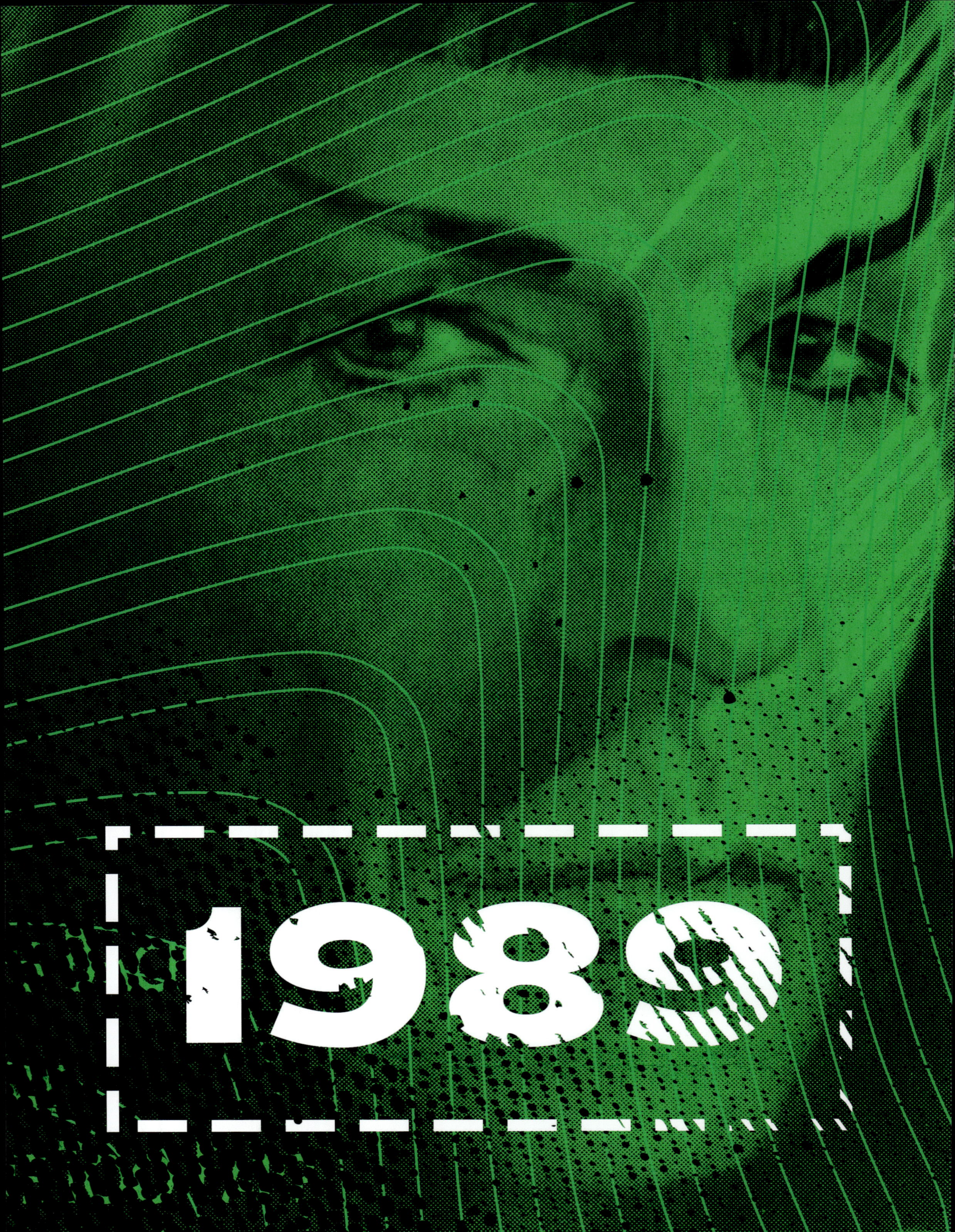
1989

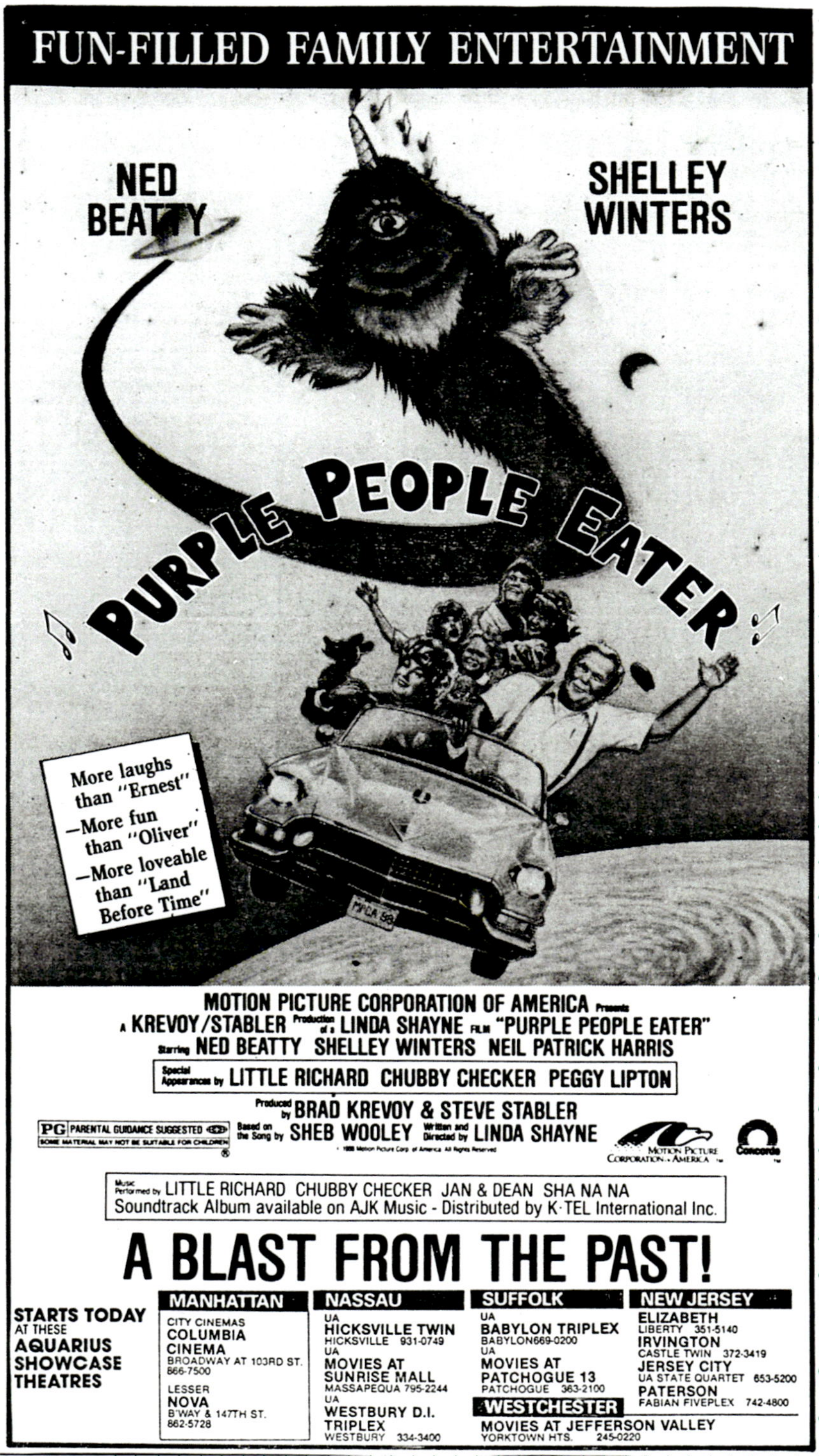

FUN-FILLED FAMILY ENTERTAINMENT
NED BEATTY
SHELLEY WINTERS
PURPLE PEOPLE EATER
More laughs than "Ernest" —More fun than "Oliver" —More loveable than "Land Before Time"
MOTION PICTURE CORPORATION OF AMERICA Presents
A KREVOY/STABLER Production of a LINDA SHAYNE FILM "PURPLE PEOPLE EATER"
Starring NED BEATTY SHELLEY WINTERS NEIL PATRICK HARRIS
Special Appearances by LITTLE RICHARD CHUBBY CHECKER PEGGY LIPTON
Produced by BRAD KREVOY & STEVE STABLER
Based on the Song by SHEB WOOLEY Written and Directed by LINDA SHAYNE
PG PARENTAL GUIDANCE SUGGESTED SOME MATERIAL MAY NOT BE SUITABLE FOR CHILDREN
Music Performed by LITTLE RICHARD CHUBBY CHECKER JAN & DEAN SHA NA NA
Soundtrack Album available on AJK Music - Distributed by K-TEL International Inc.
A BLAST FROM THE PAST!
STARTS TODAY AT THESE AQUARIUS SHOWCASE THEATRES
MANHATTAN
CITY CINEMAS COLUMBIA CINEMA BROADWAY AT 103RD ST. 866-7500
LESSER NOVA B'WAY & 147TH ST. 862-5728
NASSAU
UA HICKSVILLE TWIN HICKSVILLE 931-0749
UA MOVIES AT SUNRISE MALL MASSAPEQUA 795-2244
UA WESTBURY D.I. TRIPLEX WESTBURY 334-3400
SUFFOLK
UA BABYLON TRIPLEX BABYLON669-0200
UA MOVIES AT PATCHOGUE 13 PATCHOGUE 363-2100
WESTCHESTER
MOVIES AT JEFFERSON VALLEY YORKTOWN HTS. 245-0220
NEW JERSEY
ELIZABETH LIBERTY 351-5140
IRVINGTON CASTLE TWIN 372-3419
JERSEY CITY UA STATE QUARTET 653-5200
PATERSON FABIAN FIVEPLEX 742-4800

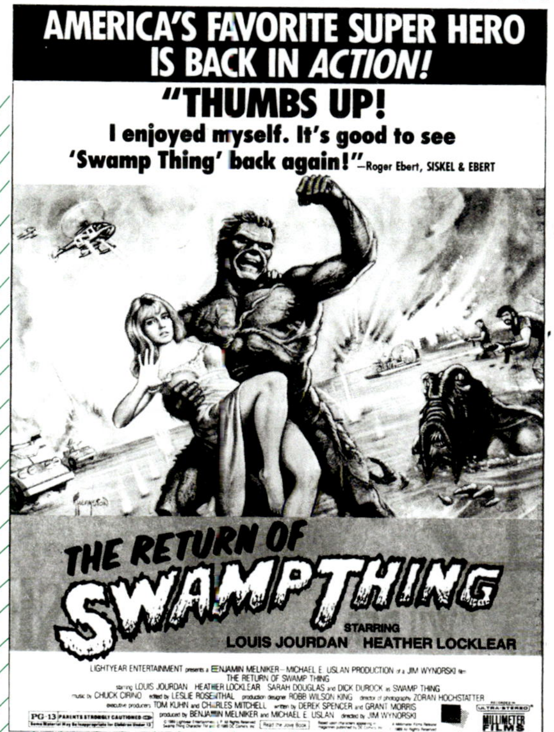

AMERICA'S FAVORITE SUPER HERO IS BACK IN ACTION!
"THUMBS UP! I enjoyed myself. It's good to see 'Swamp Thing' back again!" —Roger Ebert, SISKEL & EBERT
THE RETURN OF SWAMPTHING
STARRING LOUIS JOURDAN HEATHER LOCKLEAR
MILLIMETER FILMS

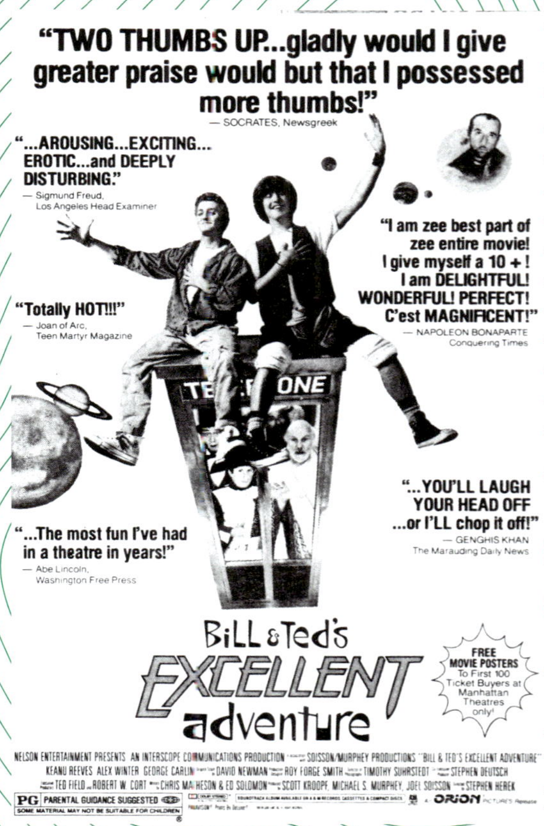

"TWO THUMBS UP...gladly would I give greater praise would but that I possessed more thumbs!" — SOCRATES, Newsgreek
"...AROUSING...EXCITING...EROTIC...and DEEPLY DISTURBING." — Sigmund Freud, Los Angeles Head Examiner
"I am zee best part of zee entire movie! I give myself a 10 + ! I am DELIGHTFUL! WONDERFUL! PERFECT! C'est MAGNIFICENT!" — NAPOLEON BONAPARTE Conquering Times
"Totally HOT!!!" — Joan of Arc, Teen Martyr Magazine
"...YOU'LL LAUGH YOUR HEAD OFF ...or I'LL chop it off!" — GENGHIS KHAN The Marauding Daily News
"...The most fun I've had in a theatre in years!" — Abe Lincoln, Washington Free Press
Bill & Ted's EXCELLENT adventure
FREE MOVIE POSTERS To First 100 Ticket Buyers at Manhattan Theatres only!
PG PARENTAL GUIDANCE SUGGESTED SOME MATERIAL MAY NOT BE SUITABLE FOR CHILDREN
ORION

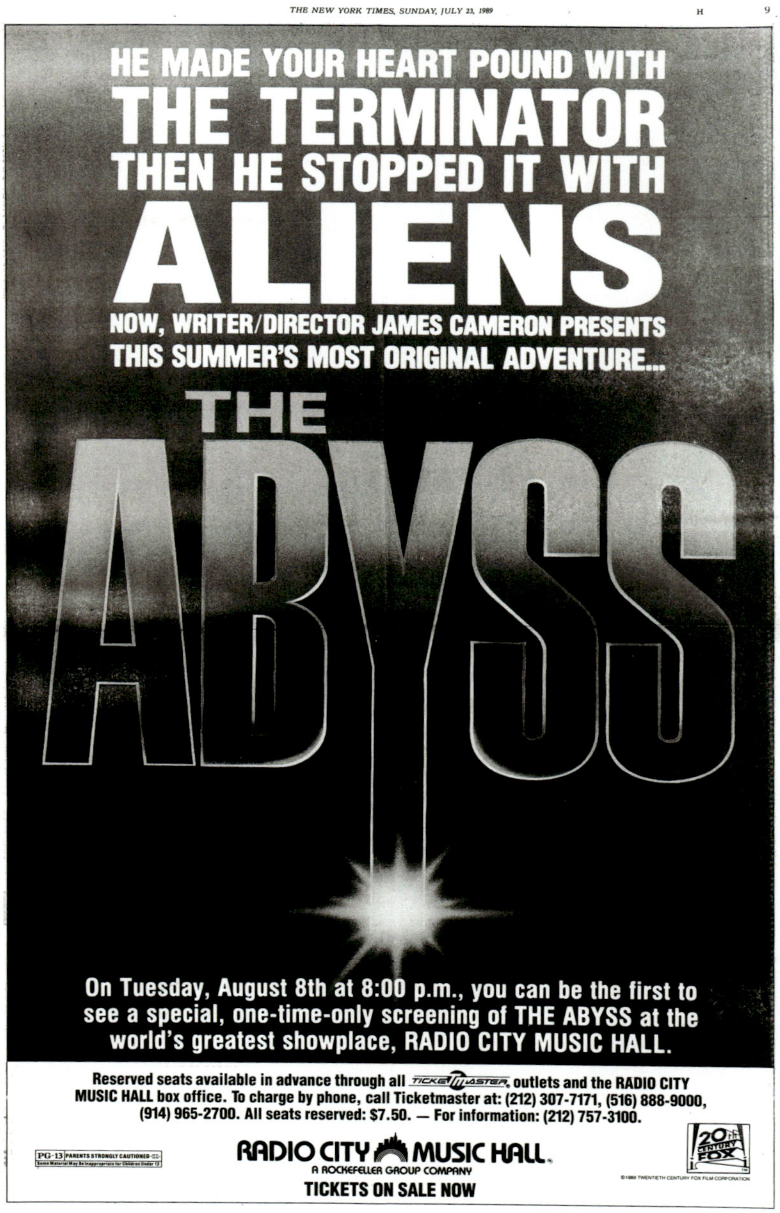

THE ABYSS

The one-two punch of *The Terminator* and *Aliens* left everyone salivating to see what would result when James Cameron traded outer space for the ocean's depths. Shooting nearly half the picture underwater entailed all manner of logistical hurdles, not to mention Cameron and producer Gale Anne Hurd's biggest budget yet, and while some found all the expenditure and effort was worth it, others found the story lacking, particularly when it came to the ending. It wasn't the one Cameron wanted, and in 1993, a Special Edition release allowed him to unveil his preferred conclusion, winning *The Abyss* a new appreciation.

"James Cameron's *The Abyss* is a marvel of a movie – an adventure-fantasy that combines state-of-the-art technique with high-intensity storytelling."

–Jack Garner, Gannett News Service

"Perhaps the secret of Cameron's appeal is that he combines a macho, military-hardware style with a reverence for things feminine. ... That heart compensates for some leaden film making, while his testosterone-heavy technique gives heft to his amazingly infantile fantasies."

–DAVID EDELSTEIN, *NEW YORK POST*

"The blissed-out ending is the downside of *The Abyss*. While Cameron's film is a life-and-death struggle in the darkness of the deep, however, it creates an absorbing world of danger and tension."

–Malcolm L. Johnson, *Hartford Courant*

"The plot, which defies all logic, becomes increasingly bewildering as *The Abyss* lurches from one murky scene to the next with all the grace of a leaking oil tanker."

–Kathleen Carroll, New York *Daily News*

AN INSTANT CLASSIC!

—Jeff Craig, SIXTY SECOND PREVIEW

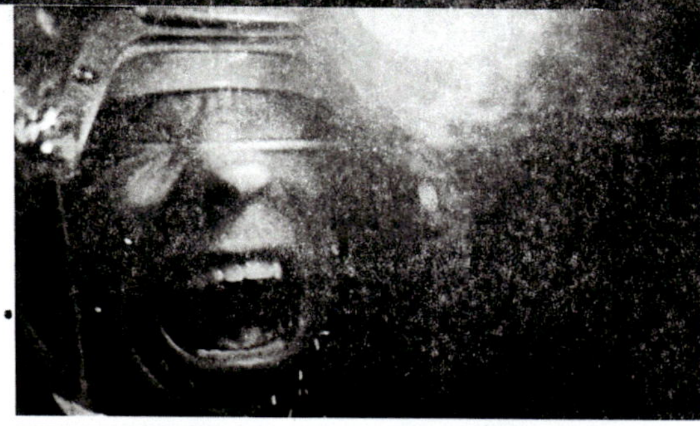

WOW!

The richest, most elaborate action/adventure ever made...it builds up the momentum of a runaway freight train early on, and never lets up!

—Jeff Craig, SIXTY SECOND PREVIEW

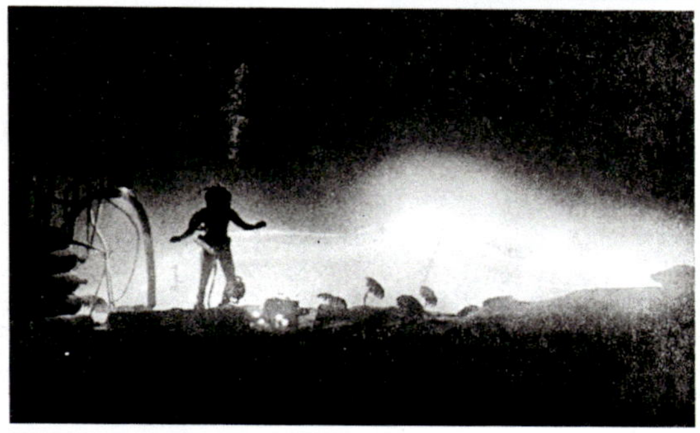

OUT-E.T.'S "E.T."

Out-Aliens "ALIEN." It's a feeding-frenzy for those who dig high-tech. It'll have you inhaling and exhaling faster than the panic-stricken divers on-screen. **It's a 10!**

—Gary Franklin, KABC TV, LOS ANGELES

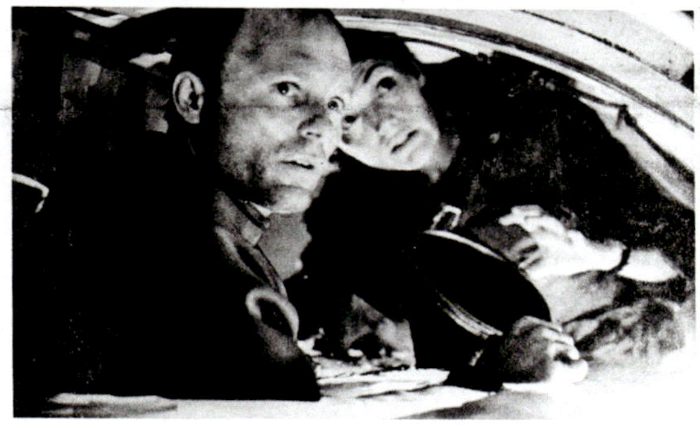

A LOVE STORY OF SHATTERING IMPACT

The Abyss is monumental mold-breaking entertainment. It is an experience like no other. **One of the best pictures of the year!**

—Peter Travers, ROLLING STONE MAGAZINE

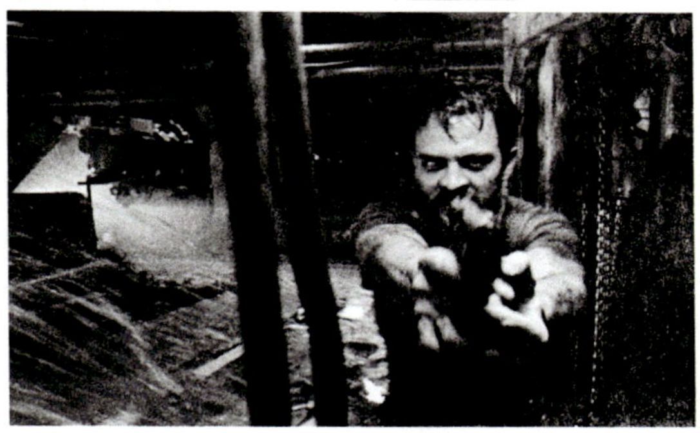

THE ABYSS

TWENTIETH CENTURY FOX PRESENTS A GALE ANNE HURD PRODUCTION A JAMES CAMERON FILM THE ABYSS ED HARRIS · MARY ELIZABETH MASTRANTONIO · MICHAEL BIEHN MUSIC BY ALAN SILVESTRI

PG-13 PARENTS STRONGLY CAUTIONED
Some Material May Be Inappropriate for Children Under 13
Original Soundtrack on Varese Sarabande Records, Cassettes and CD's

Read the Novel from Pocket Books

PRODUCTION DESIGNER LESLIE DILLEY DIRECTOR OF PHOTOGRAPHY MIKAEL SALOMON PRODUCED BY GALE ANNE HURD WRITTEN AND DIRECTED BY JAMES CAMERON PRINTS BY DELUXE® DOLBY STEREO IN SELECTED THEATRES

20th CENTURY FOX

STARTS WEDNESDAY

70MM

SIX-TRACK DOLBY STEREO IN SELECTED THEATRES PRESENTATION

CINEPLEX ODEON **ZIEGFELD** 54TH ST. NEAR 6TH AVE. 765-7600	TRANSLUX **GOTHAM CINEMA** 3RD AVE. AT 58TH ST. 759-2262	**LOEWS ORPHEUM I** 86TH ST. NEAR 3RD AVE. 289-4607	CINEPLEX ODEON **BAY CINEMA** 2ND AVE. AT 32ND ST. 679-0160

CINEPLEX ODEON
✓OLYMPIA CINEMAS
B'WAY & 107TH ST. 865-8128

UA/B.S. MOSS THEATRES
✓ MOVIELAND 8TH STREET TRIPLEX
8TH ST. & UNIVERSITY PLACE 477-6600

CINEPLEX ODEON
✓CHELSEA CINEMAS
23RD ST. BET. 7TH & 8TH AVES. 691-4744

AND AT THEATRES EVERYWHERE.

✓ DOLBY STEREO ®

Watch previews of "THE ABYSS" on your Fox Station in New York. WNYW. channel 5.

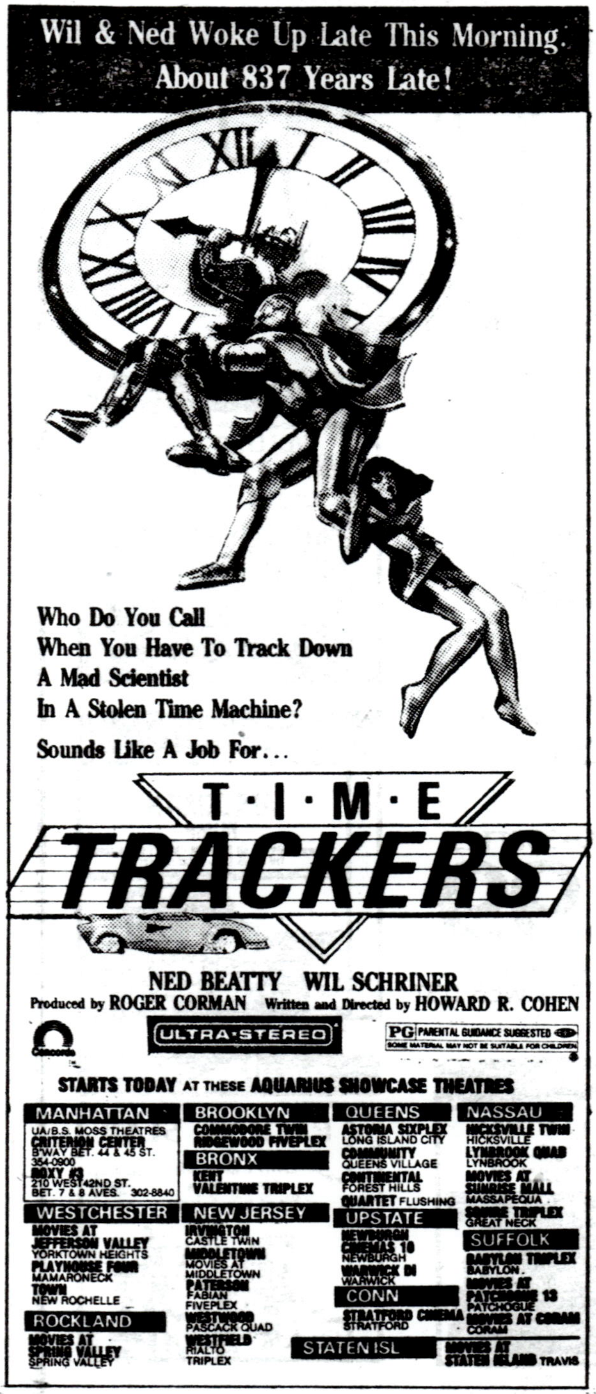

THE ADVENTURES OF BARON MUNCHAUSEN

Another costly venture by a visionary, risk-taking director, Terry Gilliam's elaborately whimsical concoction was dogged during and after its production by reports of on-set problems and budget overruns – stories that (appropriately enough, given that its title character is given to tall tales) Gilliam has claimed were untrue or blown out of proportion. One truth was that the movie fell victim to a regime change at Columbia and was tossed out in a negligible U.S. release that didn't take advantage of the many positive notices *Baron Munchausen* received.

"...*Baron Munchausen* is full of moments that dazzle, just for the fun of seeing the impossible come to life on screen. ... Nothing much happens, but you can't easily tear your eyes away from it."

–Vincent Canby, *The New York Times*

"For adults, this is a 'special effects movie,' and we approach it in that spirit, also appreciating the sly wit and satire that sneak in here and there from director Terry Gilliam and his collaborators. ... They have not made a 'children's movie,' but children may find it fascinating."

–Roger Ebert, *Chicago Sun-Times*

"One of the most voluptuously beautiful films ever imagined, *Munchausen* naturally assumes that surrealism is preferable, that through make-believe we find the way to true beliefs."

–CARRIE RICKEY, *PHILADELPHIA INQUIRER*

"*The Adventures of Baron Munchausen* is like a grand but gimcrack dirigible. In this brash, original, deluxe, and undeniably rickety fantasy, there are surprises, or at least jolts, behind each portal. Despite the billows of hot air that escape from gaping holes, it somehow manages to soar."

–Michael Sragow, *San Francisco Examiner*

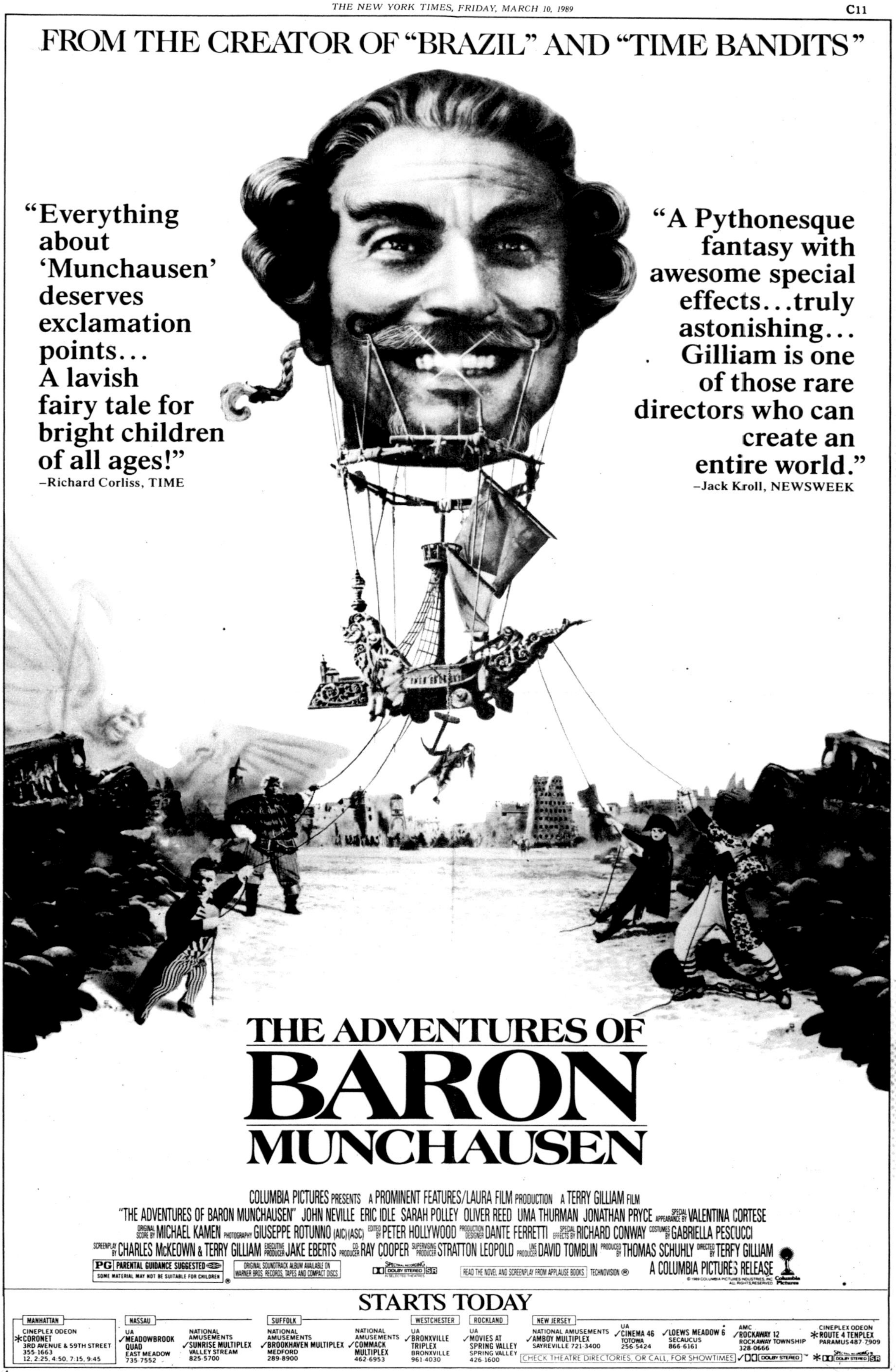

FROM THE CREATOR OF "BRAZIL" AND "TIME BANDITS"
"Everything about 'Munchausen' deserves exclamation points... A lavish fairy tale for bright children of all ages!"
–Richard Corliss, TIME
"A Pythonesque fantasy with awesome special effects...truly astonishing... Gilliam is one of those rare directors who can create an entire world."
–Jack Kroll, NEWSWEEK
THE ADVENTURES OF
BARON
MUNCHAUSEN
COLUMBIA PICTURES PRESENTS A PROMINENT FEATURES/LAURA FILM PRODUCTION A TERRY GILLIAM FILM
"THE ADVENTURES OF BARON MUNCHAUSEN" JOHN NEVILLE ERIC IDLE SARAH POLLEY OLIVER REED UMA THURMAN JONATHAN PRYCE SPECIAL APPEARANCE BY VALENTINA CORTESE
ORIGINAL SCORE BY MICHAEL KAMEN PHOTOGRAPHY GIUSEPPE ROTUNNO (AIC)(ASC) EDITED BY PETER HOLLYWOOD PRODUCTION DESIGNER DANTE FERRETTI SPECIAL EFFECTS BY RICHARD CONWAY COSTUMES BY GABRIELLA PESCUCCI
SCREENPLAY BY CHARLES McKEOWN & TERRY GILLIAM EXECUTIVE PRODUCER JAKE EBERTS CO-PRODUCER RAY COOPER SUPERVISING PRODUCER STRATTON LEOPOLD LINE PRODUCER DAVID TOMBLIN PRODUCED BY THOMAS SCHUHLY DIRECTED BY TERFY GILLIAM
PG PARENTAL GUIDANCE SUGGESTED
SOME MATERIAL MAY NOT BE SUITABLE FOR CHILDREN
ORIGINAL SOUNDTRACK ALBUM AVAILABLE ON WARNER BROS. RECORDS, TAPES AND COMPACT DISCS
DOLBY STEREO SR
READ THE NOVEL AND SCREENPLAY FROM APPLAUSE BOOKS
TECHNOVISION ®
A COLUMBIA PICTURES RELEASE
© 1989 COLUMBIA PICTURES INDUSTRIES, INC. ALL RIGHTS RESERVED
Columbia Pictures
STARTS TODAY
MANHATTAN
CINEPLEX ODEON
*CORONET
3RD AVENUE & 59TH STREET
355-1663
12, 2:25, 4:50, 7:15, 9:45
NASSAU
UA
✓MEADOWBROOK QUAD
EAST MEADOW
735-7552
NATIONAL AMUSEMENTS
✓SUNRISE MULTIPLEX
VALLEY STREAM
825-5700
SUFFOLK
NATIONAL AMUSEMENTS
✓BROOKHAVEN MULTIPLEX
MEDFORD
289-8900
NATIONAL AMUSEMENTS
✓COMMACK MULTIPLEX
462-6953
WESTCHESTER
UA
✓BRONXVILLE TRIPLEX
BRONXVILLE
961-4030
ROCKLAND
UA
✓MOVIES AT SPRING VALLEY
SPRING VALLEY
426-1600
NEW JERSEY
NATIONAL AMUSEMENTS
✓AMBOY MULTIPLEX
SAYREVILLE 721-3400
UA
✓CINEMA 46
TOTOWA
256-5424
✓LOEWS MEADOW 6
SECAUCUS
866-6161
AMC
✓ROCKAWAY 12
ROCKAWAY TOWNSHIP
328-0666
CINEPLEX ODEON
*ROUTE 4 TENPLEX
PARAMUS 487-7909
CHECK THEATRE DIRECTORIES, OR CALL, FOR SHOWTIMES
✓DOLBY STEREO
*DOLBY STEREO SR

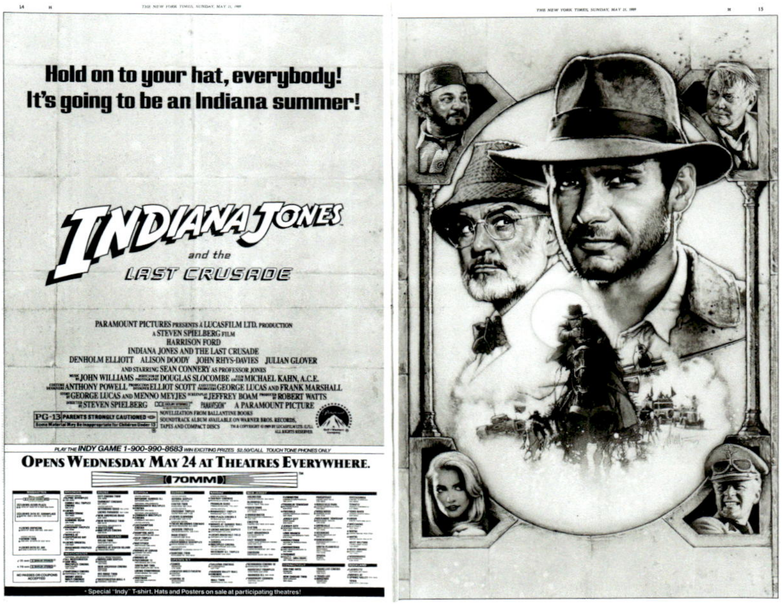

BACK TO THE FUTURE PART II

The original *Back to the Future* won praise for, among many other things, making perfect sense in the way it approached time travel and its inherent paradoxes. For the first of two sequels shot back to back, director Robert Zemeckis and scriptwriter Bob Gale went for broke, concocting a story that keeps doubling back on itself and changing the game throughout the running time. How viewers – and critics – responded to *Back to the Future Part II* depended on whether they were capable of keeping up with all the twists and reversals; some reviewers found the less frantic *Back to the Future III*, which opened six months later, a preferable experience.

"[I]t manages to be giddily and merrily mind-boggling rather than confusing. ... *Back to the Future* deserved a chance to come back, especially under the cheerful, enterprising, mathematically minded stewardship of Mr. Zemeckis and Mr. Gale."

–Janet Maslin, *The New York Times*

"As the movie ricochets all over the calendar, Gale and Zemeckis are profligate with throwaway sight gags...and a vast improvement over the sometimes skimpy invention of *Future I*."

–Sheila Benson, *Los Angeles Times*

"The plot is so absurdly convoluted even those familiar with the original should bring a personal time chart just to keep track of the shifting dates and the character transformations."

–KATHLEEN CARROLL, NEW YORK *DAILY NEWS*

"[T]he novelties, nostalgia and pace wear thin. Long before the finale. ... you find yourself pining for the bittersweet tone and charm of the original. And not getting them."

–David Armstrong, *San Francisco Examiner*

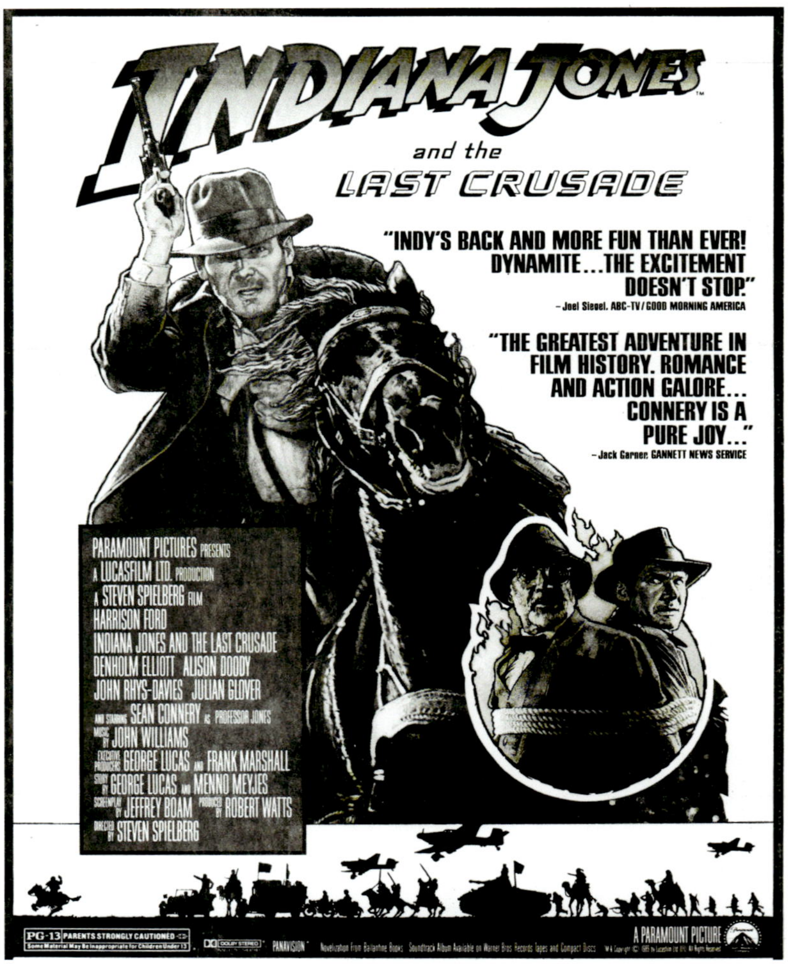

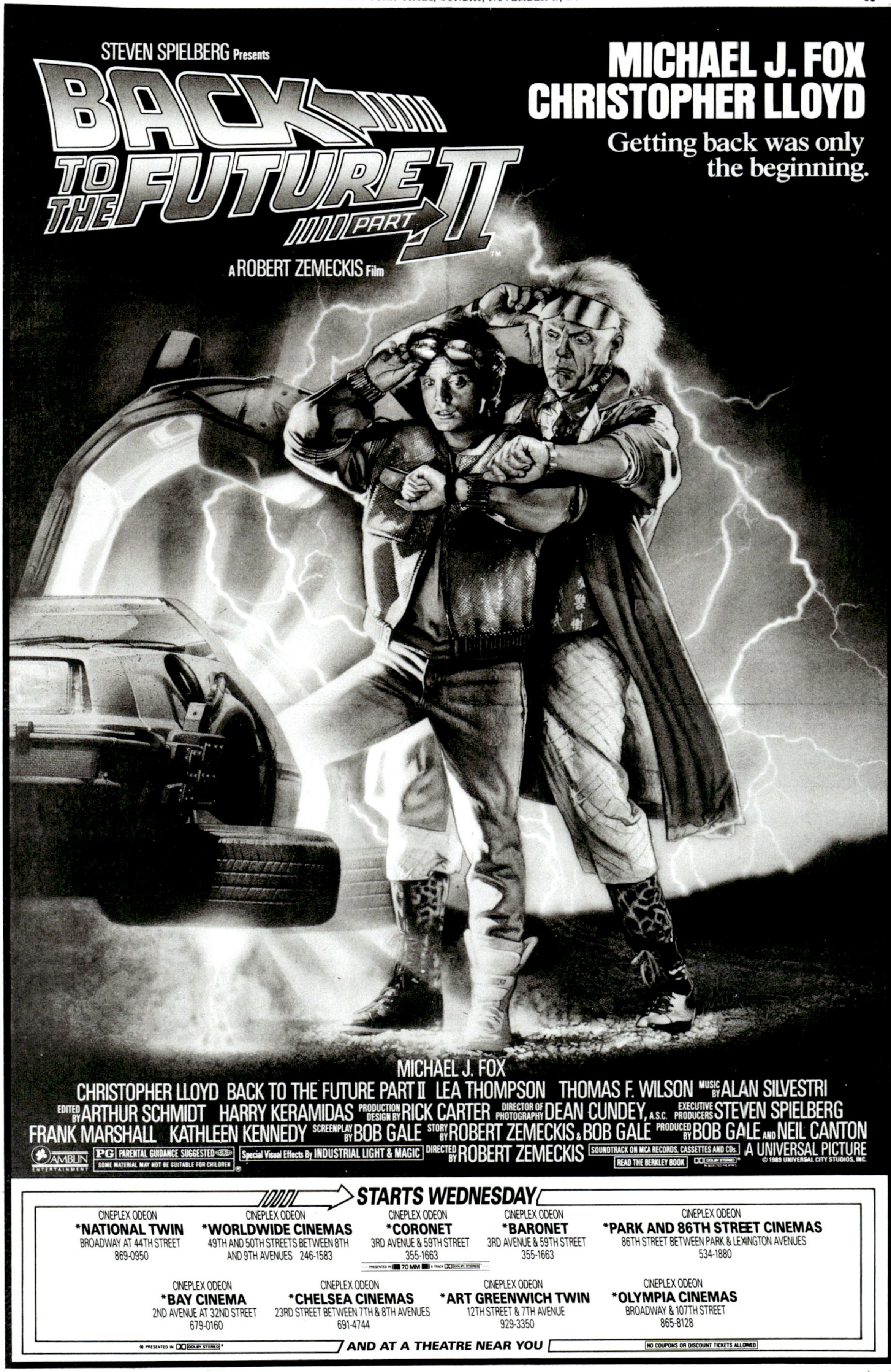
STEVEN SPIELBERG Presents
BACK TO THE FUTURE PART II
A ROBERT ZEMECKIS Film
MICHAEL J. FOX
CHRISTOPHER LLOYD
Getting back was only the beginning.
MICHAEL J. FOX
CHRISTOPHER LLOYD BACK TO THE FUTURE PART II LEA THOMPSON THOMAS F. WILSON MUSIC BY ALAN SILVESTRI
EDITED BY ARTHUR SCHMIDT HARRY KERAMIDAS PRODUCTION DESIGN BY RICK CARTER DIRECTOR OF PHOTOGRAPHY DEAN CUNDEY, A.S.C. EXECUTIVE PRODUCERS STEVEN SPIELBERG
FRANK MARSHALL KATHLEEN KENNEDY SCREENPLAY BY BOB GALE STORY BY ROBERT ZEMECKIS & BOB GALE PRODUCED BY BOB GALE AND NEIL CANTON
AMBLIN ENTERTAINMENT
PG PARENTAL GUIDANCE SUGGESTED
SOME MATERIAL MAY NOT BE SUITABLE FOR CHILDREN
Special Visual Effects By INDUSTRIAL LIGHT & MAGIC
DIRECTED BY ROBERT ZEMECKIS
SOUNDTRACK ON MCA RECORDS, CASSETTES AND CDs.
READ THE BERKLEY BOOK
A UNIVERSAL PICTURE
© 1989 UNIVERSAL CITY STUDIOS, INC.
STARTS WEDNESDAY
CINEPLEX ODEON *NATIONAL TWIN BROADWAY AT 44TH STREET 869-0950
CINEPLEX ODEON *WORLDWIDE CINEMAS 49TH AND 50TH STREETS BETWEEN 8TH AND 9TH AVENUES 246-1583
CINEPLEX ODEON *CORONET 3RD AVENUE & 59TH STREET 355-1663
PRESENTED IN 70 MM 6 TRACK DOLBY STEREO
CINEPLEX ODEON *BARONET 3RD AVENUE & 59TH STREET 355-1663
CINEPLEX ODEON *PARK AND 86TH STREET CINEMAS 86TH STREET BETWEEN PARK & LEXINGTON AVENUES 534-1880
CINEPLEX ODEON *BAY CINEMA 2ND AVENUE AT 32ND STREET 679-0160
CINEPLEX ODEON *CHELSEA CINEMAS 23RD STREET BETWEEN 7TH & 8TH AVENUES 691-4744
CINEPLEX ODEON *ART GREENWICH TWIN 12TH STREET & 7TH AVENUE 929-3350
CINEPLEX ODEON *OLYMPIA CINEMAS BROADWAY & 107TH STREET 865-8128
* PRESENTED IN DOLBY STEREO
AND AT A THEATRE NEAR YOU
NO COUPONS OR DISCOUNT TICKETS ALLOWED

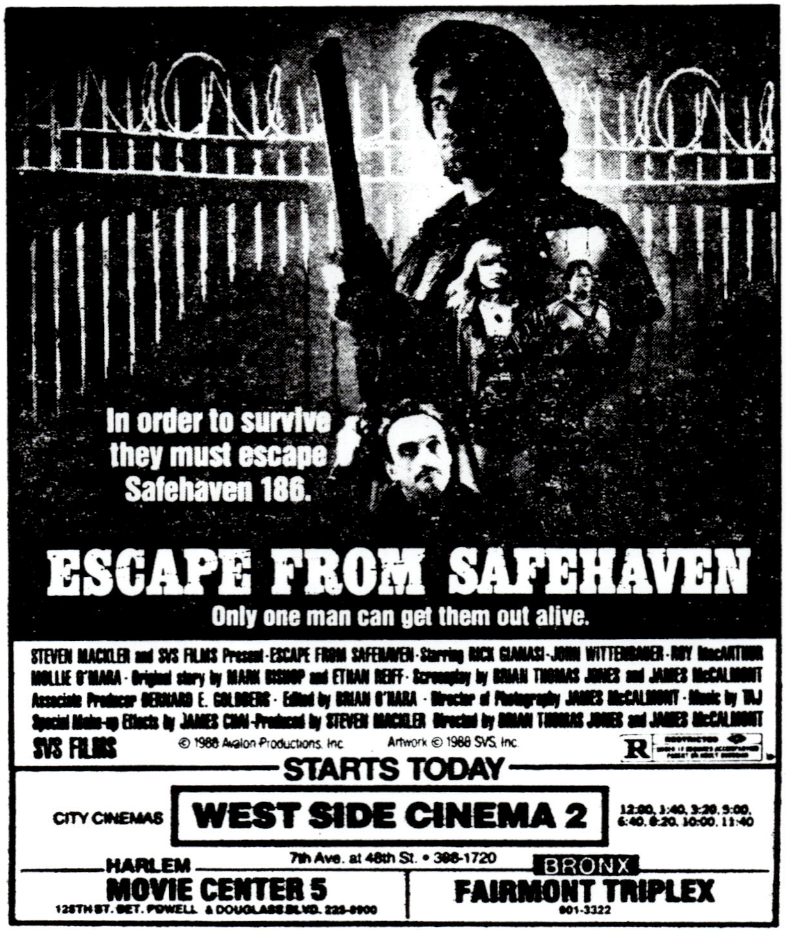

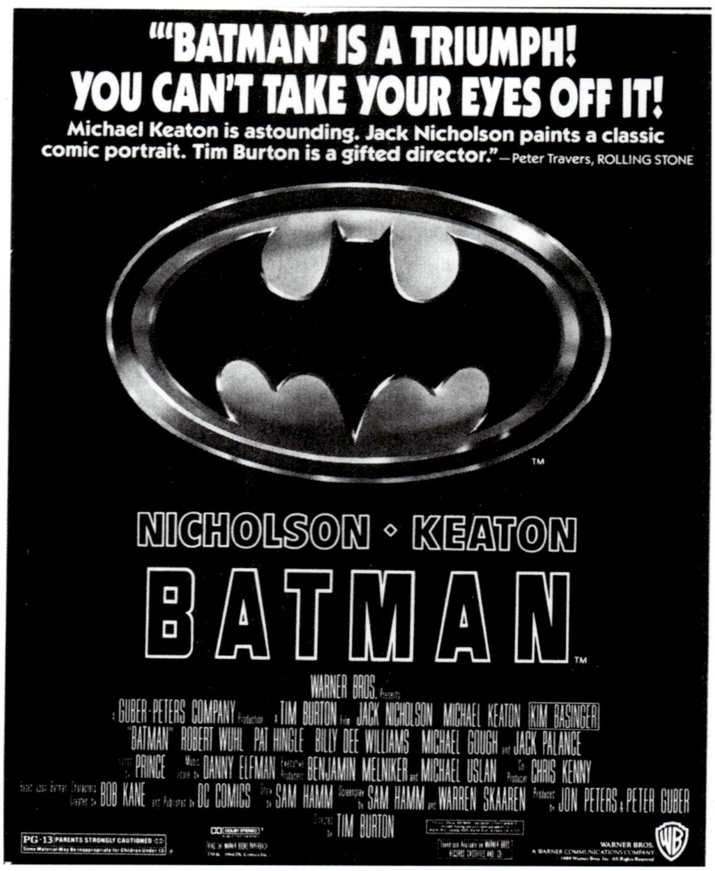

BATMAN

If *Jaws* and *Star Wars* "invented" the summer blockbuster, then *Batman* can be seen as the one that took marketing such movies to the next level. Excitement over the perfect casting of Jack Nicholson as the Joker and dismay over what many fans saw as the imperfect casting of Michael Keaton as Batman fueled Warner Bros. resolve to build enthusiasm early and as powerfully as possible, with the first trailer issued half a year in advance and all manner of tie-in materials stoking Batmania. This is the first time I can recall everyone knowing a film's release date so far in advance, and when it finally opened, Keaton silenced the doubters, and director Tim Burton became a brand name. The reviews? They were probably incidental, and very mixed.

"[The] tension between lunacy and superheroism is the core of director Tim Burton's freakily magnificent new movie. ... It revels in ambiguity, which is dangerous in the blockbuster business. ... But *Batman* feeds other, more subterranean cravings, and every frame is haunting, visionary."

–David Edelstein, *New York Post*

"It flops about, unsure of which of its scarred protagonists it finds the most seductive, and it's disastrously low on the sort of wit that can make a gargantuan movie lovable."

–SHEILA BENSON, *LOS ANGELES TIMES*

"Even on its woefully rickety story level, the movie has emotional force and conviction; it acquires a haunting aura and a pop Wagnerian ring. This *Batman* takes a tonal middle road – between seriousness and frivolity – that also proves to be the artistic high road."

–Michael Sragow, *San Francisco Examiner*

"...*Batman* is a movie without any dominant tone or style other than that provided by [production designer Anton] Furst. It's neither funny nor solemn. It has the personality not of a particular movie but of a product, of something arrived at by corporate decision."

–Vincent Canby, *The New York Times*

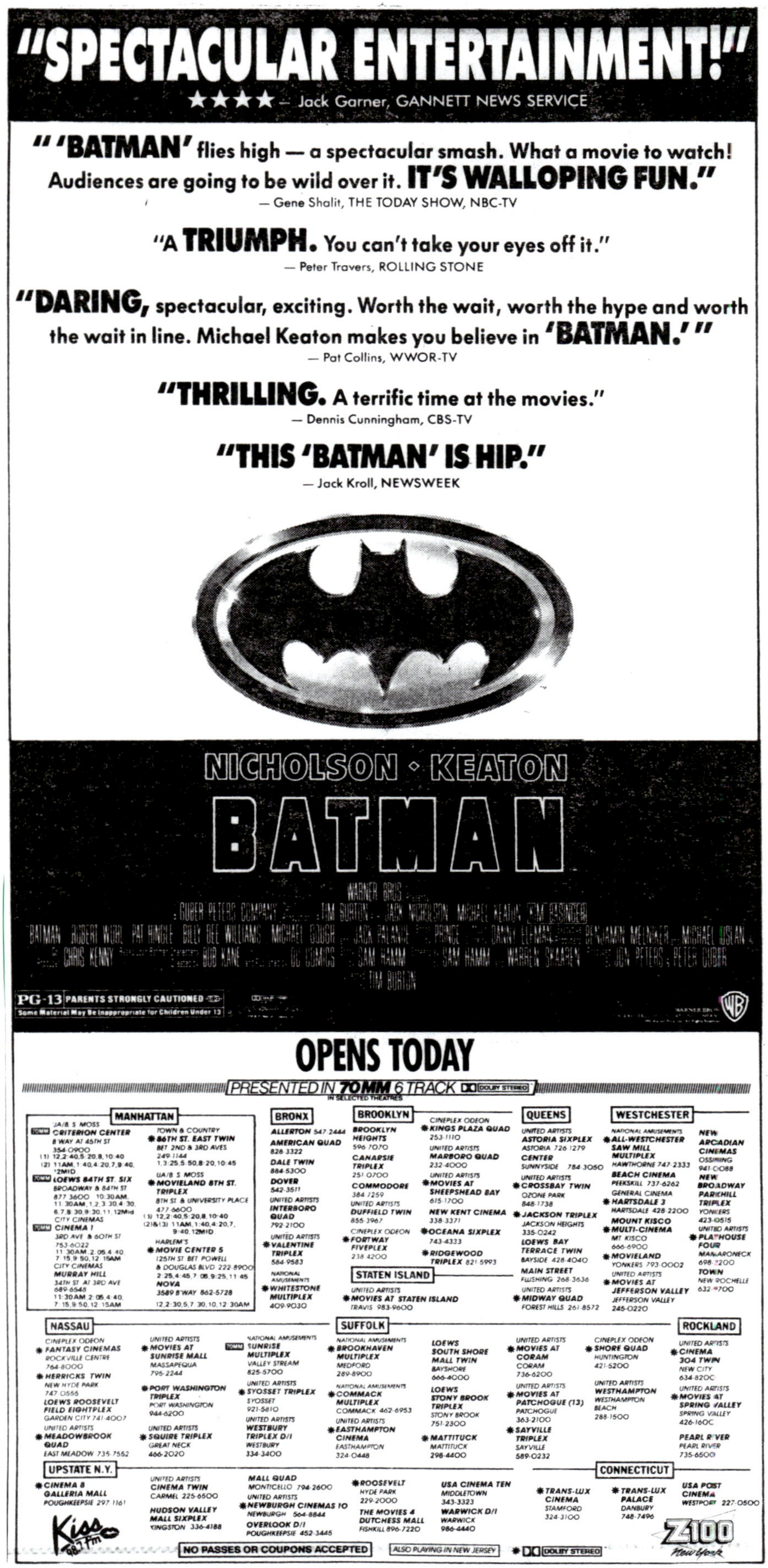
"SPECTACULAR ENTERTAINMENT!"
★★★★ — Jack Garner, GANNETT NEWS SERVICE
"'BATMAN' flies high — a spectacular smash. What a movie to watch! Audiences are going to be wild over it. IT'S WALLOPING FUN."
— Gene Shalit, THE TODAY SHOW, NBC-TV
"A TRIUMPH. You can't take your eyes off it."
— Peter Travers, ROLLING STONE
"DARING, spectacular, exciting. Worth the wait, worth the hype and worth the wait in line. Michael Keaton makes you believe in 'BATMAN.'"
— Pat Collins, WWOR-TV
"THRILLING. A terrific time at the movies."
— Dennis Cunningham, CBS-TV
"THIS 'BATMAN' IS HIP."
— Jack Kroll, NEWSWEEK
NICHOLSON • KEATON
BATMAN
WARNER BROS.
PG-13 PARENTS STRONGLY CAUTIONED
Some Material May Be Inappropriate for Children Under 13
OPENS TODAY
PRESENTED IN 70MM 6 TRACK DOLBY STEREO
IN SELECTED THEATRES
MANHATTAN
UA/B. S. MOSS
70MM CRITERION CENTER
B'WAY AT 45TH ST
354-0900
(1) 12,2:40,5:20,8,10:40
(2) 11AM,1:40,4:20,7,9:40, 12MID
70MM LOEWS 84TH ST. SIX
BROADWAY & 84TH ST
877-3600 10:30AM, 11:30AM,1,2,3:30,4:30, 6,7,8:30,9:30,11,12Mid
CITY CINEMAS
70MM CINEMA I
3RD AVE & 60TH ST
753-6022
11:30AM,2:05,4:40, 7:15,9:50,12:15AM
CITY CINEMAS
MURRAY HILL
34TH ST AT 3RD AVE
689-6548
11:30AM,2:05,4:40, 7:15,9:50,12:15AM
TOWN & COUNTRY
✱ 86TH ST. EAST TWIN
BET 2ND & 3RD AVES
249-1144
1,3:25,5:50,8:20,10:45
UA/B. S. MOSS
✱ MOVIELAND 8TH ST. TRIPLEX
8TH ST & UNIVERSITY PLACE
477-6600
(1) 12,2:40,5:20,8,10:40
(2)&(3) 11AM,1:40,4:20,7, 9:40,12MID
HARLEM'S
✱ MOVIE CENTER 5
125TH ST BET POWELL & DOUGLAS BLVD 222-8900
2:25,4:45,7:05,9:25,11:45
NOVA
3589 B'WAY 862-5728
12,2:30,5,7:30,10,12:30AM
BRONX
ALLERTON 547-2444
AMERICAN QUAD 828-3322
DALE TWIN 884-5300
DOVER 542-3511
UNITED ARTISTS
INTERBORO QUAD 792-2100
UNITED ARTISTS
✱ VALENTINE TRIPLEX 584-9583
NATIONAL AMUSEMENTS
✱ WHITESTONE MULTIPLEX 409-9030
BROOKLYN
BROOKLYN HEIGHTS 596-7070
CANARSIE TRIPLEX 251-0700
COMMODORE 384-7259
UNITED ARTISTS
DUFFIELD TWIN 855-3967
CINEPLEX ODEON
✱ FORTWAY FIVEPLEX 238-4200
CINEPLEX ODEON
✱ KINGS PLAZA QUAD 253-1110
UNITED ARTISTS
MARBORO QUAD 232-4000
UNITED ARTISTS
✱ MOVIES AT SHEEPSHEAD BAY 615-1700
NEW KENT CINEMA 338-3371
✱ OCEANA SIXPLEX 743-4333
✱ RIDGEWOOD TRIPLEX 821-5993
STATEN ISLAND
UNITED ARTISTS
✱ MOVIES AT STATEN ISLAND
TRAVIS 983-9600
QUEENS
UNITED ARTISTS
ASTORIA SIXPLEX
ASTORIA 726-1279
CENTER
SUNNYSIDE 784-3050
UNITED ARTISTS
✱ CROSSBAY TWIN
OZONE PARK 848-1738
✱ JACKSON TRIPLEX
JACKSON HEIGHTS 335-0242
LOEWS BAY TERRACE TWIN
BAYSIDE 428-4040
MAIN STREET
FLUSHING 268-3636
UNITED ARTISTS
✱ MIDWAY QUAD
FOREST HILLS 261-8572
WESTCHESTER
NATIONAL AMUSEMENTS
✱ ALL-WESTCHESTER SAW MILL MULTIPLEX
HAWTHORNE 747-2333
BEACH CINEMA
PEEKSKILL 737-6262
GENERAL CINEMA
✱ HARTSDALE 3
HARTSDALE 428-2200
MOUNT KISCO
✱ MULTI-CINEMA
MT. KISCO 666-6900
✱ MOVIELAND
YONKERS 793-0002
UNITED ARTISTS
✱ MOVIES AT JEFFERSON VALLEY
JEFFERSON VALLEY 245-0220
NEW ARCADIAN CINEMAS
OSSINING 941-0088
NEW BROADWAY PARKHILL TRIPLEX
YONKERS 423-0515
UNITED ARTISTS
✱ PLAYHOUSE FOUR
MAMARONECK 698-2200
TOWN
NEW ROCHELLE 632-1700
NASSAU
CINEPLEX ODEON
✱ FANTASY CINEMAS
ROCKVILLE CENTRE 764-8000
✱ HERRICKS TWIN
NEW HYDE PARK 747-0555
LOEWS ROOSEVELT FIELD EIGHTPLEX
GARDEN CITY 741-4007
UNITED ARTISTS
✱ MEADOWBROOK QUAD
EAST MEADOW 735-7552
UNITED ARTISTS
✱ MOVIES AT SUNRISE MALL
MASSAPEQUA 795-2244
✱ PORT WASHINGTON TRIPLEX
PORT WASHINGTON 944-6200
UNITED ARTISTS
✱ SQUIRE TRIPLEX
GREAT NECK 466-2020
NATIONAL AMUSEMENTS
70MM SUNRISE MULTIPLEX
VALLEY STREAM 825-5700
UNITED ARTISTS
✱ SYOSSET TRIPLEX
SYOSSET 921-5810
UNITED ARTISTS
WESTBURY TRIPLEX D/I
WESTBURY 334-3400
SUFFOLK
NATIONAL AMUSEMENTS
✱ BROOKHAVEN MULTIPLEX
MEDFORD 289-8900
NATIONAL AMUSEMENTS
✱ COMMACK MULTIPLEX
COMMACK 462-6953
UNITED ARTISTS
✱ EASTHAMPTON CINEMA
EASTHAMPTON 324-0448
LOEWS SOUTH SHORE MALL TWIN
BAYSHORE 666-4000
LOEWS STONY BROOK TRIPLEX
STONY BROOK 751-2300
✱ MATTITUCK
MATTITUCK 298-4400
UNITED ARTISTS
✱ MOVIES AT CORAM
CORAM 736-6200
UNITED ARTISTS
✱ MOVIES AT PATCHOGUE (13)
PATCHOGUE 363-2100
✱ SAYVILLE TRIPLEX
SAYVILLE 589-0232
CINEPLEX ODEON
✱ SHORE QUAD
HUNTINGTON 421-5200
UNITED ARTISTS
WESTHAMPTON
WESTHAMPTON BEACH 288-1500
ROCKLAND
UNITED ARTISTS
✱ CINEMA 304 TWIN
NEW CITY 634-8200
UNITED ARTISTS
✱ MOVIES AT SPRING VALLEY
SPRING VALLEY 426-1600
PEARL RIVER
PEARL RIVER 735-6500
UPSTATE N.Y.
✱ CINEMA 8 GALLERIA MALL
POUGHKEEPSIE 297-1161
UNITED ARTISTS
CINEMA TWIN
CARMEL 225-6500
HUDSON VALLEY MALL SIXPLEX
KINGSTON 336-4188
MALL QUAD
MONTICELLO 794-2600
UNITED ARTISTS
✱ NEWBURGH CINEMAS 10
NEWBURGH 564-8844
OVERLOOK D/I
POUGHKEEPSIE 452-3445
✱ ROOSEVELT
HYDE PARK 229-2000
THE MOVIES 4 DUTCHESS MALL
FISHKILL 896-7220
USA CINEMA TEN
MIDDLETOWN 343-3323
WARWICK D/I
WARWICK 986-4440
CONNECTICUT
✱ TRANS-LUX CINEMA
STAMFORD 324-3100
✱ TRANS-LUX PALACE
DANBURY 748-7496
USA POST CINEMA
WESTPORT 227-0500
Kiss 98.7 fm
Z100 New York
NO PASSES OR COUPONS ACCEPTED
ALSO PLAYING IN NEW JERSEY
✱ DOLBY STEREO

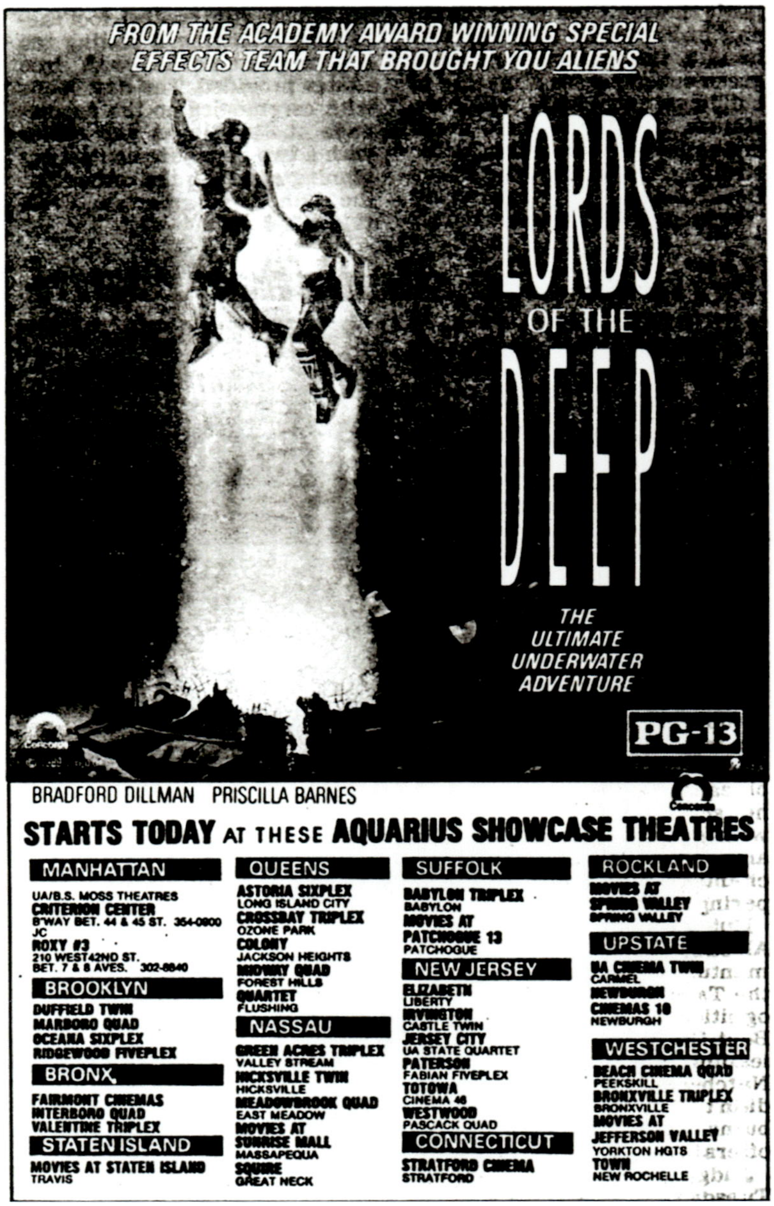

EARTH GIRLS ARE EASY

Actress/singer Julie Brown intended to star in *Earth Girls Are Easy*, which she co-wrote and was inspired by a song from her debut album *Goddess in Progress*, but the producers wanted a bigger name in the lead. So Geena Davis landed the part of a manicurist who falls in love with one of three aliens who crash-land in her swimming pool – an amorous visitor played by her then-husband and *The Fly* co-star Jeff Goldblum. Brown took the part of Davis' Valley Girl pal, and the other two spacemen were played by up-and-comers Jim Carrey and Damon Wayans. Whether the result was good, bouncy fun was up for debate across the critical spectrum.

"The movie's sense of fun is infectious and saves the material when it starts to sag. Davis is, at this point in her career, manifestly a happy young woman, and her joy of performance spills over into her character and inspires the actors around her."

–Roger Ebert, *Chicago Sun-Times*

"*Earth Girls Are Easy* is sometimes so cotton-candy fluffy it threatens to float off the screen. ... Nonetheless, there's plenty of entertainment value in this agreeably wacky comedy."

–Jack Garner, Gannett News Service

"*Earth Girls Are Easy* is a candy-colored, air-headed, empty plate of a comedy that is so cheerful about so many stupid things that you cannot, in good conscience, endorse it, but you may be tempted to adopt it."

–George Anderson, *Pittsburgh Post-Gazette*

"The Valley Girl musical *Earth Girls Are Easy* is like a beach ball with a slow leak – plastic and colorful and bouncy and fun until you notice it's not staying airborne."

–DAVID EDELSTEIN, *NEW YORK POST*

"It's a nice idea that's drowned early and often in a serious [sic] of glitzy production numbers that only the most die-hard fans of MTV can love."

–Lynn Darling, New York *Newsday*

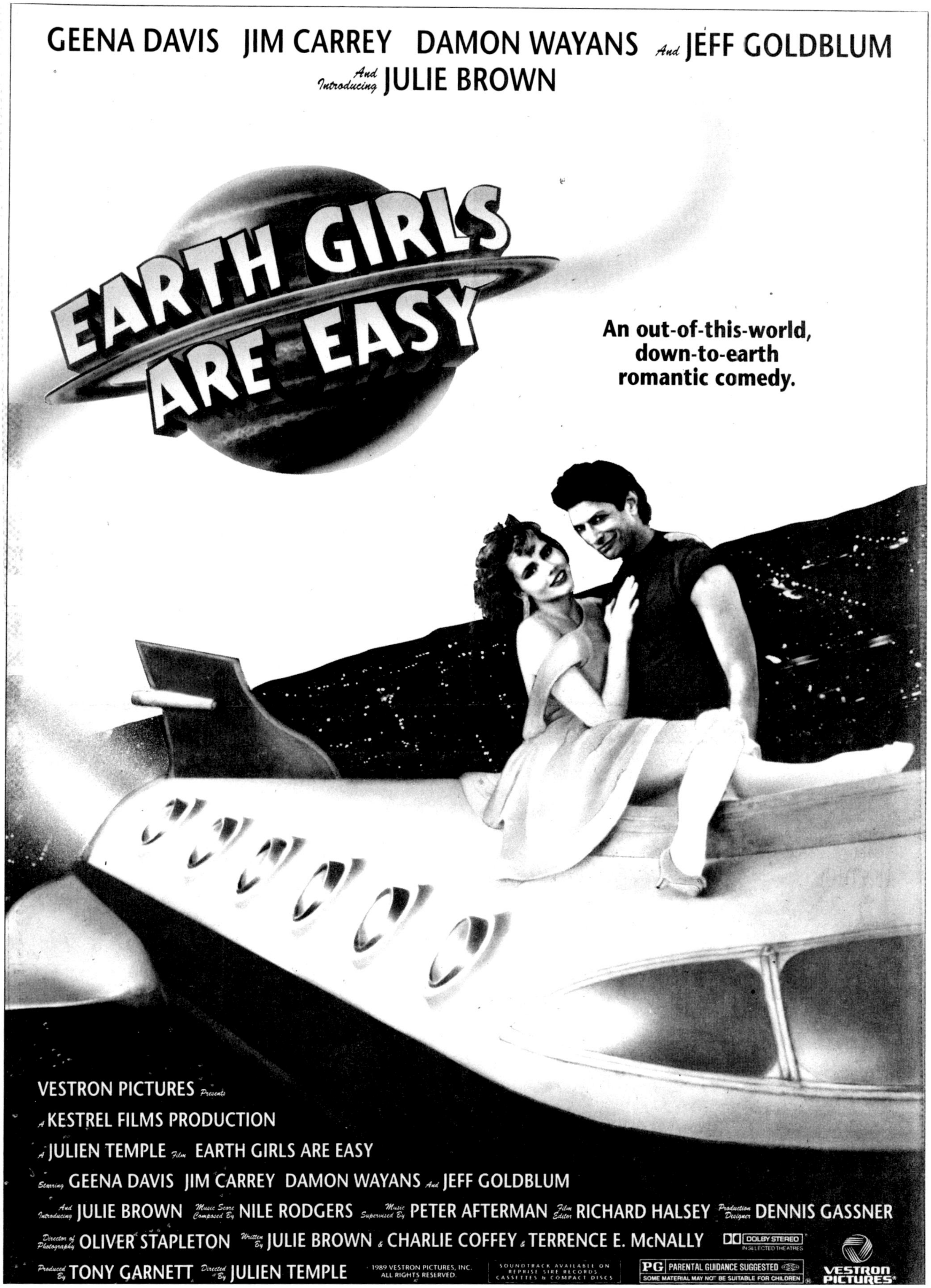
GEENA DAVIS JIM CARREY DAMON WAYANS And JEFF GOLDBLUM
And Introducing JULIE BROWN
EARTH GIRLS ARE EASY
An out-of-this-world, down-to-earth romantic comedy.
VESTRON PICTURES Presents
A KESTREL FILMS PRODUCTION
A JULIEN TEMPLE Film EARTH GIRLS ARE EASY
Starring GEENA DAVIS JIM CARREY DAMON WAYANS And JEFF GOLDBLUM
And Introducing JULIE BROWN Music Score Composed By NILE RODGERS Music Supervised By PETER AFTERMAN Film Editor RICHARD HALSEY Production Designer DENNIS GASSNER
Director of Photography OLIVER STAPLETON Written By JULIE BROWN & CHARLIE COFFEY & TERRENCE E. McNALLY
DOLBY STEREO
IN SELECTED THEATRES
Produced By TONY GARNETT Directed By JULIEN TEMPLE
1989 VESTRON PICTURES, INC. ALL RIGHTS RESERVED.
SOUNDTRACK AVAILABLE ON REPRISE SIRE RECORDS CASSETTES & COMPACT DISCS
PG PARENTAL GUIDANCE SUGGESTED
SOME MATERIAL MAY NOT BE SUITABLE FOR CHILDREN
VESTRON PICTURES

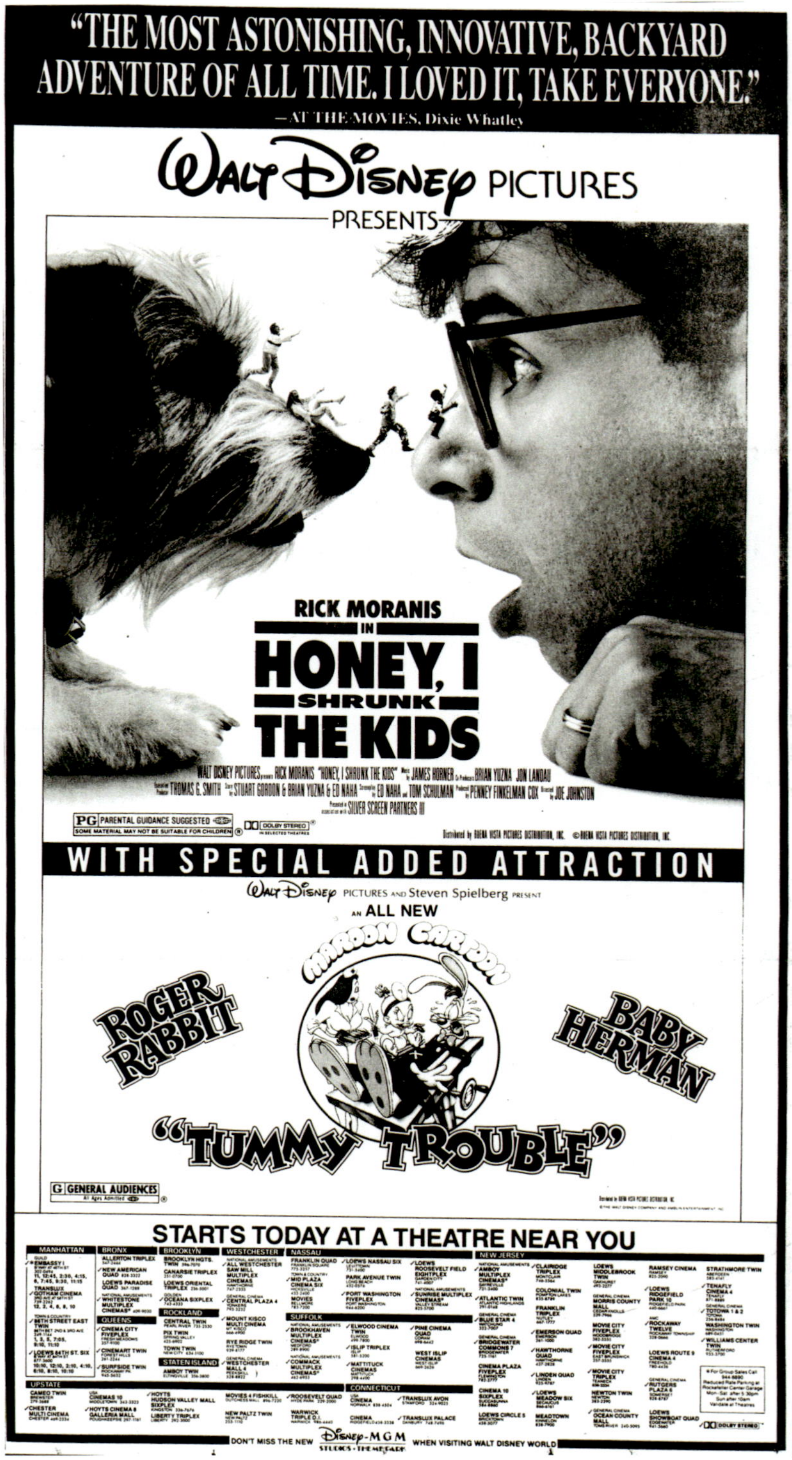

GHOSTBUSTERS II

"It's not going to be called *Ghostbusters II*," Bill Murray told *Starlog* magazine shortly before filming on the sequel began. "We'll burn in hell if we call it *Ghostbusters II*." That blazing fate didn't await the actor and the rest of the returning team when the movie opened with that Roman numeral in the title; instead, the general reaction from critics and audiences is best described as lukewarm.

"[It] strikes me as being far easier to take, funnier even, than the first film, which seemed overproduced and sloppy. *Ghostbusters II* seems more modest, less aggressive, not so oppressively extravagant."

–Vincent Canby, *The New York Times*

"[I]t's nice to discover that the makers of *Ghostbusters II* have worked hard to keep their movie's edge sharp. ... The movie's style is meticulous, beginning with Ivan Reitman's producing and directing."

–Sheila Benson, *Los Angeles Times*

"Since Ramis and Aykroyd wrote the script, they have only themselves to blame for the fact that their characters are so vacuous. And Ivan Reitman's directorial touch is, as usual, anything but ectoplasmic."

–JAY CARR,
THE BOSTON GLOBE

"It's reasonably enjoyable, although there are so many low-impact scenes it might have been wiser to avoid comparisons with the original by simply calling it *Four Ghostbusters and a Baby*."

–Kathleen Carroll, New York *Daily News*

"...Reitman doesn't have the pacing or the visual imagination to give the paranormal an out-of-this-world zing. *Ghostbusters* was a funny picture, but it was still a formula picture. *Ghostbusters II* is smoother, but it's even more formulaic."

–Michael Sragow, *San Francisco Examiner*

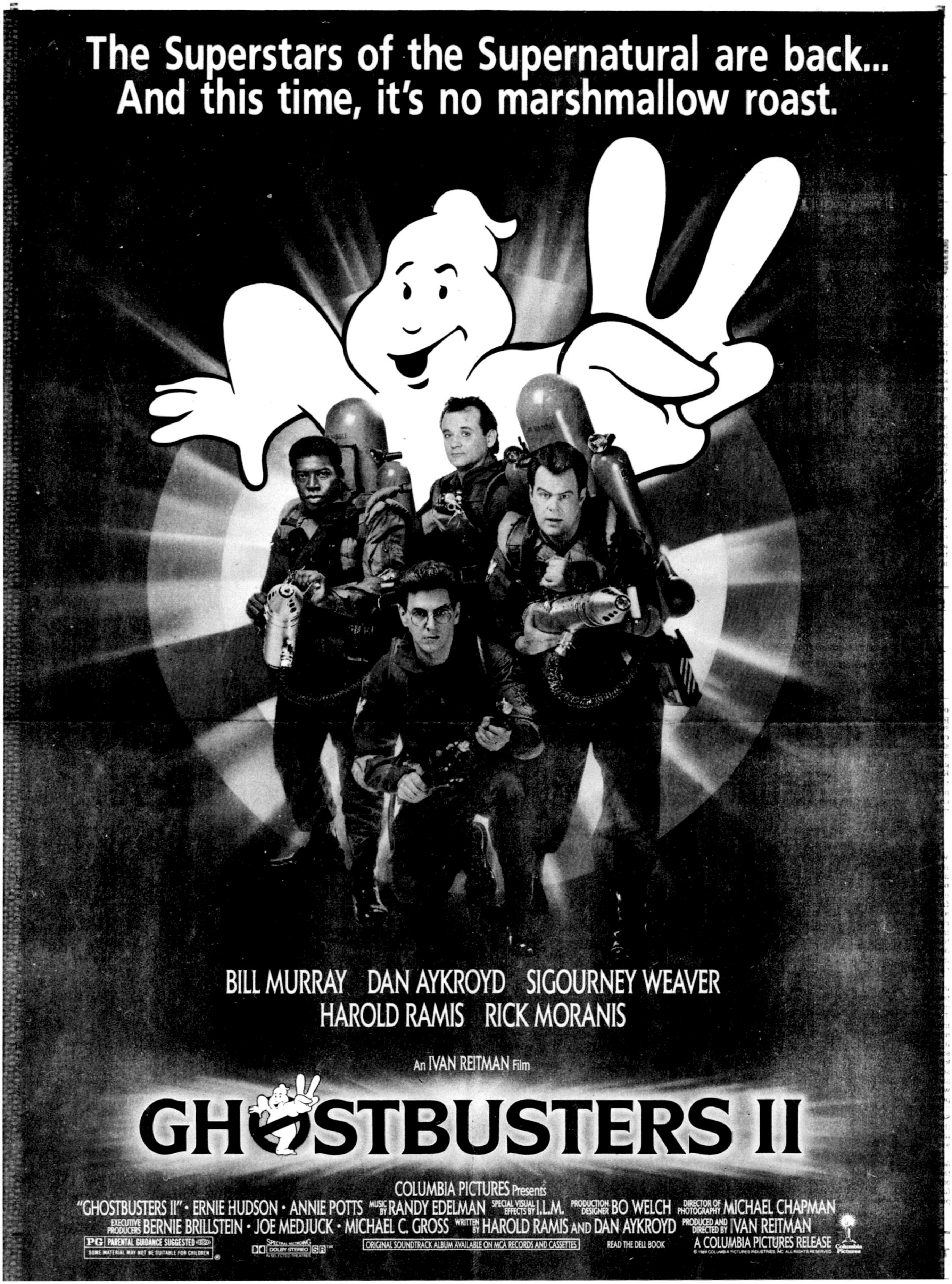
The Superstars of the Supernatural are back...
And this time, it's no marshmallow roast.
BILL MURRAY DAN AYKROYD SIGOURNEY WEAVER
HAROLD RAMIS RICK MORANIS
An IVAN REITMAN Film
GHOSTBUSTERS II
COLUMBIA PICTURES Presents
"GHOSTBUSTERS II" · ERNIE HUDSON · ANNIE POTTS MUSIC BY RANDY EDELMAN SPECIAL VISUAL EFFECTS BY I.L.M. PRODUCTION DESIGNER BO WELCH DIRECTOR OF PHOTOGRAPHY MICHAEL CHAPMAN
EXECUTIVE PRODUCERS BERNIE BRILLSTEIN · JOE MEDJUCK · MICHAEL C. GROSS WRITTEN BY HAROLD RAMIS AND DAN AYKROYD PRODUCED AND DIRECTED BY IVAN REITMAN
PG PARENTAL GUIDANCE SUGGESTED
SOME MATERIAL MAY NOT BE SUITABLE FOR CHILDREN
DOLBY STEREO SR
ORIGINAL SOUNDTRACK ALBUM AVAILABLE ON MCA RECORDS AND CASSETTES
READ THE DELL BOOK
A COLUMBIA PICTURES RELEASE
Columbia Pictures

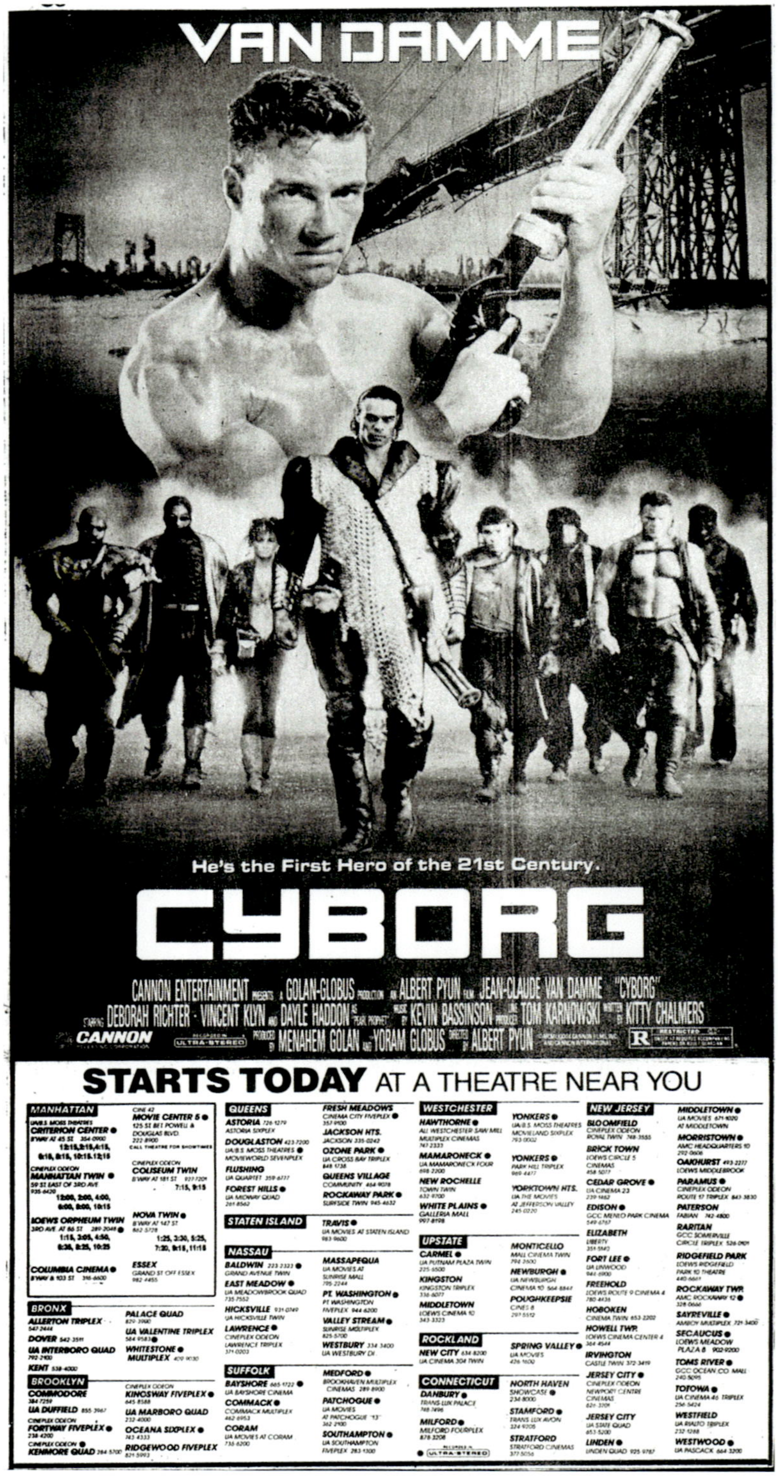

STAR TREK V: THE FINAL FRONTIER

Since Leonard Nimoy had piloted the third and fourth *Star Treks*, it seemed only logical that William Shatner should get his turn in the captain's chair for the fifth. His mission was not nearly as successful, though; *Star Trek V* opened big but faded fast, and most of the reviews chided the awkward mix of spiritualism and broad comedy. Some onlookers thought it was enough to kill the franchise, but the next entry, 1991's *Star Trek VI: The Undiscovered Country* – with *II*'s Nicholas Meyer back at the helm – got it back on course.

"*Star Trek V: The Final Frontier*...is as much a spiritual odyssey as a space adventure, and it's all the richer for it. It has high adventure, nifty special effects, and much good humor, but it also has a wonderful resonance to it."

–Kevin Thomas, *Los Angeles Times*

"Scene for scene, Mr. Shatner's direction is smooth and sharply focused. ... But he pays dearly for abandoning the Enterprise's mission: 'To boldly go where no man has gone before.'"

–Caryn James, *The New York Times*

"This reconvening of the old boys generates all the excitement of a Sunday school movie about an obscure Old Testament prophet."

–MALCOLM L. JOHNSON, *HARTFORD COURANT*

"After the pointless opening scenes, the movie begins to develop a plot of sorts, but it is so confused and inadequately explained that there are times when we simply give up and wait for what's next."

–Roger Ebert, *Chicago Sun-Times*

"Much of the blame for what's wrong with the picture must be place on William Shatner. ... The man isn't much of a thinker, though he seems to think he is."

–Jay Boyar, *Orlando Sentinel*

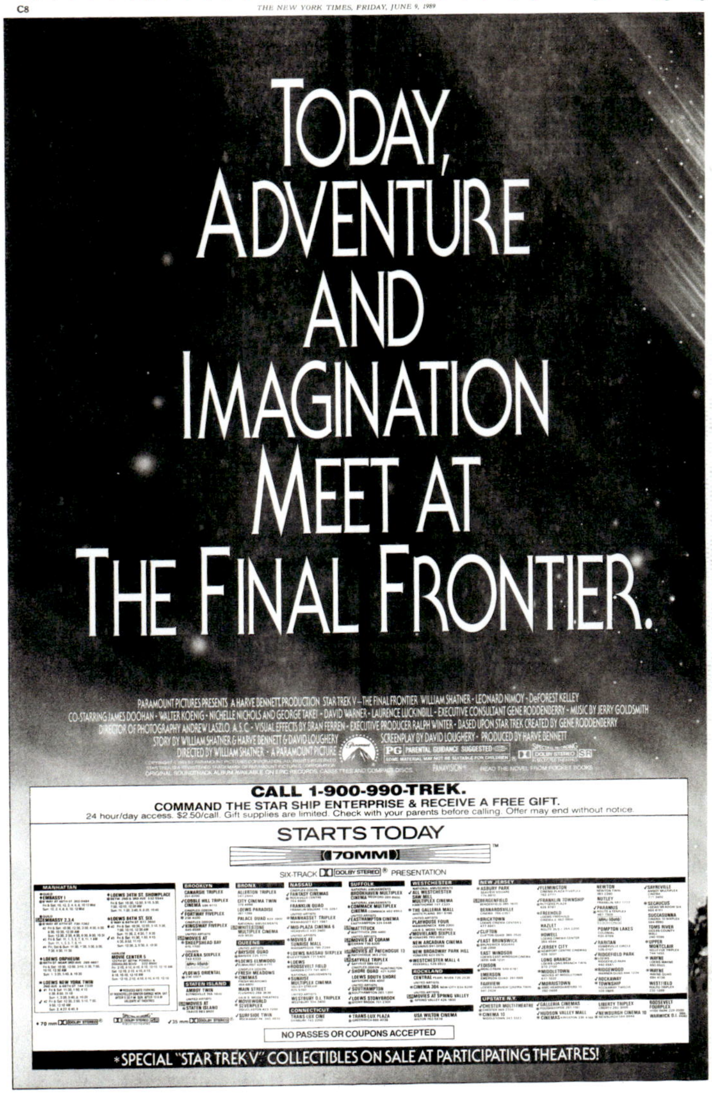
C8
THE NEW YORK TIMES, FRIDAY, JUNE 9, 1989
TODAY, ADVENTURE AND IMAGINATION MEET AT THE FINAL FRONTIER.
PARAMOUNT PICTURES PRESENTS A HARVE BENNETT PRODUCTION STAR TREK V – THE FINAL FRONTIER WILLIAM SHATNER · LEONARD NIMOY · DeFOREST KELLEY
CO-STARRING JAMES DOOHAN · WALTER KOENIG · NICHELLE NICHOLS AND GEORGE TAKEI · DAVID WARNER · LAURENCE LUCKINBILL · EXECUTIVE CONSULTANT GENE RODDENBERRY · MUSIC BY JERRY GOLDSMITH
DIRECTOR OF PHOTOGRAPHY ANDREW LASZLO, A.S.C. · VISUAL EFFECTS BY BRAN FERREN · EXECUTIVE PRODUCER RALPH WINTER · BASED UPON STAR TREK CREATED BY GENE RODDENBERRY
STORY BY WILLIAM SHATNER & HARVE BENNETT & DAVID LOUGHERY · SCREENPLAY BY DAVID LOUGHERY · PRODUCED BY HARVE BENNETT
DIRECTED BY WILLIAM SHATNER · A PARAMOUNT PICTURE
PG PARENTAL GUIDANCE SUGGESTED
SOME MATERIAL MAY NOT BE SUITABLE FOR CHILDREN
DOLBY STEREO SR
PANAVISION
READ THE NOVEL FROM POCKET BOOKS
ORIGINAL SOUNDTRACK ALBUM AVAILABLE ON EPIC RECORDS, CASSETTES AND COMPACT DISCS
CALL 1-900-990-TREK.
COMMAND THE STAR SHIP ENTERPRISE & RECEIVE A FREE GIFT.
24 hour/day access. $2.50/call. Gift supplies are limited. Check with your parents before calling. Offer may end without notice.
STARTS TODAY
70MM
SIX-TRACK DOLBY STEREO PRESENTATION
MANHATTAN
BROOKLYN
BRONX
NASSAU
SUFFOLK
WESTCHESTER
NEW JERSEY
QUEENS
ROCKLAND
CONNECTICUT
NO PASSES OR COUPONS ACCEPTED
*SPECIAL "STAR TREK V" COLLECTIBLES ON SALE AT PARTICIPATING THEATRES!

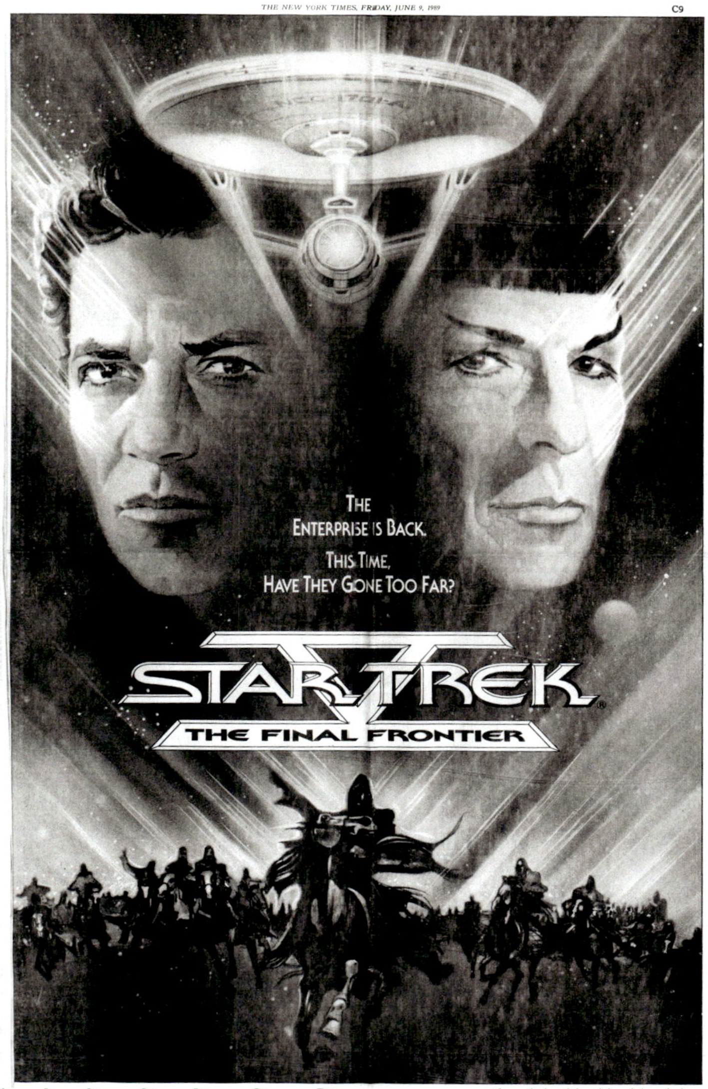
THE NEW YORK TIMES, FRIDAY, JUNE 9, 1989
C9
THE ENTERPRISE IS BACK.
THIS TIME, HAVE THEY GONE TOO FAR?
STAR TREK V
THE FINAL FRONTIER

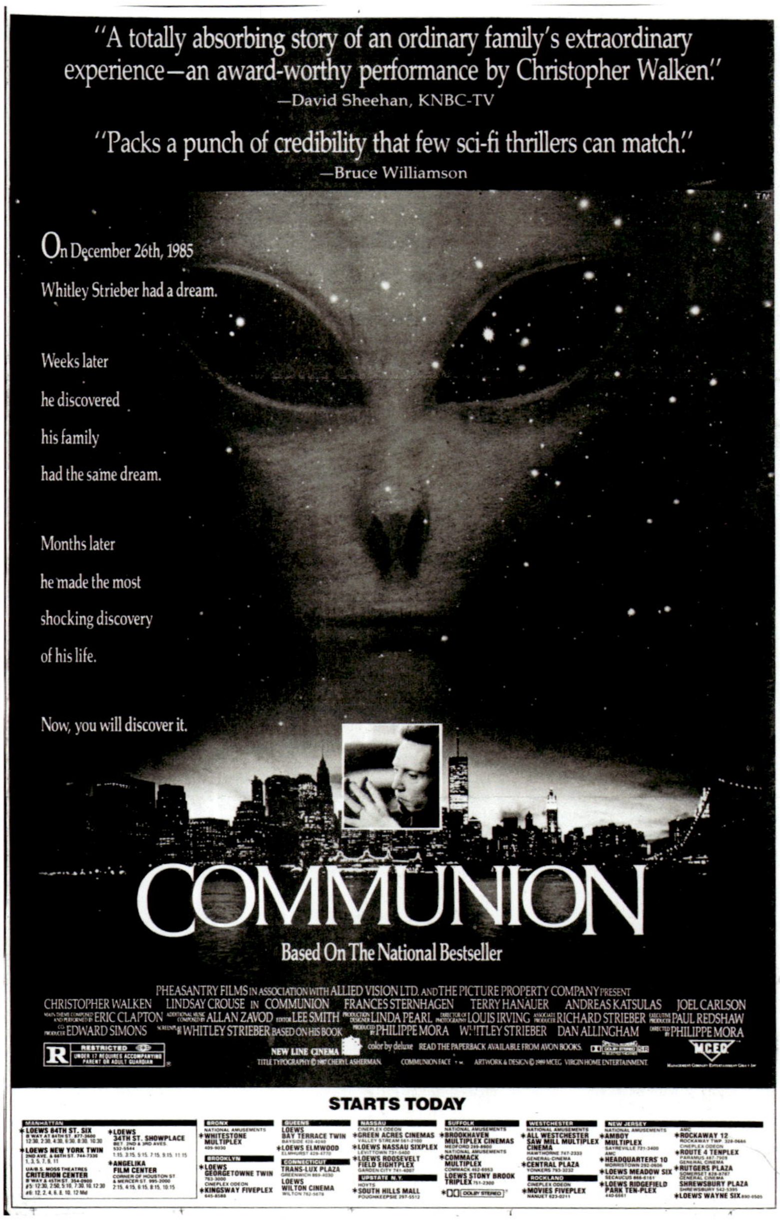

TEEN WITCH

For a while, this mix of comedy, light sorcery, and musical numbers (including rapping that's memorable for the wrong reasons) was just another low-budget youth film that barely made a blip in theaters on its way to videoland. But through the magic of heavy rotation on cable-TV and special screenings (particularly at Alamo Drafthouse Cinemas), it ascended to cult status, proving that even a movie that receives reviews like these can bewitch its share of viewers.

"*Teen Witch* sounds rather sophomoric and it is – literally. The movie is aimed at pre-teens and teens who long for popularity. ... This, in fact, would be the perfect movie for a slumber party of 11-year-olds."

–Barbara Vancheri, *Pittsburgh Post-Gazette*

"Once Louise turns 16 and has the world at her feet, the considerable early charm of the movie begins seeping away. And that's too bad, because the movie starts out as a happy cross between *Sixteen Candles* and a modern *Bye Bye Birdie*."

–Jami Bernard, *New York Post*

"Director Dorian Walker seems to have put this thing together the way artists who can't paint make pictures. ... If you want to have a good time watching an absolutely awful movie, this is one."

–BILL O'CONNOR, *AKRON* (OH) *BEACON JOURNAL*

"Be forewarned that this a high school where, bewitched or not, the youth occasionally break into song (or white rap) and dance – including a memorably ghastly 'I Like Boys' production number in a locker room that might have poor Busby Berkeley doing about 1,600 RPM in his grave."

–Chris Willman, *Los Angeles Times*

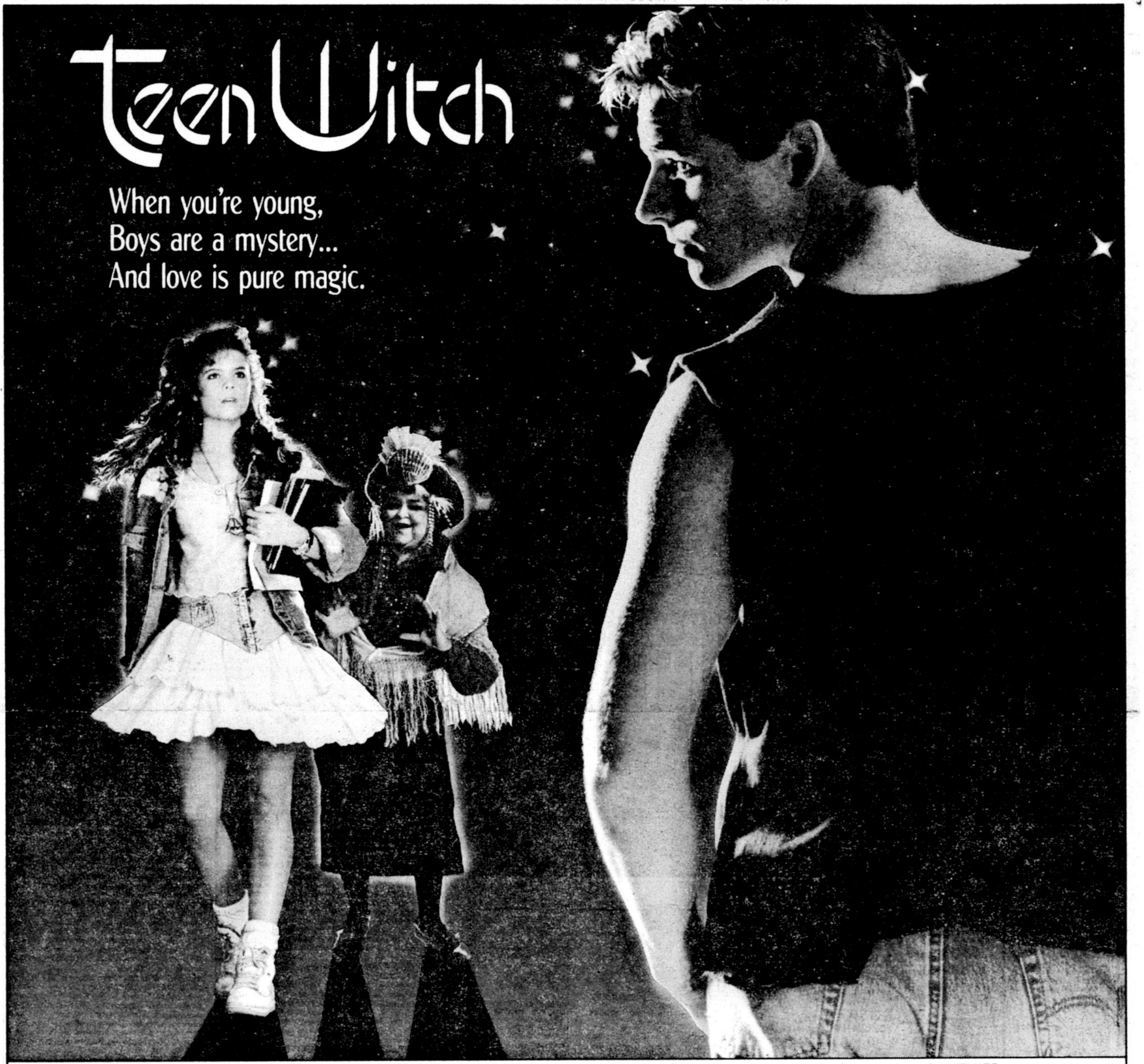

TRANS WORLD ENTERTAINMENT PRESENTS "TEEN WITCH" STARRING ROBYN LIVELY • ZELDA RUBINSTEIN • DAN GAUTHIER JOSHUA MILLER • DICK SARGENT SONGS COMPOSED BY LARRY WEIR ORIGINAL MUSIC COMPOSED BY RICHARD ELLIOT DIRECTOR OF PHOTOGRAPHY MARC RESHOVSKY EXECUTIVES IN CHARGE OF PRODUCTION PAUL MASON AND HELEN SARLUI-TUCKER EXECUTIVE PRODUCERS MOSHE DIAMANT AND EDUARD SARLUI WRITTEN BY ROBIN MENKEN & VERNON ZIMMERMAN PRODUCED BY ALANA LAMBROS AND RAFAEL EISENMAN DIRECTED BY DORIAN WALKER

PG-13 PARENTS STRONGLY CAUTIONED
Some Material May Be Inappropriate for Children Under 13

TRANS WORLD ENTERTAINMENT

RECORDED IN ULTRA·STEREO

STARTS TODAY
AT A THEATRE NEAR YOU

MANHATTAN
CITY CINEMAS
WEST SIDE CINEMA 1 & 2
7TH AVE. AT 48 ST. 398-1720
12:00, 1:50, 3:40, 5:30, 7:20, 9:10, 11:00, 12:50
CINE 42
MOVIE CENTER 5
125 ST. BET. POWELL & DOUGLAS BLVD. 222-8900
2:20, 4:15, 6:10, 8:05, 10:00, 11:55
CINE 42 TWIN
42 ST. BET. 7TH & 8TH AVES. 221-1992
11:50, 3:20, 6:55, 10:30

BRONX
FAIRMONT CINEMAS 901-3322
KENT 538-4000
UA VALENTINE TRIPLEX 584-9583

BROOKLYN
RIDGEWOOD FIVEPLEX 821-5993

QUEENS
JACKSON HTS.
COLONY TWIN 478-6777

NASSAU
VALLEY STREAM
CINEPLEX ODEON
GREEN ACRES CINEMAS 561-2100

SUFFOLK
PATCHOGUE
UA MOVIES
AT PATCHOGUE "13" 363-2100

ROCKLAND
SPRING VALLEY
UA MOVIES 426-1600

WESTCHESTER
HARRISON
CINEMA 835-5952
PEEKSKILL 528-8822
GCC WESTCHESTER MALL 4

UPSTATE
DOVER PLAINS
DOVER 877-9951
MONTICELLO
MALL CINEMA TWIN 794-2600
NEWBURGH
UA NEWBURGH
CINEMA 10 564-8844

NEW JERSEY
ELIZABETH
LIBERTY 351-5140
IRVINGTON
CASTLE TWIN 372-3419
JERSEY CITY
UA STATE QUAD 653-5200
MONTCLAIR
WELLMONT TRIPLEX 783-9500
MORRISTOWN
AMC HEADQUARTERS 10 292-0606
PATERSON
FABIAN 742-4800
ROCKAWAY TWP.
AMC ROCKAWAY 12 328-0666
TEANECK
MOVIE CITY TRIPLEX 836-3334
TOTOWA
GCC TOTOWA CINEMA 1 & 2 256-8484

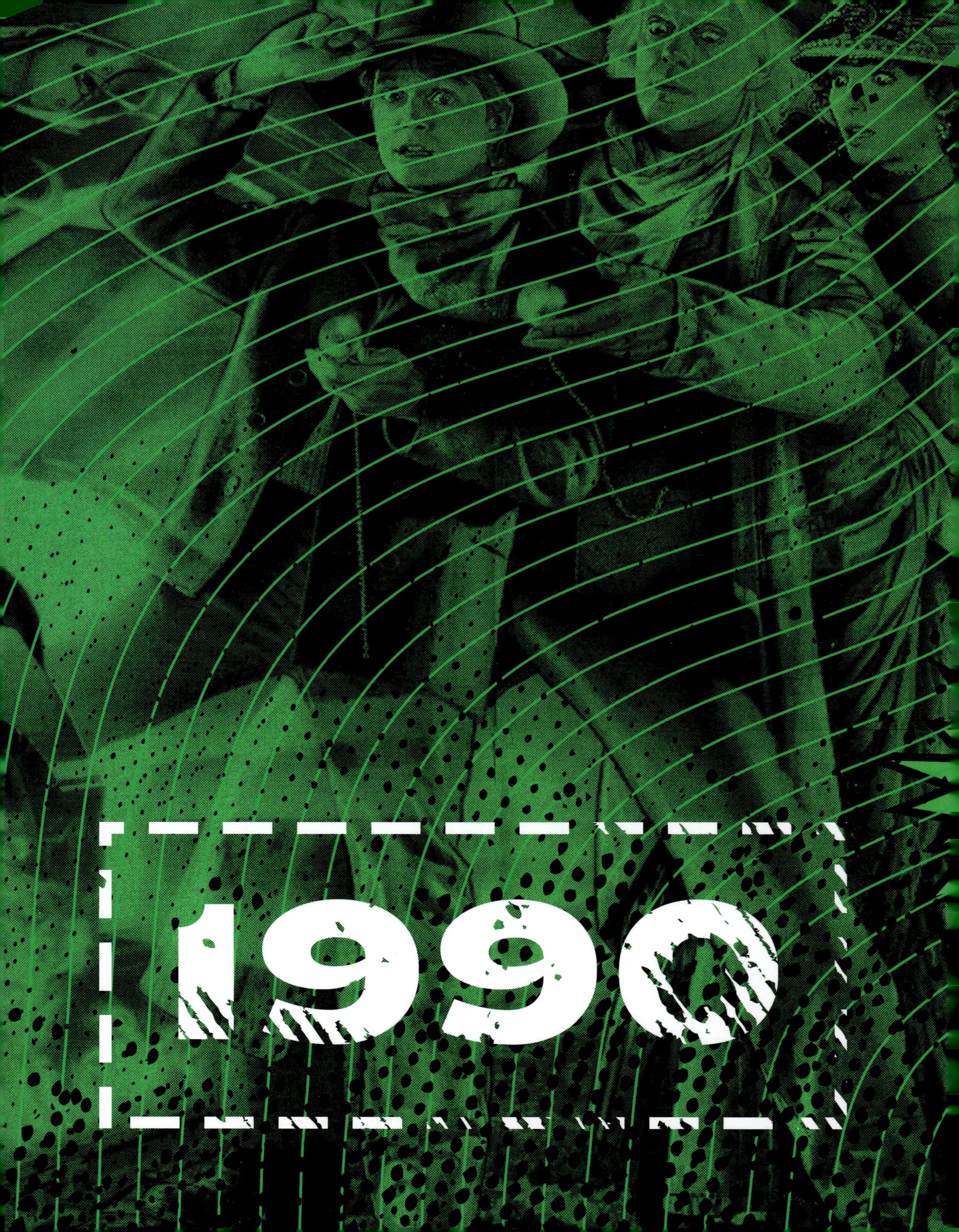
1990

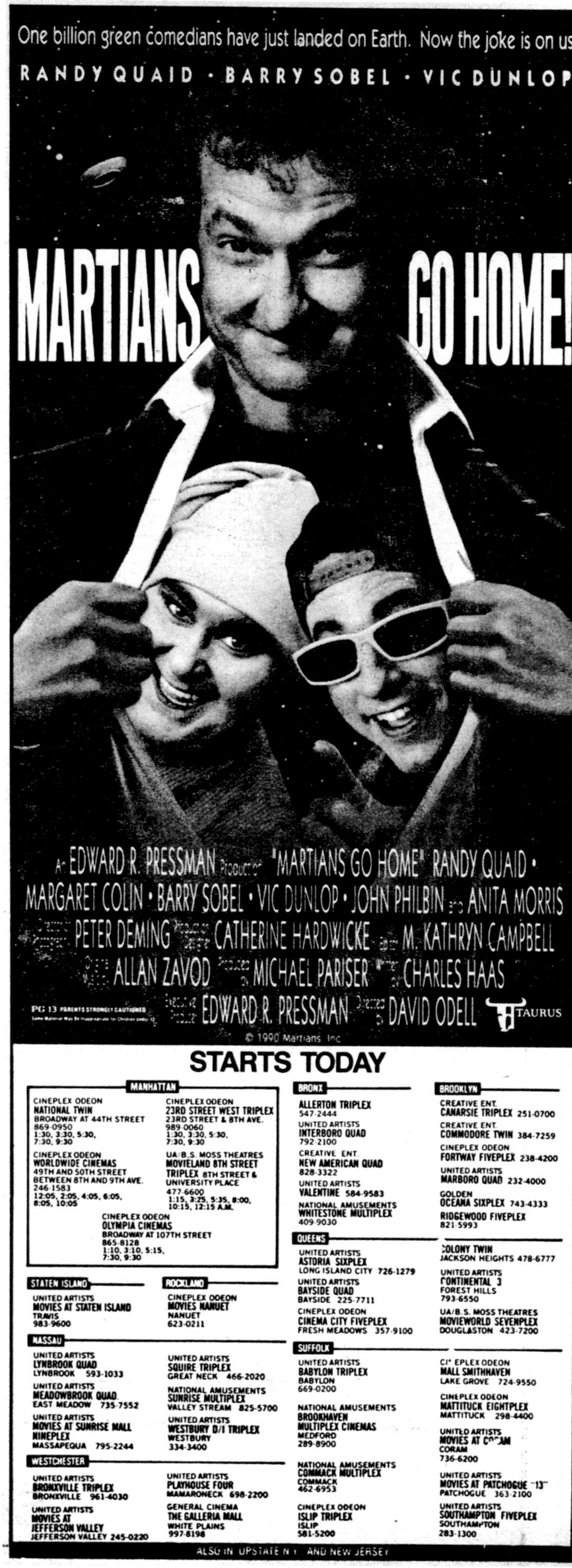
One billion green comedians have just landed on Earth. Now the joke is on us!
RANDY QUAID · BARRY SOBEL · VIC DUNLOP
MARTIANS GO HOME!
EDWARD R. PRESSMAN "MARTIANS GO HOME" RANDY QUAID ·
MARGARET COLIN · BARRY SOBEL · VIC DUNLOP · JOHN PHILBIN ANITA MORRIS
PETER DEMING CATHERINE HARDWICKE M. KATHRYN CAMPBELL
ALLAN ZAVOD MICHAEL PARISER CHARLES HAAS
PG 13 PARENTS STRONGLY CAUTIONED
EDWARD R. PRESSMAN DAVID ODELL
TAURUS
© 1990 Martians Inc
STARTS TODAY
MANHATTAN
CINEPLEX ODEON NATIONAL TWIN BROADWAY AT 44TH STREET 869-0950 1:30, 3:30, 5:30, 7:30, 9:30
CINEPLEX ODEON 23RD STREET WEST TRIPLEX 23RD STREET & 8TH AVE. 989-0060 1:30, 3:30, 5:30, 7:30, 9:30
CINEPLEX ODEON WORLDWIDE CINEMAS 49TH AND 50TH STREET BETWEEN 8TH AND 9TH AVE. 246-1583 12:05, 2:05, 4:05, 6:05, 8:05, 10:05
UA/B.S. MOSS THEATRES MOVIELAND 8TH STREET TRIPLEX 8TH STREET & UNIVERSITY PLACE 477-6600 1:15, 3:25, 5:35, 8:00, 10:15, 12:15 A.M.
CINEPLEX ODEON OLYMPIA CINEMAS BROADWAY AT 107TH STREET 865-8128 1:10, 3:10, 5:15, 7:30, 9:30
STATEN ISLAND
UNITED ARTISTS MOVIES AT STATEN ISLAND TRAVIS 983-9600
ROCKLAND
CINEPLEX ODEON MOVIES NANUET NANUET 623-0211
NASSAU
UNITED ARTISTS LYNBROOK QUAD LYNBROOK 593-1033
UNITED ARTISTS MEADOWBROOK QUAD EAST MEADOW 735-7552
UNITED ARTISTS MOVIES AT SUNRISE MALL NINEPLEX MASSAPEQUA 795-2244
UNITED ARTISTS SQUIRE TRIPLEX GREAT NECK 466-2020
NATIONAL AMUSEMENTS SUNRISE MULTIPLEX VALLEY STREAM 825-5700
UNITED ARTISTS WESTBURY D/I TRIPLEX WESTBURY 334-3400
WESTCHESTER
UNITED ARTISTS BRONXVILLE TRIPLEX BRONXVILLE 961-4030
UNITED ARTISTS MOVIES AT JEFFERSON VALLEY JEFFERSON VALLEY 245-0220
UNITED ARTISTS PLAYHOUSE FOUR MAMARONECK 698-2200
GENERAL CINEMA THE GALLERIA MALL WHITE PLAINS 997-8198
BRONX
ALLERTON TRIPLEX 547-2444
UNITED ARTISTS INTERBORO QUAD 792-2100
CREATIVE ENT. NEW AMERICAN QUAD 828-3322
UNITED ARTISTS VALENTINE 584-9583
NATIONAL AMUSEMENTS WHITESTONE MULTIPLEX 409-9030
QUEENS
UNITED ARTISTS ASTORIA SIXPLEX LONG ISLAND CITY 726-1279
UNITED ARTISTS BAYSIDE QUAD BAYSIDE 225-7711
CINEPLEX ODEON CINEMA CITY FIVEPLEX FRESH MEADOWS 357-9100
SUFFOLK
UNITED ARTISTS BABYLON TRIPLEX BABYLON 669-0200
NATIONAL AMUSEMENTS BROOKHAVEN MULTIPLEX CINEMAS MEDFORD 289-8900
NATIONAL AMUSEMENTS COMMACK MULTIPLEX COMMACK 462-6953
CINEPLEX ODEON ISLIP TRIPLEX ISLIP 581-5200
BROOKLYN
CREATIVE ENT. CANARSIE TRIPLEX 251-0700
CREATIVE ENT. COMMODORE TWIN 384-7259
CINEPLEX ODEON FORTWAY FIVEPLEX 238-4200
UNITED ARTISTS MARBORO QUAD 232-4000
GOLDEN OCEANA SIXPLEX 743-4333
RIDGEWOOD FIVEPLEX 821-5993
COLONY TWIN JACKSON HEIGHTS 478-6777
UNITED ARTISTS CONTINENTAL 3 FOREST HILLS 793-6550
UA/B.S. MOSS THEATRES MOVIEWORLD SEVENPLEX DOUGLASTON 423-7200
CINEPLEX ODEON MALL SMITHHAVEN LAKE GROVE 724-9550
CINEPLEX ODEON MATTITUCK EIGHTPLEX MATTITUCK 298-4400
UNITED ARTISTS MOVIES AT CORAM CORAM 736-6200
UNITED ARTISTS MOVIES AT PATCHOGUE "13" PATCHOGUE 363-2100
UNITED ARTISTS SOUTHAMPTON FIVEPLEX SOUTHAMPTON 283-1300
ALSO IN UPSTATE N.Y. AND NEW JERSEY

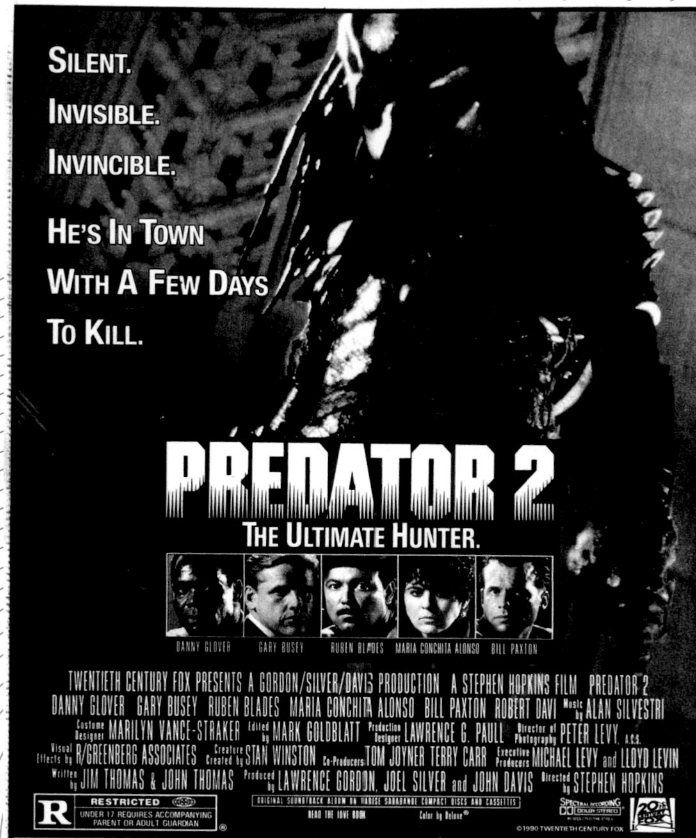
SILENT.
INVISIBLE.
INVINCIBLE.
HE'S IN TOWN WITH A FEW DAYS TO KILL.
PREDATOR 2
THE ULTIMATE HUNTER.
DANNY GLOVER GARY BUSEY RUBEN BLADES MARIA CONCHITA ALONSO BILL PAXTON
TWENTIETH CENTURY FOX PRESENTS A GORDON/SILVER/DAVIS PRODUCTION A STEPHEN HOPKINS FILM PREDATOR 2
DANNY GLOVER GARY BUSEY RUBEN BLADES MARIA CONCHITA ALONSO BILL PAXTON ROBERT DAVI Music by ALAN SILVESTRI
Costume Designer MARILYN VANCE-STRAKER Edited by MARK GOLDBLATT Production Designer LAWRENCE G. PAULL Director of Photography PETER LEVY, A.C.S.
Visual Effects by R/GREENBERG ASSOCIATES Creature Created by STAN WINSTON Co-Producers TOM JOYNER TERRY CARR Executive Producers MICHAEL LEVY and LLOYD LEVIN
Written by JIM THOMAS & JOHN THOMAS Produced by LAWRENCE GORDON, JOEL SILVER and JOHN DAVIS Directed by STEPHEN HOPKINS
R RESTRICTED UNDER 17 REQUIRES ACCOMPANYING PARENT OR ADULT GUARDIAN
READ THE JOVE BOOK
Color by Deluxe®
©1990 TWENTIETH CENTURY FOX

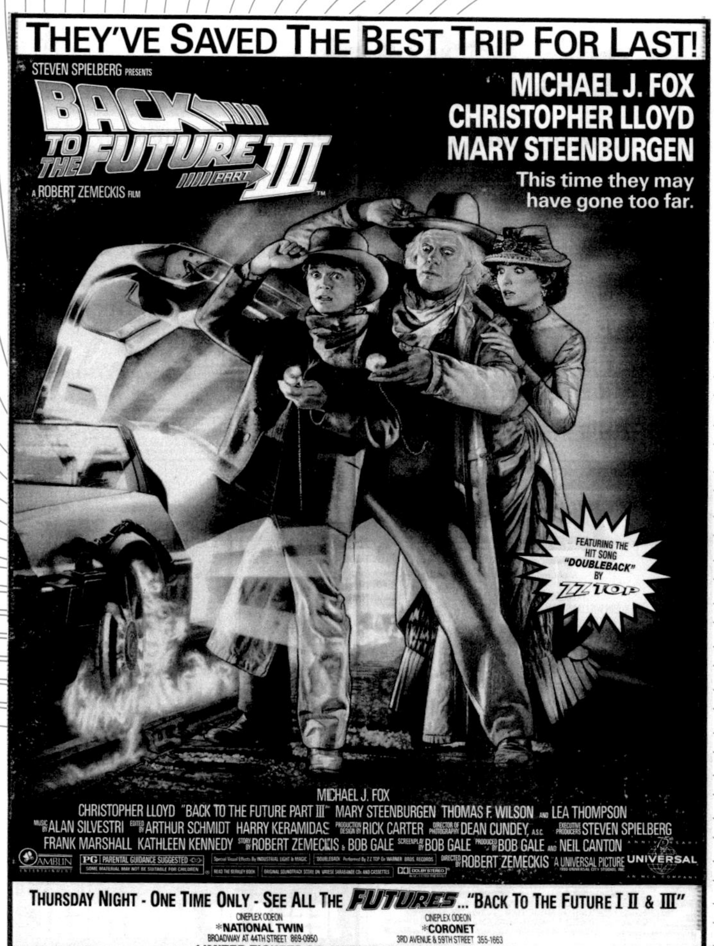
THEY'VE SAVED THE BEST TRIP FOR LAST!
STEVEN SPIELBERG PRESENTS
BACK TO THE FUTURE PART III
A ROBERT ZEMECKIS FILM
MICHAEL J. FOX
CHRISTOPHER LLOYD
MARY STEENBURGEN
This time they may have gone too far.
FEATURING THE HIT SONG "DOUBLEBACK" BY ZZ TOP
MICHAEL J. FOX
CHRISTOPHER LLOYD "BACK TO THE FUTURE PART III" MARY STEENBURGEN THOMAS F. WILSON AND LEA THOMPSON
MUSIC BY ALAN SILVESTRI EDITED BY ARTHUR SCHMIDT HARRY KERAMIDAS PRODUCTION DESIGN BY RICK CARTER DIRECTOR OF PHOTOGRAPHY DEAN CUNDEY, A.S.C. EXECUTIVE PRODUCERS STEVEN SPIELBERG
FRANK MARSHALL KATHLEEN KENNEDY STORY BY ROBERT ZEMECKIS & BOB GALE SCREENPLAY BY BOB GALE PRODUCED BY BOB GALE AND NEIL CANTON
AMBLIN
PG PARENTAL GUIDANCE SUGGESTED
DIRECTED BY ROBERT ZEMECKIS A UNIVERSAL PICTURE
UNIVERSAL
THURSDAY NIGHT - ONE TIME ONLY - SEE ALL THE FUTURES..."BACK TO THE FUTURE I II & III"
CINEPLEX ODEON *NATIONAL TWIN BROADWAY AT 44TH STREET 869-0950
CINEPLEX ODEON *CORONET 3RD AVENUE & 59TH STREET 355-1663
LIMITED TICKETS GO ON SALE THURSDAY AT 4:00 PM

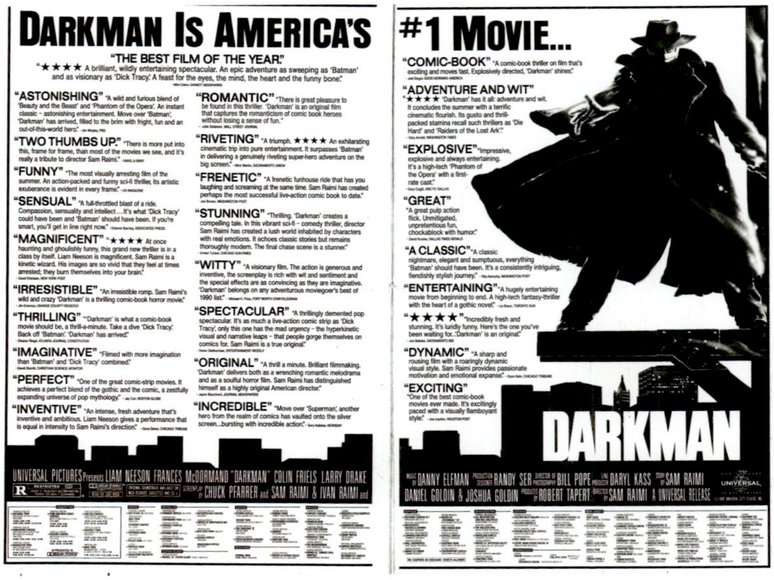

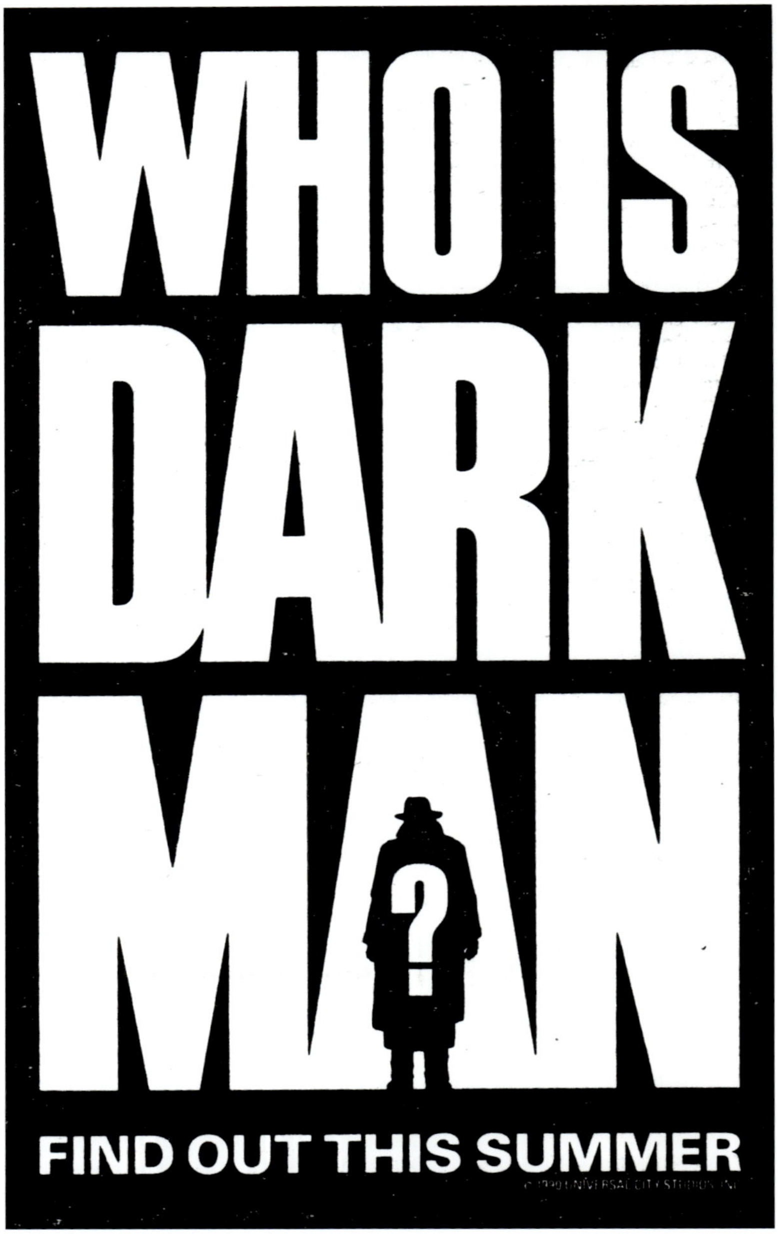

DARKMAN

A year after *Batman*'s release, Sam Raimi moved on from the *Evil Dead* trilogy to create his own shadowy superhero, bringing his usual kinetic camerawork to the project. Though inspired by comic books, *Darkman* was an original, so Universal launched an advance "Who is Darkman?" campaign to pique audience interest in this new crimefighter. It succeeded, and *Darkman* became Raimi's first box-office hit, and won him some of his most favorable reviews yet.

"*Darkman*, as unnerving as a gargoyle, is a classic nightmare, elegant, and sumptuous, everything *Batman* should have been. ... [Raimi's] work is beautiful in its scary way, and never only skin deep."

–Rita Kempley, *The Washington Post*

"Just when you think Hollywood has exhausted every possible variation on murder and mayhem, along comes Sam Raimi's *Darkman*, a first-rate horror-adventure flick crackling with slam-bang action and zappy dialogue of a comic book."

–Owen McNally, *Hartford Courant*

"In the recent flurry of comics-derived movies, *Darkman* may not be the most popular. But, in some ways, it's the best: the only one that successfully captures the graphic look, rhythm, and style of the superhero books."

–MICHAEL WILMINGTON, *THE NEW YORK TIMES*

"It's a zippy, furious yet endearing little big film – ragged as any comic-book 'secret origins' story, and erratically acted, but with its own strange poignancy and manic comic charge."

–Michael Sragow, *San Francisco Examiner*

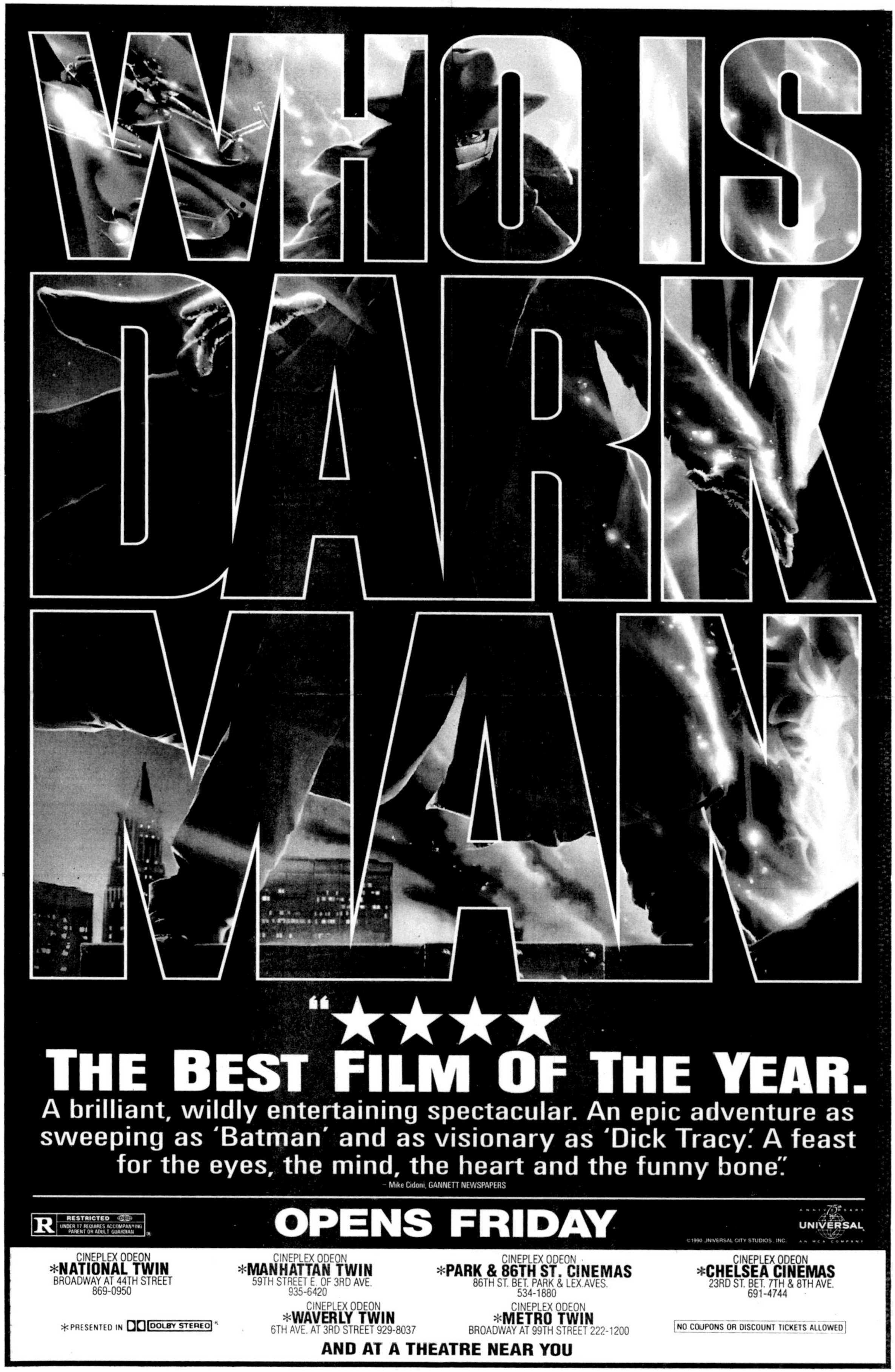
WHO IS
DARK
MAN
"★★★★
THE BEST FILM OF THE YEAR.
A brilliant, wildly entertaining spectacular. An epic adventure as sweeping as 'Batman' and as visionary as 'Dick Tracy.' A feast for the eyes, the mind, the heart and the funny bone."
– Mike Cidoni, GANNETT NEWSPAPERS
R RESTRICTED UNDER 17 REQUIRES ACCOMPANYING PARENT OR ADULT GUARDIAN
OPENS FRIDAY
75th ANNIVERSARY UNIVERSAL AN MCA COMPANY
©1990 UNIVERSAL CITY STUDIOS, INC.
CINEPLEX ODEON *NATIONAL TWIN BROADWAY AT 44TH STREET 869-0950
CINEPLEX ODEON *MANHATTAN TWIN 59TH STREET E. OF 3RD AVE. 935-6420
CINEPLEX ODEON *PARK & 86TH ST. CINEMAS 86TH ST. BET. PARK & LEX.AVES. 534-1880
CINEPLEX ODEON *CHELSEA CINEMAS 23RD ST. BET. 7TH & 8TH AVE. 691-4744
CINEPLEX ODEON *WAVERLY TWIN 6TH AVE. AT 3RD STREET 929-8037
CINEPLEX ODEON *METRO TWIN BROADWAY AT 99TH STREET 222-1200
*PRESENTED IN DOLBY STEREO
NO COUPONS OR DISCOUNT TICKETS ALLOWED
AND AT A THEATRE NEAR YOU

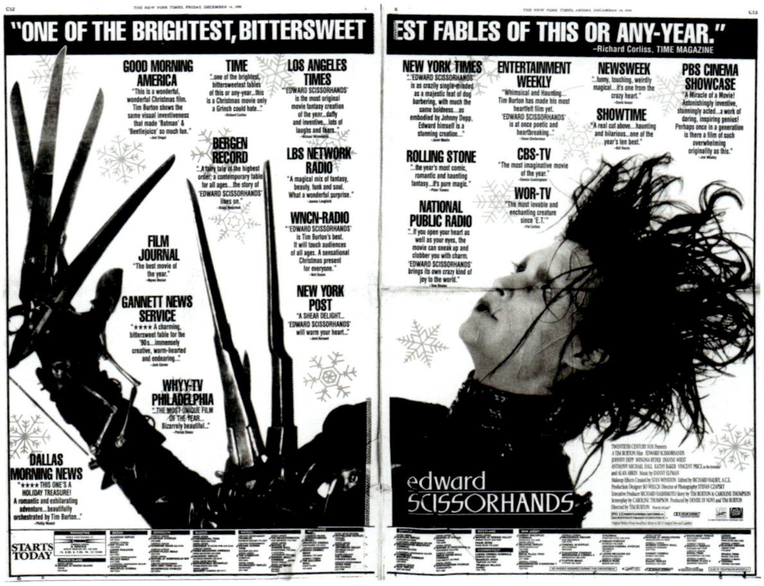

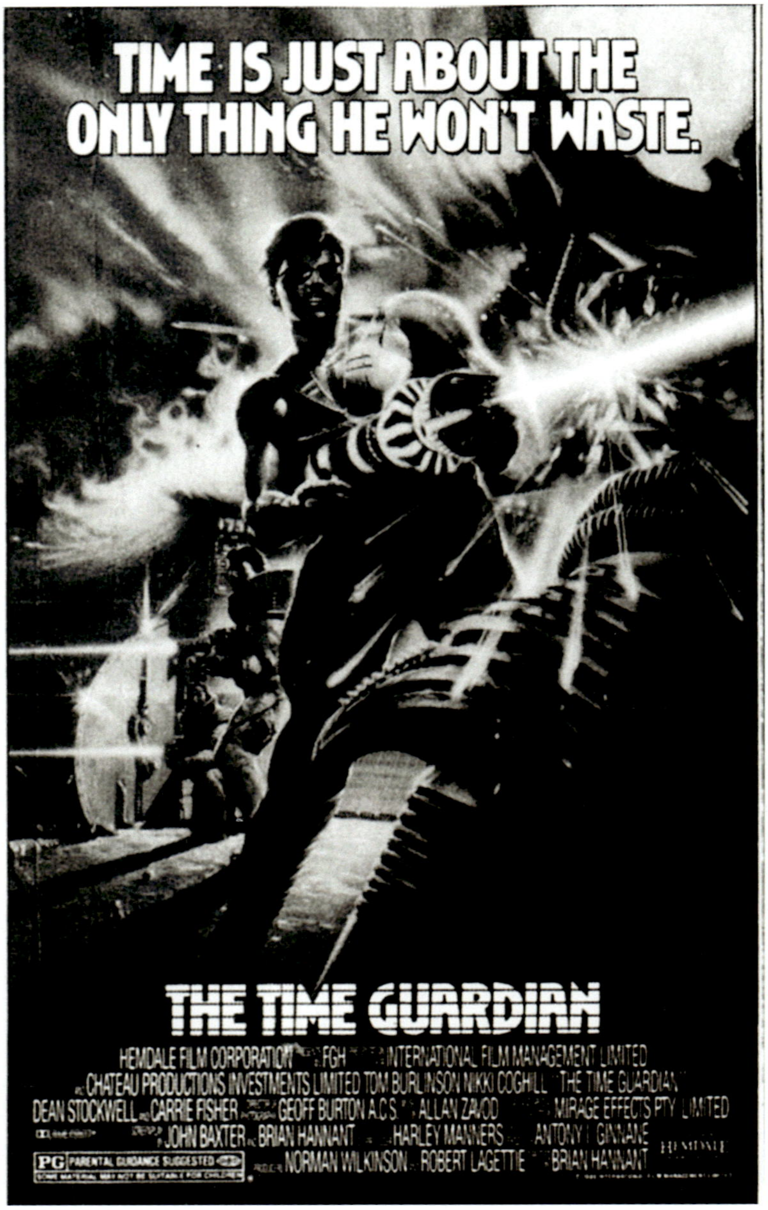

EDWARD SCISSORHANDS

After the doom and gloom of *Batman*, Tim Burton collaborated with Johnny Depp for the first time, reunited with *Beetlejuice*'s Winona Ryder, and captured one of Vincent Price's final performances in *Edward Scissorhands*, his romantic fairy tale of a Goth-suburban Frankenstein's monster. Yet, just as with his vision of the Caped Crusader, critics were split when it came to style versus substance.

"Burton's new film contains his most visually delicate camera work ever, and Danny Elfman's musical score...has the cold, gentle beauty of a snowflake. The acting is wonderful, an ensemble of eccentric performances that collectively support the movie's tone and themes."

–Jay Boyar, *Orlando Sentinel*

"Like a great chef concocting an exquisite peanut butter-and-jelly sandwich, Mr. Burton invests awe-inspiring ingenuity into the process of reinventing something very small."

–Janet Maslin, *The New York Times*

"[Edward is] perhaps the most original movie fantasy creation of the year: an icon of tenderness and artistic ambition that clings, stickum-like, to your mind's eye and the softest, most woundable parts of your mass-culture heart."

–MICHAEL WILMINGTON, *LOS ANGELES TIMES*

"One problem is that the other people are as weird, in their ways, as [Edward] is: everyone in this film is stylized and peculiar, so he becomes another exhibit in the menagerie, instead of a commentary on it."

–Roger Ebert, *Chicago Sun-Times*

"...Tim Burton's slight follow up to *Batman* is a witty collection of sets and props just waiting for a movie to come along. When one finally does, it's so skimpy that it gets lost amid all that scenery."

–John Leland, New York *Newsday*

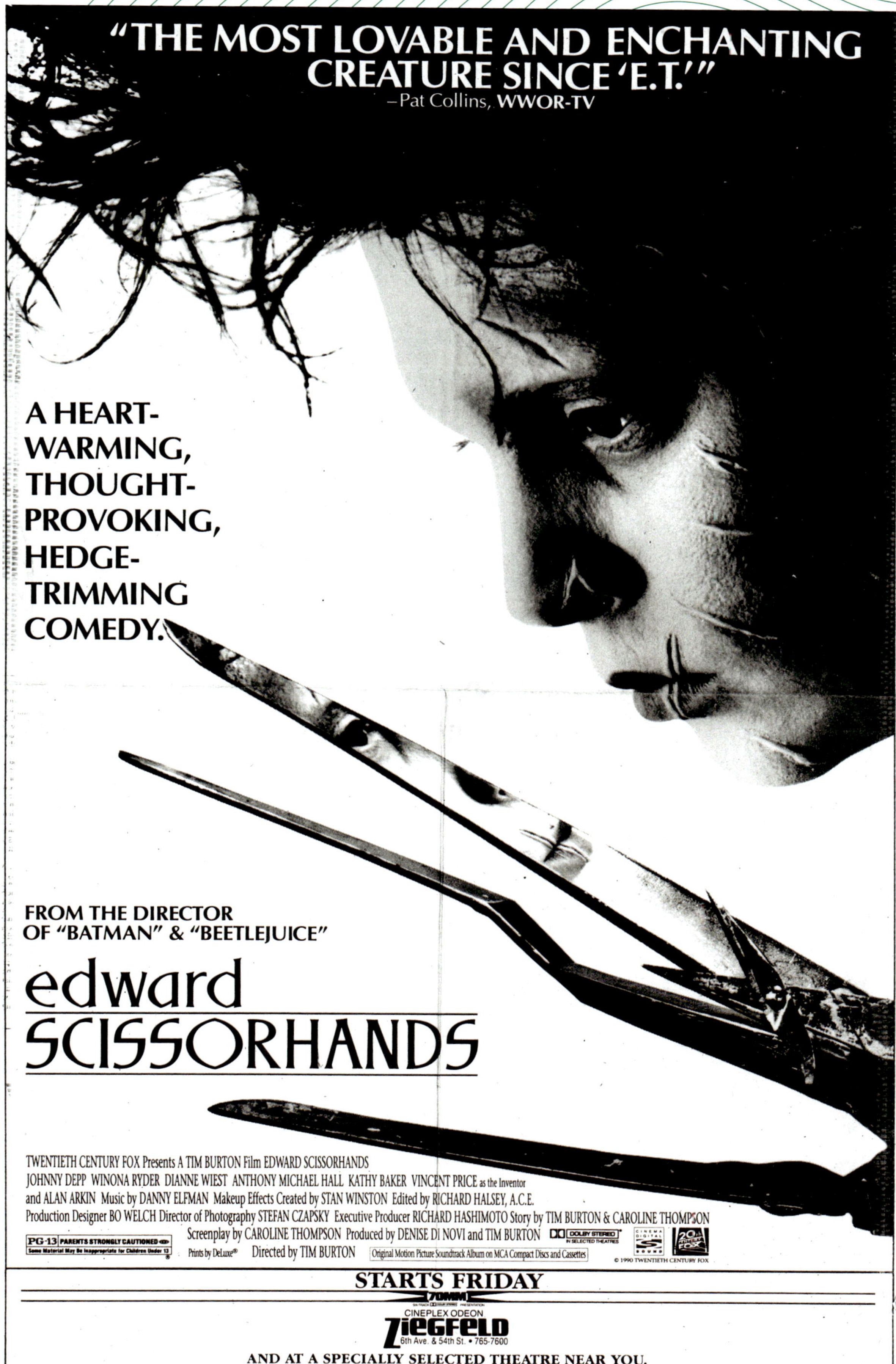
"THE MOST LOVABLE AND ENCHANTING CREATURE SINCE 'E.T.'"
–Pat Collins, WWOR-TV
A HEART-WARMING, THOUGHT-PROVOKING, HEDGE-TRIMMING COMEDY.
FROM THE DIRECTOR OF "BATMAN" & "BEETLEJUICE"
edward SCISSORHANDS
TWENTIETH CENTURY FOX Presents A TIM BURTON Film EDWARD SCISSORHANDS
JOHNNY DEPP WINONA RYDER DIANNE WIEST ANTHONY MICHAEL HALL KATHY BAKER VINCENT PRICE as the Inventor
and ALAN ARKIN Music by DANNY ELFMAN Makeup Effects Created by STAN WINSTON Edited by RICHARD HALSEY, A.C.E.
Production Designer BO WELCH Director of Photography STEFAN CZAPSKY Executive Producer RICHARD HASHIMOTO Story by TIM BURTON & CAROLINE THOMPSON
Screenplay by CAROLINE THOMPSON Produced by DENISE DI NOVI and TIM BURTON
PG-13 PARENTS STRONGLY CAUTIONED
Some Material May Be Inappropriate for Children Under 13
Prints by DeLuxe®
Directed by TIM BURTON
Original Motion Picture Soundtrack Album on MCA Compact Discs and Cassettes
DOLBY STEREO IN SELECTED THEATRES
CINEMA DIGITAL SOUND
© 1990 TWENTIETH CENTURY FOX
STARTS FRIDAY
70MM
CINEPLEX ODEON
ZIEGFELD
6th Ave. & 54th St. • 765-7600
AND AT A SPECIALLY SELECTED THEATRE NEAR YOU.

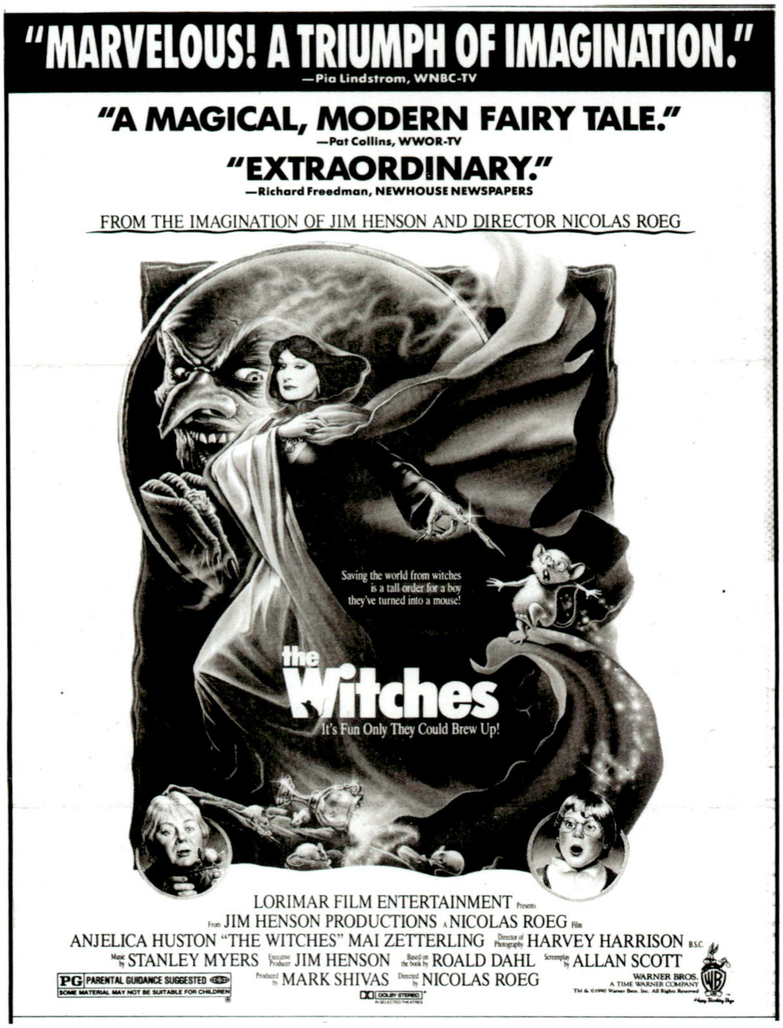

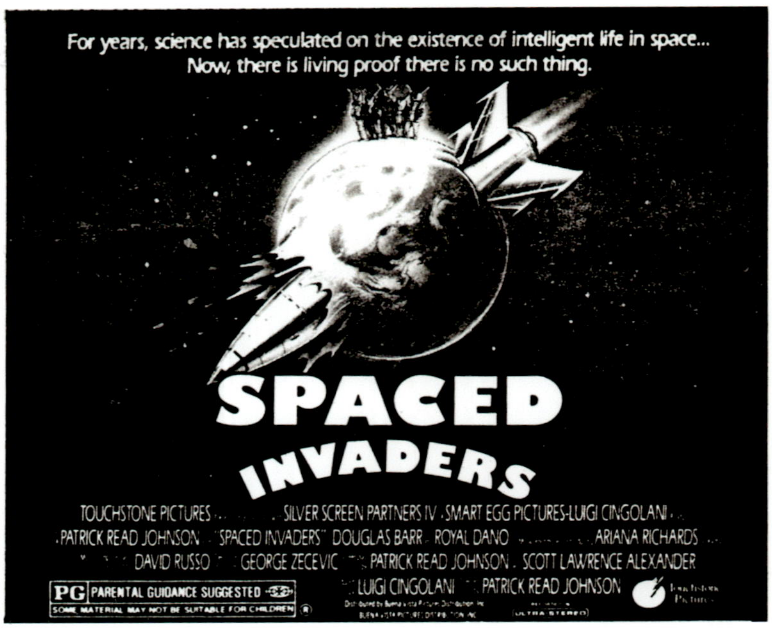

GHOST

In the summer of '90, the big box-office battle was supposed to be between Warren Beatty's *Dick Tracy* and the Tom Cruise racing drama *Days of Thunder*. Both underperformed, outdone by the mega-actioners *Total Recall* and *Die Hard 2* – but easily the season's biggest hit was a medium-budgeted genre-blender mixing romance, comedy, and supernatural fantasy. *Ghost* became a word-of-mouth smash, launched Jerry Zucker (of the Zucker-Abrahams-Zucker team behind *Airplane!* and *Ruthless People*) as a solo director, won an Oscar for Whoopi Goldberg (as psychic Oda Mae Brown, a role the producers had originally intended to cast with an unknown), and boosted attendance at pottery classes everywhere. Reviews of the movie itself were more varied.

"Don't let cloying memories of Steven Spielberg's very similar *Always* keep you from this movie. *Ghost* is tender, funny, and exciting, with much more dimension than its predecessor."

–Jami Bernard, *New York Post*

"...*Ghost* passes between genres as smoothly as its characters pass between worlds, provoking sighs at one moment and belly laughs the next."

–DAVE KEHR, *CHICAGO TRIBUNE*

"The rambling supernatural comedy/thriller/romance *Ghost* is so unfocused that it should be a transparently silly flop. Instead, it's well-crafted enough to scare up respectability as a pleasant summer sleeper."

–Joe DeChick, *The Cincinnati Enquirer*

"The movie's slogan is 'Believe,' not an unreasonable request. But even those who'd be happy to comply must get past *Ghost*'s one casting jaw-dropper [Swayze], a certain woolly-mindedness to its script and a production prettified to the point of stickiness."

–Sheila Benson, *Los Angeles Times*

"All right, a fantasy film is entitled to be inconsistent on a plot point or two. It's the inconsistency of tone that's fatal to *Ghost*."

–Terry Kelleher, New York *Newsday*

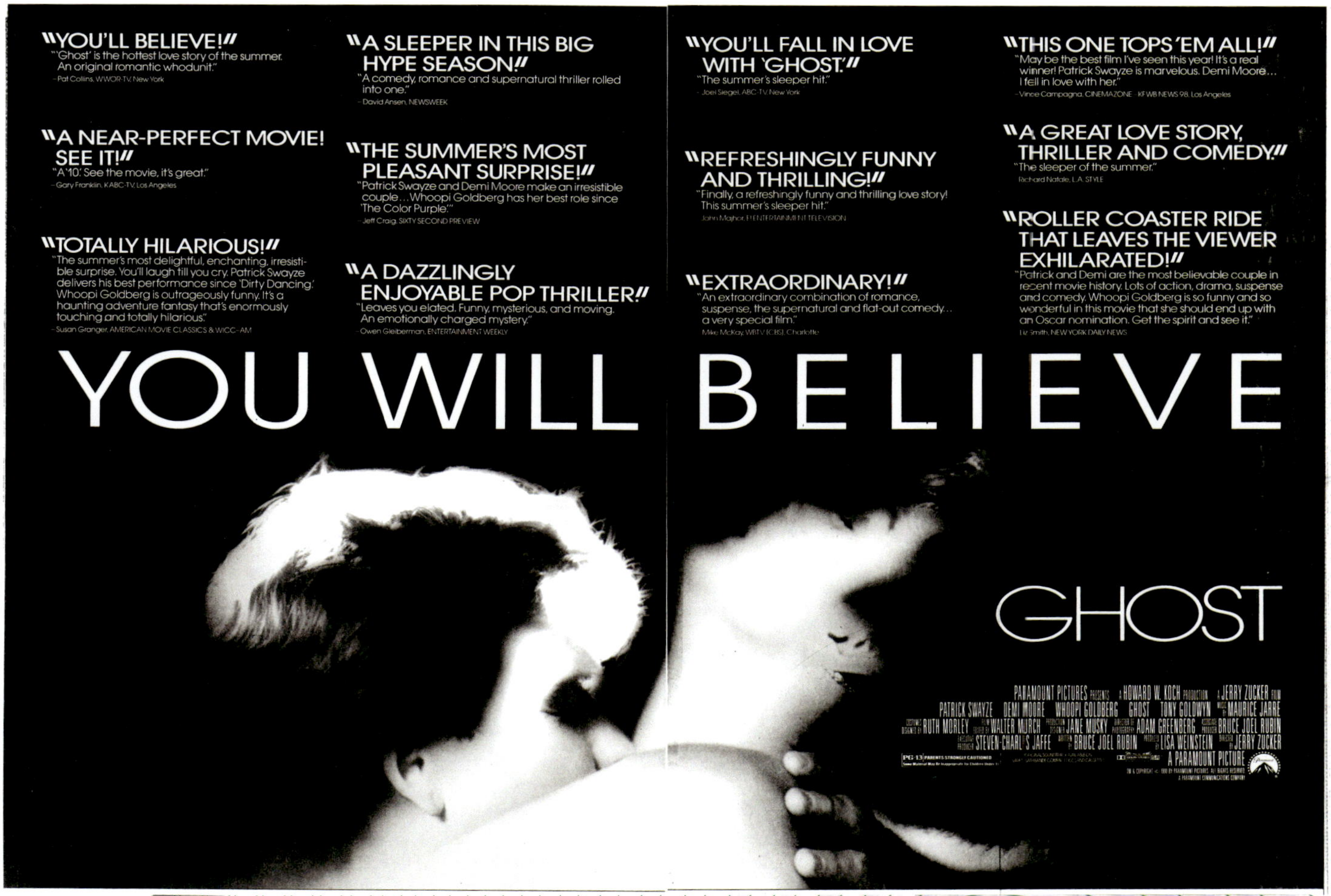
"YOU'LL BELIEVE!"
"'Ghost' is the hottest love story of the summer. An original romantic whodunit."
- Pat Collins, WWOR-TV, New York
"A NEAR-PERFECT MOVIE! SEE IT!"
"A '10.' See the movie, it's great."
- Gary Franklin, KABC-TV, Los Angeles
"TOTALLY HILARIOUS!"
"The summer's most delightful, enchanting, irresistible surprise. You'll laugh till you cry. Patrick Swayze delivers his best performance since 'Dirty Dancing.' Whoopi Goldberg is outrageously funny. It's a haunting adventure fantasy that's enormously touching and totally hilarious."
- Susan Granger, AMERICAN MOVIE CLASSICS & WICC-AM
"A SLEEPER IN THIS BIG HYPE SEASON."
"A comedy, romance and supernatural thriller rolled into one."
- David Ansen, NEWSWEEK
"THE SUMMER'S MOST PLEASANT SURPRISE!"
"Patrick Swayze and Demi Moore make an irresistible couple... Whoopi Goldberg has her best role since 'The Color Purple.'"
- Jeff Craig, SIXTY SECOND PREVIEW
"A DAZZLINGLY ENJOYABLE POP THRILLER."
"Leaves you elated. Funny, mysterious, and moving. An emotionally charged mystery."
- Owen Gleiberman, ENTERTAINMENT WEEKLY
"YOU'LL FALL IN LOVE WITH 'GHOST.'"
"The summer's sleeper hit."
- Joel Siegel, ABC-TV, New York
"REFRESHINGLY FUNNY AND THRILLING!"
"Finally, a refreshingly funny and thrilling love story! This summer's sleeper hit."
- John Mayhor, ENTERTAINMENT TELEVISION
"EXTRAORDINARY!"
"An extraordinary combination of romance, suspense, the supernatural and flat-out comedy... a very special film."
- Mike McKay, WBTV (CBS), Charlotte
"THIS ONE TOPS 'EM ALL!"
"May be the best film I've seen this year! It's a real winner! Patrick Swayze is marvelous. Demi Moore... I fell in love with her."
- Vince Campagna, CINEMAZONE - KFWB NEWS 98, Los Angeles
"A GREAT LOVE STORY, THRILLER AND COMEDY."
"The sleeper of the summer."
Richard Natale, L.A. STYLE
"ROLLER COASTER RIDE THAT LEAVES THE VIEWER EXHILARATED!"
"Patrick and Demi are the most believable couple in recent movie history. Lots of action, drama, suspense and comedy. Whoopi Goldberg is so funny and so wonderful in this movie that she should end up with an Oscar nomination. Get the spirit and see it."
- Liz Smith, NEW YORK DAILY NEWS
YOU WILL BELIEVE
GHOST
PARAMOUNT PICTURES PRESENTS A HOWARD W. KOCH PRODUCTION A JERRY ZUCKER FILM
PATRICK SWAYZE DEMI MOORE WHOOPI GOLDBERG GHOST TONY GOLDWYN MUSIC BY MAURICE JARRE
COSTUMES DESIGNED BY RUTH MORLEY FILM EDITED BY WALTER MURCH PRODUCTION DESIGNER JANE MUSKY DIRECTOR OF PHOTOGRAPHY ADAM GREENBERG ASSOCIATE PRODUCER BRUCE JOEL RUBIN
EXECUTIVE PRODUCER STEVEN-CHARLES JAFFE WRITTEN BY BRUCE JOEL RUBIN PRODUCED BY LISA WEINSTEIN DIRECTED BY JERRY ZUCKER
PG-13 PARENTS STRONGLY CAUTIONED
A PARAMOUNT PICTURE

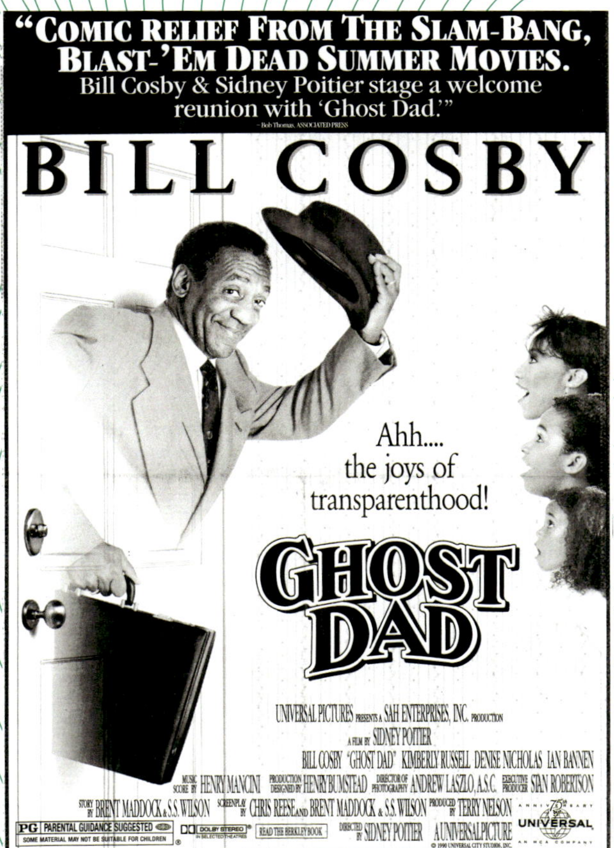
"COMIC RELIEF FROM THE SLAM-BANG, BLAST-'EM DEAD SUMMER MOVIES.
Bill Cosby & Sidney Poitier stage a welcome reunion with 'Ghost Dad.'"
- Bob Thomas, ASSOCIATED PRESS
BILL COSBY
Ahh.... the joys of transparenthood!
GHOST DAD
UNIVERSAL PICTURES PRESENTS A SAH ENTERPRISES, INC. PRODUCTION
A FILM BY SIDNEY POITIER
BILL COSBY "GHOST DAD" KIMBERLY RUSSELL DENISE NICHOLAS IAN BANNEN
MUSIC SCORE BY HENRY MANCINI PRODUCTION DESIGNED BY HENRY BUMSTEAD DIRECTOR OF PHOTOGRAPHY ANDREW LASZLO, A.S.C. EXECUTIVE PRODUCER STAN ROBERTSON
STORY BY BRENT MADDOCK & S.S. WILSON SCREENPLAY BY CHRIS REESE AND BRENT MADDOCK & S.S. WILSON PRODUCED BY TERRY NELSON
PG PARENTAL GUIDANCE SUGGESTED
SOME MATERIAL MAY NOT BE SUITABLE FOR CHILDREN
READ THE BERKLEY BOOK
DIRECTED BY SIDNEY POITIER
A UNIVERSAL PICTURE
UNIVERSAL
© 1990 UNIVERSAL CITY STUDIOS, INC.

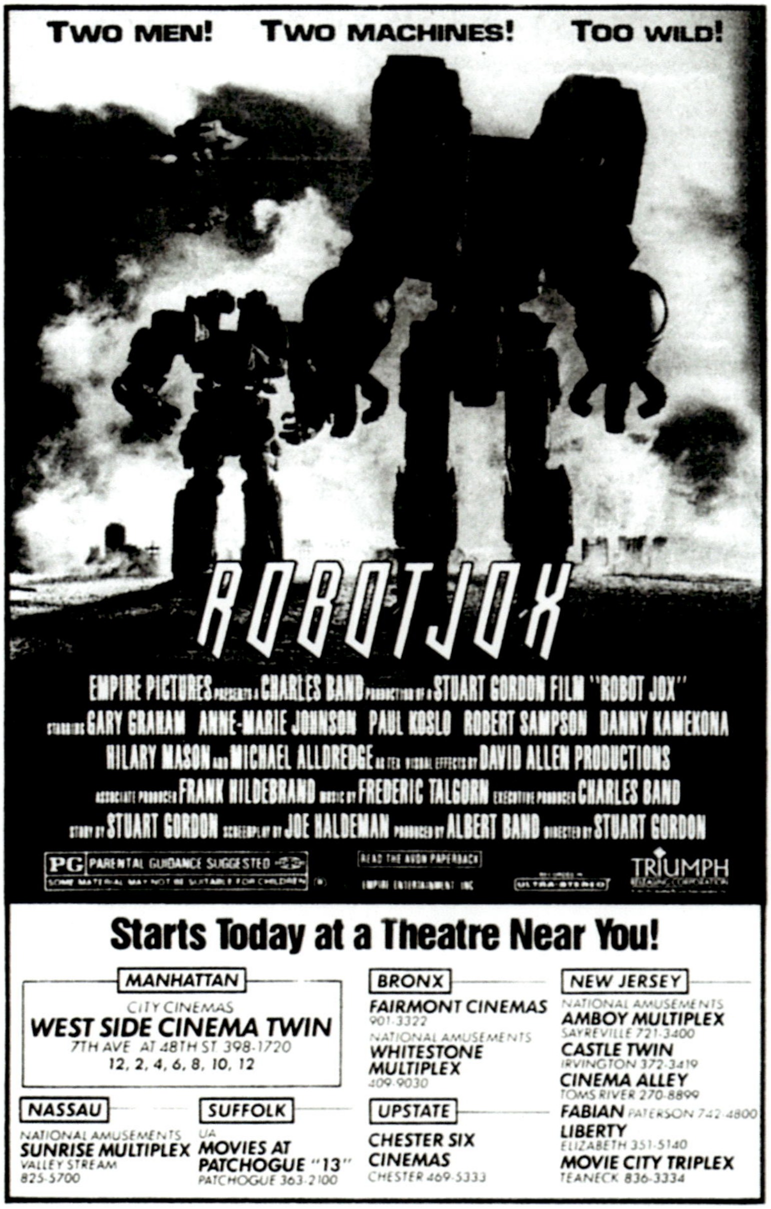

ROBOT JOX

Horror filmmaker Stuart Gordon was inspired to venture into the sci-fi realm by the wildly popular Transformers toy line, and hoped to make the first live-action feature about giant battling robots. Originally titled *Robojox*, it was to be Empire Pictures' biggest-budgeted production and potentially its widest release yet. But Empire's ongoing financial woes prevented the company from bringing the movie, which lensed in 1987, to theaters. It was eventually sold off to Triumph Films, which slightly altered the title and gave it only a limited break in late '90.

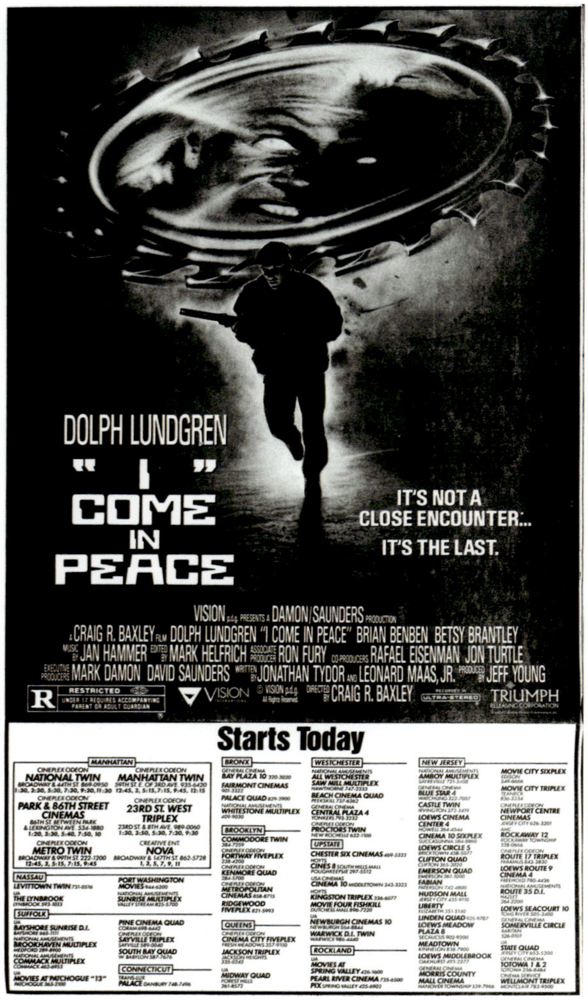

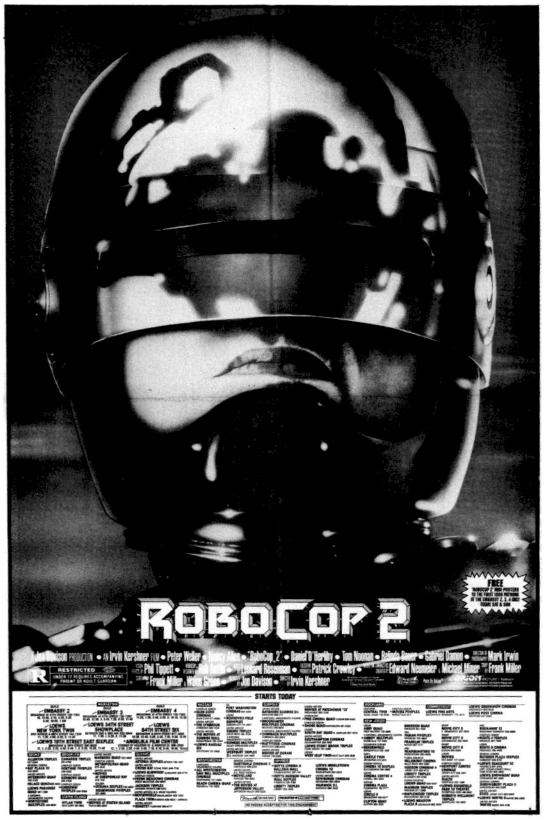
ROBOCOP 2
R RESTRICTED

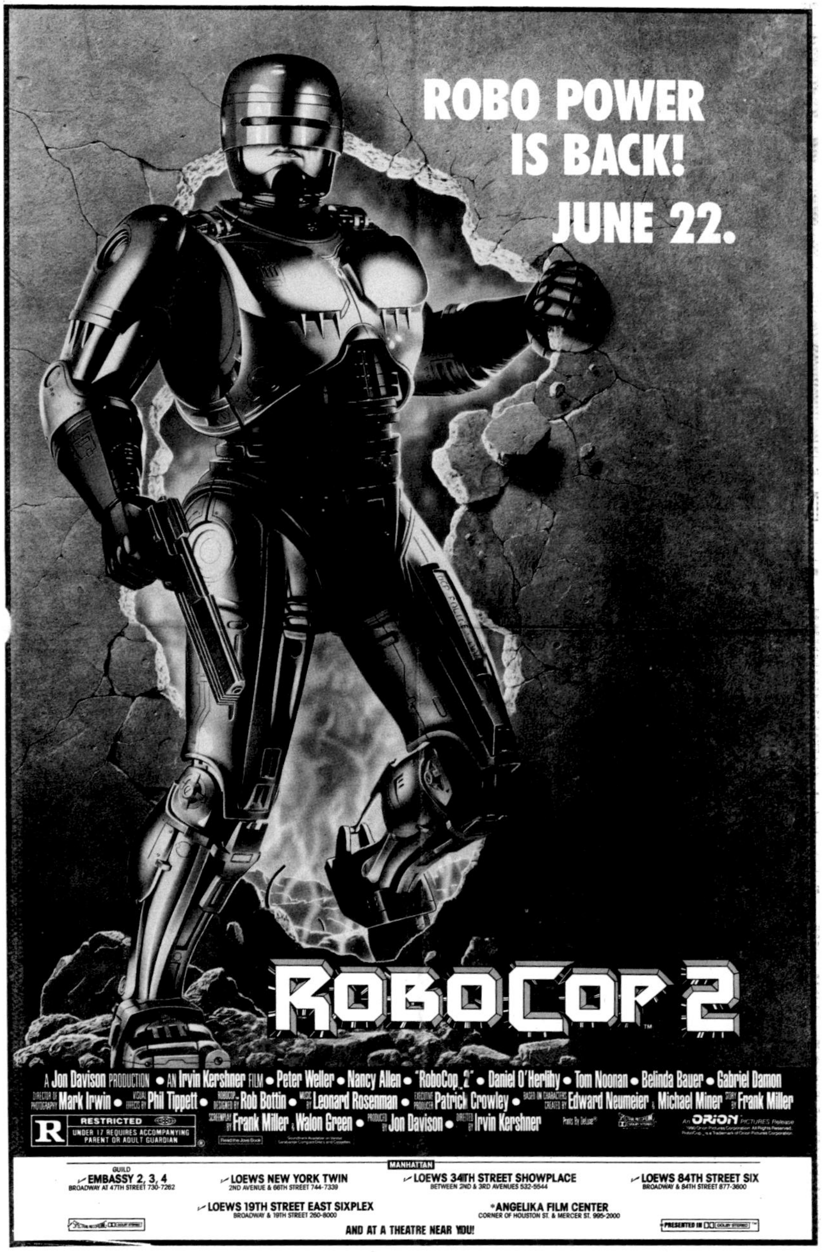
ROBO POWER IS BACK!
JUNE 22.
ROBOCOP 2
A Jon Davison PRODUCTION • AN Irvin Kershner FILM • Peter Weller • Nancy Allen • "RoboCop 2" • Daniel O'Herlihy • Tom Noonan • Belinda Bauer • Gabriel Damon
DIRECTOR OF PHOTOGRAPHY Mark Irwin • VISUAL EFFECTS BY Phil Tippett • ROBOCOP DESIGNED BY Rob Bottin • MUSIC BY Leonard Rosenman • EXECUTIVE PRODUCER Patrick Crowley • BASED ON CHARACTERS CREATED BY Edward Neumeier & Michael Miner STORY BY Frank Miller
SCREENPLAY BY Frank Miller & Walon Green • PRODUCED BY Jon Davison • DIRECTED BY Irvin Kershner
R RESTRICTED UNDER 17 REQUIRES ACCOMPANYING PARENT OR ADULT GUARDIAN
An ORION PICTURES Release
MANHATTAN
GUILD EMBASSY 2, 3, 4
BROADWAY AT 47TH STREET 730-7262
LOEWS NEW YORK TWIN
2ND AVENUE & 66TH STREET 744-7339
LOEWS 34TH STREET SHOWPLACE
BETWEEN 2ND & 3RD AVENUES 532-5544
LOEWS 84TH STREET SIX
BROADWAY & 84TH STREET 877-3600
LOEWS 19TH STREET EAST SIXPLEX
BROADWAY & 19TH STREET 260-8000
*ANGELIKA FILM CENTER
CORNER OF HOUSTON ST. & MERCER ST. 995-2000
AND AT A THEATRE NEAR YOU!

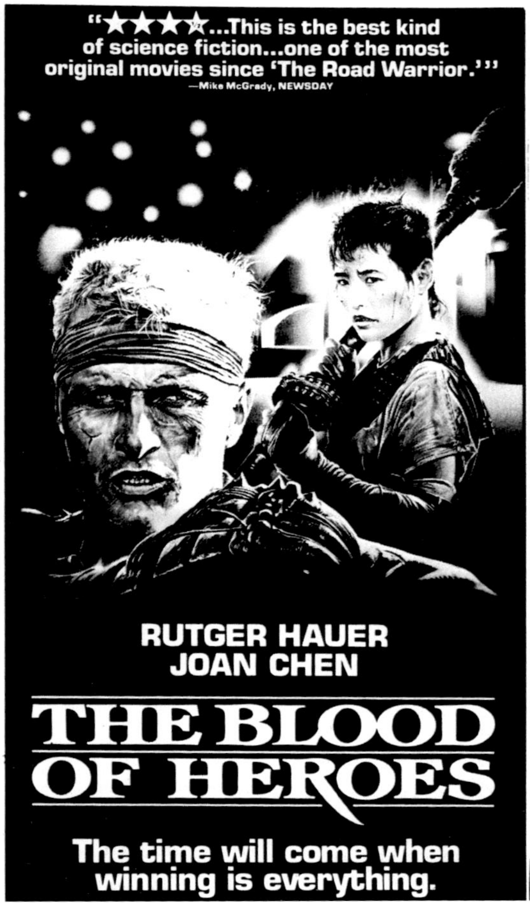
"★★★½...This is the best kind of science fiction...one of the most original movies since 'The Road Warrior.'"
—Mike McGrady, NEWSDAY
RUTGER HAUER
JOAN CHEN
THE BLOOD OF HEROES
The time will come when winning is everything.

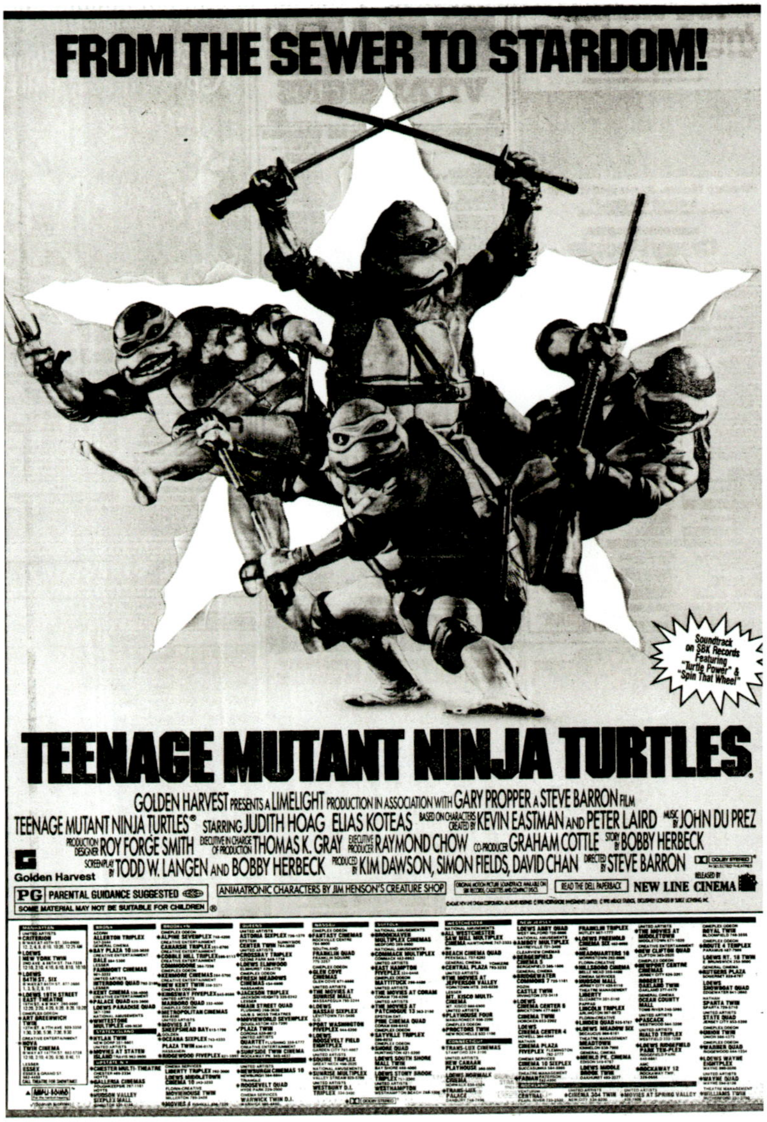

TEENAGE MUTANT NINJA TURTLES

With a multitude of fans from the previous comic-book and TV-cartoon incarnations, the Heroes in a Half Shell didn't need reviews to make their big-screen debut a major hit. Good thing, too, as most of the notices were negative, many decrying the high level of martial-arts brawling for a film aimed at kids. *Teenage Mutant Ninja Turtles* topped the box-office charts for four weeks; in the fifth, *Pretty Woman*, which had opened at #1 the week before Turtles opened, reclaimed that spot, and distributor Touchstone Pictures had some fun with the victory in a subsequent ad.

"I did not walk into the screening with a light step and a heart that sang. For that matter, I did not walk out afterward with my spirits renewed. But this movie is nowhere near as bad as it might have been, and probably is the best possible Teenage Mutant Ninja Turtle movie."

–Roger Ebert, *Chicago Sun-Times*

"On [its] level, the movie works just fine. After all, they don't call it 'Teenage Mutant Brain Surgeons."

–DAVID INMAN, LOUISVILLE, KY *COURIER-JOURNAL*

"If you wouldn't expose small fry to a chopfest starring Chuck Norris or Steven Seagal, why would you want them thrilling to the head-cracking prowess of 'heroes on the half shell'? [*The preferred tagline, of course, is* '*heroes* in a *half shell*.']"

–Terry Kelleher, New York *Newsday*

"What troubles me about *Teenage Mutant Ninja Turtles* is that it's basically an exploitation movie aimed at young children. Like any martial-arts flick, this one features a great deal of mindless violence."

–Jay Boyar, *Orlando Sentinel*

"The millions who made *Howard the Duck* one of the movie disasters of the '80s will really hate [these] mock turtles and the tacky movie that marks their big screen debut. By comparison, Howard was a living, breathing, charismatic superstar."

–Malcolm L. Johnson, *Hartford Courant*

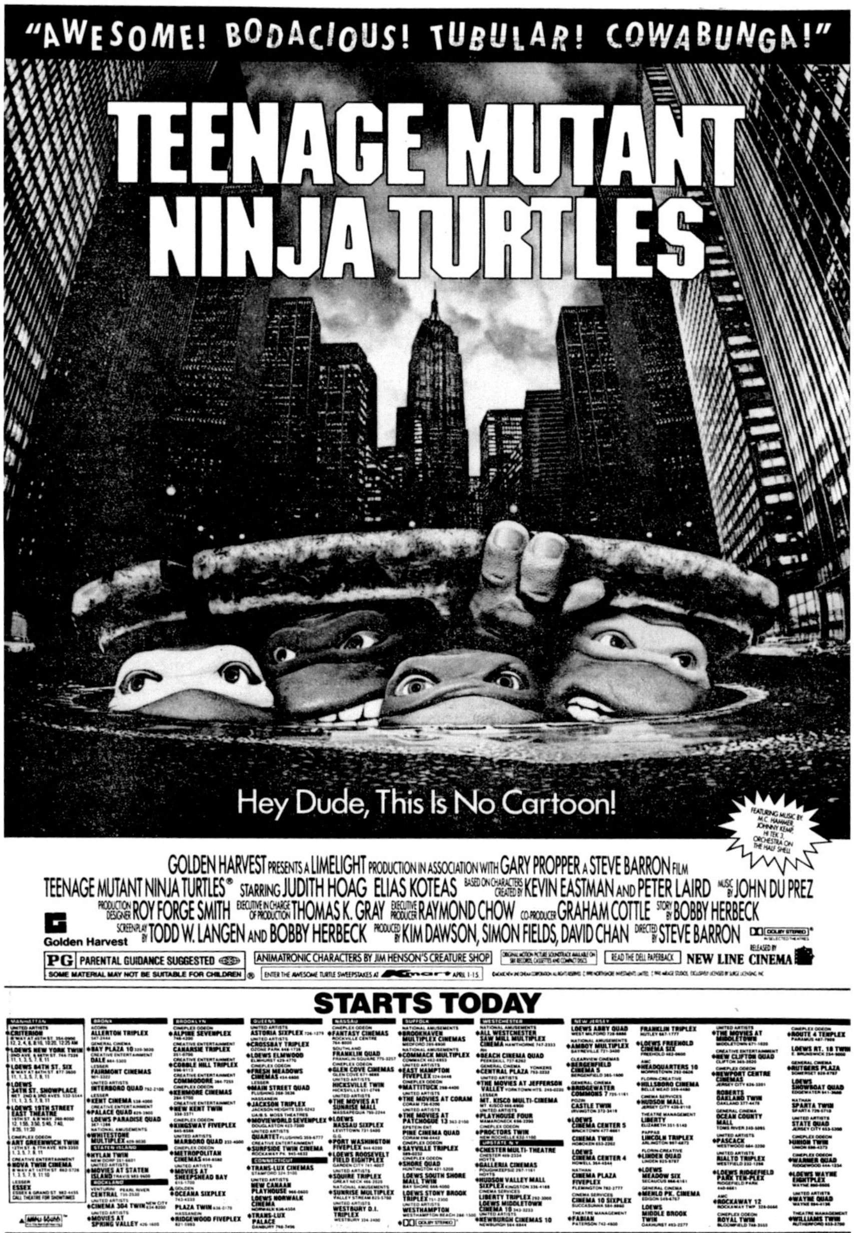
"AWESOME! BODACIOUS! TUBULAR! COWABUNGA!"
TEENAGE MUTANT NINJA TURTLES
Hey Dude, This Is No Cartoon!
FEATURING MUSIC BY M.C. HAMMER, JOHNNY KEMP, HI TEK 3, ORCHESTRA ON THE HALF SHELL
GOLDEN HARVEST PRESENTS A LIMELIGHT PRODUCTION IN ASSOCIATION WITH GARY PROPPER A STEVE BARRON FILM
TEENAGE MUTANT NINJA TURTLES® STARRING JUDITH HOAG ELIAS KOTEAS BASED ON CHARACTERS CREATED BY KEVIN EASTMAN AND PETER LAIRD MUSIC BY JOHN DU PREZ
PRODUCTION DESIGNER ROY FORGE SMITH EXECUTIVE IN CHARGE OF PRODUCTION THOMAS K. GRAY EXECUTIVE PRODUCER RAYMOND CHOW CO-PRODUCER GRAHAM COTTLE STORY BY BOBBY HERBECK
SCREENPLAY BY TODD W. LANGEN AND BOBBY HERBECK PRODUCED BY KIM DAWSON, SIMON FIELDS, DAVID CHAN DIRECTED BY STEVE BARRON
Golden Harvest
PG PARENTAL GUIDANCE SUGGESTED
SOME MATERIAL MAY NOT BE SUITABLE FOR CHILDREN
ANIMATRONIC CHARACTERS BY JIM HENSON'S CREATURE SHOP
READ THE DELL PAPERBACK
RELEASED BY NEW LINE CINEMA
ENTER THE AWESOME TURTLE SWEEPSTAKES AT Kmart APRIL 1-15
STARTS TODAY

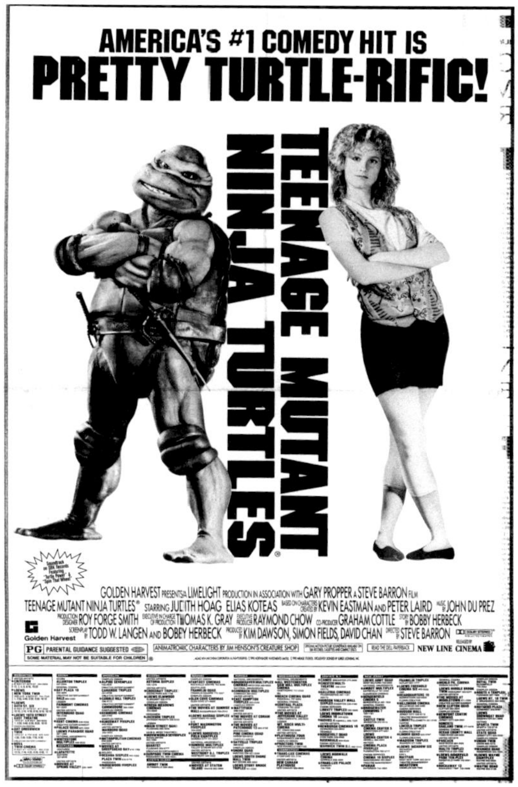
AMERICA'S #1 COMEDY HIT IS
PRETTY TURTLE-RIFIC!
TEENAGE MUTANT NINJA TURTLES
GOLDEN HARVEST PRESENTS A LIMELIGHT PRODUCTION IN ASSOCIATION WITH GARY PROPPER A STEVE BARRON FILM
TEENAGE MUTANT NINJA TURTLES® STARRING JUDITH HOAG ELIAS KOTEAS BASED ON CHARACTERS CREATED BY KEVIN EASTMAN AND PETER LAIRD MUSIC BY JOHN DU PREZ
PRODUCTION DESIGNER ROY FORGE SMITH EXECUTIVE IN CHARGE OF PRODUCTION THOMAS K. GRAY EXECUTIVE PRODUCER RAYMOND CHOW CO-PRODUCER GRAHAM COTTLE STORY BY BOBBY HERBECK
SCREENPLAY BY TODD W. LANGEN AND BOBEY HERBECK PRODUCED BY KIM DAWSON, SIMON FIELDS, DAVID CHAN DIRECTED BY STEVE BARRON
Golden Harvest
PG PARENTAL GUIDANCE SUGGESTED
SOME MATERIAL MAY NOT BE SUITABLE FOR CHILDREN
ANIMATRONIC CHARACTERS BY JIM HENSON'S CREATURE SHOP
READ THE DELL PAPERBACK
RELEASED BY NEW LINE CINEMA

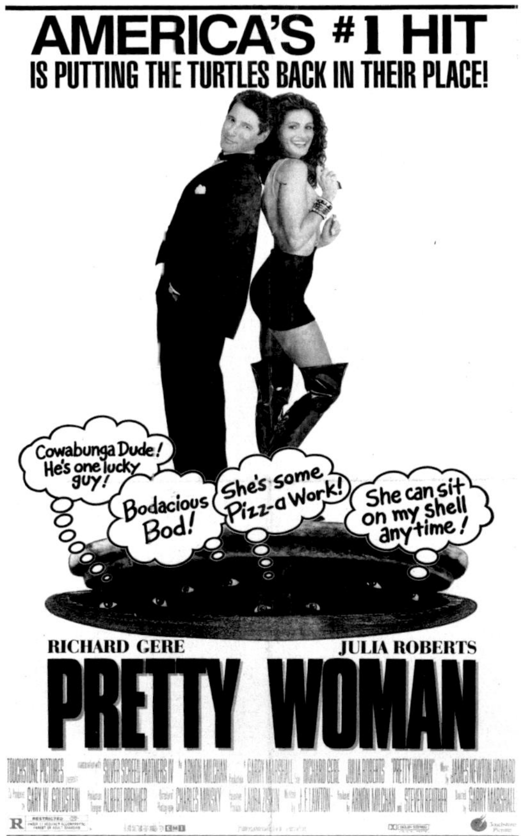
AMERICA'S #1 HIT
IS PUTTING THE TURTLES BACK IN THEIR PLACE!
Cowabunga Dude! He's one lucky guy!
Bodacious Bod!
She's some Pizz-a Work!
She can sit on my shell any time!
RICHARD GERE
JULIA ROBERTS
PRETTY WOMAN

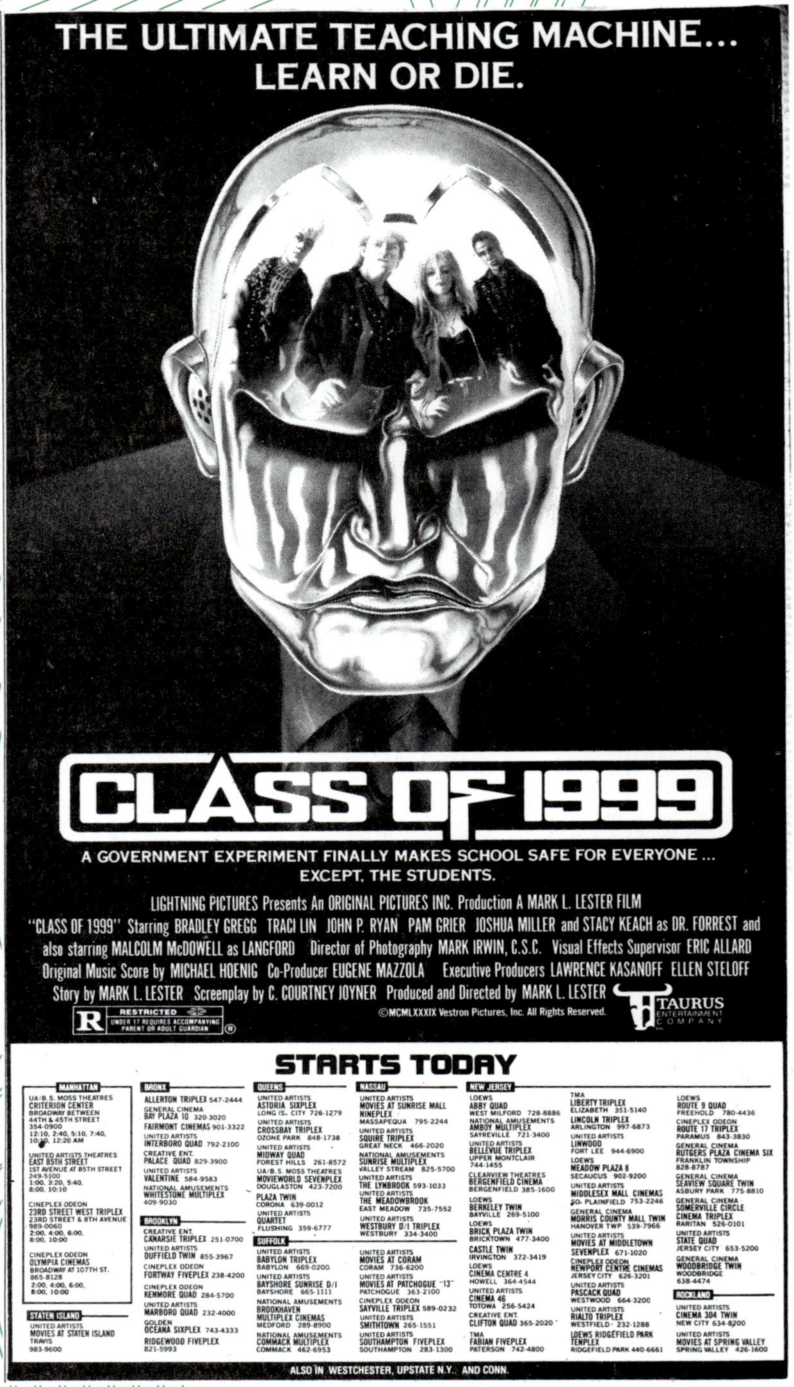

TOTAL RECALL

Arnold Schwarzenegger had several action and sci-fi hits over the course of the 1980s, but he didn't land a $100-million smash until he turned to comedy with '88's *Twins*. Then he grossed even better with *Total Recall*, his most thematically ambitious genre outing yet. As with director Paul Verhoeven's previous *RoboCop*, many reviews lauded *Recall* as a smarter-than-the-average actioner while some of them also called the movie out for its ultraviolence.

"This is one of the most complex and visually interesting science fiction movies in a long time. But the plot, based on a story by the great science fiction writer Phillip [sic] K. Dick, centers on an intriguing idea."

–Roger Ebert, *Chicago Sun-Times*

"If the movie, with its concentration on deformed mutants, popping eyes and kicked groins, were more mean-spirited, it would be unwatchable. But with Verhoeven's pounding fast pace and controlling sense of irony, *Total Recall* emerges as a real winner."

–George Anderson, *Pittsburgh Post-Gazette*

"To bring off action at this level—and there are some stunning set pieces in *Total Recall*—is a rare and underrated gift. To goad the audience into thinking at the same time is an even rarer talent."

–Desmond Ryan, *Philadelphia Inquirer*

"Let me be clear on this – *Total Recall* is not only the best bad movie of 1990, it's one of history's all-time best bad movies."

–MIKE MCGRADY, NEW YORK *NEWSDAY*

"In any emotional or imaginative sense, this stuff is as sloppy as the second 'l' the credits add to Philip K. Dick's first name."

–Michael Sragow, *San Francisco Examiner*

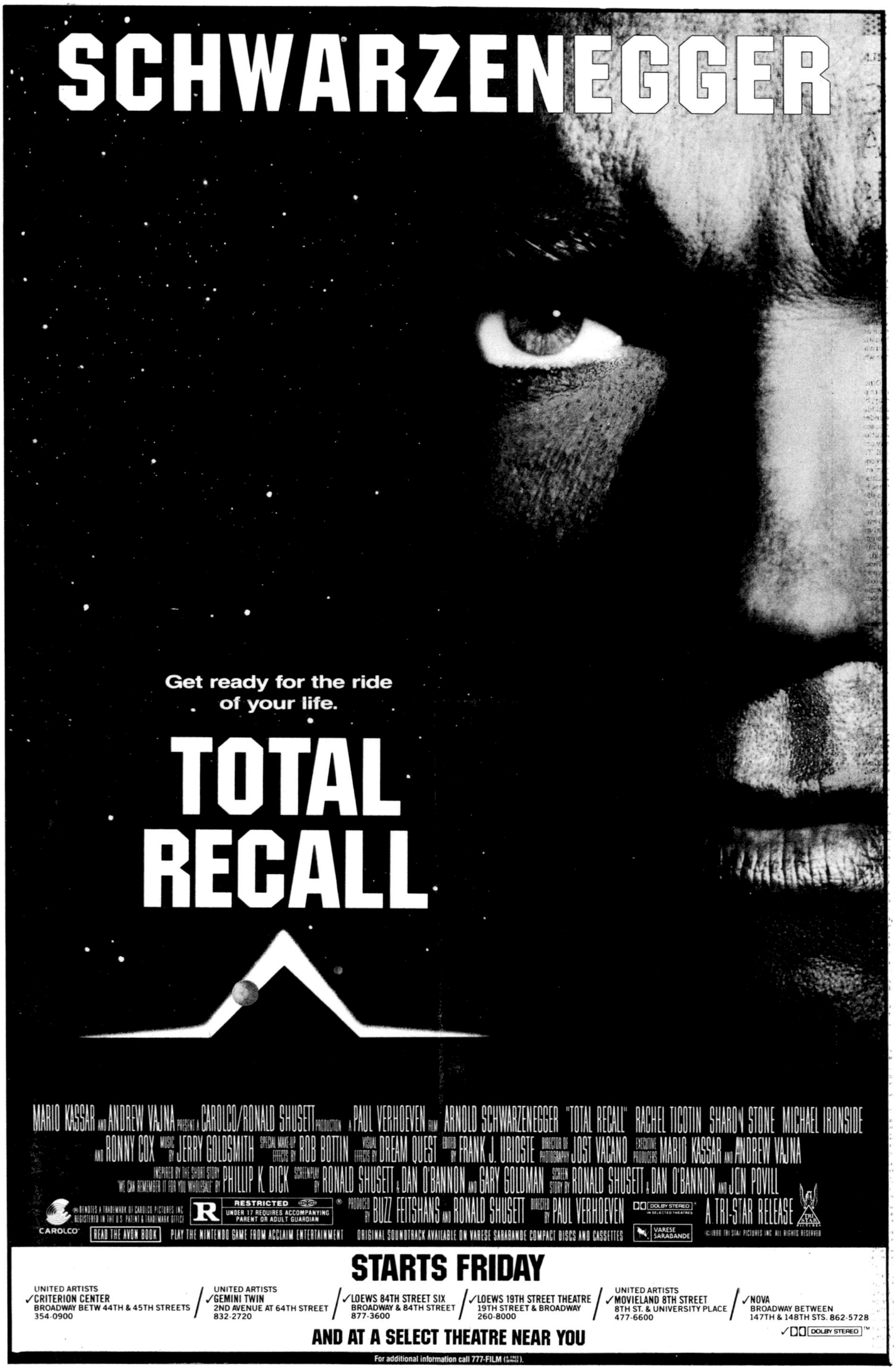

SCHWARZENEGGER
Get ready for the ride of your life.
TOTAL RECALL
MARIO KASSAR AND ANDREW VAJNA PRESENT A CAROLCO/RONALD SHUSETT PRODUCTION A PAUL VERHOEVEN FILM ARNOLD SCHWARZENEGGER "TOTAL RECALL" RACHEL TICOTIN SHARON STONE MICHAEL IRONSIDE
AND RONNY COX MUSIC BY JERRY GOLDSMITH SPECIAL MAKE-UP EFFECTS BY ROB BOTTIN VISUAL EFFECTS BY DREAM QUEST EDITED BY FRANK J. URIOSTE DIRECTOR OF PHOTOGRAPHY JOST VACANO EXECUTIVE PRODUCERS MARIO KASSAR AND ANDREW VAJNA
INSPIRED BY THE SHORT STORY "WE CAN REMEMBER IT FOR YOU WHOLESALE" BY PHILLIP K. DICK SCREENPLAY BY RONALD SHUSETT & DAN O'BANNON AND GARY GOLDMAN SCREEN STORY BY RONALD SHUSETT & DAN O'BANNON AND JON POVILL
® DENOTES A TRADEMARK OF CAROLCO PICTURES INC REGISTERED IN THE U.S. PATENT & TRADEMARK OFFICE
CAROLCO
R RESTRICTED UNDER 17 REQUIRES ACCOMPANYING PARENT OR ADULT GUARDIAN
PRODUCED BY BUZZ FEITSHANS AND RONALD SHUSETT DIRECTED BY PAUL VERHOEVEN
DOLBY STEREO IN SELECTED THEATRES
A TRI-STAR RELEASE
TRI STAR PICTURES
READ THE AVON BOOK
PLAY THE NINTENDO GAME FROM ACCLAIM ENTERTAINMENT
ORIGINAL SOUNDTRACK AVAILABLE ON VARESE SARABANDE COMPACT DISCS AND CASSETTES
VARESE SARABANDE
©1990 TRI STAR PICTURES INC ALL RIGHTS RESERVED
STARTS FRIDAY
UNITED ARTISTS ✓CRITERION CENTER BROADWAY BETW 44TH & 45TH STREETS 354-0900
UNITED ARTISTS ✓GEMINI TWIN 2ND AVENUE AT 64TH STREET 832-2720
✓LOEWS 84TH STREET SIX BROADWAY & 84TH STREET 877-3600
✓LOEWS 19TH STREET THEATRE 19TH STREET & BROADWAY 260-8000
UNITED ARTISTS ✓MOVIELAND 8TH STREET 8TH ST. & UNIVERSITY PLACE 477-6600
✓NOVA BROADWAY BETWEEN 147TH & 148TH STS. 862-5728
✓ DOLBY STEREO™
AND AT A SELECT THEATRE NEAR YOU
For additional information call 777-FILM

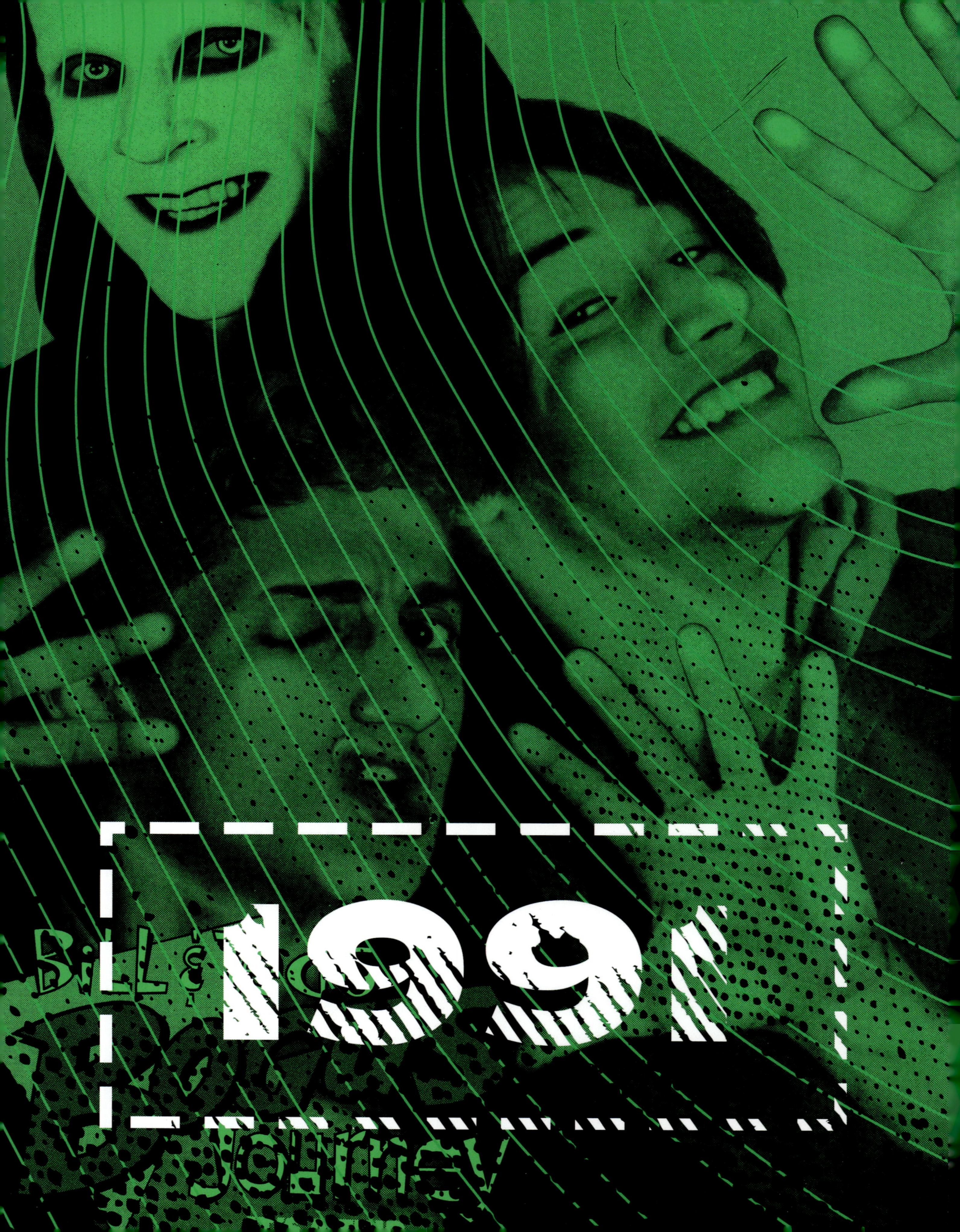
199

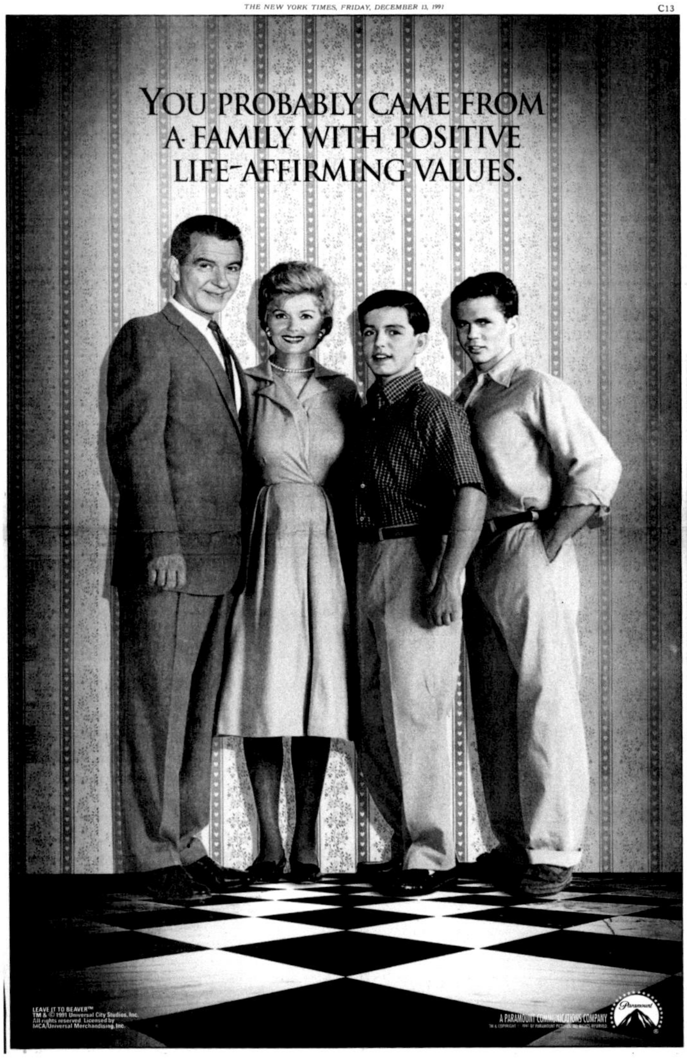
THE NEW YORK TIMES, FRIDAY, DECEMBER 13, 1991
C13
YOU PROBABLY CAME FROM
A FAMILY WITH POSITIVE
LIFE-AFFIRMING VALUES.
A PARAMOUNT COMMUNICATIONS COMPANY

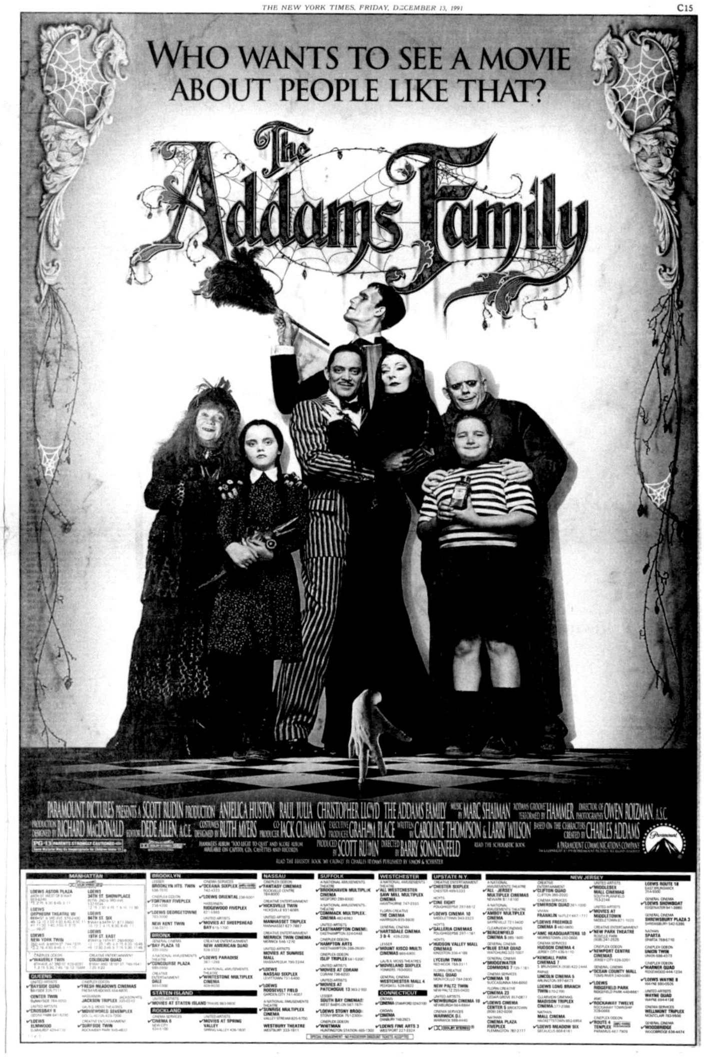
THE NEW YORK TIMES, FRIDAY, DECEMBER 13, 1991
C15
WHO WANTS TO SEE A MOVIE
ABOUT PEOPLE LIKE THAT?
The Addams Family
PARAMOUNT PICTURES PRESENTS A SCOTT RUDIN PRODUCTION ANJELICA HUSTON RAUL JULIA CHRISTOPHER LLOYD THE ADDAMS FAMILY
MARC SHAIMAN
OWEN ROIZMAN
RICHARD MacDONALD
DEDE ALLEN
RUTH MYERS
JACK CUMMINS
GRAHAM PLACE
CAROLINE THOMPSON & LARRY WILSON
CHARLES ADDAMS
SCOTT RUDIN
BARRY SONNENFELD
PG-13

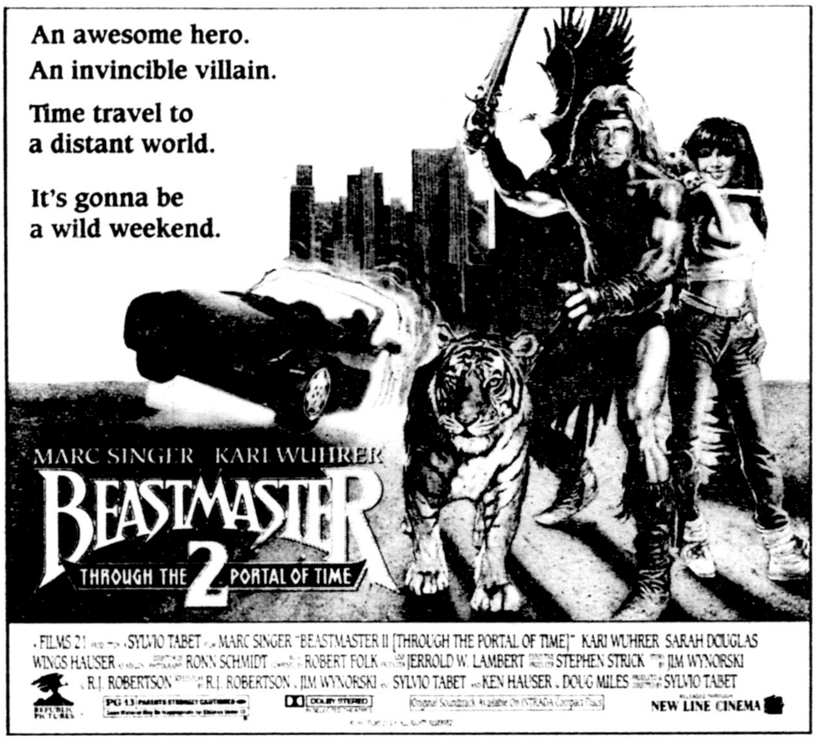
An awesome hero.
An invincible villain.
Time travel to
a distant world.
It's gonna be
a wild weekend.
MARC SINGER KARI WUHRER
BEASTMASTER
THROUGH THE 2 PORTAL OF TIME
FILMS 21
SYLVIO TABET
MARC SINGER "BEASTMASTER II [THROUGH THE PORTAL OF TIME]" KARI WUHRER SARAH DOUGLAS
WINGS HAUSER
RONN SCHMIDT
ROBERT FOLK
JERROLD W. LAMBERT
STEPHEN STRICK
JIM WYNORSKI
R.J. ROBERTSON
R.J. ROBERTSON
JIM WYNORSKI
SYLVIO TABET
KEN HAUSER
DOUG MILES
SYLVIO TABET
PG-13
NEW LINE CINEMA

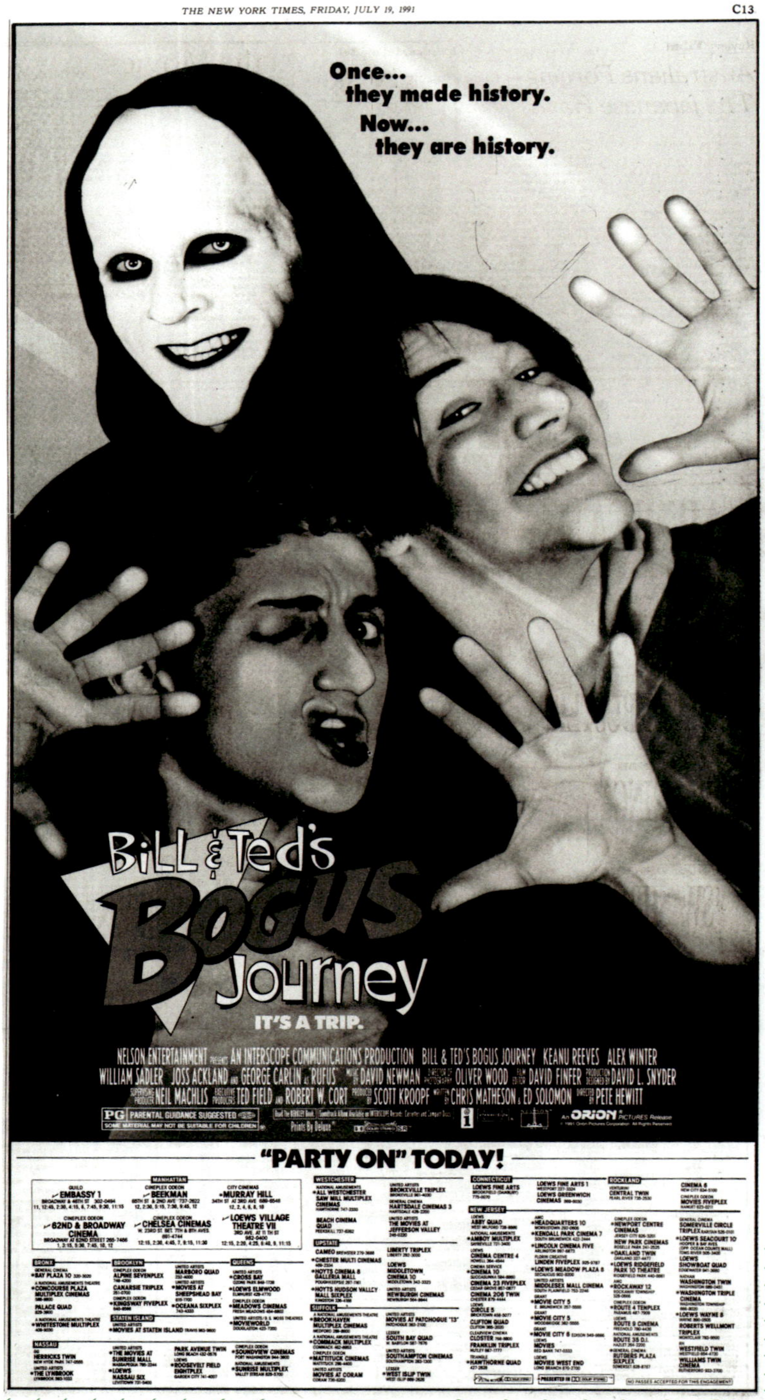

BILL & TED'S BOGUS JOURNEY

It may be hard to believe today, but there was once a time when studios were cautious about putting the word "hell" in movie titles – and by extension the advertising materials – for fear of offending people in certain parts of America. Thus, the sequel originally called *Bill and Ted Go to Hell* (which they do as part of an adventure that's even more sci-fi/fantasy-tinged than their first one) was rechristened to something milder. But really, though, those who might be turned off by the reference to the hot place probably wouldn't bother with this movie in the first place.

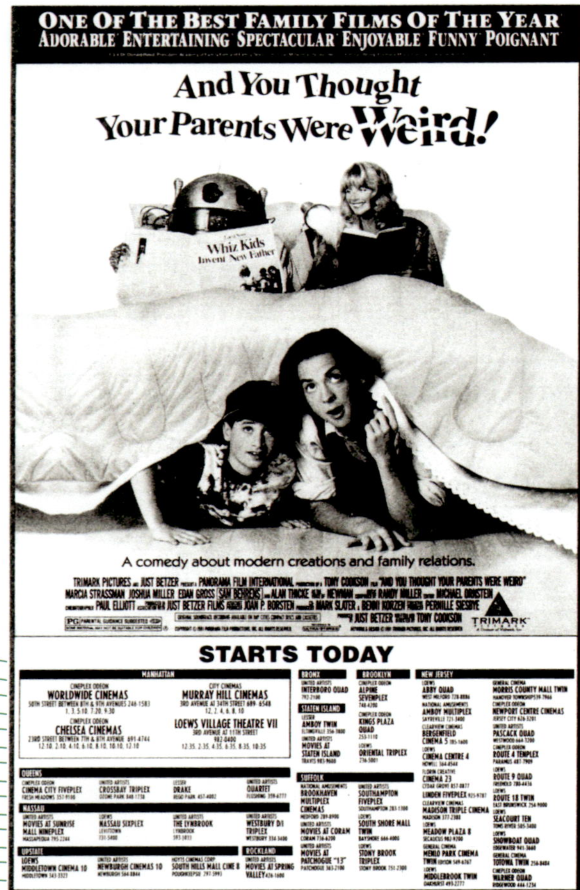

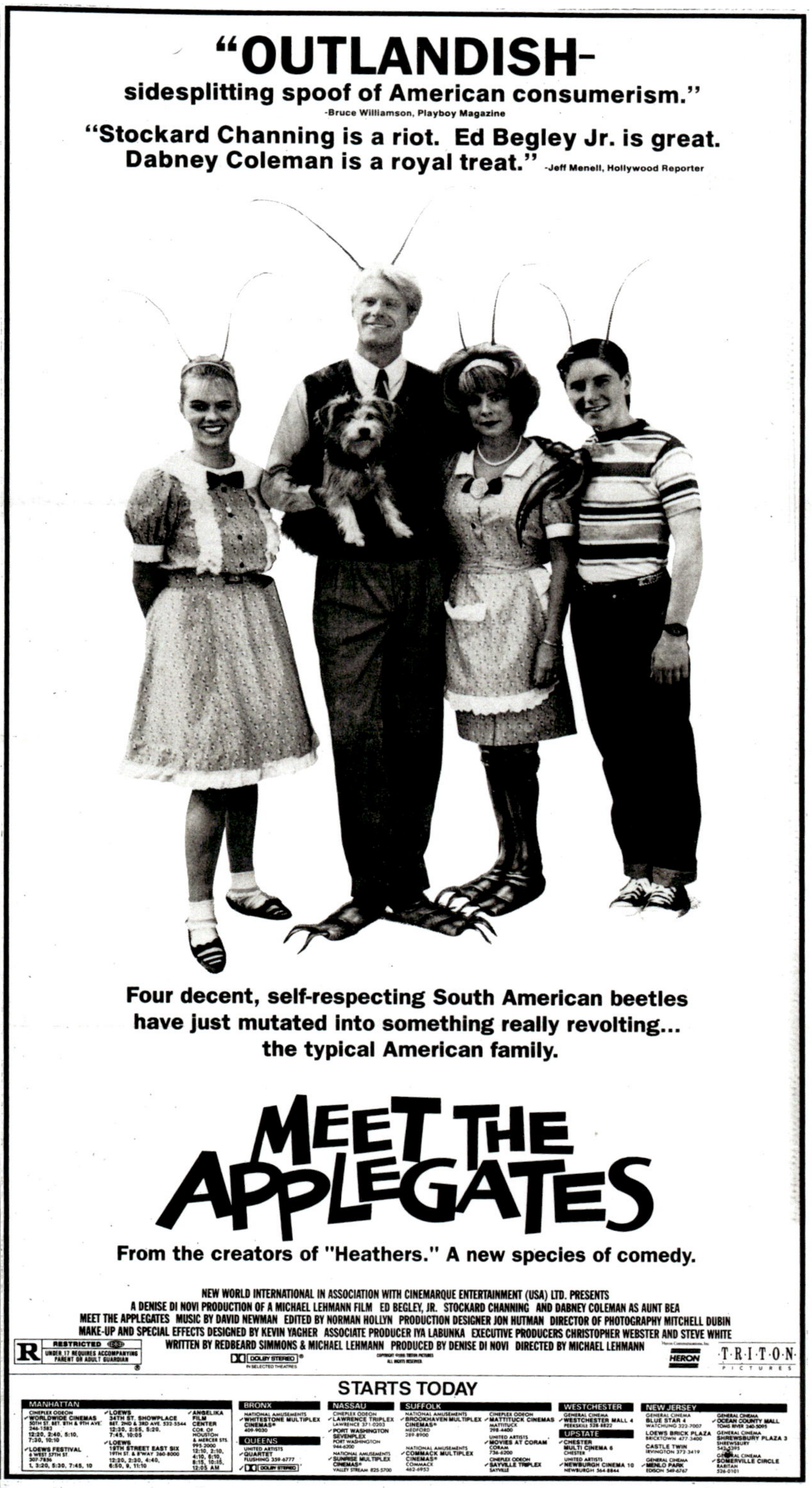
"OUTLANDISH–
sidesplitting spoof of American consumerism."
-Bruce Williamson, Playboy Magazine
"Stockard Channing is a riot. Ed Begley Jr. is great.
Dabney Coleman is a royal treat." -Jeff Menell, Hollywood Reporter
Four decent, self-respecting South American beetles
have just mutated into something really revolting...
the typical American family.
MEET THE APPLEGATES
From the creators of "Heathers." A new species of comedy.
NEW WORLD INTERNATIONAL IN ASSOCIATION WITH CINEMARQUE ENTERTAINMENT (USA) LTD. PRESENTS
A DENISE DI NOVI PRODUCTION OF A MICHAEL LEHMANN FILM ED BEGLEY, JR. STOCKARD CHANNING AND DABNEY COLEMAN AS AUNT BEA
MEET THE APPLEGATES MUSIC BY DAVID NEWMAN EDITED BY NORMAN HOLLYN PRODUCTION DESIGNER JON HUTMAN DIRECTOR OF PHOTOGRAPHY MITCHELL DUBIN
MAKE-UP AND SPECIAL EFFECTS DESIGNED BY KEVIN YAGHER ASSOCIATE PRODUCER IYA LABUNKA EXECUTIVE PRODUCERS CHRISTOPHER WEBSTER AND STEVE WHITE
WRITTEN BY REDBEARD SIMMONS & MICHAEL LEHMANN PRODUCED BY DENISE DI NOVI DIRECTED BY MICHAEL LEHMANN
R RESTRICTED
TRITON PICTURES
STARTS TODAY
MANHATTAN
BRONX
NASSAU
SUFFOLK
WESTCHESTER
NEW JERSEY
QUEENS
UPSTATE

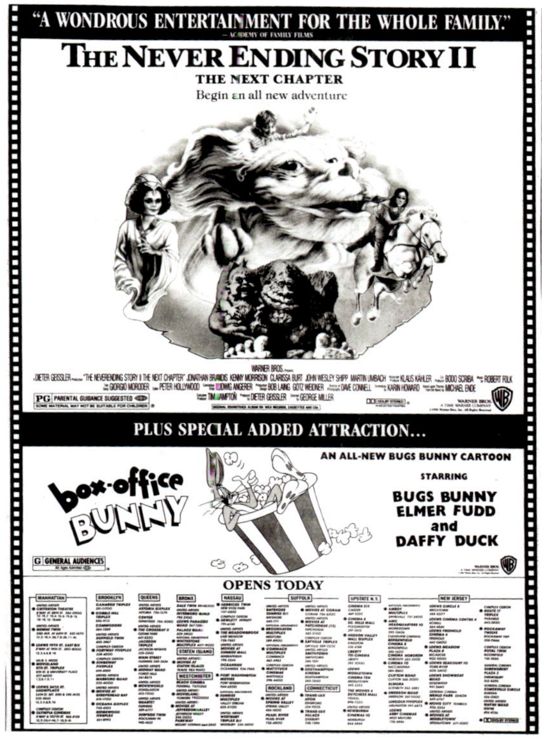
"A WONDROUS ENTERTAINMENT FOR THE WHOLE FAMILY."
THE NEVER ENDING STORY II
THE NEXT CHAPTER
Begin an all new adventure
PG PARENTAL GUIDANCE SUGGESTED
PLUS SPECIAL ADDED ATTRACTION...
AN ALL-NEW BUGS BUNNY CARTOON
box-office BUNNY
STARRING
BUGS BUNNY
ELMER FUDD
and
DAFFY DUCK
G GENERAL AUDIENCES
OPENS TODAY

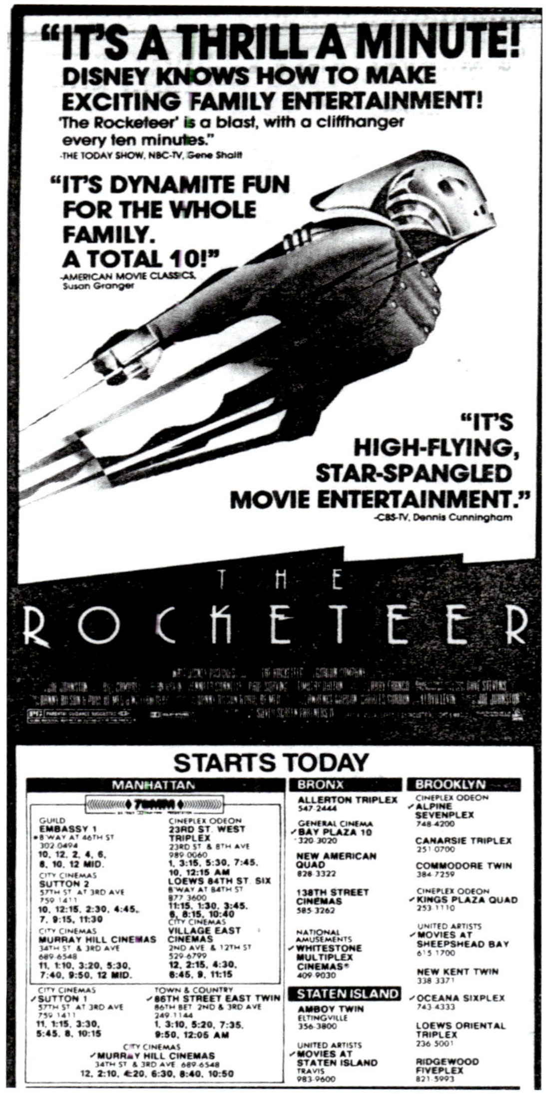
"IT'S A THRILL A MINUTE!
DISNEY KNOWS HOW TO MAKE
EXCITING FAMILY ENTERTAINMENT!
'The Rocketeer' is a blast, with a cliffhanger
every ten minutes."
-THE TODAY SHOW, NBC-TV, Gene Shalit
"IT'S DYNAMITE FUN
FOR THE WHOLE
FAMILY.
A TOTAL 10!"
-AMERICAN MOVIE CLASSICS, Susan Granger
"IT'S
HIGH-FLYING,
STAR-SPANGLED
MOVIE ENTERTAINMENT."
-CBS-TV, Dennis Cunningham
THE
ROCKETEER
STARTS TODAY
MANHATTAN
GUILD
EMBASSY 1
B'WAY AT 46TH ST
302 0494
10, 12, 2, 4, 6,
8, 10, 12 MID.
CITY CINEMAS
SUTTON 2
57TH ST AT 3RD AVE
759 1411
10, 12:15, 2:30, 4:45,
7, 9:15, 11:30
CITY CINEMAS
MURRAY HILL CINEMAS
34TH ST & 3RD AVE
689 6548
11, 1:10, 3:20, 5:30,
7:40, 9:50, 12 MID.
CINEPLEX ODEON
23RD ST. WEST
TRIPLEX
23RD ST & 8TH AVE
989 0060
1, 3:15, 5:30, 7:45,
10, 12:15 AM
LOEWS 84TH ST. SIX
B'WAY AT 84TH ST
877 3600
11:15, 1:30, 3:45,
6, 8:15, 10:40
CITY CINEMAS
VILLAGE EAST
CINEMAS
2ND AVE & 12TH ST
529 6799
12, 2:15, 4:30,
6:45, 9, 11:15
CITY CINEMAS
SUTTON 1
57TH ST AT 3RD AVE
759 1411
11, 1:15, 3:30,
5:45, 8, 10:15
TOWN & COUNTRY
86TH STREET EAST TWIN
86TH BET 2ND & 3RD AVE
249 1144
1, 3:10, 5:20, 7:35,
9:50, 12:05 AM
CITY CINEMAS
MURRAY HILL CINEMAS
34TH ST & 3RD AVE 689 6548
12, 2:10, 4:20, 6:30, 8:40, 10:50
BRONX
ALLERTON TRIPLEX
547 2444
GENERAL CINEMA
BAY PLAZA 10
320 3020
NEW AMERICAN
QUAD
828 3322
138TH STREET
CINEMAS
585 3262
NATIONAL AMUSEMENTS
WHITESTONE
MULTIPLEX
CINEMAS
409 9030
STATEN ISLAND
AMBOY TWIN
ELTINGVILLE
356 3800
UNITED ARTISTS
MOVIES AT
STATEN ISLAND
TRAVIS
983 9600
BROOKLYN
CINEPLEX ODEON
ALPINE
SEVENPLEX
748 4200
CANARSIE TRIPLEX
251 0700
COMMODORE TWIN
384 7259
CINEPLEX ODEON
KINGS PLAZA QUAD
253 1110
UNITED ARTISTS
MOVIES AT
SHEEPSHEAD BAY
615 1700
NEW KENT TWIN
338 3371
OCEANA SIXPLEX
743 4333
LOEWS ORIENTAL
TRIPLEX
236 5001
RIDGEWOOD
FIVEPLEX
821 5993

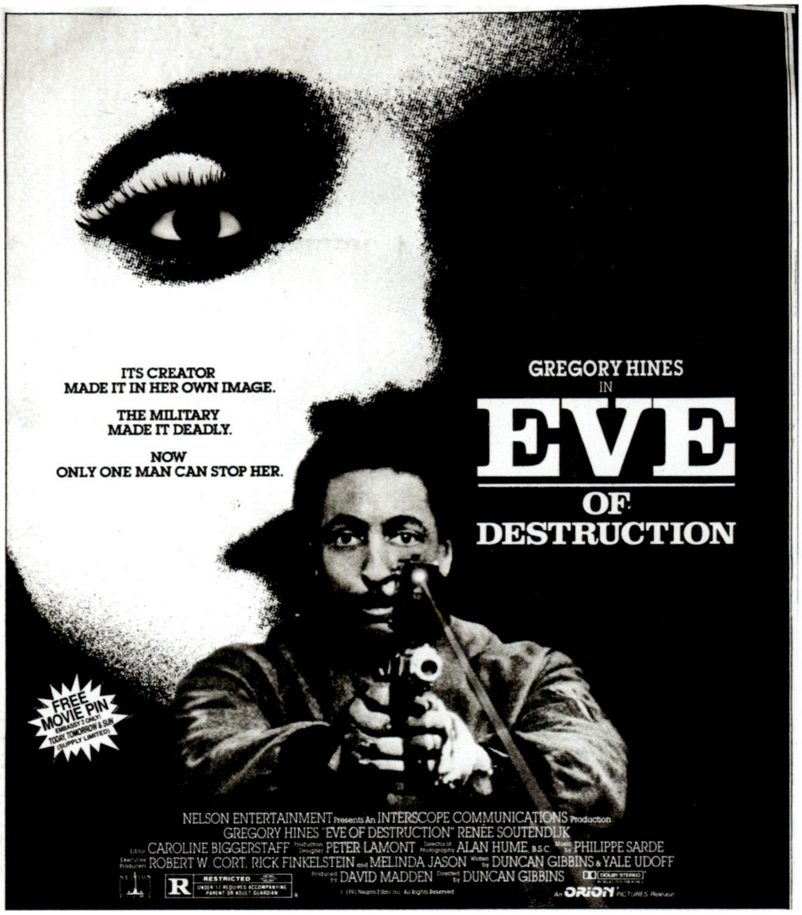

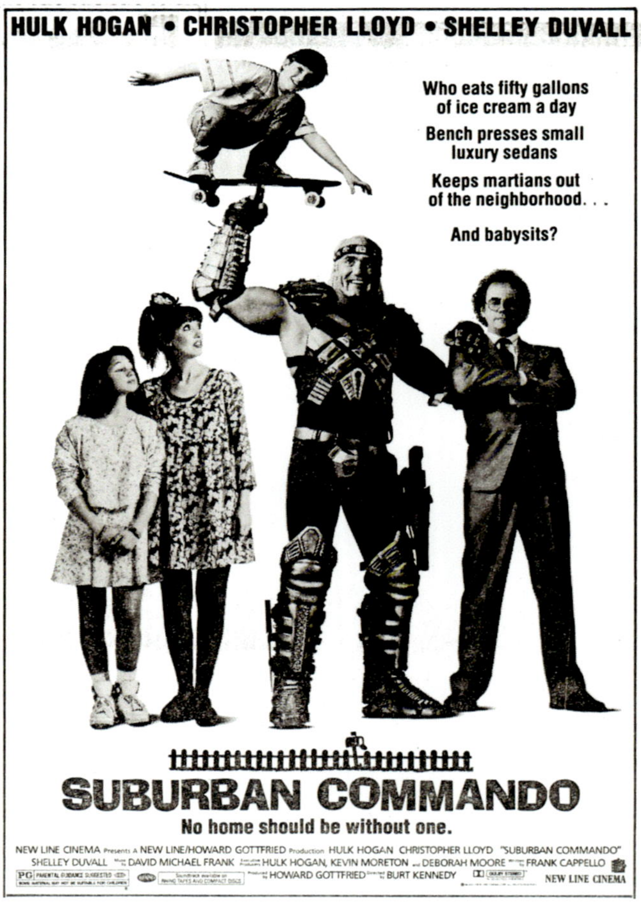

HIGHLANDER 2: THE QUICKENING

The first *Highlander* didn't make big waves at the box office but won enough fans on cable TV and video for director Russell Mulcahy and stars Christopher Lambert and Sean Connery to return for a sequel. Perhaps keeping in mind the critical brickbats the original received, short-lived distributor InterStar Releasing (which only opened three other features, including the Lambert-starrer *Knight Moves*) didn't screen *Highlander 2* in advance. New York reviewers mostly ignored the film, there was the odd positive review, and the rest… ouch.

"*Highlander 2: The Quickening* improves upon the original. This doesn't mean that it's anywhere near a classic of time-travel fantasy adventure. Rather, as both prequel and sequel, it makes clearer much that was so vague in the original; it even jokes about how confusing its premise is."

–Kevin Thomas, *Los Angeles Times*

"[A] movie almost awesome in its badness. Wherever science fiction fans gather, in decades and generations to come, this film will be remembered in hushed tones as one of the immortal low points of the genre."

–ROGER EBERT, *CHICAGO SUN-TIMES*

"It is as though the producers, realizing they had a bomb at their disposal, tried to save the film by having the principals crack wise. It doesn't work, but then nothing really works in this film, not even the special effects, which, after a time, become tiresome."

–Lou Cedrone, *The Baltimore Sun*

"Mulcahy and company don't ask us to suspend disbelief; they ask us to pretend we've all had weed-whacker lobotomies. Of course, the plot is of no more relevance to the movie than Lambert's histrionic impairments."

–Rita Kempley, *Washington Post*

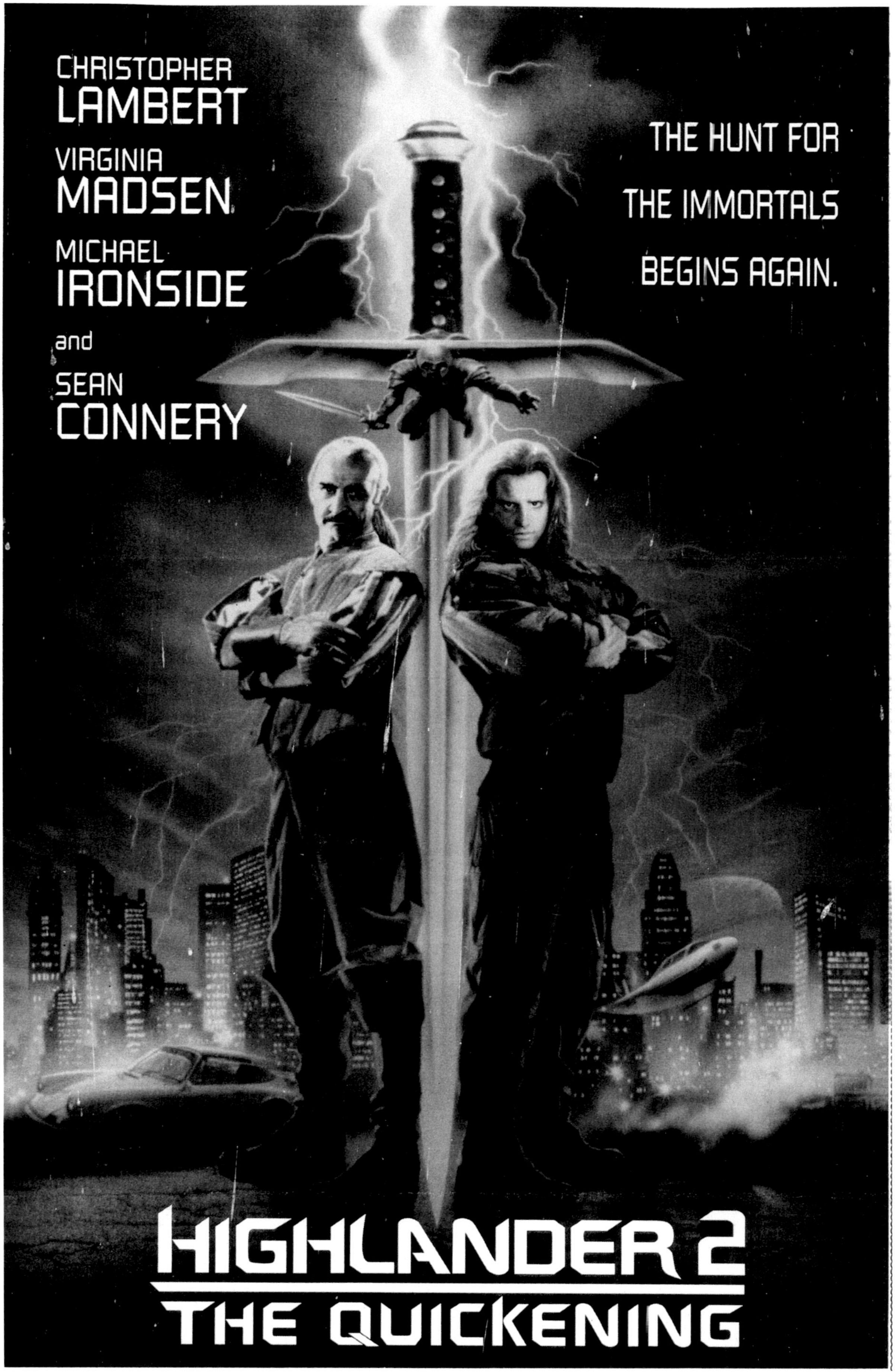
CHRISTOPHER
LAMBERT
VIRGINIA
MADSEN
MICHAEL
IRONSIDE
and
SEAN
CONNERY
THE HUNT FOR
THE IMMORTALS
BEGINS AGAIN.
HIGHLANDER 2
THE QUICKENING

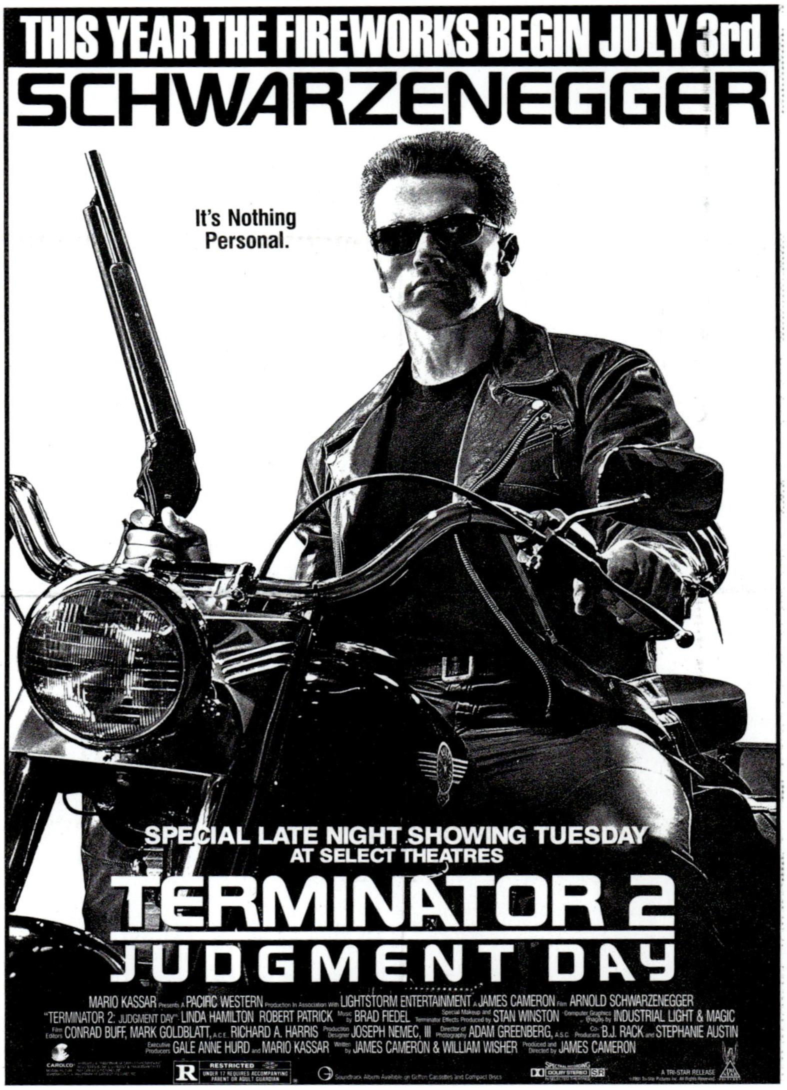

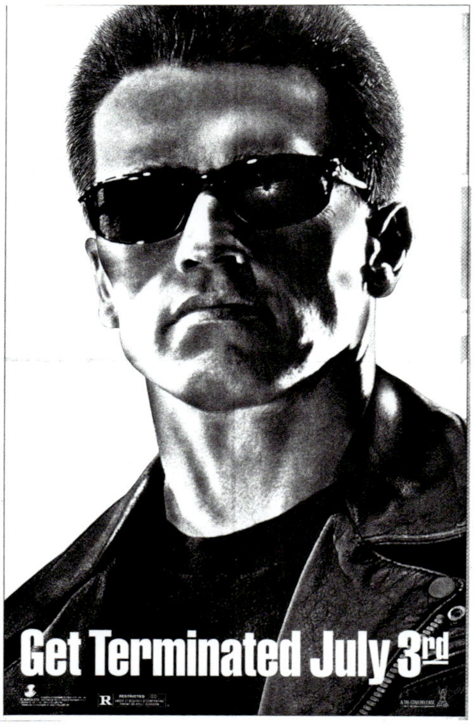

HOOK

Who better to tell the story of a grown-up Peter Pan than Steven Spielberg, and who better to play that role than Robin Williams? *Hook* seemed to have everything going for it when it opened for Christmas season '91… annnd then the reviews came in. Some were appreciative but many opined that the film lacked the typical Spielberg magic. (In later interviews, Spielberg himself would admit he wasn't happy with the film.)

"The news about *Hook* is mostly good: it's a lot of fun to watch – over two hours of thrills, spills, elaborate sets, and special effects, all tied together by a pleasingly varied (and lighter than usual) musical score by John Williams."

–Jay Boyar, *Orlando Sentinel*

"Unfortunately, a little wonder is all *Hook* has to offer. Somewhere between La-La Land and Never-Never Land, Spielberg overshot the runway and ended up at a theme park near Robin Williams' house."

–JACK MATHEWS, NEW YORK *NEWSDAY*

"For the first hour or so, it is an up and down thing, excessive, cluttered, alternately exciting and listless. By the time the film is half finished, however, it all comes together. The director, the cast, and the set designers find the right key, and then the film is a pleasure."

–Lou Cedrone, *The Baltimore Sun*

"In order to fly again, Peter has to recover the boy in himself, and, interestingly enough, that is what Spielberg has to do as well in order to finally lift this top-heavy movie off the ground for a satisfying finale. It is no easy task, for if ever there was a project that came close to being crushed by its own visual splendors, this is it."

–Kenneth Turan, *Los Angeles Times*

"The movie is about happy thoughts, but it takes a somewhat mechanical approach to happiness. It's hard to be elated about a machine, and that's what *Hook* is – an $80 million Happy Thought machine."

–Hal Hinson, *Washington Post*

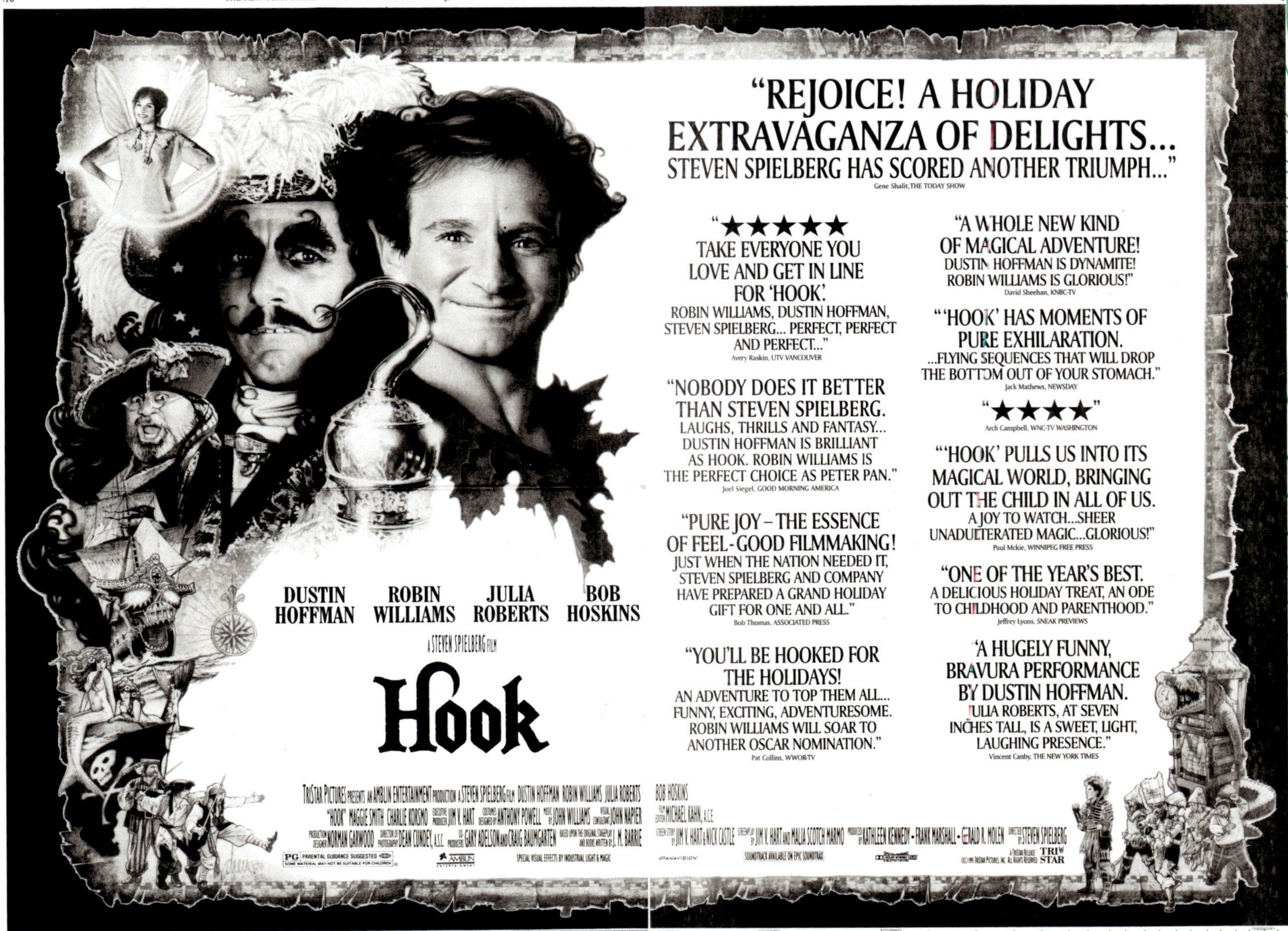

THE NEW YORK TIMES, FRIDAY, DECEMBER 20, 1991
THE NEW YORK TIMES, FRIDAY, DECEMBER 20, 1991
"REJOICE! A HOLIDAY EXTRAVAGANZA OF DELIGHTS... STEVEN SPIELBERG HAS SCORED ANOTHER TRIUMPH..."
Gene Shalit, THE TODAY SHOW
"★★★★★ TAKE EVERYONE YOU LOVE AND GET IN LINE FOR 'HOOK'. ROBIN WILLIAMS, DUSTIN HOFFMAN, STEVEN SPIELBERG... PERFECT, PERFECT AND PERFECT..."
Avery Raskin, UTV VANCOUVER
"NOBODY DOES IT BETTER THAN STEVEN SPIELBERG. LAUGHS, THRILLS AND FANTASY... DUSTIN HOFFMAN IS BRILLIANT AS HOOK. ROBIN WILLIAMS IS THE PERFECT CHOICE AS PETER PAN."
Joel Siegel, GOOD MORNING AMERICA
"PURE JOY – THE ESSENCE OF FEEL-GOOD FILMMAKING! JUST WHEN THE NATION NEEDED IT, STEVEN SPIELBERG AND COMPANY HAVE PREPARED A GRAND HOLIDAY GIFT FOR ONE AND ALL."
Bob Thomas, ASSOCIATED PRESS
"YOU'LL BE HOOKED FOR THE HOLIDAYS! AN ADVENTURE TO TOP THEM ALL... FUNNY, EXCITING, ADVENTURESOME. ROBIN WILLIAMS WILL SOAR TO ANOTHER OSCAR NOMINATION."
Pat Collins, WWOR-TV
"A WHOLE NEW KIND OF MAGICAL ADVENTURE! DUSTIN HOFFMAN IS DYNAMITE! ROBIN WILLIAMS IS GLORIOUS!"
David Sheehan, KNBC-TV
"'HOOK' HAS MOMENTS OF PURE EXHILARATION. ...FLYING SEQUENCES THAT WILL DROP THE BOTTOM OUT OF YOUR STOMACH."
Jack Mathews, NEWSDAY
"★★★★"
Arch Campbell, WNC-TV WASHINGTON
"'HOOK' PULLS US INTO ITS MAGICAL WORLD, BRINGING OUT THE CHILD IN ALL OF US. A JOY TO WATCH...SHEER UNADULTERATED MAGIC...GLORIOUS!"
Paul Mckie, WINNIPEG FREE PRESS
"ONE OF THE YEAR'S BEST. A DELICIOUS HOLIDAY TREAT, AN ODE TO CHILDHOOD AND PARENTHOOD."
Jeffrey Lyons, SNEAK PREVIEWS
'A HUGELY FUNNY, BRAVURA PERFORMANCE BY DUSTIN HOFFMAN. JULIA ROBERTS, AT SEVEN INCHES TALL, IS A SWEET, LIGHT, LAUGHING PRESENCE."
Vincent Canby, THE NEW YORK TIMES
DUSTIN HOFFMAN
ROBIN WILLIAMS
JULIA ROBERTS
BOB HOSKINS
A STEVEN SPIELBERG FILM
Hook
TRISTAR PICTURES PRESENTS AN AMBLIN ENTERTAINMENT PRODUCTION A STEVEN SPIELBERG FILM DUSTIN HOFFMAN ROBIN WILLIAMS JULIA ROBERTS BOB HOSKINS
"HOOK" MAGGIE SMITH CHARLIE KORSMO EXECUTIVE PRODUCER JIM V. HART COSTUMES DESIGNED BY ANTHONY POWELL MUSIC BY JOHN WILLIAMS VISUAL CONSULTANT JOHN NAPIER FILM EDITOR MICHAEL KAHN, A.C.E.
PRODUCTION DESIGNER NORMAN GARWOOD DIRECTOR OF PHOTOGRAPHY DEAN CUNDEY, A.S.C. CO-PRODUCERS GARY ADELSON AND CRAIG BAUMGARTEN BASED UPON THE ORIGINAL STAGEPLAY AND BOOKS WRITTEN BY J. M. BARRIE SCREEN STORY BY JIM V. HART & NICK CASTLE SCREENPLAY BY JIM V. HART AND MALIA SCOTCH MARMO PRODUCED BY KATHLEEN KENNEDY • FRANK MARSHALL • GERALD R. MOLEN DIRECTED BY STEVEN SPIELBERG
PG PARENTAL GUIDANCE SUGGESTED
SOME MATERIAL MAY NOT BE SUITABLE FOR CHILDREN
AMBLIN ENTERTAINMENT
SPECIAL VISUAL EFFECTS BY INDUSTRIAL LIGHT & MAGIC
PANAVISION
SOUNDTRACK AVAILABLE ON EPIC SOUNDTRAX
A TRISTAR RELEASE
TRISTAR
© 1991 TRISTAR PICTURES, INC. ALL RIGHTS RESERVED.

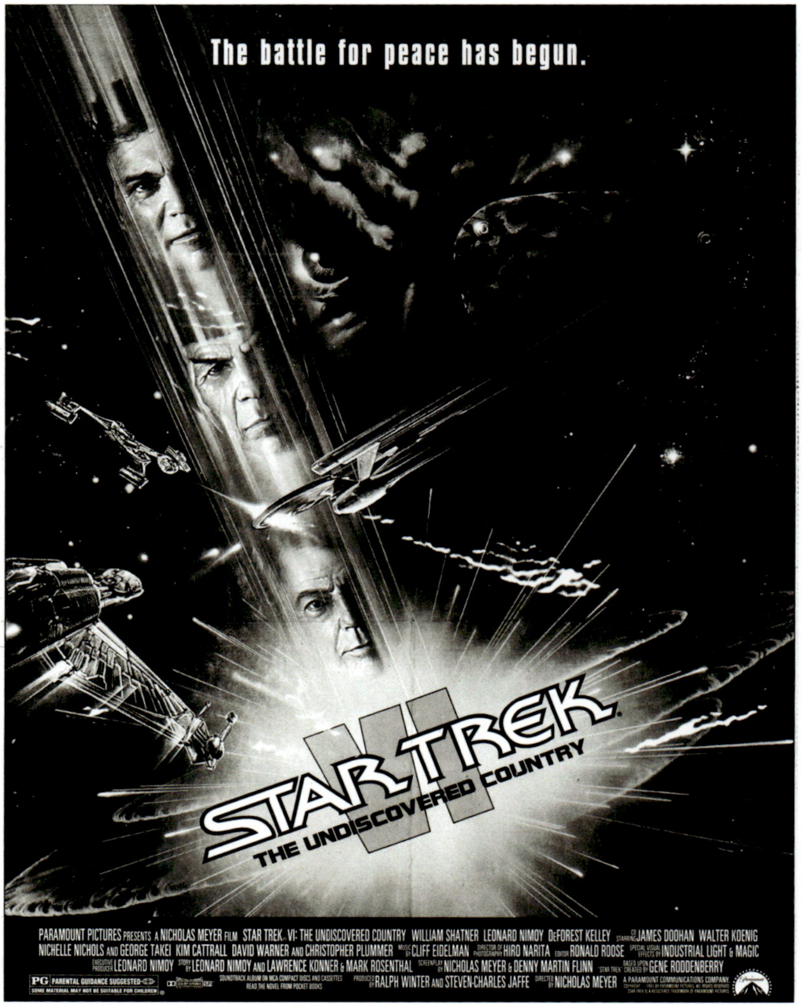

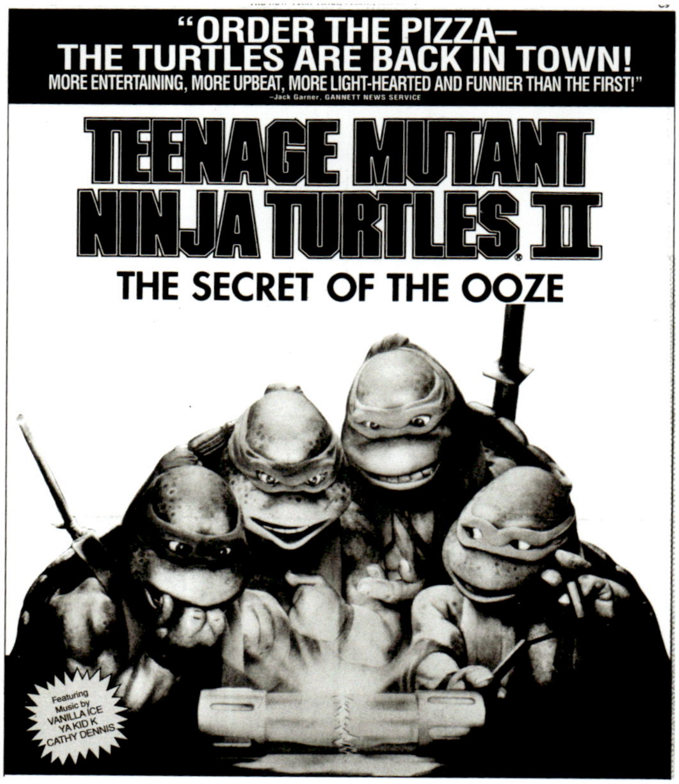

NOTHING BUT TROUBLE

Dan Aykroyd's directorial debut was originally called *Valkenvania*, after the remote New Jersey town where a yuppie couple (played by Chevy Chase and Demi Moore) become prisoners in the bizarre, trap-filled compound of a deranged 106-year-old judge. But after cost overruns (final budget: over $40 million), re-shoots in an attempt to fix the ending, and two changes in release date – from Thanksgiving '90 to that Christmas, and finally to February '91 – it's no surprise that Warner Bros. changed the title to *Nothing But Trouble*. The studio opened it without press screenings, and the reviews were nothing but calamitous.

"[I]f you're in the mood to be clobbered with stale jokes, it might seem fitfully amusing. Occasionally, the talents of the cast burn through the haze of misfires and remembered routines."

–Peter Rainer, *Los Angeles Times*

"I'll admit that Aykroyd, who directed the movie, really made it look weird. But you can only laugh at something strange once, not throughout the whole movie. What he should have done is just let go and have John and Chevy do what they do best, instead of nothing."

–Rene Carlos, *Chicago Tribune*

"If you think it's a little early in the year to be declaring the worst film of 1991, then you probably haven't seen *Nothing But Trouble*."

–JOY BOYAR, *ORLANDO SENTINEL*

"Never has a movie been more appropriately titled. The comedy, which features the directorial debut of Dan Aykroyd, is the cinematic equivalent of a nervous breakdown – complete with catatonic script, twitchy direction and split-personality performances."

–Hank Gallo, New York *Daily News*

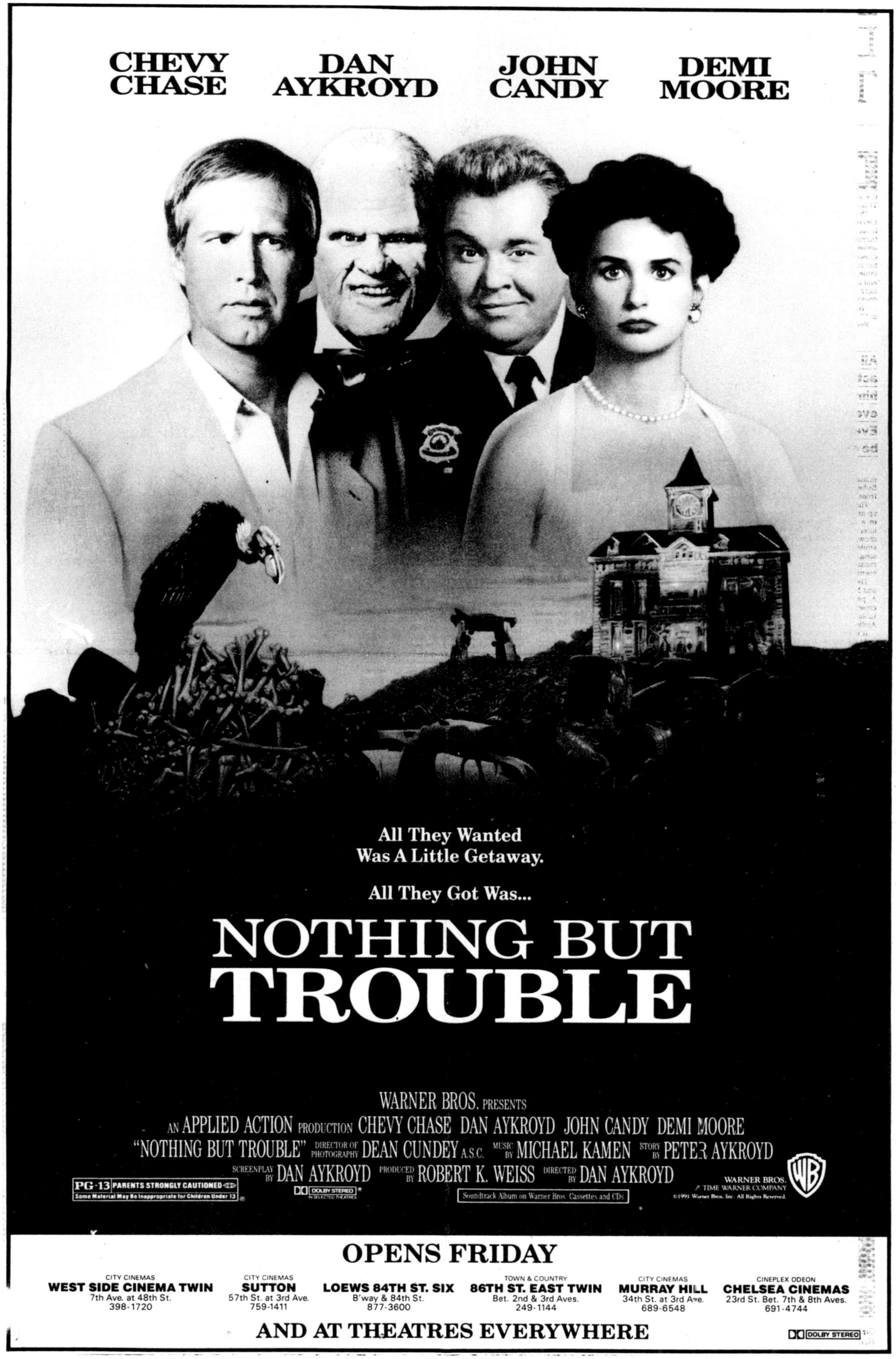
CHEVY CHASE
DAN AYKROYD
JOHN CANDY
DEMI MOORE
All They Wanted
Was A Little Getaway.
All They Got Was...
NOTHING BUT TROUBLE
WARNER BROS. PRESENTS
AN APPLIED ACTION PRODUCTION CHEVY CHASE DAN AYKROYD JOHN CANDY DEMI MOORE
"NOTHING BUT TROUBLE" DIRECTOR OF PHOTOGRAPHY DEAN CUNDEY A.S.C. MUSIC BY MICHAEL KAMEN STORY BY PETER AYKROYD
SCREENPLAY BY DAN AYKROYD PRODUCED BY ROBERT K. WEISS DIRECTED BY DAN AYKROYD
PG-13 PARENTS STRONGLY CAUTIONED
Some Material May Be Inappropriate for Children Under 13
DOLBY STEREO
Soundtrack Album on Warner Bros. Cassettes and CDs
WARNER BROS.
A TIME WARNER COMPANY
©1991 Warner Bros. Inc. All Rights Reserved.
OPENS FRIDAY
CITY CINEMAS
WEST SIDE CINEMA TWIN
7th Ave. at 48th St.
398-1720
CITY CINEMAS
SUTTON
57th St. at 3rd Ave.
759-1411
LOEWS 84TH ST. SIX
B'way & 84th St.
877-3600
TOWN & COUNTRY
86TH ST. EAST TWIN
Bet. 2nd & 3rd Aves.
249-1144
CITY CINEMAS
MURRAY HILL
34th St. at 3rd Ave.
689-6548
CINEPLEX ODEON
CHELSEA CINEMAS
23rd St. Bet. 7th & 8th Aves.
691-4744
AND AT THEATRES EVERYWHERE
DOLBY STEREO

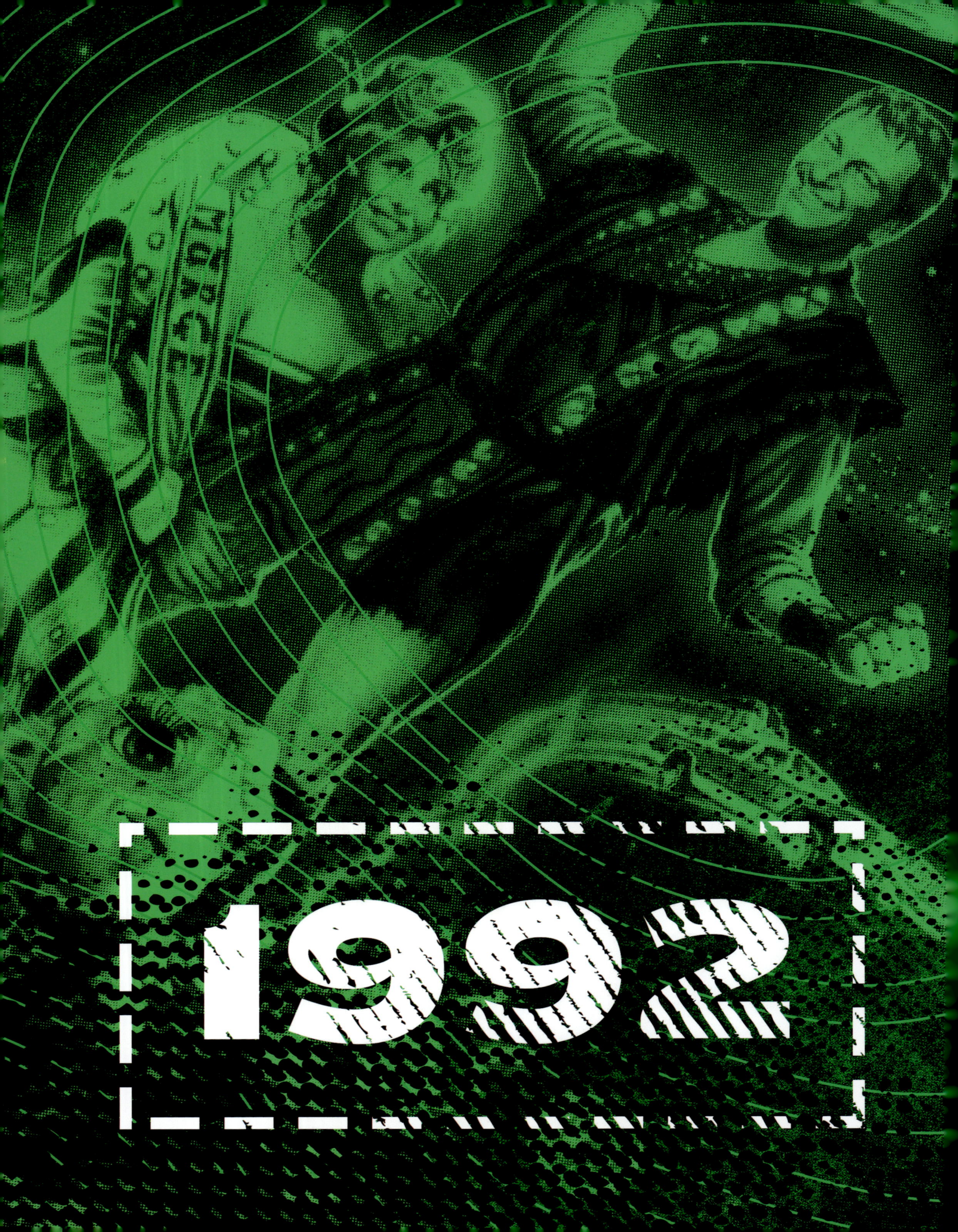

1992

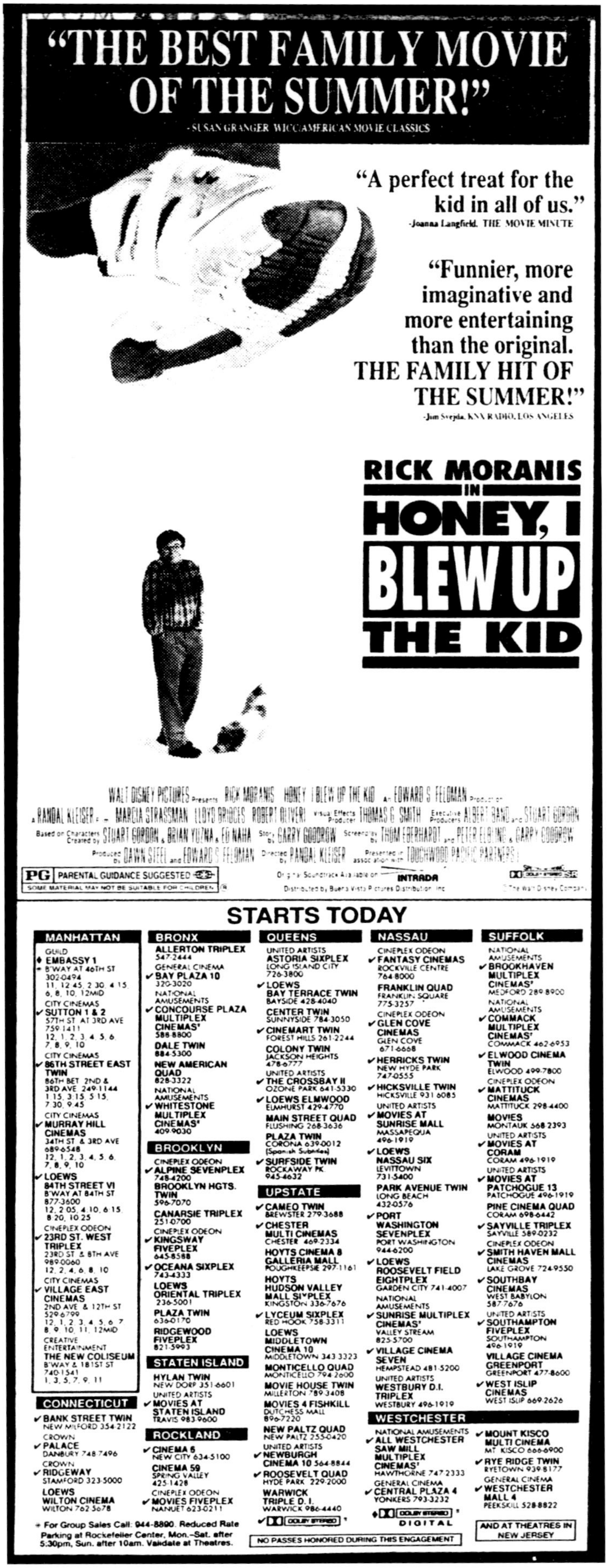
"THE BEST FAMILY MOVIE OF THE SUMMER!"
- SUSAN GRANGER WICC/AMERICAN MOVIE CLASSICS
"A perfect treat for the kid in all of us."
-Joanna Langfield, THE MOVIE MINUTE
"Funnier, more imaginative and more entertaining than the original. THE FAMILY HIT OF THE SUMMER!"
-Jim Svejda, KNX RADIO, LOS ANGELES
RICK MORANIS
IN
HONEY, I BLEW UP THE KID
WALT DISNEY PICTURES Presents RICK MORANIS "HONEY, I BLEW UP THE KID" An EDWARD S. FELDMAN Production
A RANDAL KLEISER Film MARCIA STRASSMAN LLOYD BRIDGES ROBERT OLIVERI Visual Effects Producer THOMAS G. SMITH Executive Producers ALBERT BAND and STUART GORDON
Based on Characters Created by STUART GORDON, BRIAN YUZNA & ED NAHA Story by GARRY GOODROW Screenplay by THOM EBERHARDT and PETER ELBLING & GARRY GOODROW
Produced by DAWN STEEL and EDWARD S. FELDMAN Directed by RANDAL KLEISER Presented in association with TOUCHWOOD PACIFIC PARTNERS I
PG PARENTAL GUIDANCE SUGGESTED
SOME MATERIAL MAY NOT BE SUITABLE FOR CHILDREN
Original Soundtrack Available on INTRADA
Distributed by Buena Vista Pictures Distribution, Inc.
© The Walt Disney Company
STARTS TODAY
MANHATTAN
GUILD
♦ EMBASSY 1
✦ B'WAY AT 46TH ST
302-0494
11, 12:45, 2:30, 4:15, 6, 8, 10, 12MID
CITY CINEMAS
✔ SUTTON 1 & 2
57TH ST. AT 3RD AVE
759-1411
12, 1, 2, 3, 4, 5, 6, 7, 8, 9, 10
CITY CINEMAS
✔ 86TH STREET EAST TWIN
86TH BET. 2ND & 3RD AVE. 249-1144
1:15, 3:15, 5:15, 7:30, 9:45
CITY CINEMAS
✔ MURRAY HILL CINEMAS
34TH ST. & 3RD AVE
689-6548
12, 1, 2, 3, 4, 5, 6, 7, 8, 9, 10
✔ LOEWS 84TH STREET VI
B'WAY AT 84TH ST
877-3600
12, 2:05, 4:10, 6:15, 8:20, 10:25
CINEPLEX ODEON
✔ 23RD ST. WEST TRIPLEX
23RD ST. & 8TH AVE
989-0060
12, 2, 4, 6, 8, 10
CITY CINEMAS
✔ VILLAGE EAST CINEMAS
2ND AVE. & 12TH ST
529-6799
12, 1, 2, 3, 4, 5, 6, 7, 8, 9, 10, 11, 12MID
CREATIVE ENTERTAINMENT
THE NEW COLISEUM
B'WAY & 181ST ST
740-1541
1, 3, 5, 7, 9, 11
CONNECTICUT
✔ BANK STREET TWIN
NEW MILFORD 354-2122
CROWN
✔ PALACE
DANBURY 748-7496
CROWN
✔ RIDGEWAY
STAMFORD 323-5000
LOEWS
WILTON CINEMA
WILTON 762-5678
BRONX
ALLERTON TRIPLEX
547-2444
GENERAL CINEMA
✔ BAY PLAZA 10
320-3020
NATIONAL AMUSEMENTS
✔ CONCOURSE PLAZA MULTIPLEX CINEMAS'
588-8800
DALE TWIN
884-5300
NEW AMERICAN QUAD
828-3322
NATIONAL AMUSEMENTS
✔ WHITESTONE MULTIPLEX CINEMAS'
409-9030
BROOKLYN
CINEPLEX ODEON
✔ ALPINE SEVENPLEX
748-4200
BROOKLYN HGTS. TWIN
596-7070
CANARSIE TRIPLEX
251-0700
CINEPLEX ODEON
✔ KINGSWAY FIVEPLEX
645-8588
✔ OCEANA SIXPLEX
743-4333
LOEWS ORIENTAL TRIPLEX
236-5001
PLAZA TWIN
636-0170
RIDGEWOOD FIVEPLEX
821-5993
STATEN ISLAND
HYLAN TWIN
NEW DORP 351-6601
UNITED ARTISTS
✔ MOVIES AT STATEN ISLAND
TRAVIS 983-9600
ROCKLAND
✔ CINEMA 6
NEW CITY 634-5100
CINEMA 59
SPRING VALLEY 425-1428
CINEPLEX ODEON
✔ MOVIES FIVEPLEX
NANUET 623-0211
QUEENS
UNITED ARTISTS
ASTORIA SIXPLEX
LONG ISLAND CITY 726-3800
✔ LOEWS BAY TERRACE TWIN
BAYSIDE 428-4040
CENTER TWIN
SUNNYSIDE 784-3050
✔ CINEMART TWIN
FOREST HILLS 261-2244
COLONY TWIN
JACKSON HEIGHTS 478-6777
UNITED ARTISTS
✔ THE CROSSBAY II
OZONE PARK 641-5330
✔ LOEWS ELMWOOD
ELMHURST 429-4770
MAIN STREET QUAD
FLUSHING 268-3636
PLAZA TWIN
CORONA 639-0012
(Spanish Subtitles)
✔ SURFSIDE TWIN
ROCKAWAY PK. 945-4632
UPSTATE
✔ CAMEO TWIN
BREWSTER 279-3688
✔ CHESTER MULTI CINEMAS
CHESTER 469-2334
HOYTS CINEMA 8 GALLERIA MALL
POUGHKEEPSIE 297-1161
HOYTS HUDSON VALLEY MALL SIXPLEX
KINGSTON 336-7676
✔ LYCEUM SIXPLEX
RED HOOK 758-3311
LOEWS MIDDLETOWN CINEMA 10
MIDDLETOWN 343-3323
MONTICELLO QUAD
MONTICELLO 794-2600
MOVIE HOUSE TWIN
MILLERTON 789-3408
MOVIES 4 FISHKILL
DUTCHESS MALL 896-7220
NEW PALTZ QUAD
NEW PALTZ 255-0420
UNITED ARTISTS
✔ NEWBURGH CINEMA 10
564-8844
✔ ROOSEVELT QUAD
HYDE PARK 229-2000
WARWICK TRIPLE D.I.
WARWICK 986-4440
NASSAU
CINEPLEX ODEON
✔ FANTASY CINEMAS
ROCKVILLE CENTRE 764-8000
FRANKLIN QUAD
FRANKLIN SQUARE 775-3257
CINEPLEX ODEON
✔ GLEN COVE CINEMAS
GLEN COVE 671-6668
✔ HERRICKS TWIN
NEW HYDE PARK 747-0555
✔ HICKSVILLE TWIN
HICKSVILLE 931-6085
UNITED ARTISTS
✔ MOVIES AT SUNRISE MALL
MASSAPEQUA 496-1919
✔ LOEWS NASSAU SIX
LEVITTOWN 731-5400
PARK AVENUE TWIN
LONG BEACH 432-0576
✔ PORT WASHINGTON SEVENPLEX
PORT WASHINGTON 944-6200
✔ LOEWS ROOSEVELT FIELD EIGHTPLEX
GARDEN CITY 741-4007
NATIONAL AMUSEMENTS
✔ SUNRISE MULTIPLEX CINEMAS'
VALLEY STREAM 825-5700
✔ VILLAGE CINEMA SEVEN
HEMPSTEAD 481-5200
UNITED ARTISTS
WESTBURY D.I. TRIPLEX
WESTBURY 496-1919
SUFFOLK
NATIONAL AMUSEMENTS
✔ BROOKHAVEN MULTIPLEX CINEMAS'
MEDFORD 289-8900
NATIONAL AMUSEMENTS
✔ COMMACK MULTIPLEX CINEMAS'
COMMACK 462-6953
✔ ELWOOD CINEMA TWIN
ELWOOD 499-7800
CINEPLEX ODEON
✔ MATTITUCK CINEMAS
MATTITUCK 298-4400
MOVIES
MONTAUK 668-2393
UNITED ARTISTS
✔ MOVIES AT CORAM
CORAM 496-1919
UNITED ARTISTS
✔ MOVIES AT PATCHOGUE 13
PATCHOGUE 496-1919
PINE CINEMA QUAD
CORAM 698-6442
✔ SAYVILLE TRIPLEX
SAYVILLE 589-0232
CINEPLEX ODEON
✔ SMITH HAVEN MALL CINEMAS
LAKE GROVE 724-9550
✔ SOUTHBAY CINEMAS
WEST BABYLON 587-7676
UNITED ARTISTS
✔ SOUTHAMPTON FIVEPLEX
SOUTHAMPTON 496-1919
VILLAGE CINEMA GREENPORT
GREENPORT 477-8600
✔ WEST ISLIP CINEMAS
WEST ISLIP 669-2626
WESTCHESTER
NATIONAL AMUSEMENTS
✔ ALL WESTCHESTER SAW MILL MULTIPLEX CINEMAS'
HAWTHORNE 747-2333
GENERAL CINEMA
✔ CENTRAL PLAZA 4
YONKERS 793-3232
✔ MOUNT KISCO MULTI CINEMA
MT. KISCO 666-6900
✔ RYE RIDGE TWIN
RYETOWN 939-8177
GENERAL CINEMA
✔ WESTCHESTER MALL 4
PEEKSKILL 528-8822
✔ DOLBY STEREO
♦ DOLBY STEREO DIGITAL
✦ For Group Sales Call: 944-8890. Reduced Rate Parking at Rockefeller Center, Mon.–Sat. after 5:30pm, Sun. after 10am. Validate at Theatres.
NO PASSES HONORED DURING THIS ENGAGEMENT
AND AT THEATRES IN NEW JERSEY

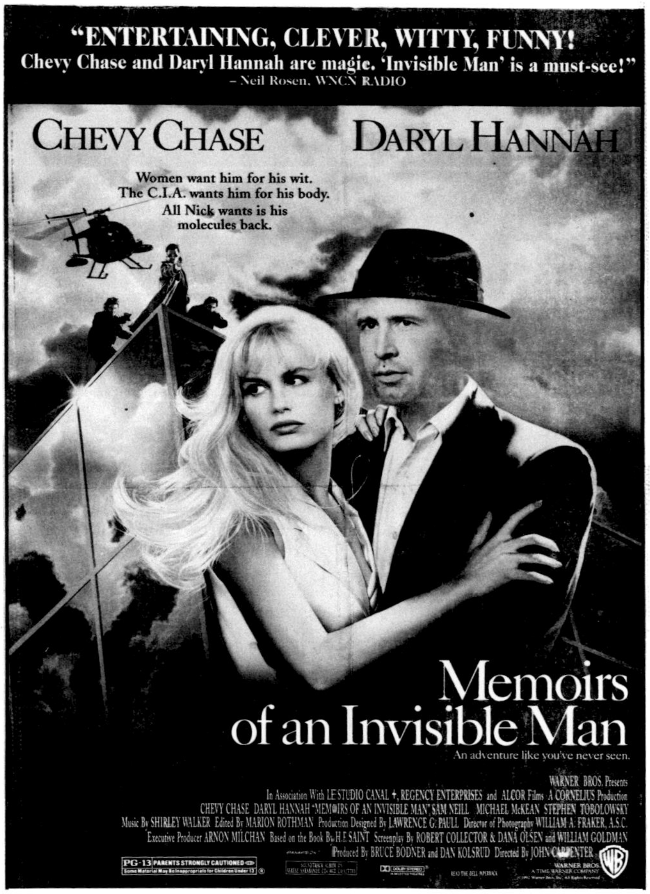
"ENTERTAINING, CLEVER, WITTY, FUNNY!
Chevy Chase and Daryl Hannah are magic. 'Invisible Man' is a must-see!"
– Neil Rosen, WNCN RADIO
CHEVY CHASE
DARYL HANNAH
Women want him for his wit.
The C.I.A. wants him for his body.
All Nick wants is his molecules back.
Memoirs of an Invisible Man
An adventure like you've never seen.
WARNER BROS. Presents
In Association With LE STUDIO CANAL +, REGENCY ENTERPRISES and ALCOR Films A CORNELIUS Production
CHEVY CHASE DARYL HANNAH "MEMOIRS OF AN INVISIBLE MAN" SAM NEILL MICHAEL McKEAN STEPHEN TOBOLOWSKY
Music By SHIRLEY WALKER Edited By MARION ROTHMAN Production Designed By LAWRENCE G. PAULL Director of Photography WILLIAM A. FRAKER, A.S.C.
Executive Producer ARNON MILCHAN Based on the Book By H.F. SAINT Screenplay By ROBERT COLLECTOR & DANA OLSEN and WILLIAM GOLDMAN
Produced By BRUCE BODNER and DAN KOLSRUD Directed By JOHN CARPENTER
PG-13 PARENTS STRONGLY CAUTIONED
Some Material May Be Inappropriate for Children Under 13

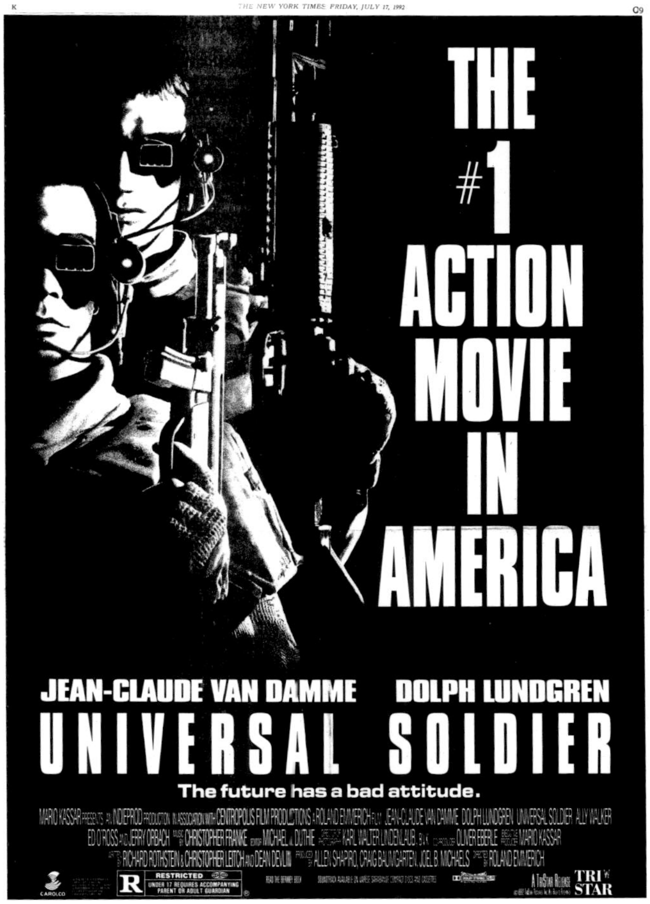
THE NEW YORK TIMES, FRIDAY, JULY 17, 1992
THE #1 ACTION MOVIE IN AMERICA
JEAN-CLAUDE VAN DAMME
DOLPH LUNDGREN
UNIVERSAL SOLDIER
The future has a bad attitude.
RESTRICTED
UNDER 17 REQUIRES ACCOMPANYING PARENT OR ADULT GUARDIAN
TRI STAR

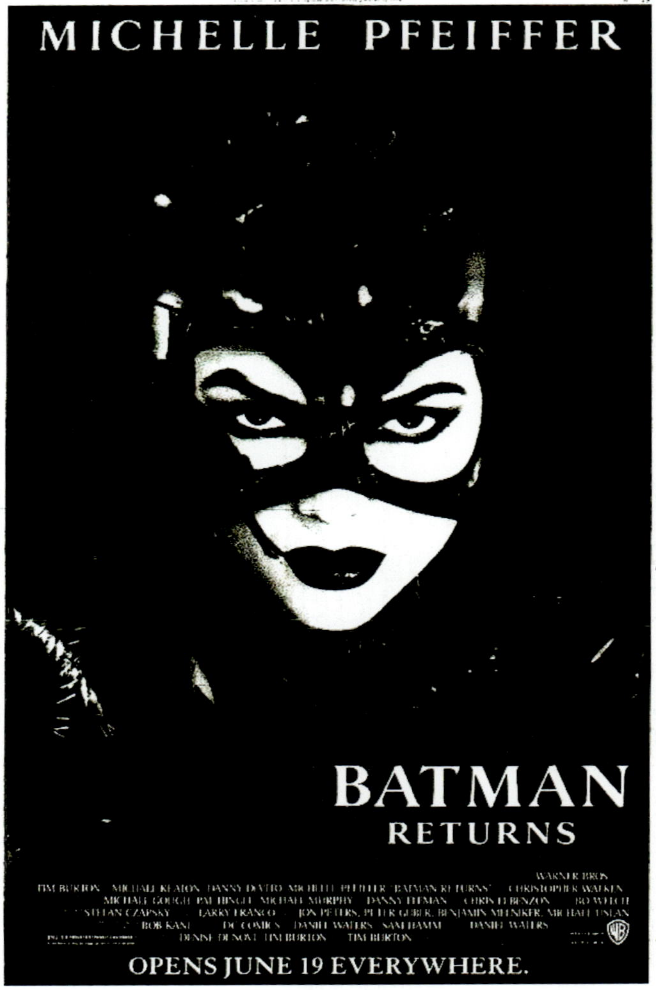

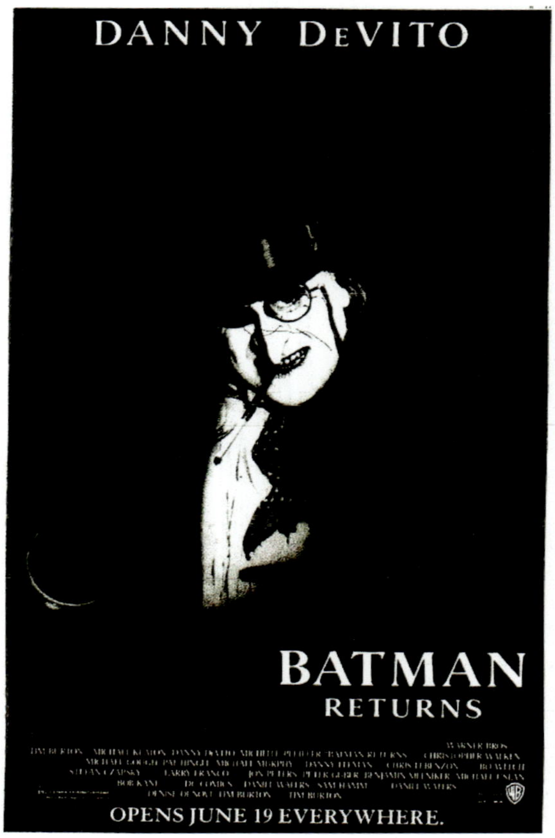

BATMAN RETURNS

While Tim Burton's first *Batman* became a blockbuster, some observers felt it was just too dark and weird. So for the sequel – teased with ads spotlighting its villains – Burton went... even darker and weirder. Quite a few critics were impressed, with Michelle Pfeiffer as Catwoman singled out for praise, though once again, some felt story was an afterthought.

"Great efforts have been made to keep up (and exceed) the visual wonder and oomph of the original, and it shows. ... Director Burton not only re-creates his one-of-a-kind atmosphere, he one-ups it, even two-ups it."

–Desson Howe, *Washington Post*

"[I]t should be a pleasure for non-adolescents to encounter a comic-book action picture in which the characters are more important than their gadgets. In other words, I liked *Batman Returns* because I found myself thinking more about Bruce Wayne than the Batmobile, more about the Penguin's childhood than his aerodynamic umbrella."

–GENE SISKEL, *CHICAGO TRIBUNE*

"[Pfeiffer's] scenes with Keaton, who renders the Caped Crusader with the same effective and subdued reticence, boast the film's best dialogue – and a charged ambivalence and subtlety missing from the rest of *Batman Returns*."

–Desmond Ryan, *Philadelphia Inquirer*

"It's very messy, at least in the narrative sense. ... But then it's not really a movie. It's a painting and Burton is a painter, a Hieronymus Bosch for our time. ... As pure visual spectacle, *Batman Returns* never lets up."

–Stephen Hunter, *The Baltimore Sun*

"I can admire the movie on many levels, but I cannot accept it as Batman. And I was disappointed that the disjointed plot advanced so unsteadily, depriving us of the luxury of really caring about the outcome."

—Roger Ebert, *Chicago Sun-Times*

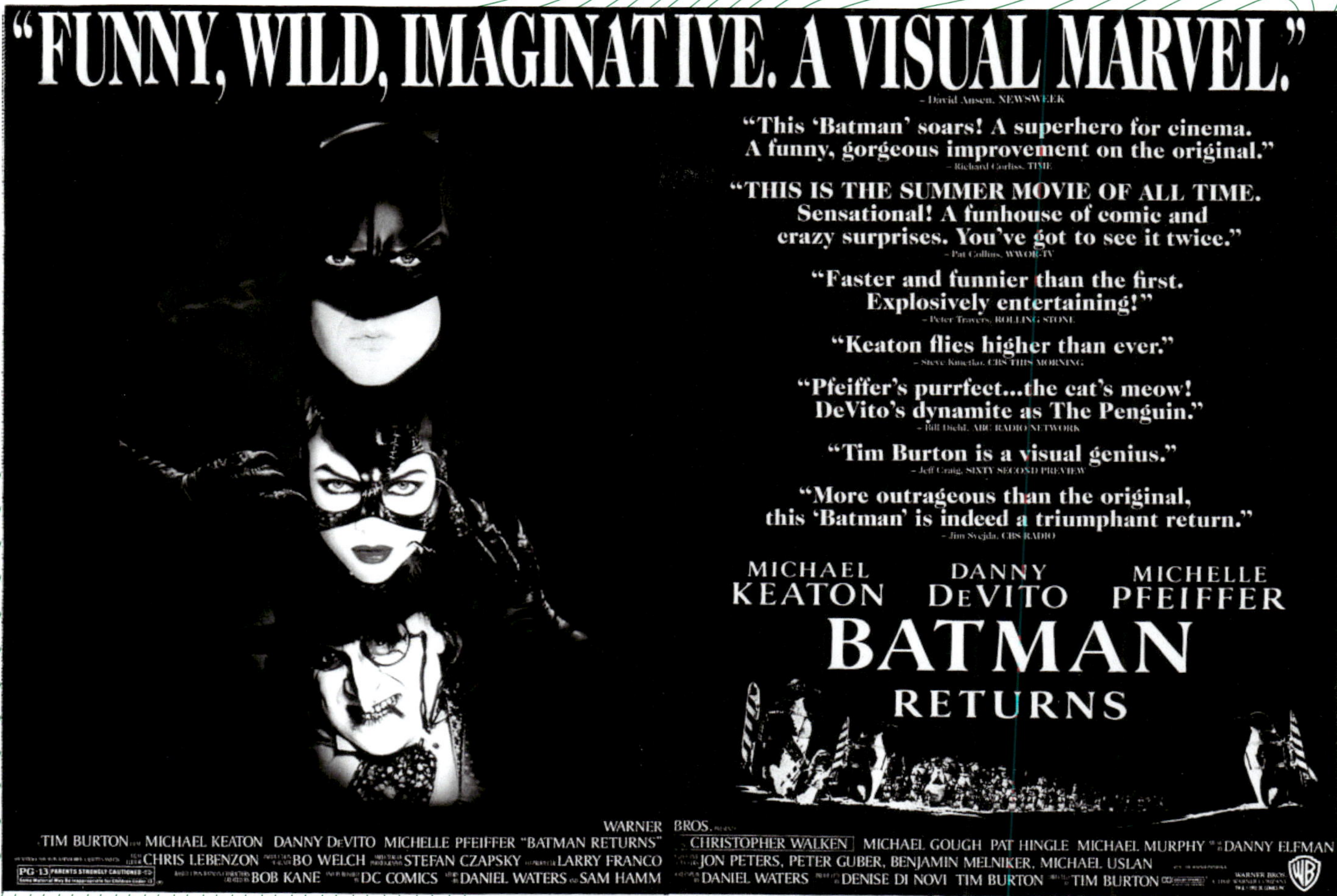
"FUNNY, WILD, IMAGINATIVE. A VISUAL MARVEL."
– David Ansen, NEWSWEEK
"This 'Batman' soars! A superhero for cinema. A funny, gorgeous improvement on the original."
– Richard Corliss, TIME
"THIS IS THE SUMMER MOVIE OF ALL TIME. Sensational! A funhouse of comic and crazy surprises. You've got to see it twice."
– Pat Collins, WWOR-TV
"Faster and funnier than the first. Explosively entertaining!"
– Peter Travers, ROLLING STONE
"Keaton flies higher than ever."
"Pfeiffer's purrfect...the cat's meow! DeVito's dynamite as The Penguin."
– Bill Diehl, ABC RADIO NETWORK
"Tim Burton is a visual genius."
– Jeff Craig, SIXTY SECOND PREVIEW
"More outrageous than the original, this 'Batman' is indeed a triumphant return."
– Jim Svejda, CBS RADIO
MICHAEL KEATON
DANNY DeVITO
MICHELLE PFEIFFER
BATMAN RETURNS
WARNER BROS.
TIM BURTON MICHAEL KEATON DANNY DeVITO MICHELLE PFEIFFER "BATMAN RETURNS" CHRISTOPHER WALKEN MICHAEL GOUGH PAT HINGLE MICHAEL MURPHY DANNY ELFMAN
CHRIS LEBENZON BO WELCH STEFAN CZAPSKY LARRY FRANCO JON PETERS, PETER GUBER, BENJAMIN MELNIKER, MICHAEL USLAN
BOB KANE DC COMICS DANIEL WATERS SAM HAMM DANIEL WATERS DENISE DI NOVI TIM BURTON TIM BURTON
PG-13 PARENTS STRONGLY CAUTIONED

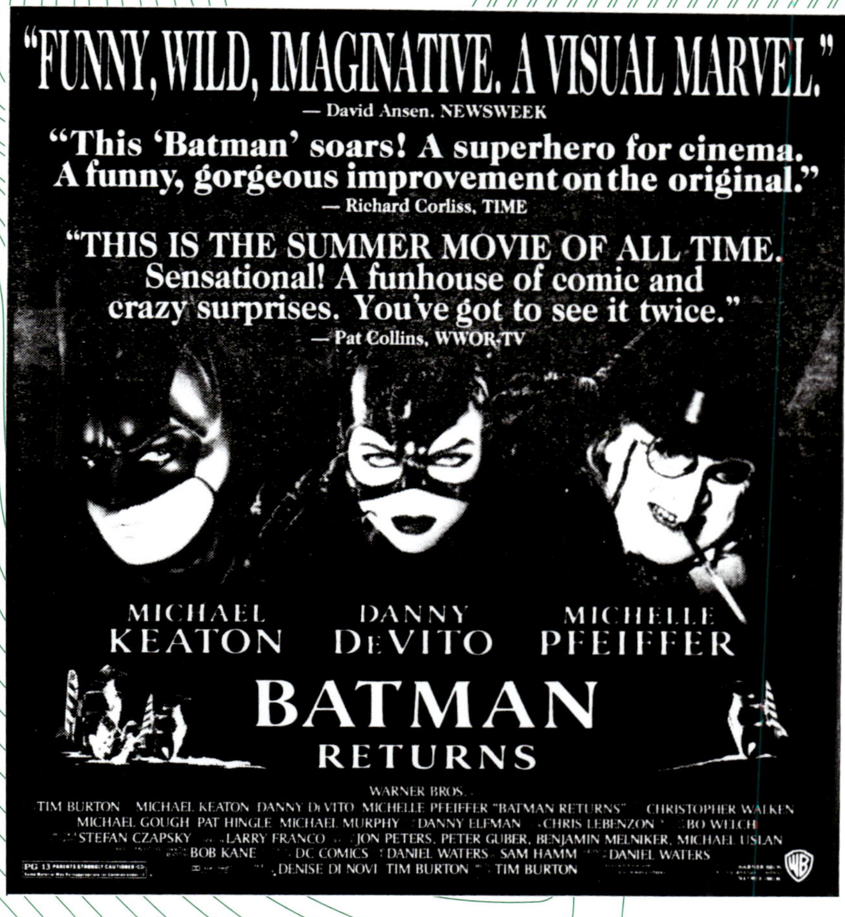
"FUNNY, WILD, IMAGINATIVE. A VISUAL MARVEL."
— David Ansen, NEWSWEEK
"This 'Batman' soars! A superhero for cinema. A funny, gorgeous improvement on the original."
— Richard Corliss, TIME
"THIS IS THE SUMMER MOVIE OF ALL TIME. Sensational! A funhouse of comic and crazy surprises. You've got to see it twice."
— Pat Collins, WWOR-TV
MICHAEL KEATON
DANNY DeVITO
MICHELLE PFEIFFER
BATMAN RETURNS
WARNER BROS.
TIM BURTON MICHAEL KEATON DANNY DeVITO MICHELLE PFEIFFER "BATMAN RETURNS" CHRISTOPHER WALKEN
MICHAEL GOUGH PAT HINGLE MICHAEL MURPHY DANNY ELFMAN CHRIS LEBENZON BO WELCH
STEFAN CZAPSKY LARRY FRANCO JON PETERS, PETER GUBER, BENJAMIN MELNIKER, MICHAEL USLAN
BOB KANE DC COMICS DANIEL WATERS SAM HAMM DANIEL WATERS
DENISE DI NOVI TIM BURTON TIM BURTON
PG-13 PARENTS STRONGLY CAUTIONED

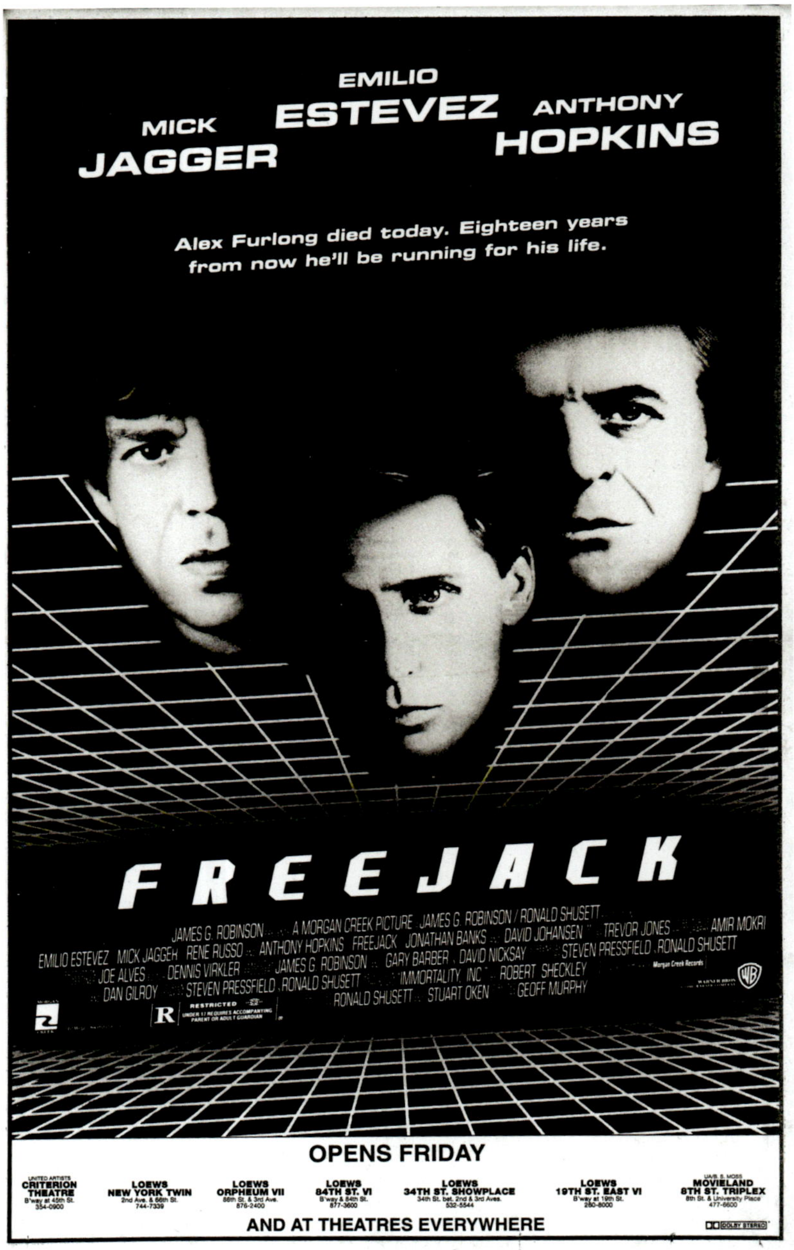

THE LAWNMOWER MAN

Handed the gig of making a film version of Stephen King's short story, writer/director Brett Leonard and writer/producer Gimel Everett inserted the author's setpiece into their existing virtual-reality script *Cyber God*. The result displeased a lot of hardcore King fans, as well as the man himself, who sued to have his billing removed from the title. Regardless, the movie rode its then-cutting-edge visual effects to a higher gross than more faithful King adaptations of the period, such as *The Dark Half* and *Needful Things*, and his original film *Sleepwalkers*. The box office was unaffected by mixed reviews, including at least one whose author apparently didn't take the time to read King's tale and realize the film had almost nothing to do with his prose.

"As a visual adventure, *The Lawnmower Man* is great fun. ... [But the] usual melodramatic excesses are committed, first by King who cannot imagine a relationship that is not cheesy and hostile, and second by director-adapter Brett Leonard, who punches up everything as far as it can go."

–Stephen Hunter, *The Baltimore Sun*

"*Lawnmower Man* will probably be a cult hit. It's been all the buzz on the 'net' (electronic bulletin boards like CompuServe, Genie, or Prodigy) for some months now, but if as much care had been taken with the human elements – the actors, the story – it would have been a much better ride."

–KATHLEEN MAHER, *THE AUSTIN CHRONICLE*

"The only thing *The Lawnmower Man* accomplishes is to remind you how boring it is to watch someone else play a video game. If they ever start marketing this virtual reality stuff, however, someone's going to get very rich."

–Rene Rodriguez, *Miami Herald*

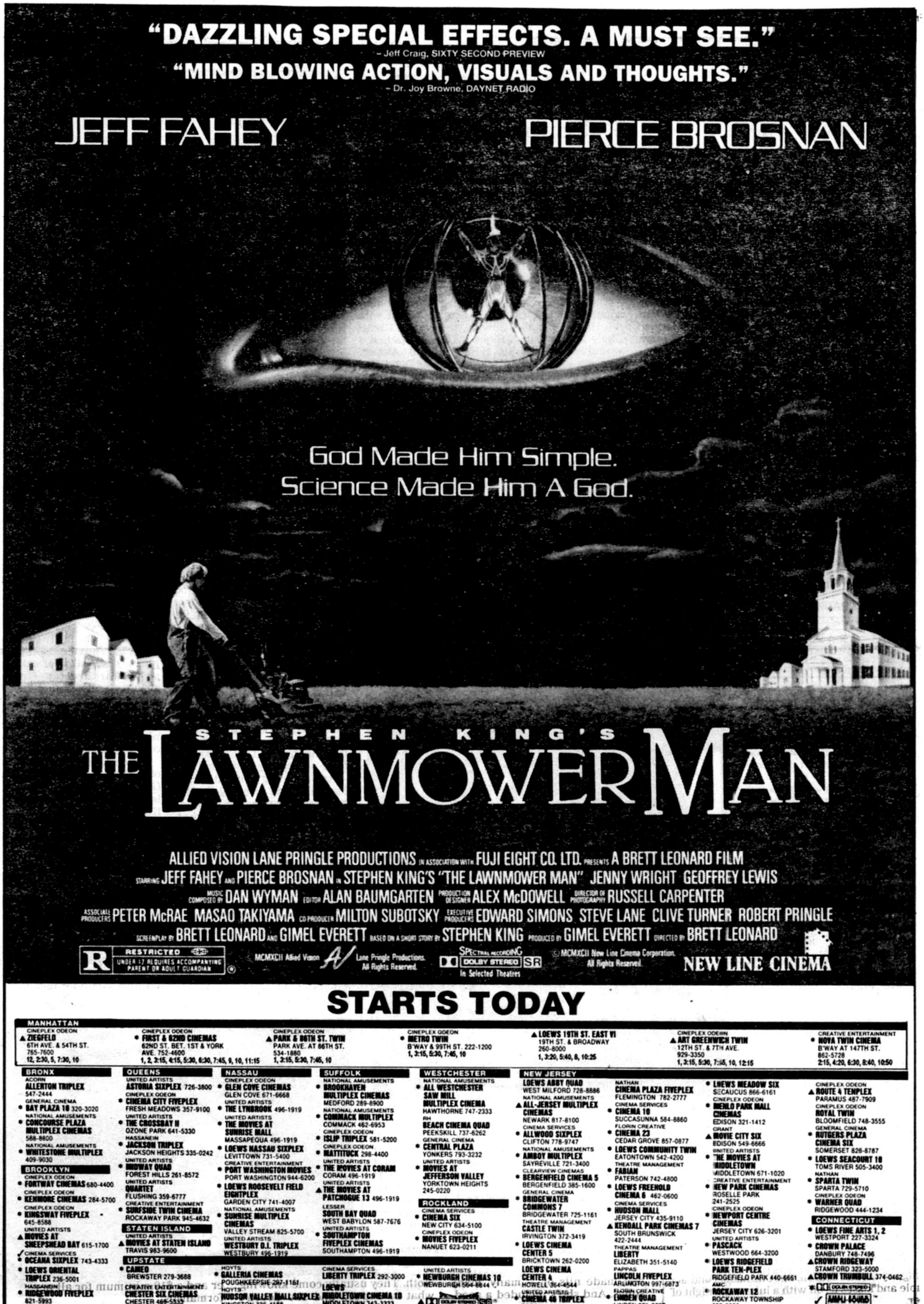
"DAZZLING SPECIAL EFFECTS. A MUST SEE."
– Jeff Craig, SIXTY SECOND PREVIEW
"MIND BLOWING ACTION, VISUALS AND THOUGHTS."
– Dr. Joy Browne, DAYNET RADIO
JEFF FAHEY
PIERCE BROSNAN
God Made Him Simple.
Science Made Him A God.
STEPHEN KING'S
THE LAWNMOWER MAN
ALLIED VISION LANE PRINGLE PRODUCTIONS IN ASSOCIATION WITH FUJI EIGHT CO. LTD. PRESENTS A BRETT LEONARD FILM
STARRING JEFF FAHEY AND PIERCE BROSNAN IN STEPHEN KING'S "THE LAWNMOWER MAN" JENNY WRIGHT GEOFFREY LEWIS
MUSIC COMPOSED BY DAN WYMAN EDITOR ALAN BAUMGARTEN PRODUCTION DESIGNER ALEX McDOWELL DIRECTOR OF PHOTOGRAPHY RUSSELL CARPENTER
ASSOCIATE PRODUCERS PETER McRAE MASAO TAKIYAMA CO-PRODUCER MILTON SUBOTSKY EXECUTIVE PRODUCERS EDWARD SIMONS STEVE LANE CLIVE TURNER ROBERT PRINGLE
SCREENPLAY BY BRETT LEONARD AND GIMEL EVERETT BASED ON A SHORT STORY BY STEPHEN KING PRODUCED BY GIMEL EVERETT DIRECTED BY BRETT LEONARD
R RESTRICTED UNDER 17 REQUIRES ACCOMPANYING PARENT OR ADULT GUARDIAN
MCMXCII Allied Vision Lane Pringle Productions. All Rights Reserved.
SPECTRAL RECORDING DOLBY STEREO SR In Selected Theatres
© MCMXCII New Line Cinema Corporation. All Rights Reserved.
NEW LINE CINEMA
STARTS TODAY
MANHATTAN
BRONX
QUEENS
NASSAU
SUFFOLK
WESTCHESTER
NEW JERSEY
BROOKLYN
STATEN ISLAND
ROCKLAND
CONNECTICUT
UPSTATE

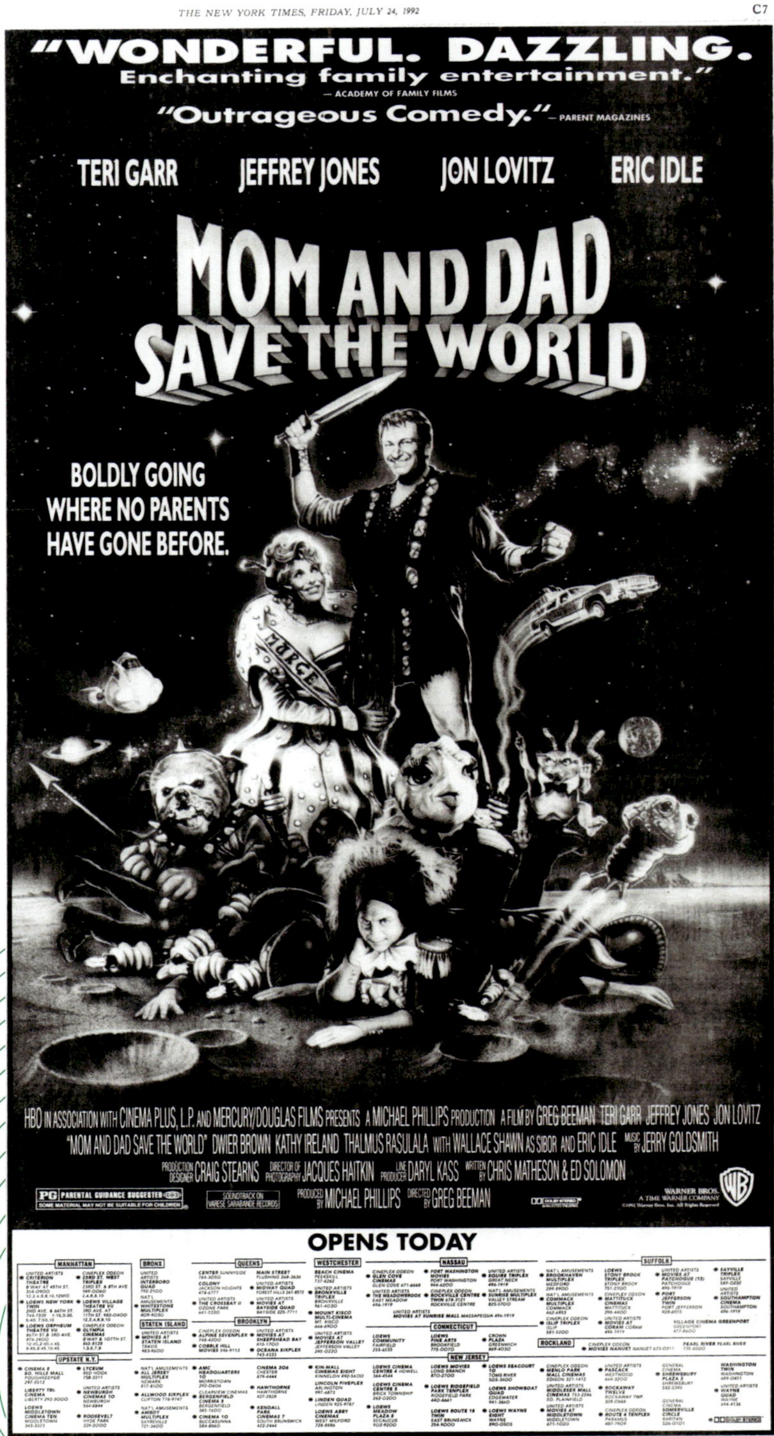

MOM AND DAD SAVE THE WORLD

Warner Bros. apparently had trouble figuring out what to call this kids-oriented sci-fi comedy, flipflopping between *Mom and Dad Save the World* and *Dick and Marge Save the World.* (Based on a couple of online accounts, the movie appears to have had theatrical test runs under the latter title.) They finally settled on *Mom and Dad*...but the box office wound up being so bad, it's unlikely any title change could have saved it.

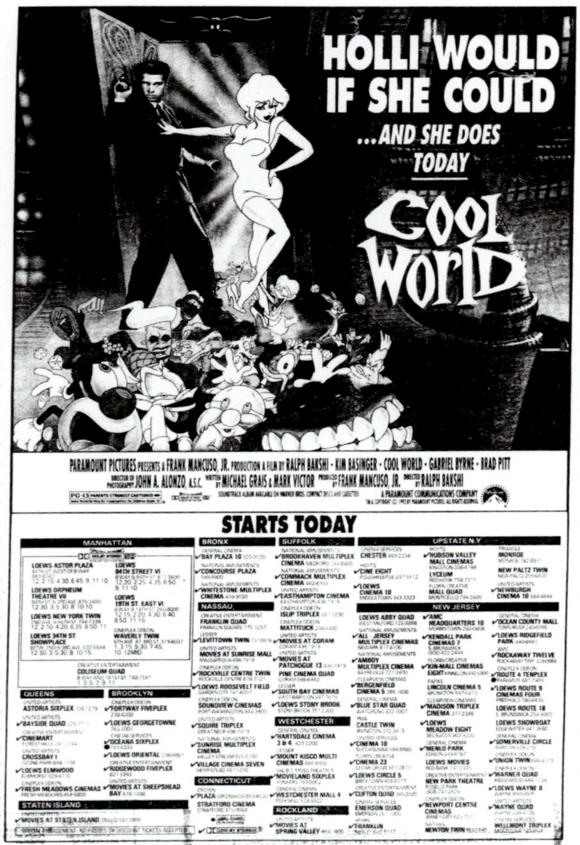

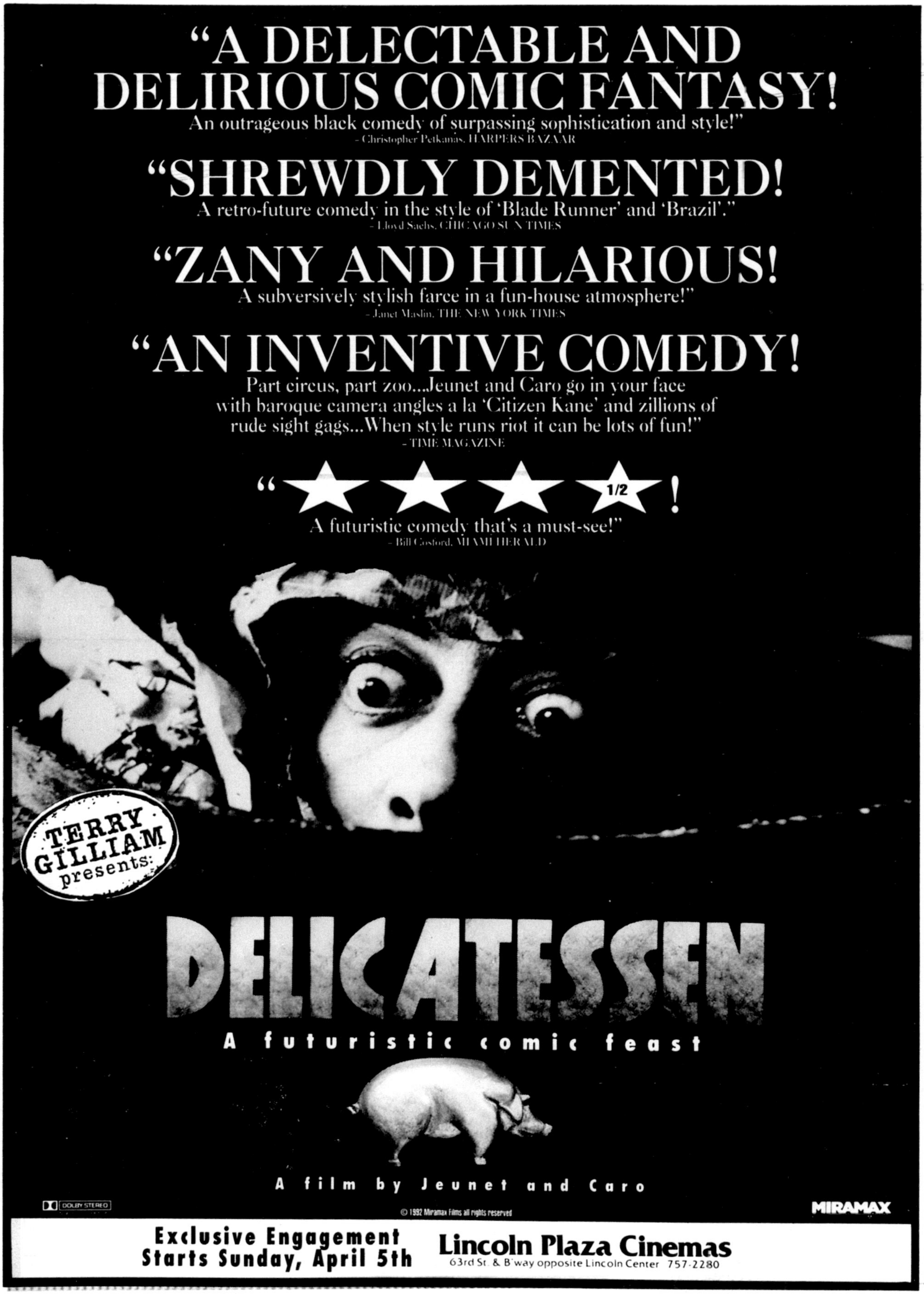

"A DELECTABLE AND DELIRIOUS COMIC FANTASY!
An outrageous black comedy of surpassing sophistication and style!"
- Christopher Petkanas, HARPERS BAZAAR
"SHREWDLY DEMENTED!
A retro-future comedy in the style of 'Blade Runner' and 'Brazil'."
- Lloyd Sachs, CHICAGO SUN TIMES
"ZANY AND HILARIOUS!
A subversively stylish farce in a fun-house atmosphere!"
- Janet Maslin, THE NEW YORK TIMES
"AN INVENTIVE COMEDY!
Part circus, part zoo...Jeunet and Caro go in your face with baroque camera angles a la 'Citizen Kane' and zillions of rude sight gags...When style runs riot it can be lots of fun!"
- TIME MAGAZINE
"★★★★1/2!
A futuristic comedy that's a must-see!"
- Bill Cosford, MIAMI HERALD
TERRY GILLIAM presents:
DELICATESSEN
A futuristic comic feast
A film by Jeunet and Caro
DOLBY STEREO
© 1992 Miramax Films all rights reserved
MIRAMAX
Exclusive Engagement
Starts Sunday, April 5th
Lincoln Plaza Cinemas
63rd St. & B'way opposite Lincoln Center 757-2280

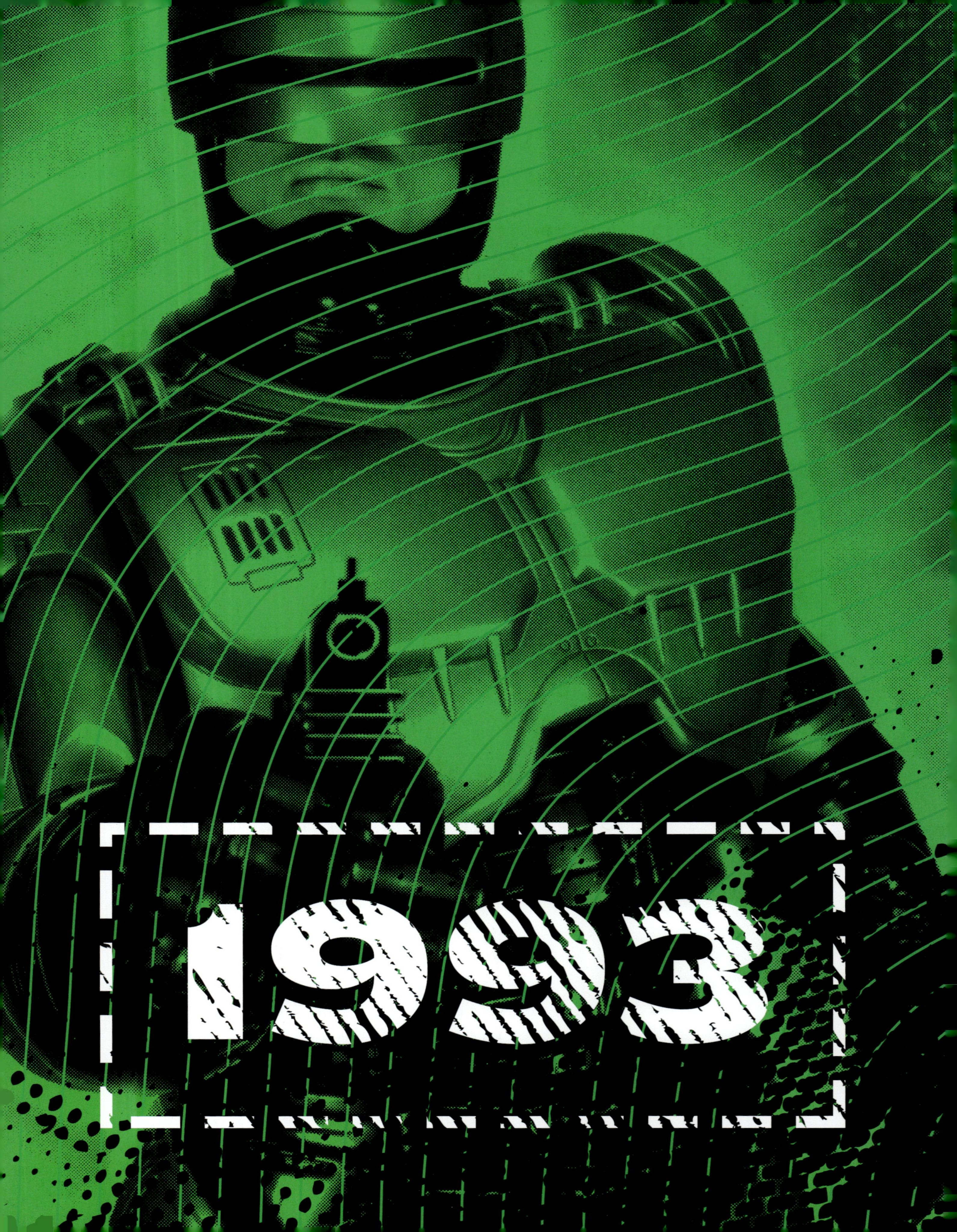
1993

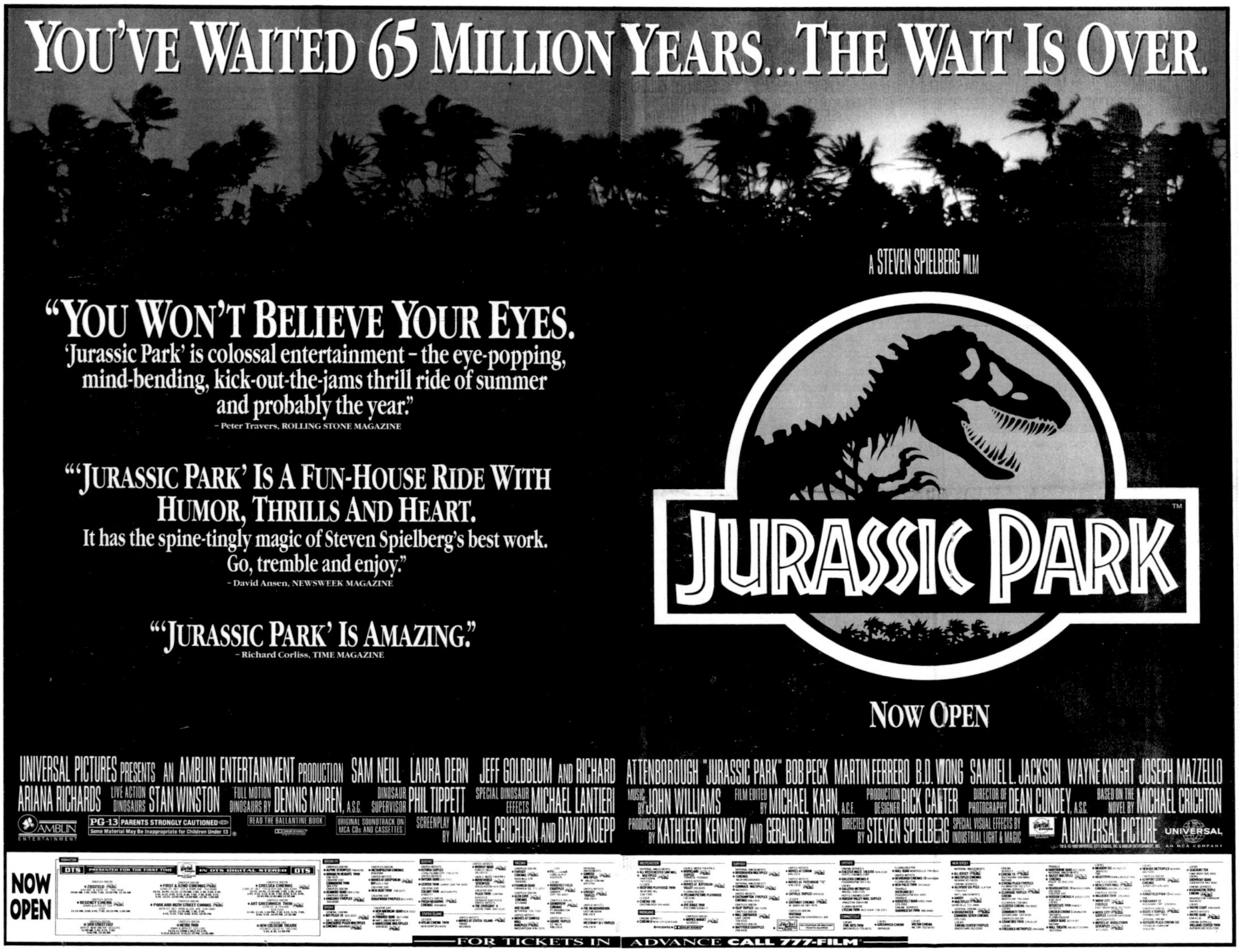
YOU'VE WAITED 65 MILLION YEARS...THE WAIT IS OVER.
A STEVEN SPIELBERG FILM
"YOU WON'T BELIEVE YOUR EYES.
'Jurassic Park' is colossal entertainment – the eye-popping, mind-bending, kick-out-the-jams thrill ride of summer and probably the year."
– Peter Travers, ROLLING STONE MAGAZINE
"'JURASSIC PARK' IS A FUN-HOUSE RIDE WITH HUMOR, THRILLS AND HEART.
It has the spine-tingly magic of Steven Spielberg's best work. Go, tremble and enjoy."
– David Ansen, NEWSWEEK MAGAZINE
"'JURASSIC PARK' IS AMAZING."
– Richard Corliss, TIME MAGAZINE
JURASSIC PARK
NOW OPEN
UNIVERSAL PICTURES PRESENTS AN AMBLIN ENTERTAINMENT PRODUCTION SAM NEILL LAURA DERN JEFF GOLDBLUM AND RICHARD ATTENBOROUGH "JURASSIC PARK" BOB PECK MARTIN FERRERO B.D. WONG SAMUEL L. JACKSON WAYNE KNIGHT JOSEPH MAZZELLO ARIANA RICHARDS LIVE ACTION DINOSAURS STAN WINSTON FULL MOTION DINOSAURS BY DENNIS MUREN, A.S.C. DINOSAUR SUPERVISOR PHIL TIPPETT SPECIAL DINOSAUR EFFECTS MICHAEL LANTIERI MUSIC BY JOHN WILLIAMS FILM EDITED BY MICHAEL KAHN, A.C.E. PRODUCTION DESIGNER RICK CARTER DIRECTOR OF PHOTOGRAPHY DEAN CUNDEY, A.S.C. BASED ON THE NOVEL BY MICHAEL CRICHTON
SCREENPLAY BY MICHAEL CRICHTON AND DAVID KOEPP PRODUCED BY KATHLEEN KENNEDY AND GERALD R. MOLEN DIRECTED BY STEVEN SPIELBERG SPECIAL VISUAL EFFECTS BY INDUSTRIAL LIGHT & MAGIC A UNIVERSAL PICTURE
AMBLIN ENTERTAINMENT
PG-13 PARENTS STRONGLY CAUTIONED
Some Material May Be Inappropriate for Children Under 13
READ THE BALLANTINE BOOK
ORIGINAL SOUNDTRACK ON MCA CDs AND CASSETTES
UNIVERSAL
NOW OPEN
FOR TICKETS IN ADVANCE CALL 777-FILM

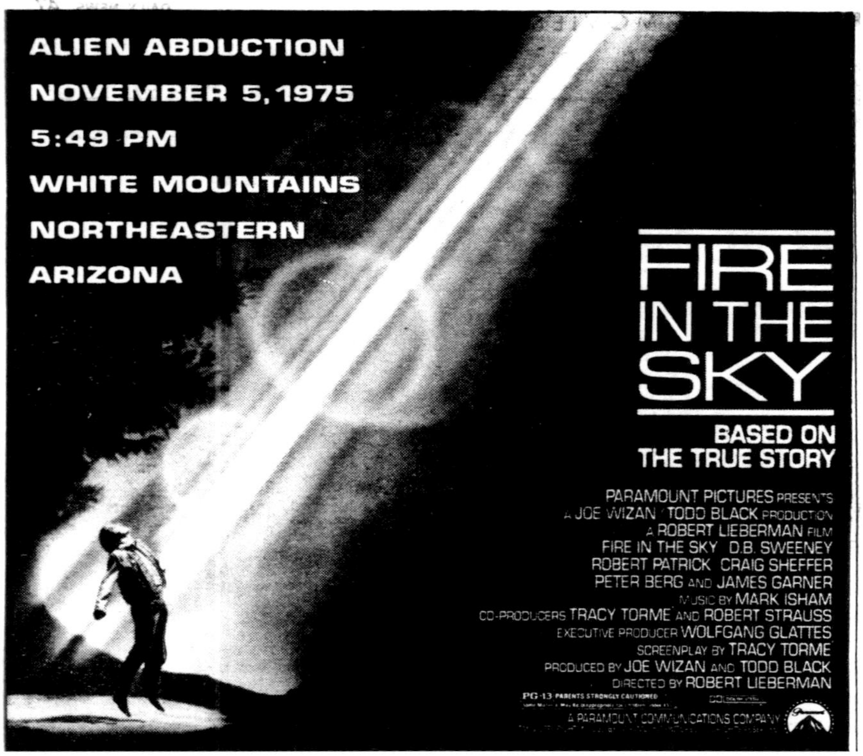
ALIEN ABDUCTION
NOVEMBER 5, 1975
5:49 PM
WHITE MOUNTAINS
NORTHEASTERN
ARIZONA
FIRE IN THE SKY
BASED ON THE TRUE STORY
PARAMOUNT PICTURES PRESENTS
A JOE WIZAN / TODD BLACK PRODUCTION
A ROBERT LIEBERMAN FILM
FIRE IN THE SKY D.B. SWEENEY
ROBERT PATRICK CRAIG SHEFFER
PETER BERG AND JAMES GARNER
MUSIC BY MARK ISHAM
CO-PRODUCERS TRACY TORME AND ROBERT STRAUSS
EXECUTIVE PRODUCER WOLFGANG GLATTES
SCREENPLAY BY TRACY TORME
PRODUCED BY JOE WIZAN AND TODD BLACK
DIRECTED BY ROBERT LIEBERMAN
PG-13 PARENTS STRONGLY CAUTIONED
A PARAMOUNT COMMUNICATIONS COMPANY

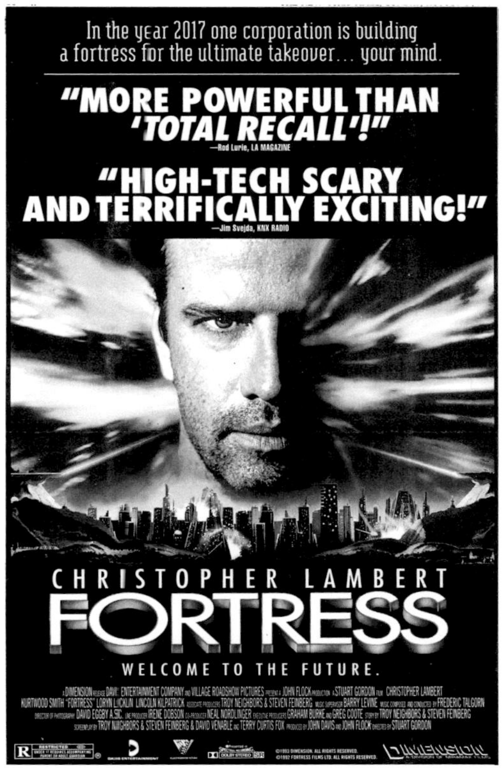
In the year 2017 one corporation is building a fortress for the ultimate takeover... your mind.
"MORE POWERFUL THAN 'TOTAL RECALL'!"
—Rod Lurie, LA MAGAZINE
"HIGH-TECH SCARY AND TERRIFICALLY EXCITING!"
—Jim Svejda, KNX RADIO
CHRISTOPHER LAMBERT
FORTRESS
WELCOME TO THE FUTURE.
DIMENSION

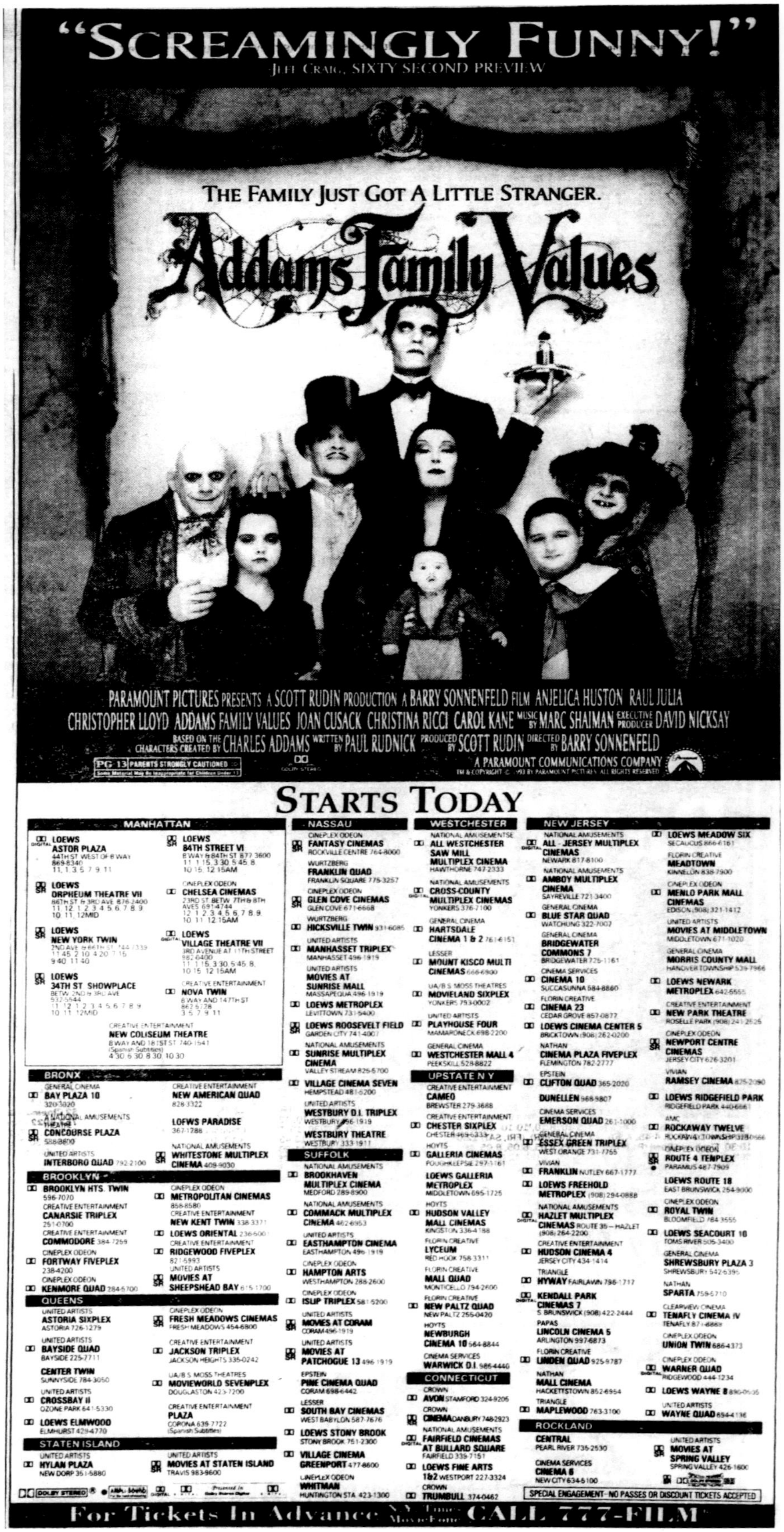

"SCREAMINGLY FUNNY!"
JEFF CRAIG, SIXTY SECOND PREVIEW
THE FAMILY JUST GOT A LITTLE STRANGER.
Addams Family Values
PARAMOUNT PICTURES PRESENTS A SCOTT RUDIN PRODUCTION A BARRY SONNENFELD FILM ANJELICA HUSTON RAUL JULIA
CHRISTOPHER LLOYD ADDAMS FAMILY VALUES JOAN CUSACK CHRISTINA RICCI CAROL KANE MUSIC BY MARC SHAIMAN EXECUTIVE PRODUCER DAVID NICKSAY
BASED ON THE CHARACTERS CREATED BY CHARLES ADDAMS WRITTEN BY PAUL RUDNICK PRODUCED BY SCOTT RUDIN DIRECTED BY BARRY SONNENFELD
PG-13 PARENTS STRONGLY CAUTIONED
A PARAMOUNT COMMUNICATIONS COMPANY
STARTS TODAY
MANHATTAN
NASSAU
WESTCHESTER
NEW JERSEY
BRONX
BROOKLYN
QUEENS
STATEN ISLAND
SUFFOLK
UPSTATE N.Y.
CONNECTICUT
ROCKLAND
SPECIAL ENGAGEMENT - NO PASSES OR DISCOUNT TICKETS ACCEPTED
For Tickets In Advance CALL 777-FILM

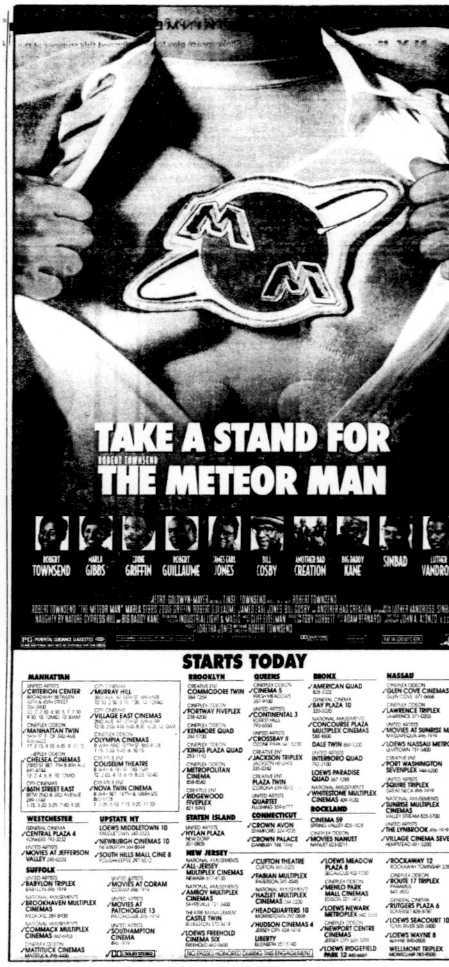

TAKE A STAND FOR
ROBERT TOWNSEND
THE METEOR MAN
ROBERT TOWNSEND
MARLA GIBBS
EDDIE GRIFFIN
ROBERT GUILLAUME
JAMES EARL JONES
BILL COSBY
ANOTHER BAD CREATION
BIG DADDY KANE
SINBAD
LUTHER VANDROSS
STARTS TODAY
MANHATTAN
BROOKLYN
QUEENS
BRONX
NASSAU
WESTCHESTER
UPSTATE NY
STATEN ISLAND
CONNECTICUT
ROCKLAND
SUFFOLK
NEW JERSEY

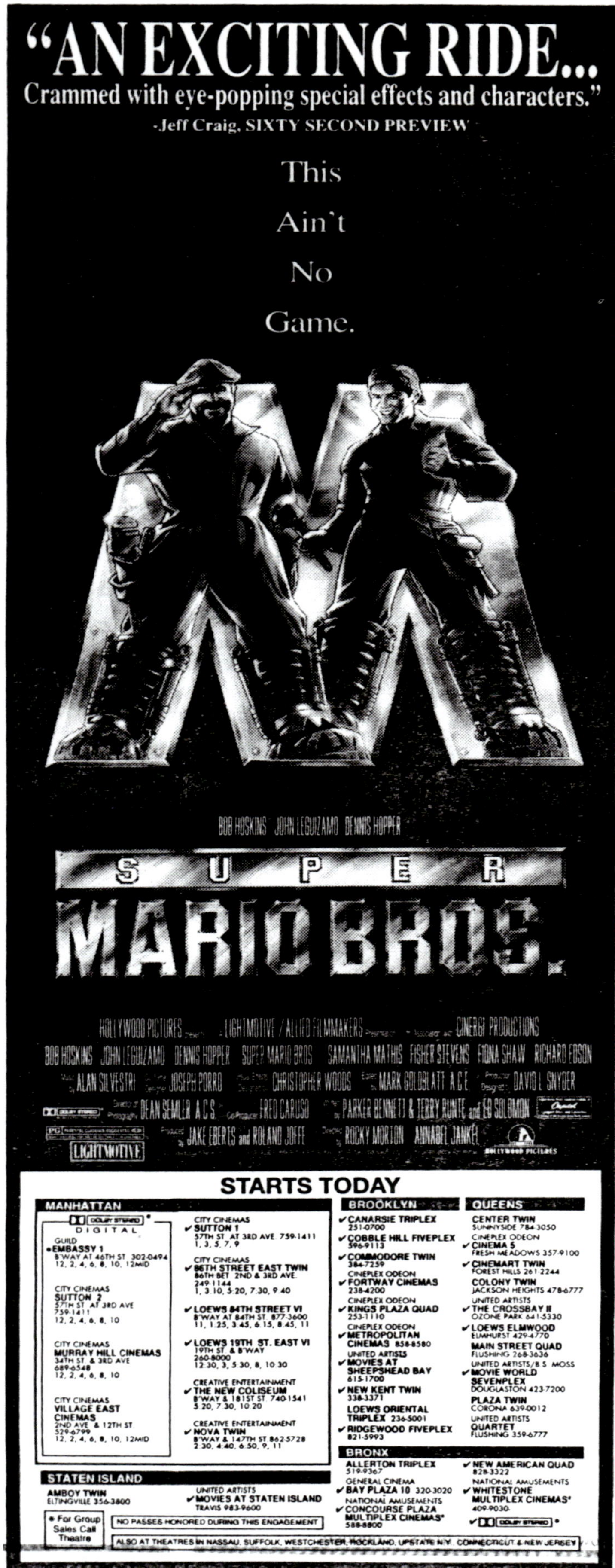
"AN EXCITING RIDE...
Crammed with eye-popping special effects and characters."
-Jeff Craig, SIXTY SECOND PREVIEW
This Ain't No Game.
BOB HOSKINS JOHN LEGUIZAMO DENNIS HOPPER
SUPER MARIO BROS.
HOLLYWOOD PICTURES presents LIGHTMOTIVE / ALLIED FILMMAKERS presentation CINERGI PRODUCTIONS
BOB HOSKINS JOHN LEGUIZAMO DENNIS HOPPER SUPER MARIO BROS SAMANTHA MATHIS FISHER STEVENS FIONA SHAW RICHARD EDSON
ALAN SILVESTRI JOSEPH PORRO CHRISTOPHER WOODS MARK GOLDBLATT A.C.E. DAVID L. SNYDER
DEAN SEMLER A.C.S. FRED CARUSO PARKER BENNETT & TERRY RUNTE and ED SOLOMON
JAKE EBERTS and ROLAND JOFFE ROCKY MORTON ANNABEL JANKEL
LIGHTMOTIVE
HOLLYWOOD PICTURES
STARTS TODAY
MANHATTAN
DOLBY STEREO DIGITAL
GUILD EMBASSY 1 B'WAY AT 46TH ST 302-0494 12, 2, 4, 6, 8, 10, 12MID
CITY CINEMAS SUTTON 2 57TH ST AT 3RD AVE 759-1411 12, 2, 4, 6, 8, 10
CITY CINEMAS MURRAY HILL CINEMAS 34TH ST & 3RD AVE 689-6548 12, 2, 4, 6, 8, 10
CITY CINEMAS VILLAGE EAST CINEMAS 2ND AVE & 12TH ST 529-6799 12, 2, 4, 6, 8, 10, 12MID
CITY CINEMAS SUTTON 1 57TH ST AT 3RD AVE 759-1411 1, 3, 5, 7, 9
CITY CINEMAS 86TH STREET EAST TWIN 86TH BET 2ND & 3RD AVE 249-1144 1, 3:10, 5:20, 7:30, 9:40
LOEWS 84TH STREET VI B'WAY AT 84TH ST 877-3600 11, 1:25, 3:45, 6:15, 8:45, 11
LOEWS 19TH ST. EAST VI 19TH ST & B'WAY 260-8000 12:30, 3, 5:30, 8, 10:30
CREATIVE ENTERTAINMENT THE NEW COLISEUM B'WAY & 181ST ST 740-1541 3:20, 7:30, 10:20
CREATIVE ENTERTAINMENT NOVA TWIN B'WAY & 147TH ST 862-5728 2:30, 4:40, 6:50, 9, 11
BROOKLYN
CANARSIE TRIPLEX 251-0700
COBBLE HILL FIVEPLEX 596-9113
COMMODORE TWIN 384-7259
CINEPLEX ODEON FORTWAY CINEMAS 238-4200
CINEPLEX ODEON KINGS PLAZA QUAD 253-1110
CINEPLEX ODEON METROPOLITAN CINEMAS 858-8580
UNITED ARTISTS MOVIES AT SHEEPSHEAD BAY 615-1700
NEW KENT TWIN 338-3371
LOEWS ORIENTAL TRIPLEX 236-5001
RIDGEWOOD FIVEPLEX 821-5993
QUEENS
CENTER TWIN SUNNYSIDE 784-3050
CINEPLEX ODEON CINEMA 5 FRESH MEADOWS 357-9100
CINEMART TWIN FOREST HILLS 261-2244
COLONY TWIN JACKSON HEIGHTS 478-6777
UNITED ARTISTS THE CROSSBAY II OZONE PARK 641-5330
LOEWS ELMWOOD ELMHURST 429-4770
MAIN STREET QUAD FLUSHING 268-3636
UNITED ARTISTS/B.S. MOSS MOVIE WORLD SEVENPLEX DOUGLASTON 423-7200
PLAZA TWIN CORONA 639-0012
UNITED ARTISTS QUARTET FLUSHING 359-6777
BRONX
ALLERTON TRIPLEX 519-9367
GENERAL CINEMA BAY PLAZA 10 320-3020
NATIONAL AMUSEMENTS CONCOURSE PLAZA MULTIPLEX CINEMAS* 588-8800
NEW AMERICAN QUAD 828-3322
NATIONAL AMUSEMENTS WHITESTONE MULTIPLEX CINEMAS* 409-9030
DOLBY STEREO
STATEN ISLAND
AMBOY TWIN ELTINGVILLE 356-3800
UNITED ARTISTS MOVIES AT STATEN ISLAND TRAVIS 983-9600
* For Group Sales Call Theatre
NO PASSES HONORED DURING THIS ENGAGEMENT
ALSO AT THEATRES IN NASSAU, SUFFOLK, WESTCHESTER, ROCKLAND, UPSTATE N.Y., CONNECTICUT & NEW JERSEY

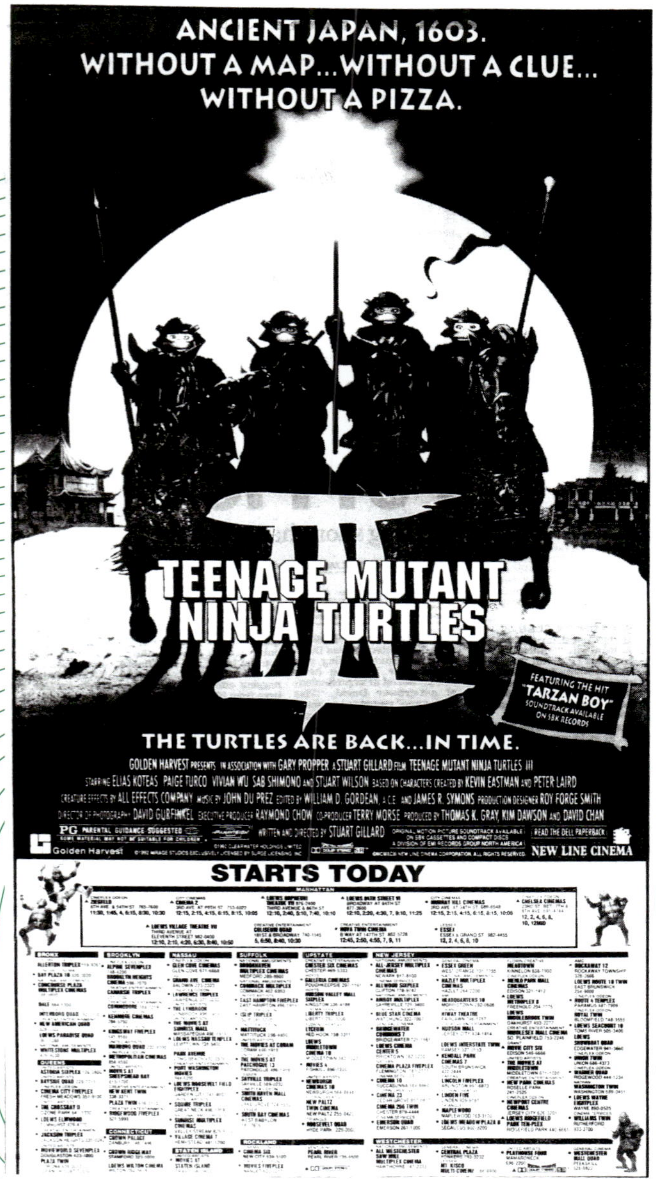
ANCIENT JAPAN, 1603.
WITHOUT A MAP...WITHOUT A CLUE...
WITHOUT A PIZZA.
TEENAGE MUTANT NINJA TURTLES III
FEATURING THE HIT "TARZAN BOY" SOUNDTRACK AVAILABLE ON SBK RECORDS
THE TURTLES ARE BACK...IN TIME.
GOLDEN HARVEST PRESENTS IN ASSOCIATION WITH GARY PROPPER A STUART GILLARD FILM TEENAGE MUTANT NINJA TURTLES III
STARRING ELIAS KOTEAS PAIGE TURCO VIVIAN WU SAB SHIMONO AND STUART WILSON BASED ON CHARACTERS CREATED BY KEVIN EASTMAN AND PETER LAIRD
CREATURE EFFECTS BY ALL EFFECTS COMPANY MUSIC BY JOHN DU PREZ EDITED BY WILLIAM D. GORDEAN, A.C.E. AND JAMES R. SYMONS PRODUCTION DESIGNER ROY FORGE SMITH
DIRECTOR OF PHOTOGRAPHY DAVID GURFINKEL EXECUTIVE PRODUCER RAYMOND CHOW CO-PRODUCER TERRY MORSE PRODUCED BY THOMAS K. GRAY, KIM DAWSON AND DAVID CHAN
PG PARENTAL GUIDANCE SUGGESTED
WRITTEN AND DIRECTED BY STUART GILLARD
READ THE DELL PAPERBACK
Golden Harvest
NEW LINE CINEMA
STARTS TODAY
MANHATTAN
BRONX
BROOKLYN
NASSAU
SUFFOLK
UPSTATE
NEW JERSEY
QUEENS
CONNECTICUT
ROCKLAND
STATEN ISLAND
WESTCHESTER

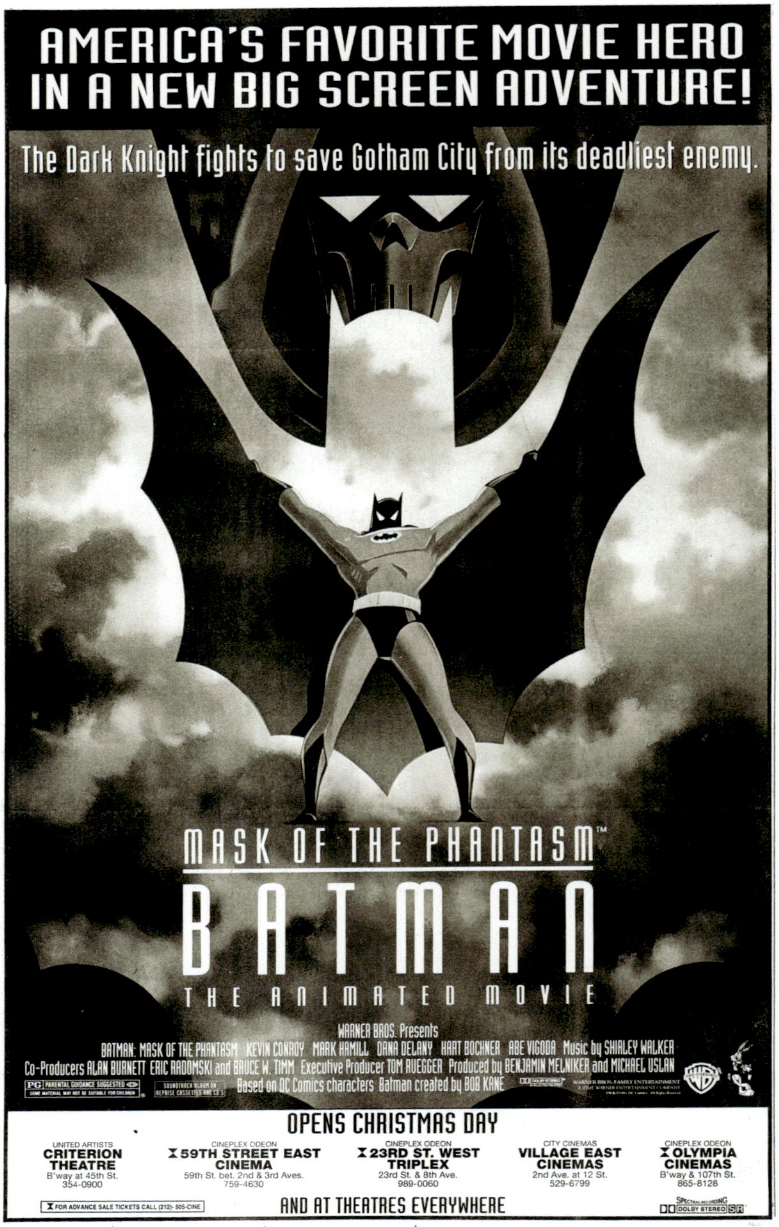

DEMOLITION MAN

No doubt due to the popularity of Arnold Schwarzenegger's *Terminator* films and *Total Recall*, studio sci-fi in the first half of the 1990s shifted from *Star Wars*-esque space opera to heavier action-oriented fare featuring the likes of Sylvester Stallone. This was one of the more entertaining entries, thanks to rewrites by Daniel Waters (*Heathers*, *Batman Returns*) that brought a satirical edge to the saga of a brutish 20th-century cop (Stallone) released from a cryogenic prison in 2032 to capture his similarly unfrozen nemesis (Wesley Snipes). Some reviewers appreciated the film's more humorous bent, while for others it was business as usual.

"Stallone tosses every line away with an ironic shrug, not taking himself or any of the nonsense seriously. And Snipes wisely follows suit, though at a markedly higher, crazier level of energy."

–Hal Hinson, *The Washington Post*

"The script is fueled by genuine wit, everyone turns in fine performances and, beginning to end, the film actually shows some thought, if little originality. Let's not get carried away here: we're saying that for a soulless, unimaginative film that must have cost $50 million to make, *Demolition Man*, if you don't really think about it, isn't a bad ride."

–Louis Black, *The Austin Chronicle*

"Clearly undecided about whether to be a loud movie or a dopey movie, *Demolition Man*...has ended up being both a loud movie and a dopey movie, a resolution that does not give the art of compromise a very good name."

–KENNETH TURAN, *LOS ANGELES TIMES*

"So this is a science-fiction film? Not quite, for good sci-fi involves believable science and plausible fiction. *Demolition Man* offers merely a future fantasy, whose cartoon outlines seem highly unlikely."

–Steve McKerrow, *The Baltimore Sun*

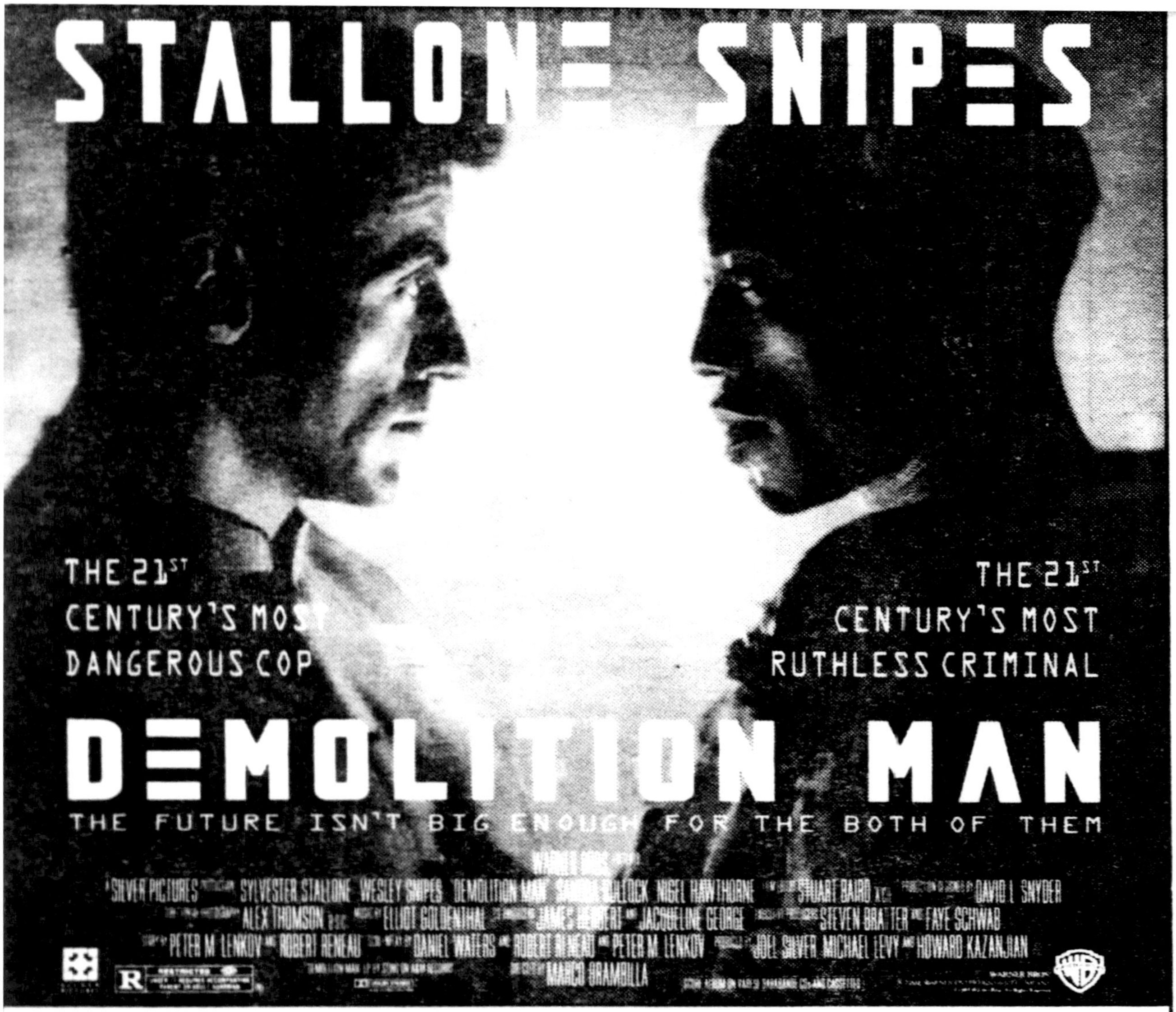

OPENS TODAY

MANHATTAN

UNITED ARTISTS
◆ **CRITERION THEATRE**
B'WAY AT 45TH ST
354-0900

△ **LOEWS 84TH STREET VI**
BROADWAY & 84TH ST

△ **LOEWS ORPHEUM THEATRE VII**
86TH ST & 3RD AVE
876-2400

CINEPLEX ODEON
I **FIRST & 62ND CINEMAS**
62ND ST BET 1ST & YORK AVE
752-4600

△ **LOEWS 34TH ST. SHOWPLACE**
34TH ST BET 2ND & 3RD AVES

CINEPLEX ODEON
I **CHELSEA CINEMAS**
23RD ST BET 7TH & 8TH AVES

◆ △ **LOEWS VILLAGE THEATRE VII**
3RD AVE AT 11TH ST

✱ **ESSEX**
GRAND ST AT ESSEX
982-4455

✱ **NEW COLISEUM THEATRE**
701 WEST 181ST ST
740-1541

✱ **NOVA TWIN CINEMA**
3589 B'WAY

FOR ADVANCE SALE TICKETS CALL
△ (212)-59-LOEWS I (212)-505-CINE

BRONX

AMERICAN QUAD
828-3322

GENERAL CINEMA
✱ **BAY PLAZA 10**
320-3020

NAT'L AMUSEMENTS
✱ **CONCOURSE PLAZA MULTIPLEX CINEMAS**
588-8800

UNITED ARTISTS
INTERBORO QUAD
792-2100

LOEWS PARADISE QUAD
367-1288

NAT'L AMUSEMENTS
✱ **WHITESTONE MULTIPLEX**
409-9030

BROOKLYN

BROOKLYN HEIGHTS 596-7070

CANARSIE TRIPLEX
251-0700

COMMODORE
384-7259

CINEPLEX ODEON
✱ **FORTWAY FIVEPLEX** 238-4200

CINEPLEX ODEON
KENMORE QUAD
284-5700

CINEPLEX ODEON
✱ **KINGS PLAZA QUAD** 253-1110

UNITED ARTISTS
MARBORO QUAD
232-4000

CINEPLEX ODEON
✱ **METROPOLITAN CINEMAS**
858-8580

UNITED ARTISTS
✱ **MOVIES AT SHEEPSHEAD BAY**
615-1700

NEW KENT CINEMA 338-3371

RIDGEWOOD FIVEPLEX 821-5993

QUEENS

CINEPLEX ODEON
✱ **CINEMA CITY**
FRESH MEADOWS
357-9100

UNITED ARTISTS
✱ **CROSSBAY TRIPLEX**
OZONE PARK
848-1738

JACKSON TRIPLEX
JACKSON HEIGHTS
335-0242

✱ **MAIN STREET**
FLUSHING
268-3636

UNITED ARTISTS
✱ **MIDWAY QUAD**
FOREST HILLS
261-8572

UNITED ARTISTS
MOVIEWORLD
DOUGLASTON
423-7200

PLAZA
CORONA 639-0012
(Spanish Subtitles)

✱ **SURFSIDE TWIN**
ROCKAWAY PK
945-4632

STATEN ISLAND

UNITED ARTISTS
✱ **HYLAN PLAZA**
NEW DORP
351-0805

UNITED ARTISTS
✱ **MOVIES AT STATEN ISLAND**
TRAVIS
983-9600

WESTCHESTER

NAT'L AMUSEMENTS
✱ **ALL-WESTCHESTER SAW MILL MULTIPLEX**
HAWTHORNE
747-2333

✱ **BEACH CINEMA**
PEEKSKILL
737-6262

GENERAL CINEMA
✱ **HARTSDALE 3 & 4**
HARTSDALE
428-2200

UNITED ARTISTS
✱ **MOVIELAND**
YONKERS
793-0002

UNITED ARTISTS
✱ **MOVIES AT JEFFERSON VALLEY**
JEFFERSON VALLEY
245-0220

UNITED ARTISTS
✱ **PLAYHOUSE FOUR**
MAMARONECK
698-2200

ROCKLAND

UNITED ARTISTS
✱ **CINEMA 304 TWIN**
NEW CITY
634-8200

CINEPLEX ODEON
✱ **MOVIES NANUET**
NANUET
623-0211

NASSAU

CINEPLEX ODEON
✱ **GLEN COVE CINEMAS**
GLEN COVE 671-6668

✱ **HERRICKS TWIN**
NEW HYDE PARK
747-0555

✱ **LOEWS NASSAU SIX**
LEVITTOWN
731-5400

✱ **LOEWS ROOSEVELT FIELD EIGHTPLEX**
GARDEN CITY
741-4007

UNITED ARTISTS
MOVIES AT SUNRISE MALL
MASSAPEQUA
496-1919

✱ **PORT WASHINGTON MOVIES**
PORT WASHINGTON
944-6200

CINEPLEX ODEON
✱ **ROCKVILLE CENTRE TWIN**
ROCKVILLE CENTRE
678-3121

UNITED ARTISTS
✱ **SQUIRE TRIPLEX**
GREAT NECK
496-1919

NAT'L AMUSEMENTS
✱ **SUNRISE MULTIPLEX**
VALLEY STREAM
825-5700

UNITED ARTISTS
✱ **THE SYOSSET**
WOODBURY 496-1919

VILLAGE CINEMA SEVEN
HEMPSTEAD
481-5200

UNITED ARTISTS
WESTBURY TRIPLEX D/I
WESTBURY 496-1919

SUFFOLK

NAT'L AMUSEMENTS
✱ **BROOKHAVEN MULTIPLEX**
MEDFORD
289-8900

NAT'L AMUSEMENTS
✱ **COMMACK MULTIPLEX**
COMMACK
462-6953

✱ **LOEWS SOUTH SHORE MALL TWIN**
BAYSHORE
666-4000

CINEPLEX ODEON
✱ **MATTITUCK CINEMAS**
MATTITUCK
298-4400

UNITED ARTISTS
✱ **MOVIES AT CORAM**
CORAM
496-1919

UNITED ARTISTS
✱ **MOVIES AT PATCHOGUE (13)**
PATCHOGUE
496-1919

UNITED ARTISTS
✱ **SOUTHAMPTON CINEMA**
SOUTHAMPTON
496-1919

VILLAGE CINEMA GREENPORT
GREENPORT
477-8600

CINEPLEX ODEON
WHITMAN
HUNTINGTON STATION
423-1300

CONNECTICUT

CROWN
✱ **CINEMA**
STAMFORD 324-3100

LOEWS CINEMA NORWALK 1 & 2
NORWALK 838-4504

CROWN
✱ **PALACE** DANBURY
748-7496

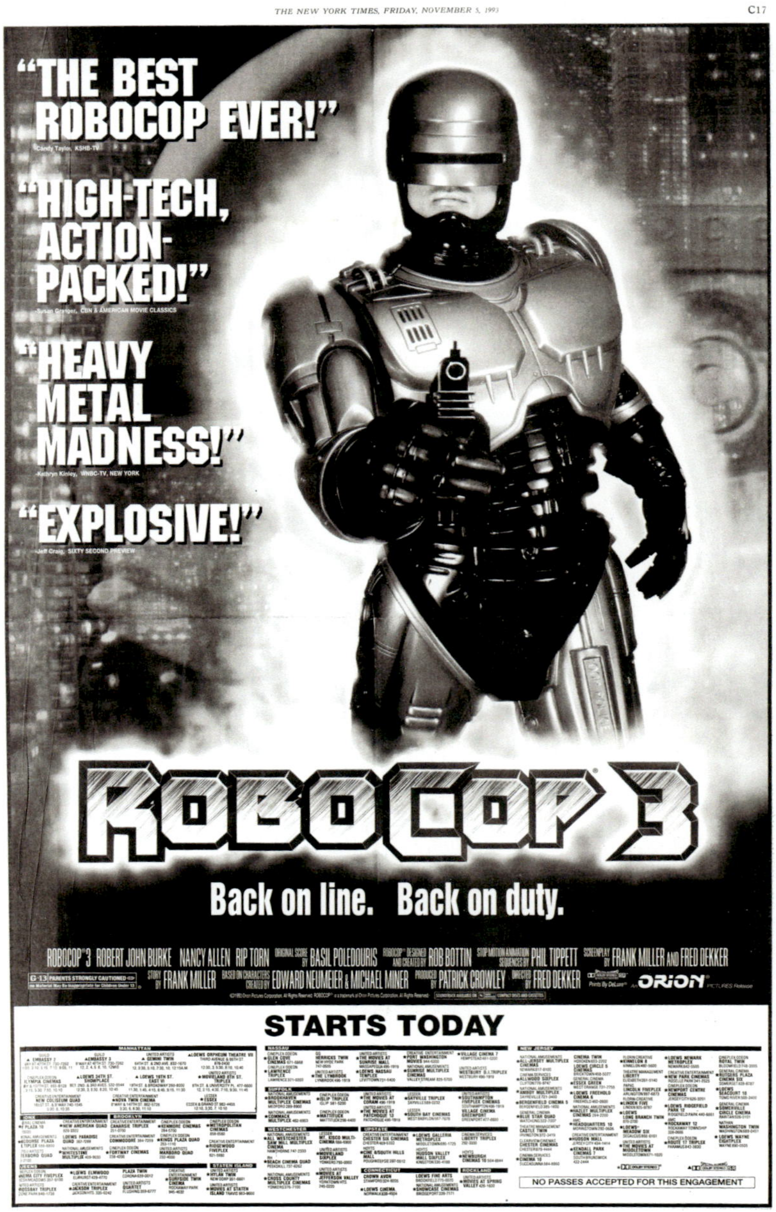

HOCUS POCUS

When Disney opened this youth-oriented comedy about Salem sorceresses reviving in the present day, a group of self-proclaimed witches protested, denouncing it as a "silly witch movie" that perpetuated negative stereotypes about their kind. They weren't the only ones who looked down on the film; critics largely sneered. Today, however, *Hocus Pocus* is beloved by a generation who enjoyed it as kids.

"All three actresses, most especially [Bette] Midler, clearly had a fine time as the sisters of Satan. ... But though children may be satisfied (if the witch stuff doesn't scare them), adults will have a harder time with the by-the-numbers confrontations between the witches and the plucky youths."

–Kenneth Turan, *Los Angeles Times*

"*Hocus Pocus* is harmless, but it's about as much fun as celebrating Mardi Gras under the influence of candy corn."

–Johanna Steinmetz, *Chicago Tribune*

"All things considered, *Hocus Pocus* is much more entertaining than a pimple-people picture has a right to be. In addition to the delightful witches and the delightful Thora Birch, the film's bag of tricks and treats also includes a cat that – thanks to the magic of computer graphics – really seems to talk."

–Jay Boyar, *Orlando Sentinel*

"Of the film's many problems, the greatest may be that all three witches are thoroughly unpleasant. They don't have personalities; they have behavior patterns and decibel levels."

–ROGER EBERT, *CHICAGO SUN-TIMES*

"The movie begins with its foot in the bucket and never gets out. I mean, it is somewhat difficult to do a frothy musical parody when the first scene depicts the comical murder of a darling little girl whose 'life vapors' are sucked out of her by a trio of third-rate actresses."

–Stephen Hunter, *The Baltimore Sun*

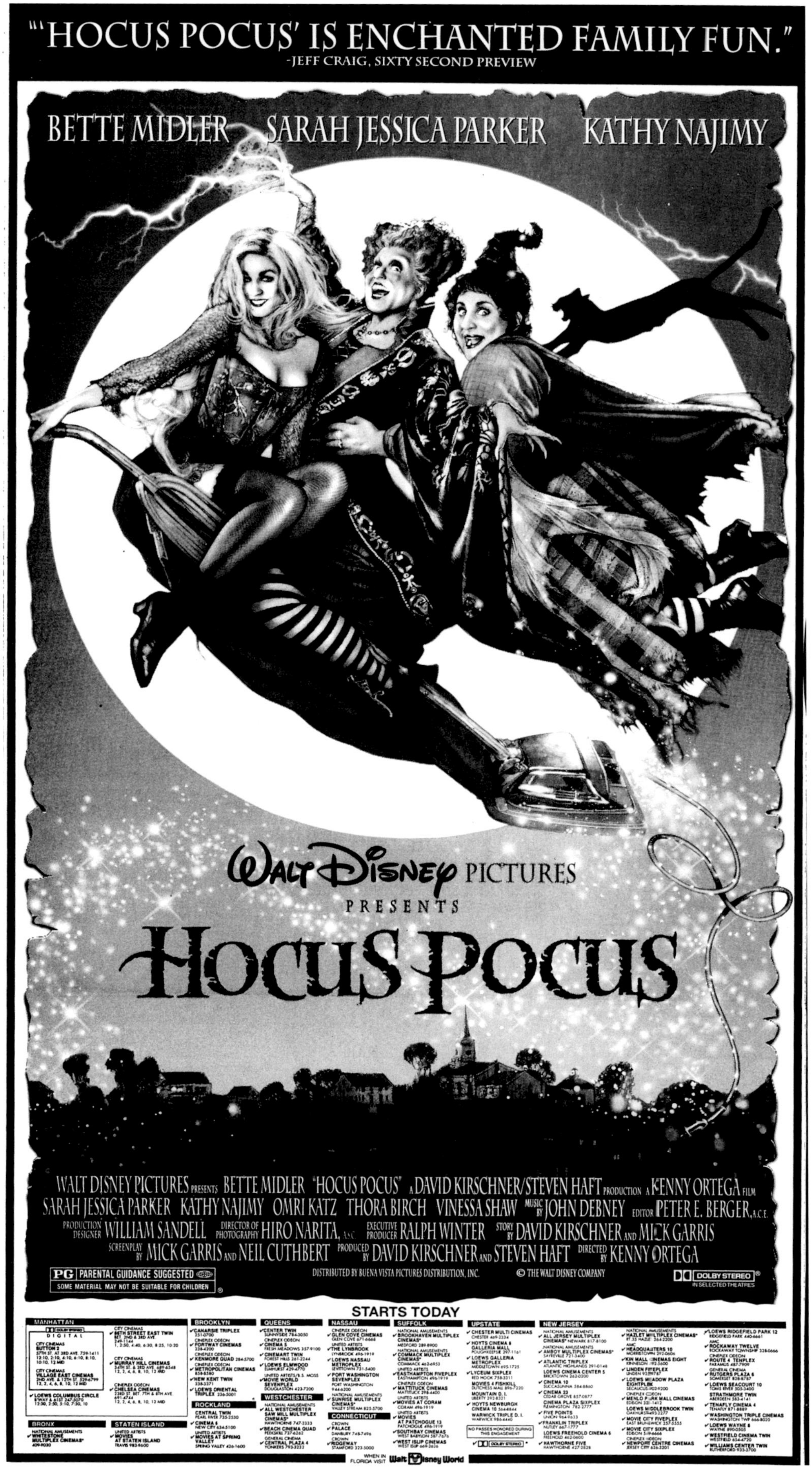

"'HOCUS POCUS' IS ENCHANTED FAMILY FUN."
-JEFF CRAIG, SIXTY SECOND PREVIEW
BETTE MIDLER SARAH JESSICA PARKER KATHY NAJIMY
WALT DISNEY PICTURES
PRESENTS
HOCUS POCUS
WALT DISNEY PICTURES PRESENTS BETTE MIDLER "HOCUS POCUS" A DAVID KIRSCHNER/STEVEN HAFT PRODUCTION A KENNY ORTEGA FILM
SARAH JESSICA PARKER KATHY NAJIMY OMRI KATZ THORA BIRCH VINESSA SHAW MUSIC BY JOHN DEBNEY EDITOR PETER E. BERGER, A.C.E.
PRODUCTION DESIGNER WILLIAM SANDELL DIRECTOR OF PHOTOGRAPHY HIRO NARITA, A.S.C. EXECUTIVE PRODUCER RALPH WINTER STORY BY DAVID KIRSCHNER AND MICK GARRIS
SCREENPLAY BY MICK GARRIS AND NEIL CUTHBERT PRODUCED BY DAVID KIRSCHNER AND STEVEN HAFT DIRECTED BY KENNY ORTEGA
PG PARENTAL GUIDANCE SUGGESTED
SOME MATERIAL MAY NOT BE SUITABLE FOR CHILDREN
DISTRIBUTED BY BUENA VISTA PICTURES DISTRIBUTION, INC.
© THE WALT DISNEY COMPANY
DOLBY STEREO
IN SELECTED THEATRES
STARTS TODAY
MANHATTAN
BROOKLYN
QUEENS
NASSAU
SUFFOLK
UPSTATE
NEW JERSEY
WESTCHESTER
ROCKLAND
CONNECTICUT
BRONX
STATEN ISLAND
NO PASSES HONORED DURING THIS ENGAGEMENT
WHEN IN FLORIDA VISIT Walt Disney World

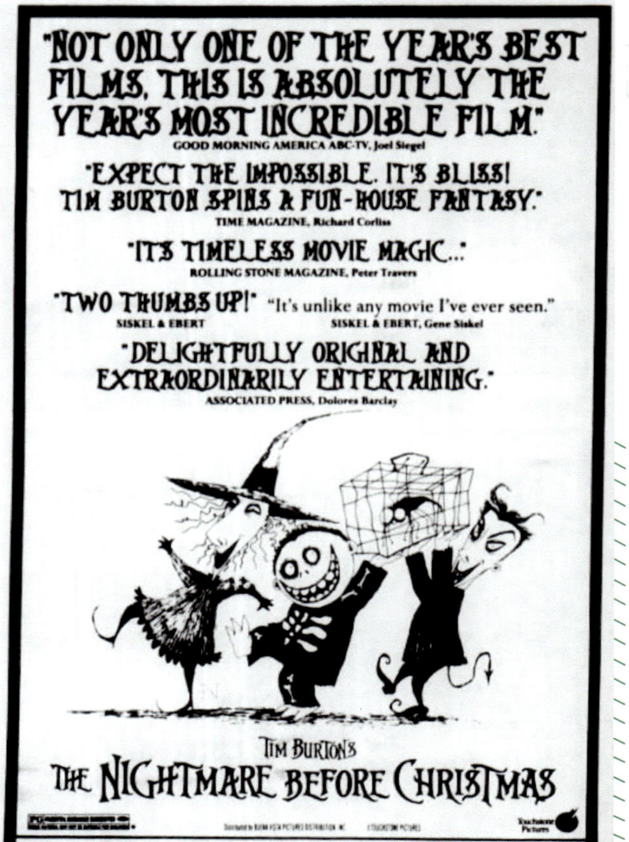
"NOT ONLY ONE OF THE YEAR'S BEST FILMS, THIS IS ABSOLUTELY THE YEAR'S MOST INCREDIBLE FILM."
GOOD MORNING AMERICA ABC-TV, Joel Siegel
"EXPECT THE IMPOSSIBLE. IT'S BLISS! TIM BURTON SPINS A FUN-HOUSE FANTASY."
TIME MAGAZINE, Richard Corliss
"IT'S TIMELESS MOVIE MAGIC..."
ROLLING STONE MAGAZINE, Peter Travers
"TWO THUMBS UP!"
SISKEL & EBERT
"It's unlike any movie I've ever seen."
SISKEL & EBERT, Gene Siskel
"DELIGHTFULLY ORIGINAL AND EXTRAORDINARILY ENTERTAINING."
ASSOCIATED PRESS, Dolores Barclay
TIM BURTON'S
THE NIGHTMARE BEFORE CHRISTMAS
Touchstone Pictures

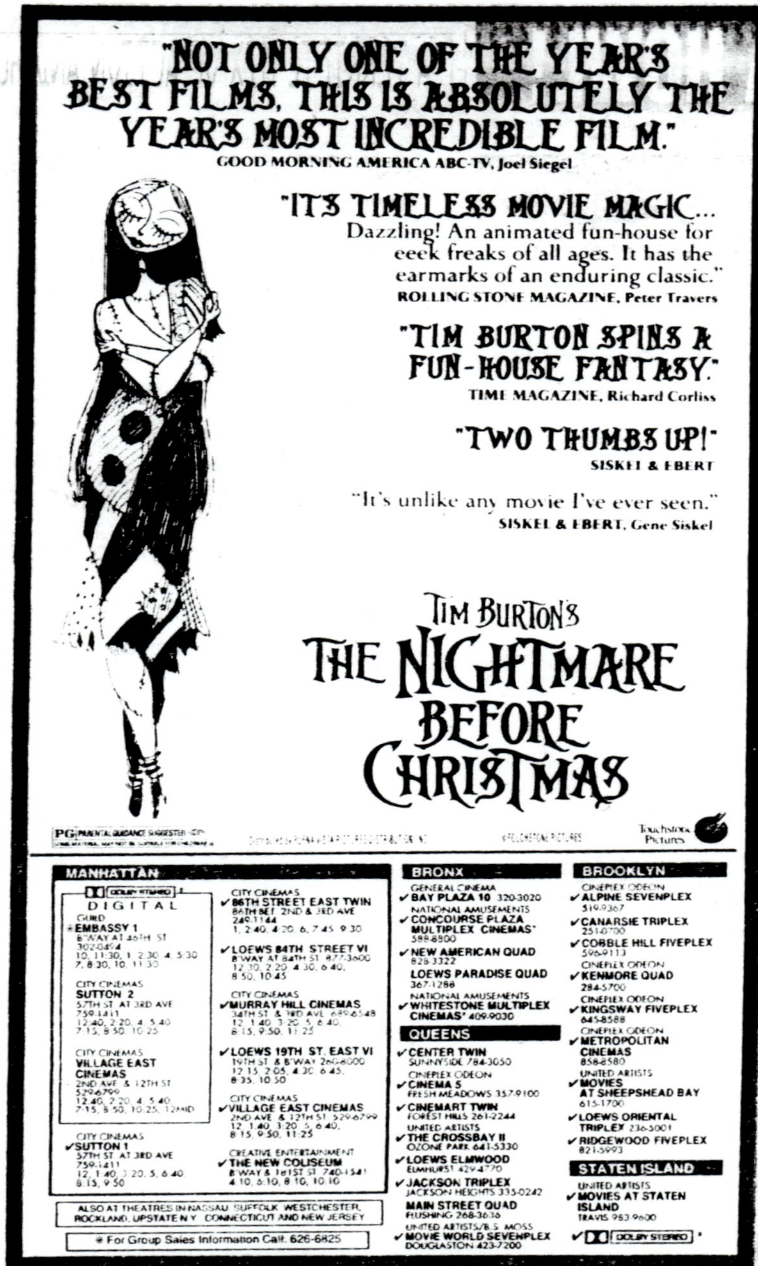
"NOT ONLY ONE OF THE YEAR'S BEST FILMS, THIS IS ABSOLUTELY THE YEAR'S MOST INCREDIBLE FILM."
GOOD MORNING AMERICA ABC-TV, Joel Siegel
"IT'S TIMELESS MOVIE MAGIC... Dazzling! An animated fun-house for eeek freaks of all ages. It has the earmarks of an enduring classic."
ROLLING STONE MAGAZINE, Peter Travers
"TIM BURTON SPINS A FUN-HOUSE FANTASY."
TIME MAGAZINE, Richard Corliss
"TWO THUMBS UP!"
SISKEL & EBERT
"It's unlike any movie I've ever seen."
SISKEL & EBERT, Gene Siskel
TIM BURTON'S
THE NIGHTMARE BEFORE CHRISTMAS
PG PARENTAL GUIDANCE SUGGESTED
Touchstone Pictures
MANHATTAN
DOLBY STEREO DIGITAL
GUILD
EMBASSY 1
B'WAY AT 46TH ST
302-0494
10, 11:30, 1, 2:30, 4, 5:30, 7, 8:30, 10, 11:30
CITY CINEMAS
SUTTON 2
57TH ST. AT 3RD AVE
759-1411
12:40, 2:20, 4, 5:40, 7:15, 8:50, 10:25
CITY CINEMAS
VILLAGE EAST CINEMAS
2ND AVE & 12TH ST
529-6799
12:40, 2:20, 4, 5:40, 7:15, 8:50, 10:25, 12MID
CITY CINEMAS
SUTTON 1
57TH ST. AT 3RD AVE
759-1411
12, 1:40, 3:20, 5, 6:40, 8:15, 9:50
CITY CINEMAS
86TH STREET EAST TWIN
86TH BET. 2ND & 3RD AVE
249-1144
1, 2:40, 4:20, 6, 7:45, 9:30
LOEWS 84TH STREET VI
B'WAY AT 84TH ST. 877-3600
12:30, 2:20, 4:30, 6:40, 8:50, 10:45
CITY CINEMAS
MURRAY HILL CINEMAS
34TH ST. & 3RD AVE. 689-6548
12, 1:40, 3:20, 5, 6:40, 8:15, 9:50, 11:25
LOEWS 19TH ST. EAST VI
19TH ST. & B'WAY 260-8000
12:15, 2:05, 4:30, 6:45, 8:35, 10:50
CITY CINEMAS
VILLAGE EAST CINEMAS
2ND AVE. & 12TH ST. 529-6799
12, 1:40, 3:20, 5, 6:40, 8:15, 9:50, 11:25
CREATIVE ENTERTAINMENT
THE NEW COLISEUM
B'WAY & 181ST ST. 740-1541
4:10, 6:10, 8:10, 10:10
ALSO AT THEATRES IN NASSAU, SUFFOLK, WESTCHESTER, ROCKLAND, UPSTATE N.Y., CONNECTICUT AND NEW JERSEY
* For Group Sales Information Call: 626-6825
BRONX
GENERAL CINEMA
BAY PLAZA 10 320-3020
NATIONAL AMUSEMENTS
CONCOURSE PLAZA MULTIPLEX CINEMAS' 588-8900
NEW AMERICAN QUAD
828-3322
LOEWS PARADISE QUAD
367-1288
NATIONAL AMUSEMENTS
WHITESTONE MULTIPLEX CINEMAS' 409-9030
QUEENS
CENTER TWIN
SUNNYSIDE 784-3050
CINEPLEX ODEON
CINEMA 5
FRESH MEADOWS 357-9100
CINEMART TWIN
FOREST HILLS 261-2244
UNITED ARTISTS
THE CROSSBAY II
OZONE PARK 641-5330
LOEWS ELMWOOD
ELMHURST 429-4770
JACKSON TRIPLEX
JACKSON HEIGHTS 335-0242
MAIN STREET QUAD
FLUSHING 268-3636
UNITED ARTISTS/B.S. MOSS
MOVIE WORLD SEVENPLEX
DOUGLASTON 423-7200
BROOKLYN
CINEPLEX ODEON
ALPINE SEVENPLEX
519-9367
CANARSIE TRIPLEX
251-0700
COBBLE HILL FIVEPLEX
596-9113
CINEPLEX ODEON
KENMORE QUAD
284-5700
CINEPLEX ODEON
KINGSWAY FIVEPLEX
645-8588
CINEPLEX ODEON
METROPOLITAN CINEMAS
858-8580
UNITED ARTISTS
MOVIES AT SHEEPSHEAD BAY
615-1700
LOEWS ORIENTAL TRIPLEX 236-5001
RIDGEWOOD FIVEPLEX
821-5993
STATEN ISLAND
UNITED ARTISTS
MOVIES AT STATEN ISLAND
TRAVIS 983-9600
DOLBY STEREO

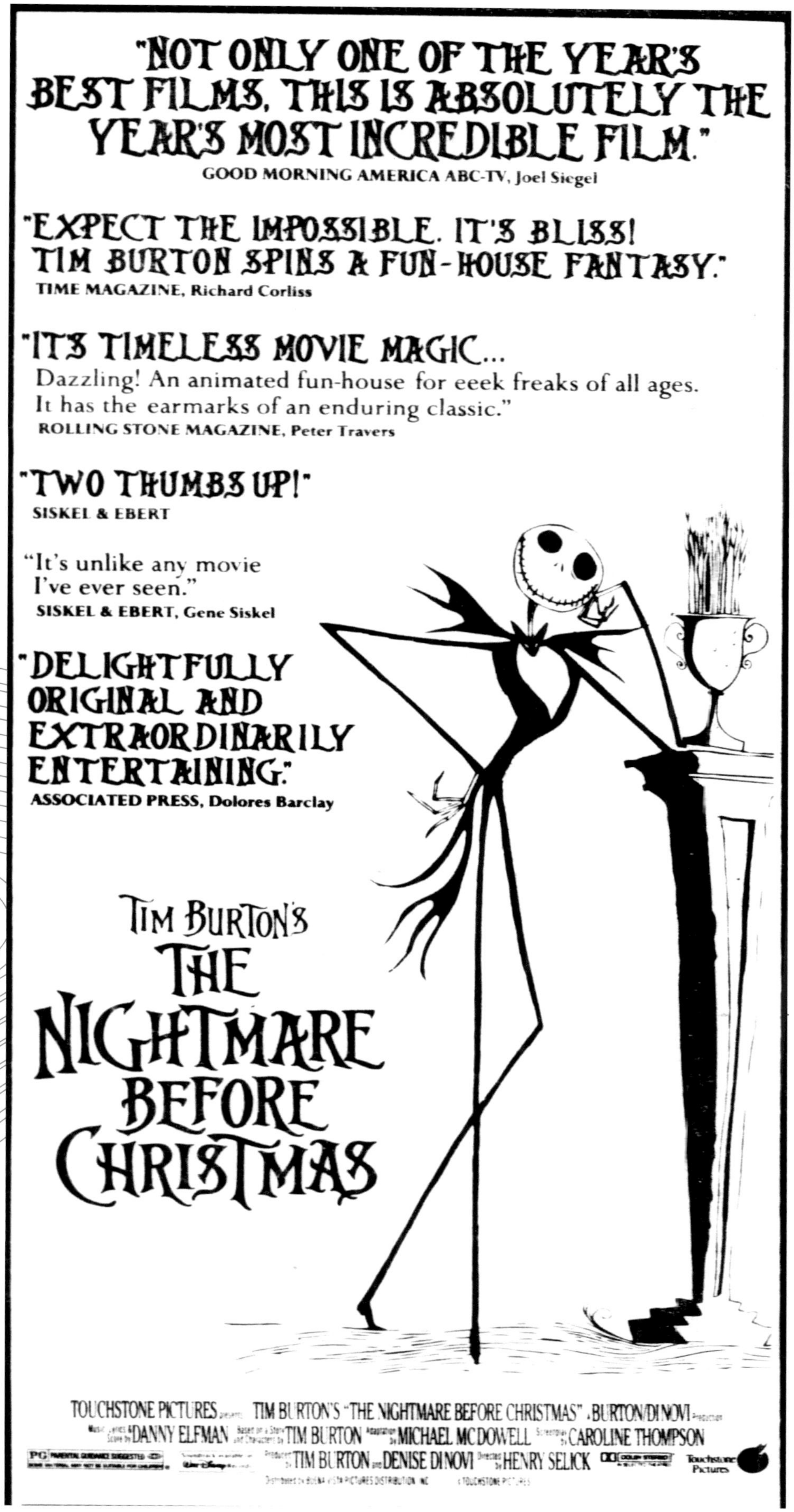
"NOT ONLY ONE OF THE YEAR'S BEST FILMS, THIS IS ABSOLUTELY THE YEAR'S MOST INCREDIBLE FILM."
GOOD MORNING AMERICA ABC-TV, Joel Siegel
"EXPECT THE IMPOSSIBLE. IT'S BLISS! TIM BURTON SPINS A FUN-HOUSE FANTASY."
TIME MAGAZINE, Richard Corliss
"IT'S TIMELESS MOVIE MAGIC... Dazzling! An animated fun-house for eeek freaks of all ages. It has the earmarks of an enduring classic."
ROLLING STONE MAGAZINE, Peter Travers
"TWO THUMBS UP!"
SISKEL & EBERT
"It's unlike any movie I've ever seen."
SISKEL & EBERT, Gene Siskel
"DELIGHTFULLY ORIGINAL AND EXTRAORDINARILY ENTERTAINING."
ASSOCIATED PRESS, Dolores Barclay
TIM BURTON'S
THE NIGHTMARE BEFORE CHRISTMAS
TOUCHSTONE PICTURES presents TIM BURTON'S "THE NIGHTMARE BEFORE CHRISTMAS" A BURTON/DI NOVI Production
DANNY ELFMAN
TIM BURTON
MICHAEL MCDOWELL
CAROLINE THOMPSON
PG PARENTAL GUIDANCE SUGGESTED
TIM BURTON and DENISE DI NOVI
Directed by HENRY SELICK
Touchstone Pictures

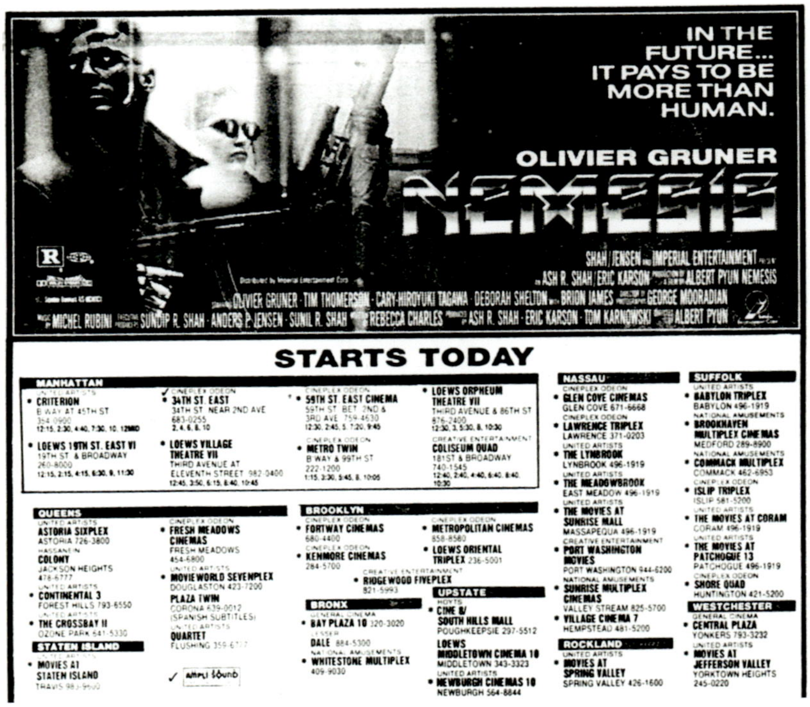

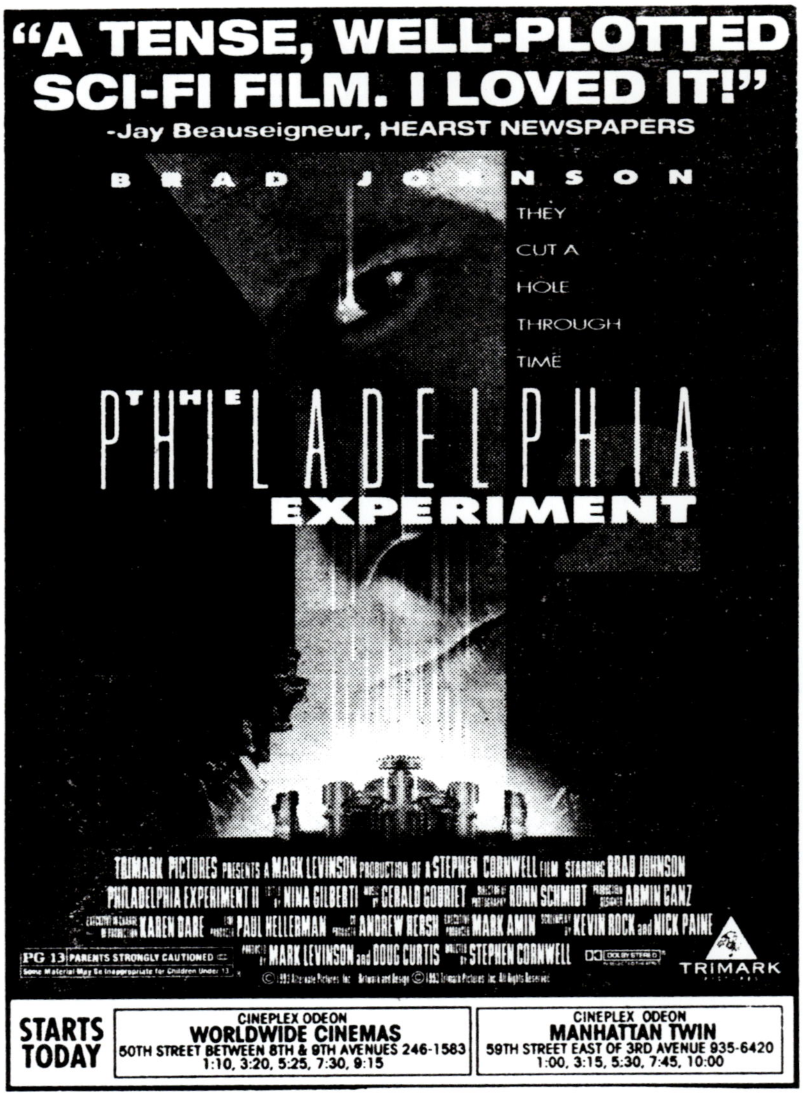

MATINEE

Universal didn't have much faith in Joe Dante's heartfelt homage to classic creature features, their young fans and the producers who sold the hell out of them in the '50s and '60s. The studio gave *Matinee* a negligible release, and by the time the good reviews started rolling in (including raves from Gene Siskel and Roger Ebert both in print and on their syndicated TV show), it was too late to give the film the treatment it deserved. While not every critic was taken with *Matinee*, to this day it's viewed fondly by many a "monster kid."

"They say if you go to the movies long enough you will finally see yourself on the screen. I had that experience during *Matinee*. ... There are a lot of big laughs in *Matinee*, and not many moments when I didn't have a wide smile on my face."

–Roger Ebert, *Chicago Sun-Times*

"*Matinee* is one of those rare, unifying, movie experiences that cuts across generation groupings to provide a rich and merry experience. It's the best at this game since *Back to the Future*."

–Stephen Hunter, *The Baltimore Sun*

"[T]he first pleasant surprise of the new year, as filmmaker Joe Dante pays affectionate tribute to B-grade horror films of the Atomic Age and their old-fashioned showman creators. ... What we get in *Matinee* is a movie within a movie, and both work."

–Gene Siskel, *Chicago Tribune*

"Period-perfect and photographed in faded family-snapshot hues, *Matinee* isn't ironic or kitschy-coy about its period. Director Joe Dante sweetly celebrates 1962, a time when kids had names like Sherry and Dwight and Stan."

–JOE BROWN, *THE WASHINGTON POST*

"*Matinee*...is funny and ingenious up to a point. Eventually, it becomes much too cluttered, with an oversupply of minor characters and a labored bomb-and-horror-film parallel."

–Janet Maslin, *The New York Times*

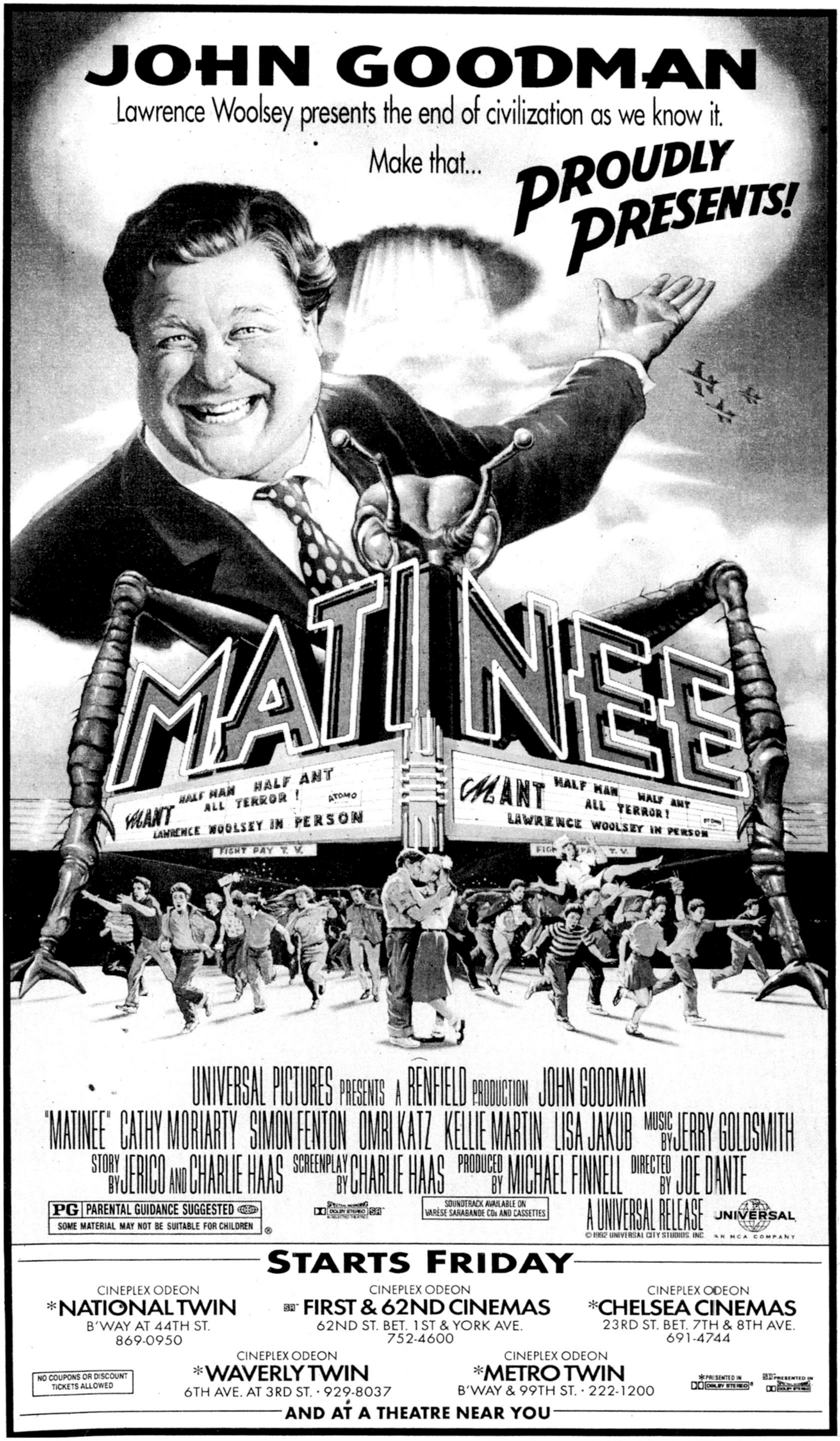

JOHN GOODMAN
Lawrence Woolsey presents the end of civilization as we know it.
Make that... PROUDLY PRESENTS!
MATINEE
MANT HALF MAN HALF ANT ALL TERROR! LAWRENCE WOOLSEY IN PERSON
UNIVERSAL PICTURES PRESENTS A RENFIELD PRODUCTION JOHN GOODMAN
"MATINEE" CATHY MORIARTY SIMON FENTON OMRI KATZ KELLIE MARTIN LISA JAKUB MUSIC BY JERRY GOLDSMITH
STORY BY JERICO AND CHARLIE HAAS SCREENPLAY BY CHARLIE HAAS PRODUCED BY MICHAEL FINNELL DIRECTED BY JOE DANTE
PG PARENTAL GUIDANCE SUGGESTED
SOME MATERIAL MAY NOT BE SUITABLE FOR CHILDREN
SOUNDTRACK AVAILABLE ON VARÈSE SARABANDE CDs AND CASSETTES
A UNIVERSAL RELEASE
UNIVERSAL
AN MCA COMPANY
©1992 UNIVERSAL CITY STUDIOS, INC.
STARTS FRIDAY
CINEPLEX ODEON
*NATIONAL TWIN
B'WAY AT 44TH ST.
869-0950
CINEPLEX ODEON
FIRST & 62ND CINEMAS
62ND ST. BET. 1ST & YORK AVE.
752-4600
CINEPLEX ODEON
*CHELSEA CINEMAS
23RD ST. BET. 7TH & 8TH AVE.
691-4744
NO COUPONS OR DISCOUNT TICKETS ALLOWED
CINEPLEX ODEON
*WAVERLY TWIN
6TH AVE. AT 3RD ST. · 929-8037
CINEPLEX ODEON
*METRO TWIN
B'WAY & 99TH ST. · 222-1200
AND AT A THEATRE NEAR YOU

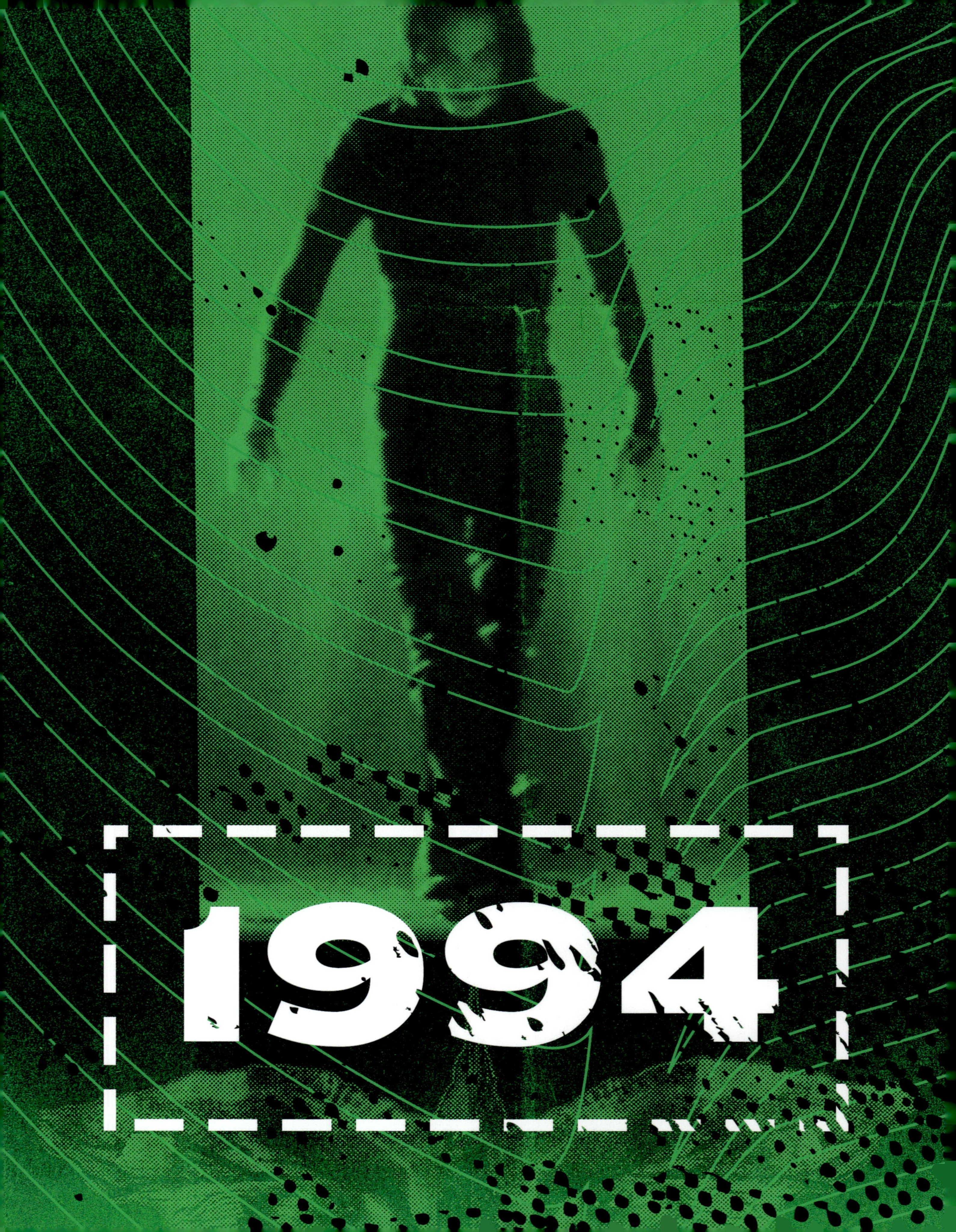
1994

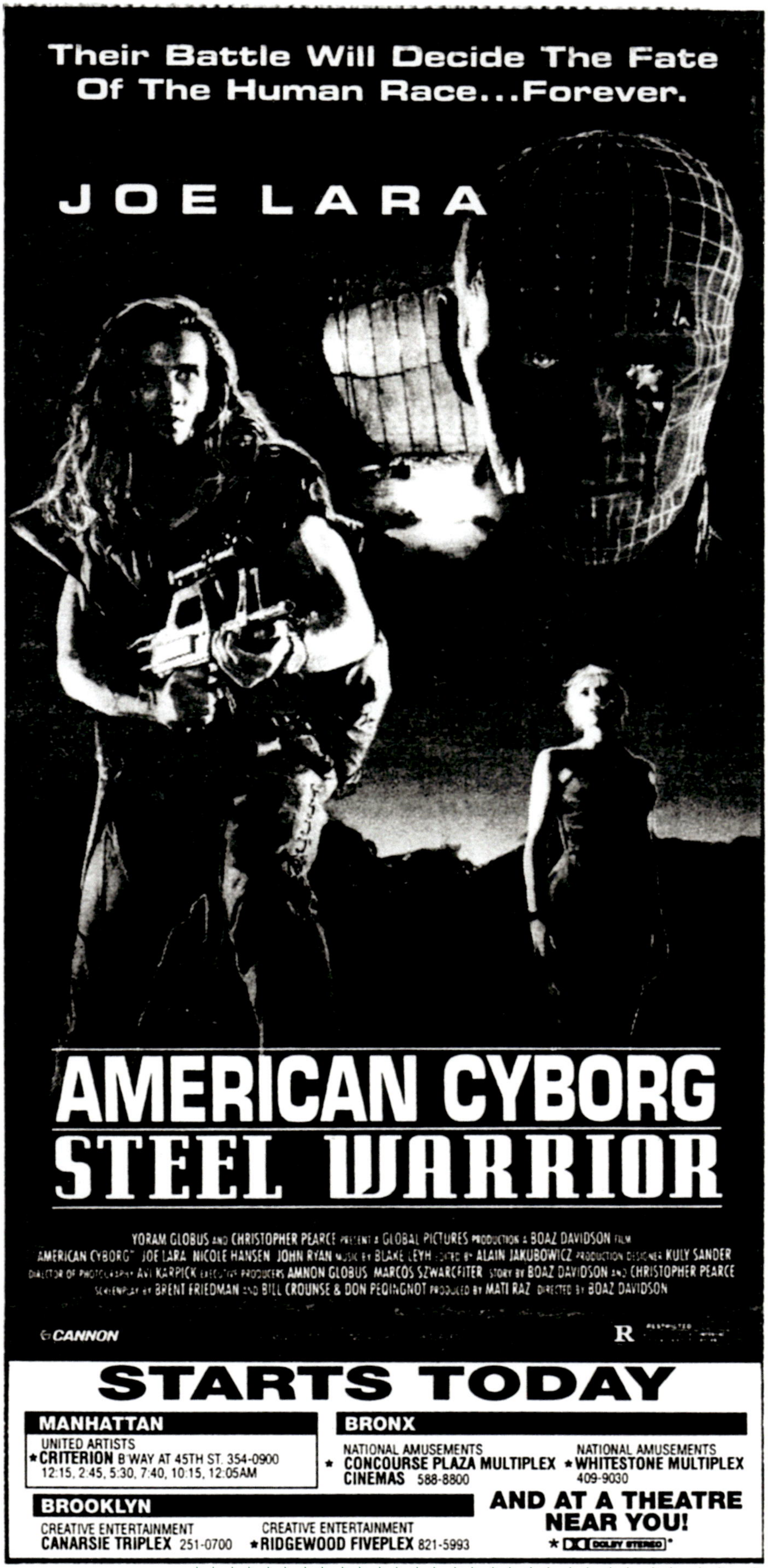
Their Battle Will Decide The Fate Of The Human Race...Forever.
JOE LARA
AMERICAN CYBORG
STEEL WARRIOR
YORAM GLOBUS AND CHRISTOPHER PEARCE PRESENT A GLOBAL PICTURES PRODUCTION A BOAZ DAVIDSON FILM
AMERICAN CYBORG™ JOE LARA NICOLE HANSEN JOHN RYAN MUSIC BY BLAKE LEYH EDITED BY ALAIN JAKUBOWICZ PRODUCTION DESIGNER KULY SANDER
DIRECTOR OF PHOTOGRAPHY AVI KARPICK EXECUTIVE PRODUCERS AMNON GLOBUS MARCOS SZWARCFITER STORY BY BOAZ DAVIDSON AND CHRISTOPHER PEARCE
SCREENPLAY BY BRENT FRIEDMAN AND BILL CROUNSE & DON PEQINGNOT PRODUCED BY MATI RAZ DIRECTED BY BOAZ DAVIDSON
CANNON
R
STARTS TODAY
MANHATTAN
UNITED ARTISTS
★CRITERION B'WAY AT 45TH ST. 354-0900
12:15, 2:45, 5:30, 7:40, 10:15, 12:05AM
BRONX
NATIONAL AMUSEMENTS
★ CONCOURSE PLAZA MULTIPLEX CINEMAS 588-8800
NATIONAL AMUSEMENTS
★WHITESTONE MULTIPLEX 409-9030
BROOKLYN
CREATIVE ENTERTAINMENT
CANARSIE TRIPLEX 251-0700
CREATIVE ENTERTAINMENT
★RIDGEWOOD FIVEPLEX 821-5993
AND AT A THEATRE NEAR YOU!
★ DOLBY STEREO

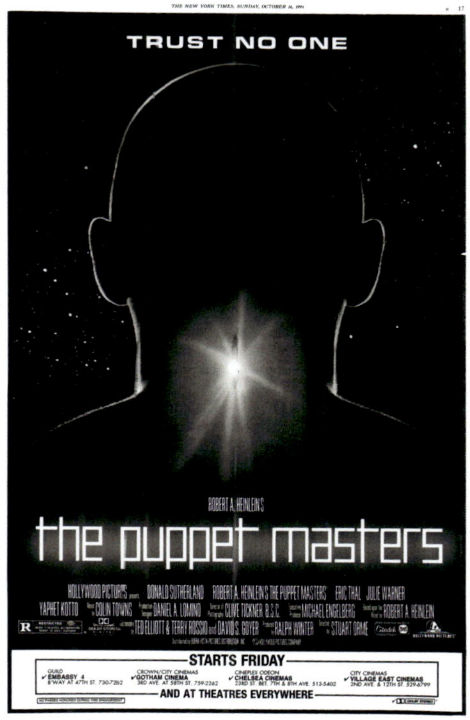
TRUST NO ONE
ROBERT A. HEINLEIN'S
the puppet masters
HOLLYWOOD PICTURES presents DONALD SUTHERLAND "ROBERT A. HEINLEIN'S THE PUPPET MASTERS" ERIC THAL JULIE WARNER
YAPHET KOTTO COLIN TOWNS DANIEL A. LOMINO CLIVE TICKNER, B.S.C. MICHAEL ENGELBERG ROBERT A. HEINLEIN
TED ELLIOTT & TERRY ROSSIO and DAVID S. GOYER RALPH WINTER STUART ORME
STARTS FRIDAY
GUILD
✓EMBASSY 4
B'WAY AT 47TH ST. 730-7262
CROWN/CITY CINEMAS
✓GOTHAM CINEMA
3RD AVE. AT 58TH ST. 759-2262
CINEPLEX ODEON
✓CHELSEA CINEMAS
23RD ST. BET. 7TH & 8TH AVE. 513-5402
CITY CINEMAS
✓VILLAGE EAST CINEMAS
2ND AVE. & 12TH ST. 529-6799
AND AT THEATRES EVERYWHERE

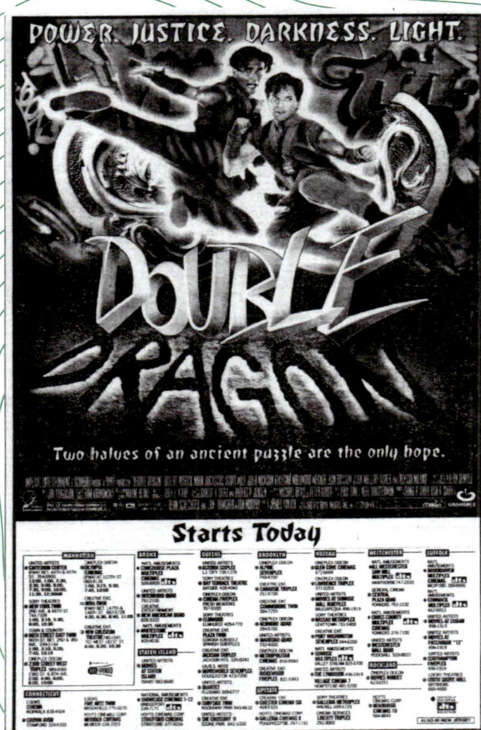
POWER. JUSTICE. DARKNESS. LIGHT.
DOUBLE DRAGON
Two halves of an ancient puzzle are the only hope.
Starts Today

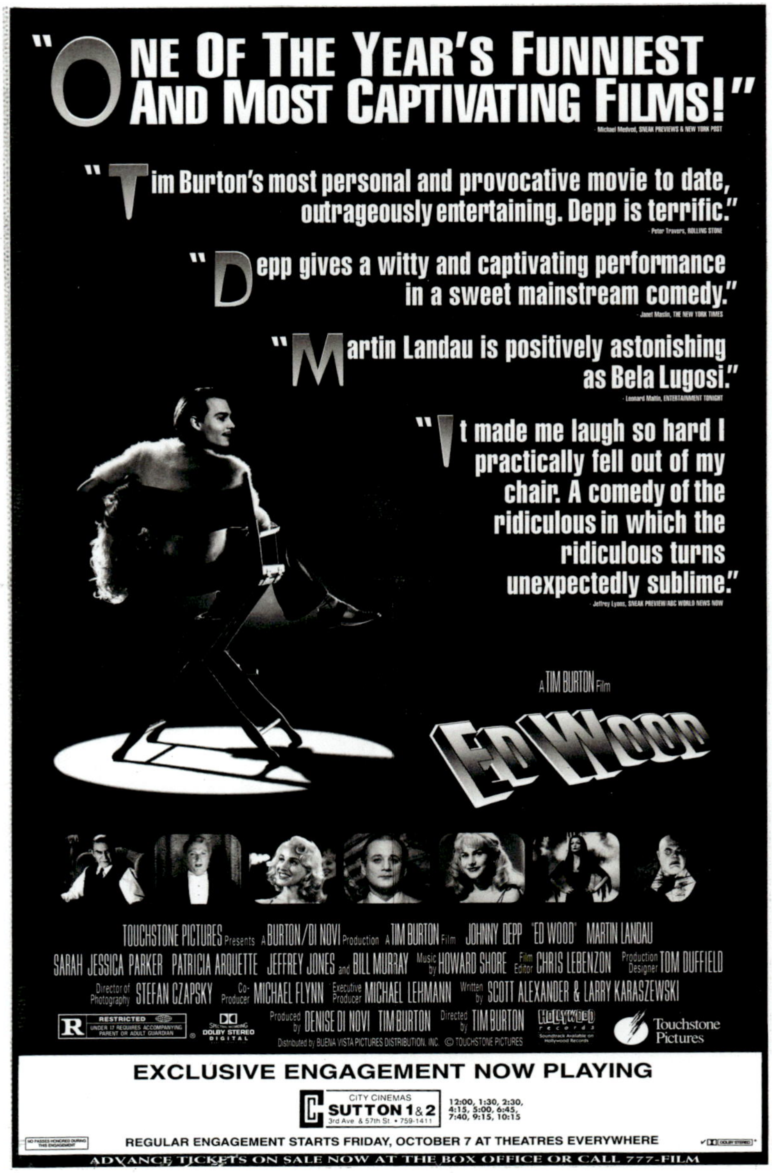

THE CROW

Alex Proyas' darkly stylish adaptation of James O'Barr's comic series would likely have grabbed attention under any circumstances. But for both moviegoers and critics, there was no way to watch this story of a murdered rock musician returning from the grave to avenge himself outside the context of star Brandon Lee's accidental death on the set. After that incident, original distributor Paramount Pictures dropped *The Crow*, which was picked up by Miramax/Dimension and became a box-office hit, partially driven by reviews that praised both the movie and Lee's performance.

"[Lee's] passing suffuses this scenario… with prescient, touching irony: an otherwise respectable pop noir is transformed into something eerie and deeply compelling."

–Desson Howe, *Washington Post*

"Like most of the bad blood-drenched thrillers of the '80s, this movie is deliberately, defiantly over-the-top. But it's clear the filmmakers want to blow away the audience with talent as much as gore. And they do."

–MICHAEL WILMINGTON, *CHICAGO TRIBUNE*

"It's one of those strange numbers that can only be classified as being of a piece, meaning that however you feel about the value of what it sets out to do, you must admit that it does it brilliantly."

–Stephen Hunter, *The Baltimore Sun*

"The only reason for a grown person to check out *The Crow* is for Lee – and not for sentimental reasons, either. What gives the movie its mite of 'heart' is that, as Lee plays him, Draven's fury comes out of an almost operatic pain."

–Peter Rainer, *Los Angeles Times*

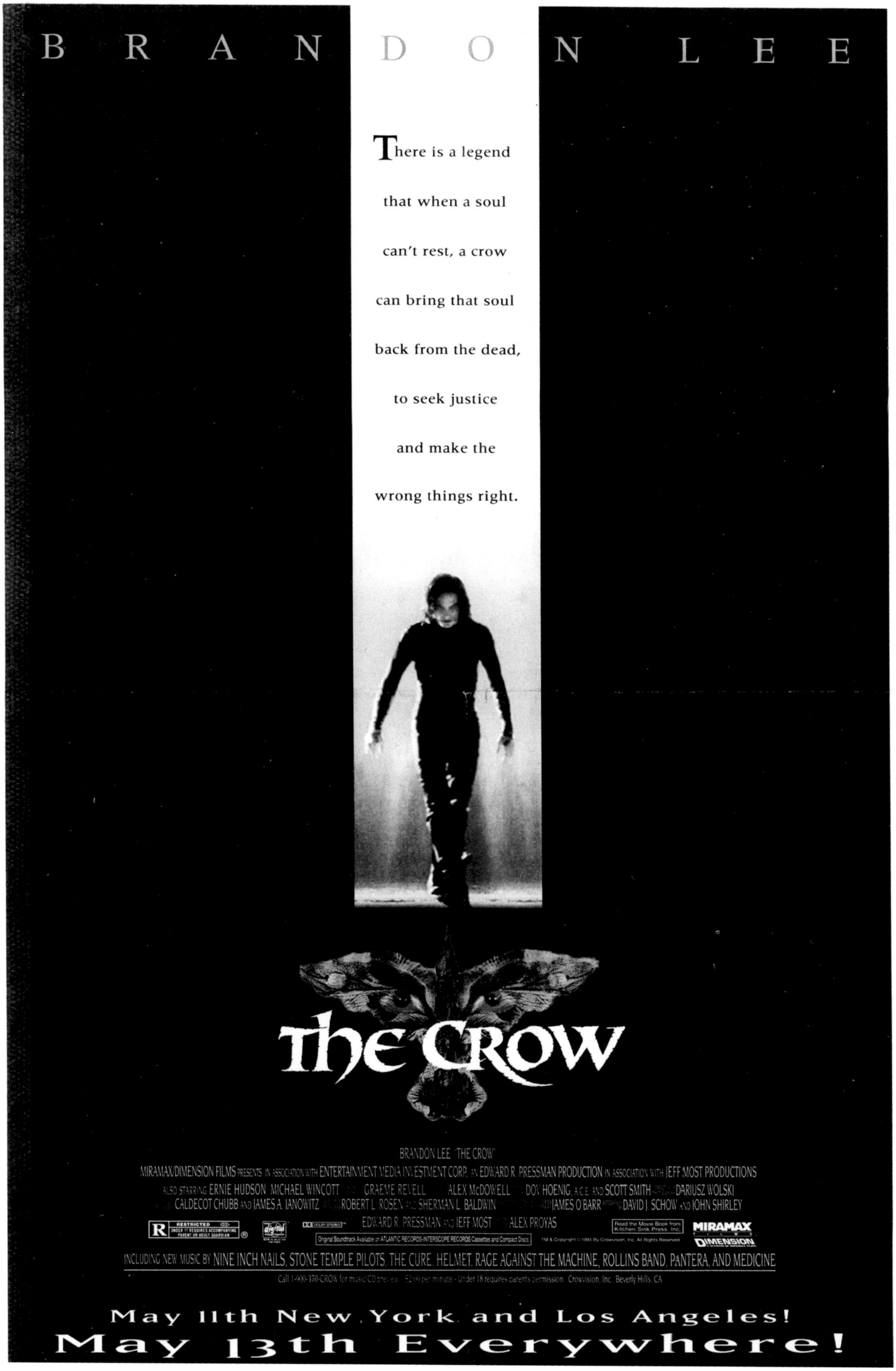

B R A N D O N L E E
There is a legend that when a soul can't rest, a crow can bring that soul back from the dead, to seek justice and make the wrong things right.
THE CROW
BRANDON LEE "THE CROW"
MIRAMAX/DIMENSION FILMS PRESENTS IN ASSOCIATION WITH ENTERTAINMENT MEDIA INVESTMENT CORP. AN EDWARD R. PRESSMAN PRODUCTION IN ASSOCIATION WITH JEFF MOST PRODUCTIONS
ALSO STARRING ERNIE HUDSON MICHAEL WINCOTT GRAEME REVELL ALEX McDOWELL DOV HOENIG, A.C.E. AND SCOTT SMITH DARIUSZ WOLSKI
CALDECOT CHUBB AND JAMES A. JANOWITZ ROBERT L. ROSEN AND SHERMAN L. BALDWIN JAMES O'BARR DAVID J. SCHOW AND JOHN SHIRLEY
EDWARD R. PRESSMAN AND JEFF MOST ALEX PROYAS
R RESTRICTED UNDER 17 REQUIRES ACCOMPANYING PARENT OR ADULT GUARDIAN
Original Soundtrack Available on ATLANTIC RECORDS-INTERSCOPE RECORDS Cassettes and Compact Discs
Read the Movie Book from Kitchen Sink Press, Inc.
MIRAMAX FILMS
DIMENSION
INCLUDING NEW MUSIC BY NINE INCH NAILS, STONE TEMPLE PILOTS, THE CURE, HELMET, RAGE AGAINST THE MACHINE, ROLLINS BAND, PANTERA, AND MEDICINE
Call 1-900-370-CROW for music CD preview · $2.00 per minute · Under 18 requires parents permission · Crowvision, Inc., Beverly Hills, CA
May 11th New York and Los Angeles!
May 13th Everywhere!

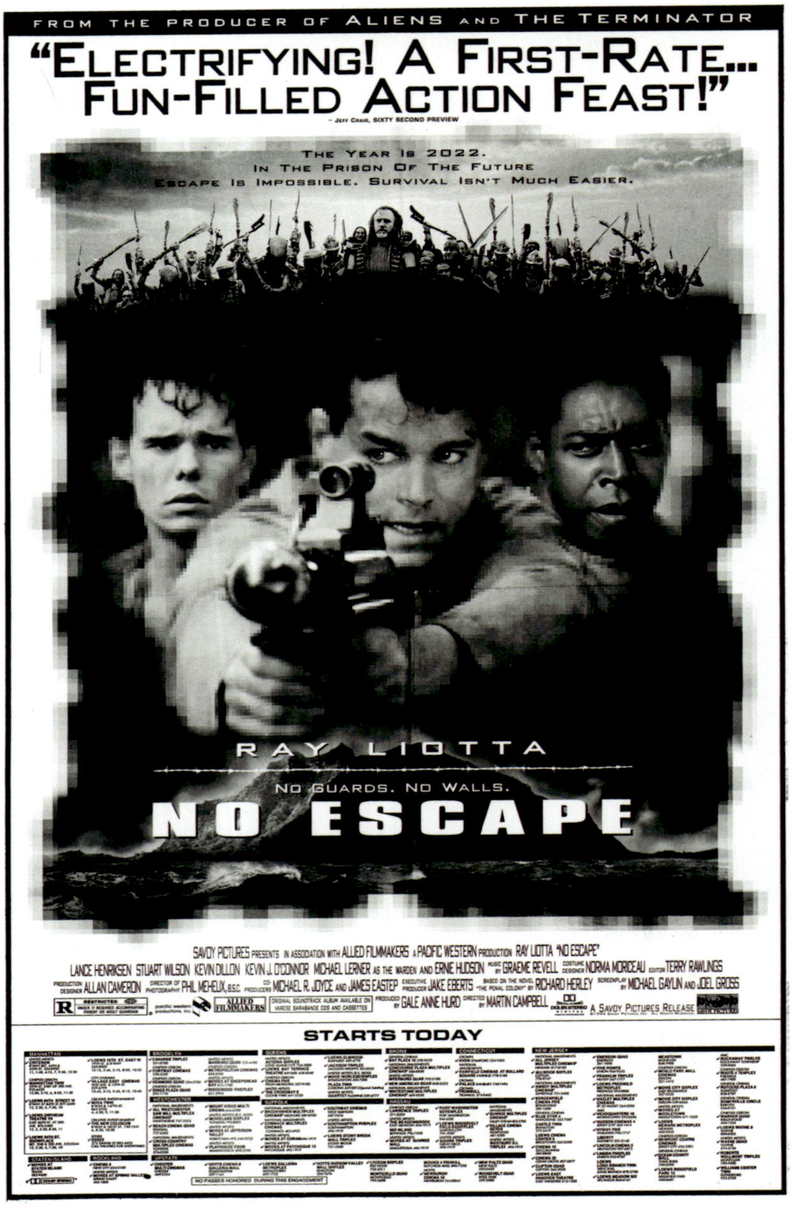

STARGATE

Prior to *Stargate*, German director Roland Emmerich cut his teeth on English-language fantasy/sci-fi flicks such as 1990's *Moon 44*, before making the jump to Hollywood with the Jean-Claude Van Damme/Dolph Lundgren matchup *Universal Soldier*. He then went much bigger with the extravagant *Stargate*, which attracted attention by showcasing Jaye Davidson's follow-up acting gig after giving audiences a big surprise in *The Crying Game*. (He never made another feature after portraying the sun god Ra here.) Although reviews were generally unkind, *Stargate* surprised Hollywood by raking in big grosses, spawning the long-running TV series *Stargate: SG-1* and pointing Emmerich toward even grander pictures.

"*Stargate* clearly doesn't take itself more seriously than it has to, of course, and this is a virtue."

–John Anderson, New York *Newsday*

"What's so dispiriting about it isn't its goofiness, but its smallness. However awful *Dune* was, it offered immense subversive pleasure in the scale, the density, the depth of its folly! Folly writ small, alas, is only stupidity; and inside *Stargate* there's a small, stupid movie struggling to get out."

–Stephen Hunter, *Baltimore Sun*

"*Stargate* is like a film school exercise. Assignment: conceive of the weirdest plot you can think of, and reduce it as quickly as possible to action movie cliches."

–ROGER EBERT, *CHICAGO SUN-TIMES*

"To [a] point, *Stargate*...holds our attention through a combination of suspense and funky wit. The latter is supplied primarily by [James] Spader. ... By the end, the film's early promise has pretty much degenerated into routine pyrotechnics."

–Hal Hinson, *Washington Post*

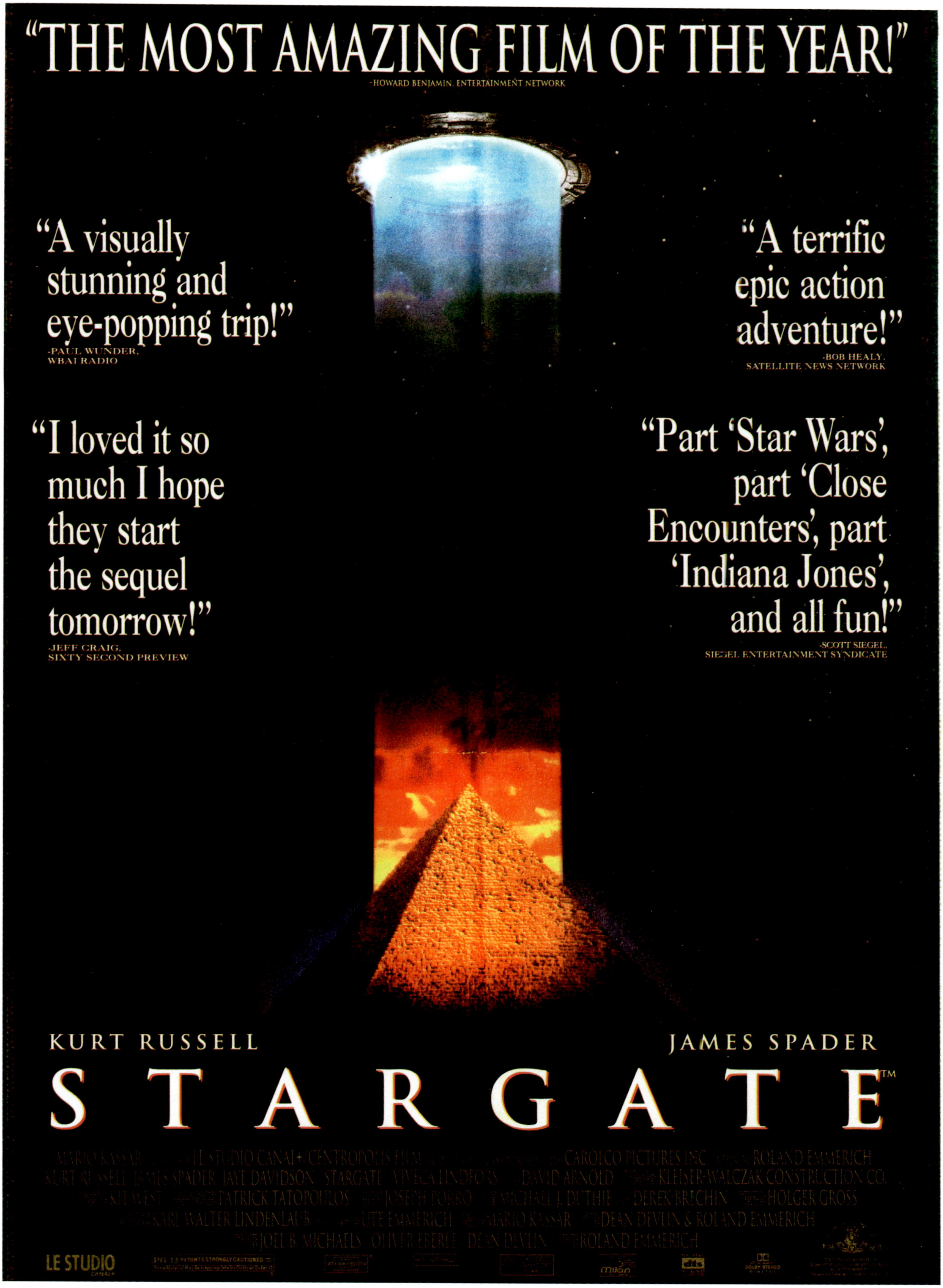
"THE MOST AMAZING FILM OF THE YEAR!"
-HOWARD BENJAMIN, ENTERTAINMENT NETWORK
"A visually stunning and eye-popping trip!"
-PAUL WUNDER, WBAI RADIO
"A terrific epic action adventure!"
-BOB HEALY, SATELLITE NEWS NETWORK
"I loved it so much I hope they start the sequel tomorrow!"
-JEFF CRAIG, SIXTY SECOND PREVIEW
"Part 'Star Wars', part 'Close Encounters', part 'Indiana Jones', and all fun!"
-SCOTT SIEGEL, SIEGEL ENTERTAINMENT SYNDICATE
KURT RUSSELL
JAMES SPADER
STARGATE™
LE STUDIO CANAL+

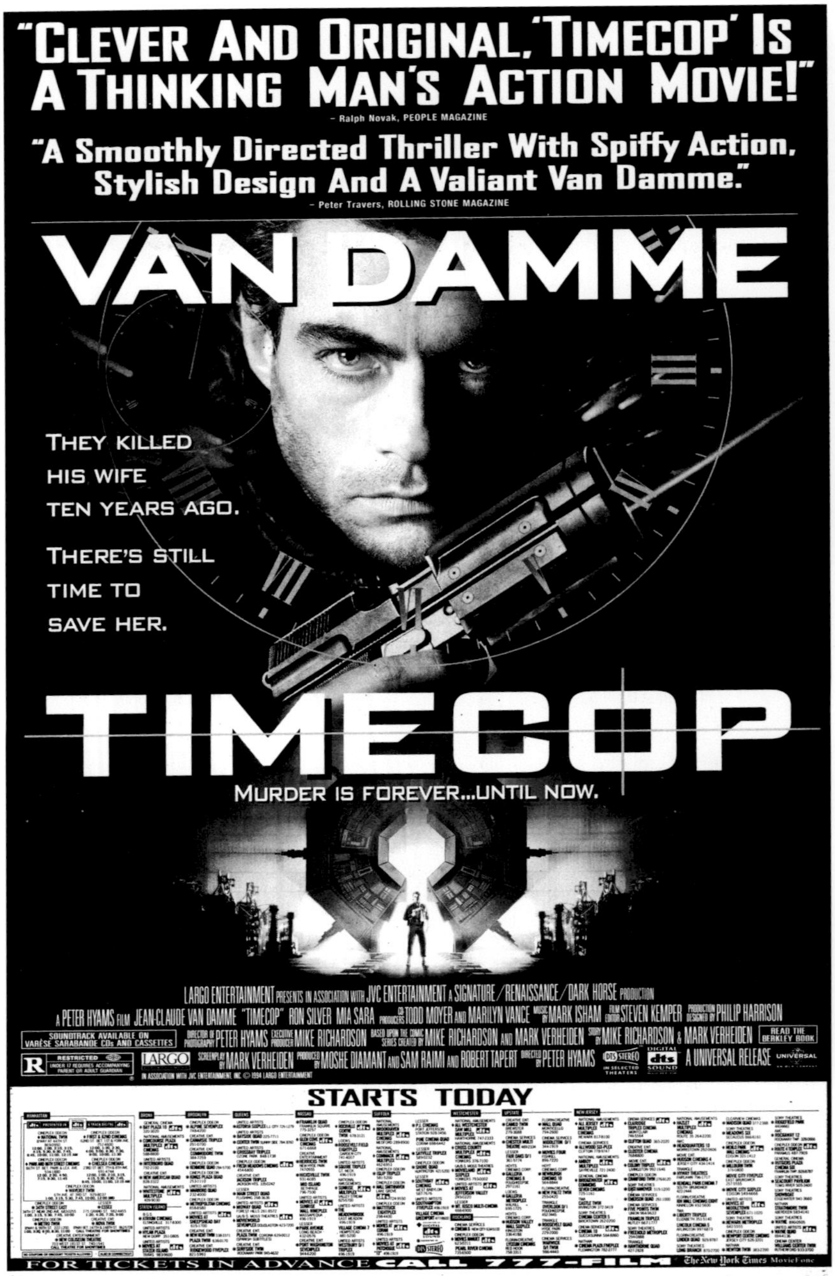

"CLEVER AND ORIGINAL. 'TIMECOP' IS A THINKING MAN'S ACTION MOVIE!"
– Ralph Novak, PEOPLE MAGAZINE
"A Smoothly Directed Thriller With Spiffy Action, Stylish Design And A Valiant Van Damme."
– Peter Travers, ROLLING STONE MAGAZINE
VAN DAMME
THEY KILLED HIS WIFE TEN YEARS AGO.
THERE'S STILL TIME TO SAVE HER.
TIMECOP
MURDER IS FOREVER...UNTIL NOW.
A UNIVERSAL RELEASE
STARTS TODAY
FOR TICKETS IN ADVANCE CALL 777-FILM

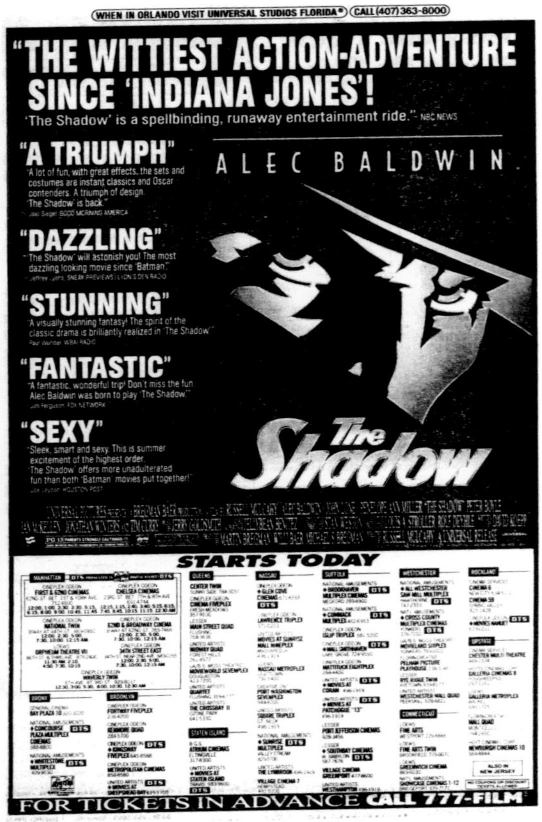

WHEN IN ORLANDO VISIT UNIVERSAL STUDIOS FLORIDA® CALL (407) 363-8000
"THE WITTIEST ACTION-ADVENTURE SINCE 'INDIANA JONES'!
'The Shadow' is a spellbinding, runaway entertainment ride." – NBC NEWS
"A TRIUMPH"
"DAZZLING"
"STUNNING"
"FANTASTIC"
"SEXY"
ALEC BALDWIN
The Shadow
STARTS TODAY
FOR TICKETS IN ADVANCE CALL 777-FILM

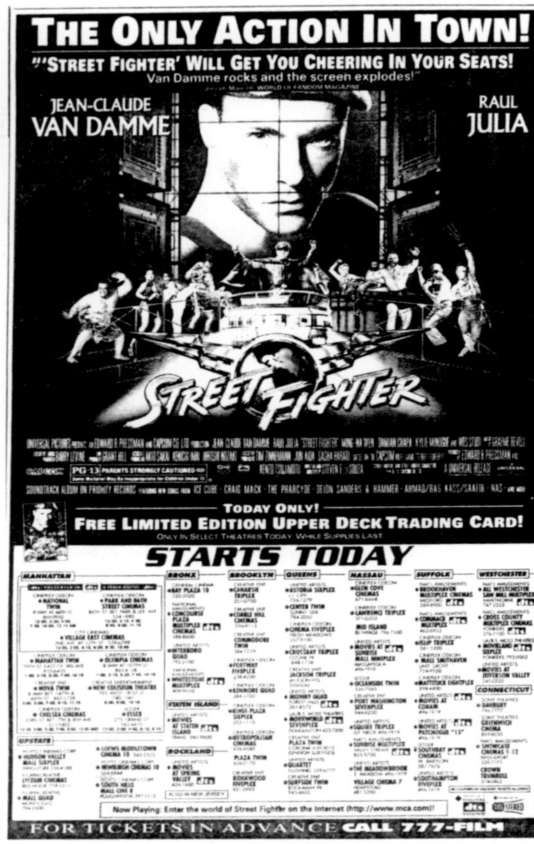

THE ONLY ACTION IN TOWN!
"'STREET FIGHTER' WILL GET YOU CHEERING IN YOUR SEATS! Van Damme rocks and the screen explodes!"
JEAN-CLAUDE VAN DAMME
RAUL JULIA
STREET FIGHTER
TODAY ONLY!
FREE LIMITED EDITION UPPER DECK TRADING CARD!
STARTS TODAY
FOR TICKETS IN ADVANCE CALL 777-FILM

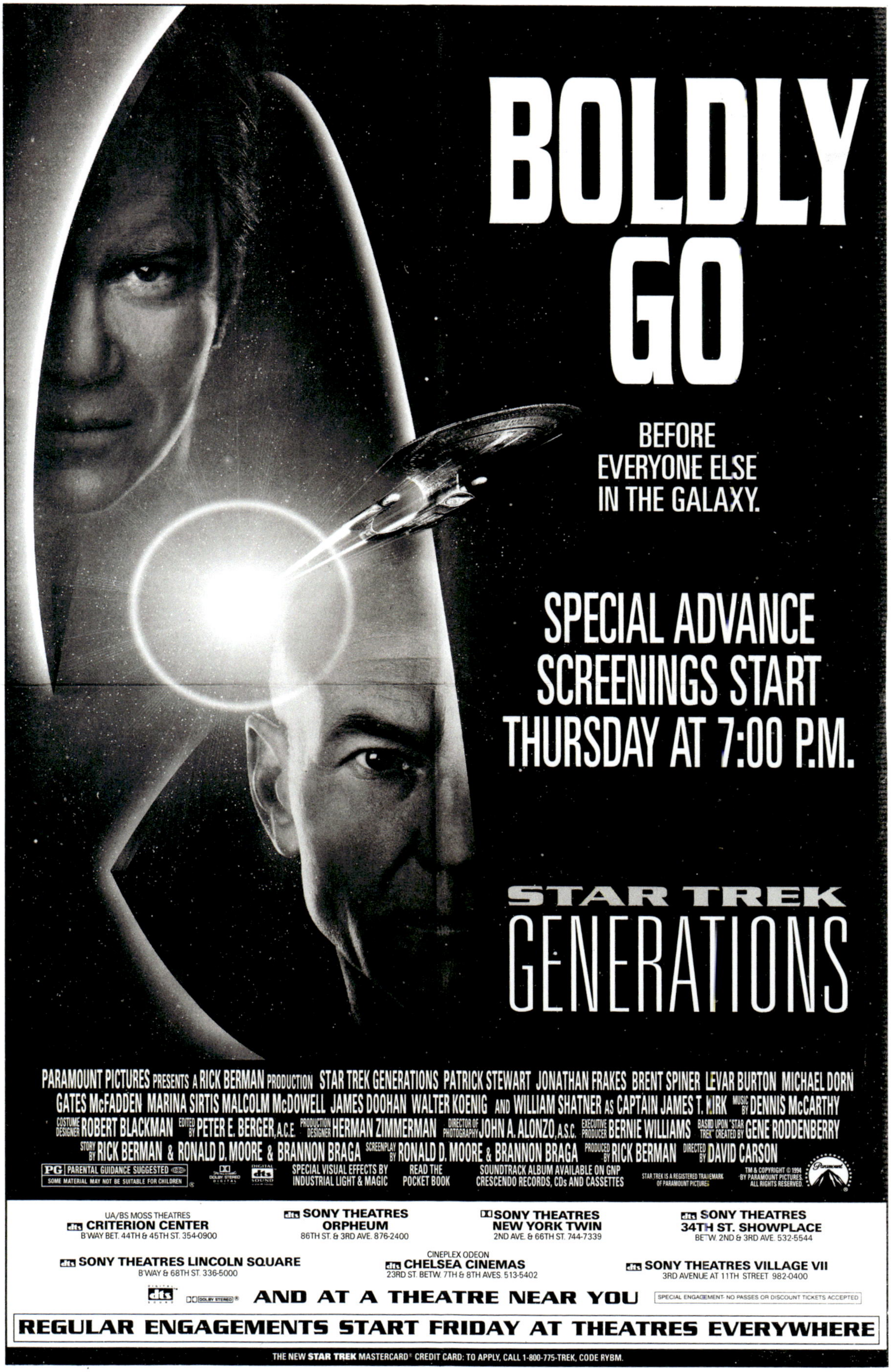
BOLDLY GO
BEFORE EVERYONE ELSE IN THE GALAXY.
SPECIAL ADVANCE SCREENINGS START THURSDAY AT 7:00 P.M.
STAR TREK
GENERATIONS
PARAMOUNT PICTURES PRESENTS A RICK BERMAN PRODUCTION STAR TREK GENERATIONS PATRICK STEWART JONATHAN FRAKES BRENT SPINER LEVAR BURTON MICHAEL DORN GATES McFADDEN MARINA SIRTIS MALCOLM McDOWELL JAMES DOOHAN WALTER KOENIG AND WILLIAM SHATNER AS CAPTAIN JAMES T. KIRK MUSIC BY DENNIS McCARTHY COSTUME DESIGNER ROBERT BLACKMAN EDITED BY PETER E. BERGER, A.C.E. PRODUCTION DESIGNER HERMAN ZIMMERMAN DIRECTOR OF PHOTOGRAPHY JOHN A. ALONZO, A.S.C. EXECUTIVE PRODUCER BERNIE WILLIAMS BASED UPON "STAR TREK" CREATED BY GENE RODDENBERRY STORY BY RICK BERMAN & RONALD D. MOORE & BRANNON BRAGA SCREENPLAY BY RONALD D. MOORE & BRANNON BRAGA PRODUCED BY RICK BERMAN DIRECTED BY DAVID CARSON
PG PARENTAL GUIDANCE SUGGESTED
SOME MATERIAL MAY NOT BE SUITABLE FOR CHILDREN
SPECIAL VISUAL EFFECTS BY INDUSTRIAL LIGHT & MAGIC
READ THE POCKET BOOK
SOUNDTRACK ALBUM AVAILABLE ON GNP CRESCENDO RECORDS, CDs AND CASSETTES
STAR TREK IS A REGISTERED TRADEMARK OF PARAMOUNT PICTURES
TM & COPYRIGHT © 1994 BY PARAMOUNT PICTURES. ALL RIGHTS RESERVED.
UA/BS MOSS THEATRES
CRITERION CENTER
B'WAY BET. 44TH & 45TH ST. 354-0900
SONY THEATRES ORPHEUM
86TH ST. & 3RD AVE. 876-2400
SONY THEATRES NEW YORK TWIN
2ND AVE. & 66TH ST. 744-7339
SONY THEATRES 34TH ST. SHOWPLACE
BETW. 2ND & 3RD AVE. 532-5544
SONY THEATRES LINCOLN SQUARE
B'WAY & 68TH ST. 336-5000
CINEPLEX ODEON
CHELSEA CINEMAS
23RD ST. BETW. 7TH & 8TH AVES. 513-5402
SONY THEATRES VILLAGE VII
3RD AVENUE AT 11TH STREET 982-0400
AND AT A THEATRE NEAR YOU
SPECIAL ENGAGEMENT- NO PASSES OR DISCOUNT TICKETS ACCEPTED
REGULAR ENGAGEMENTS START FRIDAY AT THEATRES EVERYWHERE
THE NEW STAR TREK MASTERCARD® CREDIT CARD: TO APPLY, CALL 1-800-775-TREK, CODE RYBM.

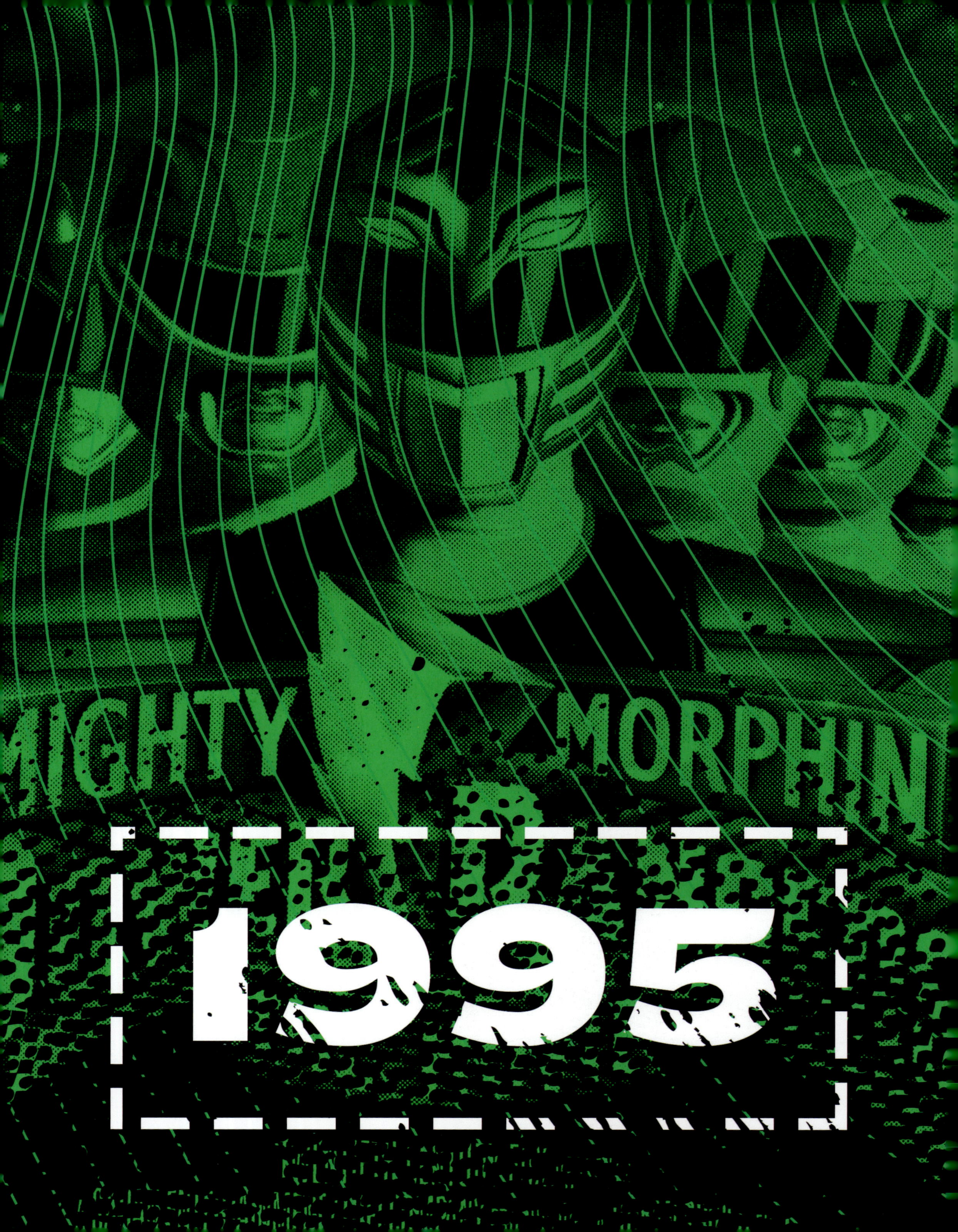
MORPHIN
1995

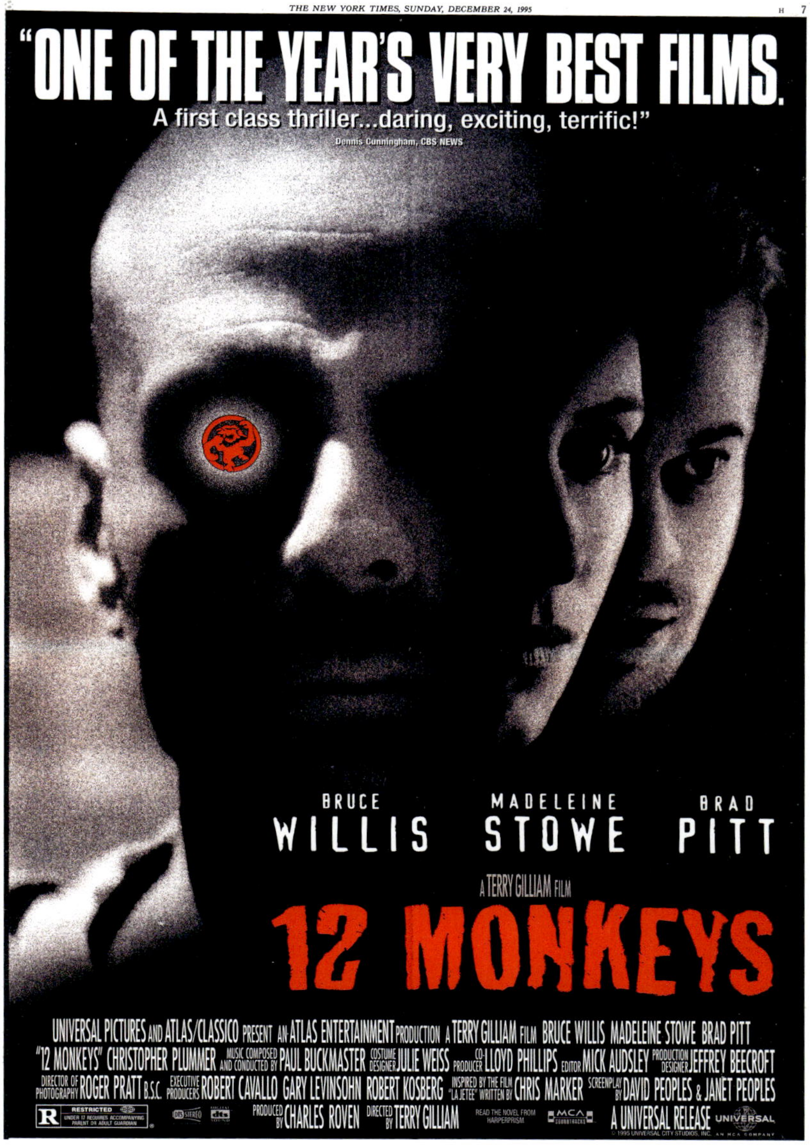
THE NEW YORK TIMES, SUNDAY, DECEMBER 24, 1995 H 7
"ONE OF THE YEAR'S VERY BEST FILMS.
A first class thriller...daring, exciting, terrific!"
Dennis Cunningham, CBS NEWS
BRUCE WILLIS
MADELEINE STOWE
BRAD PITT
A TERRY GILLIAM FILM
12 MONKEYS
UNIVERSAL PICTURES AND ATLAS/CLASSICO PRESENT AN ATLAS ENTERTAINMENT PRODUCTION A TERRY GILLIAM FILM BRUCE WILLIS MADELEINE STOWE BRAD PITT
"12 MONKEYS" CHRISTOPHER PLUMMER MUSIC COMPOSED AND CONDUCTED BY PAUL BUCKMASTER COSTUME DESIGNER JULIE WEISS CO-PRODUCER LLOYD PHILLIPS EDITOR MICK AUDSLEY PRODUCTION DESIGNER JEFFREY BEECROFT
DIRECTOR OF PHOTOGRAPHY ROGER PRATT B.S.C. EXECUTIVE PRODUCERS ROBERT CAVALLO GARY LEVINSOHN ROBERT KOSBERG INSPIRED BY THE FILM "LA JETEE" WRITTEN BY CHRIS MARKER SCREENPLAY BY DAVID PEOPLES & JANET PEOPLES
R RESTRICTED
PRODUCED BY CHARLES ROVEN DIRECTED BY TERRY GILLIAM
READ THE NOVEL FROM HARPERPRISM
A UNIVERSAL RELEASE
UNIVERSAL

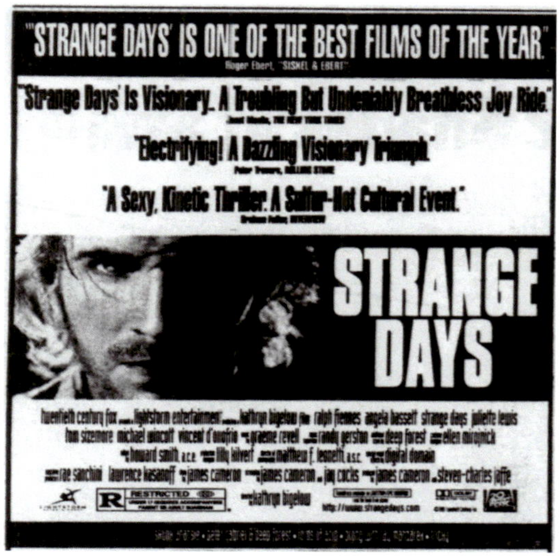
"STRANGE DAYS" IS ONE OF THE BEST FILMS OF THE YEAR.
Roger Ebert, "SISKEL & EBERT"
"Strange Days' Is Visionary. A Troubling But Undeniably Breathless Joy Ride."
"Electrifying! A Dazzling Visionary Triumph."
"A Sexy, Kinetic Thriller. A Sulfur-Hot Cultural Event."
STRANGE DAYS
twentieth century fox lightstorm entertainment kathryn bigelow ralph fiennes angela bassett strange days juliette lewis
tom sizemore michael wincott vincent d'onofrio
R RESTRICTED

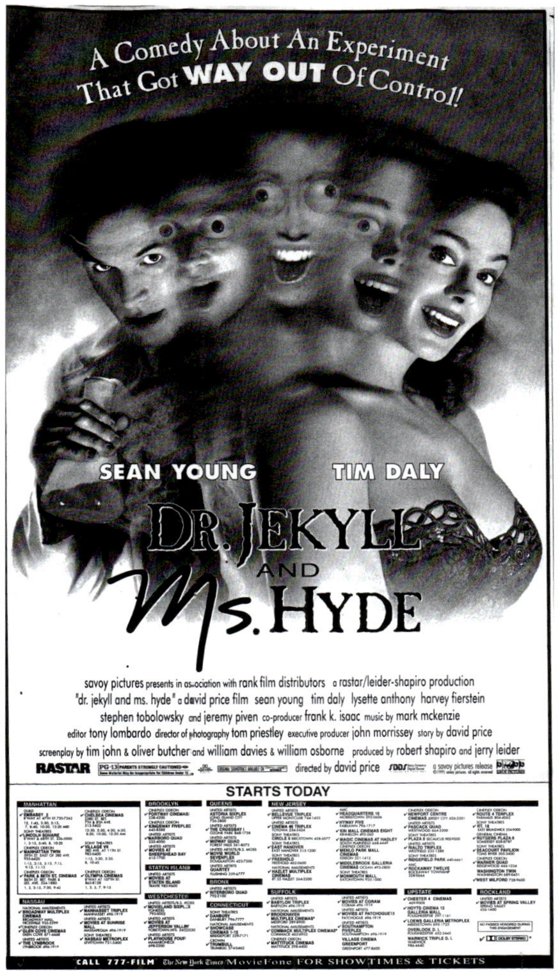
A Comedy About An Experiment That Got WAY OUT Of Control!
SEAN YOUNG
TIM DALY
DR. JEKYLL AND MS. HYDE
savoy pictures presents in association with rank film distributors a rastar/leider-shapiro production
"dr. jekyll and ms. hyde" a david price film sean young tim daly lysette anthony harvey fierstein
stephen tobolowsky and jeremy piven co-producer frank k. isaac music by mark mckenzie
editor tony lombardo director of photography tom priestley executive producer john morrissey story by david price
screenplay by tim john & oliver butcher and william davies & william osborne produced by robert shapiro and jerry leider
RASTAR
directed by david price
STARTS TODAY
MANHATTAN
BROOKLYN
QUEENS
NEW JERSEY
STATEN ISLAND
BRONX
WESTCHESTER
CONNECTICUT
NASSAU
SUFFOLK
UPSTATE
ROCKLAND
CALL 777-FILM The New York Times MovieFone FOR SHOWTIMES & TICKETS

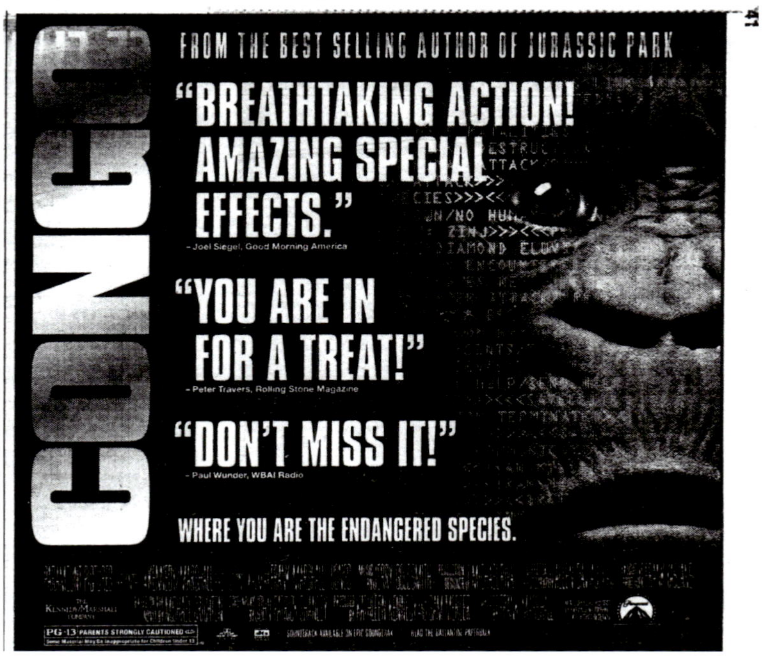
CONGO
FROM THE BEST SELLING AUTHOR OF JURASSIC PARK
"BREATHTAKING ACTION! AMAZING SPECIAL EFFECTS."
- Joel Siegel, Good Morning America
"YOU ARE IN FOR A TREAT!"
- Peter Travers, Rolling Stone Magazine
"DON'T MISS IT!"
- Paul Wunder, WBAI Radio
WHERE YOU ARE THE ENDANGERED SPECIES.
PG-13 PARENTS STRONGLY CAUTIONED

JUDGE DREDD

In his second futuristic flick of the '90s, Sylvester Stallone stepped into the boots of the ruthless lawman first popularized by the British comic book *2000 A.D.* But he took off the character's trademark helmet, which angered Dredd's die-hard fans, as did other changes such as the inclusion of a comic-relief sidekick played by Rob Schneider. *Judge Dredd*'s release was heralded the previous Christmas by a teaser trailer backed with rousing original music by Jerry Goldsmith, but the film itself (on which Stallone and director Danny Cannon repeatedly clashed) flopped upon its release in summer '95, not helped by withering reviews.

"*Judge Dredd* never slows down enough to make much sense; it's a *Blade Runner* for audiences with Attention Deficit Disorder."

–Roger Ebert, *Chicago Sun-Times*

"The director doesn't provide much kinetic movie-making pleasure but he knows enough to jam the screen with clamor. It's not excitement, exactly. It's simulated excitement."

–Peter Rainer, *Los Angeles Times*

> "Just dreadful is more like it. In fact, if Sylvester Stallone's new slam-bam sci-fi travesty were just a tad dumber, it would qualify as an instant camp classic."
>
> **–JAY BOYAR, *ORLANDO SENTINEL***

"Stallone delivers his lines through a mouth seemingly weighted with pulleys. Despite a hastily re-shot ending after test audiences hooted at one character's fate, the audience still giggles at inappropriate moments."

–Jami Bernard, New York *Daily News*

"Usually engaging and sympathetic, Stallone is blank and tongue-tied here, an immovable slab in the midst of 95 minutes of gunfire, explosions, and Gothic excess."

–Mick LaSalle, *San Francisco Chronicle*

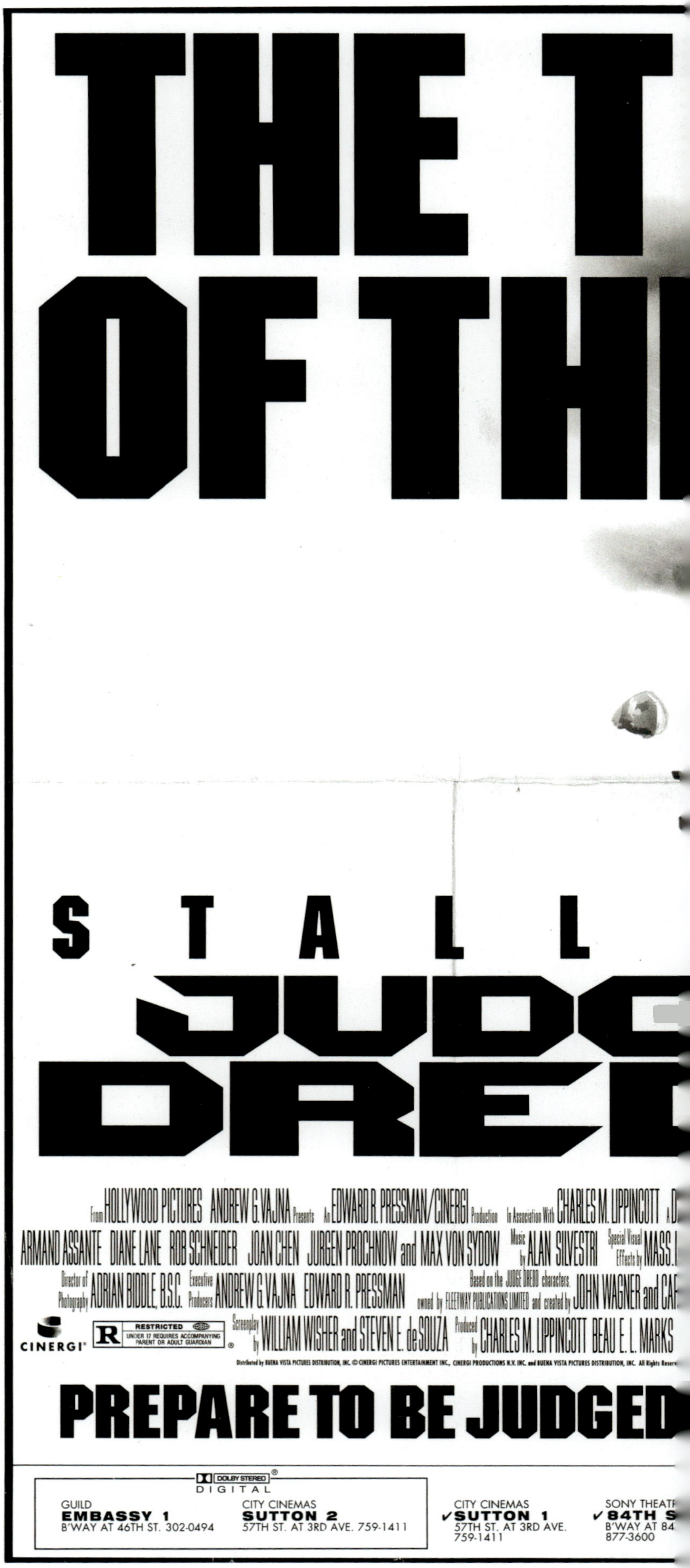

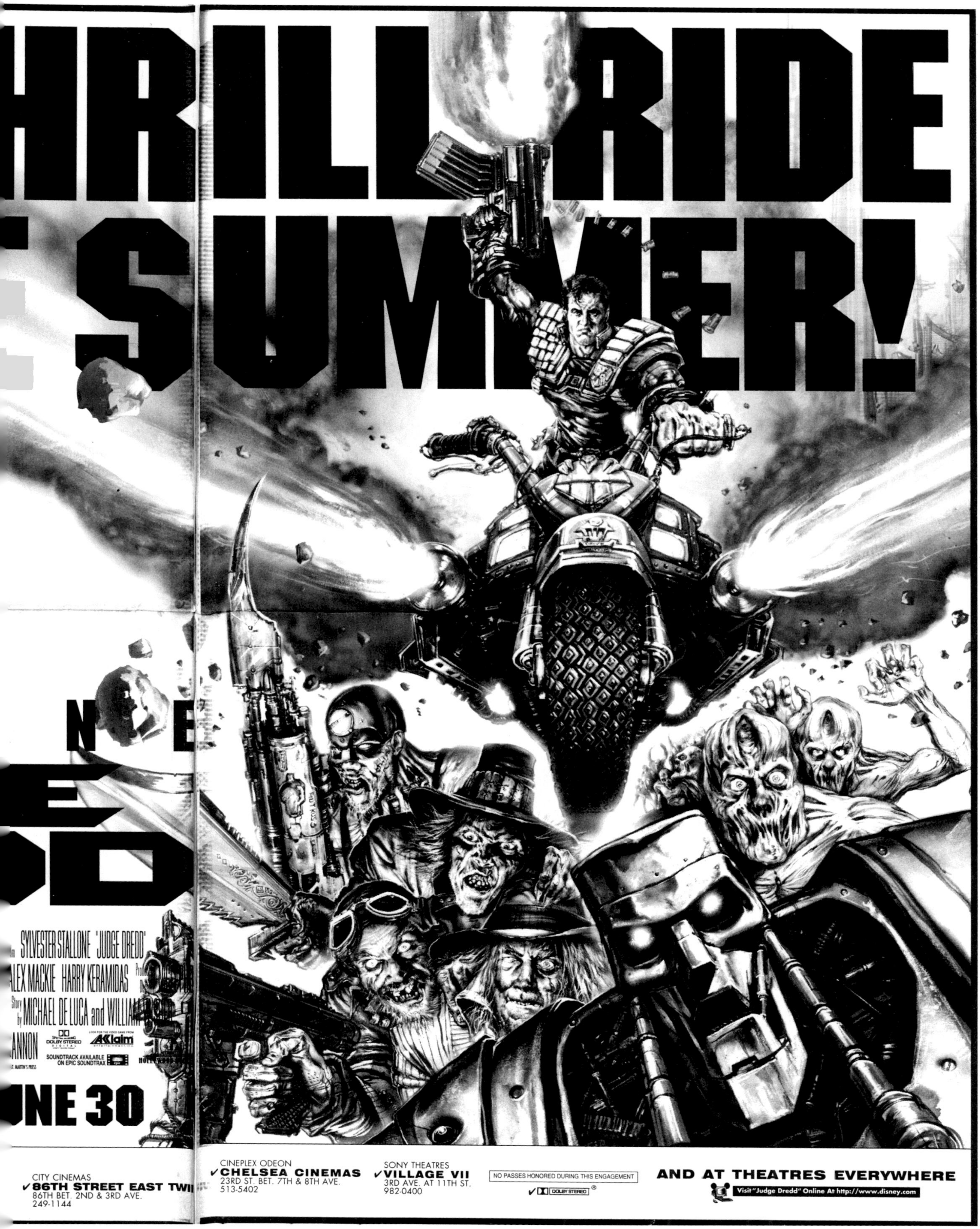
HRILL RIDE
SUMMER!
SYLVESTER STALLONE "JUDGE DREDD"
ALEX MACKIE HARRY KERAMIDAS
Story by MICHAEL DE LUCA and WILLIAM
ANNON
DOLBY STEREO DIGITAL
Akklaim
SOUNDTRACK AVAILABLE ON EPIC SOUNDTRAX
UNE 30
CITY CINEMAS
✓86TH STREET EAST TWI
86TH BET. 2ND & 3RD AVE.
249-1144
CINEPLEX ODEON
✓CHELSEA CINEMAS
23RD ST. BET. 7TH & 8TH AVE.
513-5402
SONY THEATRES
✓VILLAGE VII
3RD AVE. AT 11TH ST.
982-0400
NO PASSES HONORED DURING THIS ENGAGEMENT
DOLBY STEREO
AND AT THEATRES EVERYWHERE
Visit "Judge Dredd" Online At http://www.disney.com

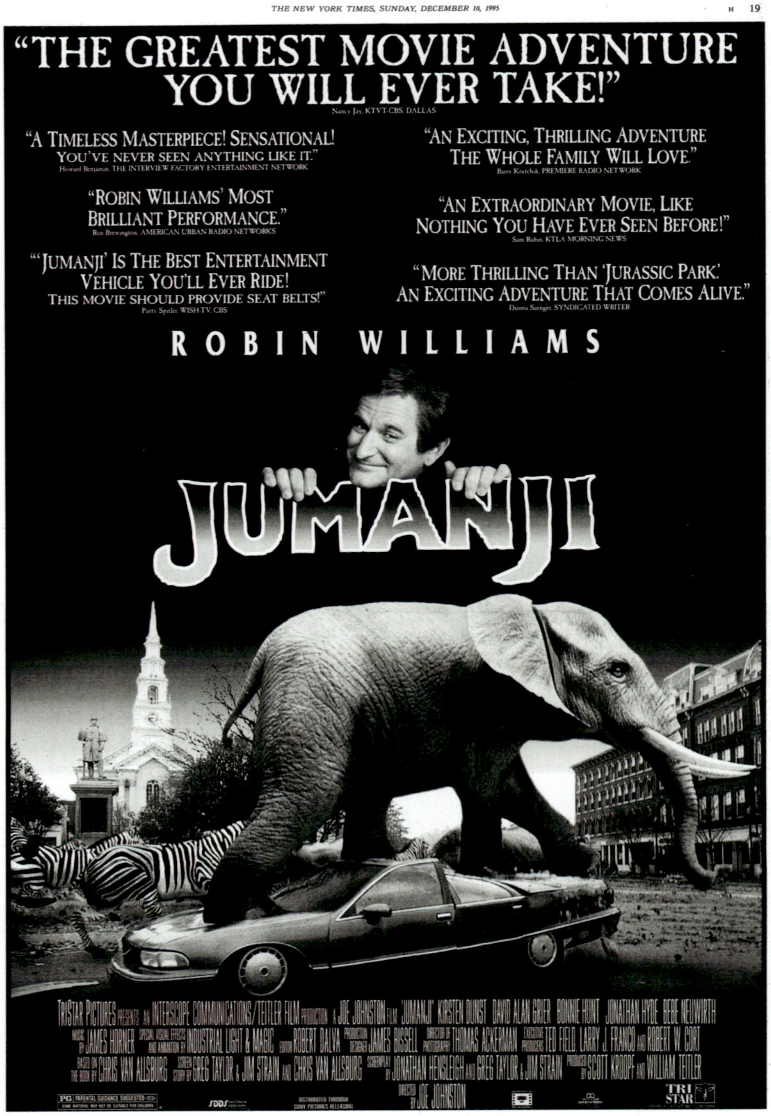

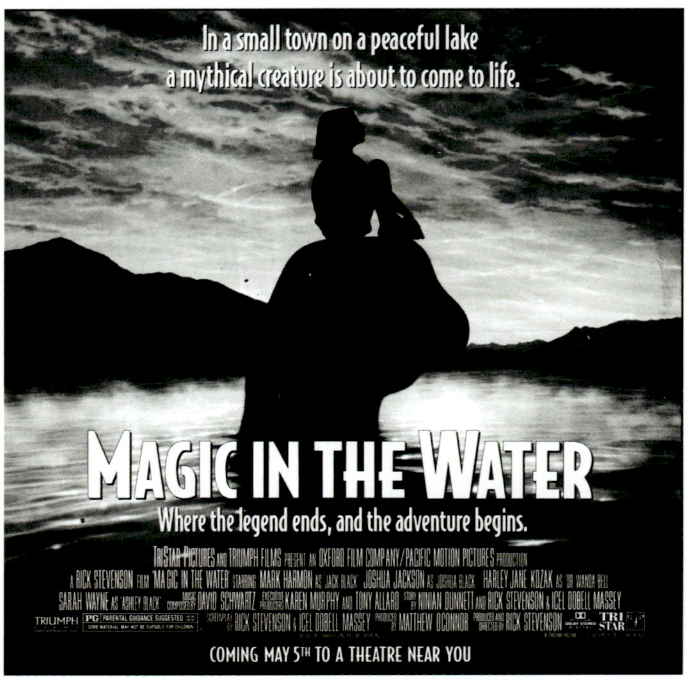

TANK GIRL

Judge Dredd wasn't the only British comics character to get a Hollywood vehicle in '95. Rachel Talalay, who had produced some *Nightmare on Elm Street* and John Waters films for New Line Cinema before making her directorial debut on *Freddy's Dead: The Final Nightmare*, pitched a *Tank Girl* movie all over Hollywood before settling at MGM/UA. Open casting calls were held for the title role before Lori Petty won the part, and Australian Naomi Watts got her first significant role in a Hollywood feature (after a bit part in *Matinee*) as Jet Girl. Also featuring Ice-T and others in Stan Winston-created prosthetic suits as the kangaroo-like Rippers, the eccentric *Tank Girl* made little impression at the time on audiences or critics, but has endured as a cult favorite.

"Since this is thoroughly tongue in cheek, *Tank Girl* has a likable brashness, even when breathless, pointless plotting threatens to eclipse the movie's charms."

–Janet Maslin, *The New York Times*

"Working from a generally faithful script by Teri [*actually Tedi*] Sarafian, director Rachel Talalay opts for an approach that emphasizes surface and flash at the expense of depth and coherence – much like its source."

–Richard Harrington, *Washington Post*

"I hate to attack one of the rare major studio movies featuring a dominant female character, especially one with the even rarer distinction of being directed by a woman. But if the genders are ever balanced in Hollywood, no one is going to look back on *Tank Girl* and its bawdy, beer-guzzling heroine as a landmark."

–JACK MATHEWS, NEW YORK *NEWSDAY*

"Watching *Tank Girl* is as disorienting as waking up in someone else's bad dream. You want to get out as fast as possible, but all the exits seem to be blocked."

–Kenneth Turan, *Los Angeles Times*

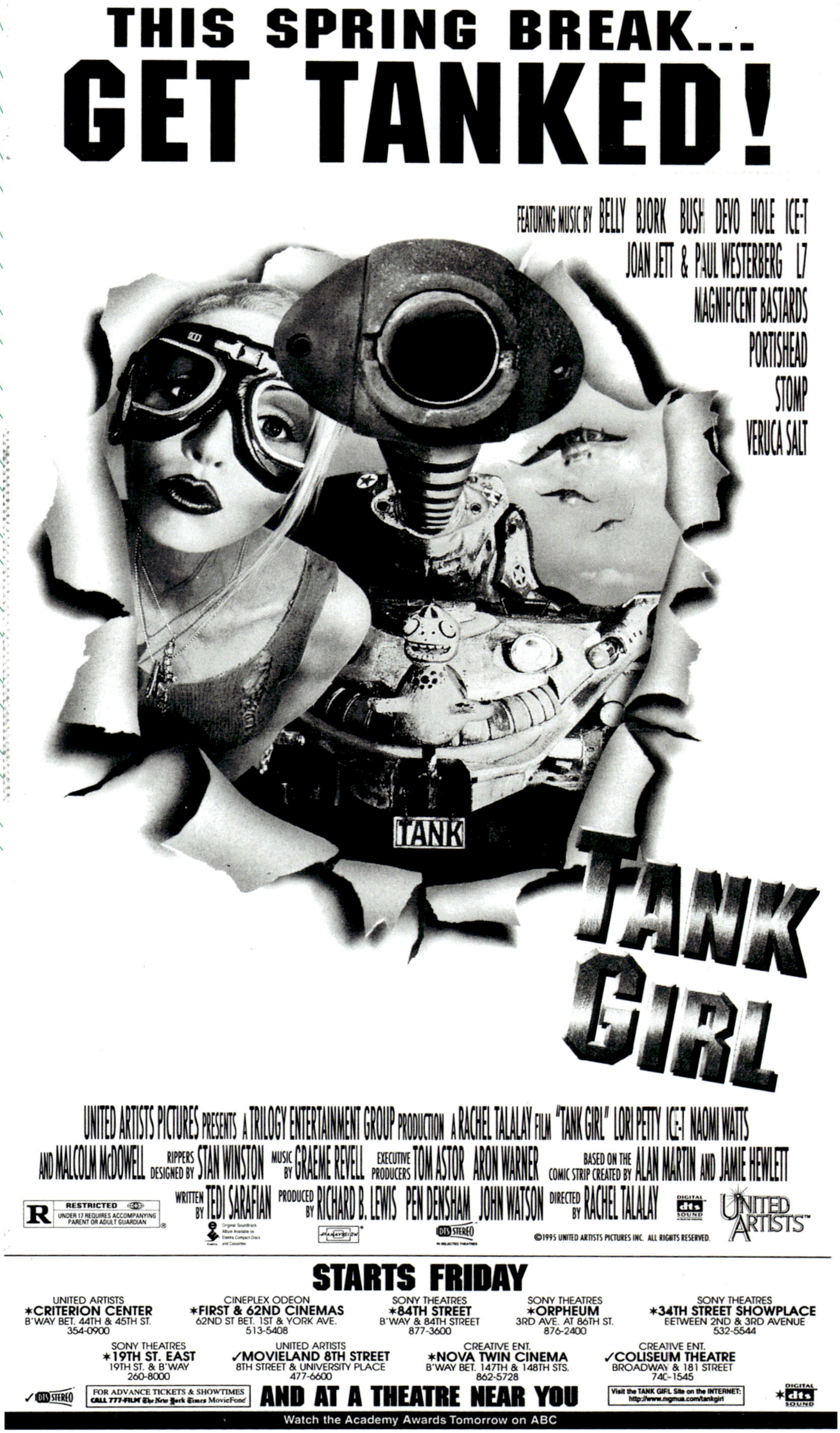
THIS SPRING BREAK...
GET TANKED!
FEATURING MUSIC BY BELLY BJORK BUSH DEVO HOLE ICE-T
JOAN JETT & PAUL WESTERBERG L7
MAGNIFICENT BASTARDS
PORTISHEAD
STOMP
VERUCA SALT
TANK
TANK GIRL
UNITED ARTISTS PICTURES PRESENTS A TRILOGY ENTERTAINMENT GROUP PRODUCTION A RACHEL TALALAY FILM "TANK GIRL" LORI PETTY ICE-T NAOMI WATTS
AND MALCOLM McDOWELL RIPPERS DESIGNED BY STAN WINSTON MUSIC BY GRAEME REVELL EXECUTIVE PRODUCERS TOM ASTOR ARON WARNER BASED ON THE COMIC STRIP CREATED BY ALAN MARTIN AND JAMIE HEWLETT
WRITTEN BY TEDI SARAFIAN PRODUCED BY RICHARD B. LEWIS PEN DENSHAM JOHN WATSON DIRECTED BY RACHEL TALALAY
R RESTRICTED
UNDER 17 REQUIRES ACCOMPANYING PARENT OR ADULT GUARDIAN
DTS STEREO
©1995 UNITED ARTISTS PICTURES INC. ALL RIGHTS RESERVED.
UNITED ARTISTS
STARTS FRIDAY
UNITED ARTISTS ∗CRITERION CENTER B'WAY BET. 44TH & 45TH ST. 354-0900
CINEPLEX ODEON ∗FIRST & 62ND CINEMAS 62ND ST BET. 1ST & YORK AVE. 513-5408
SONY THEATRES ∗84TH STREET B'WAY & 84TH STREET 877-3600
SONY THEATRES ∗ORPHEUM 3RD AVE. AT 86TH ST. 876-2400
SONY THEATRES ∗34TH STREET SHOWPLACE BETWEEN 2ND & 3RD AVENUE 532-5544
SONY THEATRES ∗19TH ST. EAST 19TH ST. & B'WAY 260-8000
UNITED ARTISTS ✓MOVIELAND 8TH STREET 8TH STREET & UNIVERSITY PLACE 477-6600
CREATIVE ENT. ∗NOVA TWIN CINEMA B'WAY BET. 147TH & 148TH STS. 862-5728
CREATIVE ENT. ✓COLISEUM THEATRE BROADWAY & 181 STREET 740-1545
✓DTS STEREO
FOR ADVANCE TICKETS & SHOWTIMES CALL 777-FILM The New York Times MovieFone
AND AT A THEATRE NEAR YOU
Visit the TANK GIRL Site on the INTERNET: http://www.mgmua.com/tankgirl
∗DIGITAL dts SOUND
Watch the Academy Awards Tomorrow on ABC

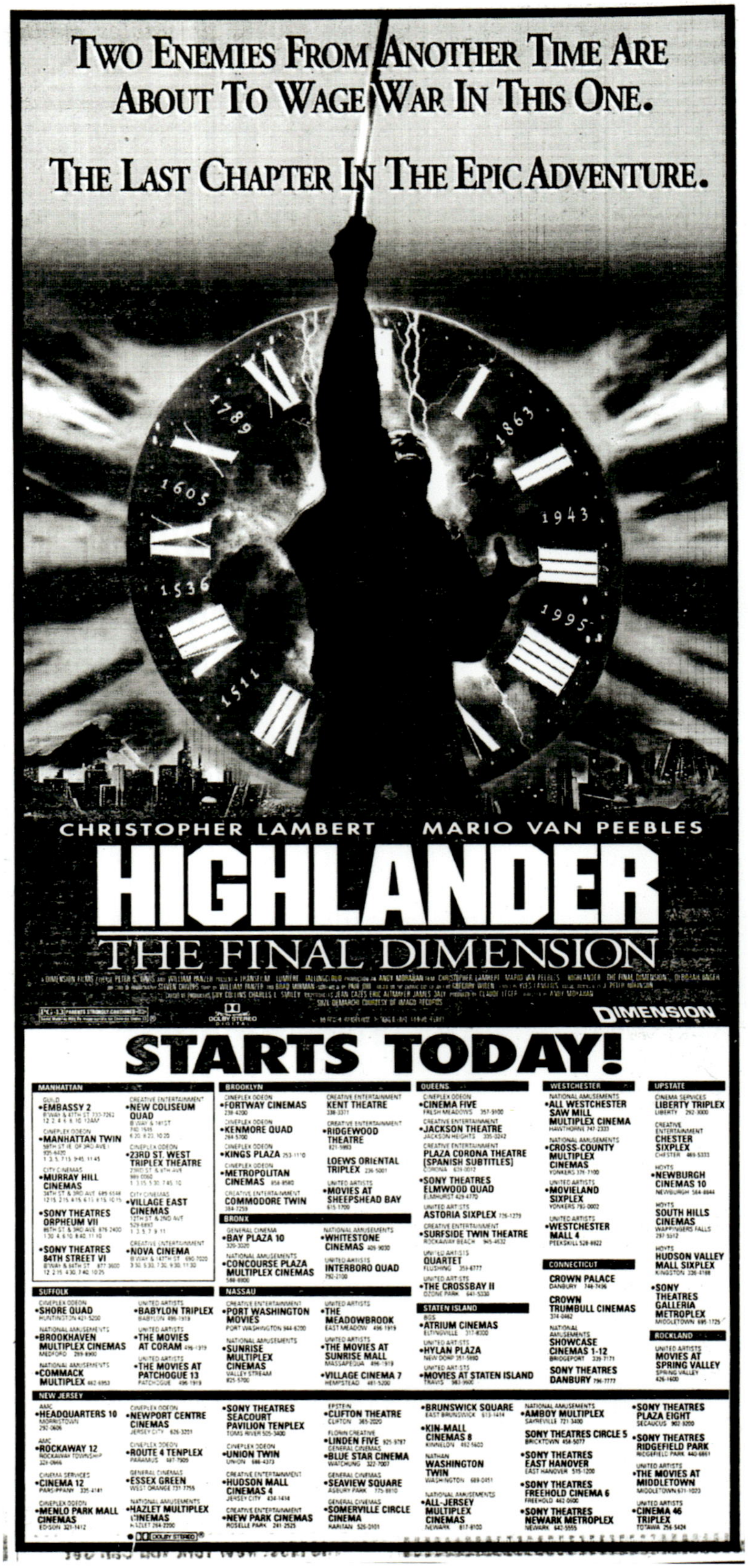

WATERWORLD

Once upon a time, scriptwriter Peter Rader conceived a postapocalyptic action story set on the ocean for Roger Corman and producer Brad Krevoy, who responded that they could never do it, as it would cost at least $5 million. Years later, after rewrites by David Twohy, the project reunited *Robin Hood: Prince of Thieves* star Kevin Costner and director Kevin Reynolds, and won infamy as the most expensive movie ever made at the time. Thanks to difficulties shooting on the water, the budget ballooned to $175 million, inspiring nicknames like "*Fishtar*" and "*Kevin's Gate*," to the point where some critics couldn't help but review the production circumstances along with the film. And some of them even liked it.

"If you're looking for some harmonic combination of art and entertainment…you're treading water in the wrong sea park. This $150-million (and counting) production…has been budgeted chiefly for spectacle. And if the story…seems a little waterlogged, it's still big, loud, and fun to watch."

–Desson Howe, *Washington Post*

"In fact, *Waterworld* is quite entertaining and thought-provoking. Despite its mediocre script, uneven direction, choppy editing, and bloated self-importance, the movie offers a multitude of unusual thrills."

–JAMI BERNARD, NEW YORK *DAILY NEWS*

"Unlike *Batman Forever* and some of the other summer blockbusters, *Waterworld* is not a cynically made film designed to pander to the public's fickle taste. It's a genuine vault at greatness that misses the mark – but survives."

–Mick LaSalle, *San Francisco Chronicle*

"It lacks the coherent fantasy of truly enveloping science fiction, preferring to concentrate on flashy, isolated stunts that say more about expense than expertise. Its storytelling, remarkably crude for such an elaborate production, takes a back seat to its enthusiasm for post-apocalyptic rust and rubble."

–Janet Maslin, *The New York Times*

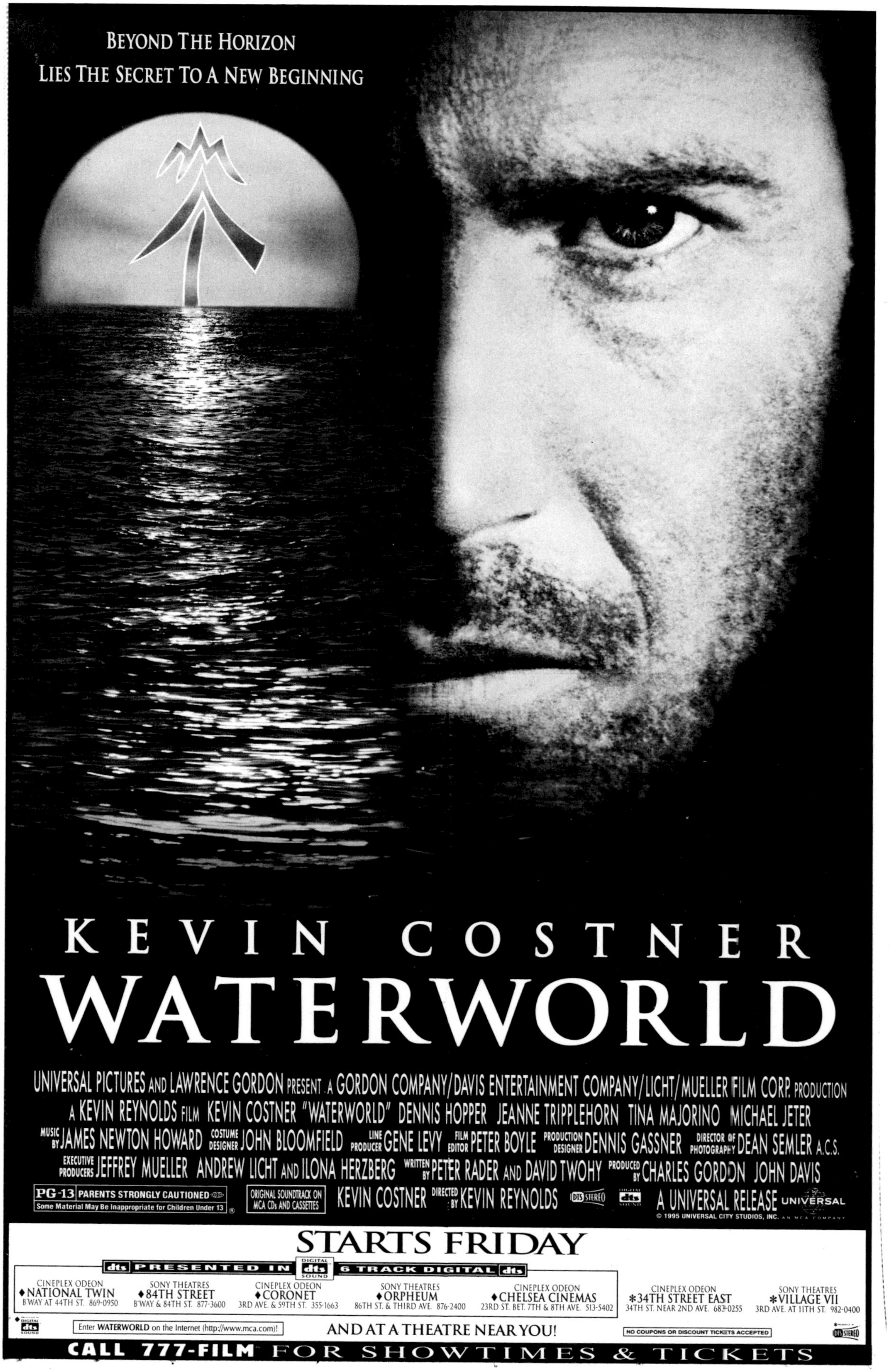
BEYOND THE HORIZON
LIES THE SECRET TO A NEW BEGINNING
KEVIN COSTNER
WATERWORLD
UNIVERSAL PICTURES AND LAWRENCE GORDON PRESENT A GORDON COMPANY/DAVIS ENTERTAINMENT COMPANY/LICHT/MUELLER FILM CORP. PRODUCTION
A KEVIN REYNOLDS FILM KEVIN COSTNER "WATERWORLD" DENNIS HOPPER JEANNE TRIPPLEHORN TINA MAJORINO MICHAEL JETER
MUSIC BY JAMES NEWTON HOWARD COSTUME DESIGNER JOHN BLOOMFIELD LINE PRODUCER GENE LEVY FILM EDITOR PETER BOYLE PRODUCTION DESIGNER DENNIS GASSNER DIRECTOR OF PHOTOGRAPHY DEAN SEMLER A.C.S.
EXECUTIVE PRODUCERS JEFFREY MUELLER ANDREW LICHT AND ILONA HERZBERG WRITTEN BY PETER RADER AND DAVID TWOHY PRODUCED BY CHARLES GORDON JOHN DAVIS
PG-13 PARENTS STRONGLY CAUTIONED
Some Material May Be Inappropriate for Children Under 13
ORIGINAL SOUNDTRACK ON MCA CDs AND CASSETTES
KEVIN COSTNER DIRECTED BY KEVIN REYNOLDS
A UNIVERSAL RELEASE UNIVERSAL
© 1995 UNIVERSAL CITY STUDIOS, INC.
STARTS FRIDAY
PRESENTED IN DIGITAL dts SOUND 6 TRACK DIGITAL
CINEPLEX ODEON ♦NATIONAL TWIN B'WAY AT 44TH ST. 869-0950
SONY THEATRES ♦84TH STREET B'WAY & 84TH ST. 877-3600
CINEPLEX ODEON ♦CORONET 3RD AVE. & 59TH ST. 355-1663
SONY THEATRES ♦ORPHEUM 86TH ST. & THIRD AVE. 876-2400
CINEPLEX ODEON ♦CHELSEA CINEMAS 23RD ST. BET. 7TH & 8TH AVE. 513-5402
CINEPLEX ODEON ✻34TH STREET EAST 34TH ST. NEAR 2ND AVE. 683-0255
SONY THEATRES ✻VILLAGE VII 3RD AVE. AT 11TH ST. 982-0400
Enter WATERWORLD on the Internet (http://www.mca.com)!
AND AT A THEATRE NEAR YOU!
NO COUPONS OR DISCOUNT TICKETS ACCEPTED
CALL 777-FILM FOR SHOWTIMES & TICKETS

THE NEW YORK TIMES, FRIDAY, AUGUST 18, 1995 C15

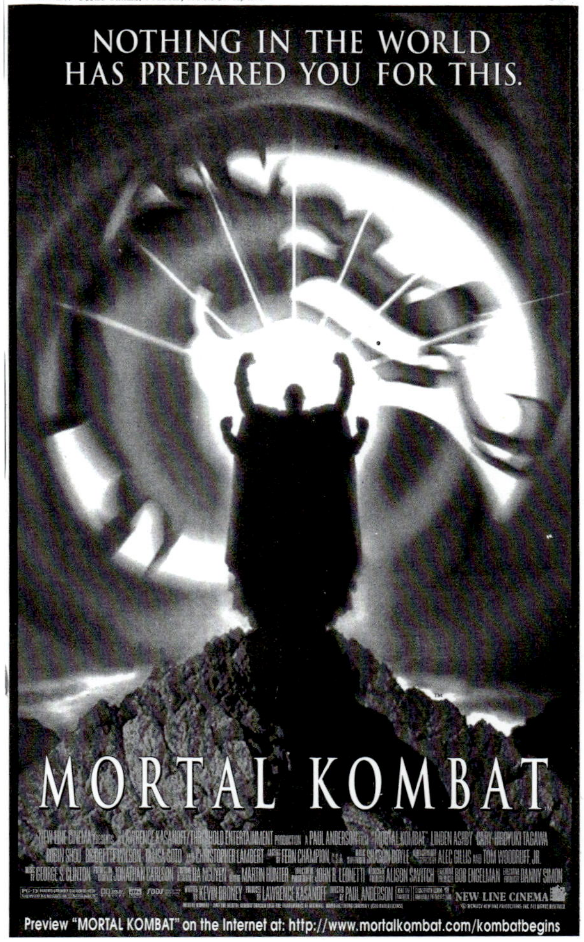

THE NEW YORK TIMES, SUNDAY, JUNE 11, 1995 17

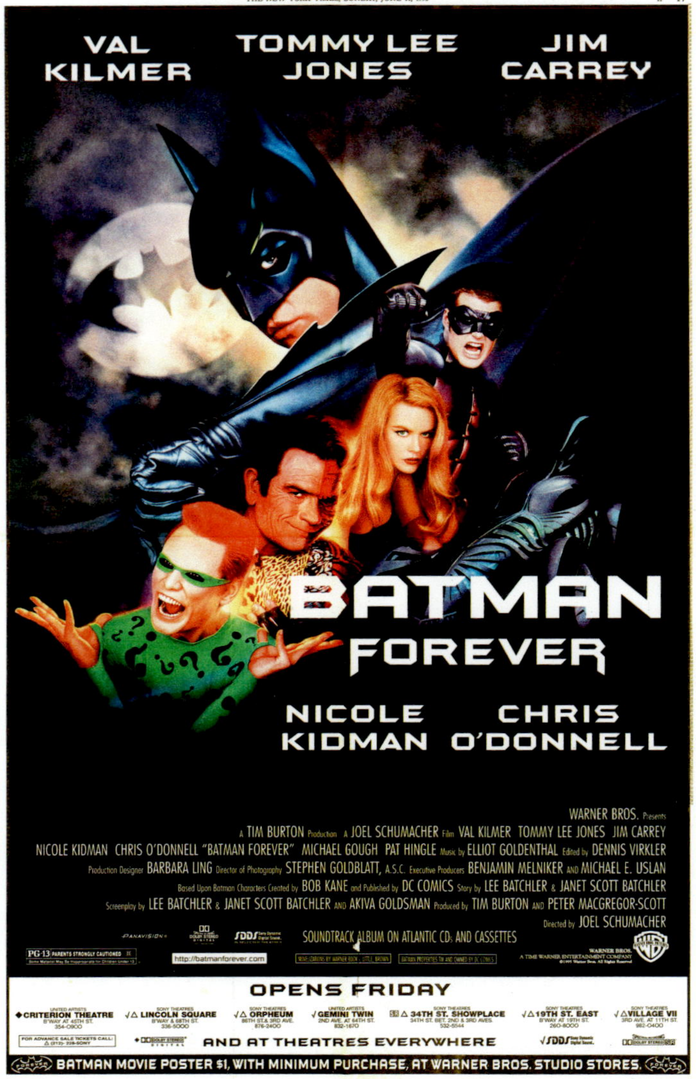

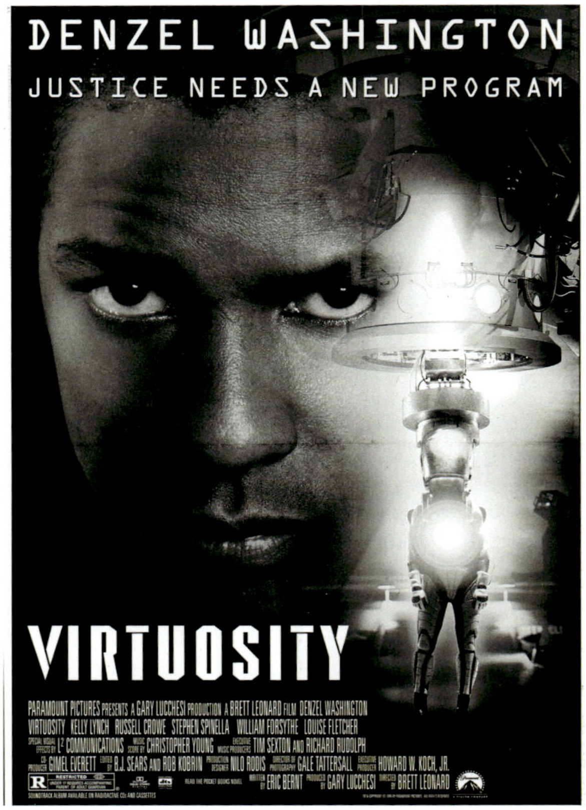

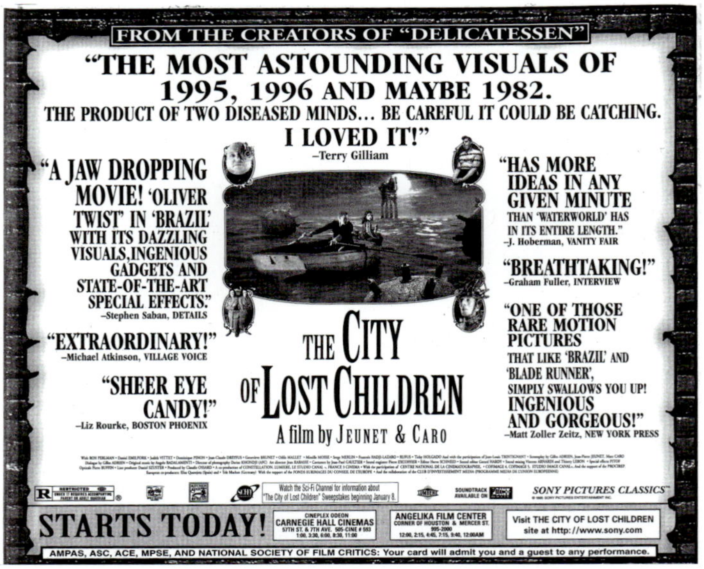

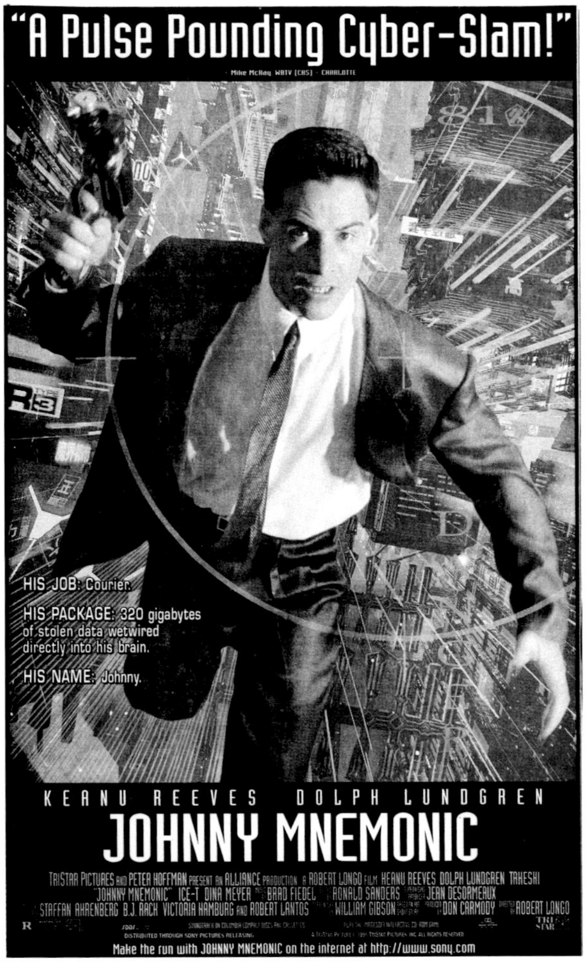
"A Pulse Pounding Cyber-Slam!"
Mike McRay WBTV (CBS) - CHARLOTTE
HIS JOB: Courier.
HIS PACKAGE: 320 gigabytes of stolen data wetwired directly into his brain.
HIS NAME: Johnny.
KEANU REEVES DOLPH LUNDGREN
JOHNNY MNEMONIC
TRISTAR PICTURES AND PETER HOFFMAN PRESENT AN ALLIANCE PRODUCTION A ROBERT LONGO FILM KEANU REEVES DOLPH LUNDGREN TAKESHI
"JOHNNY MNEMONIC" ICE-T DINA MEYER BRAD FIEDEL RONALD SANDERS JEAN DESORMEAUX
STAFFAN AHRENBERG B.J. RACK VICTORIA HAMBURG AND ROBERT LANTOS WILLIAM GIBSON DON CARMODY ROBERT LONGO
DISTRIBUTED THROUGH SONY PICTURES RELEASING
Make the run with JOHNNY MNEMONIC on the internet at http://www.sony.com

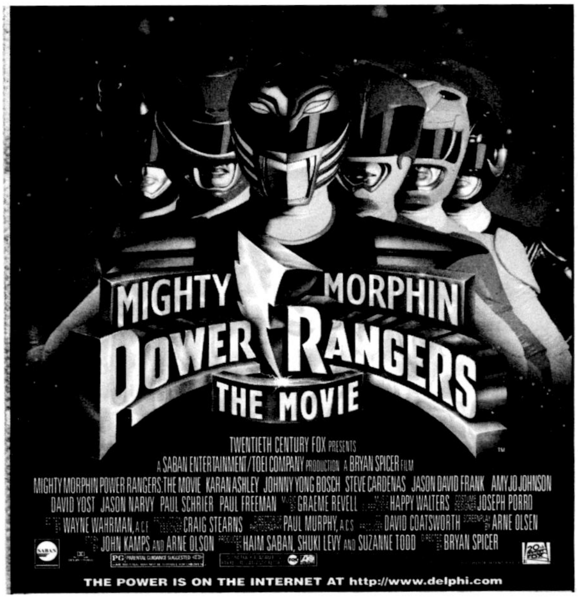
MIGHTY MORPHIN
POWER RANGERS
THE MOVIE
TWENTIETH CENTURY FOX PRESENTS
A SABAN ENTERTAINMENT/TOEI COMPANY PRODUCTION A BRYAN SPICER FILM
MIGHTY MORPHIN POWER RANGERS: THE MOVIE KARAN ASHLEY JOHNNY YONG BOSCH STEVE CARDENAS JASON DAVID FRANK AMY JO JOHNSON
DAVID YOST JASON NARVY PAUL SCHRIER PAUL FREEMAN MUSIC BY GRAEME REVELL HAPPY WALTERS COSTUME DESIGNER JOSEPH PORRO
WAYNE WAHRMAN, A.C.E. CRAIG STEARNS DIRECTOR OF PHOTOGRAPHY PAUL MURPHY, A.C.S. DAVID COATSWORTH SCREENPLAY BY ARNE OLSEN
JOHN KAMPS AND ARNE OLSON PRODUCED BY HAIM SABAN, SHUKI LEVY AND SUZANNE TODD DIRECTED BY BRYAN SPICER
PG PARENTAL GUIDANCE SUGGESTED
THE POWER IS ON THE INTERNET AT http://www.delphi.com

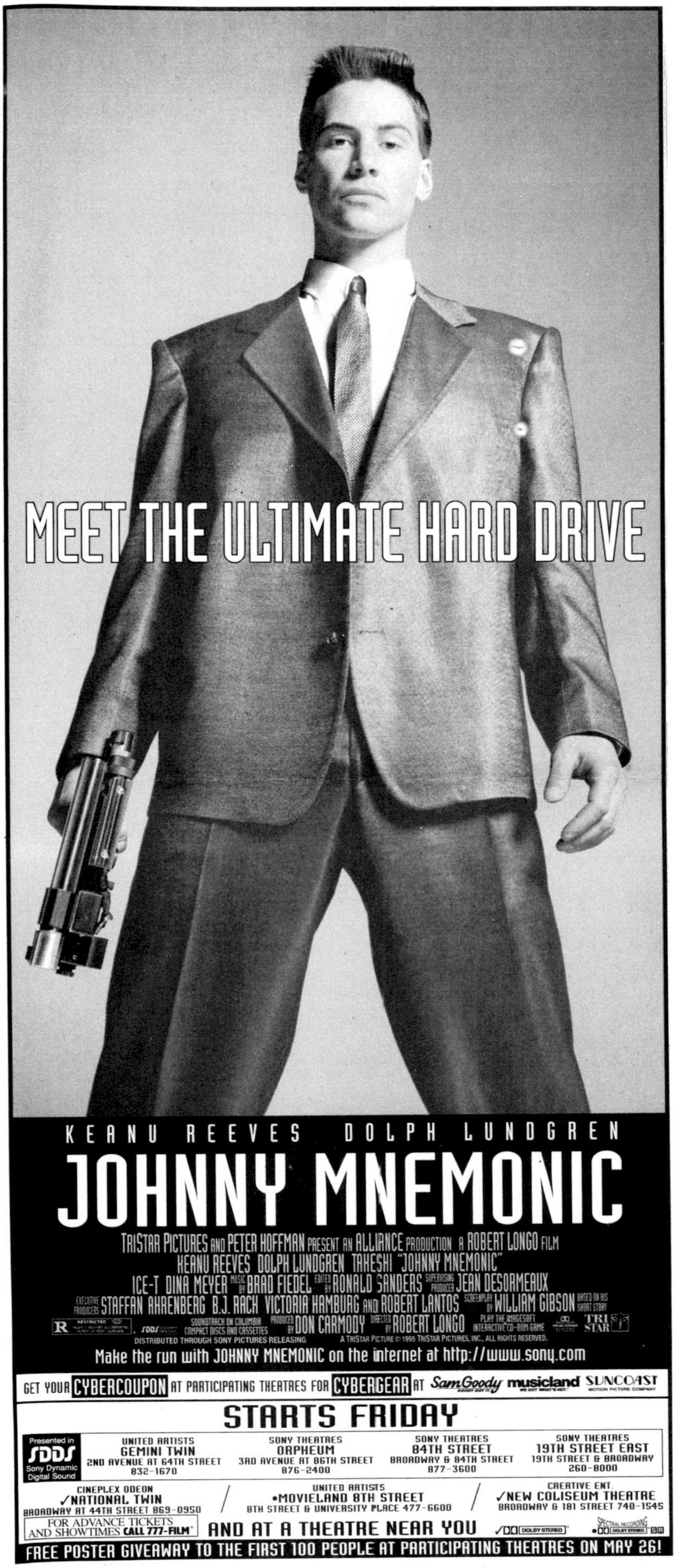
MEET THE ULTIMATE HARD DRIVE
KEANU REEVES DOLPH LUNDGREN
JOHNNY MNEMONIC
TRISTAR PICTURES AND PETER HOFFMAN PRESENT AN ALLIANCE PRODUCTION A ROBERT LONGO FILM
KEANU REEVES DOLPH LUNDGREN TAKESHI "JOHNNY MNEMONIC"
ICE-T DINA MEYER MUSIC BY BRAD FIEDEL EDITED BY RONALD SANDERS SUPERVISING PRODUCER JEAN DESORMEAUX
EXECUTIVE PRODUCERS STAFFAN AHRENBERG B.J. RACK VICTORIA HAMBURG AND ROBERT LANTOS SCREENPLAY BY WILLIAM GIBSON BASED ON HIS SHORT STORY
SOUNDTRACK ON COLUMBIA COMPACT DISCS AND CASSETTES PRODUCED BY DON CARMODY DIRECTED BY ROBERT LONGO PLAY THE IMAGESOFT INTERACTIVE CD-ROM GAME
DISTRIBUTED THROUGH SONY PICTURES RELEASING
A TRISTAR PICTURE © 1995 TRISTAR PICTURES, INC., ALL RIGHTS RESERVED.
Make the run with JOHNNY MNEMONIC on the internet at http://www.sony.com
GET YOUR CYBERCOUPON AT PARTICIPATING THEATRES FOR CYBERGEAR AT Sam Goody musicland SUNCOAST MOTION PICTURE COMPANY
STARTS FRIDAY
Presented in SDDS Sony Dynamic Digital Sound
UNITED ARTISTS GEMINI TWIN 2ND AVENUE AT 64TH STREET 832-1670
SONY THEATRES ORPHEUM 3RD AVENUE AT 86TH STREET 876-2400
SONY THEATRES 84TH STREET BROADWAY & 84TH STREET 877-3600
SONY THEATRES 19TH STREET EAST 19TH STREET & BROADWAY 260-8000
CINEPLEX ODEON ✓NATIONAL TWIN BROADWAY AT 44TH STREET 869-0950
UNITED ARTISTS •MOVIELAND 8TH STREET 8TH STREET & UNIVERSITY PLACE 477-6600
CREATIVE ENT. ✓NEW COLISEUM THEATRE BROADWAY & 181 STREET 740-1545
FOR ADVANCE TICKETS AND SHOWTIMES CALL 777-FILM
AND AT A THEATRE NEAR YOU
FREE POSTER GIVEAWAY TO THE FIRST 100 PEOPLE AT PARTICIPATING THEATRES ON MAY 26!

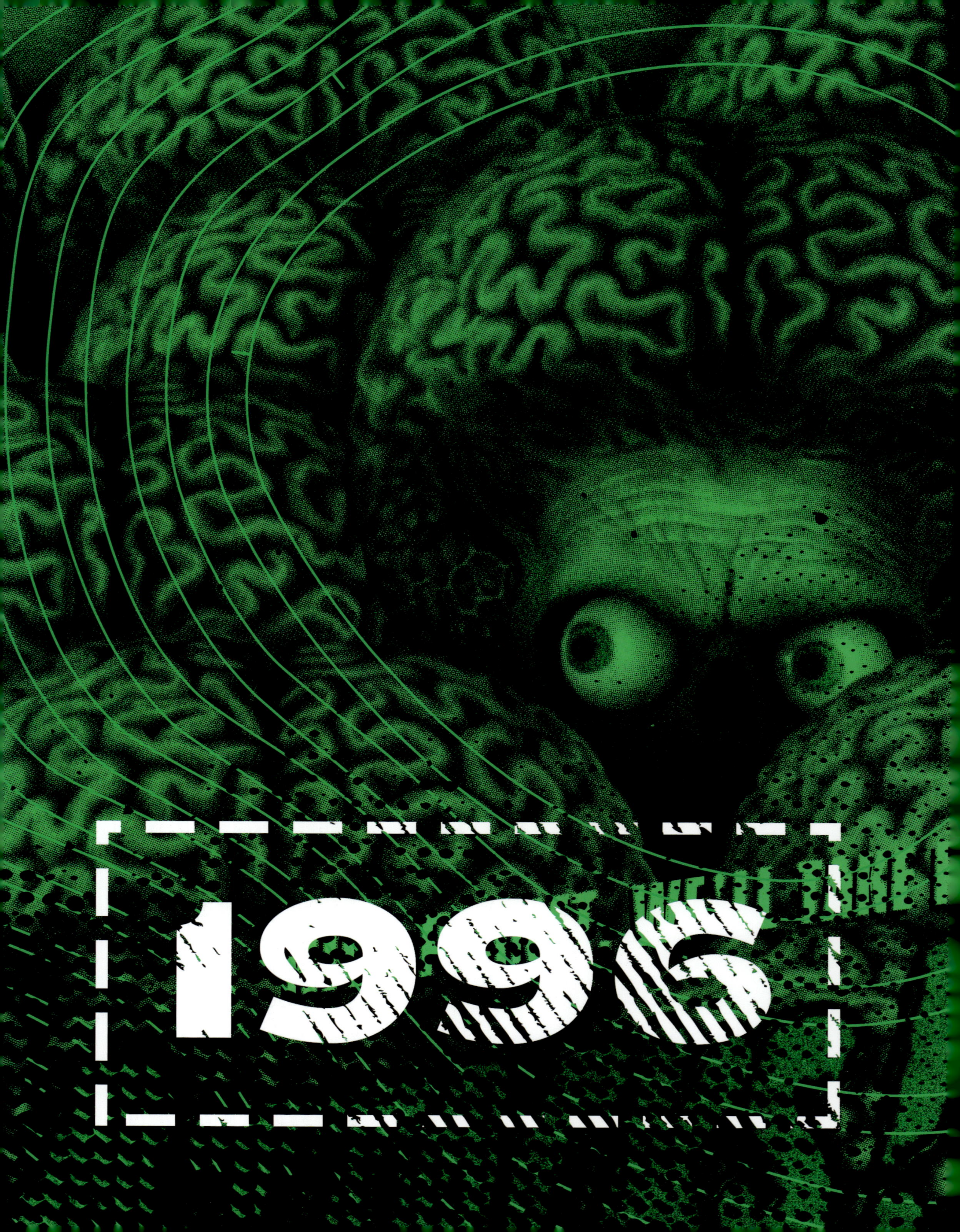
1996

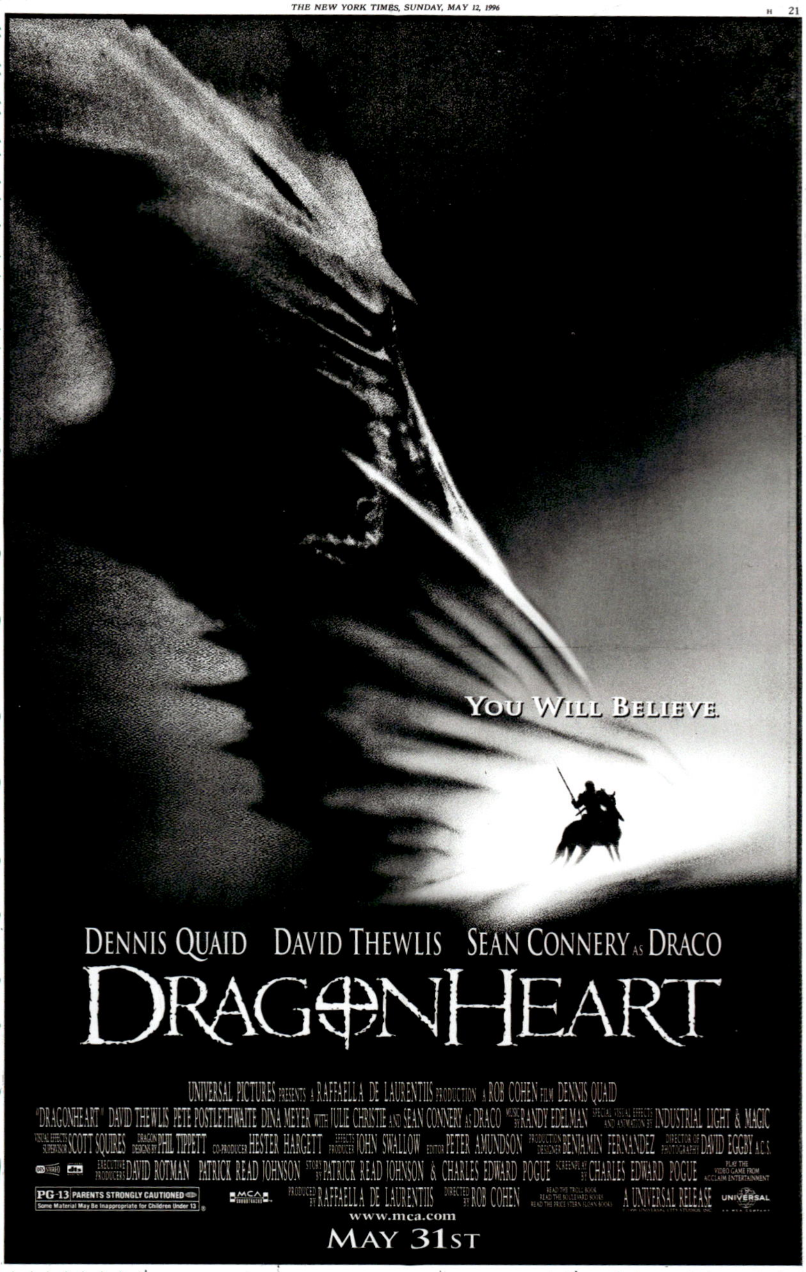

THE NEW YORK TIMES, SUNDAY, MAY 12, 1996
H 21
YOU WILL BELIEVE.
DENNIS QUAID DAVID THEWLIS SEAN CONNERY AS DRACO
DRAGONHEART
UNIVERSAL PICTURES PRESENTS A RAFFAELLA DE LAURENTIIS PRODUCTION A ROB COHEN FILM DENNIS QUAID
PG-13 PARENTS STRONGLY CAUTIONED
A UNIVERSAL RELEASE
www.mca.com
MAY 31ST

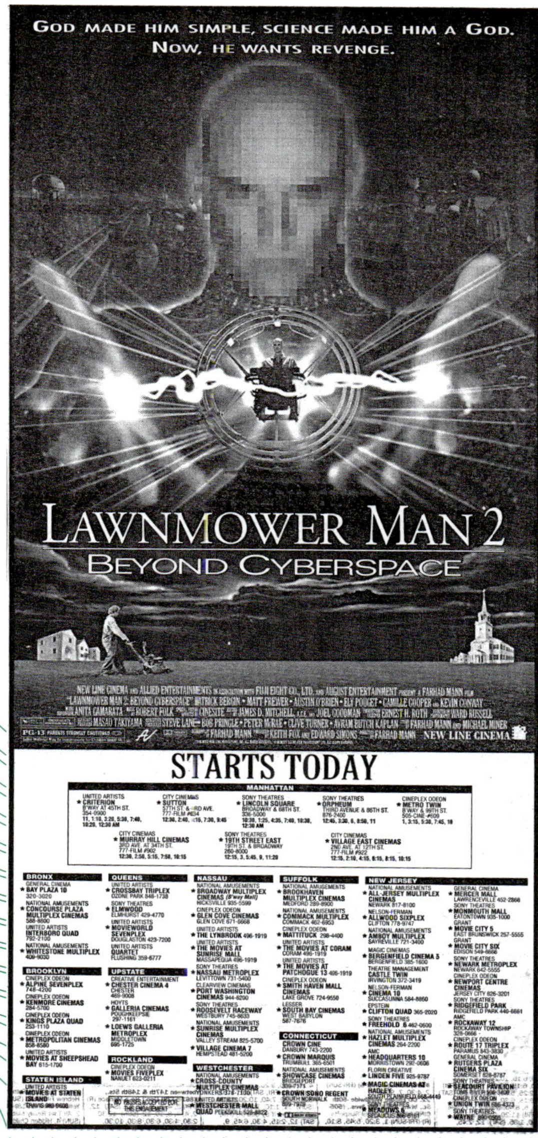

GOD MADE HIM SIMPLE, SCIENCE MADE HIM A GOD.
NOW, HE WANTS REVENGE.
LAWNMOWER MAN 2
BEYOND CYBERSPACE
NEW LINE CINEMA
STARTS TODAY
MANHATTAN
BRONX
QUEENS
NASSAU
SUFFOLK
NEW JERSEY
BROOKLYN
UPSTATE
WESTCHESTER
ROCKLAND
CONNECTICUT
STATEN ISLAND

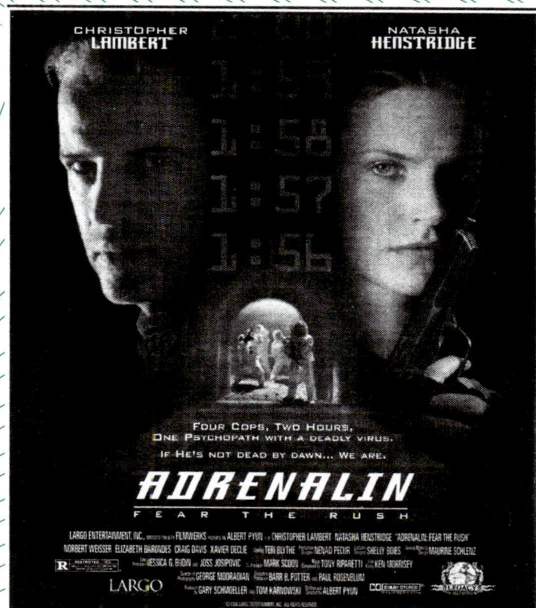

CHRISTOPHER LAMBERT
NATASHA HENSTRIDGE
1:58
1:57
1:56
FOUR COPS, TWO HOURS,
ONE PSYCHOPATH WITH A DEADLY VIRUS.
IF HE'S NOT DEAD BY DAWN... WE ARE.
ADRENALIN
FEAR THE RUSH
LARGO

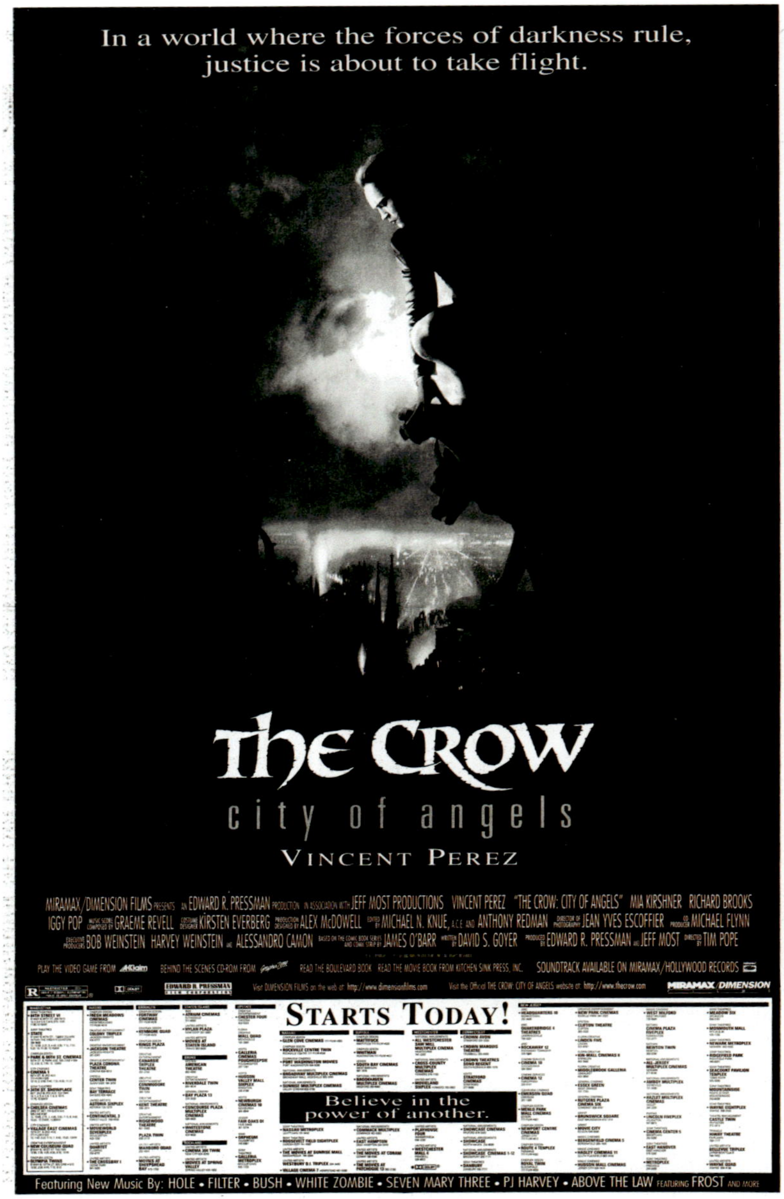

BARB WIRE

The second attempt in as many years, after *Tank Girl*, to bring a female comic book hero to the screen, *Barb Wire* wasn't done any credibility favors by the casting of *Playboy* model/*Baywatch* babe Pamela Anderson (then billed as Pamela Anderson Lee, as she was married at the time to Mötley Crüe's Tommy Lee – her co-star in an infamous sex tape). Yet surprisingly, a few critics responded favorably to the film – which adapted the plot of *Casablanca*, of all things, into its action-packed futuristic world of 2017.

"The movie carries its cyberpunk variation [of *Casablanca*] right through to the end, and usually with enough wit and craziness to freshen the mix. Then, there is Pamela, whose tight, disciplined performance deserves more respect than it will almost certainly get."

–Hal Hinson, *Washington Post*

"This is not great sci-fi or even great camp. But it is trash with a definite attitude, and thanks to some slick-looking visuals and a handful of strong supporting performances, it works better than it should."

–John Petrakis, *Chicago Tribune*

"...Lee is a direct rebuke to Mother Nature, a creature about as likely to occur in the wild as a Lincoln Continental. But in *Barb Wire*, she's strangely likable, blessed with an ironic self-consciousness that suggests she's in on the joke."

–DAVE KEHR, NEW YORK *DAILY NEWS*

"Ms. Lee's makeup is painted on so heavily that she may not even be able to change expression. On the other hand, there's not much about *Barb Wire* to make her want to."

–Janet Maslin, *The New York Times*

"The hypocrisy level is annoying. Barb may be a pseudo-feminist icon, but, I assure you, she is not using her brains or convictions (either of them) to litter the set with corpses."

–Allan Ulrich, *San Francisco Examiner*

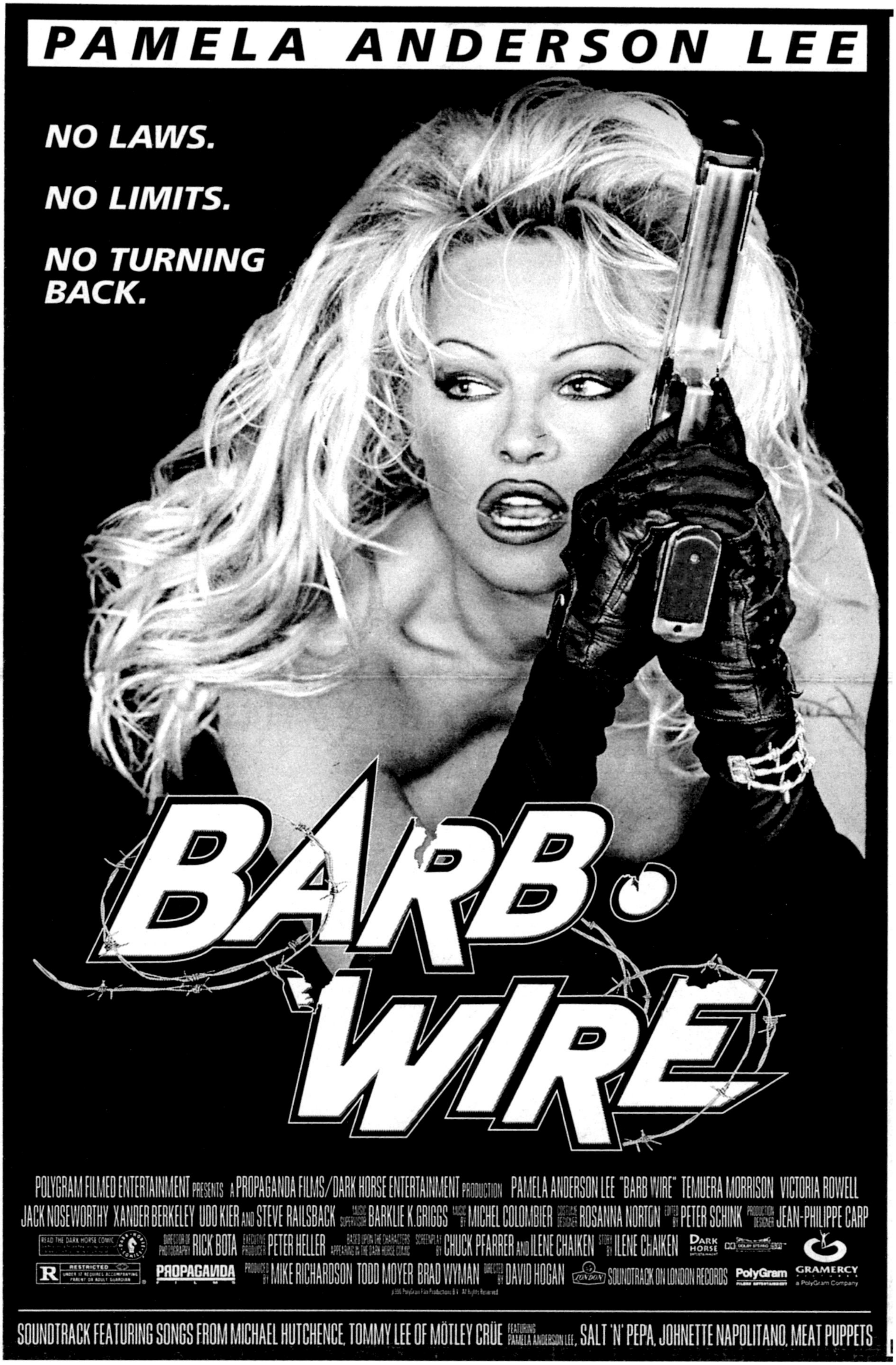
PAMELA ANDERSON LEE
NO LAWS.
NO LIMITS.
NO TURNING BACK.
BARB WIRE
POLYGRAM FILMED ENTERTAINMENT PRESENTS A PROPAGANDA FILMS/DARK HORSE ENTERTAINMENT PRODUCTION PAMELA ANDERSON LEE "BARB WIRE" TEMUERA MORRISON VICTORIA ROWELL
JACK NOSEWORTHY XANDER BERKELEY UDO KIER AND STEVE RAILSBACK MUSIC SUPERVISOR BARKLIE K. GRIGGS MUSIC BY MICHEL COLOMBIER COSTUME DESIGNER ROSANNA NORTON EDITED BY PETER SCHINK PRODUCTION DESIGNER JEAN-PHILIPPE CARP
READ THE DARK HORSE COMIC
DIRECTOR OF PHOTOGRAPHY RICK BOTA EXECUTIVE PRODUCER PETER HELLER BASED UPON THE CHARACTERS APPEARING IN THE DARK HORSE COMIC SCREENPLAY BY CHUCK PFARRER AND ILENE CHAIKEN STORY BY ILENE CHAIKEN
DARK HORSE
R RESTRICTED UNDER 17 REQUIRES ACCOMPANYING PARENT OR ADULT GUARDIAN
PROPAGANDA FILMS
PRODUCED BY MIKE RICHARDSON TODD MOYER BRAD WYMAN DIRECTED BY DAVID HOGAN
LONDON SOUNDTRACK ON LONDON RECORDS
PolyGram FILMED ENTERTAINMENT
GRAMERCY PICTURES a PolyGram Company
SOUNDTRACK FEATURING SONGS FROM MICHAEL HUTCHENCE, TOMMY LEE OF MÖTLEY CRÜE FEATURING PAMELA ANDERSON LEE, SALT 'N' PEPA, JOHNETTE NAPOLITANO, MEAT PUPPETS

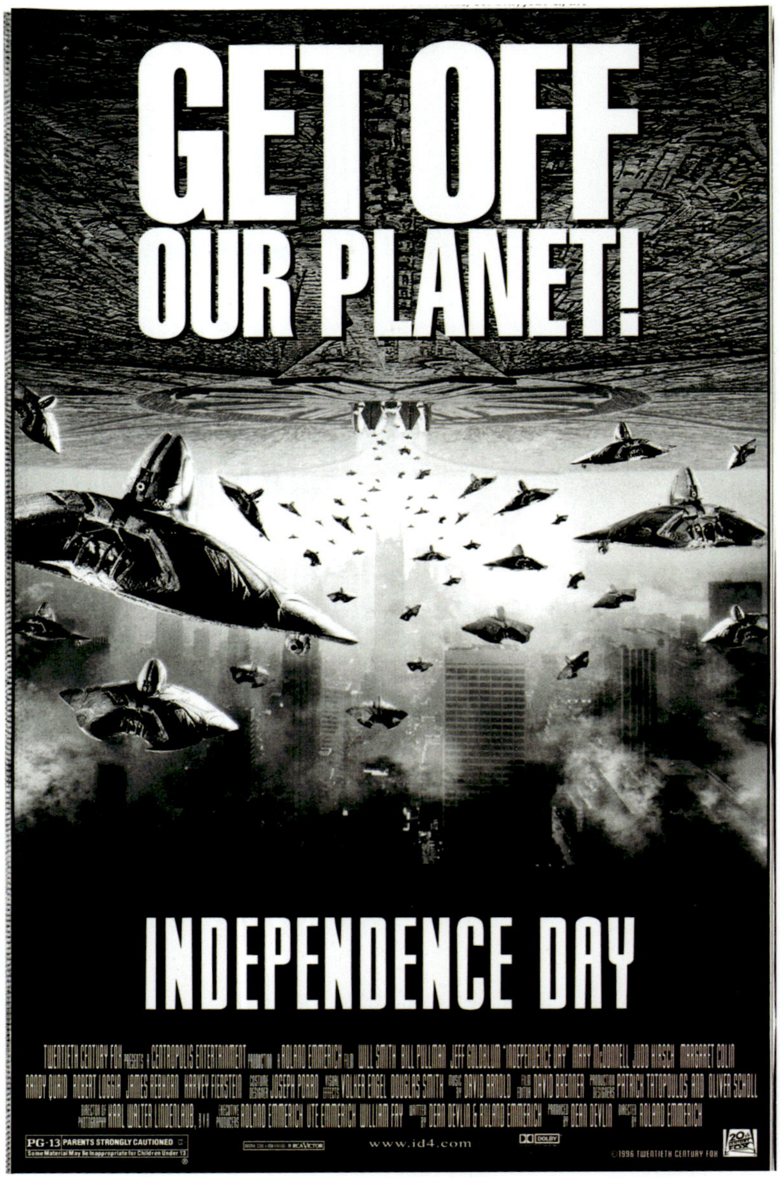

INDEPENDENCE DAY

With its titular tie to a prime summer box-office holiday, Roland Emmerich's update of '50s alien-invasion thrillers was as surefire a hit as Hollywood had in summer '96. And so it came to pass: *Independence Day* became the year's highest grosser and set trends in blockbuster marketing, such as the now-common airing of teaser trailers during the Super Bowl. Who cared if most critics wrote that the film was all about the spectacle and not about the story or characters?

"This is a movie that combines overwhelming scope and almost lunatic notions with enough surprising good humor and technical ingenuity to make most of them palatable and entertaining."

–Michael Wilmington, *Chicago Tribune*

"*Independence Day* is in the tradition of silly summer fun, and on that level I kind of liked it, as, indeed, I kind of like any movie with the courage to use the line, 'It's the end of the world as we know it.'"

–Roger Ebert, *Chicago Sun-Times*

"In an act as astonishing in its own way as the visual wonders, *ID4*, as it's come to be known, has consciously duplicated the cornball dramatic sensibility of those lost days. This is not a 1990s version of a 1950s movie, this is a 1950s movie, period."

–KENNETH TURAN, *LOS ANGELES TIMES*

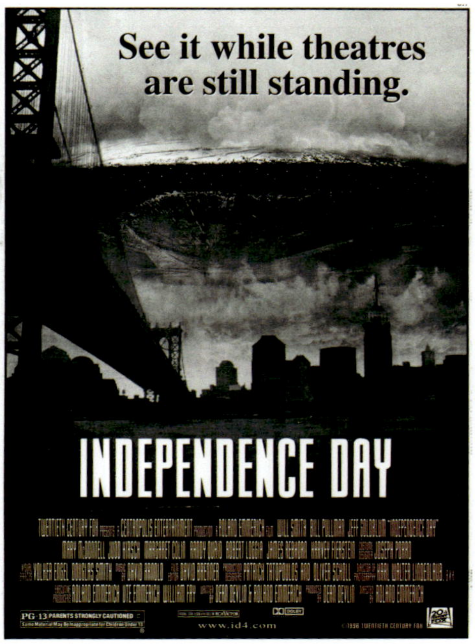

"While there's been much hoopla over the movie's stupefying effects, *Independence Day* makes no perceptible leap forward in computer-generated bedazzlements. ... Unfortunately, there is a vast expanse of dead time in which to ponder this sieve of a plot."

–Rita Kempley, *Washington Post*

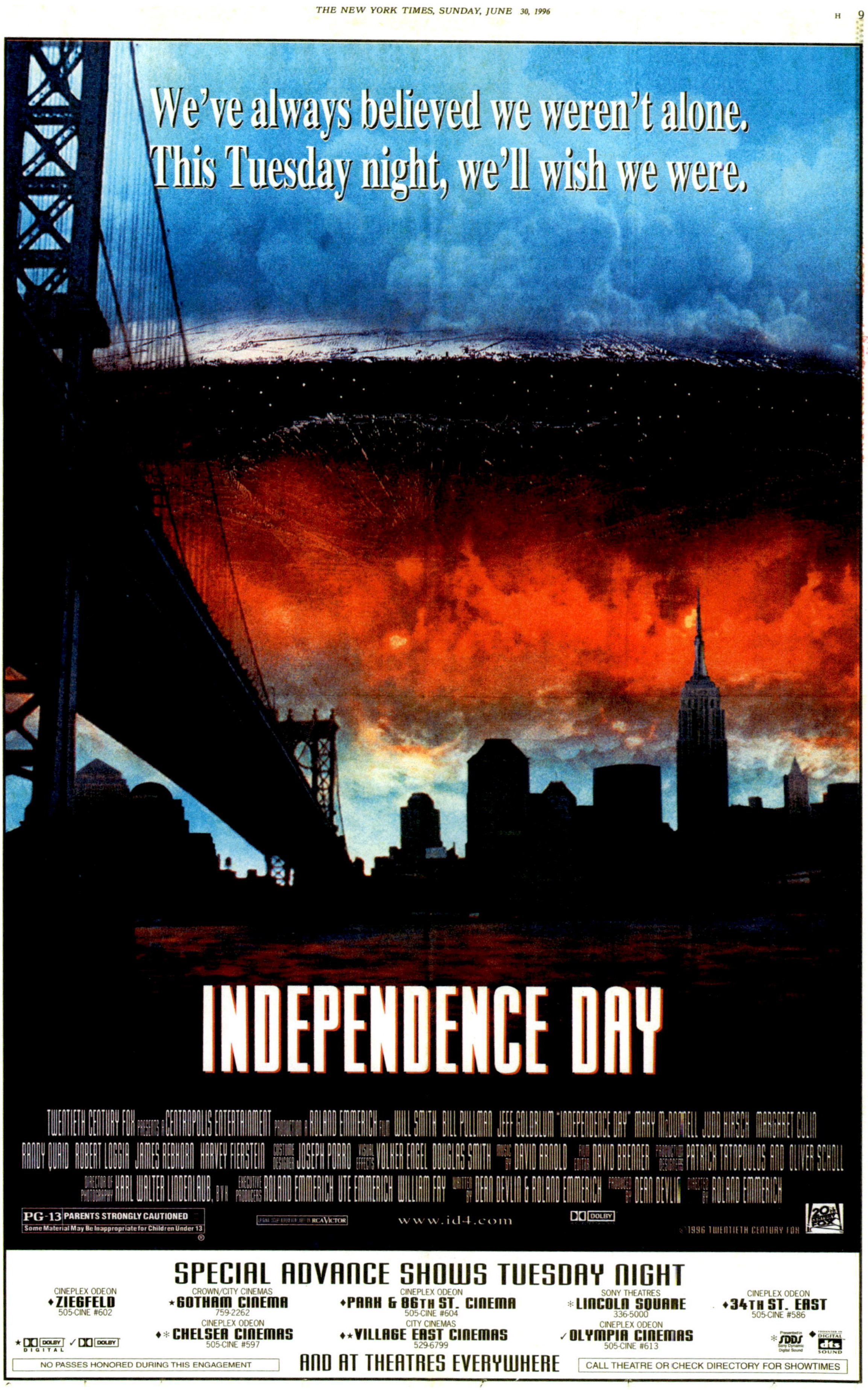
THE NEW YORK TIMES, SUNDAY, JUNE 30, 1996
H 9
We've always believed we weren't alone.
This Tuesday night, we'll wish we were.
INDEPENDENCE DAY
TWENTIETH CENTURY FOX PRESENTS A CENTROPOLIS ENTERTAINMENT PRODUCTION A ROLAND EMMERICH FILM WILL SMITH BILL PULLMAN JEFF GOLDBLUM "INDEPENDENCE DAY" MARY McDONNELL JUDD HIRSCH MARGARET COLIN
RANDY QUAID ROBERT LOGGIA JAMES REBHORN HARVEY FIERSTEIN COSTUME DESIGNER JOSEPH PORRO VISUAL EFFECTS VOLKER ENGEL DOUGLAS SMITH MUSIC BY DAVID ARNOLD FILM EDITOR DAVID BRENNER PRODUCTION DESIGNERS PATRICK TATOPOULOS AND OLIVER SCHOLL
DIRECTOR OF PHOTOGRAPHY KARL WALTER LINDENLAUB, BVK EXECUTIVE PRODUCERS ROLAND EMMERICH UTE EMMERICH WILLIAM FAY WRITTEN BY DEAN DEVLIN & ROLAND EMMERICH PRODUCED BY DEAN DEVLIN DIRECTED BY ROLAND EMMERICH
PG-13 PARENTS STRONGLY CAUTIONED
Some Material May Be Inappropriate for Children Under 13
RCA VICTOR
www.id4.com
DOLBY
©1996 TWENTIETH CENTURY FOX
SPECIAL ADVANCE SHOWS TUESDAY NIGHT
CINEPLEX ODEON ♦ZIEGFELD 505-CINE #602
CROWN/CITY CINEMAS ★GOTHAM CINEMA 759-2262
CINEPLEX ODEON ♦PARK & 86TH ST. CINEMA 505-CINE #604
SONY THEATRES ✻LINCOLN SQUARE 336-5000
CINEPLEX ODEON ♦34TH ST. EAST 505-CINE #586
CINEPLEX ODEON ♦✻CHELSEA CINEMAS 505-CINE #597
CITY CINEMAS ♦★VILLAGE EAST CINEMAS 529-6799
CINEPLEX ODEON ✓OLYMPIA CINEMAS 505-CINE #613
NO PASSES HONORED DURING THIS ENGAGEMENT
AND AT THEATRES EVERYWHERE
CALL THEATRE OR CHECK DIRECTORY FOR SHOWTIMES

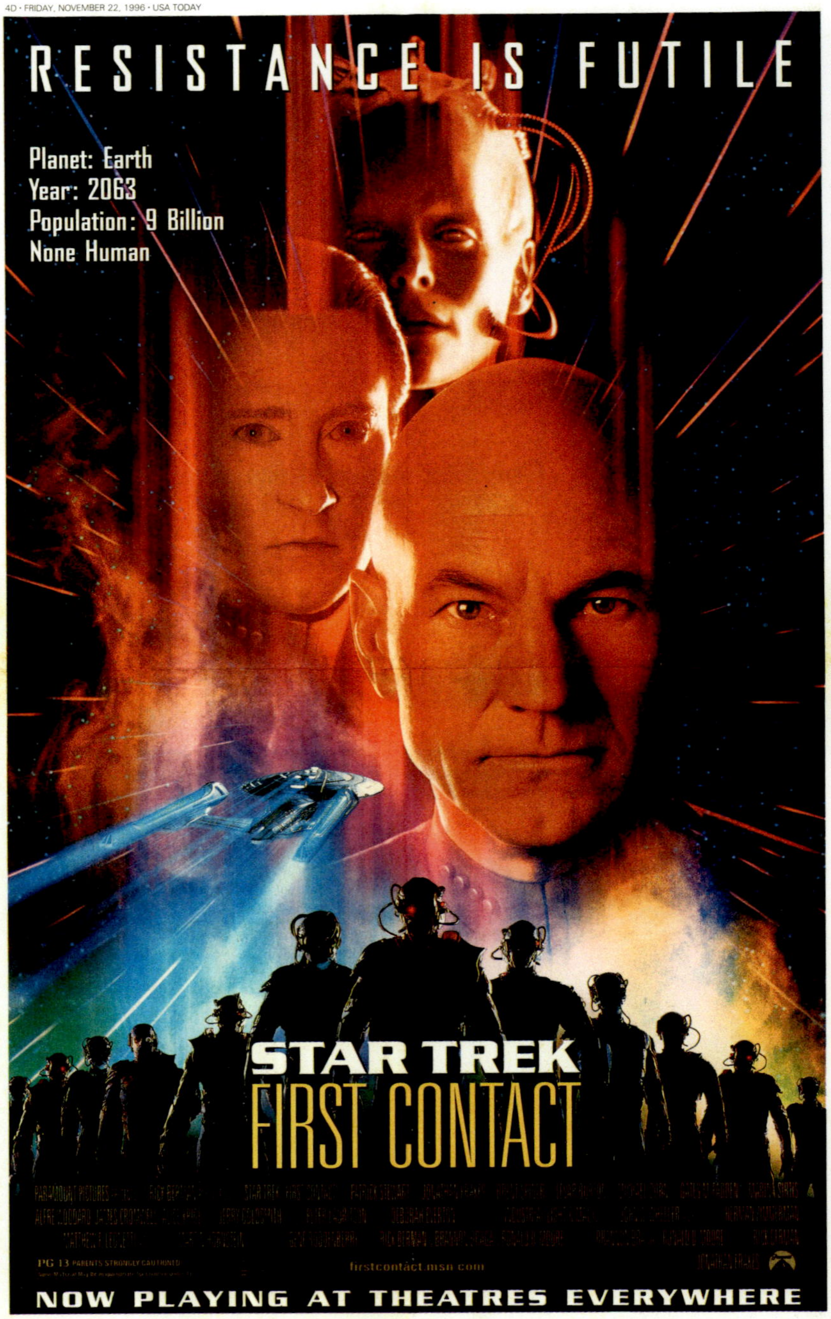
4D • FRIDAY, NOVEMBER 22, 1996 • USA TODAY
RESISTANCE IS FUTILE
Planet: Earth
Year: 2063
Population: 9 Billion
None Human
STAR TREK
FIRST CONTACT
firstcontact.msn.com
NOW PLAYING AT THEATRES EVERYWHERE

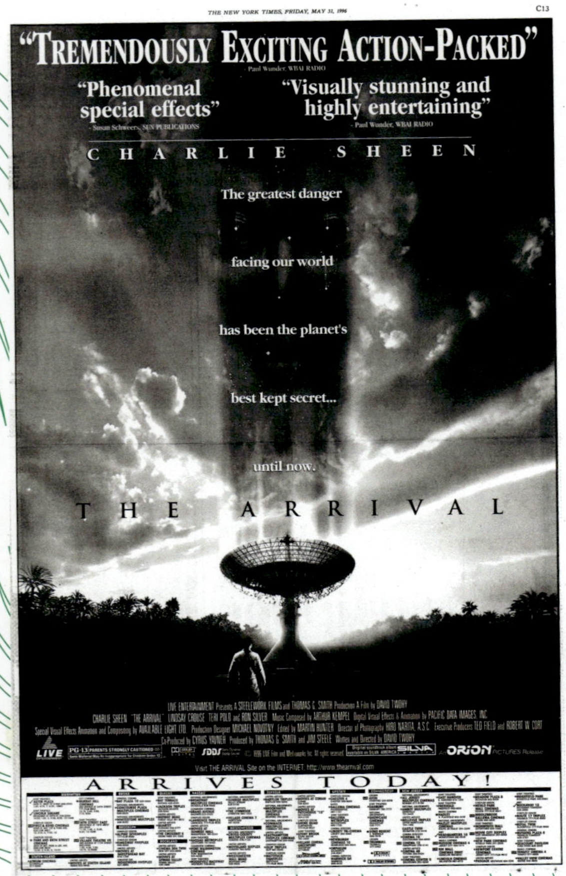
THE NEW YORK TIMES, FRIDAY, MAY 31, 1996
C13
"TREMENDOUSLY EXCITING ACTION-PACKED"
"Phenomenal special effects"
"Visually stunning and highly entertaining"
CHARLIE SHEEN
The greatest danger
facing our world
has been the planet's
best kept secret...
until now.
THE ARRIVAL
ARRIVES TODAY!

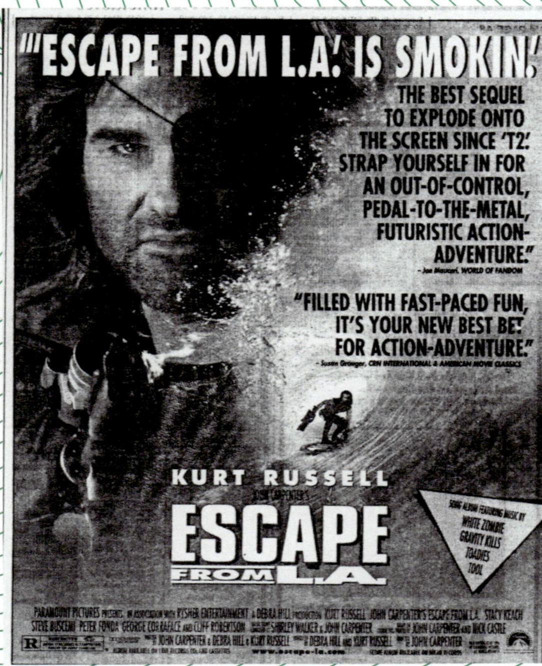
"'ESCAPE FROM L.A.' IS SMOKIN'!
THE BEST SEQUEL TO EXPLODE ONTO THE SCREEN SINCE 'T2.' STRAP YOURSELF IN FOR AN OUT-OF-CONTROL, PEDAL-TO-THE-METAL, FUTURISTIC ACTION-ADVENTURE."
"FILLED WITH FAST-PACED FUN, IT'S YOUR NEW BEST BET FOR ACTION-ADVENTURE."
KURT RUSSELL
ESCAPE FROM L.A.
WHITE ZOMBIE
GRAVITY KILLS
TOADIES
TOOL

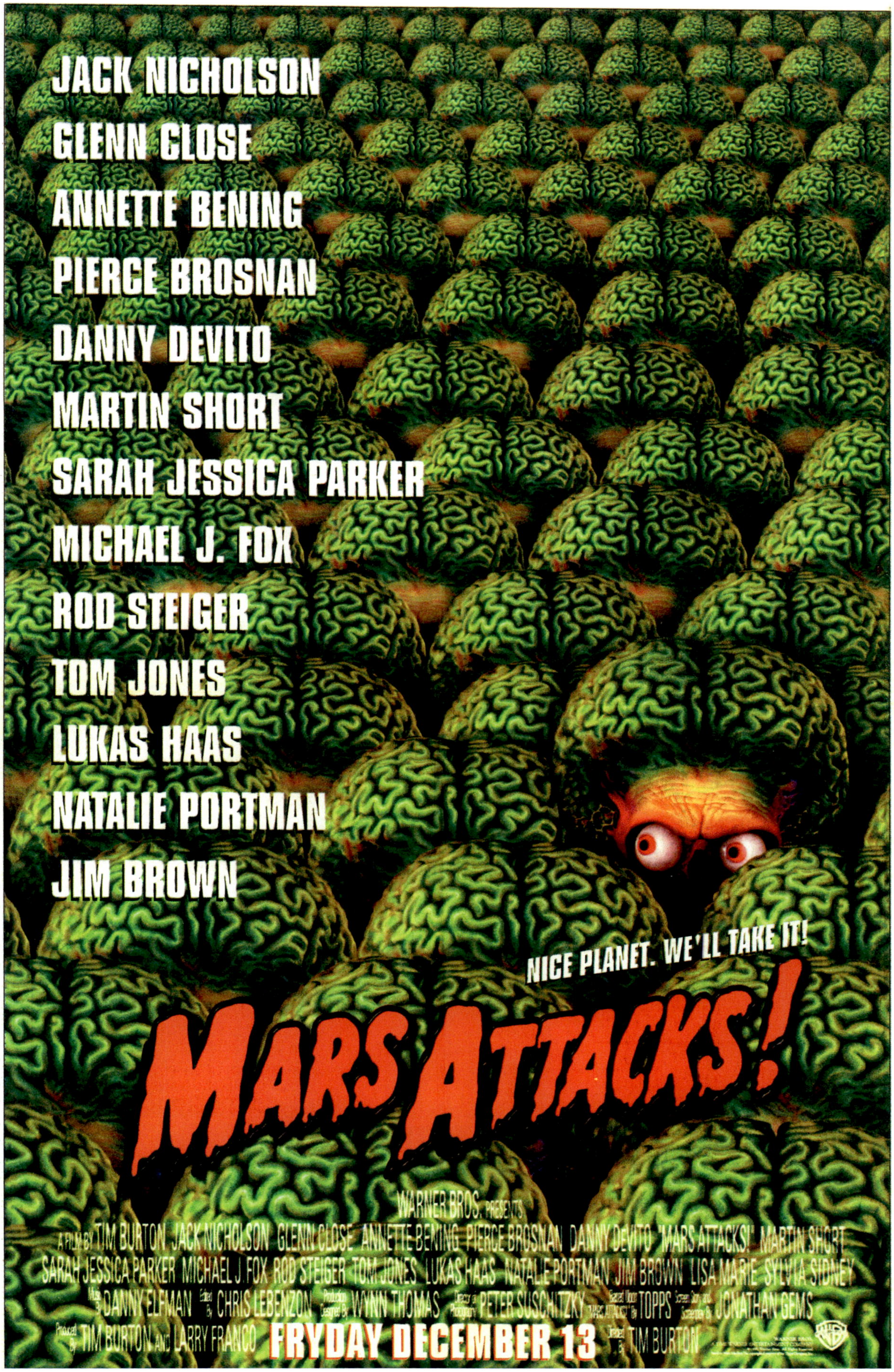
JACK NICHOLSON
GLENN CLOSE
ANNETTE BENING
PIERCE BROSNAN
DANNY DEVITO
MARTIN SHORT
SARAH JESSICA PARKER
MICHAEL J. FOX
ROD STEIGER
TOM JONES
LUKAS HAAS
NATALIE PORTMAN
JIM BROWN
NICE PLANET. WE'LL TAKE IT!
MARS ATTACKS!
WARNER BROS. PRESENTS
A FILM BY TIM BURTON JACK NICHOLSON GLENN CLOSE ANNETTE BENING PIERCE BROSNAN DANNY DEVITO "MARS ATTACKS!" MARTIN SHORT
SARAH JESSICA PARKER MICHAEL J. FOX ROD STEIGER TOM JONES LUKAS HAAS NATALIE PORTMAN JIM BROWN LISA MARIE SYLVIA SIDNEY
Music By DANNY ELFMAN Edited By CHRIS LEBENZON Production Designed By WYNN THOMAS Director of Photography PETER SUSCHITZKY Based Upon "MARS ATTACKS" By TOPPS Screen Story and Screenplay By JONATHAN GEMS
Produced By TIM BURTON AND LARRY FRANCO
FRYDAY DECEMBER 13
Directed By TIM BURTON

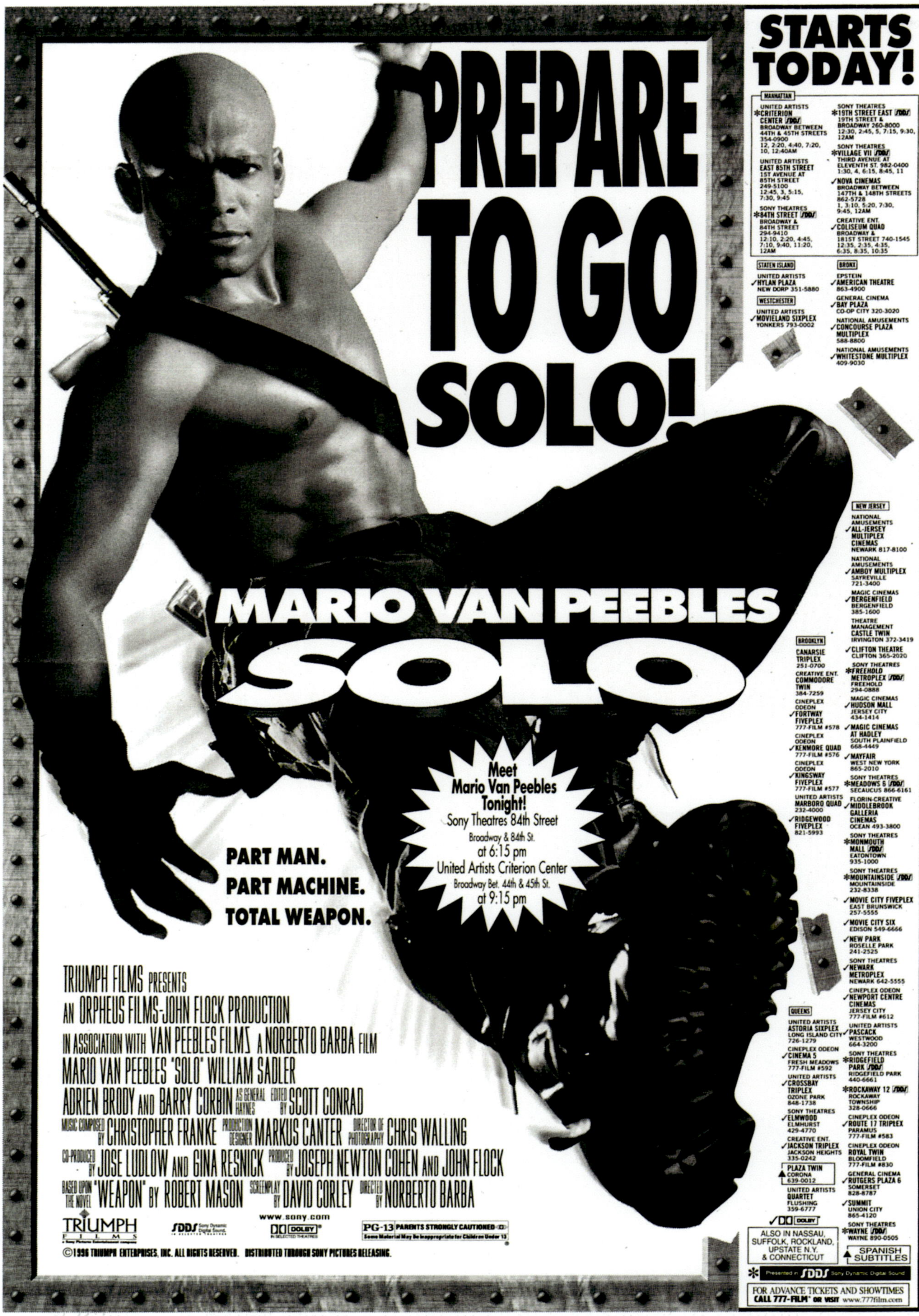

PREPARE TO GO SOLO!
MARIO VAN PEEBLES
SOLO
PART MAN. PART MACHINE. TOTAL WEAPON.
Meet Mario Van Peebles Tonight!
Sony Theatres 84th Street
Broadway & 84th St.
at 6:15 pm
United Artists Criterion Center
Broadway Bet. 44th & 45th St.
at 9:15 pm
TRIUMPH FILMS PRESENTS
AN ORPHEUS FILMS-JOHN FLOCK PRODUCTION
IN ASSOCIATION WITH VAN PEEBLES FILMS A NORBERTO BARBA FILM
MARIO VAN PEEBLES "SOLO" WILLIAM SADLER
ADRIEN BRODY AND BARRY CORBIN AS GENERAL HAYNES EDITED BY SCOTT CONRAD
MUSIC COMPOSED BY CHRISTOPHER FRANKE PRODUCTION DESIGNER MARKUS CANTER DIRECTOR OF PHOTOGRAPHY CHRIS WALLING
CO-PRODUCED BY JOSE LUDLOW AND GINA RESNICK PRODUCED BY JOSEPH NEWTON COHEN AND JOHN FLOCK
BASED UPON THE NOVEL "WEAPON" BY ROBERT MASON SCREENPLAY BY DAVID CORLEY DIRECTED BY NORBERTO BARBA
TRIUMPH FILMS
www.sony.com
PG-13 PARENTS STRONGLY CAUTIONED
©1996 TRIUMPH ENTERPRISES, INC. ALL RIGHTS RESERVED. DISTRIBUTED THROUGH SONY PICTURES RELEASING.
STARTS TODAY!
MANHATTAN
UNITED ARTISTS *CRITERION CENTER SDDS BROADWAY BETWEEN 44TH & 45TH STREETS 354-0900 12, 2:20, 4:40, 7:20, 10, 12:40AM
UNITED ARTISTS EAST 85TH STREET 1ST AVENUE AT 85TH STREET 249-5100 12:45, 3, 5:15, 7:30, 9:45
SONY THEATRES *84TH STREET SDDS BROADWAY & 84TH STREET 294-9410 12:10, 2:20, 4:45, 7:10, 9:40, 11:20, 12AM
SONY THEATRES *19TH STREET EAST SDDS 19TH STREET & BROADWAY 260-8000 12:30, 2:45, 5, 7:15, 9:30, 12AM
SONY THEATRES *VILLAGE VII SDDS THIRD AVENUE AT ELEVENTH ST. 982-0400 1:30, 4, 6:15, 8:45, 11
✓NOVA CINEMAS BROADWAY BETWEEN 147TH & 148TH STREETS 862-5728 1, 3:10, 5:20, 7:30, 9:45, 12AM
CREATIVE ENT. ✓COLISEUM QUAD BROADWAY & 181ST STREET 740-1545 12:35, 2:35, 4:35, 6:35, 8:35, 10:35
STATEN ISLAND
UNITED ARTISTS ✓HYLAN PLAZA NEW DORP 351-5880
WESTCHESTER
UNITED ARTISTS ✓MOVIELAND SIXPLEX YONKERS 793-0002
BRONX
EPSTEIN ✓AMERICAN THEATRE 863-4900
GENERAL CINEMA ✓BAY PLAZA CO-OP CITY 320-3020
NATIONAL AMUSEMENTS ✓CONCOURSE PLAZA MULTIPLEX 588-8800
NATIONAL AMUSEMENTS ✓WHITESTONE MULTIPLEX 409-9030
BROOKLYN
CANARSIE TRIPLEX 251-0700
CREATIVE ENT. COMMODORE TWIN 384-7259
CINEPLEX ODEON ✓FORTWAY FIVEPLEX 777-FILM #578
CINEPLEX ODEON ✓KENMORE QUAD 777-FILM #576
CINEPLEX ODEON ✓KINGSWAY FIVEPLEX 777-FILM #577
UNITED ARTISTS MARBORO QUAD 232-4000
✓RIDGEWOOD FIVEPLEX 821-5993
QUEENS
UNITED ARTISTS ASTORIA SIXPLEX LONG ISLAND CITY 726-1279
CINEPLEX ODEON ✓CINEMA 5 FRESH MEADOWS 777-FILM #592
UNITED ARTISTS ✓CROSSBAY TRIPLEX OZONE PARK 848-1738
SONY THEATRES ✓ELMWOOD ELMHURST 429-4770
CREATIVE ENT. ✓JACKSON TRIPLEX JACKSON HEIGHTS 335-0242
▲PLAZA TWIN CORONA 639-0012
UNITED ARTISTS QUARTET FLUSHING 359-6777
NEW JERSEY
NATIONAL AMUSEMENTS ✓ALL-JERSEY MULTIPLEX CINEMAS NEWARK 817-8100
NATIONAL AMUSEMENTS ✓AMBOY MULTIPLEX SAYREVILLE 721-3400
MAGIC CINEMAS ✓BERGENFIELD BERGENFIELD 385-1600
THEATRE MANAGEMENT CASTLE TWIN IRVINGTON 372-3419
✓CLIFTON THEATRE CLIFTON 365-2020
SONY THEATRES *FREEHOLD METROPLEX SDDS FREEHOLD 294-0888
MAGIC CINEMAS ✓HUDSON MALL JERSEY CITY 434-1414
✓MAGIC CINEMAS AT HADLEY SOUTH PLAINFIELD 668-4449
✓MAYFAIR WEST NEW YORK 865-2010
SONY THEATRES *MEADOWS 6 SDDS SECAUCUS 866-6161
FLORIN-CREATIVE ✓MIDDLEBROOK GALLERIA CINEMAS OCEAN 493-3800
SONY THEATRES *MONMOUTH MALL SDDS EATONTOWN 935-1000
SONY THEATRES *MOUNTAINSIDE SDDS MOUNTAINSIDE 232-8338
✓MOVIE CITY FIVEPLEX EAST BRUNSWICK 257-5555
✓MOVIE CITY SIX EDISON 549-6666
✓NEW PARK ROSELLE PARK 241-2525
SONY THEATRES ✓NEWARK METROPLEX NEWARK 642-5555
CINEPLEX ODEON ✓NEWPORT CENTRE CINEMAS JERSEY CITY 777-FILM #612
UNITED ARTISTS ✓PASCACK WESTWOOD 664-3200
SONY THEATRES *RIDGEFIELD PARK SDDS RIDGEFIELD PARK 440-6661
*ROCKAWAY 12 SDDS ROCKAWAY TOWNSHIP 328-0666
CINEPLEX ODEON ✓ROUTE 17 TRIPLEX PARAMUS 777-FILM #583
CINEPLEX ODEON ROYAL TWIN BLOOMFIELD 777-FILM #830
GENERAL CINEMA ✓RUTGERS PLAZA 6 SOMERSET 828-8787
✓SUMMIT UNION CITY 865-4120
SONY THEATRES *WAYNE SDDS WAYNE 890-0505
✓ DOLBY
ALSO IN NASSAU, SUFFOLK, ROCKLAND, UPSTATE N.Y. & CONNECTICUT
▲ SPANISH SUBTITLES
* Presented in SDDS Sony Dynamic Digital Sound
FOR ADVANCE TICKETS AND SHOWTIMES CALL 777-FILM OR VISIT www.777film.com

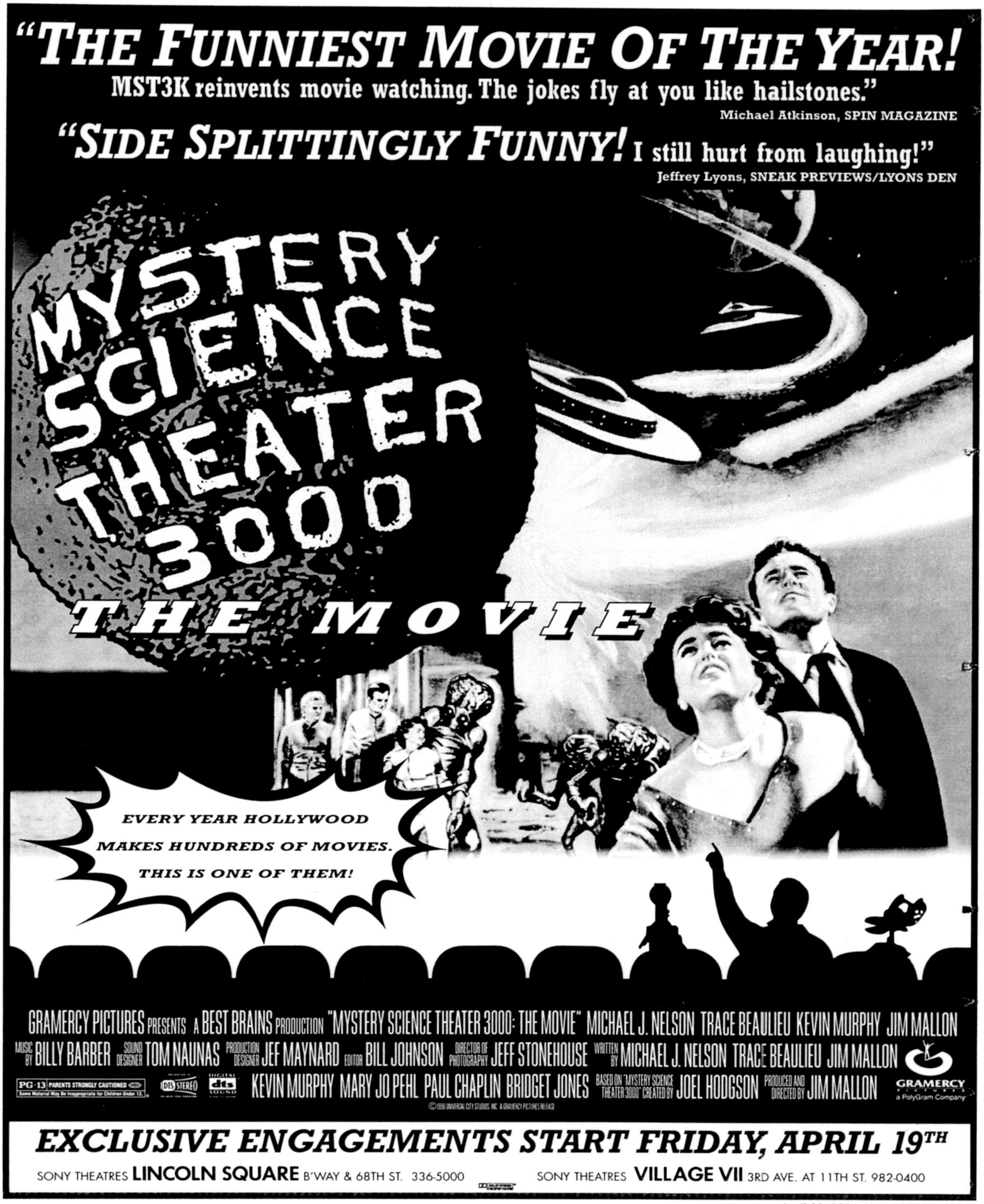
"THE FUNNIEST MOVIE OF THE YEAR!
MST3K reinvents movie watching. The jokes fly at you like hailstones."
Michael Atkinson, SPIN MAGAZINE
"SIDE SPLITTINGLY FUNNY! I still hurt from laughing!"
Jeffrey Lyons, SNEAK PREVIEWS/LYONS DEN
MYSTERY SCIENCE THEATER 3000
THE MOVIE
EVERY YEAR HOLLYWOOD MAKES HUNDREDS OF MOVIES. THIS IS ONE OF THEM!
GRAMERCY PICTURES PRESENTS A BEST BRAINS PRODUCTION "MYSTERY SCIENCE THEATER 3000: THE MOVIE" MICHAEL J. NELSON TRACE BEAULIEU KEVIN MURPHY JIM MALLON
MUSIC BY BILLY BARBER SOUND DESIGNER TOM NAUNAS PRODUCTION DESIGNER JEF MAYNARD EDITOR BILL JOHNSON DIRECTOR OF PHOTOGRAPHY JEFF STONEHOUSE WRITTEN BY MICHAEL J. NELSON TRACE BEAULIEU JIM MALLON
KEVIN MURPHY MARY JO PEHL PAUL CHAPLIN BRIDGET JONES BASED ON "MYSTERY SCIENCE THEATER 3000" CREATED BY JOEL HODGSON PRODUCED AND DIRECTED BY JIM MALLON
PG-13 PARENTS STRONGLY CAUTIONED
GRAMERCY PICTURES a PolyGram Company
EXCLUSIVE ENGAGEMENTS START FRIDAY, APRIL 19TH
SONY THEATRES LINCOLN SQUARE B'WAY & 68TH ST. 336-5000
SONY THEATRES VILLAGE VII 3RD AVE. AT 11TH ST. 982-0400

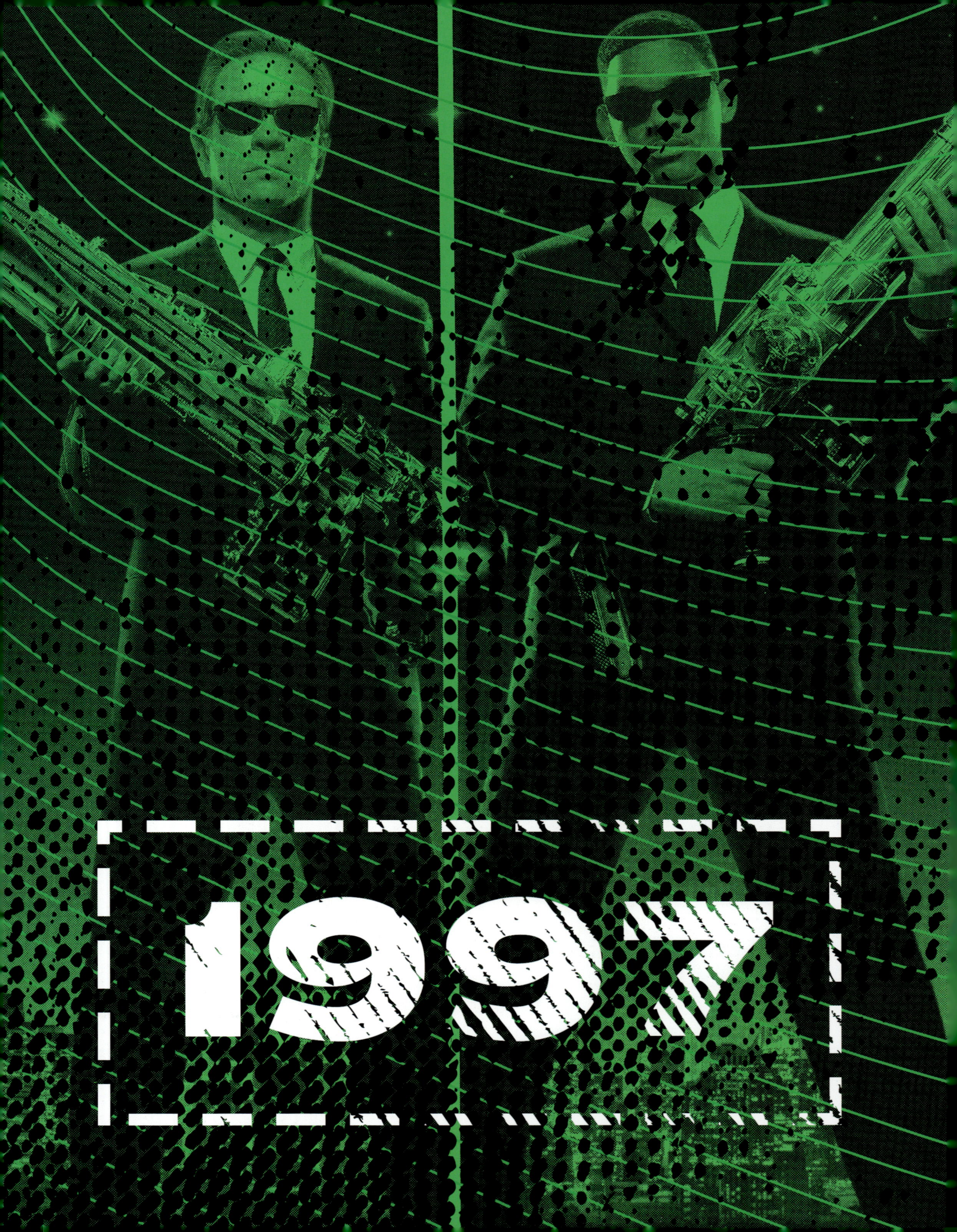
1997

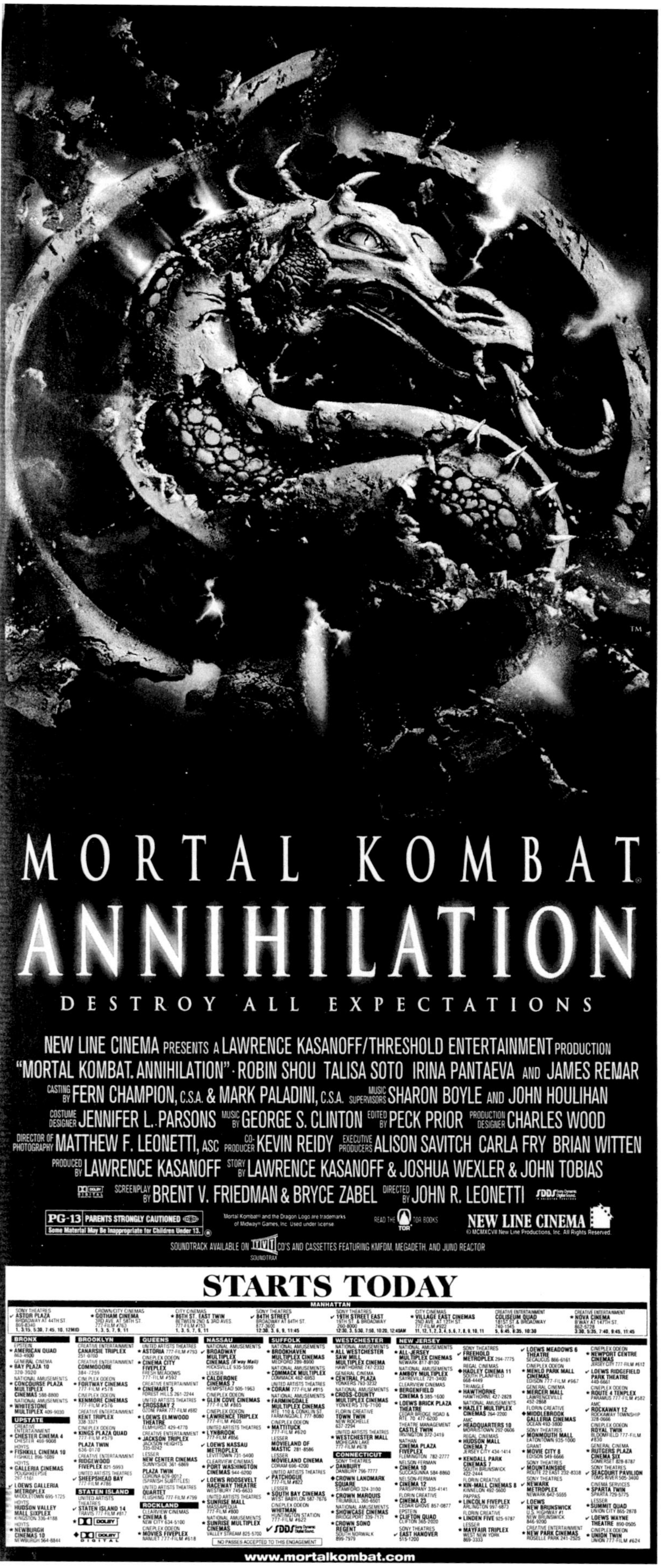
MORTAL KOMBAT
ANNIHILATION
DESTROY ALL EXPECTATIONS
NEW LINE CINEMA PRESENTS A LAWRENCE KASANOFF/THRESHOLD ENTERTAINMENT PRODUCTION
"MORTAL KOMBAT: ANNIHILATION" · ROBIN SHOU TALISA SOTO IRINA PANTAEVA AND JAMES REMAR
CASTING BY FERN CHAMPION, C.S.A. & MARK PALADINI, C.S.A. MUSIC SUPERVISORS SHARON BOYLE AND JOHN HOULIHAN
COSTUME DESIGNER JENNIFER L. PARSONS MUSIC BY GEORGE S. CLINTON EDITED BY PECK PRIOR PRODUCTION DESIGNER CHARLES WOOD
DIRECTOR OF PHOTOGRAPHY MATTHEW F. LEONETTI, ASC CO-PRODUCER KEVIN REIDY EXECUTIVE PRODUCERS ALISON SAVITCH CARLA FRY BRIAN WITTEN
PRODUCED BY LAWRENCE KASANOFF STORY BY LAWRENCE KASANOFF & JOSHUA WEXLER & JOHN TOBIAS
SCREENPLAY BY BRENT V. FRIEDMAN & BRYCE ZABEL DIRECTED BY JOHN R. LEONETTI
PG-13 PARENTS STRONGLY CAUTIONED
Some Material May Be Inappropriate for Children Under 13.
NEW LINE CINEMA
SOUNDTRACK AVAILABLE ON TVT CD'S AND CASSETTES FEATURING KMFDM, MEGADETH, AND JUNO REACTOR
STARTS TODAY
MANHATTAN
www.mortalkombat.com

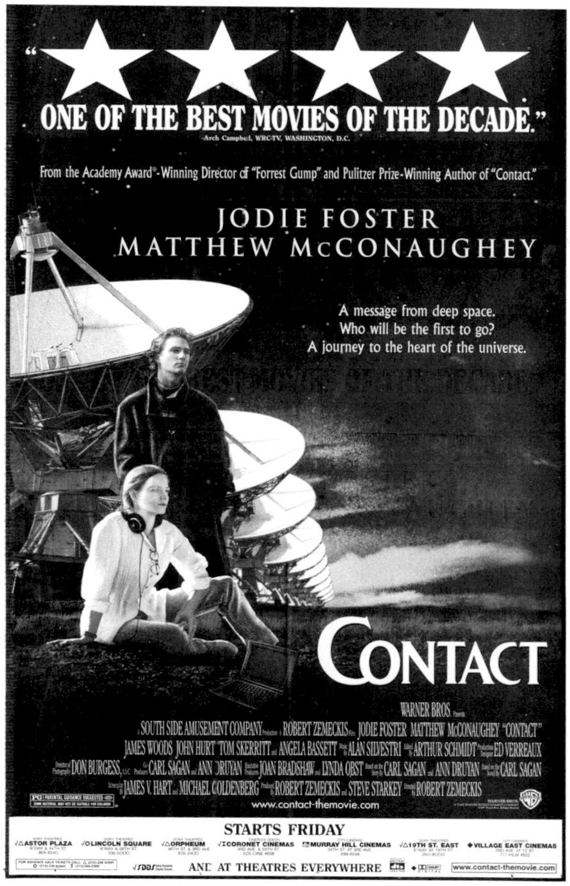
"★★★★ ONE OF THE BEST MOVIES OF THE DECADE."
-Arch Campbell, WRC-TV, WASHINGTON, D.C.
From the Academy Award®-Winning Director of "Forrest Gump" and Pulitzer Prize-Winning Author of "Contact."
JODIE FOSTER
MATTHEW McCONAUGHEY
A message from deep space.
Who will be the first to go?
A journey to the heart of the universe.
CONTACT
WARNER BROS. Presents
A SOUTH SIDE AMUSEMENT COMPANY Production A ROBERT ZEMECKIS Film JODIE FOSTER MATTHEW McCONAUGHEY "CONTACT"
JAMES WOODS JOHN HURT TOM SKERRITT and ANGELA BASSETT Music by ALAN SILVESTRI Edited by ARTHUR SCHMIDT Production Designer ED VERREAUX
Director of Photography DON BURGESS, A.S.C. Co-Producers CARL SAGAN and ANN DRUYAN Executive Producers JOAN BRADSHAW and LYNDA OBST Based on the Novel by CARL SAGAN Story by CARL SAGAN and ANN DRUYAN
Screenplay by JAMES V. HART and MICHAEL GOLDENBERG Produced by ROBERT ZEMECKIS and STEVE STARKEY Directed by ROBERT ZEMECKIS
www.contact-themovie.com
STARTS FRIDAY
ASTOR PLAZA
LINCOLN SQUARE
ORPHEUM
CORONET CINEMAS
MURRAY HILL CINEMAS
19TH ST. EAST
VILLAGE EAST CINEMAS
AND AT THEATRES EVERYWHERE
www.contact-themovie.com

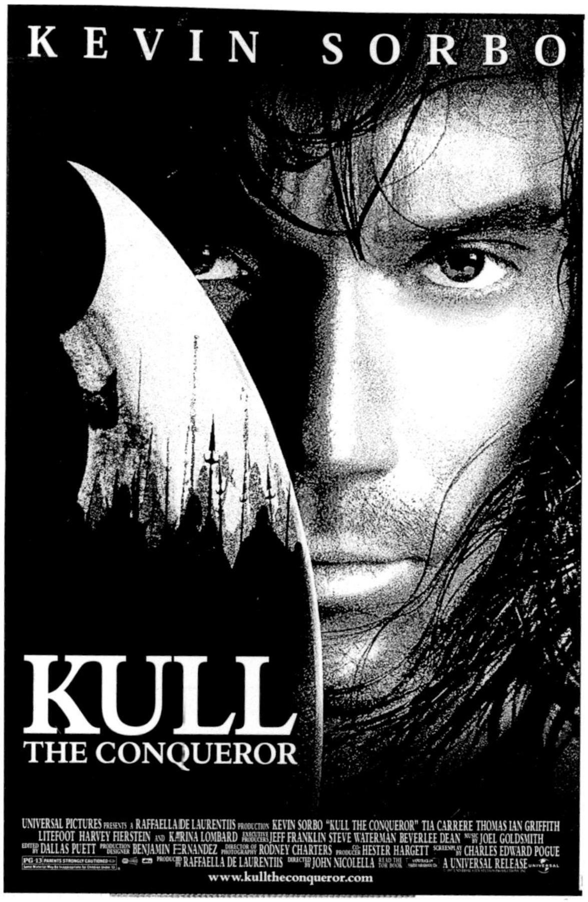
KEVIN SORBO
KULL
THE CONQUEROR
UNIVERSAL PICTURES PRESENTS A RAFFAELLA DE LAURENTIIS PRODUCTION KEVIN SORBO "KULL THE CONQUEROR" TIA CARRERE THOMAS IAN GRIFFITH
LITEFOOT HARVEY FIERSTEIN AND KARINA LOMBARD
PRODUCED BY RAFFAELLA DE LAURENTIIS DIRECTED BY JOHN NICOLELLA
A UNIVERSAL RELEASE
www.kulltheconqueror.com

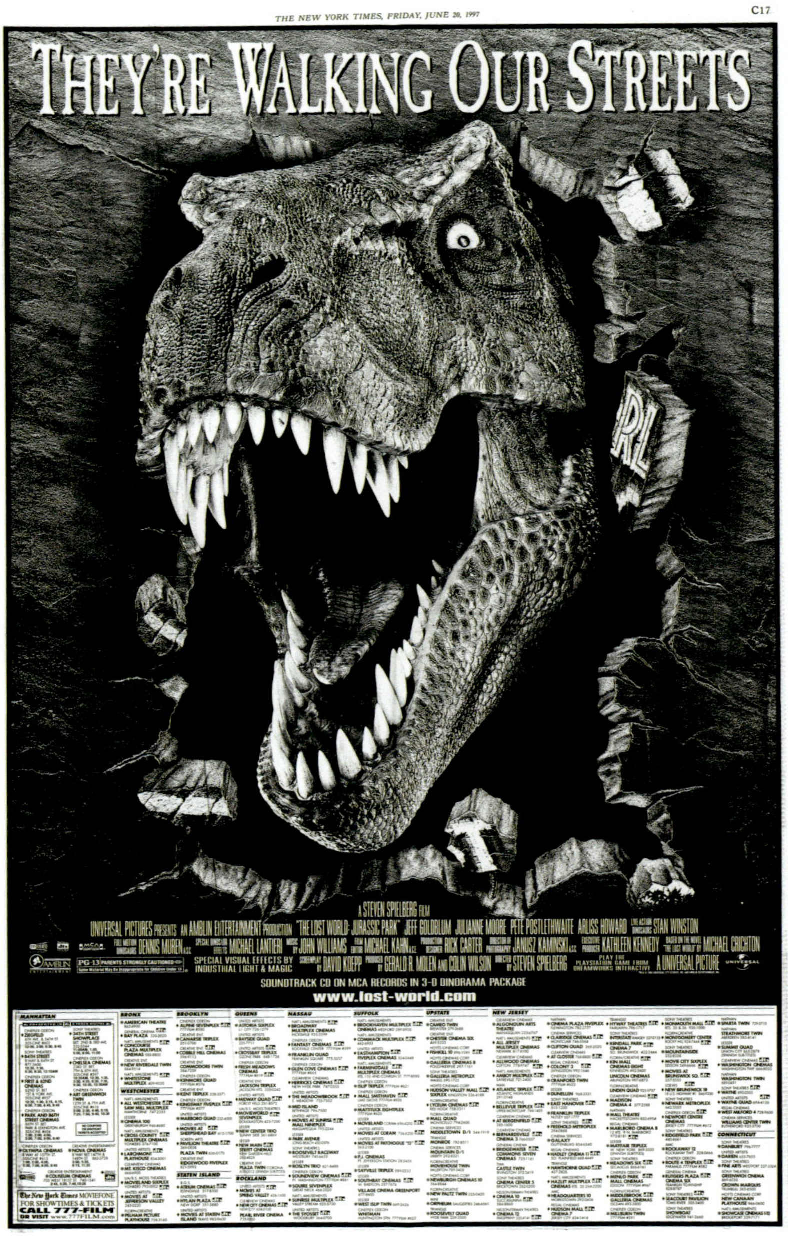

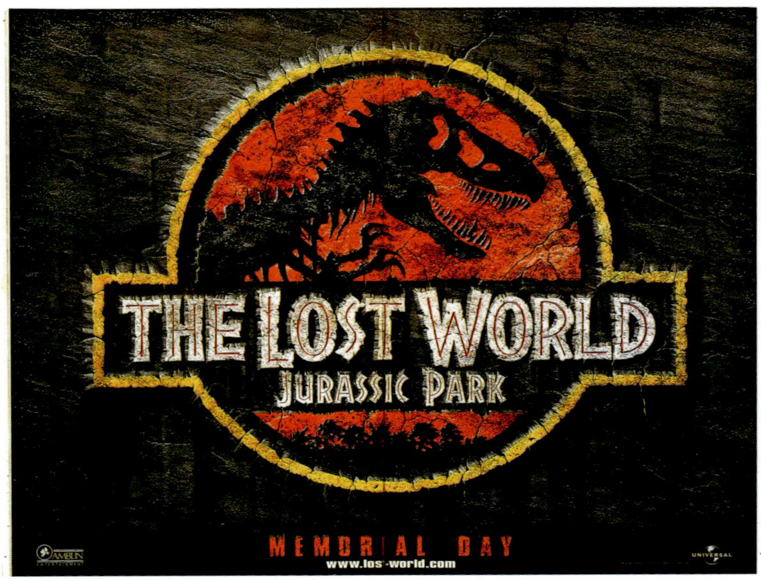

THE FIFTH ELEMENT

Long before making his flashy/gritty real-world crime thrillers *La Femme Nikita* and *The Professional* (a.k.a. *Leon*), Luc Besson drafted the idea that became *The Fifth Element* as a teenager. The eventual movie (the first of many Besson scripted with Robert Mark Kamen) showcased all manner of wild flights of fantasy, and the first ads emphasized the unique environment before the later ones showcased the cast. For the most part, Besson and his team's unusual settings and characters – both human and alien – dazzled critics to the point where they were able to forgive narrative flaws.

"Willis holds together French filmmaker Luc Besson's elaborate, even campy sci-fi extravaganza, which is nearly as hard to follow as last year's *Mission: Impossible*. But it is also a lot warmer, more fun, and boasts some of the most sophisticated, witty production and costume design you could ever hope to see."

–Kevin Thomas, *Los Angeles Times*

"A spectacular triumph of style over substance, *The Fifth Element* makes about as much sense as bras on the moon. But it's also really very sweet, and Besson honestly seems to believe the movie's message: love conquers all."

–RITA KEMPLEY, *WASHINGTON POST*

"Orson Welles once compared making movies to a boy having a wonderful electric train set to play with. But no boy ever had a train set like Besson's in *The Fifth Element*. ...Yet all the pretty pictures would mean nothing if *The Fifth Element* didn't move. It does. And it's fun, as in no-time-to-get-up-for-popcorn."

–Mick LaSalle, *San Francisco Chronicle*

"It's not that *The Fifth Element* is derivative – so are most science-fantasy movies, even the best. ... But *The Fifth Element*...doesn't really work up its derivations into any kind of style; it doesn't build into something radically new."

–Peter Rainer, *Dallas Observer*

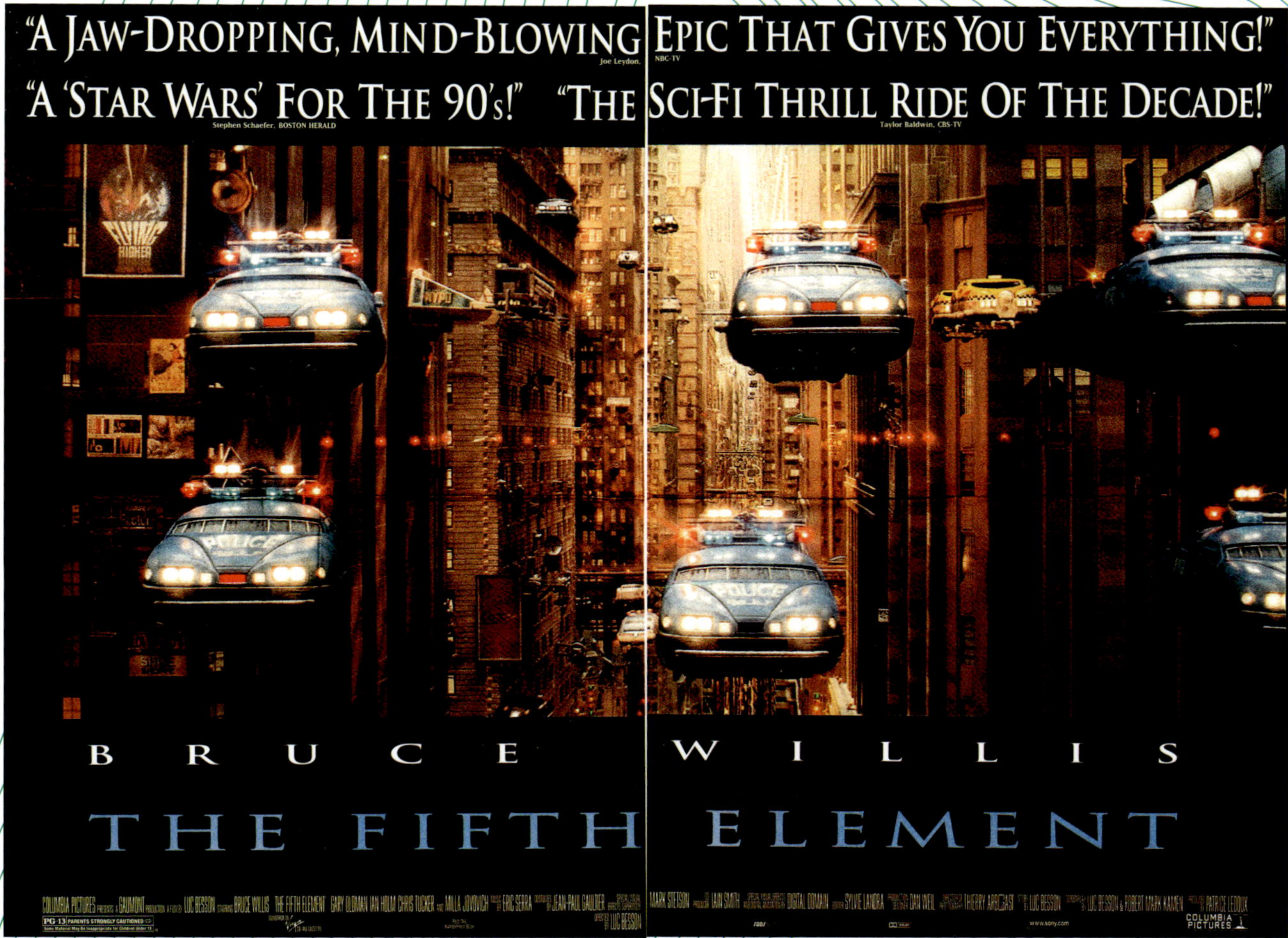

"A JAW-DROPPING, MIND-BLOWING EPIC THAT GIVES YOU EVERYTHING!"
Joe Leydon, NBC-TV
"A 'STAR WARS' FOR THE 90's!"
Stephen Schaefer, BOSTON HERALD
"THE SCI-FI THRILL RIDE OF THE DECADE!"
Taylor Baldwin, CBS-TV
B R U C E W I L L I S
THE FIFTH ELEMENT

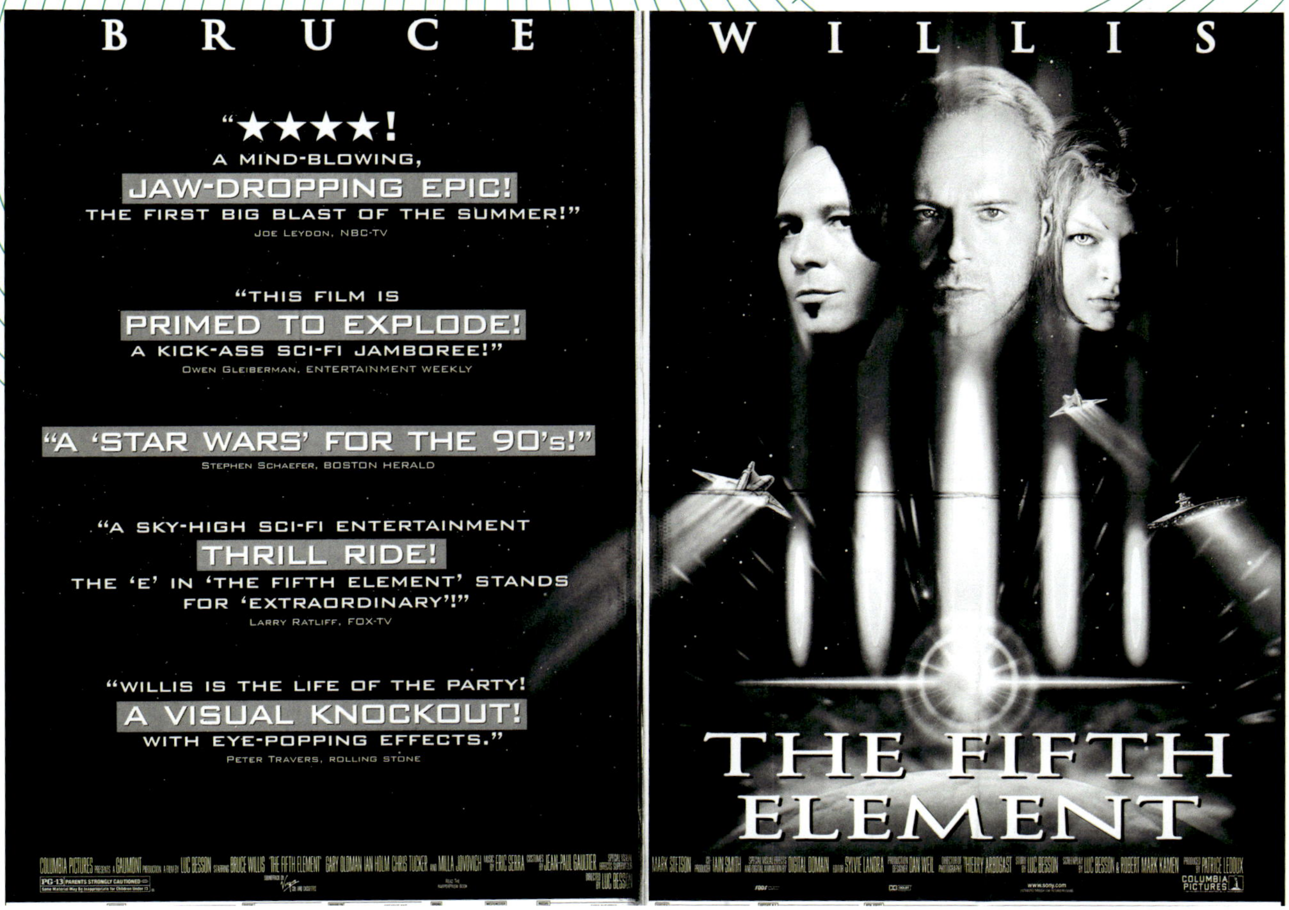

B R U C E W I L L I S
"★★★★!
A MIND-BLOWING,
JAW-DROPPING EPIC!
THE FIRST BIG BLAST OF THE SUMMER!"
JOE LEYDON, NBC-TV
"THIS FILM IS
PRIMED TO EXPLODE!
A KICK-ASS SCI-FI JAMBOREE!"
OWEN GLEIBERMAN, ENTERTAINMENT WEEKLY
"A 'STAR WARS' FOR THE 90's!"
STEPHEN SCHAEFER, BOSTON HERALD
"A SKY-HIGH SCI-FI ENTERTAINMENT
THRILL RIDE!
THE 'E' IN 'THE FIFTH ELEMENT' STANDS
FOR 'EXTRAORDINARY'!"
LARRY RATLIFF, FOX-TV
"WILLIS IS THE LIFE OF THE PARTY!
A VISUAL KNOCKOUT!
WITH EYE-POPPING EFFECTS."
PETER TRAVERS, ROLLING STONE
THE FIFTH ELEMENT

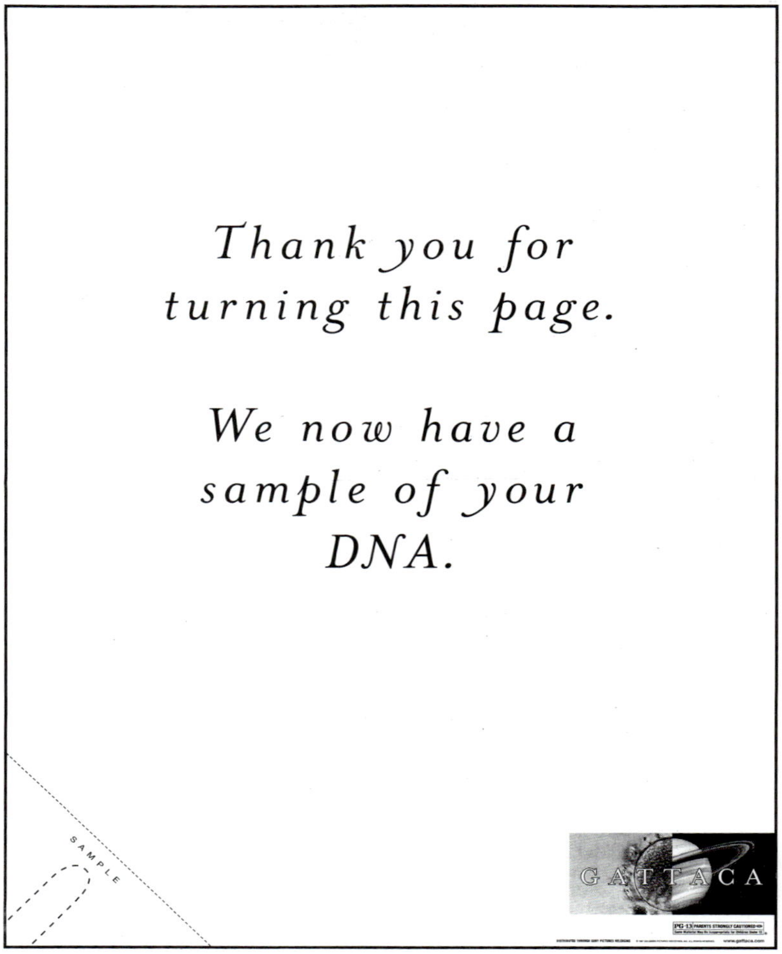

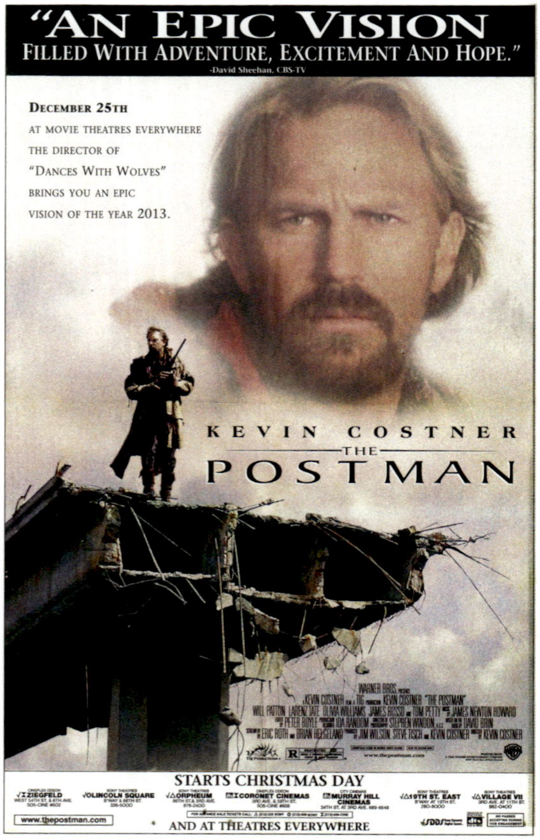

GATTACA

In the midst of the special-effects extravaganzas of the late '90s came a more thoughtful, humanistic science-fiction drama marking the feature debut of writer/director Andrew Niccol. It's set in a near-futuristic society in which people are divided between "valids," who have been bred via selective genetics, and "in-valids," those born without such manipulation. The theme of genetic detection and encoding was teased in the advance ads, and many reviews praised Niccol's intelligent handling of a topical theme.

"[A] handsome and fully imagined work of cautionary futuristic fiction. ... The film is set in 'the not-too-distant future,' and indeed it succeeds as a scarily apt extension of present-day attitudes."

–Janet Maslin, *The New York Times*

"[The] premise is more than a launching pad for action sequences. It's the very subject of the film, leading us to issues we as a society undoubtedly will encounter someday soon. *Gattaca* is also great to look at, funny and unpredictable."

–Gene Siskel, *Chicago Tribune*

"The notion of a spotless tomorrow went out with the polluted funk of *Blade Runner* and the Gothic gloom of *Batman*. But *Gattaca* offers an alternative as clean as June Cleaver's countertops in *Leave It to Beaver*. With that comes an intriguing, eerily stylish but muddled look at the hazards of bioengineering."

–RITA KEMPLEY, *WASHINGTON POST*

"Niccol has presented a future world based on genetics, but he's concentrated only on physical attributes. Wouldn't a future meritocracy be more interested in brain power rather than in people's likelihood of keeling over from a heart attack at a young age?"

–Mick LaSalle, *San Francisco Chronicle*

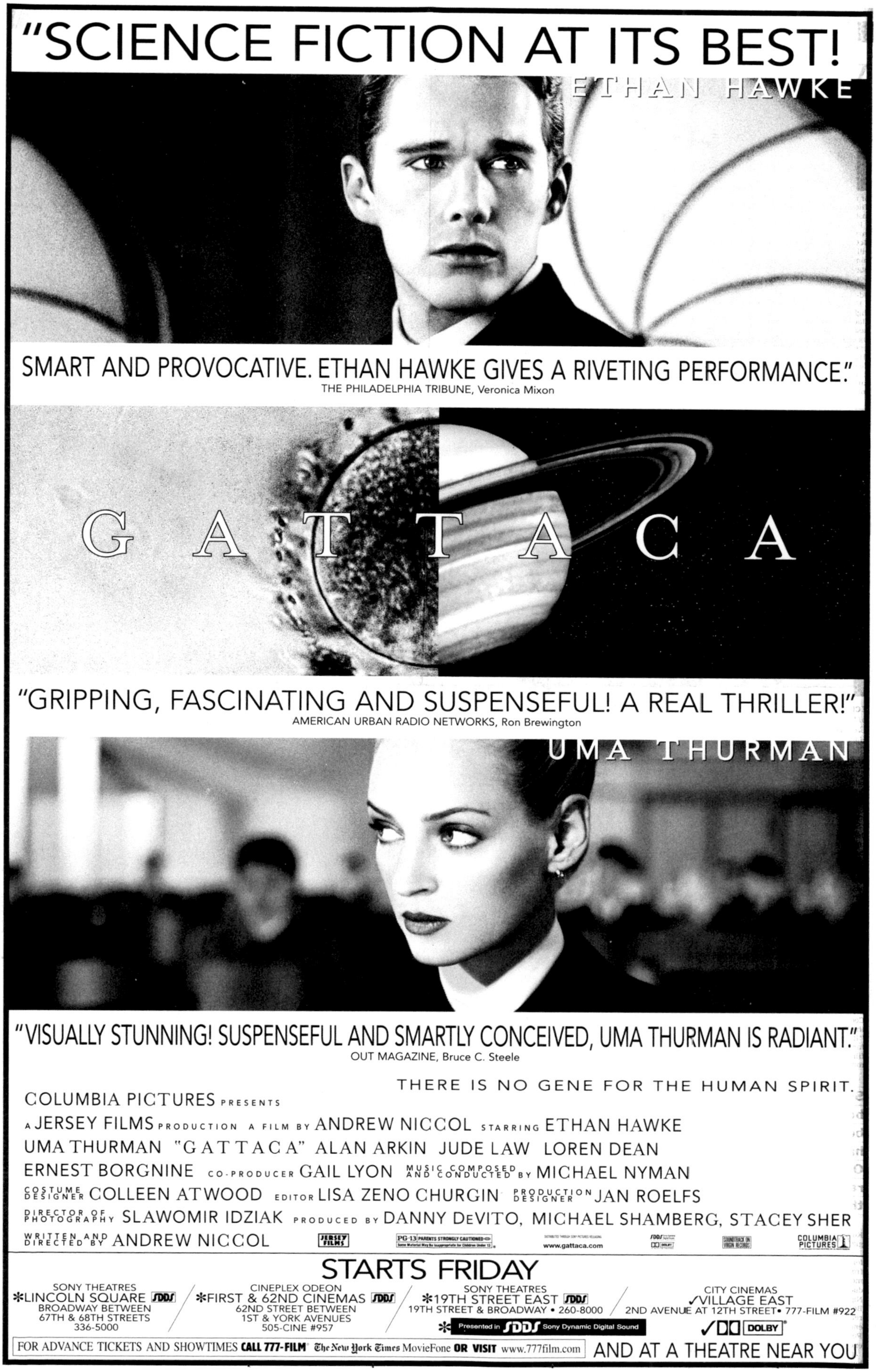
"SCIENCE FICTION AT ITS BEST!
ETHAN HAWKE
SMART AND PROVOCATIVE. ETHAN HAWKE GIVES A RIVETING PERFORMANCE."
THE PHILADELPHIA TRIBUNE, Veronica Mixon
G A T T A C A
"GRIPPING, FASCINATING AND SUSPENSEFUL! A REAL THRILLER!"
AMERICAN URBAN RADIO NETWORKS, Ron Brewington
UMA THURMAN
"VISUALLY STUNNING! SUSPENSEFUL AND SMARTLY CONCEIVED, UMA THURMAN IS RADIANT."
OUT MAGAZINE, Bruce C. Steele
THERE IS NO GENE FOR THE HUMAN SPIRIT.
COLUMBIA PICTURES PRESENTS
A JERSEY FILMS PRODUCTION A FILM BY ANDREW NICCOL STARRING ETHAN HAWKE
UMA THURMAN "GATTACA" ALAN ARKIN JUDE LAW LOREN DEAN
ERNEST BORGNINE CO-PRODUCER GAIL LYON MUSIC COMPOSED AND CONDUCTED BY MICHAEL NYMAN
COSTUME DESIGNER COLLEEN ATWOOD EDITOR LISA ZENO CHURGIN PRODUCTION DESIGNER JAN ROELFS
DIRECTOR OF PHOTOGRAPHY SLAWOMIR IDZIAK PRODUCED BY DANNY DEVITO, MICHAEL SHAMBERG, STACEY SHER
WRITTEN AND DIRECTED BY ANDREW NICCOL
JERSEY FILMS
PG-13 PARENTS STRONGLY CAUTIONED
www.gattaca.com
COLUMBIA PICTURES
STARTS FRIDAY
SONY THEATRES
*LINCOLN SQUARE SDDS
BROADWAY BETWEEN 67TH & 68TH STREETS
336-5000
CINEPLEX ODEON
*FIRST & 62ND CINEMAS SDDS
62ND STREET BETWEEN 1ST & YORK AVENUES
505-CINE #957
SONY THEATRES
*19TH STREET EAST SDDS
19TH STREET & BROADWAY • 260-8000
CITY CINEMAS
✓VILLAGE EAST
2ND AVENUE AT 12TH STREET • 777-FILM #922
* Presented in SDDS Sony Dynamic Digital Sound
✓ DOLBY
FOR ADVANCE TICKETS AND SHOWTIMES CALL 777-FILM The New York Times MovieFone OR VISIT www.777film.com
AND AT A THEATRE NEAR YOU

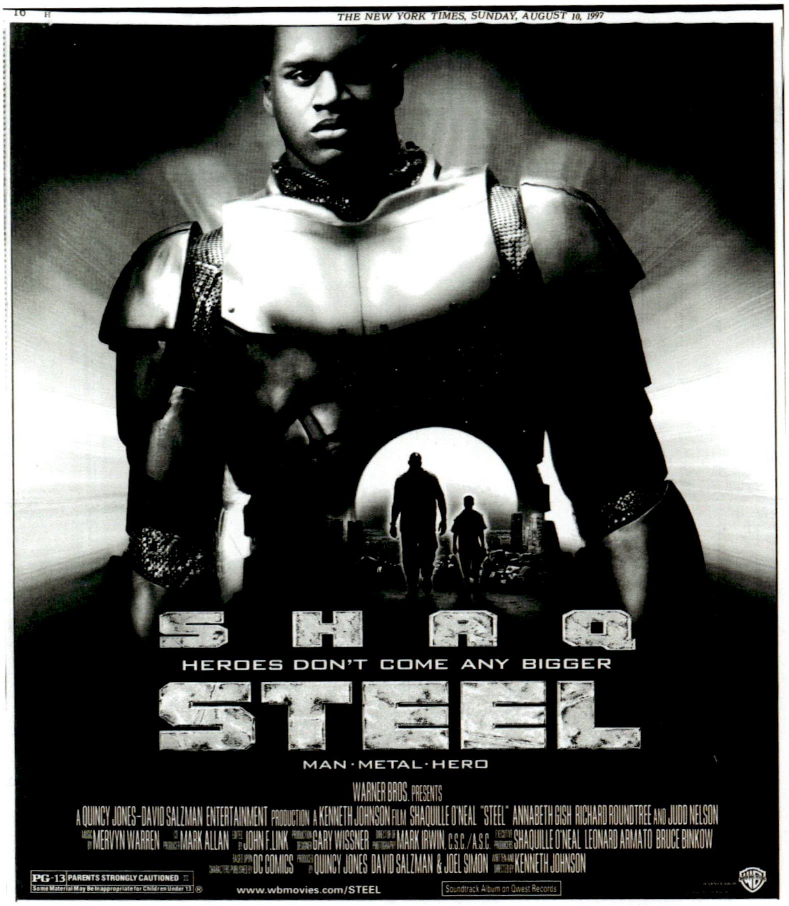

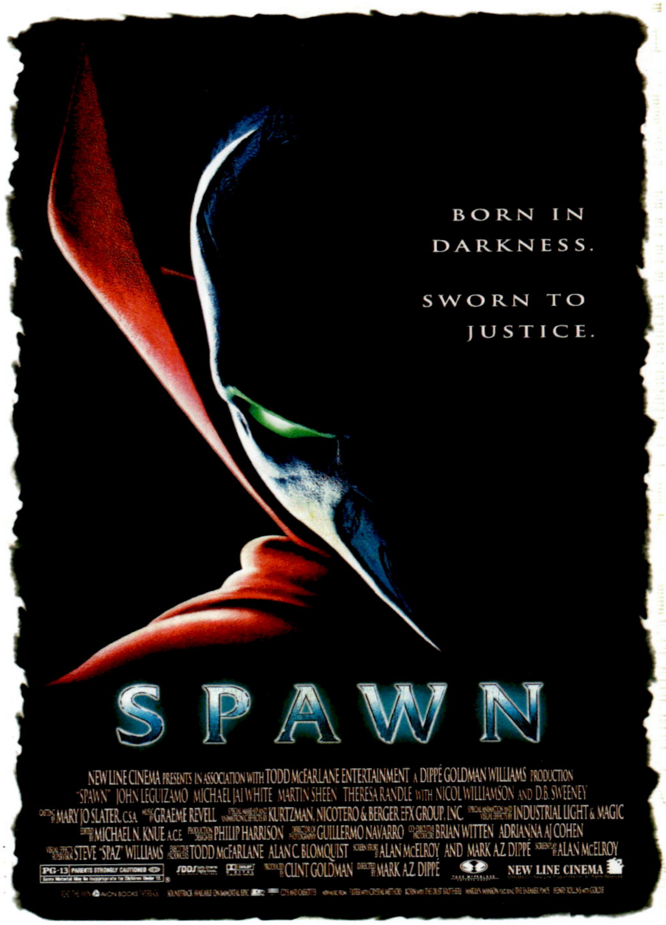

STARSHIP TROOPERS

Paul Verhoeven took a break from science fiction for most of the '90s to explore erotic drama and thrills with *Basic Instinct* and *Showgirls*. After the debacle of the latter, he returned to outer-space conflict with his most savagely satirical film yet, based on Robert Heinlein's novel and poking caustic fun at its militaristic bent and the fascist underpinnings of its story. Unfortunately, not all the critics got the dark joke Verhoeven was attempting at the time, and many of those who did, believed he didn't hit his target.

"Audiences are going to swarm to *Starship Troopers* like insane ants on a gloppy piece of honey-soaked French toast. Paul Verhoeven's stormtroopers-with-a-heart extravaganza manages to be both fun and shocking – sometimes in the same shot."

–Mick LaSalle, *San Francisco Chronicle*

"Alas, Verhoeven's tone, which varies from camp to cynical, is so inconsistent that it's impossible to decide whether he's sending up the Third Reich or in love with it. On the other hand, maybe this is just his misguided idea of a big old scary bug movie. In any case, he'd be right at home in a roach motel."

–RITA KEMPLEY, *WASHINGTON POST*

"*Starship Troopers* looks like reason to wonder how the big-ticket exploitation film mutated into its present form. ... [It] may be the finishing stroke for *Gattaca*...since the latter represents what is all but extinct: the science-fiction film made with intelligent restraint."

–Janet Maslin, *The New York Times*

"*Troopers* does not fit any reasonable definition of a quality motion picture. But it certainly is a jaw-dropping experience, so rigorously one-dimensional and free from even the pretense of intelligence it's hard not to be astonished and even mesmerized by what is on the screen."

–Kenneth Turan, *Los Angeles Times*

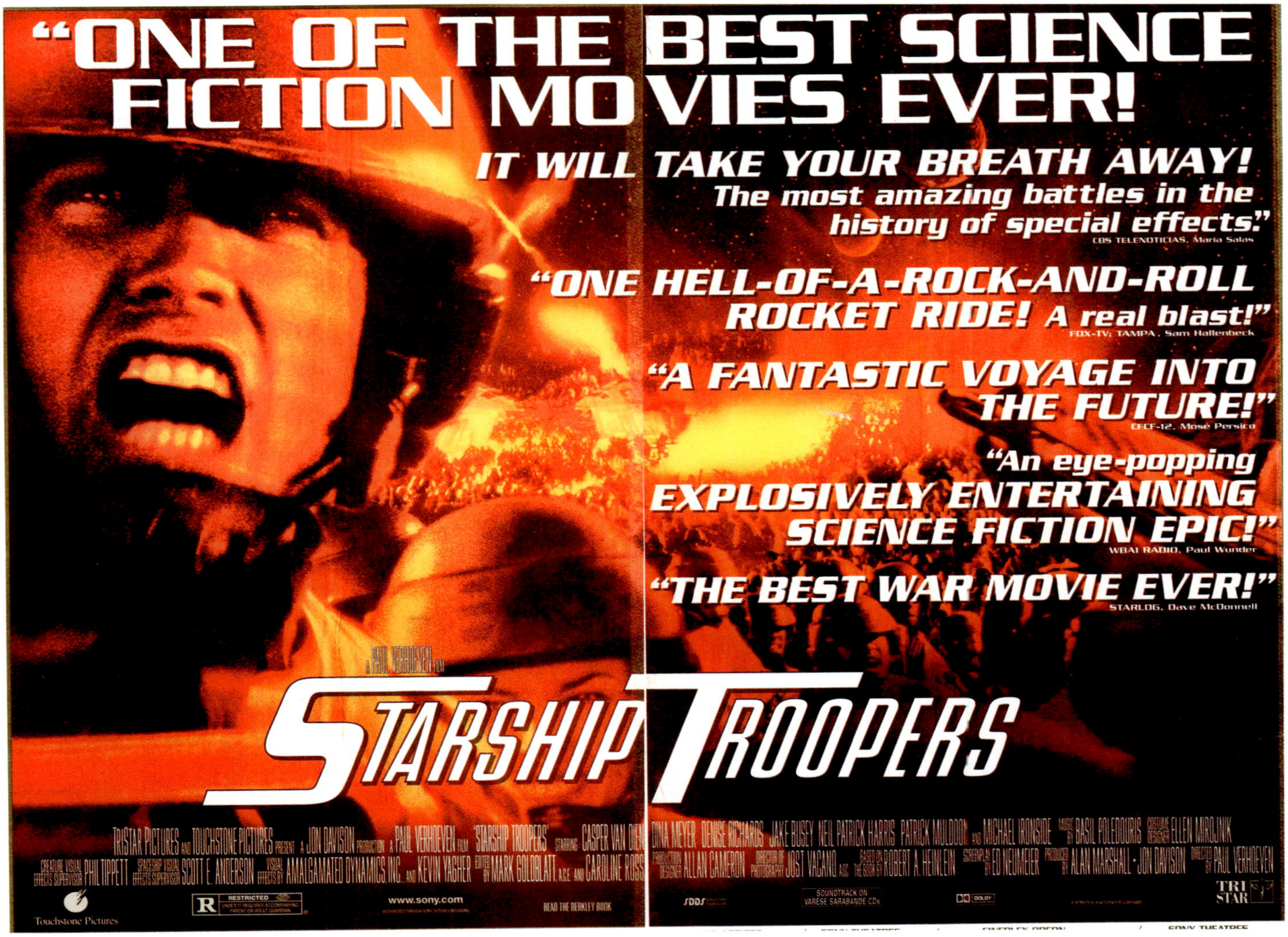

"ONE OF THE BEST SCIENCE FICTION MOVIES EVER!
IT WILL TAKE YOUR BREATH AWAY!
The most amazing battles in the history of special effects."
CBS TELENOTICIAS, Maria Salas
"ONE HELL-OF-A-ROCK-AND-ROLL ROCKET RIDE! A real blast!"
FOX-TV, TAMPA, Sam Hallenbeck
"A FANTASTIC VOYAGE INTO THE FUTURE!"
CFCF-12, Mose Persico
"An eye-popping EXPLOSIVELY ENTERTAINING SCIENCE FICTION EPIC!"
WBAI RADIO, Paul Wunder
"THE BEST WAR MOVIE EVER!"
STARLOG, Dave McDonnell
A PAUL VERHOEVEN FILM
STARSHIP TROOPERS
TRISTAR PICTURES AND TOUCHSTONE PICTURES PRESENT A JON DAVISON PRODUCTION A PAUL VERHOEVEN FILM "STARSHIP TROOPERS" STARRING CASPER VAN DIEN DINA MEYER DENISE RICHARDS JAKE BUSEY NEIL PATRICK HARRIS PATRICK MULDOON AND MICHAEL IRONSIDE MUSIC BY BASIL POLEDOURIS COSTUME DESIGNER ELLEN MIROJNICK
CREATURE VISUAL EFFECTS SUPERVISOR PHIL TIPPETT SPACESHIP VISUAL EFFECTS SUPERVISOR SCOTT E. ANDERSON VISUAL EFFECTS BY AMALGAMATED DYNAMICS, INC. AND KEVIN YAGHER EDITED BY MARK GOLDBLATT, A.C.E. AND CAROLINE ROSS PRODUCTION DESIGNER ALLAN CAMERON DIRECTOR OF PHOTOGRAPHY JOST VACANO, A.S.C. BASED ON THE BOOK BY ROBERT A. HEINLEIN SCREENPLAY BY ED NEUMEIER PRODUCED BY ALAN MARSHALL · JON DAVISON DIRECTED BY PAUL VERHOEVEN
Touchstone Pictures
R RESTRICTED
www.sony.com
READ THE BERKLEY BOOK
SOUNDTRACK ON VARESE SARABANDE CDs
TRI STAR

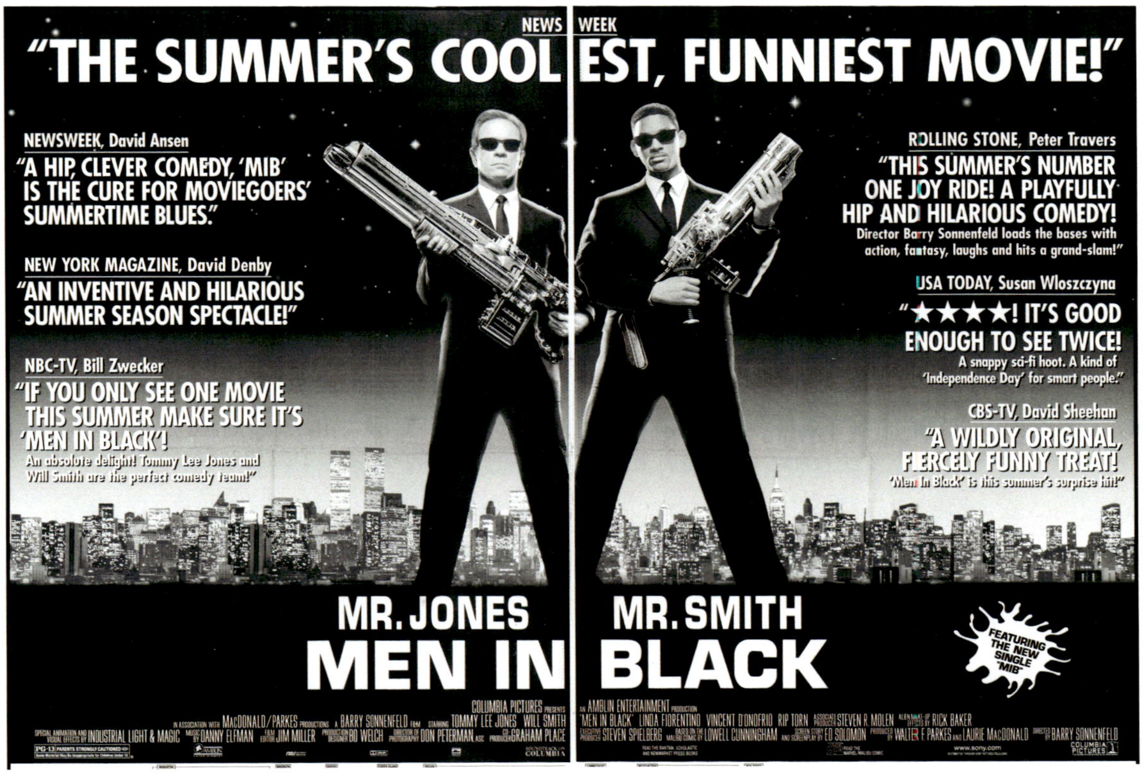

NEWSWEEK
"THE SUMMER'S COOLEST, FUNNIEST MOVIE!"
NEWSWEEK, David Ansen
"A HIP, CLEVER COMEDY, 'MIB' IS THE CURE FOR MOVIEGOERS' SUMMERTIME BLUES."
NEW YORK MAGAZINE, David Denby
"AN INVENTIVE AND HILARIOUS SUMMER SEASON SPECTACLE!"
NBC-TV, Bill Zwecker
"IF YOU ONLY SEE ONE MOVIE THIS SUMMER MAKE SURE IT'S 'MEN IN BLACK'!
An absolute delight! Tommy Lee Jones and Will Smith are the perfect comedy team!"
ROLLING STONE, Peter Travers
"THIS SUMMER'S NUMBER ONE JOY RIDE! A PLAYFULLY HIP AND HILARIOUS COMEDY!
Director Barry Sonnenfeld loads the bases with action, fantasy, laughs and hits a grand-slam!"
USA TODAY, Susan Wloszczyna
"★★★★! IT'S GOOD ENOUGH TO SEE TWICE!
A snappy sci-fi hoot. A kind of 'Independence Day' for smart people."
CBS-TV, David Sheehan
"A WILDLY ORIGINAL, FIERCELY FUNNY TREAT!
'Men In Black' is this summer's surprise hit!"
MR. JONES
MR. SMITH
MEN IN BLACK
FEATURING THE NEW SINGLE "MIB"
COLUMBIA PICTURES PRESENTS IN ASSOCIATION WITH MacDONALD/PARKES PRODUCTIONS A BARRY SONNENFELD FILM STARRING TOMMY LEE JONES WILL SMITH
AN AMBLIN ENTERTAINMENT PRODUCTION "MEN IN BLACK" LINDA FIORENTINO VINCENT D'ONOFRIO RIP TORN
SPECIAL ANIMATION AND VISUAL EFFECTS BY INDUSTRIAL LIGHT & MAGIC MUSIC BY DANNY ELFMAN FILM EDITOR JIM MILLER PRODUCTION DESIGNER BO WELCH DIRECTOR OF PHOTOGRAPHY DON PETERMAN, A.S.C. CO-PRODUCER GRAHAM PLACE EXECUTIVE PRODUCER STEVEN SPIELBERG BASED ON THE COMIC BY LOWELL CUNNINGHAM SCREEN STORY AND SCREENPLAY BY ED SOLOMON PRODUCED BY WALTER F. PARKES AND LAURIE MacDONALD DIRECTED BY BARRY SONNENFELD
PG-13 PARENTS STRONGLY CAUTIONED
www.sony.com
COLUMBIA PICTURES

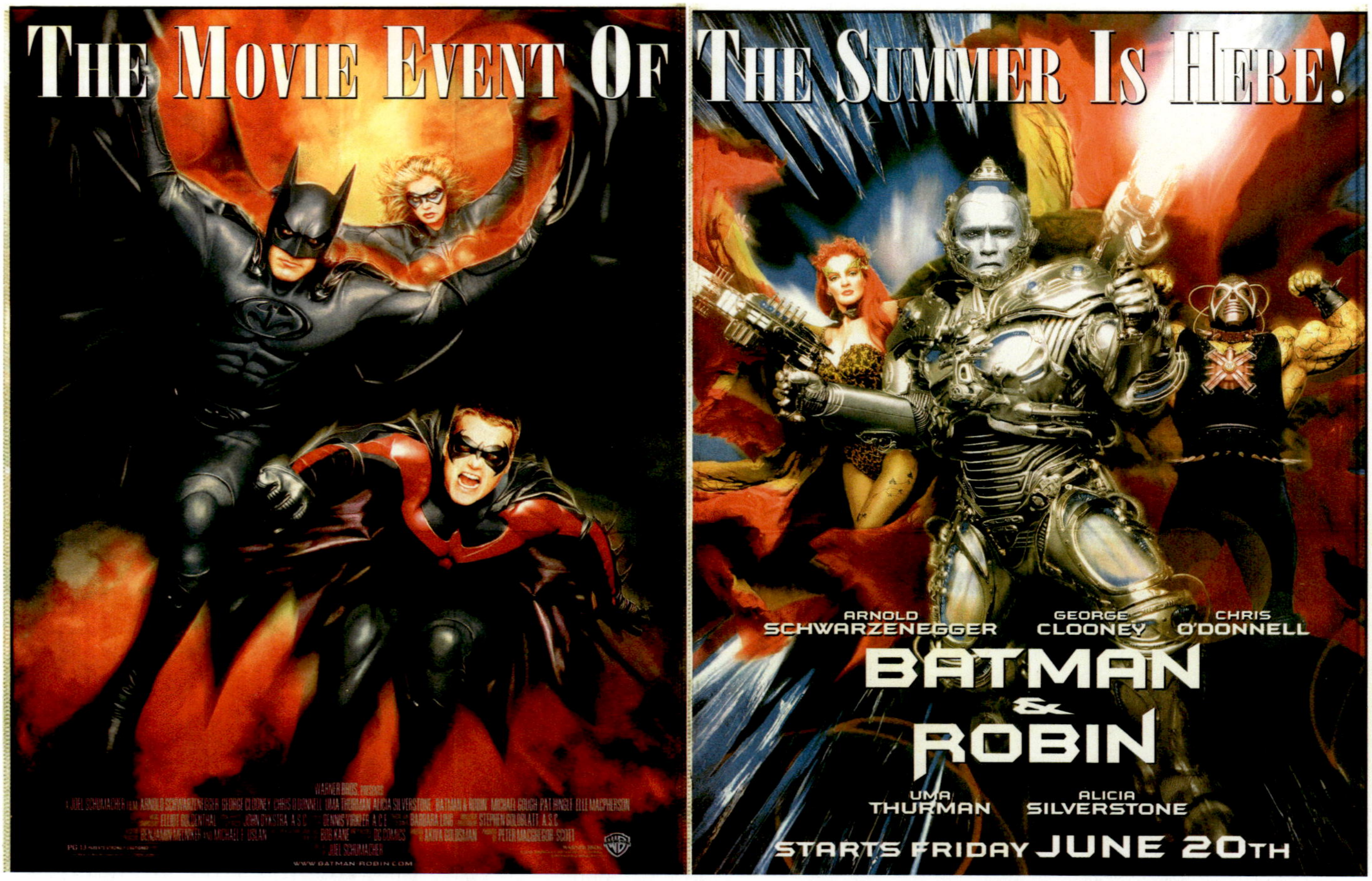
The Movie Event Of The Summer Is Here!
Arnold Schwarzenegger
George Clooney
Chris O'Donnell
Batman & Robin
Uma Thurman
Alicia Silverstone
Starts Friday June 20th
www.batman-robin.com

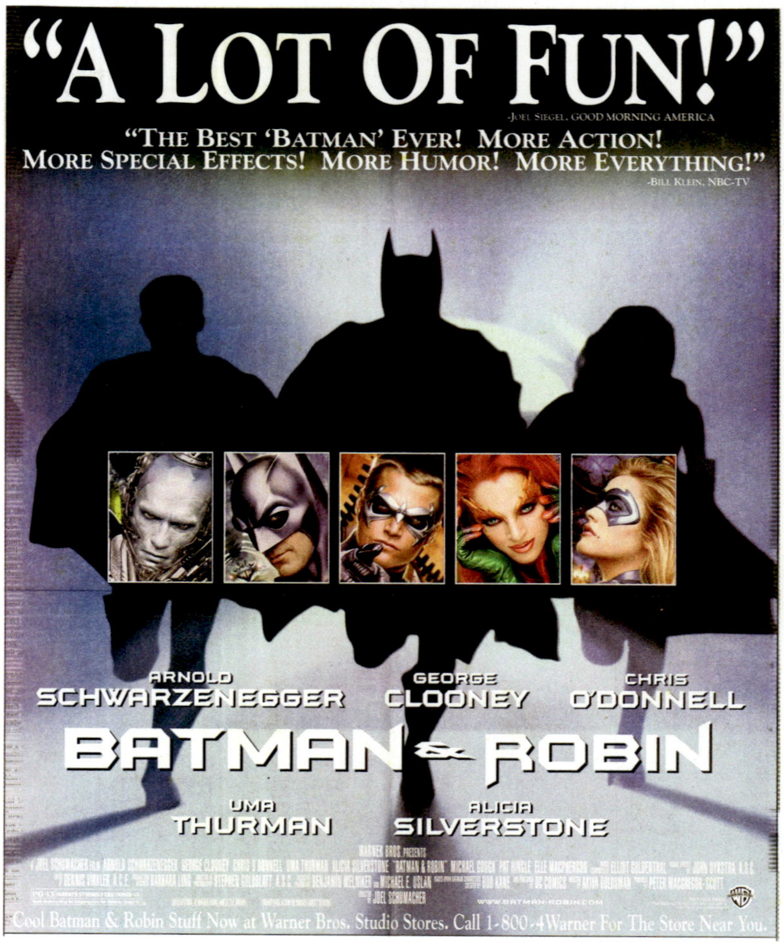
"A Lot Of Fun!"
-Joel Siegel, Good Morning America
"The Best 'Batman' Ever! More Action! More Special Effects! More Humor! More Everything!"
-Bill Klein, NBC-TV
Arnold Schwarzenegger
George Clooney
Chris O'Donnell
Batman & Robin
Uma Thurman
Alicia Silverstone
Cool Batman & Robin Stuff Now at Warner Bros. Studio Stores. Call 1-800-4Warner For The Store Near You.

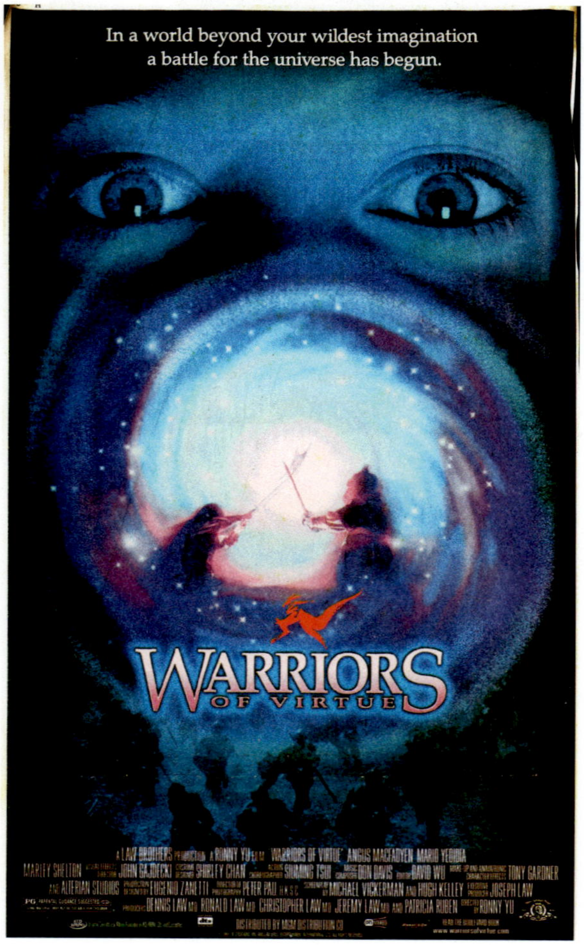
In a world beyond your wildest imagination
a battle for the universe has begun.
Warriors of Virtue

1997

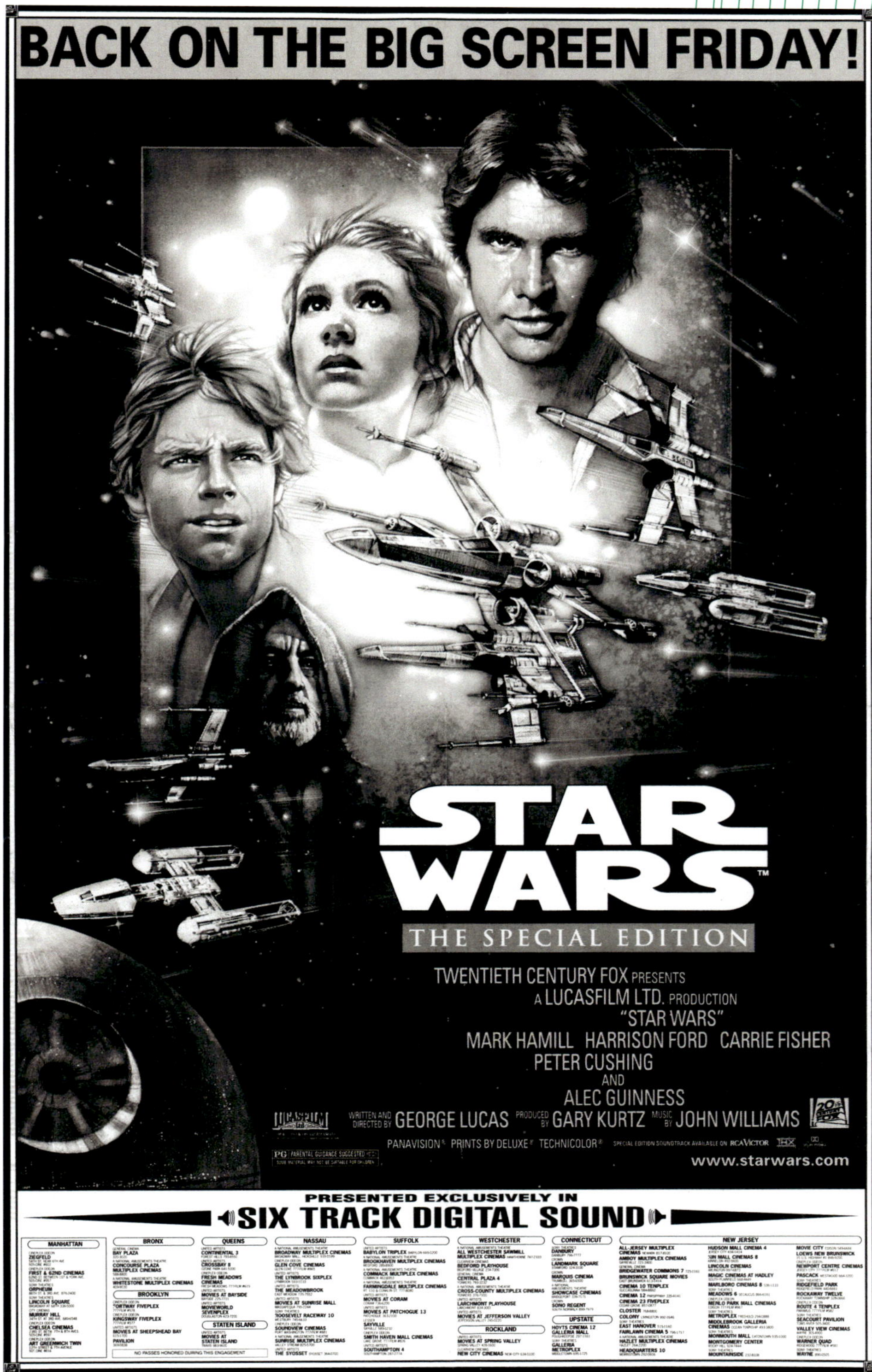
BACK ON THE BIG SCREEN FRIDAY!
STAR WARS
THE SPECIAL EDITION
TWENTIETH CENTURY FOX PRESENTS
A LUCASFILM LTD. PRODUCTION
"STAR WARS"
MARK HAMILL HARRISON FORD CARRIE FISHER
PETER CUSHING
AND
ALEC GUINNESS
WRITTEN AND DIRECTED BY GEORGE LUCAS PRODUCED BY GARY KURTZ MUSIC BY JOHN WILLIAMS
PANAVISION PRINTS BY DELUXE TECHNICOLOR
www.starwars.com
PRESENTED EXCLUSIVELY IN
SIX TRACK DIGITAL SOUND
MANHATTAN
BRONX
QUEENS
NASSAU
SUFFOLK
WESTCHESTER
CONNECTICUT
NEW JERSEY
BROOKLYN
STATEN ISLAND
ROCKLAND
UPSTATE
NO PASSES HONORED DURING THIS ENGAGEMENT

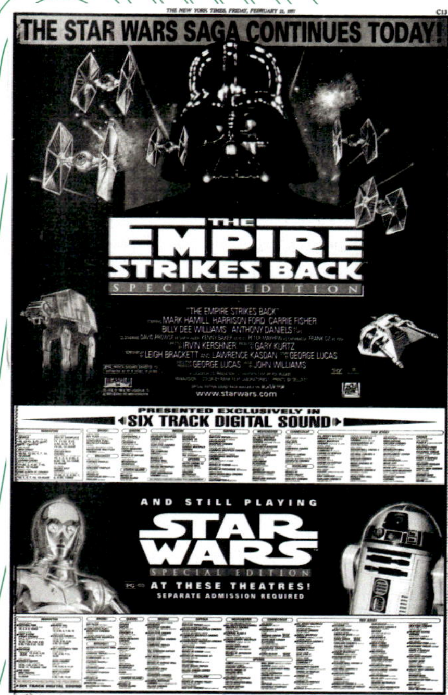
THE STAR WARS SAGA CONTINUES TODAY!
THE EMPIRE STRIKES BACK
SPECIAL EDITION
"THE EMPIRE STRIKES BACK"
MARK HAMILL HARRISON FORD CARRIE FISHER
BILLY DEE WILLIAMS ANTHONY DANIELS
IRVIN KERSHNER GARY KURTZ
LEIGH BRACKETT AND LAWRENCE KASDAN GEORGE LUCAS
GEORGE LUCAS JOHN WILLIAMS
www.starwars.com
PRESENTED EXCLUSIVELY IN
SIX TRACK DIGITAL SOUND
AND STILL PLAYING
STAR WARS
SPECIAL EDITION
AT THESE THEATRES!
SEPARATE ADMISSION REQUIRED

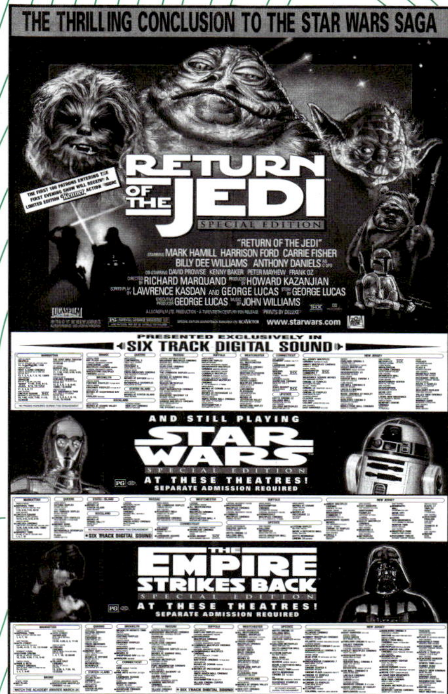
THE THRILLING CONCLUSION TO THE STAR WARS SAGA
RETURN OF THE JEDI
SPECIAL EDITION
"RETURN OF THE JEDI"
MARK HAMILL HARRISON FORD CARRIE FISHER
BILLY DEE WILLIAMS ANTHONY DANIELS
DAVID PROWSE KENNY BAKER PETER MAYHEW FRANK OZ
RICHARD MARQUAND HOWARD KAZANJIAN
LAWRENCE KASDAN AND GEORGE LUCAS GEORGE LUCAS
GEORGE LUCAS JOHN WILLIAMS
www.starwars.com
PRESENTED EXCLUSIVELY IN
SIX TRACK DIGITAL SOUND
AND STILL PLAYING
STAR WARS
SPECIAL EDITION
AT THESE THEATRES!
SEPARATE ADMISSION REQUIRED
THE EMPIRE STRIKES BACK
SPECIAL EDITION
AT THESE THEATRES!
SEPARATE ADMISSION REQUIRED

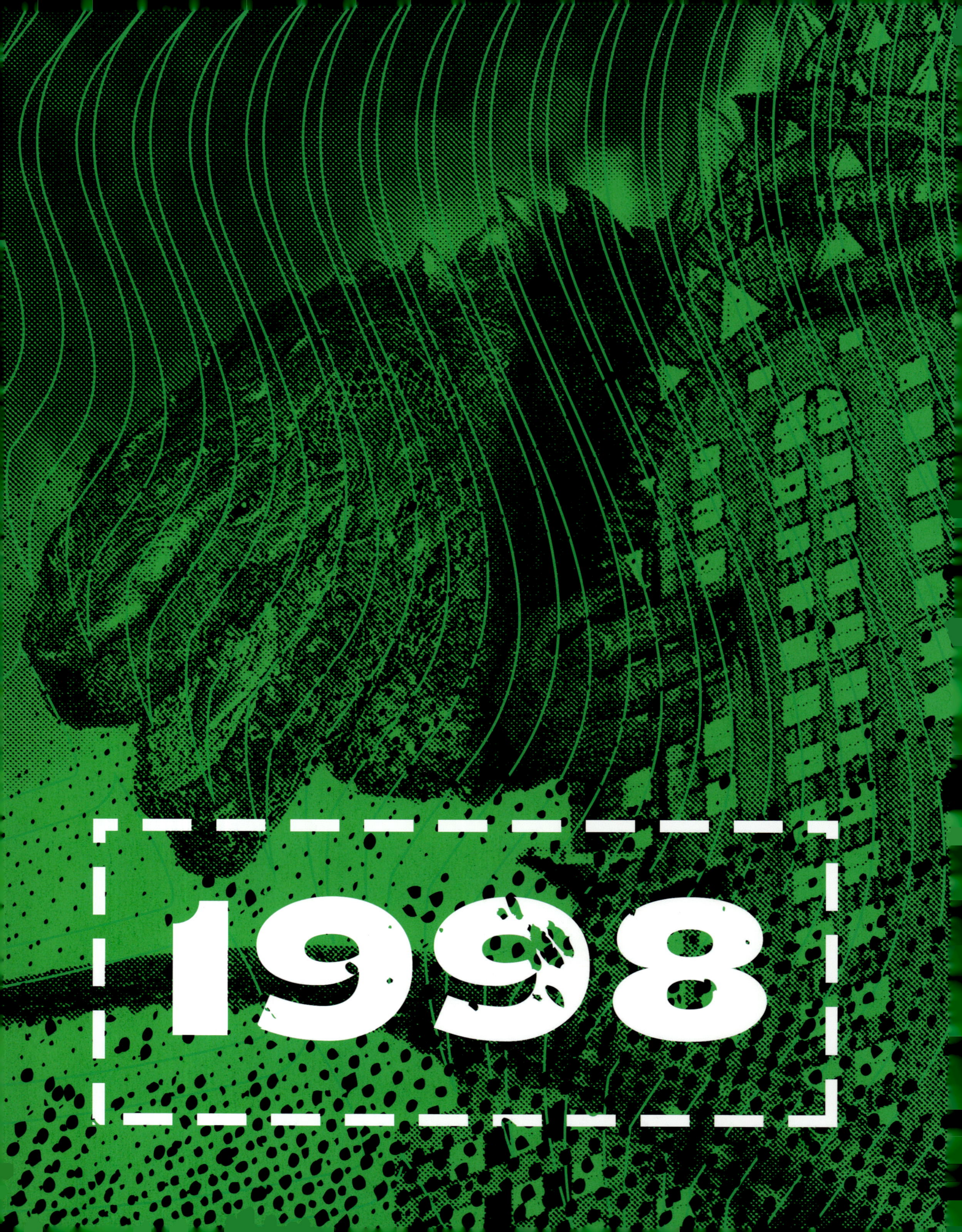
1998

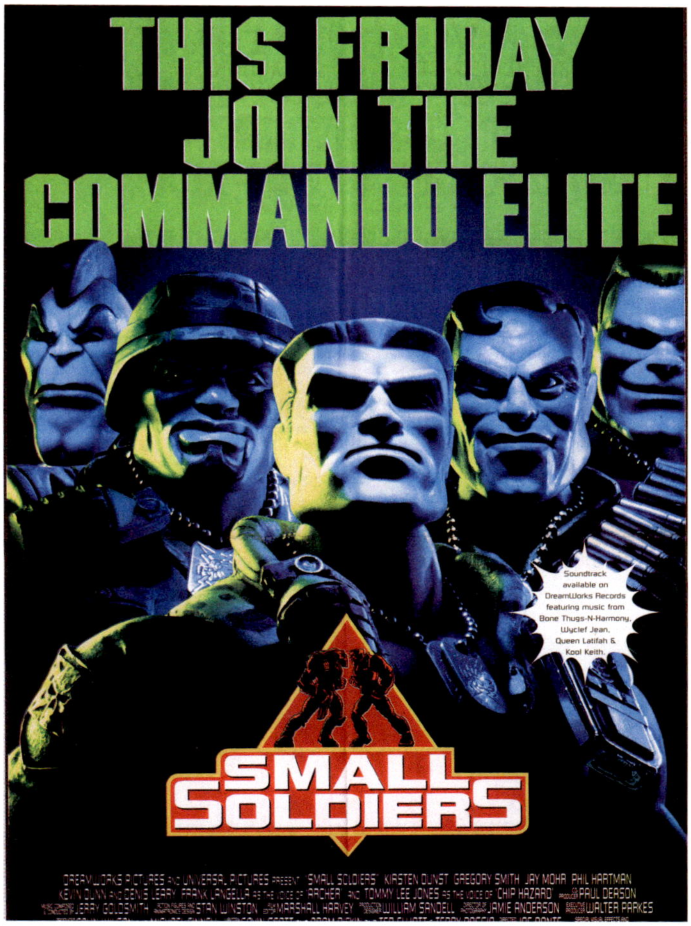
THIS FRIDAY
JOIN THE
COMMANDO ELITE
Soundtrack available on DreamWorks Records featuring music from Bone Thugs-N-Harmony, Wyclef Jean, Queen Latifah & Kool Keith.
SMALL SOLDIERS

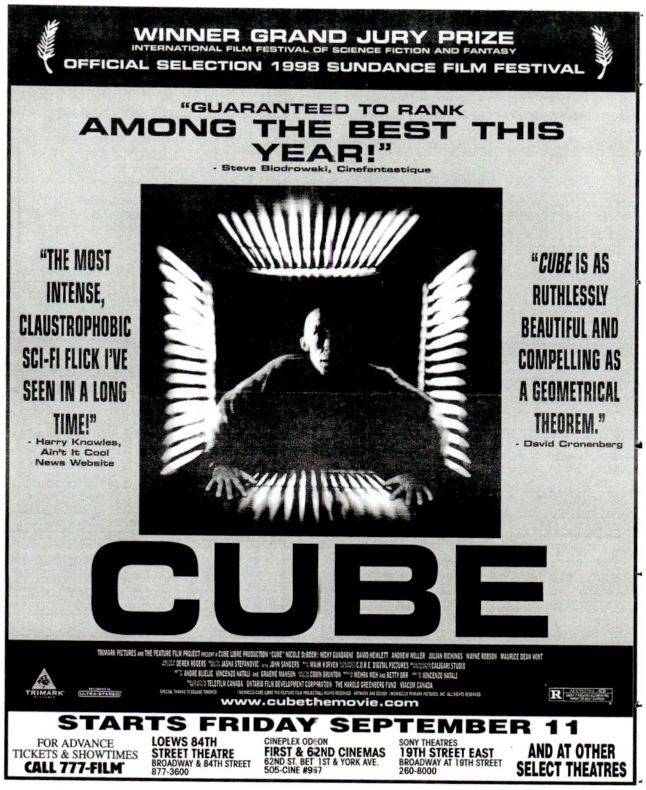
WINNER GRAND JURY PRIZE
INTERNATIONAL FILM FESTIVAL OF SCIENCE FICTION AND FANTASY
OFFICIAL SELECTION 1998 SUNDANCE FILM FESTIVAL
"GUARANTEED TO RANK AMONG THE BEST THIS YEAR!"
- Steve Biodrowski, Cinefantastique
"THE MOST INTENSE, CLAUSTROPHOBIC SCI-FI FLICK I'VE SEEN IN A LONG TIME!"
- Harry Knowles, Ain't It Cool News Website
"CUBE IS AS RUTHLESSLY BEAUTIFUL AND COMPELLING AS A GEOMETRICAL THEOREM."
- David Cronenberg
CUBE
www.cubethemovie.com
STARTS FRIDAY SEPTEMBER 11
FOR ADVANCE TICKETS & SHOWTIMES CALL 777-FILM
LOEWS 84TH STREET THEATRE
BROADWAY & 84TH STREET
877-3600
CINEPLEX ODEON FIRST & 62ND CINEMAS
62ND ST. BET. 1ST & YORK AVE.
505-CINE #957
SONY THEATRES 19TH STREET EAST
BROADWAY AT 19TH STREET
260-8000
AND AT OTHER SELECT THEATRES

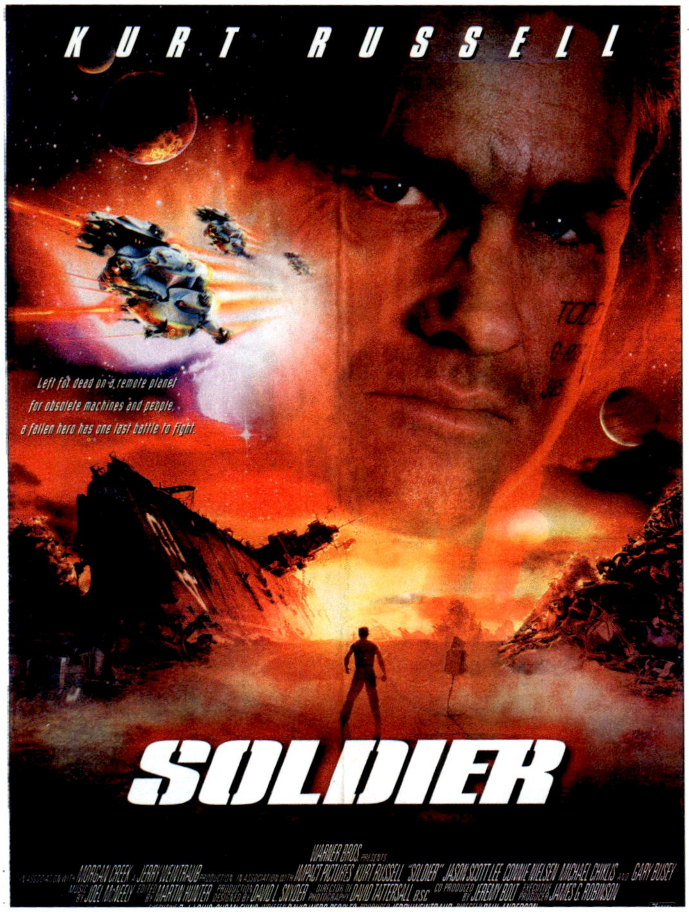
KURT RUSSELL
Left for dead on a remote planet
for obsolete machines and people,
a fallen hero has one last battle to fight.
SOLDIER

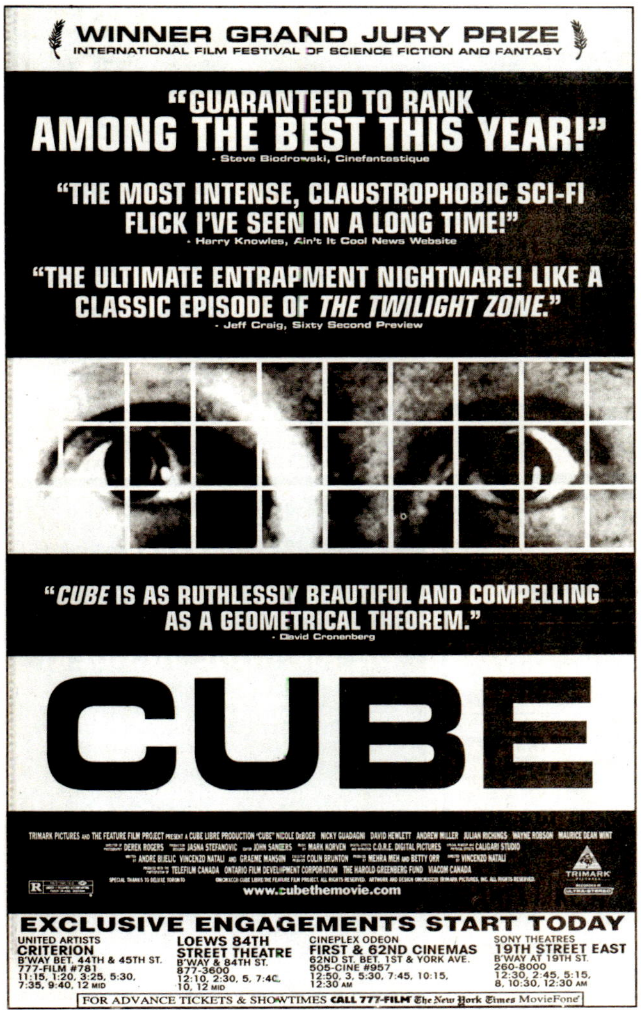
WINNER GRAND JURY PRIZE
INTERNATIONAL FILM FESTIVAL OF SCIENCE FICTION AND FANTASY
"GUARANTEED TO RANK AMONG THE BEST THIS YEAR!"
- Steve Biodrowski, Cinefantastique
"THE MOST INTENSE, CLAUSTROPHOBIC SCI-FI FLICK I'VE SEEN IN A LONG TIME!"
- Harry Knowles, Ain't It Cool News Website
"THE ULTIMATE ENTRAPMENT NIGHTMARE! LIKE A CLASSIC EPISODE OF THE TWILIGHT ZONE."
- Jeff Craig, Sixty Second Preview
"CUBE IS AS RUTHLESSLY BEAUTIFUL AND COMPELLING AS A GEOMETRICAL THEOREM."
- David Cronenberg
CUBE
www.cubethemovie.com
EXCLUSIVE ENGAGEMENTS START TODAY
UNITED ARTISTS CRITERION
B'WAY BET. 44TH & 45TH ST.
777-FILM #781
11:15, 1:20, 3:25, 5:30, 7:35, 9:40, 12 MID
LOEWS 84TH STREET THEATRE
B'WAY & 84TH ST.
877-3600
12:10, 2:30, 5, 7:40, 10, 12 MID
CINEPLEX ODEON FIRST & 62ND CINEMAS
62ND ST. BET. 1ST & YORK AVE.
505-CINE #957
12:50, 3, 5:30, 7:45, 10:15, 12:30 AM
SONY THEATRES 19TH STREET EAST
B'WAY AT 19TH ST.
260-8000
12:30, 2:45, 5:15, 8, 10:30, 12:30 AM
FOR ADVANCE TICKETS & SHOWTIMES CALL 777-FILM The New York Times MovieFone

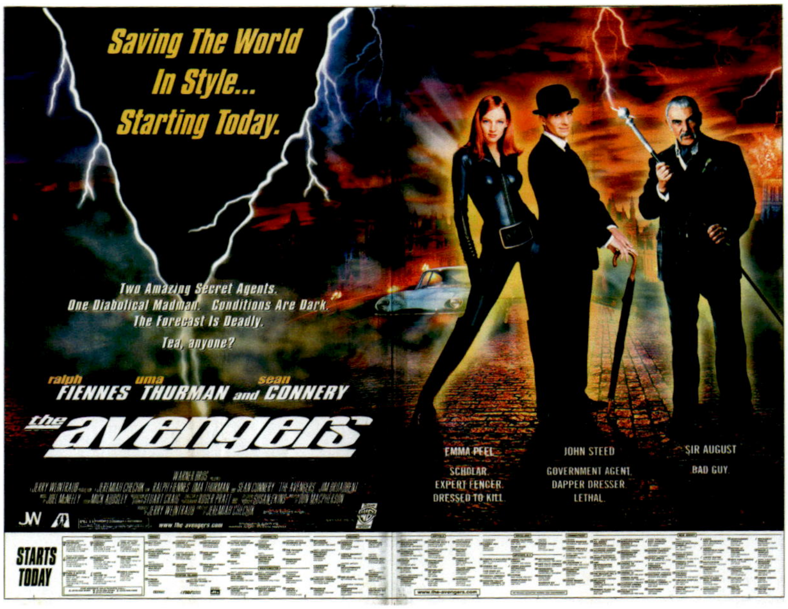

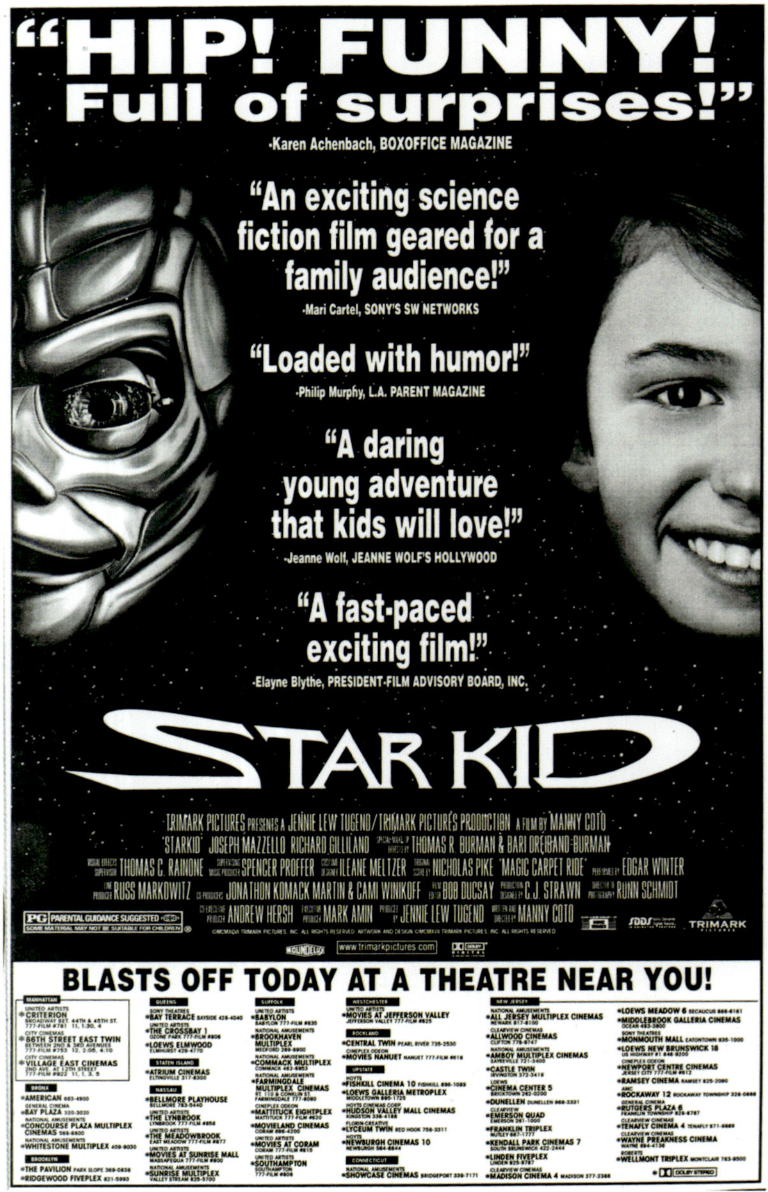

THE AVENGERS

A decade before the launch of the Marvel Cinematic Universe, many pop-culture fans most commonly associated the title *The Avengers* with a cult-favorite British television series from the '60s, starring Patrick Macnee and Diana Rigg. It was the epitome of cool, so there was no surprise when it joined the many classic TV shows turned into feature films in the '90s. It had a top cast in Ralph Fiennes, Uma Thurman, and Sean Connery, but test screenings didn't go well, resulting in nearly a half hour being trimmed by Warner Bros., which opened the bowdlerized result with no critics' screenings. Come Saturday, the reactions were inevitable.

"[How] do you duplicate a magic aura from 30 years ago? You don't. But that apparently hasn't stopped those who made this new incarnation of *The Avengers* from trying. Needless to say, they fall short – though not by as much as one might have expected. Or feared."

–Gene Seymour, *Los Angeles Times*

"If you were walking down the street and saw Fiennes and Connery brawling, which one would you root for? My guess is that half the people would stand on the sidelines rooting for Connery, while the other half would jump in to help beat up Fiennes."

–MICK LASALLE, *SAN FRANCISCO CHRONICLE*

"The movie is an idiocy-driven 90 minutes of torture dreamed up by people who have no new ideas of their own, but who believe that even when they steal old ideas, they can do them better than the smart people who thought them up first."

–Barbara Shulgasser, *San Francisco Examiner*

"In this movie, the sense of charm has been obliterated. A comet must have hit it! Maybe a dinosaur stepped on it! In any event, the new *Avengers* is dismal in dispiriting, dreary ways, and Ralph Fiennes, playing Macnee's part, is a particular disaster."

–Stephen Hunter, *Washington Post*

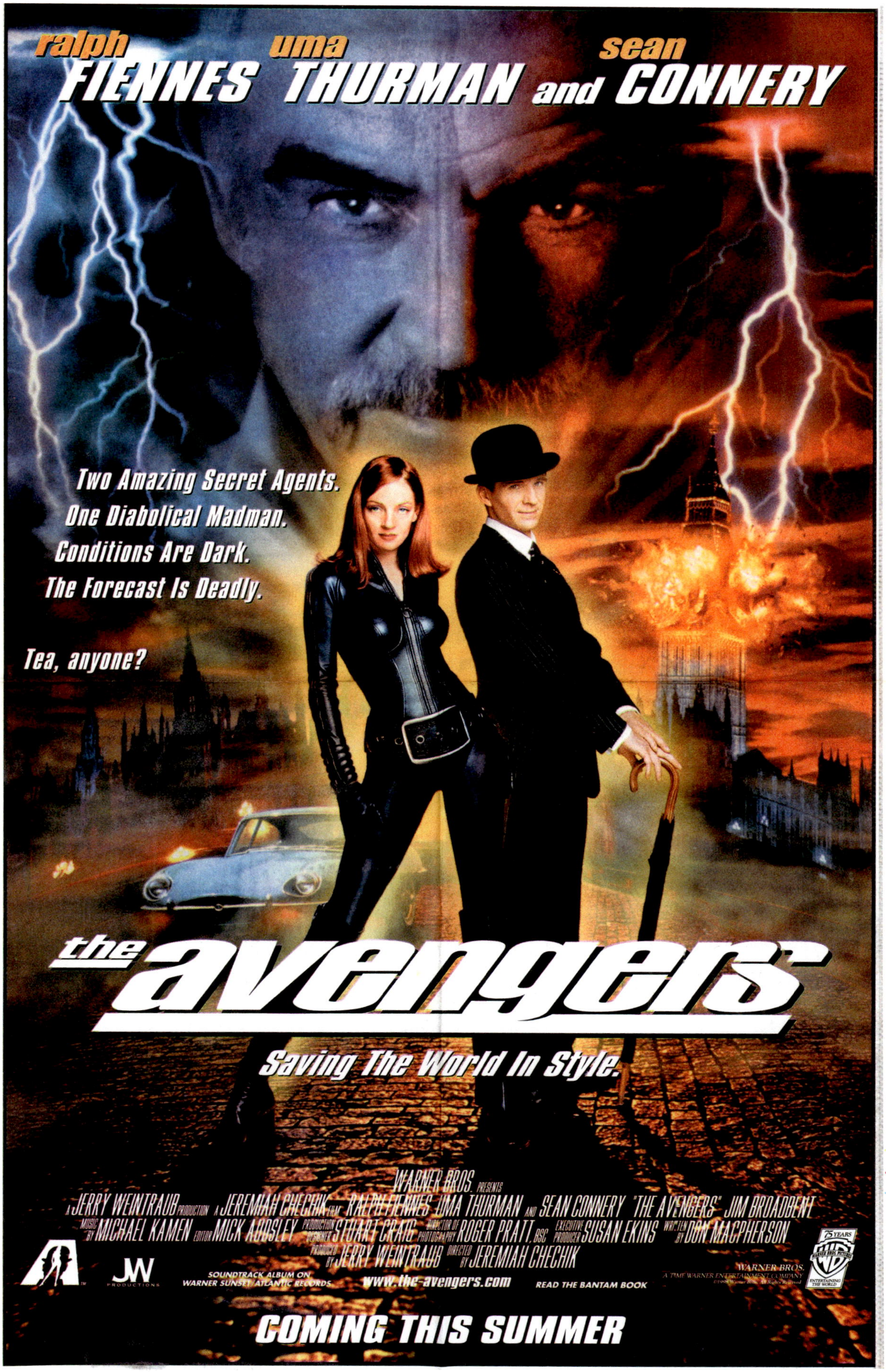
ralph FIENNES uma THURMAN and sean CONNERY
Two Amazing Secret Agents.
One Diabolical Madman.
Conditions Are Dark.
The Forecast Is Deadly.
Tea, anyone?
the avengers
Saving The World In Style.
WARNER BROS. PRESENTS
A JERRY WEINTRAUB PRODUCTION A JEREMIAH CHECHIK FILM RALPH FIENNES UMA THURMAN AND SEAN CONNERY "THE AVENGERS" JIM BROADBENT
MUSIC BY MICHAEL KAMEN EDITOR MICK AUDSLEY PRODUCTION DESIGNER STUART CRAIG DIRECTOR OF PHOTOGRAPHY ROGER PRATT, BSC EXECUTIVE PRODUCER SUSAN EKINS WRITTEN BY DON MACPHERSON
PRODUCED BY JERRY WEINTRAUB DIRECTED BY JEREMIAH CHECHIK
JW PRODUCTIONS
SOUNDTRACK ALBUM ON WARNER SUNSET/ATLANTIC RECORDS
www.the-avengers.com
READ THE BANTAM BOOK
WARNER BROS.
A TIME WARNER ENTERTAINMENT COMPANY
75 YEARS
ENTERTAINING THE WORLD
COMING THIS SUMMER

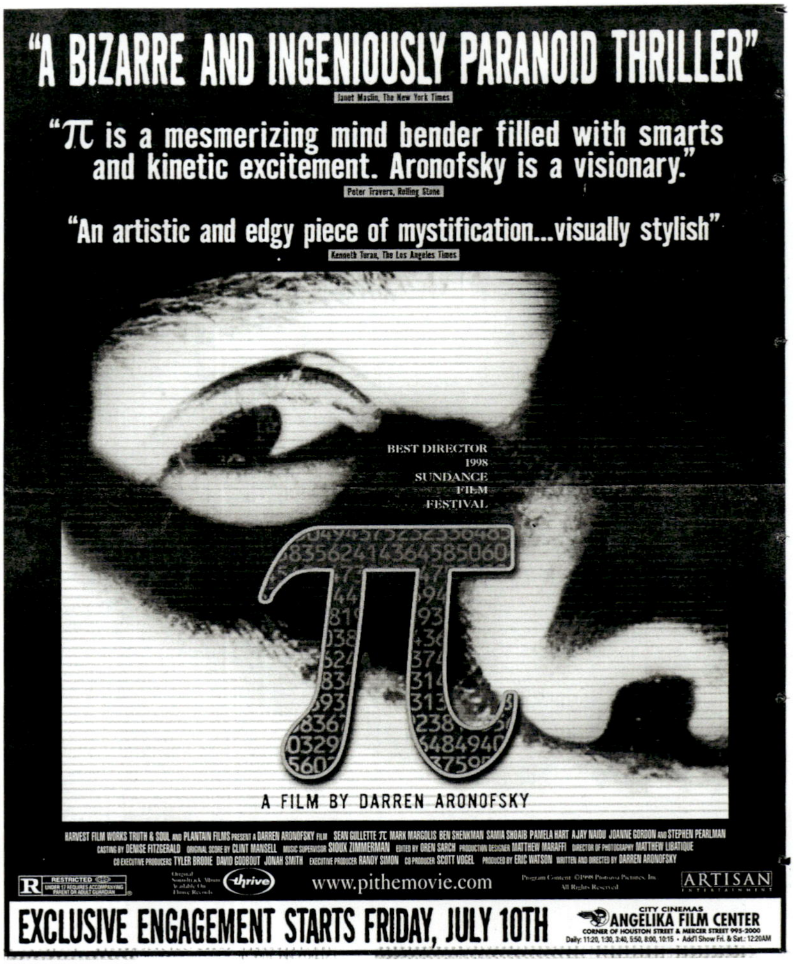

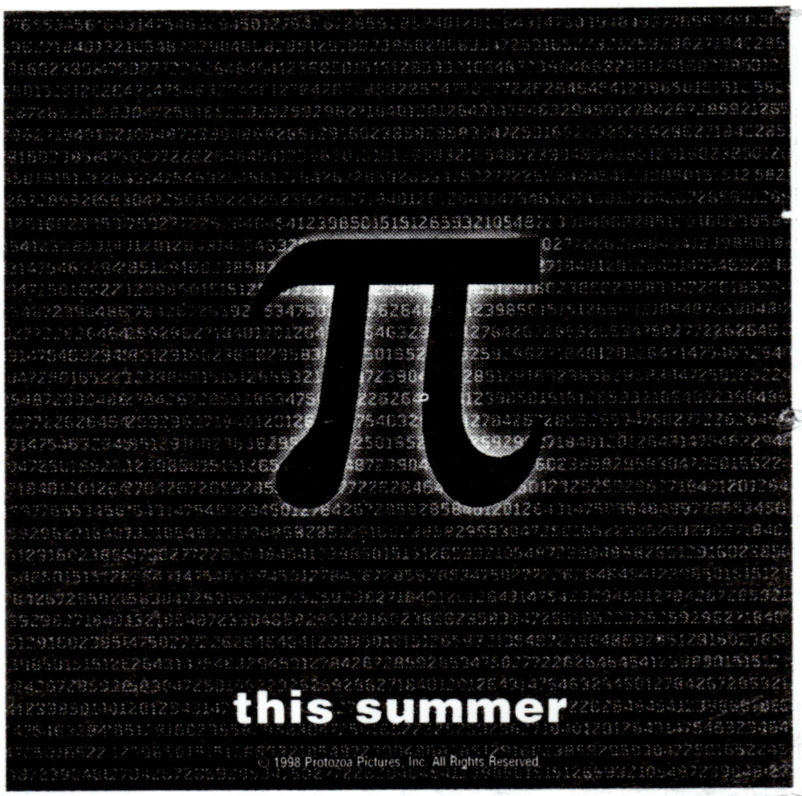

DARK CITY

In his follow-up to *The Crow*, director Alex Proyas explored another shadowy environment, as an amnesiac (Rufus Sewell) discovers the metropolis around him is being "tuned" (altered) at will by a group of mysterious Strangers. The title and release date underwent some tuning as well; the movie was first known as *Dark World*, then *Dark Empire*, and its debut shifted from October '97 to January and then February '98. It was greeted by generally favorable reviews, and a few outright raves; Roger Ebert later named it the best film of the year.

"[A] wonderfully eerie study of what makes humans human, complete with fantastically stylized sets, carefully constricted performances (maybe too constricted, but that's a minor gripe), and atmosphere to burn."

–Chris Kaltenbach, *The Baltimore Sun*

"It is hypnotic, haunting and, to be sure, dark. It is among the most memorable cinematic ventures in recent years. Maybe there's nothing wrong with a movie that is simply sensational to look at."

–Peter Stack, *San Francisco Chronicle*

"If it is true, as the German director Werner Herzog believes, that we live in an age starved of new images, then *Dark City* is a film to nourish us. Not a story so much as an experience, it is a triumph of art direction, set design, cinematography, special effects – and imagination."

–ROGER EBERT, *CHICAGO SUN-TIMES*

"Although its story doesn't add up when you analyze it afterward, the movie does take you on a visually arresting ride that offers many unsettling surprises right up to a sentimental sunburst of an ending that has a paranoid undertone."

–Stephen Holden, *The New York Times*

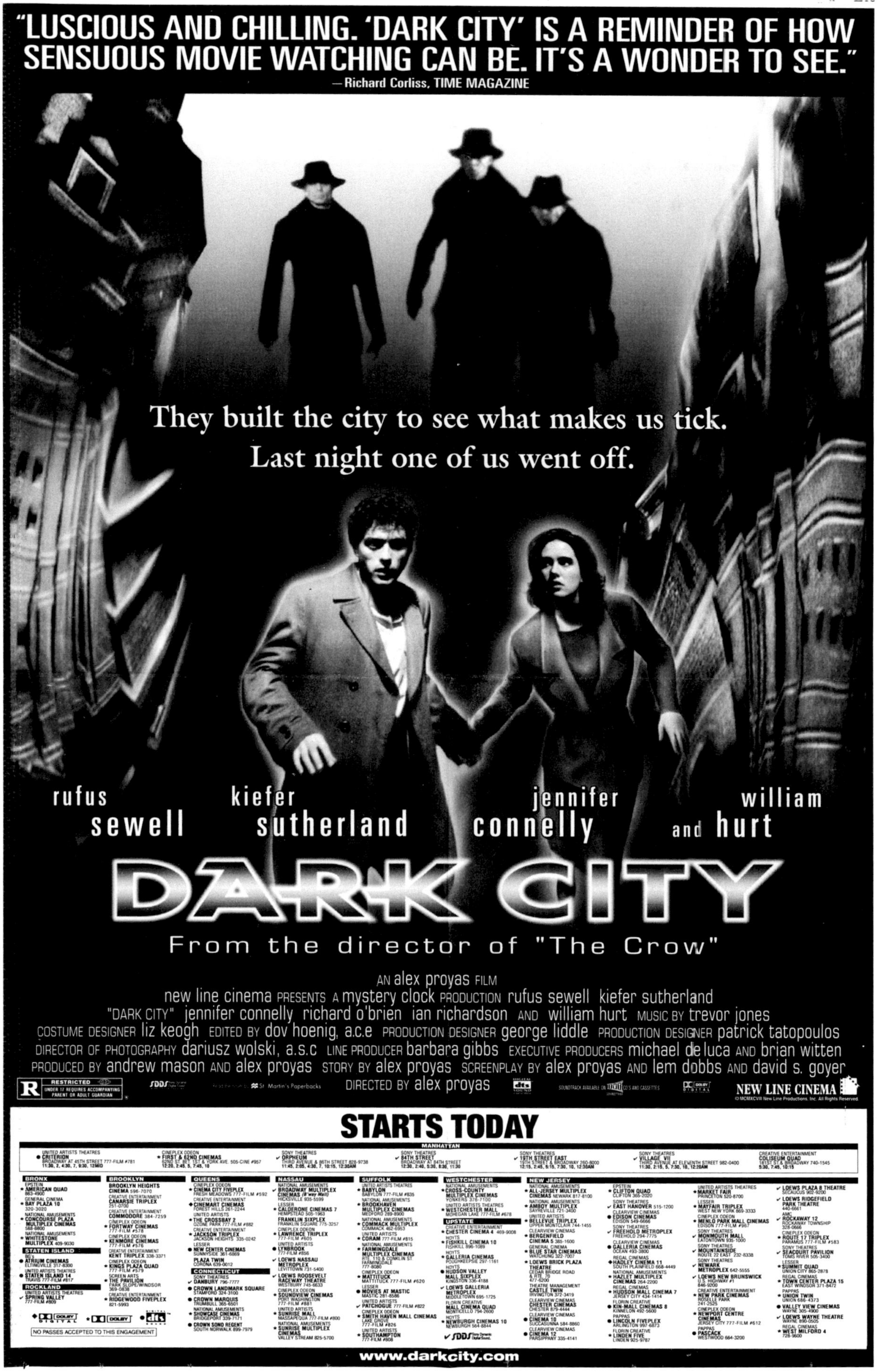
"LUSCIOUS AND CHILLING. 'DARK CITY' IS A REMINDER OF HOW SENSUOUS MOVIE WATCHING CAN BE. IT'S A WONDER TO SEE."
—Richard Corliss, TIME MAGAZINE
They built the city to see what makes us tick.
Last night one of us went off.
rufus sewell
kiefer sutherland
jennifer connelly
and william hurt
DARK CITY
From the director of "The Crow"
AN alex proyas FILM
new line cinema PRESENTS A mystery clock PRODUCTION rufus sewell kiefer sutherland
"DARK CITY" jennifer connelly richard o'brien ian richardson AND william hurt MUSIC BY trevor jones
COSTUME DESIGNER liz keogh EDITED BY dov hoenig, a.c.e PRODUCTION DESIGNER george liddle PRODUCTION DESIGNER patrick tatopoulos
DIRECTOR OF PHOTOGRAPHY dariusz wolski, a.s.c LINE PRODUCER barbara gibbs EXECUTIVE PRODUCERS michael de luca AND brian witten
PRODUCED BY andrew mason AND alex proyas STORY BY alex proyas SCREENPLAY BY alex proyas AND lem dobbs AND david s. goyer
R RESTRICTED UNDER 17 REQUIRES ACCOMPANYING PARENT OR ADULT GUARDIAN
DIRECTED BY alex proyas
NEW LINE CINEMA
STARTS TODAY
MANHATTAN
BRONX
BROOKLYN
QUEENS
NASSAU
SUFFOLK
WESTCHESTER
NEW JERSEY
STATEN ISLAND
ROCKLAND
CONNECTICUT
UPSTATE
NO PASSES ACCEPTED TO THIS ENGAGEMENT
www.darkcity.com

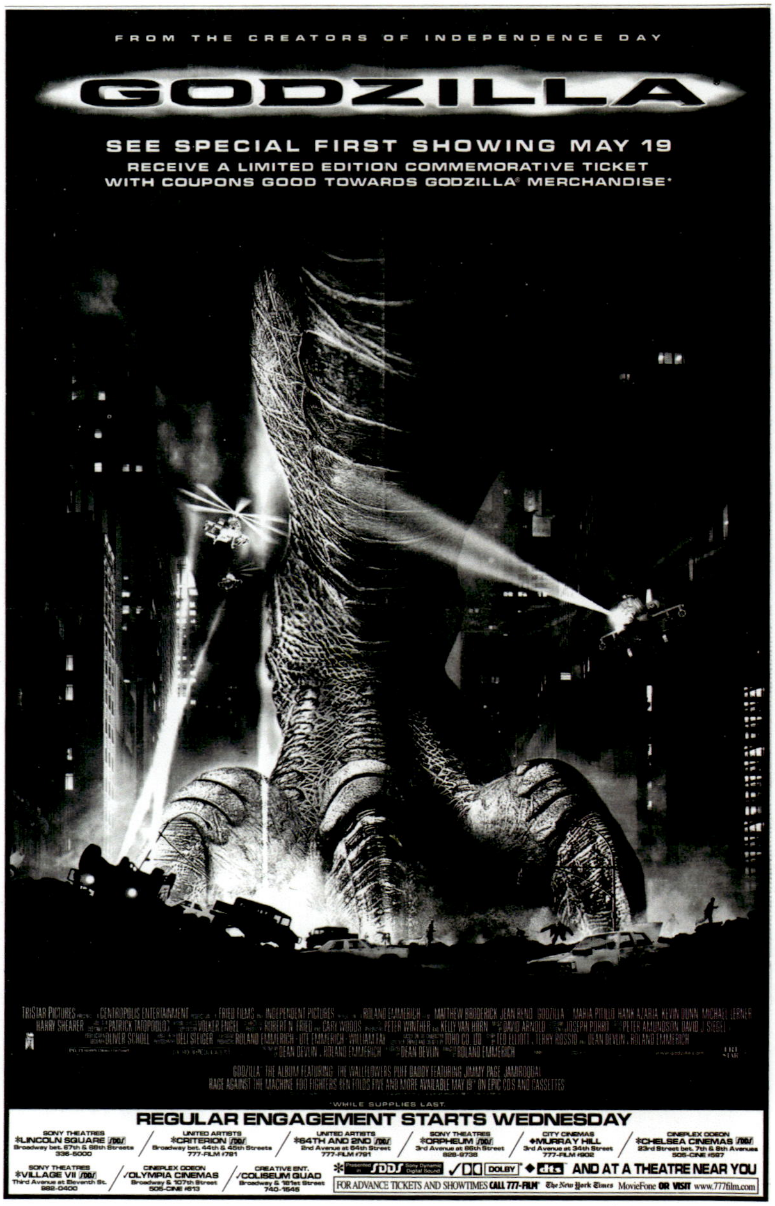

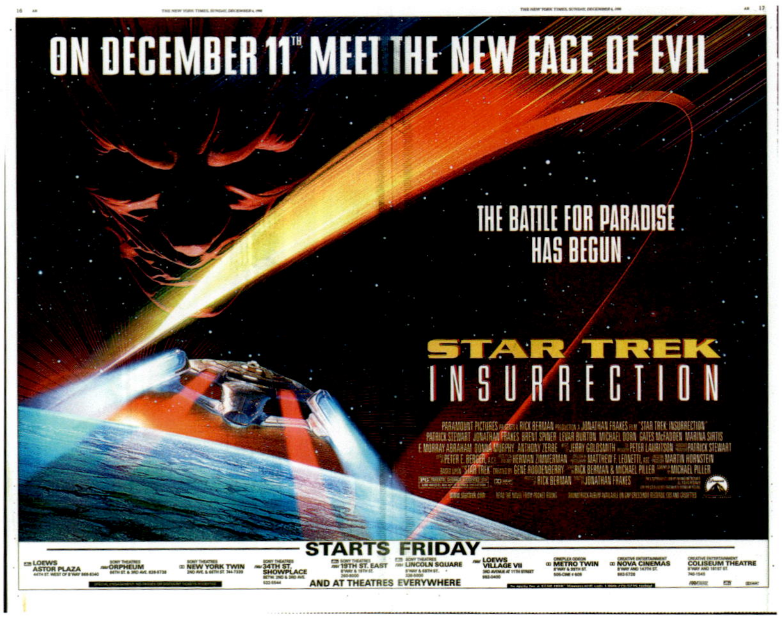

GODZILLA

One of Hollywood's best-kept secrets of the '90s was the look of TriStar and Roland Emmerich's re-imagining of the beloved king of Japanese *kaiju*. No glimpses were afforded of the monster, save the enormous foot seen in both the teaser trailer and first round of posters/ads. "Size does matter" became the cornerstone of a massive marketing campaign, with comparative slogans (e.g., "His Foot Is As Long As This Bus") plastered all over major cities. Then the reviews, followed by word of mouth, got around, and this *Godzilla* fell far short of its wannabe blockbuster status. (It also occasioned an early Internet controversy when Ain't It Cool News' Harry Knowles raved about the film after being invited to the Madison Square Garden premiere; readers cried sellout, and he quickly reversed his opinion.) Ads after opening week offered a better look at the new Godzilla, but the damage was done.

"[A]n expertly-designed theme park ride of a movie that packs nonstop thrills. Emmerich and his co-writers...are never at a loss for inspiration, and their pace is unflagging as that of old serials; wisely, they don't underline Godzilla's inherent allegorical aspect."

–Kevin Thomas, *Los Angeles Times*

"Once the beast begins his third rampage through the city's landmarks, watching New York get pummeled into a pile of rubble loses its novelty and becomes simply tedious."

–Stephen Holden, *The New York Times*

"Not only should filmgoers not bother seeing *Godzilla*, they should storm the ramparts of Tristar Pictures and demand some compensation for the time spent enduring the movie's endless marketing on television, in newspapers and in theaters. This is a rip-off on the order of New Coke, with none of the taste."

–ANN HORNADAY, *THE BALTIMORE SUN*

"The philosophy of Emmerich and co-writer Dean Devlin...seems to be if you can do something obvious and hackneyed once, why not do it twice? Why not three times?"

–Barbara Shulgasser, *San Francisco Examiner*

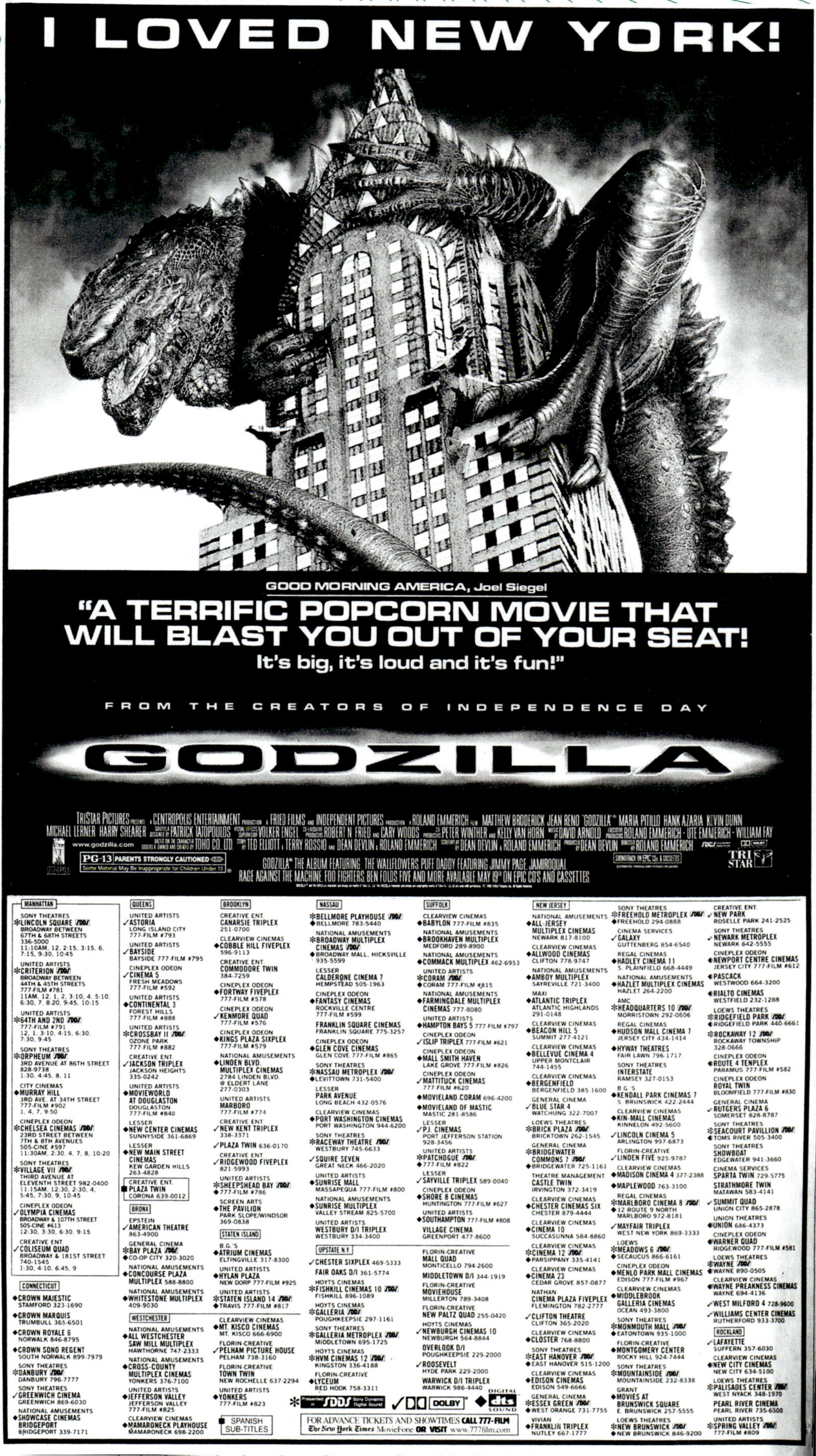
I LOVED NEW YORK!
GOOD MORNING AMERICA, Joel Siegel
"A TERRIFIC POPCORN MOVIE THAT WILL BLAST YOU OUT OF YOUR SEAT!
It's big, it's loud and it's fun!"
FROM THE CREATORS OF INDEPENDENCE DAY
GODZILLA
PG-13 PARENTS STRONGLY CAUTIONED
www.godzilla.com
FOR ADVANCE TICKETS AND SHOWTIMES CALL 777-FILM

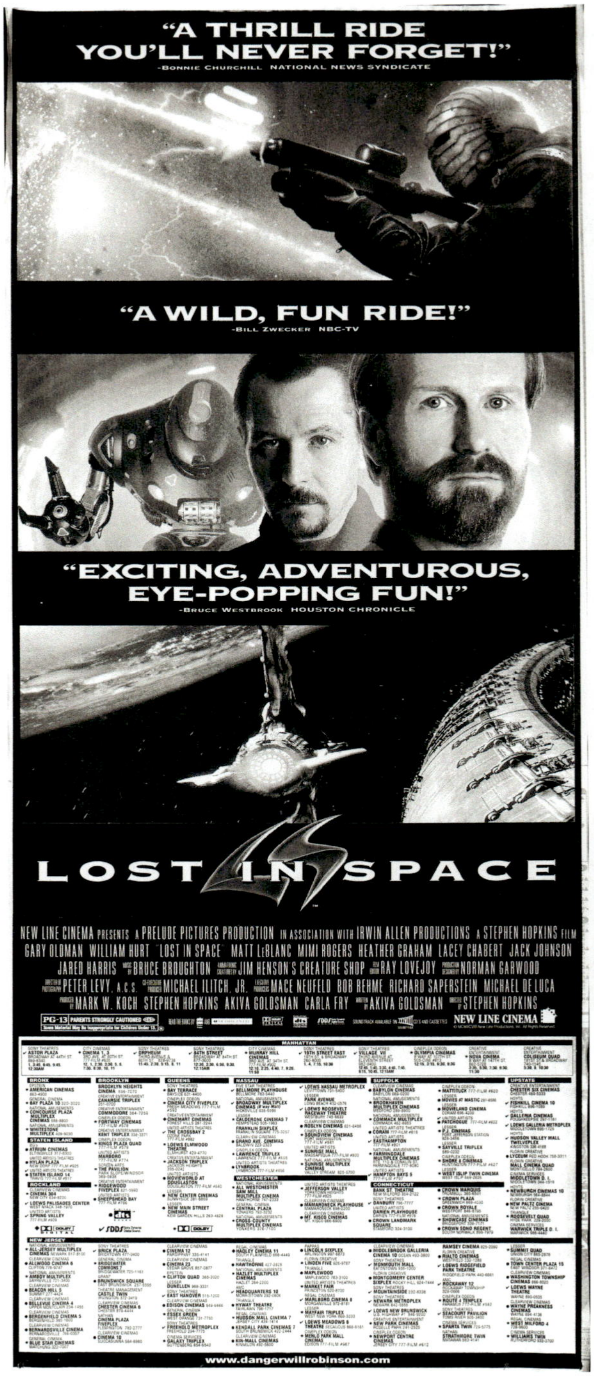
"A THRILL RIDE YOU'LL NEVER FORGET!"
-Bonnie Churchill NATIONAL NEWS SYNDICATE
"A WILD, FUN RIDE!"
-Bill Zwecker NBC-TV
"EXCITING, ADVENTUROUS, EYE-POPPING FUN!"
-Bruce Westbrook HOUSTON CHRONICLE
LOST IN SPACE
NEW LINE CINEMA PRESENTS A PRELUDE PICTURES PRODUCTION IN ASSOCIATION WITH IRWIN ALLEN PRODUCTIONS A STEPHEN HOPKINS FILM
GARY OLDMAN WILLIAM HURT "LOST IN SPACE" MATT LeBLANC MIMI ROGERS HEATHER GRAHAM LACEY CHABERT JACK JOHNSON
JARED HARRIS BRUCE BROUGHTON JIM HENSON'S CREATURE SHOP RAY LOVEJOY NORMAN GARWOOD
PETER LEVY, A.C.S. MICHAEL ILITCH, JR. MACE NEUFELD BOB REHME RICHARD SAPERSTEIN MICHAEL DE LUCA
MARK W. KOCH STEPHEN HOPKINS AKIVA GOLDSMAN CARLA FRY AKIVA GOLDSMAN STEPHEN HOPKINS
PG-13 PARENTS STRONGLY CAUTIONED
NEW LINE CINEMA
MANHATTAN
BRONX
BROOKLYN
QUEENS
NASSAU
SUFFOLK
UPSTATE
STATEN ISLAND
ROCKLAND
WESTCHESTER
CONNECTICUT
NEW JERSEY
www.dangerwillrobinson.com

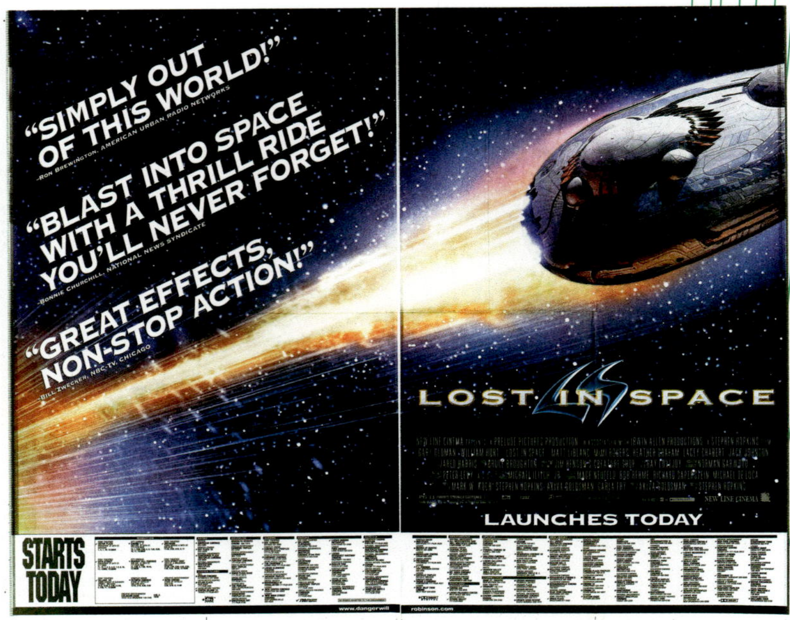
"SIMPLY OUT OF THIS WORLD!"
-Ron Brewington, AMERICAN URBAN RADIO NETWORKS
"BLAST INTO SPACE WITH A THRILL RIDE YOU'LL NEVER FORGET!"
-Bonnie Churchill, NATIONAL NEWS SYNDICATE
"GREAT EFFECTS, NON-STOP ACTION!"
-Bill Zwecker, NBC-TV, CHICAGO
LOST IN SPACE
LAUNCHES TODAY
STARTS TODAY

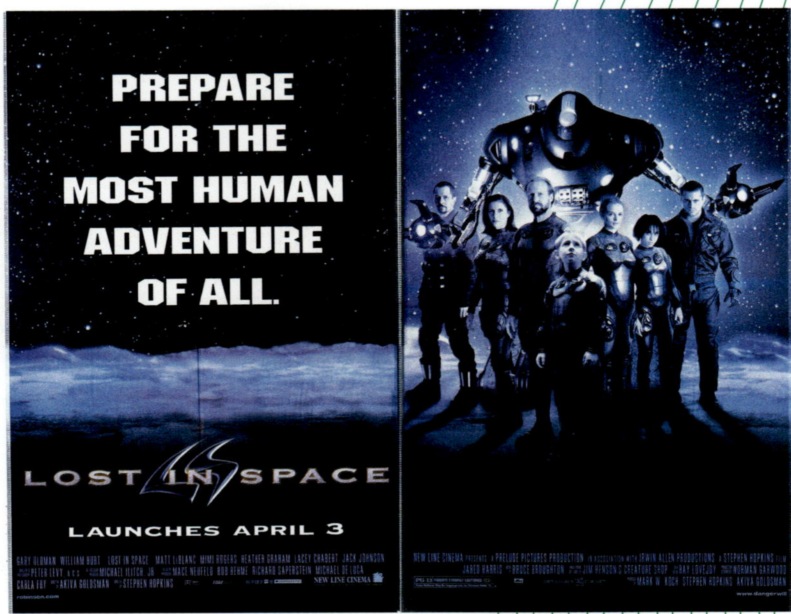
PREPARE FOR THE MOST HUMAN ADVENTURE OF ALL.
LOST IN SPACE
LAUNCHES APRIL 3
NEW LINE CINEMA

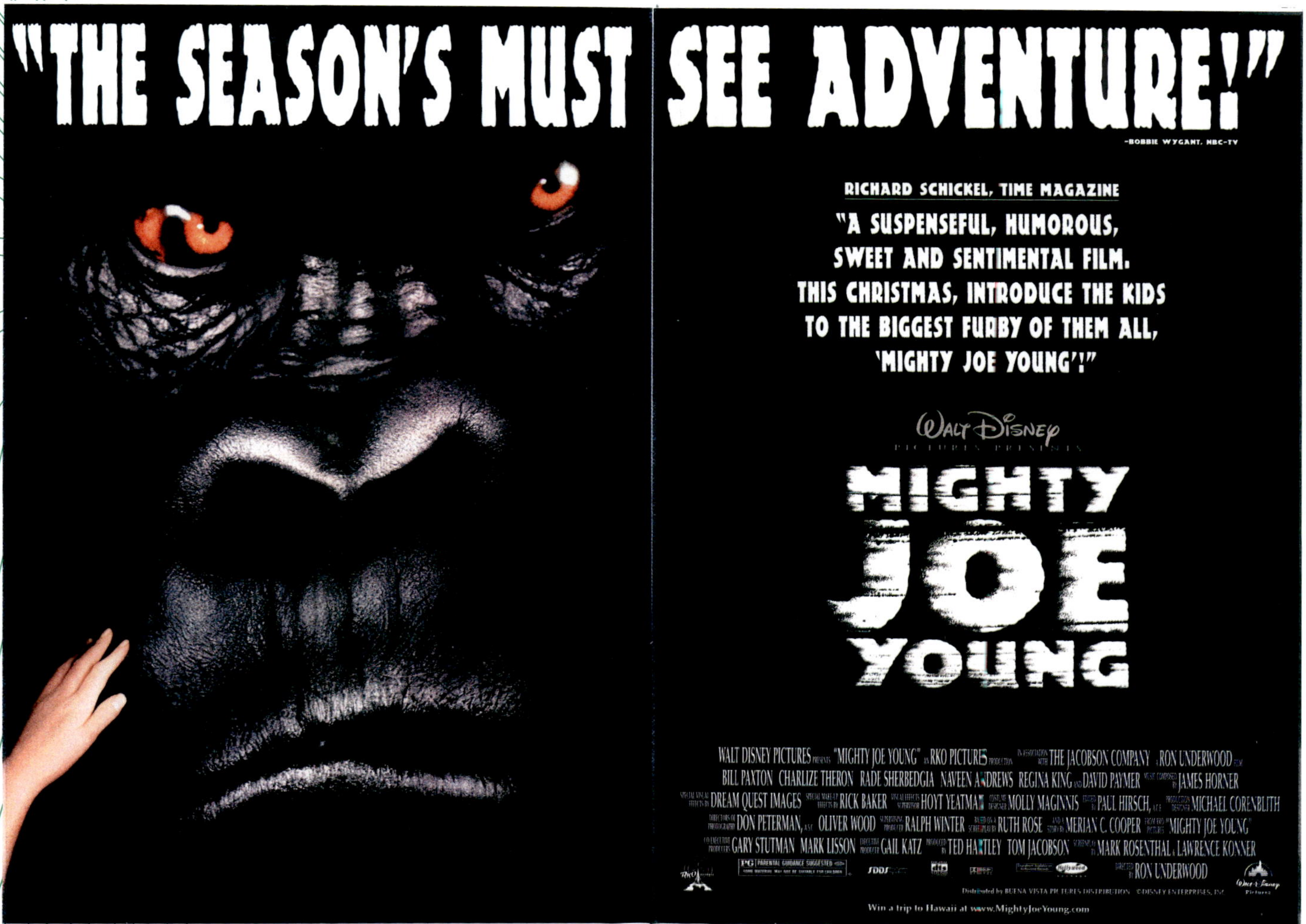
"THE SEASON'S MUST SEE ADVENTURE!"
-BOBBIE WYGANT, NBC-TV
RICHARD SCHICKEL, TIME MAGAZINE
"A SUSPENSEFUL, HUMOROUS, SWEET AND SENTIMENTAL FILM. THIS CHRISTMAS, INTRODUCE THE KIDS TO THE BIGGEST FURBY OF THEM ALL, 'MIGHTY JOE YOUNG'!"
Walt Disney PICTURES PRESENTS
MIGHTY JOE YOUNG
WALT DISNEY PICTURES PRESENTS "MIGHTY JOE YOUNG" AN RKO PICTURES PRODUCTION IN ASSOCIATION WITH THE JACOBSON COMPANY A RON UNDERWOOD FILM
BILL PAXTON CHARLIZE THERON RADE SHERBEDGIA NAVEEN ANDREWS REGINA KING AND DAVID PAYMER MUSIC COMPOSED BY JAMES HORNER
SPECIAL VISUAL EFFECTS BY DREAM QUEST IMAGES SPECIAL MAKE-UP EFFECTS BY RICK BAKER VISUAL EFFECTS SUPERVISOR HOYT YEATMAN COSTUME DESIGNER MOLLY MAGINNIS EDITED BY PAUL HIRSCH, A.C.E. PRODUCTION DESIGNER MICHAEL CORENBLITH
DIRECTORS OF PHOTOGRAPHY DON PETERMAN, A.S.C. OLIVER WOOD SUPERVISING PRODUCER RALPH WINTER BASED ON A SCREENPLAY BY RUTH ROSE AND A STORY BY MERIAN C. COOPER FROM RKO PICTURES "MIGHTY JOE YOUNG"
CO-EXECUTIVE PRODUCERS GARY STUTMAN MARK LISSON EXECUTIVE PRODUCER GAIL KATZ PRODUCED BY TED HARTLEY TOM JACOBSON SCREENPLAY BY MARK ROSENTHAL & LAWRENCE KONNER
PG PARENTAL GUIDANCE SUGGESTED
DIRECTED BY RON UNDERWOOD
Distributed by BUENA VISTA PICTURES DISTRIBUTION ©DISNEY ENTERPRISES, INC.
Win a trip to Hawaii at www.MightyJoeYoung.com

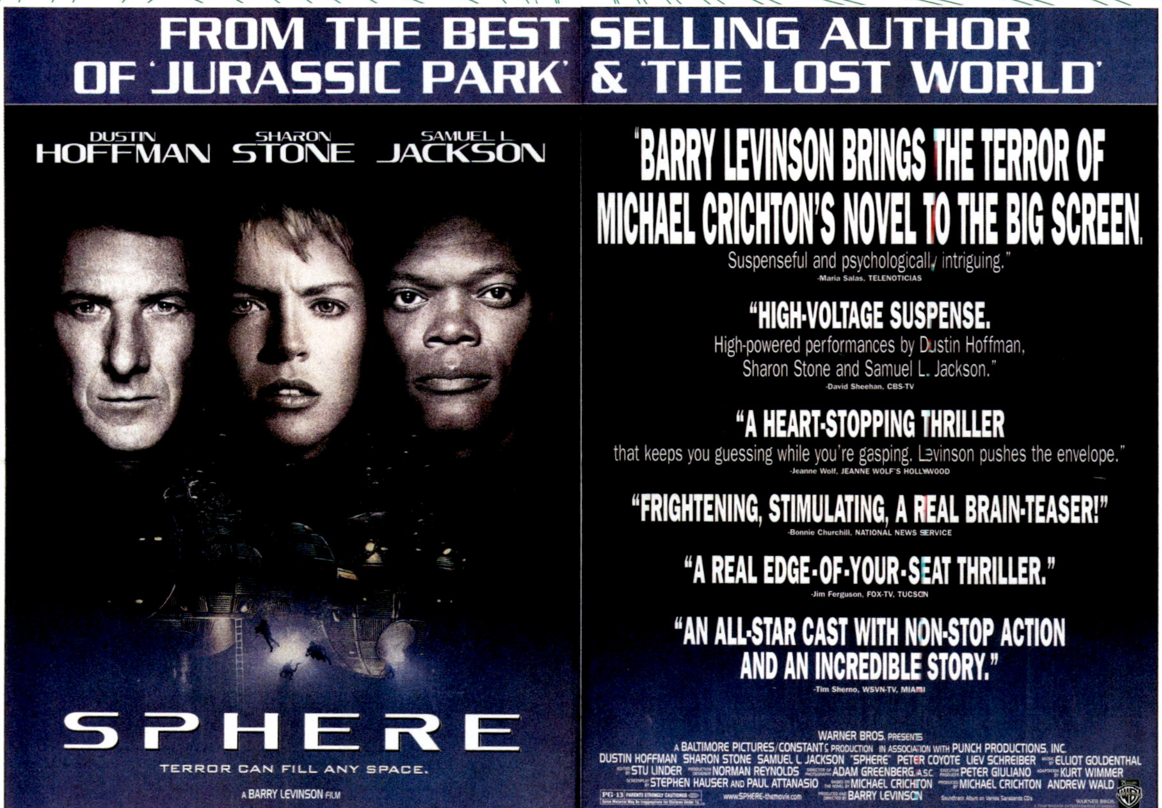
FROM THE BEST SELLING AUTHOR OF 'JURASSIC PARK' & 'THE LOST WORLD'
DUSTIN HOFFMAN SHARON STONE SAMUEL L. JACKSON
SPHERE
TERROR CAN FILL ANY SPACE.
A BARRY LEVINSON FILM
"BARRY LEVINSON BRINGS THE TERROR OF MICHAEL CRICHTON'S NOVEL TO THE BIG SCREEN.
Suspenseful and psychologically intriguing."
-Maria Salas, TELENOTICIAS
"HIGH-VOLTAGE SUSPENSE.
High-powered performances by Dustin Hoffman, Sharon Stone and Samuel L. Jackson."
-David Sheehan, CBS-TV
"A HEART-STOPPING THRILLER
that keeps you guessing while you're gasping. Levinson pushes the envelope."
-Jeanne Wolf, JEANNE WOLF'S HOLLYWOOD
"FRIGHTENING, STIMULATING, A REAL BRAIN-TEASER!"
-Bonnie Churchill, NATIONAL NEWS SERVICE
"A REAL EDGE-OF-YOUR-SEAT THRILLER."
-Jim Ferguson, FOX-TV, TUCSON
"AN ALL-STAR CAST WITH NON-STOP ACTION AND AN INCREDIBLE STORY."
-Tim Sherno, WSVN-TV, MIAMI
WARNER BROS. PRESENTS
A BALTIMORE PICTURES/CONSTANT C PRODUCTION IN ASSOCIATION WITH PUNCH PRODUCTIONS, INC.
DUSTIN HOFFMAN SHARON STONE SAMUEL L. JACKSON "SPHERE" PETER COYOTE LIEV SCHREIBER MUSIC BY ELLIOT GOLDENTHAL
EDITED BY STU LINDER PRODUCTION DESIGNER NORMAN REYNOLDS DIRECTOR OF PHOTOGRAPHY ADAM GREENBERG, A.S.C. EXECUTIVE PRODUCER PETER GIULIANO ADAPTATION BY KURT WIMMER
SCREENPLAY BY STEPHEN HAUSER AND PAUL ATTANASIO BASED ON THE NOVEL BY MICHAEL CRICHTON PRODUCED BY MICHAEL CRICHTON ANDREW WALD
PG-13 PARENTS STRONGLY CAUTIONED
www.SPHERE-themovie.com
PRODUCED AND DIRECTED BY BARRY LEVINSON

NYPRESS FILM CLOCK

An Open Letter From Abel Ferrara:

In response to the slanderous reporting in the September 14th issue of *Variety*. I would like to respond with this:

"...a remarkable composition in the genre of cerebral film noir...beautiful, strong and surprising labyrinth/hotel built by that devil Ferrara"
-LE MONDE Paris

"...a fiercely well-performed erotic drama...Argento positively lights up the screen with an electric, sensual, funny performance that has star written all over it.
-VARIETY New York

"A brilliant work...brave and funny as hell. Walken and Dafoe have never been better."
-LIBERATION, Paris

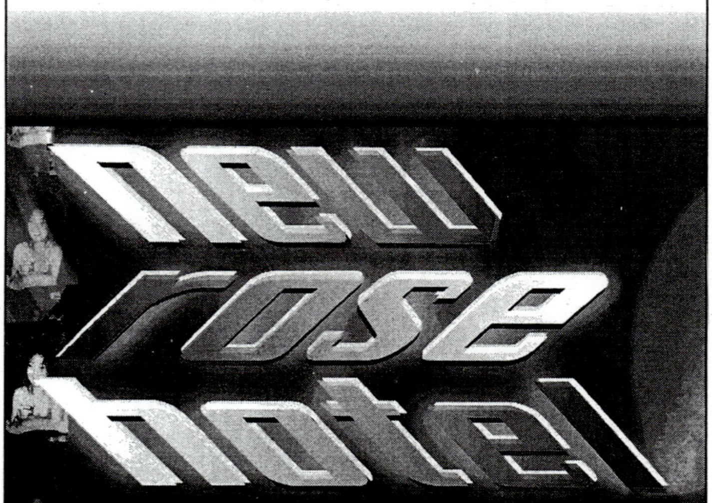

26 • NYPRESS ARTS & LISTINGS • SEPT. 30-OCT. 6, 1998

NEW ROSE HOTEL

The most noteworthy ad for Abel Ferrara's adaptation of William Gibson's cyberpunk short story appeared in a number of newspapers a year before its U.S. release. The *Variety* story it cites was filed from the Venice Film Festival, where *Hotel* played in competition; the trade reported it "confirmed everybody's lowest expectations" and that the reaction was so bad, the movie "was suddenly declared to be a 'work in progress,' taking even the film's publicists by surprise and prompting questions about why it had been entered into the competition at all." In addition to taking out the rebuttal ad, Ferrara told *The New York Post*'s Page Six, "I gotta bleepin' defend myself somehow from these bleeping pro-studio suckers, or whatever you call these journalist motherbleepers. Tell them to go bleep themselves." [*Note: He didn't actually say "bleep."*]

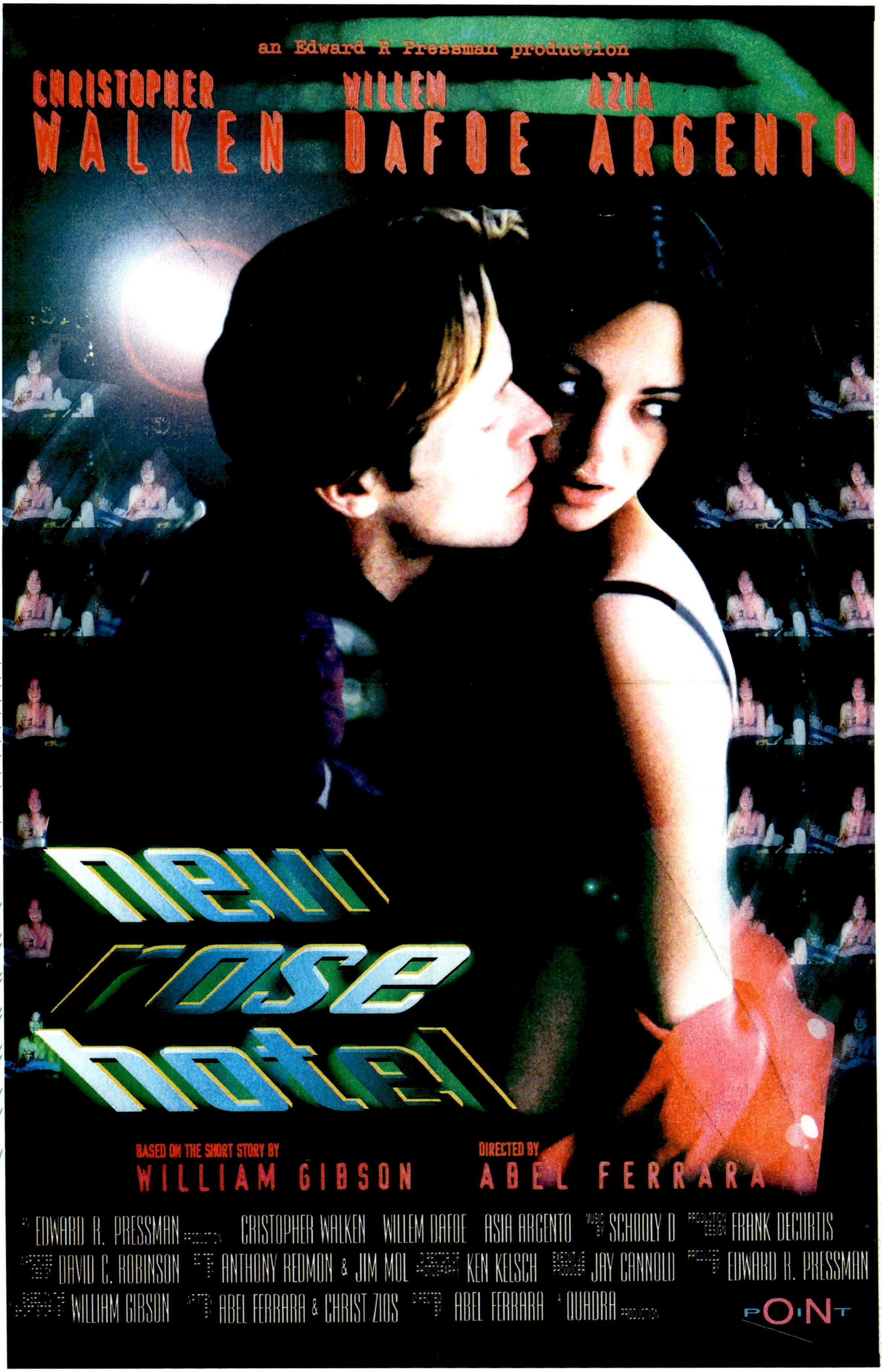

an Edward R Pressman production
CHRISTOPHER WALKEN
WILLEM DAFOE
AZIA ARGENTO
new rose hotel
BASED ON THE SHORT STORY BY
WILLIAM GIBSON
DIRECTED BY
ABEL FERRARA
EDWARD R. PRESSMAN
CRISTOPHER WALKEN WILLEM DAFOE ASIA ARGENTO
SCHOOLY D
FRANK DECURTIS
DAVID C. ROBINSON
ANTHONY REDMON & JIM MOL
KEN KELSCH
JAY CANNOLD
EDWARD R. PRESSMAN
WILLIAM GIBSON
ABEL FERRARA & CHRIST ZIOS
ABEL FERRARA
QUADRA
POINT

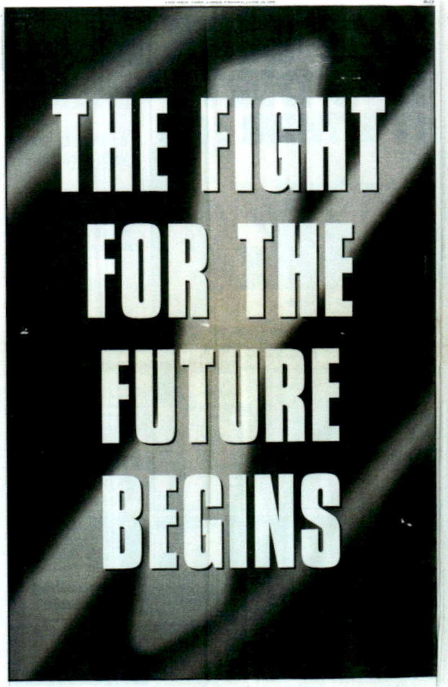

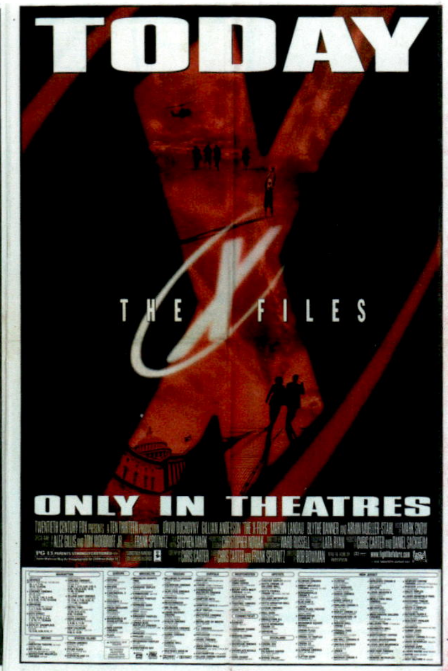

THE X FILES

As noted with *The Avengers*, big-screen reboots of small-screen properties were commonplace this decade, but *The X Files* was a special case: a movie tied to a TV counterpart that was still on the air. Series creator and the film's writer/director Chris Carter conceived the feature as a bridge between the show's fifth and six seasons, following the investigation of agents Mulder (David Duchovny) and Scully (Gillian Anderson) into the government/alien conspiracy on a bigger scale. Ads emphasized both the intrigue and the horror of the scenario, but only some critics wanted to believe...

"All of this is, of course, nonsense, and wonderfully engrossing, too. The movie is a kick to watch but just as much fun to let percolate in the mind afterward."

–Bob Graham, *San Francisco Chronicle*

"The story is challenging without depending on arbitrary plot twists, the staple of so much screenwriting these days. Mulder and Scully are in jeopardy here, and we buy it."

–Gene Siskel, *Chicago Tribune*

"People whose brains are dominated by the Mulder side, I suspect, will most enjoy this movie, an often gripping, slime-dripping amusement-park ride through a paranoid world of eerie, unexplained phenomena, and creepy coincidence. ... Scully-brained folks, on the other hand, may have a wee bit of trouble with the flaky science, inadequate explanations, and preposterous interconnectivity of all of life's mysteries."

–MICHAEL O'SULLIVAN, *WASHINGTON POST*

"If devotees of the television series come to the film with enough baggage for a six-week safari, perhaps they can deepen the experience of watching a middling, unfocused action-adventure with brand-name appeal."

–Janet Maslin, *The New York Times*

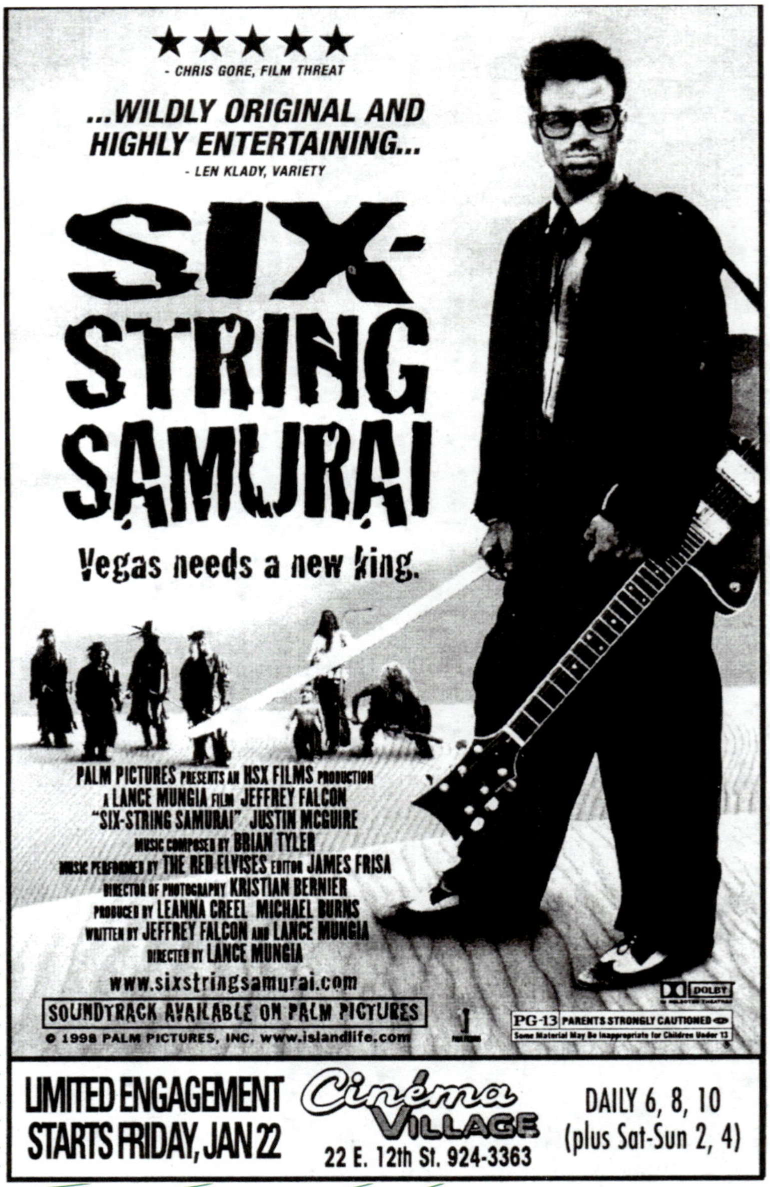

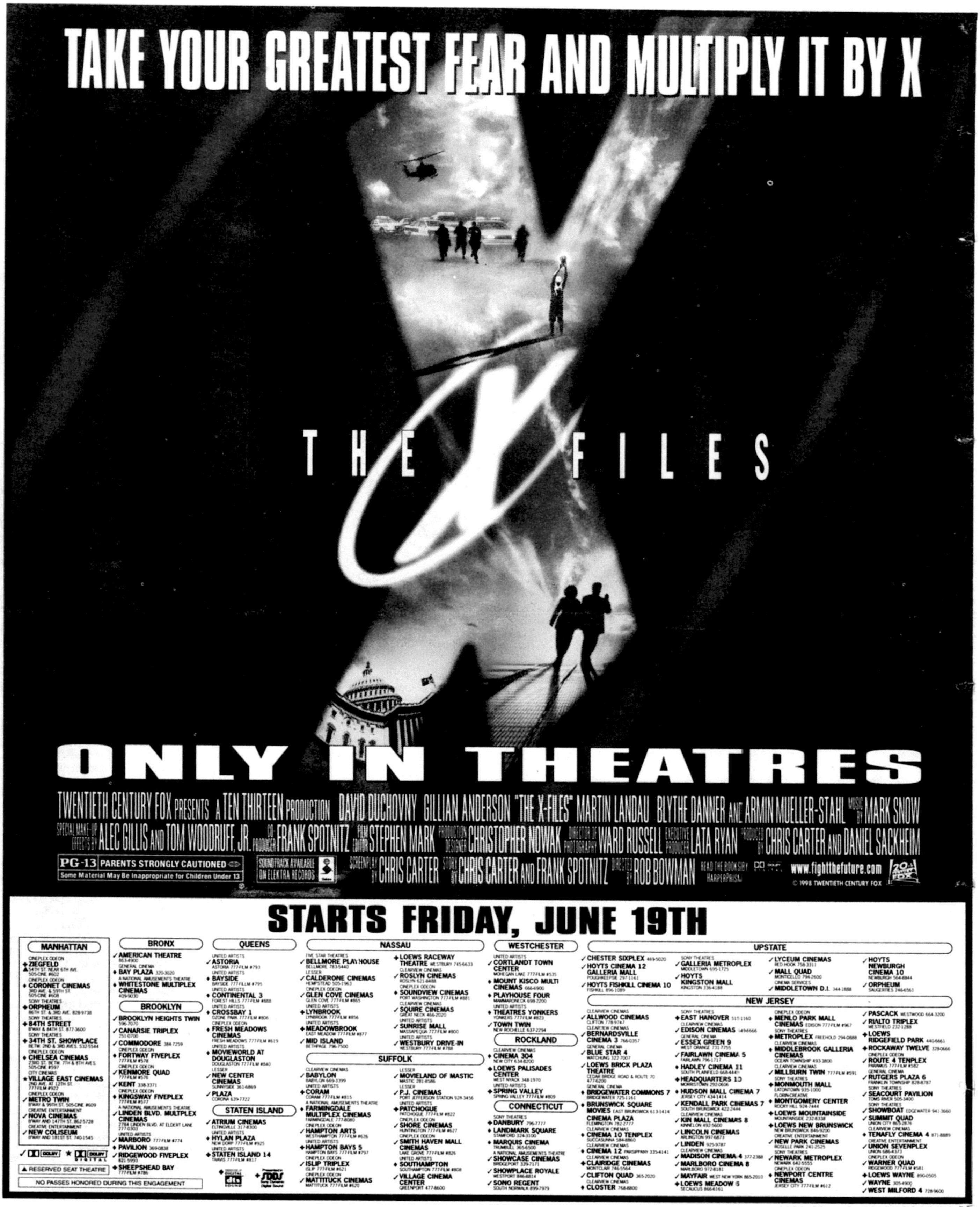
TAKE YOUR GREATEST FEAR AND MULTIPLY IT BY X
THE X FILES
ONLY IN THEATRES
TWENTIETH CENTURY FOX PRESENTS A TEN THIRTEEN PRODUCTION DAVID DUCHOVNY GILLIAN ANDERSON "THE X-FILES" MARTIN LANDAU BLYTHE DANNER AND ARMIN MUELLER-STAHL MUSIC BY MARK SNOW
SPECIAL MAKE-UP EFFECTS BY ALEC GILLIS AND TOM WOODRUFF, JR. CO-PRODUCER FRANK SPOTNITZ FILM EDITOR STEPHEN MARK PRODUCTION DESIGNER CHRISTOPHER NOWAK DIRECTOR OF PHOTOGRAPHY WARD RUSSELL EXECUTIVE PRODUCER LATA RYAN PRODUCED BY CHRIS CARTER AND DANIEL SACKHEIM
PG-13 PARENTS STRONGLY CAUTIONED
Some Material May Be Inappropriate for Children Under 13
SOUNDTRACK AVAILABLE ON ELEKTRA RECORDS
SCREENPLAY BY CHRIS CARTER STORY BY CHRIS CARTER AND FRANK SPOTNITZ DIRECTED BY ROB BOWMAN
READ THE BOOK BY HARPERPRISM
www.fightthefuture.com
© 1998 TWENTIETH CENTURY FOX
STARTS FRIDAY, JUNE 19TH
MANHATTAN
BRONX
QUEENS
NASSAU
WESTCHESTER
UPSTATE
BROOKLYN
SUFFOLK
ROCKLAND
NEW JERSEY
STATEN ISLAND
CONNECTICUT
RESERVED SEAT THEATRE
NO PASSES HONORED DURING THIS ENGAGEMENT

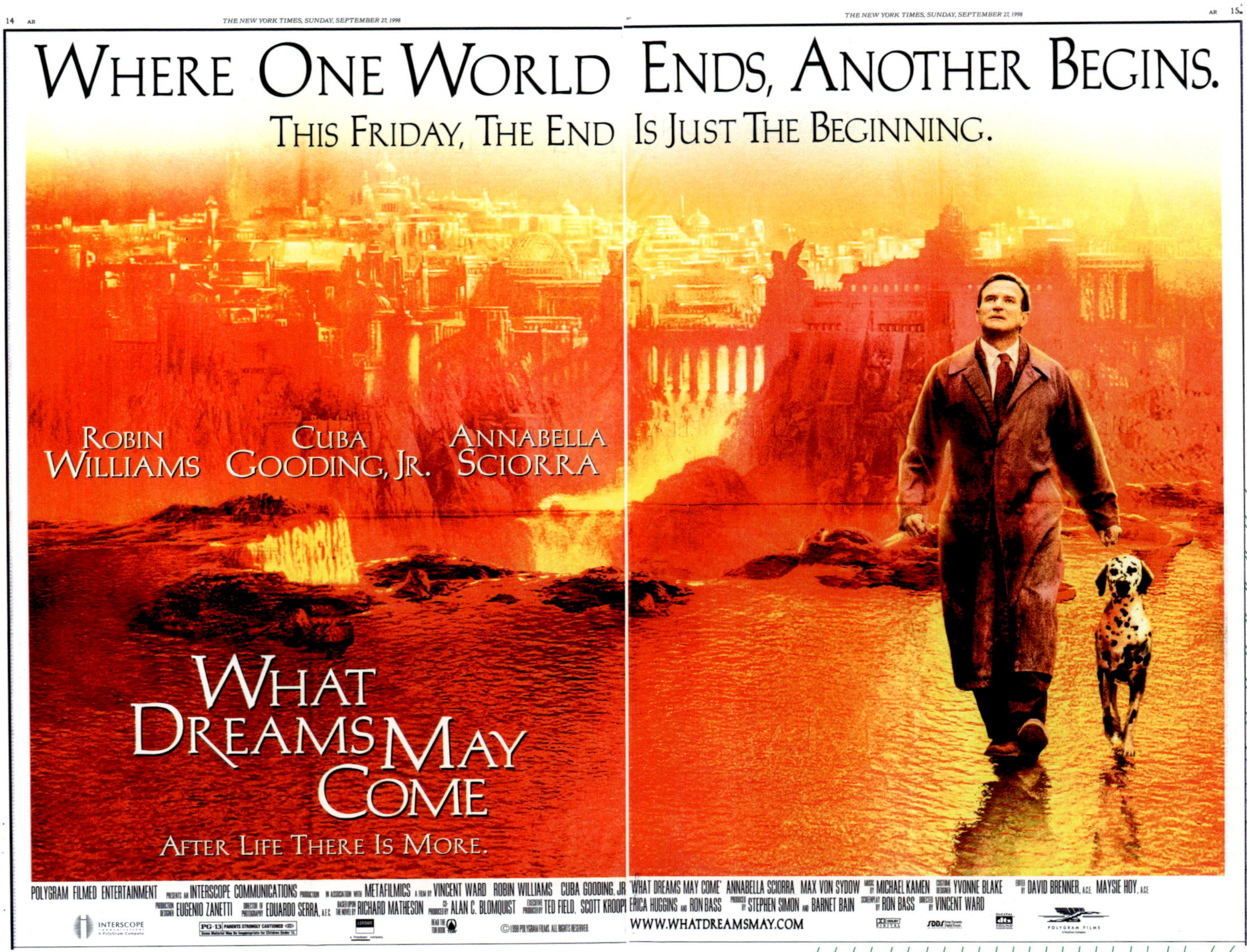
THE NEW YORK TIMES, SUNDAY, SEPTEMBER 27, 1998
WHERE ONE WORLD ENDS, ANOTHER BEGINS.
THIS FRIDAY, THE END IS JUST THE BEGINNING.
ROBIN WILLIAMS
CUBA GOODING, JR.
ANNABELLA SCIORRA
WHAT DREAMS MAY COME
AFTER LIFE THERE IS MORE.
WWW.WHATDREAMSMAY.COM

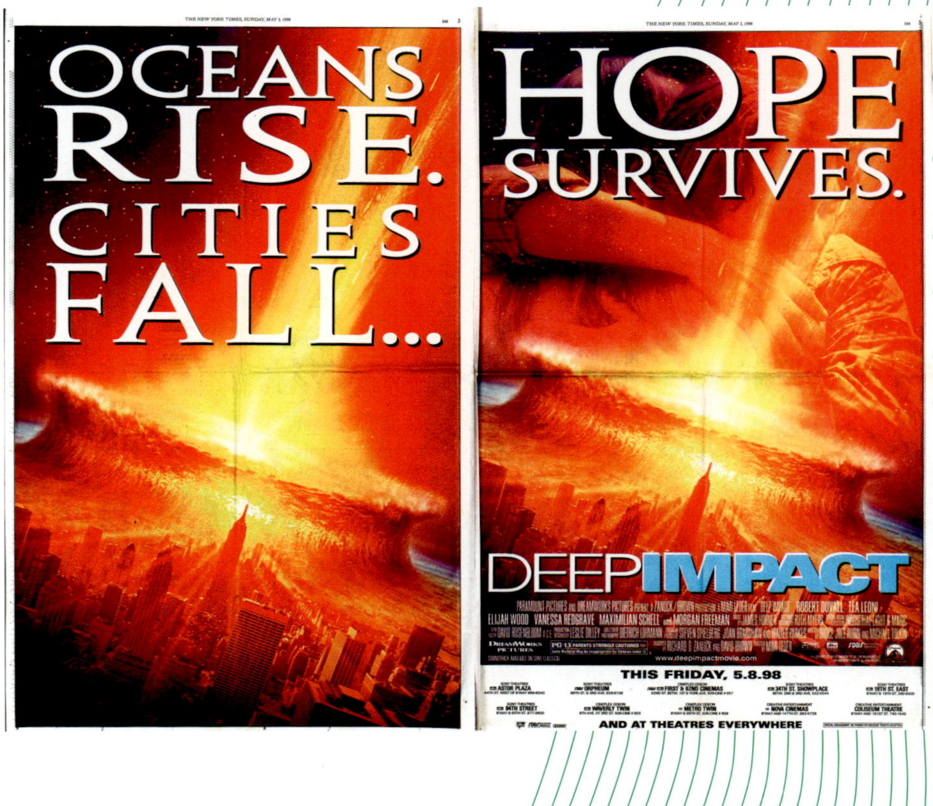
OCEANS RISE. CITIES FALL...
HOPE SURVIVES.
DEEP IMPACT
www.deepimpactmovie.com
THIS FRIDAY, 5.8.98
AND AT THEATRES EVERYWHERE

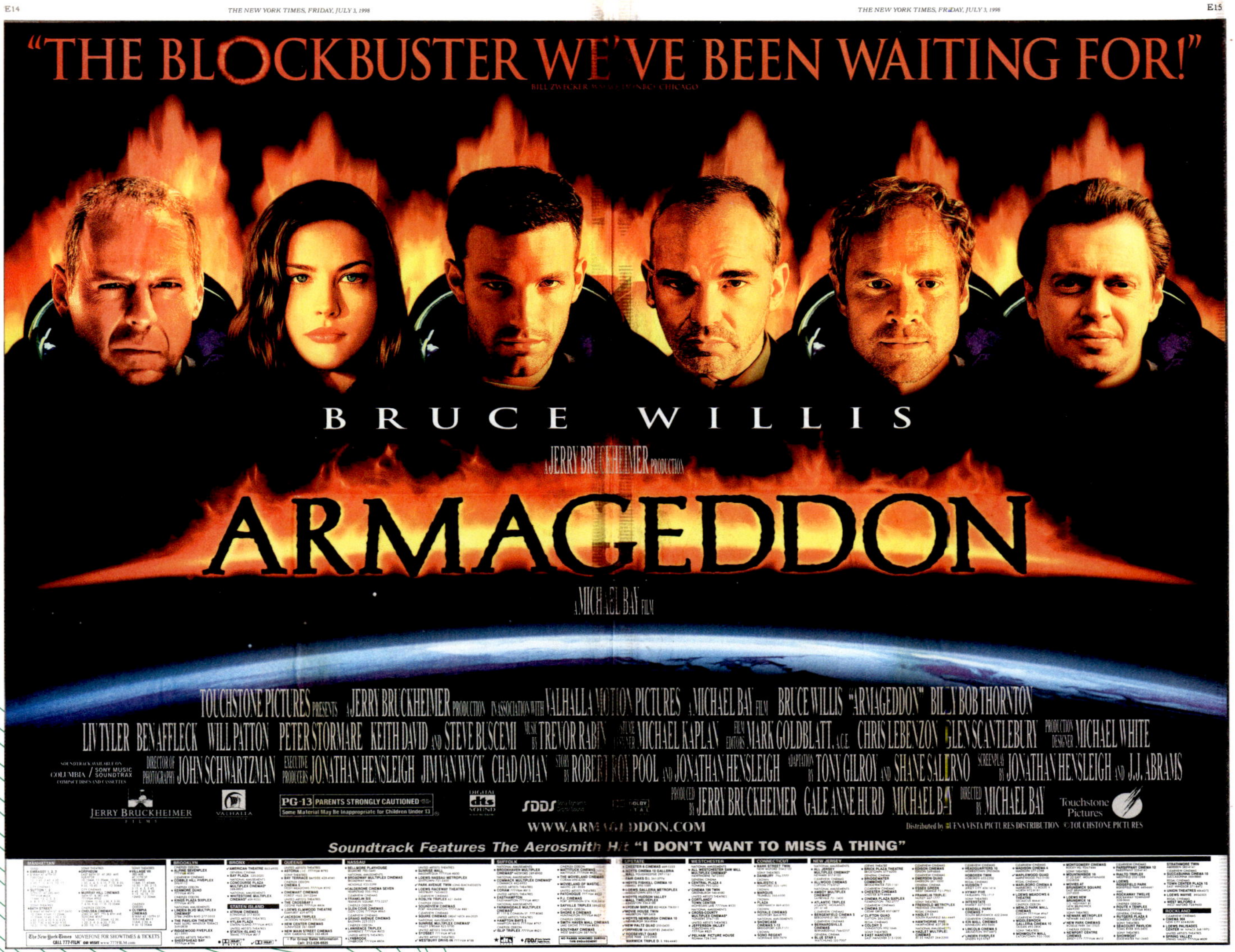
E14
THE NEW YORK TIMES, FRIDAY, JULY 3, 1998
THE NEW YORK TIMES, FRIDAY, JULY 3, 1998
E15
"THE BLOCKBUSTER WE'VE BEEN WAITING FOR!"
BRUCE WILLIS
A JERRY BRUCKHEIMER PRODUCTION
ARMAGEDDON
A MICHAEL BAY FILM
TOUCHSTONE PICTURES PRESENTS A JERRY BRUCKHEIMER PRODUCTION IN ASSOCIATION WITH VALHALLA MOTION PICTURES A MICHAEL BAY FILM BRUCE WILLIS "ARMAGEDDON" BILLY BOB THORNTON
LIV TYLER BEN AFFLECK WILL PATTON PETER STORMARE KEITH DAVID AND STEVE BUSCEMI
PG-13 PARENTS STRONGLY CAUTIONED
Some Material May Be Inappropriate for Children Under 13
WWW.ARMAGEDDON.COM
Soundtrack Features The Aerosmith Hit "I DON'T WANT TO MISS A THING"

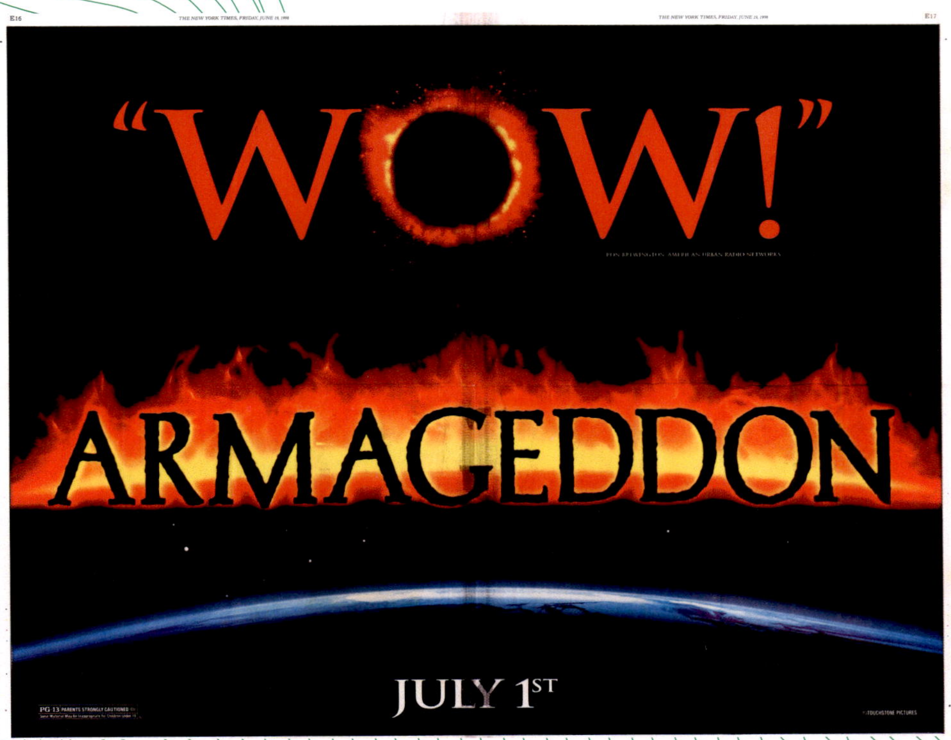
"WOW!"
ARMAGEDDON
JULY 1ST

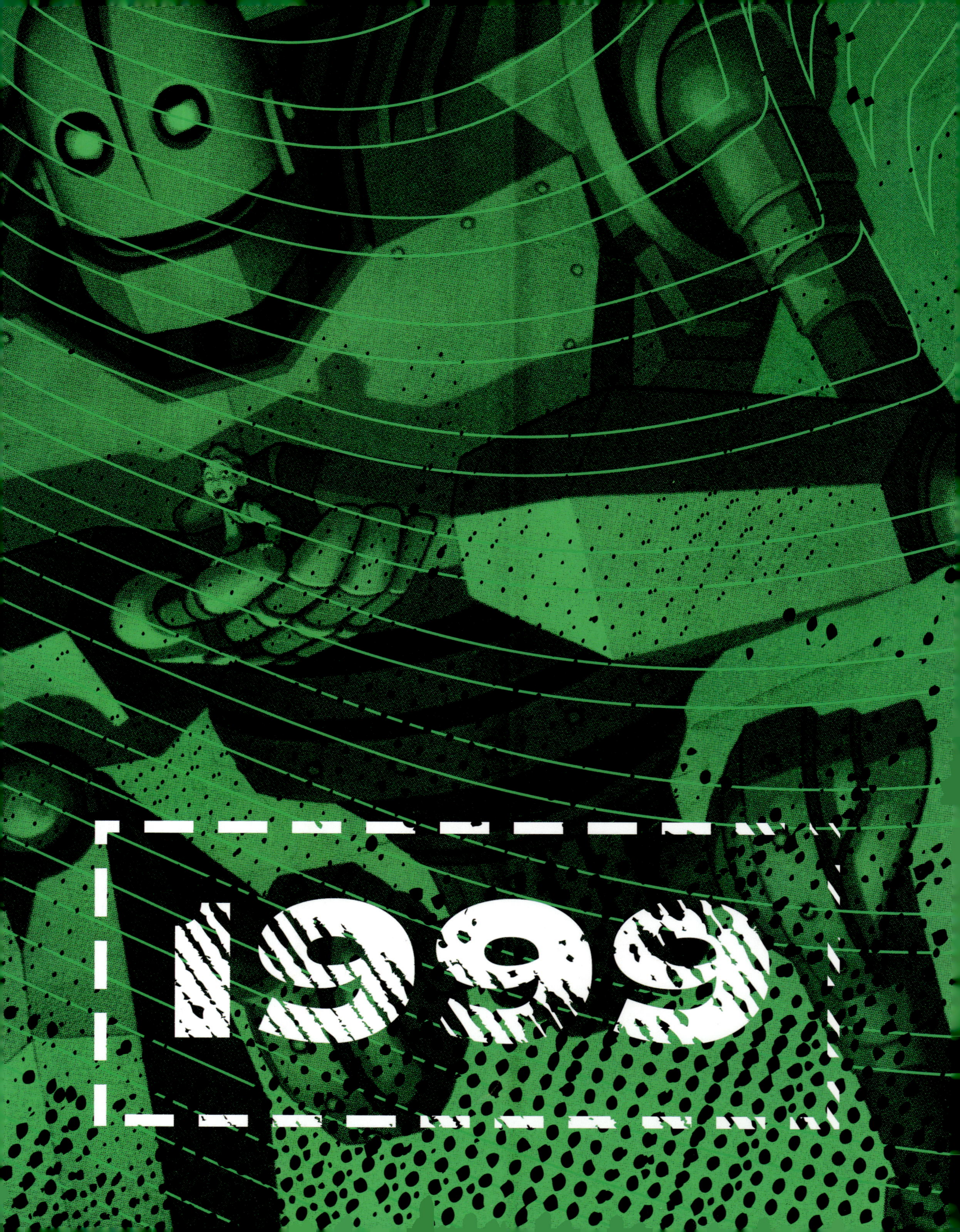
1999

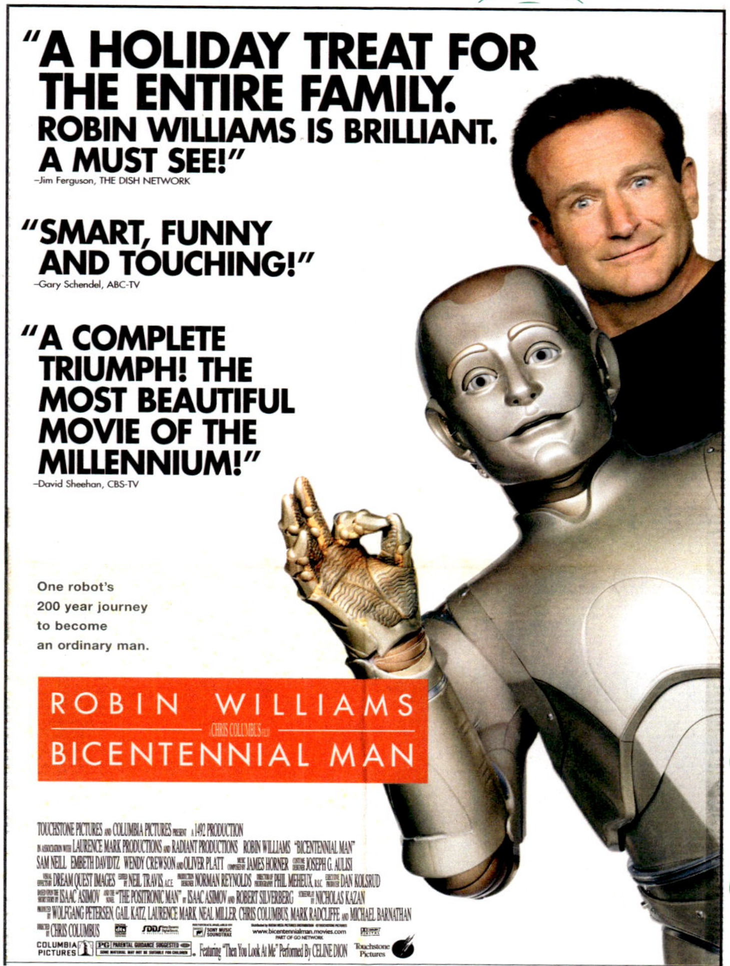
"A HOLIDAY TREAT FOR THE ENTIRE FAMILY.
ROBIN WILLIAMS IS BRILLIANT. A MUST SEE!"
–Jim Ferguson, THE DISH NETWORK
"SMART, FUNNY AND TOUCHING!"
–Gary Schendel, ABC-TV
"A COMPLETE TRIUMPH! THE MOST BEAUTIFUL MOVIE OF THE MILLENNIUM!"
–David Sheehan, CBS-TV
One robot's 200 year journey to become an ordinary man.
ROBIN WILLIAMS
CHRIS COLUMBUS FILM
BICENTENNIAL MAN
Featuring "Then You Look At Me" Performed By CELINE DION

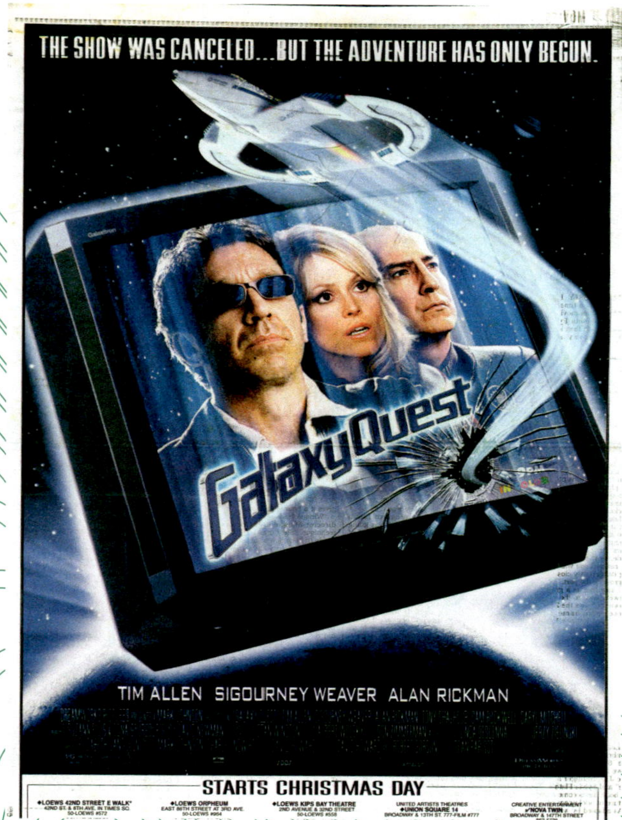
THE SHOW WAS CANCELED...BUT THE ADVENTURE HAS ONLY BEGUN.
Galaxy Quest
TIM ALLEN SIGOURNEY WEAVER ALAN RICKMAN
STARTS CHRISTMAS DAY

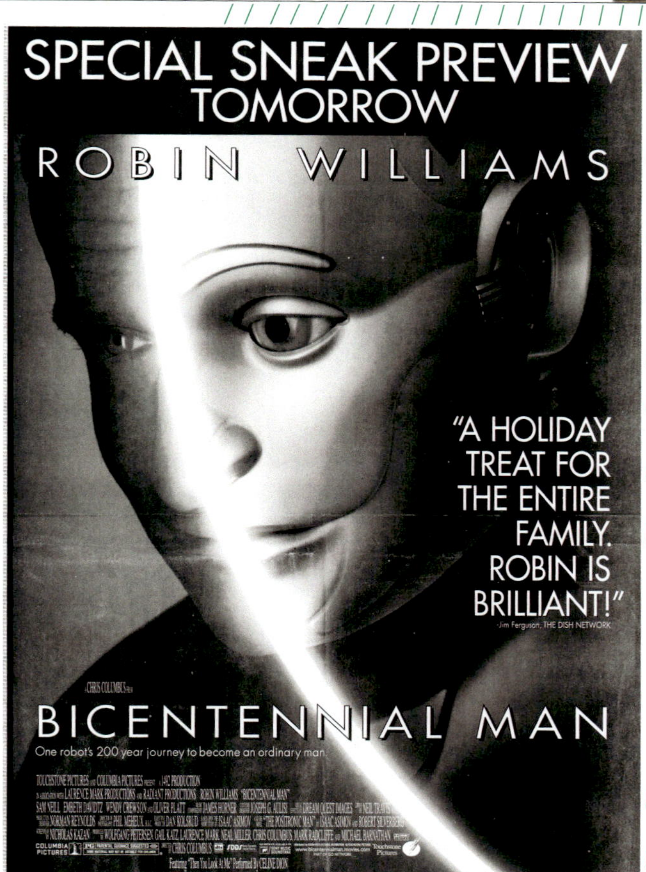
SPECIAL SNEAK PREVIEW TOMORROW
ROBIN WILLIAMS
"A HOLIDAY TREAT FOR THE ENTIRE FAMILY. ROBIN IS BRILLIANT!"
–Jim Ferguson, THE DISH NETWORK
BICENTENNIAL MAN
One robot's 200 year journey to become an ordinary man.

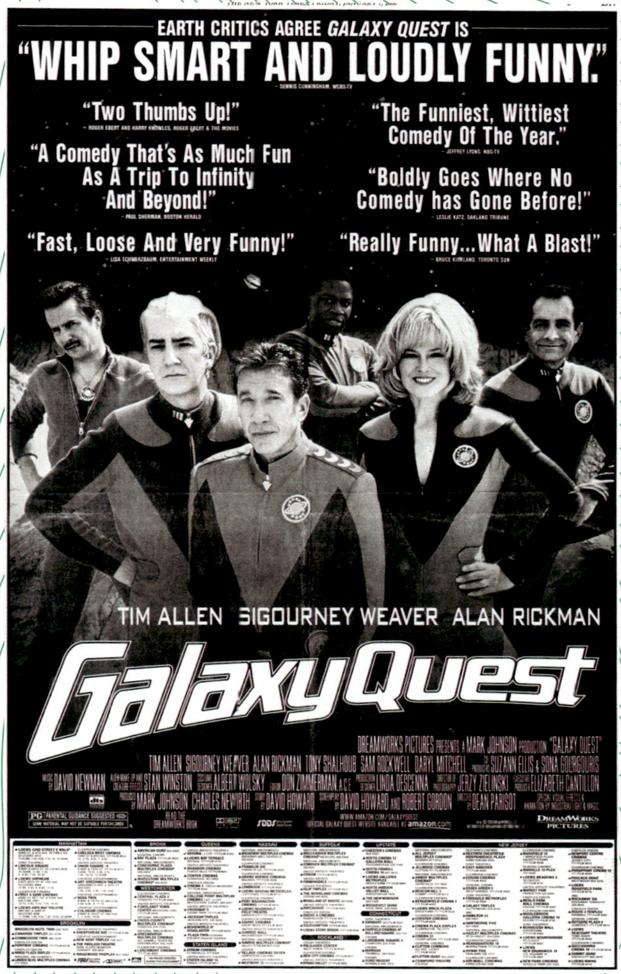
EARTH CRITICS AGREE GALAXY QUEST IS
"WHIP SMART AND LOUDLY FUNNY."
"Two Thumbs Up!"
"The Funniest, Wittiest Comedy Of The Year."
"A Comedy That's As Much Fun As A Trip To Infinity And Beyond!"
"Boldly Goes Where No Comedy has Gone Before!"
"Fast, Loose And Very Funny!"
"Really Funny...What A Blast!"
TIM ALLEN SIGOURNEY WEAVER ALAN RICKMAN
Galaxy Quest

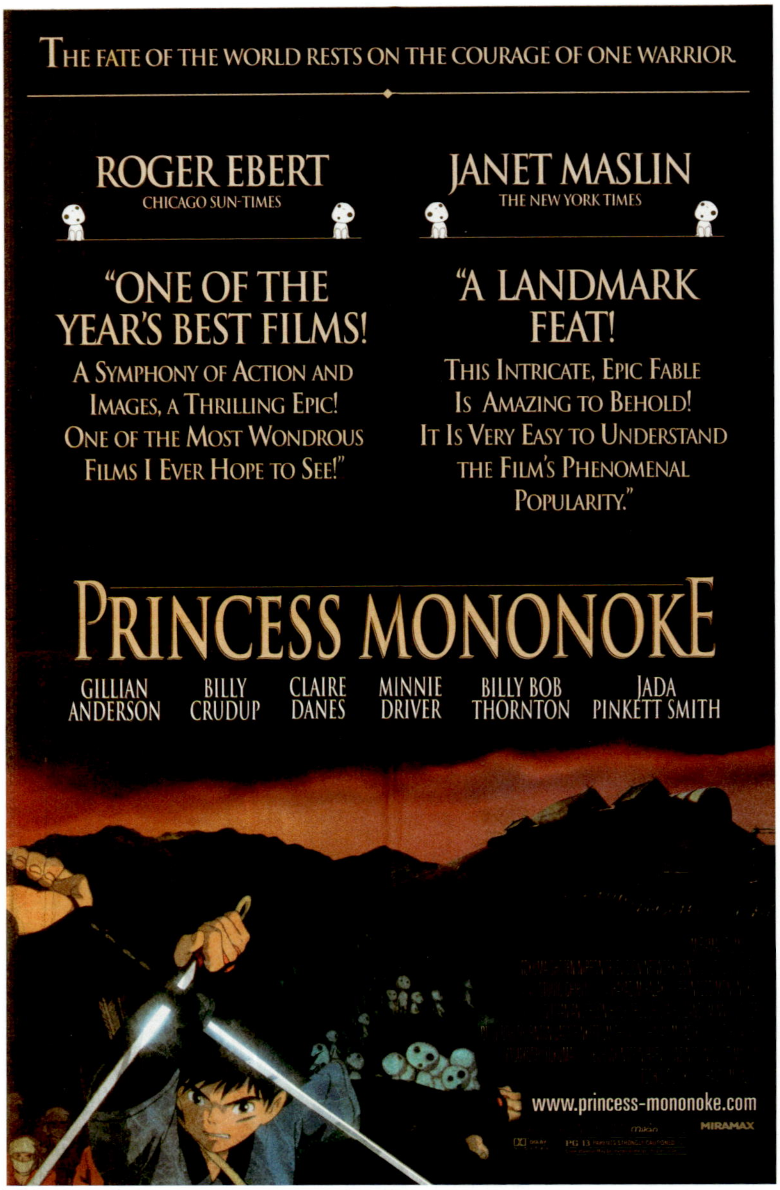

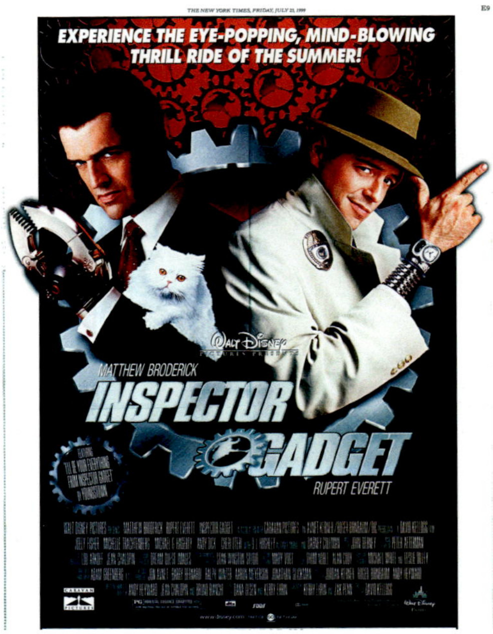

THE IRON GIANT

Walt Disney Pictures had dominated feature-film animation in the decade since the breakout success of *The Little Mermaid*, and competitor Warner Bros. Feature Animation did not impress much with its first two productions, *Space Jam* and *Quest for Camelot*. Then came *The Iron Giant*, Brad Bird's gentle and heartfelt parable about a young boy in 1957 Cold War America who befriends a towering alien robot. Though it was a box-office underperformer that would have to wait for video to find its audience, *Iron Giant*, with its appealing characters and anti-war theme, was embraced by most critics – though at least one strongly disagreed with its message.

"Animated films excel in conjuring up colorful fantasy worlds, but few evoke an actual time and place as vividly – and playfully – as *The Iron Giant* does."

–Marc Caro, *Chicago Tribune*

"Straight-arrow and subversive, made with simplicity as well as sophistication, *The Iron Giant* remembers the wonder of being a child and understands how to convey that in a media-savvy age."

–KENNETH TURAN, *LOS ANGELES TIMES*

"Adults, more than children, are likely to find stimulation, provocation, and controversy in *The Iron Giant*. ... Directed by Brad Bird, [it] is a smooth, skilled example of animated filmmaking."

–Lawrence van Gelder, *The New York Times*

"*The Iron Giant* is a fabulous animated feature, funny, touching, vivid and, best of all, humane. I hated it. ... [A]t a certain point [the film], without missing a beat in charm or artistry, skews off into TULWC. And that would be The Usual Left-Wing Crap."

–Stephen Hunter, *Washington Post*

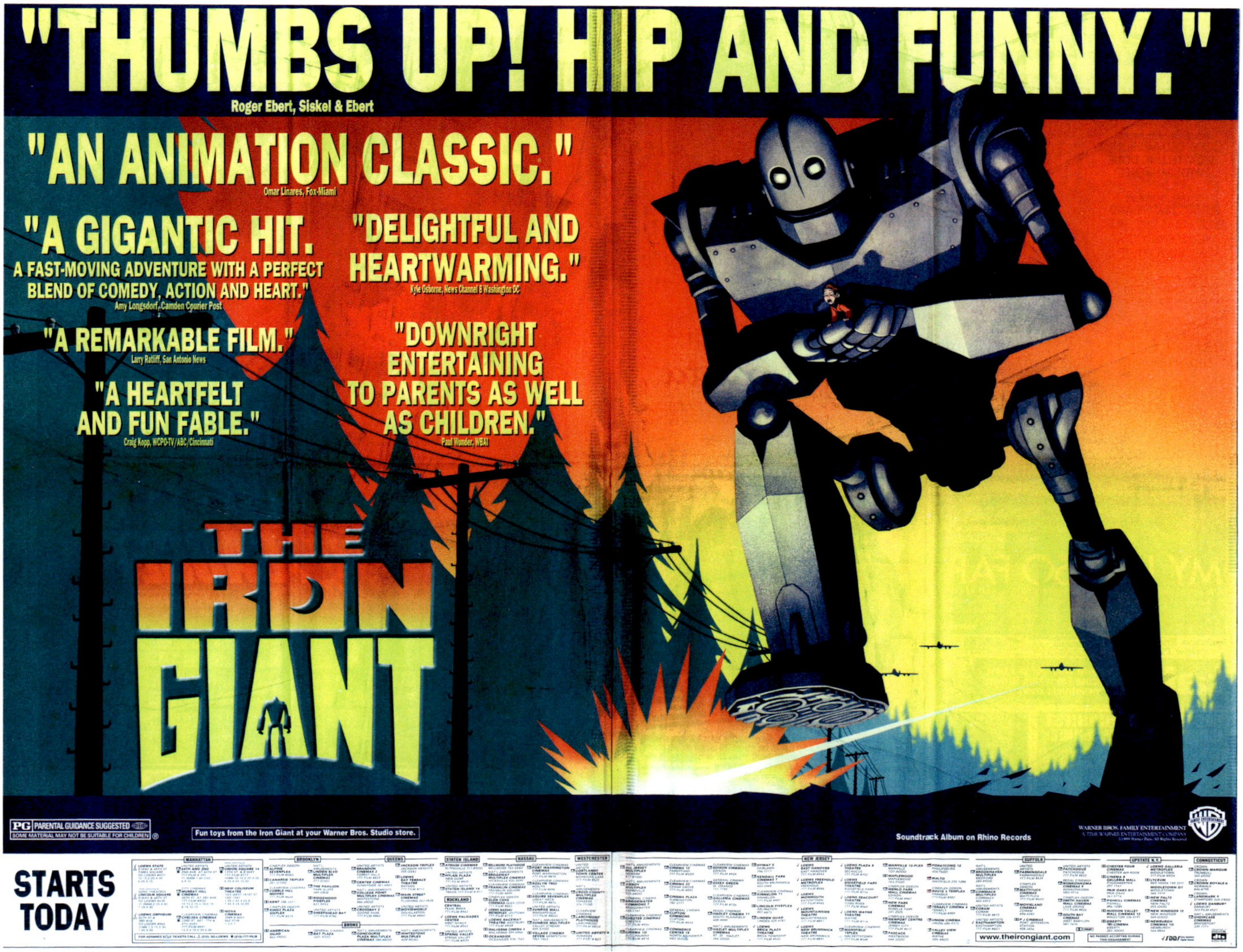
"THUMBS UP! HIP AND FUNNY."
Roger Ebert, Siskel & Ebert
"AN ANIMATION CLASSIC."
Omar Linares, Fox-Miami
"A GIGANTIC HIT. A FAST-MOVING ADVENTURE WITH A PERFECT BLEND OF COMEDY, ACTION AND HEART."
Amy Longsdorf, Camden Courier Post
"DELIGHTFUL AND HEARTWARMING."
Kyle Osborne, News Channel 8 Washington DC
"A REMARKABLE FILM."
Larry Ratliff, San Antonio News
"DOWNRIGHT ENTERTAINING TO PARENTS AS WELL AS CHILDREN."
Paul Wunder, WBAI
"A HEARTFELT AND FUN FABLE."
Craig Kopp, WCPO-TV/ABC/Cincinnati
THE IRON GIANT
PG PARENTAL GUIDANCE SUGGESTED
SOME MATERIAL MAY NOT BE SUITABLE FOR CHILDREN
Fun toys from the Iron Giant at your Warner Bros. Studio store.
Soundtrack Album on Rhino Records
WARNER BROS. FAMILY ENTERTAINMENT
STARTS TODAY
www.theirongiant.com

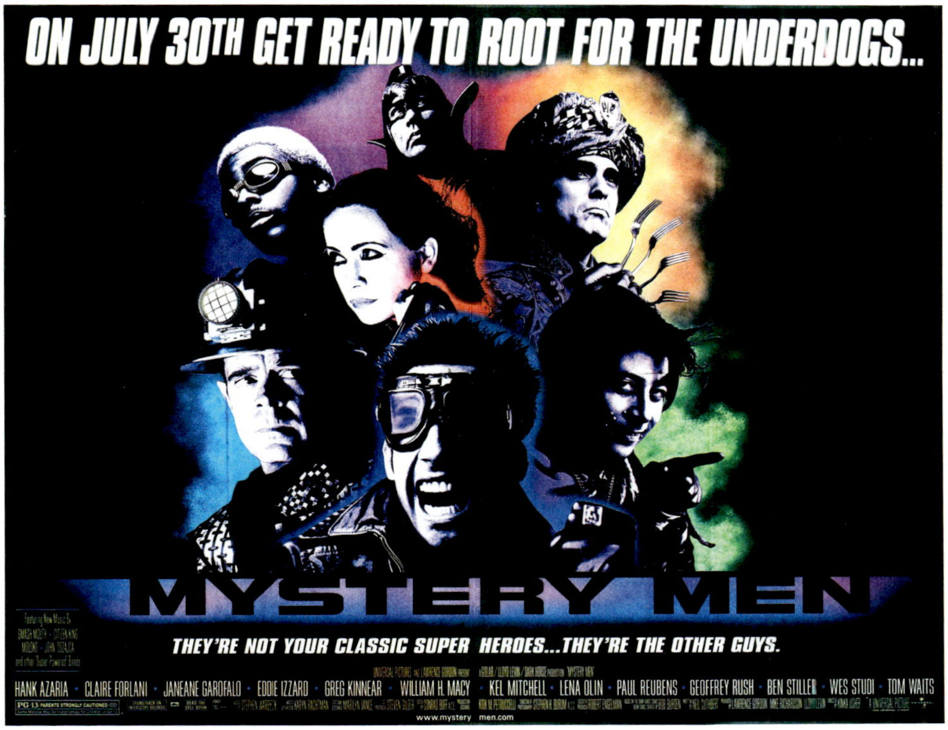
ON JULY 30TH GET READY TO ROOT FOR THE UNDERDOGS...
MYSTERY MEN
THEY'RE NOT YOUR CLASSIC SUPER HEROES...THEY'RE THE OTHER GUYS.
HANK AZARIA · CLAIRE FORLANI · JANEANE GAROFALO · EDDIE IZZARD · GREG KINNEAR · WILLIAM H. MACY · KEL MITCHELL · LENA OLIN · PAUL REUBENS · GEOFFREY RUSH · BEN STILLER · WES STUDI · TOM WAITS
PG-13 PARENTS STRONGLY CAUTIONED
www.mysterymen.com

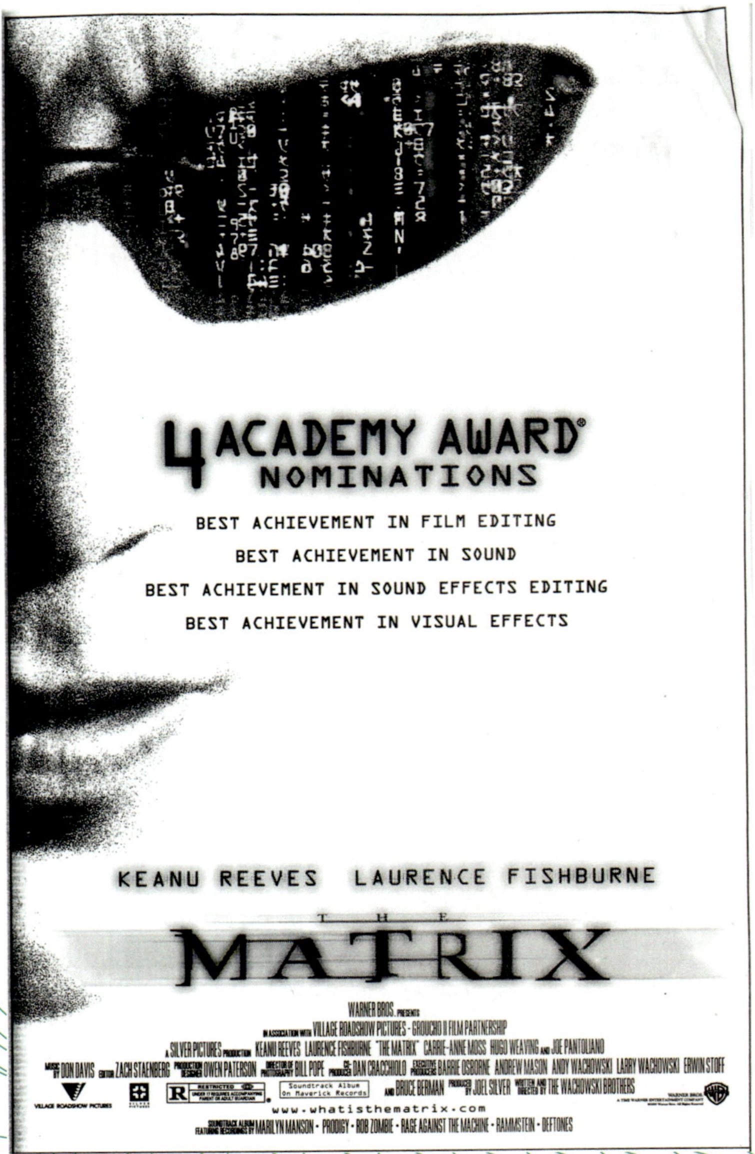

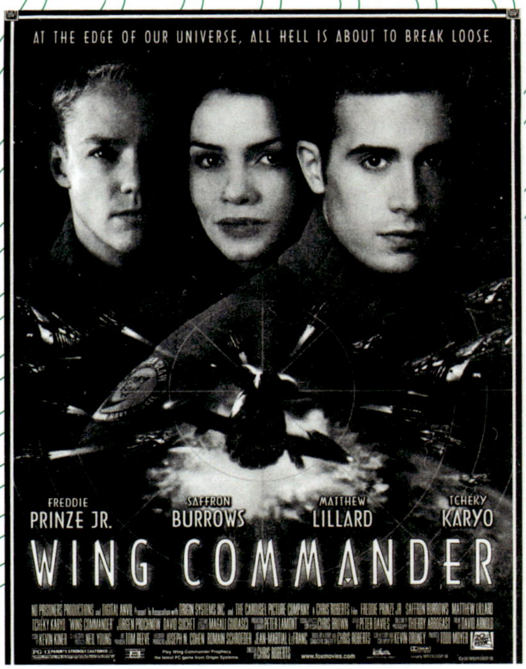

THE MATRIX

Even producer Joel Silver wasn't sure how this unusual hybrid of heady sci-fi themes and high-powered action would fare with mass audiences. He needn't have been concerned: *The Matrix*, with its intriguing plotline and eye-boggling (and soon to be much-imitated) "bullet time" effects, was an immediate hit, scoring with (most of) the critics, and becoming one of the highest-grossing R-rated movies of all time. It was also a rare science fiction film to be reissued early the following year due to Academy Awards attention.

"It's smashing entertainment, building to a rousing final hour and drenched in top-notch special effects, finely etched character acting and action sequences that will play in your head for days. Words simply don't do it justice."

–Shawn Levy, *The Oregonian*

"A wildly cinematic futuristic thriller that is determined to overpower the imagination, *The Matrix* combines traditional science-fiction premises with spanking new visual technology in a way that almost defies description."

–KENNETH TURAN, *LOS ANGELES TIMES*

"*The Matrix* is so wild and crazed it requires adult supervision. Thank God, it never got it. It rocks."

–Stephen Hunter, *Washington Post*

"*The Matrix* is a visually dazzling cyber adventure, full of kinetic excitement, but it retreats to formula just when it's getting interesting. It's kind of a letdown when a movie begins by redefining the nature of reality, and ends with a shoot-out."

–Roger Ebert, *Chicago Sun-Times*

"It's astonishing that so much money, talent, technical expertise, and visual imagination can be put in the service of something so stupid. Folly on such a monumental scale is almost exhilarating."

–Bob Graham, *San Francisco Chronicle*

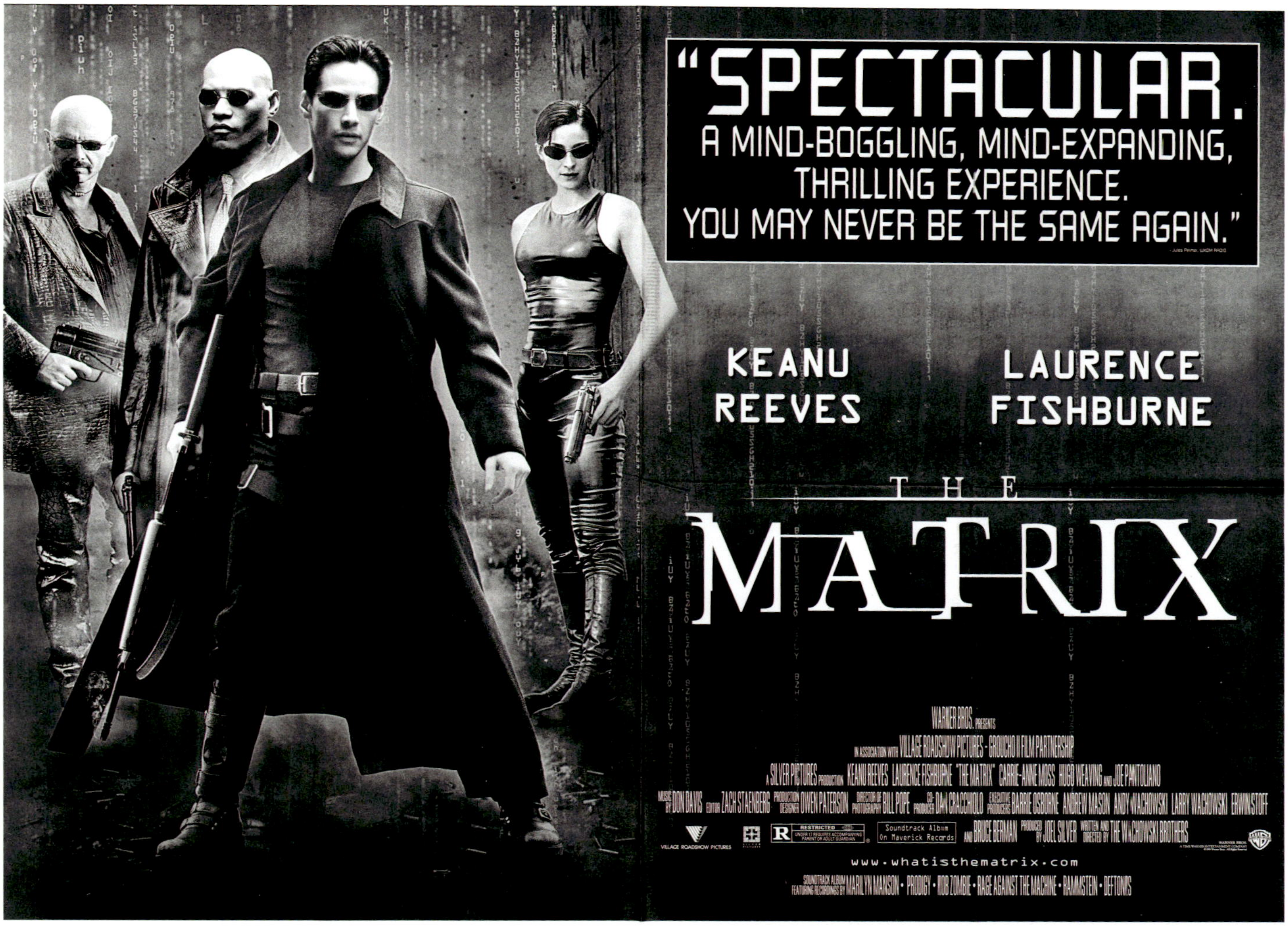
"SPECTACULAR.
A MIND-BOGGLING, MIND-EXPANDING,
THRILLING EXPERIENCE.
YOU MAY NEVER BE THE SAME AGAIN."
KEANU REEVES
LAURENCE FISHBURNE
THE MATRIX
www.whatisthematrix.com

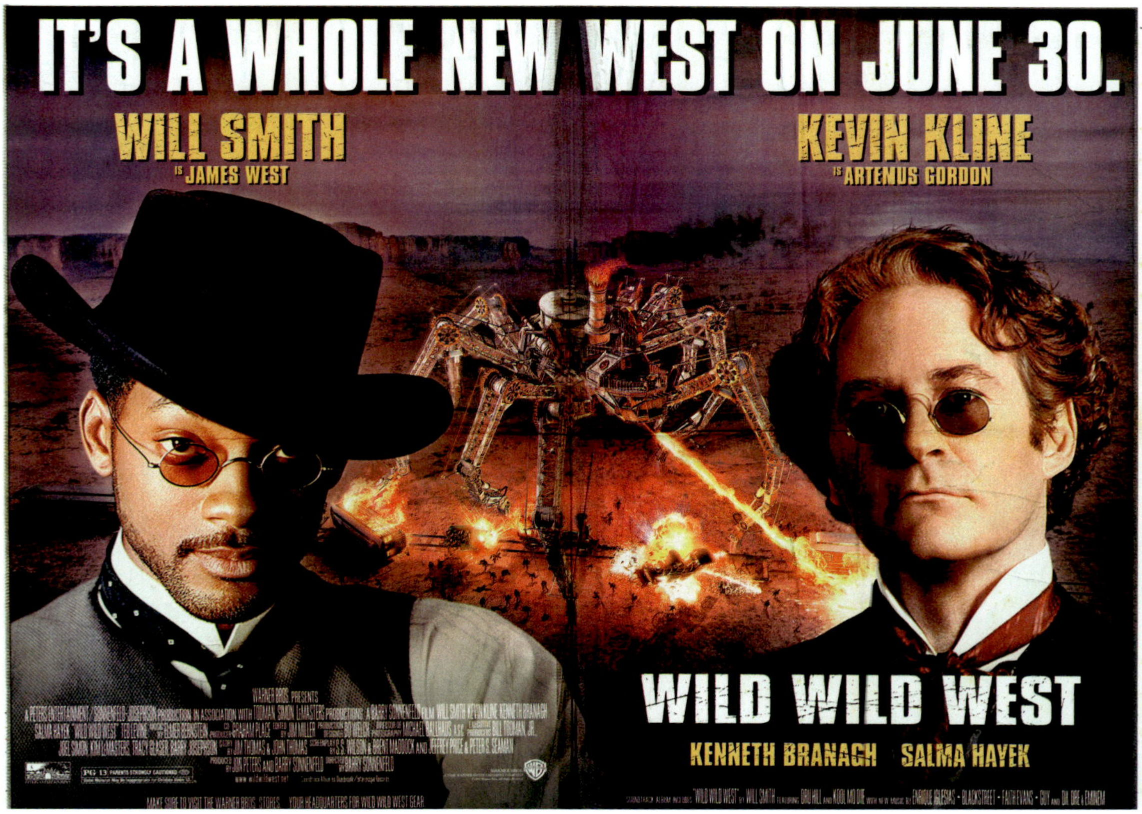
IT'S A WHOLE NEW WEST ON JUNE 30.
WILL SMITH
IS JAMES WEST
KEVIN KLINE
IS ARTEMUS GORDON
WILD WILD WEST
KENNETH BRANAGH
SALMA HAYEK

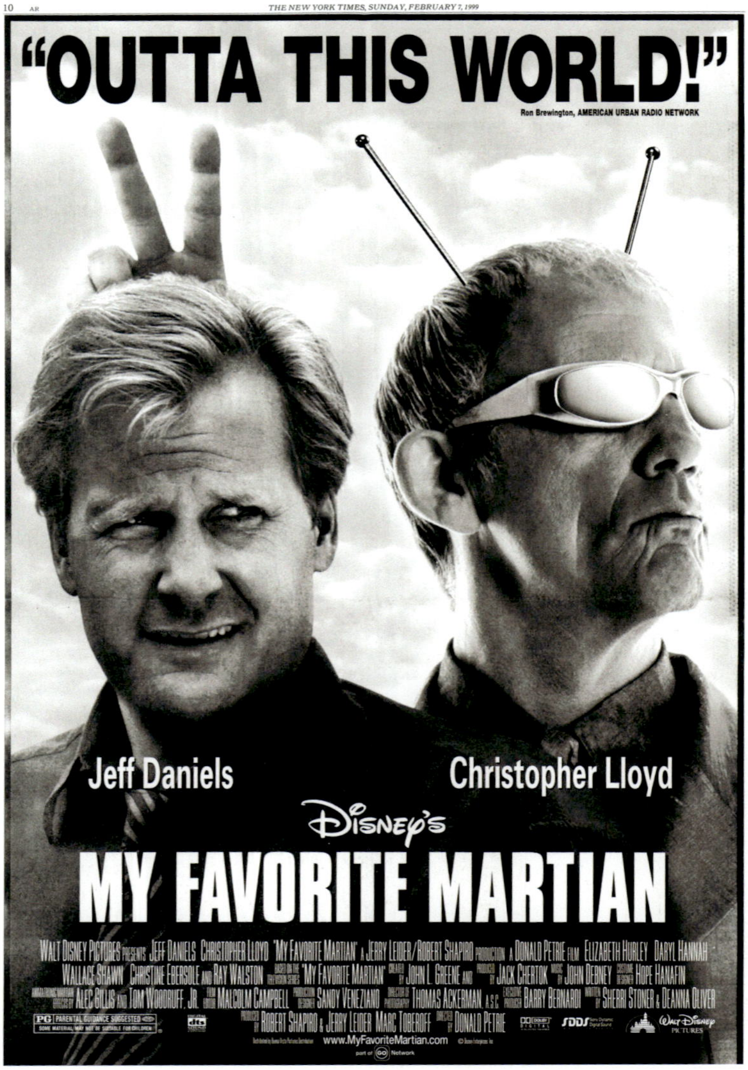

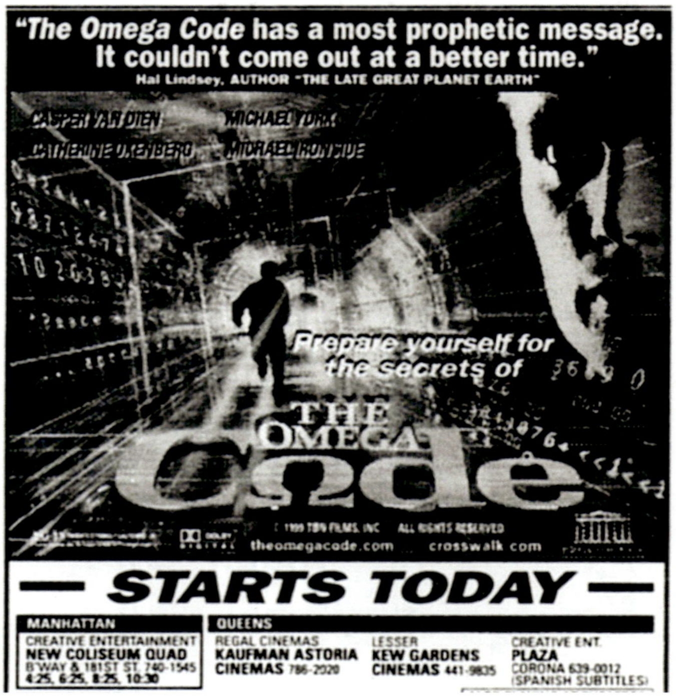

MIGHTY PEKING MAN

Nineteen years after its first Stateside release as *Goliathon*, Ho Meng-Hua's monster mash returned under the auspices of Quentin Tarantino and his Rolling Thunder Pictures, which also gave new theatrical leases on life to Lucio Fulci's *The Beyond*, Jack Hill's *Switchblade Sisters* and others. This won *Peking Man* more critical attention than it had previously received, and those notices demonstrated that one decade's trash could be another decade's guilty pleasure.

"*Mighty Peking Man* is very funny, although a shade off the high mark of *Infra-Man*, which was made a year earlier, and is my favorite Hong Kong monster film. ... I am awarding *Mighty Peking Man* three stars, for general goofiness, and a certain level of insane genius."

–Roger Ebert, *Chicago Sun-Times*

"Miniature work and process shots are painfully obvious, the dubbed English dialogue predictably dreadful, but it adds up to perfect midnight movie fun."

–Kevin Thomas, *Los Angeles Times*

"Director Ho has the Shaw Brothers' eye for ratty visuals and stunningly bad costuming (the film is particularly proud of the creature's animatronic facial expressions), but *Mighty Peking Man* triumphs by virtue of its sheer oddball charm."

–Marc Savlov, *The Austin Chronicle*

"***Mighty Peking Man* is one of those so-bad-it's-good movies that are best experienced after midnight and multiple cocktails. It's like eating Cheez Whiz out of the jar with your bare hands. ... Unspeakably awful, but undeniably fun."**

–ROD DREHER, *NEW YORK POST*

"What is it that we missed in '77 that we are going to grasp now? And why – after having spoiled us with the work of new wave Hong Kong director Wong Kar-Wai (*Chungking Express*) – does Rolling Thunder subject us to this utterly forgettable flick?"

–Serena Donadoni, *Detroit Metro Times*

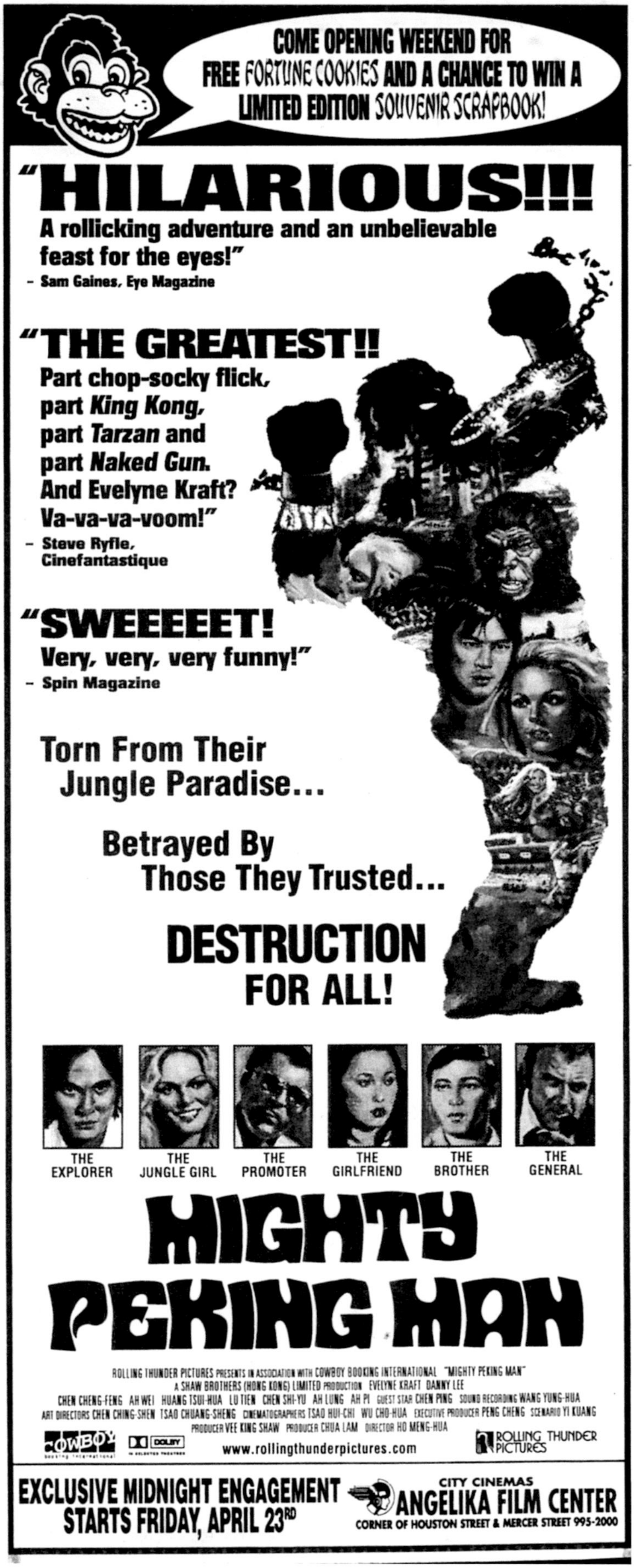
COME OPENING WEEKEND FOR FREE FORTUNE COOKIES AND A CHANCE TO WIN A LIMITED EDITION SOUVENIR SCRAPBOOK!
"HILARIOUS!!!
A rollicking adventure and an unbelievable feast for the eyes!"
- Sam Gaines, Eye Magazine
"THE GREATEST!!
Part chop-socky flick, part King Kong, part Tarzan and part Naked Gun. And Evelyne Kraft? Va-va-va-voom!"
- Steve Ryfle, Cinefantastique
"SWEEEEET!
Very, very, very funny!"
- Spin Magazine
Torn From Their Jungle Paradise...
Betrayed By Those They Trusted...
DESTRUCTION FOR ALL!
THE EXPLORER
THE JUNGLE GIRL
THE PROMOTER
THE GIRLFRIEND
THE BROTHER
THE GENERAL
MIGHTY PEKING MAN
ROLLING THUNDER PICTURES PRESENTS IN ASSOCIATION WITH COWBOY BOOKING INTERNATIONAL "MIGHTY PEKING MAN"
A SHAW BROTHERS (HONG KONG) LIMITED PRODUCTION EVELYNE KRAFT DANNY LEE
CHEN CHENG-FENG AH WEI HUANG TSUI-HUA LU TIEN CHEN SHI-YU AH LUNG AH PI GUEST STAR CHEN PING SOUND RECORDING WANG YUNG-HUA
ART DIRECTORS CHEN CHING-SHEN TSAO CHUANG-SHENG CINEMATOGRAPHERS TSAO HUI-CHI WU CHO-HUA EXECUTIVE PRODUCER PENG CHENG SCENARIO YI KUANG
PRODUCER VEE KING SHAW PRODUCER CHUA LAM DIRECTOR HO MENG-HUA
www.rollingthunderpictures.com
ROLLING THUNDER PICTURES
EXCLUSIVE MIDNIGHT ENGAGEMENT
STARTS FRIDAY, APRIL 23RD
CITY CINEMAS
ANGELIKA FILM CENTER
CORNER OF HOUSTON STREET & MERCER STREET 995-2000

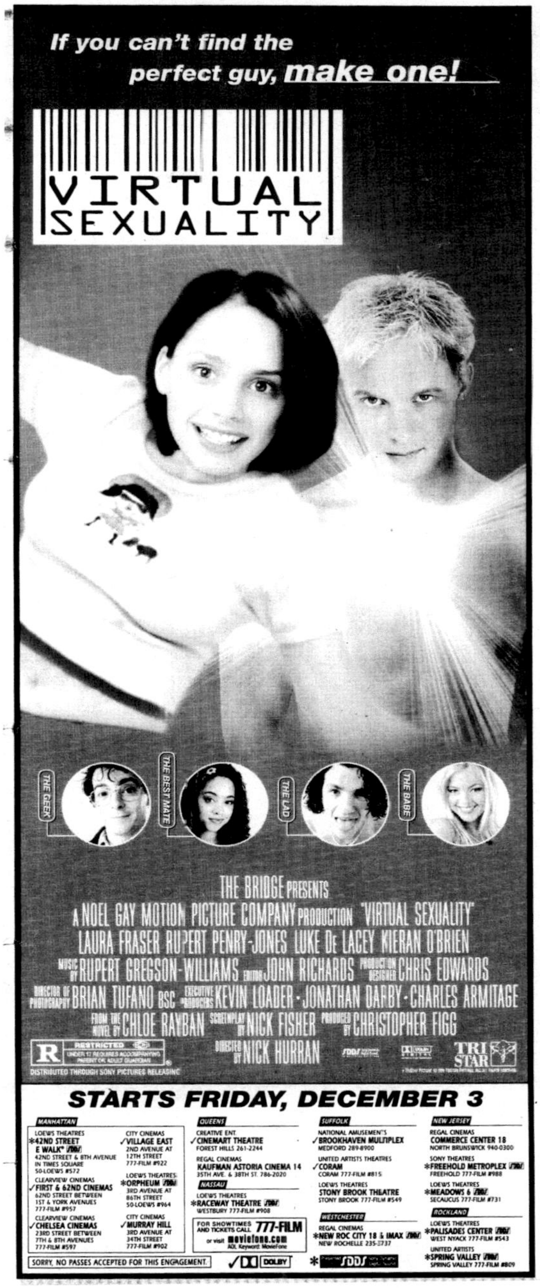
If you can't find the perfect guy, make one!
VIRTUAL SEXUALITY
THE GEEK
THE BEST MATE
THE LAD
THE BABE
THE BRIDGE PRESENTS
A NOEL GAY MOTION PICTURE COMPANY PRODUCTION "VIRTUAL SEXUALITY"
LAURA FRASER RUPERT PENRY-JONES LUKE DE LACEY KIERAN O'BRIEN
MUSIC BY RUPERT GREGSON-WILLIAMS EDITOR JOHN RICHARDS PRODUCTION DESIGNER CHRIS EDWARDS
DIRECTOR OF PHOTOGRAPHY BRIAN TUFANO BSC EXECUTIVE PRODUCERS KEVIN LOADER · JONATHAN DARBY · CHARLES ARMITAGE
FROM THE NOVEL BY CHLOE RAYBAN SCREENPLAY BY NICK FISHER PRODUCED BY CHRISTOPHER FIGG
DIRECTED BY NICK HURRAN
DISTRIBUTED THROUGH SONY PICTURES RELEASING
TRISTAR
STARTS FRIDAY, DECEMBER 3
MANHATTAN
QUEENS
NASSAU
SUFFOLK
WESTCHESTER
NEW JERSEY
ROCKLAND
SORRY, NO PASSES ACCEPTED FOR THIS ENGAGEMENT.

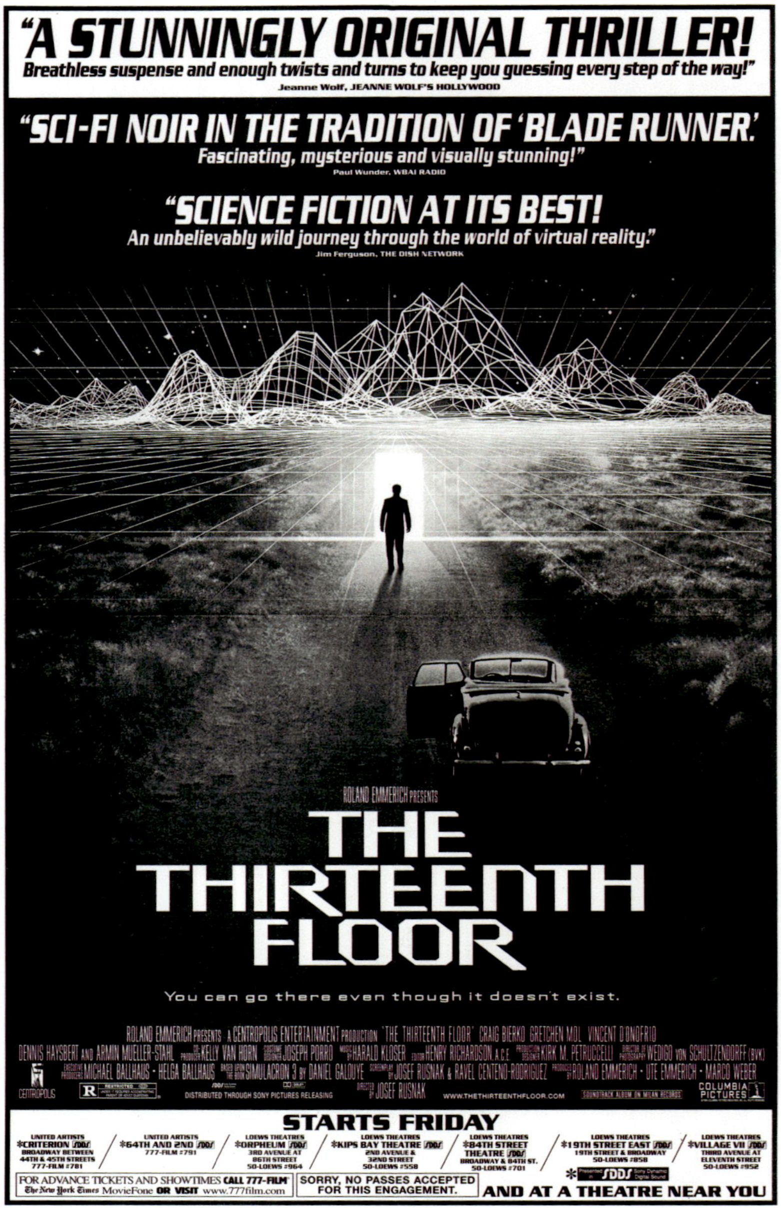

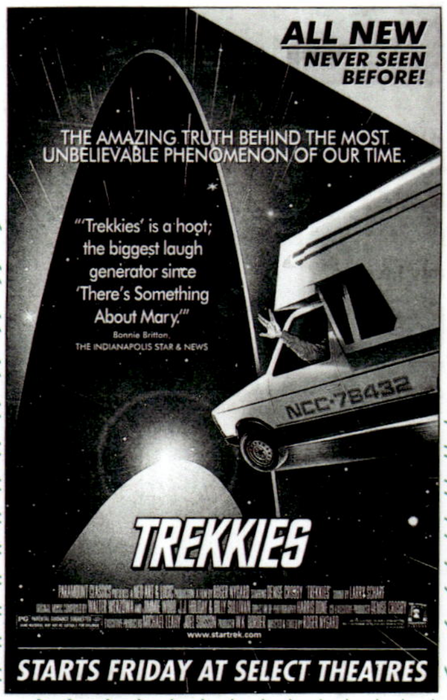

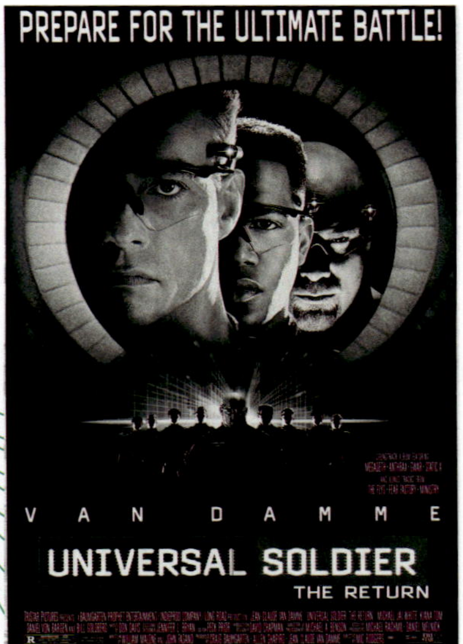

STAR WARS: EPISODE I – THE PHANTOM MENACE

As this book began with the first of the *Star Wars* sequels, so it comes to a close with the initial entry in the prequel trilogy. Anticipation built to a fever pitch in the months before *Episode I*'s release, and though it was the expected monster hit, and some found it a worthy successor to the previous films, many critics and fans felt let down – for reasons that didn't even involve the much-despised Jar Jar Binks.

"[A]n astonishing achievement in imaginative filmmaking. If some of the characters are less than compelling, perhaps that's inevitable: this is the first story in the chronology and has to set up characters who (we already know) will become more interesting with the passage of time."

–Roger Ebert, *Chicago Sun-Times*

"There's no human-scale character on the screen who can engage the audience's emotions, no Han Solo with his rough-hewn charm, not even a Chewbacca with his plaintive, affectionate howl. It's all sound and fury and special effects, signifying nothing."

–Jami Bernard, New York *Daily News*

"There's a disturbance in the Force called hype, and *Star Wars: Episode I – The Phantom Menace* doesn't begin to live up to its advance press. Even die-hard fans of the heretofore awe-inspiring saga are bound to be disappointed with this joyless, overly reverential, and impenetrably plotted prequel."

–RITA KEMPLEY, *WASHINGTON POST*

"The wonks have won. Those niggling concerns of movies past – things like story, character, and meaning – have finally been vanquished by Lucas' megalo-merchandising machine."

–Ann Hornaday, *Baltimore Sun*

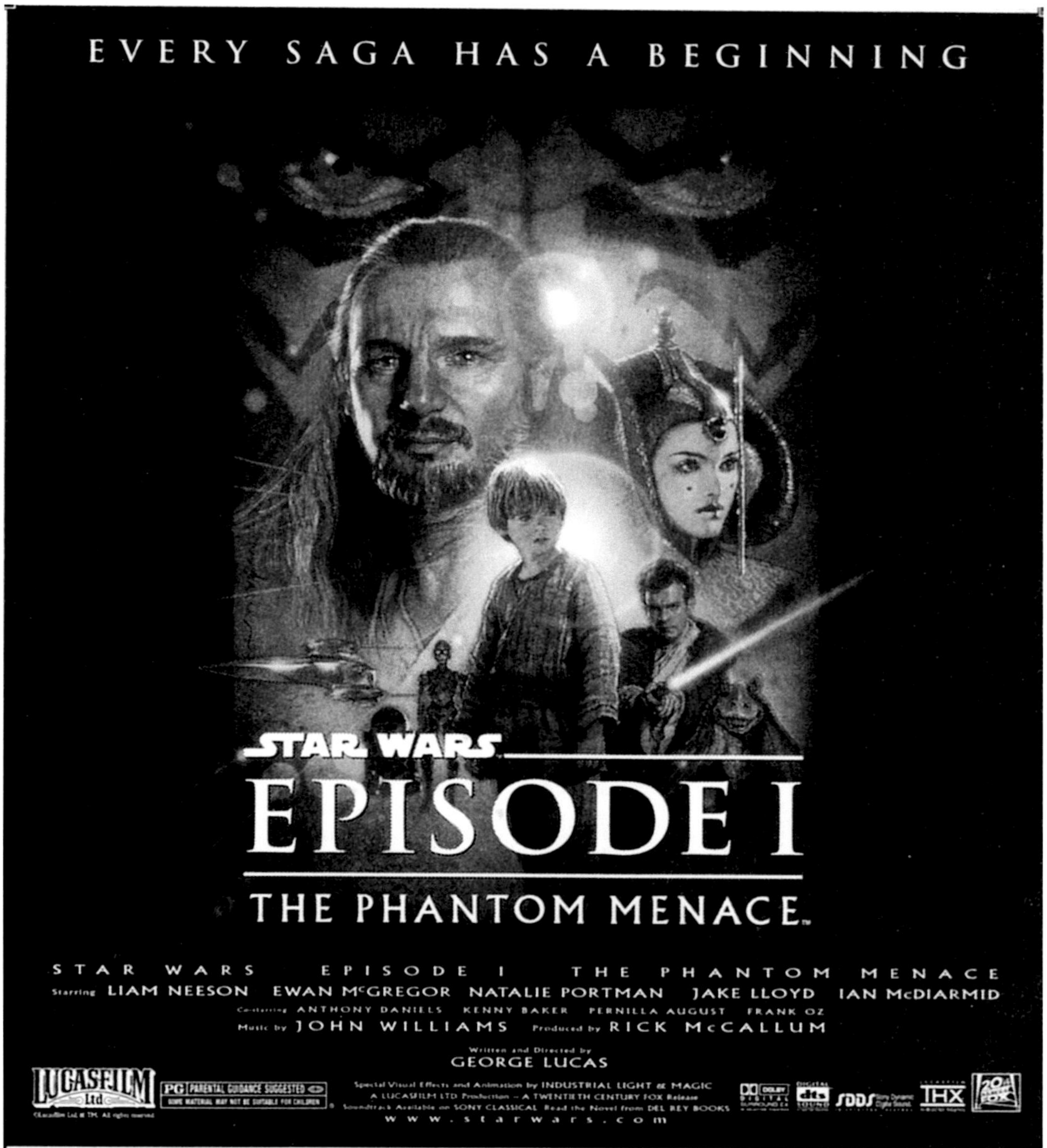

MANHATTAN

CLEARVIEW CINEMAS
ZIEGFELD
54TH ST. NEAR 6TH AVE.
777-FILM #602
12:01AM, 3:30AM, 6:30AM, 9:45AM, 1:15, 4:45, 8:15, 12:01AM

CLEARVIEW CINEMAS
FIRST & 62ND CINEMAS
62ND ST. BETW. 1ST & YORK AVES.
777-FILM #957
#1 - 12:00AM, 9:00AM, 10:00AM, 12:30, 1:30, 4:00, 5:00, 7:30, 8:30, 11:00, 12:00MID
#2 - 9:30AM, 1:00, 4:30, 8:00, 11:30

CITY CINEMAS
EAST 86TH STREET CINEMAS
EAST 86TH ST. BETW. 2ND & 3RD AVES.
777-FILM #753
#1 - 2:30AM, 11:30AM, 2:30, 5:30, 8:30, 11:30
#2 - 1:00AM, 10:00AM, 1:00, 4:00, 7:00, 10:00

CITY CINEMAS
MURRAY HILL
34TH ST. AT 3RD AVE.
689-6548
1:00AM, 2:30AM, 10:00AM, 11:30AM, 1:00, 2:30, 4:00, 5:30, 7:00, 8:30, 10:00, 11:30

UNITED ARTISTS
UNION SQUARE 14
BROADWAY & 13TH ST
777-FILM #777
#1 - 12:00AM, 12:00PM, 3:00, 6:00, 9:00, 12:00MID
#2 - 1:00AM, 10:00AM, 1:00, 4:00, 7:00, 10:00, 1:00AM
#3 - 2:00AM, 11:00AM, 2:00, 5:00, 8:00, 11:00, 2:00AM
#1 - 12:00AM, 12:00PM, 3:00, 6:00, 9:00, 12:00MID

CLEARVIEW CINEMAS
OLYMPIA CINEMAS
BROADWAY & 107TH ST
777-FILM #613
12:00AM, 11:00AM, 1:45, 4:30, 7:30, 10:30

WESTCHESTER

A NATIONAL AMUSEMENTS THEATRE
ALL WESTCHESTER SAWMILL MULTIPLEX CINEMAS HAWTHORNE 747-2333
CLEARVIEW CINEMAS
BEDFORD PLAYHOUSE
BEDFORD 777-FILM #693
UNITED ARTISTS
CORTLANDT TOWN CENTER
MOHEGAN LAKE 777-FILM #535
A NATIONAL AMUSEMENTS THEATRE
CROSS-COUNTY MULTIPLEX CINEMAS
YONKERS 376-7100
UNITED ARTISTS
JEFFERSON VALLEY
JEFFERSON VALLEY 777-FILM #825
CLEARVIEW CINEMAS
MAMARONECK PLAYHOUSE
MAMARONECK 777-FILM #810
UNITED ARTISTS
YONKERS 777-FILM #823

CONNECTICUT

SONY THEATRES
DANBURY
DANBURY 323-FILM #521
UNITED ARTISTS
DARIEN PLAYHOUSE
DARIEN 777-FILM #976
CROWN
MAJESTIC
STAMFORD 323-1690
CROWN
MARQUIS CINEMA
TRUMBULL 365-6500
CROWN
PLAZA
GREENWICH 869-4030
A NATIONAL AMUSEMENTS THEATRE
SHOWCASE CINEMAS
BRIDGEPORT 339-7171
CROWN
SHOWPLACE ROYALE
WESTPORT 846-8814
CROWN
SONO REGENT
SOUTH NORWALK 899-7979

BRONX

AMERICAN THEATRE
863-4900
GENERAL CINEMA
BAY PLAZA
320-3020
A NATIONAL AMUSEMENTS THEATRE
CONCOURSE PLAZA MULTIPLEX CINEMAS
588-8800
A NATIONAL AMUSEMENTS THEATRE
WHITESTONE MULTIPLEX CINEMAS
409-9030

BROOKLYN

CINEPLEX ODEON
ALPINE SEVENPLEX
777-FILM #580
CREATIVE ENTERTAINMENT
CANARSIE TRIPLEX
251-0700
CLEARVIEW CINEMAS
COBBLE HILL CINEMAS
777-FILM #644
CREATIVE ENTERTAINMENT
KENT 338-3371
CINEPLEX ODEON
KINGS PLAZA SIXPLEX
777-FILM #579
A NATIONAL AMUSEMENTS THEATRE
LINDEN BLVD. MULTPLEX CINEMAS 277-0303
UNITED ARTISTS
MARBORO 777-FILM #774
PAVILION 369-0838
CREATIVE ENTERTAINMENT
RIDGEWOOD FIVEPLEX
821-5993
UNITED ARTISTS
SHEEPSHEAD BAY
777-FILM #786

QUEENS

UNITED ARTISTS
ASTORIA
ASTORIA 777-FILM #793
UNITED ARTISTS
BAYSIDE
BAYSIDE 777-FILM #795
LESSER
CENTER CINEMAS
SUNNYSIDE 361-6869
A NATIONAL AMUSEMENTS THEATRE
COLLEGE POINT MULTIPLEX CINEMAS
EXIT 14 OFF THE WHITESTONE EXPWY.
COLLEGE POINT 886-4900
UNITED ARTISTS
CROSSBAY 1
OZONE PARK 777-FILM #806
CINEPLEX ODEON
FRESH MEADOWS CINEMAS
FRESH MEADOWS 777-FILM #619
JACKSON
JACKSON HEIGHTS 335-0242
LESSER
MAIN STREET CINEMAS
FLUSHING 263-4828
UNITED ARTISTS
MIDWAY
FOREST HILLS 777-FILM #819
UNITED ARTISTS
MOVIEWORLD AT DOUGLASTON
DOUGLASTON 777-FILM #840

STATEN ISLAND

ATRIUM CINEMAS
ELTINGVILLE 317-8300
UNITED ARTISTS
HYLAN PLAZA
NEW DORP 777-FILM #925
UNITED ARTISTS
STATEN ISLAND 14
TRAVIS 777-FILM #817

UPSTATE

CHESTER SIXPLEX
CHESTER 469-5020
DESTINTA'S NEW WINDSOR 12 569-0300
HOYTS CINEMA 12 GALLERIA MALL
POUGHKEEPSIE 297-1161
HOYTS FISHKILL CINEMA 10 896-1089
SONY THEATRES
GALLERIA METROPLEX
MIDDLETOWN 777-FILM #904
HOYTS KINGSTON MALL
KINGSTON 336-4188
LYCEUM CINEMAS
RED HOOK 758-3311
MALL QUAD MONTICELLO 794-2600
HOYTS NEWBURGH CINEMA 10 564-8844
NEW PALTZ QUAD 255-0420
ORPHEUM SAUGERTIES 246-6561
ROOSEVELT FOURPLEX
HYDE PARK 229-2000

NASSAU

FIVE STAR THEATRES
BELLMORE PLAYHOUSE
BELLMORE 783-5440
A NATIONAL AMUSEMENTS THEATRE
BROADWAY MULTIPLEX CINEMAS
HICKSVILLE 935-5599
CLEARVIEW CINEMAS
FRANKLIN SQUARE CINEMAS
FRANKLIN SQUARE 777-FILM #899
CINEPLEX ODEON
GLEN COVE CINEMAS
GLEN COVE 777-FILM #865
CLEARVIEW CINEMAS
GRAND AVENUE CINEMAS
BALDWIN 777-FILM #880
CLEARVIEW CINEMAS
HERRICKS CINEMA 4
NEW HYDE PARK 777-FILM #879
CINEPLEX ODEON
LAWRENCE TRIPLEX
LAWRENCE 777-FILM #605
UNITED ARTISTS
LYNBROOK
LYNBROOK 777-FILM #856
LOEWS NASSAU METROPLEX
LEVITTOWN 777-FILM #713
LOEWS RACEWAY THEATRE
WESTBURY 777-FILM #908
CLEARVIEW CINEMAS
SOUNDVIEW CINEMAS
PORT WASHINGTON 777-FILM #881
CLEARVIEW CINEMAS
SQUIRE CINEMAS
GREAT NECK 777-FILM #876
UNITED ARTISTS
SUNRISE MALL
MASSAPEQUA 777-FILM #800
A NATIONAL AMUSEMENTS THEATRE
SUNRISE MULTIPLEX CINEMAS
VALLEY STREAM 825-5700
UNITED ARTISTS
SYOSSET
SYOSSET 777-FILM #768

ROCKLAND

CLEARVIEW CINEMAS
CINEMA 304
NEW CITY 777-FILM #811
LOEWS PALISADES CENTER
WEST NYACK 777-FILM #543
UNITED ARTISTS
SPRING VALLEY
SPRING VALLEY 777-FILM #809

SUFFOLK

CLEARVIEW CINEMAS
BABYLON CINEMAS
BABYLON 777-FILM #835
A NATIONAL AMUSEMENTS THEATRE
BROOKHAVEN MULTIPLEX CINEMAS
MEDFORD 289-8900
A NATIONAL AMUSEMENTS THEATRE
COMMACK MULTIPLEX CINEMAS
COMMACK 462-6953
UNITED ARTISTS
CORAM
CORAM 777-FILM #815
UNITED ARTISTS
EASTHAMPTON
EASTHAMPTON 777-FILM #801
UNITED ARTISTS
FARMINGDALE
FARMINGDALE 777-FILM #539
CINEPLEX ODEON
HAMPTON ARTS
WESTHAMPTON 777-FILM #626
UNITED ARTISTS
HAMPTON BAYS 5
HAMPTON BAYS 777-FILM #797
CINEPLEX ODEON
ISLIP TRIPLEX
ISLIP 777-FILM #621
CINEPLEX ODEON
MATTITUCK CINEMAS
MATTITUCK 777-FILM #620
LESSER
MOVIELAND EIGHTPLEX
CORAM 696-4200
LESSER
MOVIELAND OF MASTIC
MASTIC 281-8586
LESSER
P.J. CINEMAS
PORT JEFFERSON STATION
928-3456
UNITED ARTISTS
PATCHOGUE
PATCHOGUE 777-FILM #822
HOYTS RONKONKOMA
RONKONKOMA 980-9707
LESSER
SAYVILLE
SAYVILLE 589-0232
CINEPLEX ODEON
SHORE CINEMAS
HUNTINGTON 777-FILM #627
LOEWS STONY BROOK 15
STONY BROOK 777-FILM #549

MICHAEL GINGOLD

Michael Gingold first began reproducing newspaper ads for 1980s horror films in the pages of his Xeroxed fanzine *Scareaphanalia*, which he wrote and self-published for nearly a decade. While still in college, he began contributing capsule reviews to the annual book *Movies on TV and Videocassette*, and later did the same for *The Blockbuster Video Guide*. For eight years, he wrote dozens of full-length reviews annually for CineBooks' *The Motion Picture Guide*, many of which also appear in the *TV Guide* online movie database.

In 1988, during his junior year, Michael began writing for *Fangoria* magazine, then joined the staff in 1990. He spent 26 years there, moving up quickly from associate editor to managing editor, and eventually editor-in-chief, while also serving as an editor and writer for Fangoria.com, as well as sister publication *GoreZone* and numerous one-shot publications. He rejoined *Fangoria* for its fall 2018 resurrection, and has also written for numerous other publications and websites; he currently contributes to *Rue Morgue*, *Birth.Movies. Death*, *Moviemaker*, *Time Out New York*, *Scream*, and *Delirium*, among others.

Other writings include liner notes for a number of Blu-ray and DVD releases, including lengthy essays for Anchor Bay and Shout! Factory's award-winning *Halloween: The Complete Collection* box set and Shout!'s *Creepshow*. He has directed and produced featurettes and documentary segments for discs such as *Alice, Sweet Alice*, *The Last House on the Left*, *Basket Case*, *Brain Damage*, and *C.H.U.D.* for Arrow Video and *The Children* for Vinegar Syndrome. Michael has appeared in numerous documentaries (among them David Gregory's *Lost Soul: The Doomed Journey of Richard Stanley's Island of Dr. Moreau* and Rob Galluzzo's *The Psycho Legacy*) and featurettes, and has taken part in DVD/Blu-ray audio commentaries for releases such as *The Stepfather* (Shout! Factory), *Blue Vengeance* (Vinegar Syndrome), the *42nd Street Forever* series (Synapse Films), and a pair of *Trailer Trauma* compilations (Garagehouse Pictures).

In addition to his pair of *Ad Nauseam* books on horror newspaper advertising, Michael is the author of *The FrightFest Guide to Monster Movies* (FAB Press) and *Shark Movie Mania* (*Rue Morgue*), and he's contributed to *Yuletide Terror: Christmas Horror on Film and Television* (Spectacular Optical) and *My Favorite Horror Movie* (Black Vortex). Among his screenplays are *Shadow: Dead Riot* for Fever Dreams and *Leeches!* for Rapid Heart Pictures; he also directed the "Girlkiller" segment for Alternative Cinema's *Shock Festival* DVD. He has served on juries for festivals including Montreal's Fantasia, The Boston Underground Film Festival and the Ithaca International Fantastic Film Festival, and as a programmer for the Brooklyn Horror Film Festival and the HorrorHound Film Festival.

HAVING NOW SHARED THE BULK OF HIS HORROR/SCI-FI AD TROVE WITH THE WORLD, HE HOPES TO SEE OTHER FANS AND COLLECTORS DO THE SAME FOR OTHER GENRES.

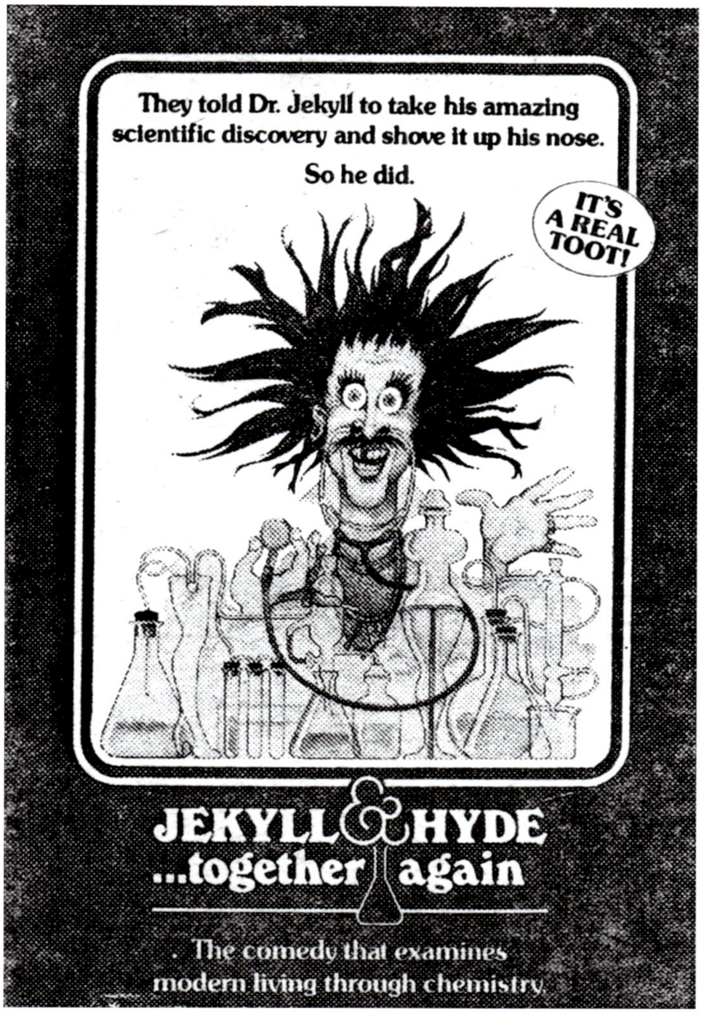

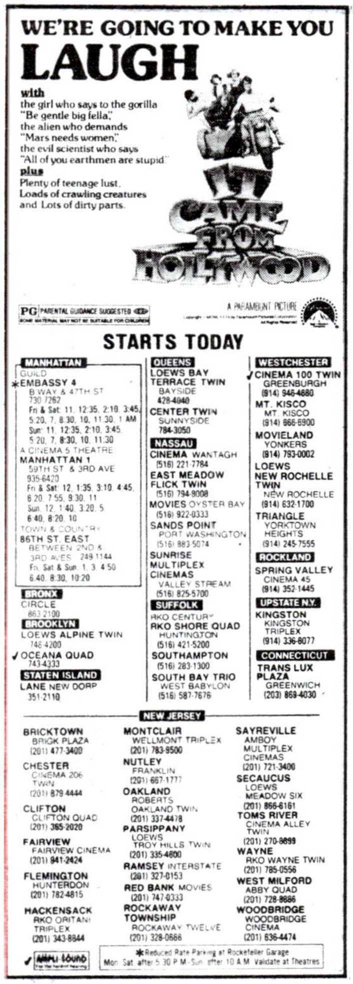

ONE LAST FLASHBACK

JEKYLL & HYDE...TOGETHER AGAIN & IT CAME FROM HOLLYWOOD

My fellow New Yorkers and I only got to see this pair of Paramount releases a couple of months after the rest of the country. The studio opened its snarky "celebration" of B-cinema and its comedic variation on the mad-scientist classic in nationwide (albeit comparatively limited) release in October '82, but bypassed the NYC area until December. Then, they each got one-week runs starting on consecutive Fridays. When a friend and I went to see *Jekyll & Hyde*, we were two of the five people in the theater, and when two pals and I went to *It Came from Hollywood*, we were the *only* people in the theater. We arrived a little early, and when we asked when the previous showing was ending, we were told there hadn't been a previous showing, because no one had come to see it!

INDEX

AD ASTRA: 20 YEARS OF NEWSPAPER ADS FOR SCI-FI & FANTASY FILMS

WRITER: Michael Gingold

FOREWORD: Larry Karaszewski

ART DIRECTION & LAYOUT DESIGN: Shane Lewis / Desiree Lewis

EDITOR: David Alexander

PUBLISHER: Matthew Chojnacki

COVER ILLUSTRATION: Andrew Wright

LIBRARY OF CONGRESS CONTROL NUMBER: 2019905335

ISBN: 978-1-948221-11-5

1984 PUBLISHING
Cleveland, Ohio / USA
1984Publishing.com
info@1984Publishing.com

PRINTED AND BOUND IN THE UNITED STATES OF AMERICA.

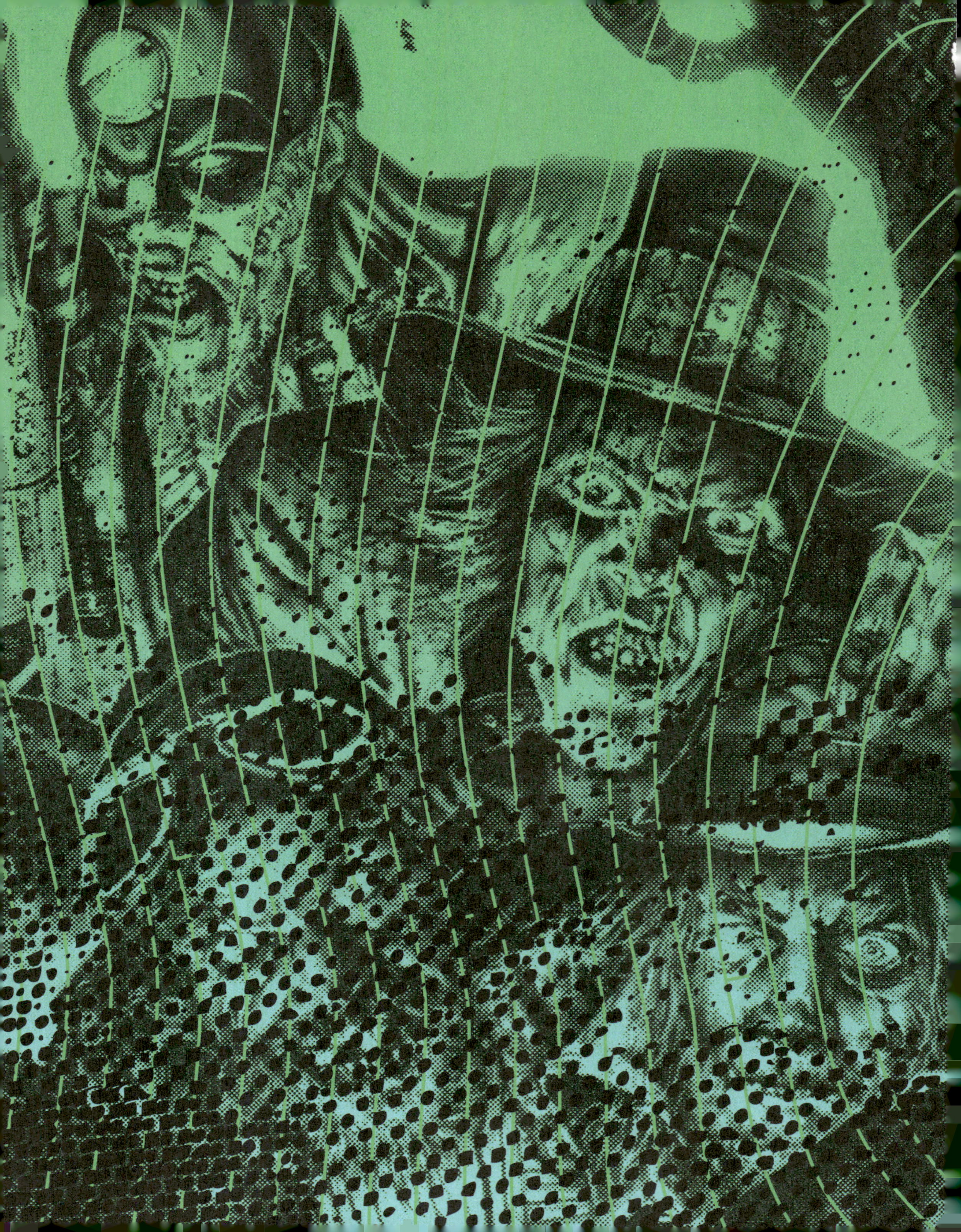